AF697137

2011 Uniform CPA Examination: CANDIDATE PERFORMANCE

Published by
National Association of State Boards of Accountancy

Editor
James Suh

Associate Editors
Matthew Wilkins
Tim Wright

NASBA

150 Fourth Avenue North, Suite 700, Nashville, TN 37219-2417
Tel/615.880.4200 Fax/615.880.4290
www.nasba.org

Table of Contents

INTRODUCTION

The National Association of State Boards of Accountancy (NASBA) began gathering data on CPA examination candidates in 1982 and has published reports on performance and selected characteristics since 1985. This edition of the book covers candidate performance for the Uniform CPA Examination (Examination) for the calendar year 2011. NASBA offers these reports through the voluntary participation of candidates and their individual boards of accountancy, which provide data, and the cooperation of the American Institute of Certified Public Accountants (AICPA), which prepares and scores the Examination for the 55 U.S. jurisdictions.

BACKGROUND DATA

The background data is obtained directly from state boards of accountancy, when they submit information about eligible candidates to NASBA's Gateway System. The Gateway System is a Web Interface which provides state boards a means to enter, review and manage candidate information. The process of entering candidate information using the Web Interface results in the eventual scheduling of an Examination by the candidate. Candidate information is transmitted through the Gateway System and stored in the National Candidate Database (NCD) where all CPA candidate information and Examination history data are maintained.

SPECIAL NOTE ABOUT THIS EDITION

This year's edition has been completely redesigned to better meet the needs of the both NASBA's stakeholders and the book's numerous end users. In addition to the summary data points, significant emphasis was placed on developing and presenting a comprehensive and graphical view of candidate performance from a variety of different viewpoints. One of the most noticeable changes is the inclusion of a 2-page dashboard for each of the jurisdictions represented in this book.

Additional improvements include:

- Enhanced demographic reporting: Age, Gender, Home Country
- International exam performance metrics
- School rankings based on program size
- Inclusion of more schools in the publication

Demographics

The reader should note that demographic data is not reported completely for all jurisdictions. This gap in data is often due to the fact that the reported information may not be critical to a given jurisdiction's application process and thus not collected. NASBA will continue to work with several of the jurisdictions to close many of the data collection gaps.

FIRST-TIME VERSUS REPEAT CANDIDATES

A candidate's initial attempt at a section is labeled as a First-Time (FT) event; all subsequent attempts to retake that particular section are labeled as Re-Exam (RE) events. It is entirely possible for a given candidate to have both FT and RE events for multiple sections of the test or to have exclusively FT events for some sections and exclusively RE events for others. Candidates often require multiple attempts (events) before passing a particular section.

A candidate's status as FT or RE is evaluated on a section-by-section basis. Candidates are considered to be FT candidates the first time they take a given section. If a candidate fails that section, then the candidate is treated as a RE candidate for all subsequent administrations of that section. By definition, candidates can have only one FT event per section but can have multiple RE events for each section. Event-level passing rates are calculated as the number of passing events (either FT, RE or combined) divided by the total number of events (either FT, RE or combined).

FEEDBACK

The changes and improvements in this book are a direct result of the feedback received from the many end users of this product. Although this edition has made significant strides over previous editions, we acknowledge that there is additional room for improvement. To get there we need your feedback, both positive and negative. Please send any questions, comments and (most importantly) suggestions to *CPB@nasba.org* .

GENERAL DISCLAIMERS / LIMITED LIABILITY:

Notwithstanding any language to the contrary, nothing contained herein constitutes nor is intended to constitute a promise of any kind. While reasonable efforts are made to insure accurate and up to date information in this Candidate Performance Book, the data contained herein is for informational purposes only and is not represented to be error free. The National Association of State Boards of Accountancy (NASBA) does not warrant that the information and materials in this handbook are adequate, accurate, current or complete, and, to the fullest extent permitted by applicable laws, expressly disclaims liability for any errors or omissions in the information and materials. No warranty of any kind, implied, express or statutory, including fitness for a particular purpose, is given in conjunction with the information and materials contained within the Candidate Performance Book. In no event will NASBA or its directors, officers, agents, representatives, employees, or volunteers be liable for any damage to you or any other party for any losses or damage including, without limitation, incidental, exemplary or consequential damage arising from the use or inability to use the data contained within the Candidate Performance Book.

2011 CANDIDATE PERFORMANCE

OVERVIEW

This section contains summary dashboards and data related to the 2011 testing windows. Both the full year and individual quarter summaries are included.

CPA Exam Performance: *All Jurisdictions*

2011

Overall Performance

Unique Candidates	**90,644**
New Candidates	**39,805**
Total Sections	**230,564**
Passing 4th Section	**23,814**
Sections/Candidate	**2.54**
Pass Rate	**45.5%**
Average Score	**70.6**

Section Performance

	Sections	Score	% Pass
First-Time	**134,831**	**70.9**	**49.8%**
Re-Exam	**95,733**	**70.1**	**39.5%**
AUD	**62,933**	**71.7**	**45.6%**
BEC	**50,478**	**71.2**	**46.9%**
FAR	**55,338**	**69.3**	**45.6%**
REG	**61,815**	**69.9**	**44.1%**

Top 3 Jurisdictions

Most Candidates

1. California	**13,344**
2. New York	**8,366**
3. Texas	**5,515**

Highest Pass Rate

1. Utah	**57.4%**
2. North Dakota	**55.1%**
3. Missouri	**54.8%**

Exam Type by Percent

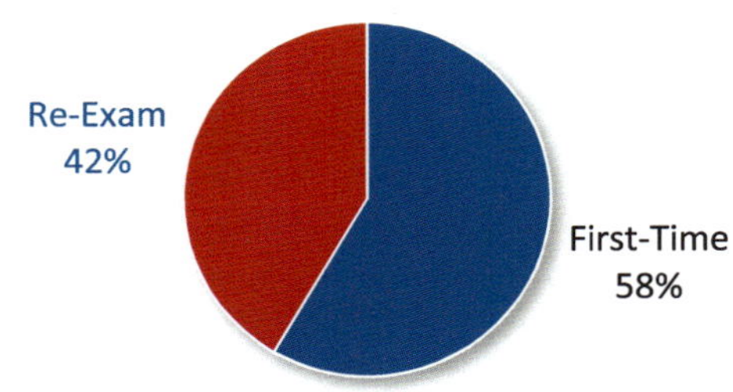

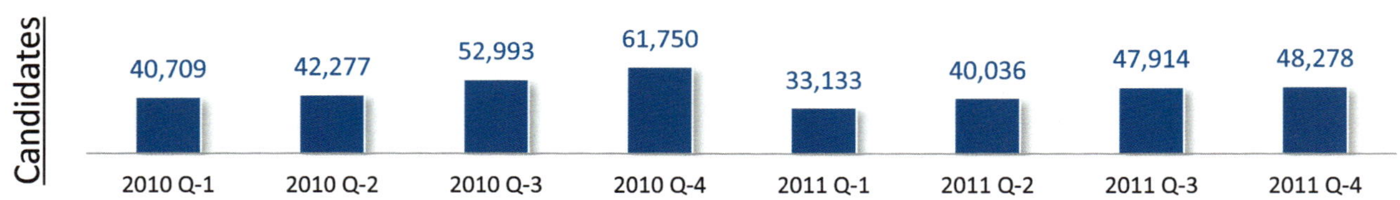

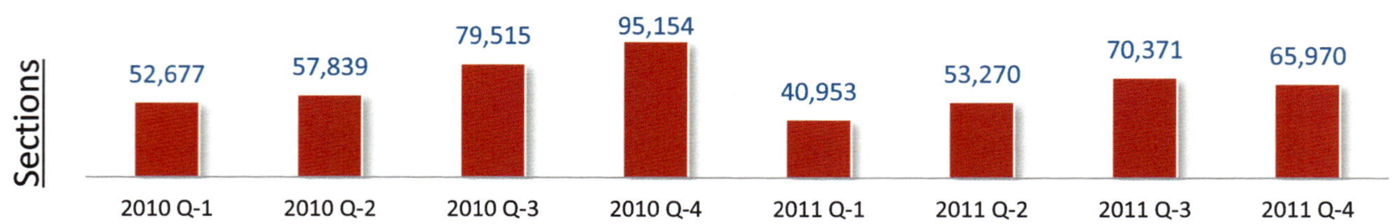

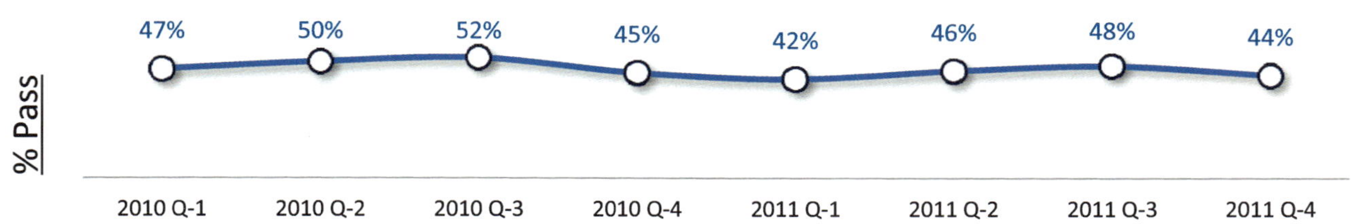

CPA Exam Performance: *All Jurisdictions*

Demographics

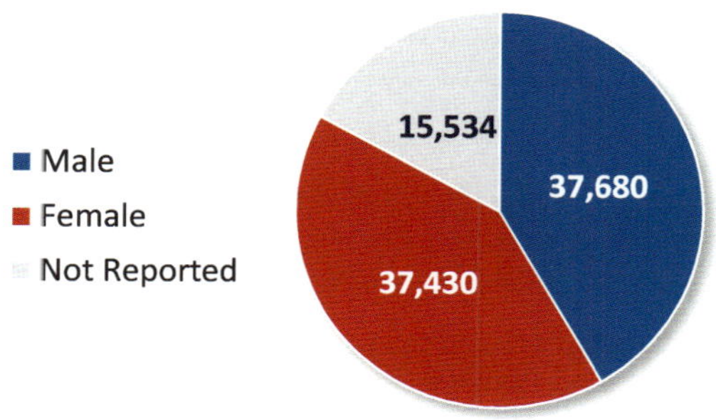

Residency

Candidate Count	
In-State Address	70,411
Out-of-State Address	12,509
International Address	7,724

% of Candidates	
In-State Address	77.7%
Out-of-State Address	13.8%
International Address	8.5%

Average Age

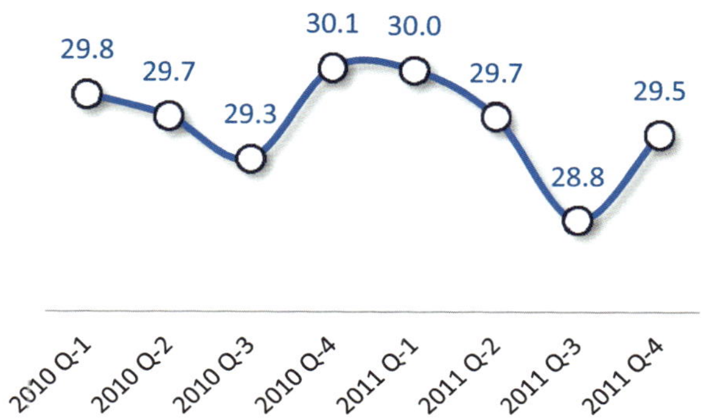

Degree Type

Candidate Count	
Bachelor's Degree	62,940
Advanced Degree	12,719
None/Other	14,985

% of Candidates	
Bachelor's Degree	69.4%
Advanced Degree	14.0%
None/Other	16.5%

New Candidates vs Candidates Passing 4th Section

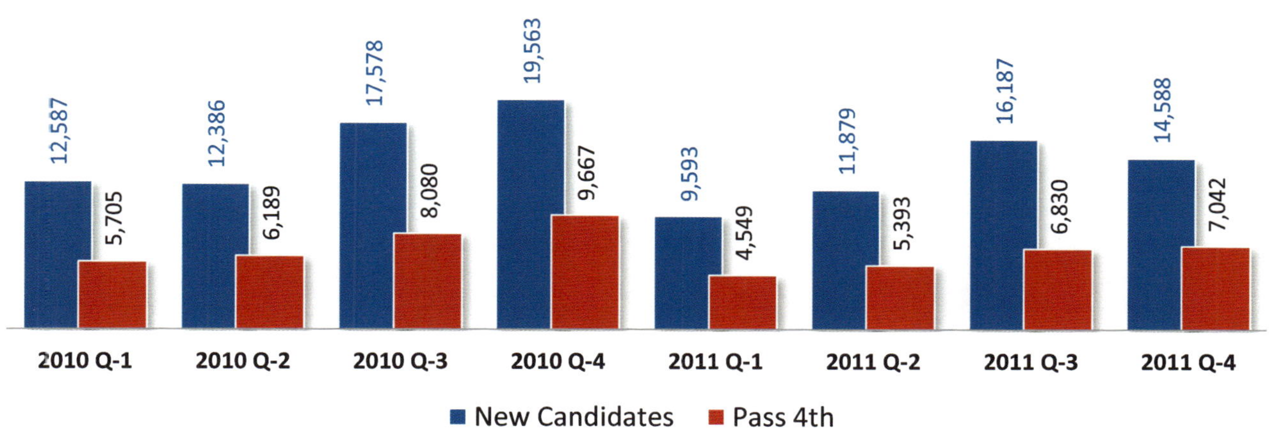

Notes about the Data

1. The data used to develop this report was pulled from NASBA's Gateway System, which houses the Uniform CPA Examination's Application and Performance information for all 55 jusrisdictions.
2. The demographic data related to Age, Gender and Degree Type is provided by the individual candidates and may not be 100% accurate.

2011

CPA Exam Performance: *All Jurisdictions*

2011 Q-1

Overall Performance

Unique Candidates	**33,133**
New Candidates	**9,593**
Total Sections	**40,953**
Passing 4th Section	**4,549**
Sections/Candidate	**1.24**
Pass Rate	**42.5%**
Average Score	**69.4**

Section Performance

	Sections	Score	% Pass
First-Time	**22,519**	**69.0**	**45.4%**
Re-Exam	**18,434**	**69.8**	**38.9%**
AUD	**11,144**	**71.0**	**43.9%**
BEC	**8,482**	**69.7**	**42.3%**
FAR	**9,494**	**67.8**	**42.4%**
REG	**11,833**	**68.8**	**41.3%**

Top 3 Jurisdictions

Most Candidates

1. California	**4,700**
2. New York	**3,056**
3. Texas	**2,234**

Highest Pass Rate

1. North Dakota	**58.7%**
2. Utah	**55.2%**
3. Texas	**50.8%**

Exam Type by Percent

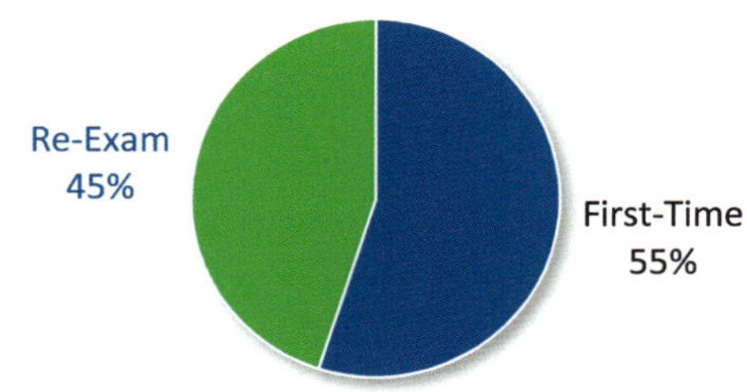

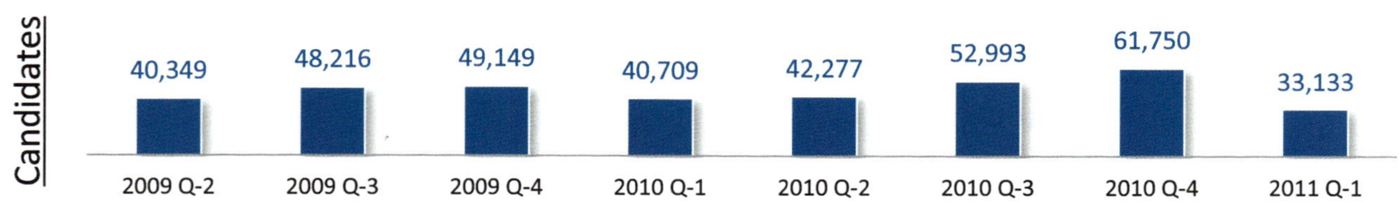

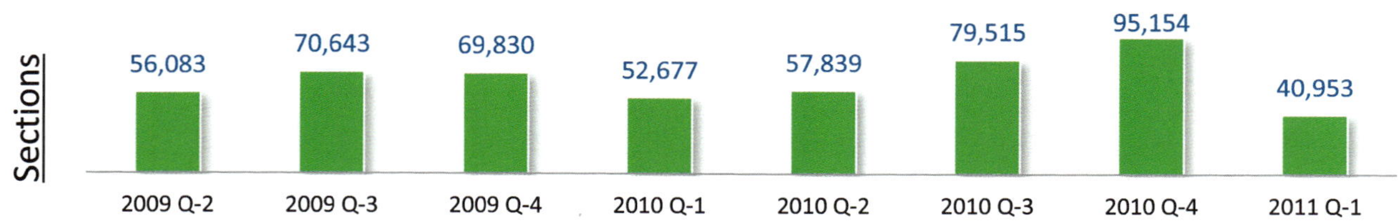

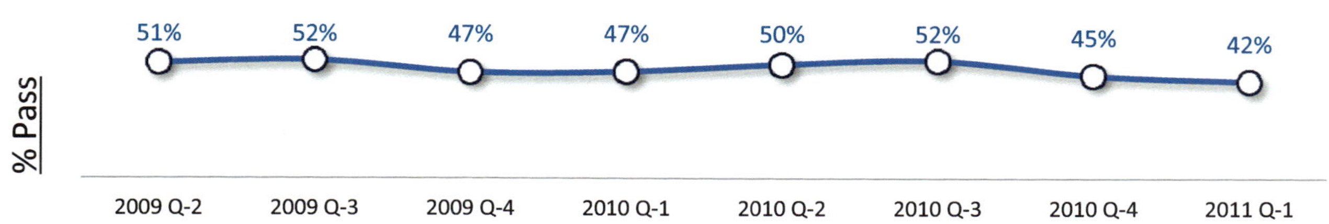

Data and Trends published by NASBA (www.nasba.org)
CPB@nasba.org

CPA Exam Performance: *All Jurisdictions*

Demographics

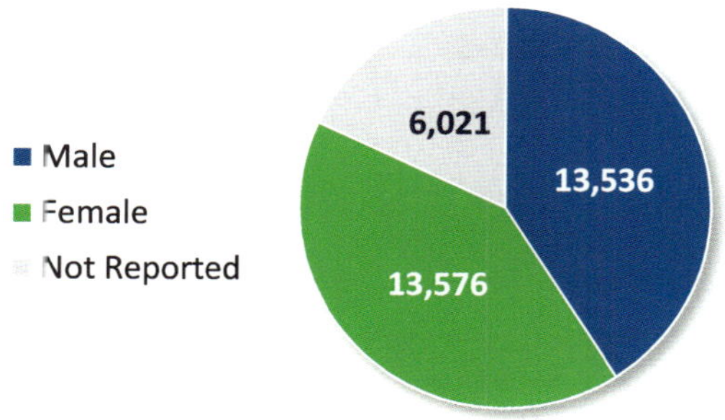

Residency

Candidate Count

In-State Address	**26,126**
Out-of-State Address	**4,608**
Foreign Address	**2,399**

% of Candidates

In-State Address	**78.9%**
Out-of-State Address	**13.9%**
Foreign Address	**7.2%**

Average Age

Degree Type

Candidate Count

Bachelor's Degree	**22,584**
Advanced Degree	**4,818**
None/Other	**6,021**

% of Candidates

Bachelor's Degree	**68.2%**
Advanced Degree	**14.5%**
None/Other	**18.2%**

New Candidates vs Candidates Passing 4th Section

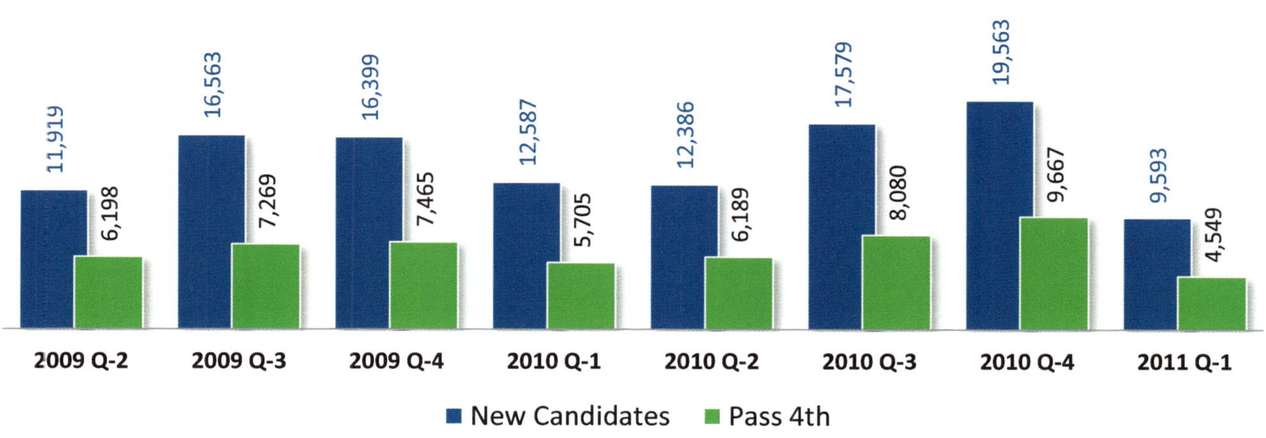

Notes about the Data

1. The data used to develop this report was pulled from NASBA's Gateway System, which houses the Uniform CPA Examination's Application and Performance information for all 55 jurisdictions.
2. The demographic data related to Age, Gender and Degree Type is provided by the individual candidates and may not be 100% accurate.

2011 Q-1

CPA Exam Performance: *All Jurisdictions*

2011 Q-2

Overall Performance

Unique Candidates	**40,036**
New Candidates	**11,879**
Total Sections	**53,270**
Passing 4th Section	**5,393**
Sections/Candidate	**1.33**
Pass Rate	**46.0%**
Average Score	**70.8**

Section Performance

	Sections	Score	% Pass
First-Time	**30,913**	**71.3**	**50.9%**
Re-Exam	**22,357**	**70.1**	**39.3%**
AUD	**15,184**	**72.7**	**48.0%**
BEC	**11,625**	**70.9**	**46.5%**
FAR	**11,988**	**69.1**	**44.3%**
REG	**14,473**	**70.1**	**45.1%**

Top 3 Jurisdictions

Most Candidates

1. California	**6,129**
2. New York	**3,499**
3. Texas	**2,749**

Highest Pass Rate

1. Missouri	**63.1%**
2. Iowa	**59.9%**
3. Utah	**58.1%**

Exam Type by Percent

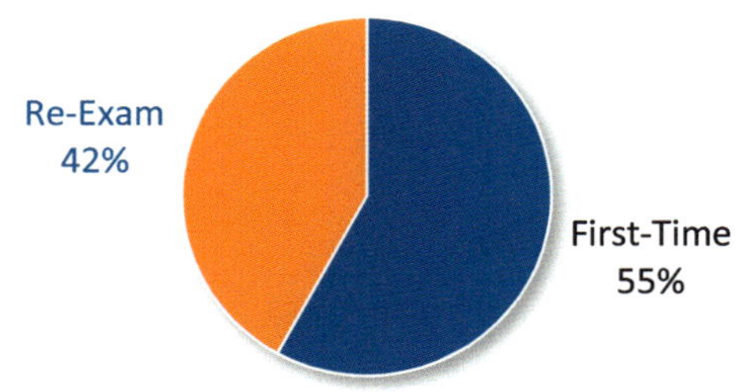

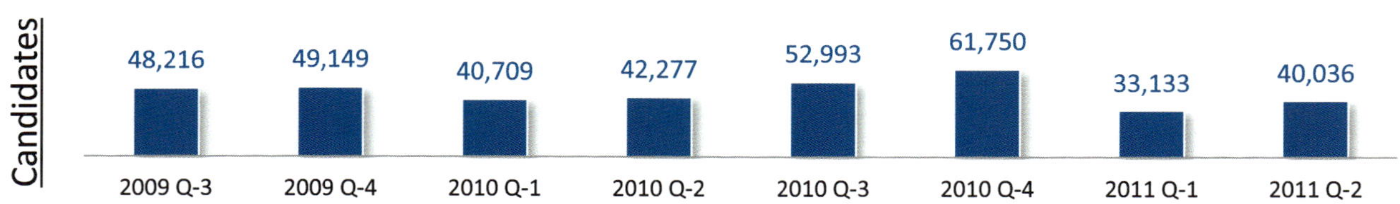

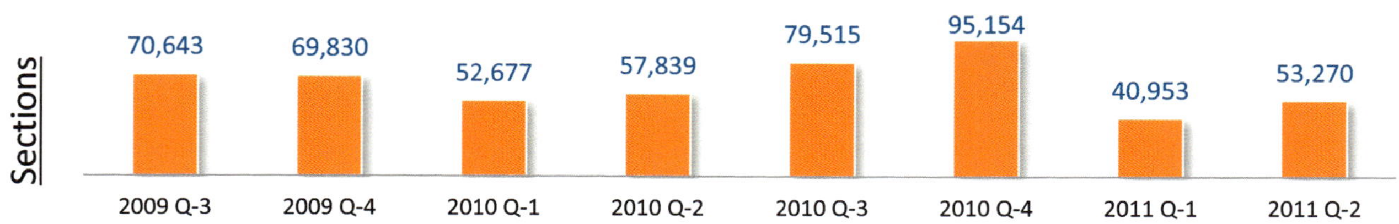

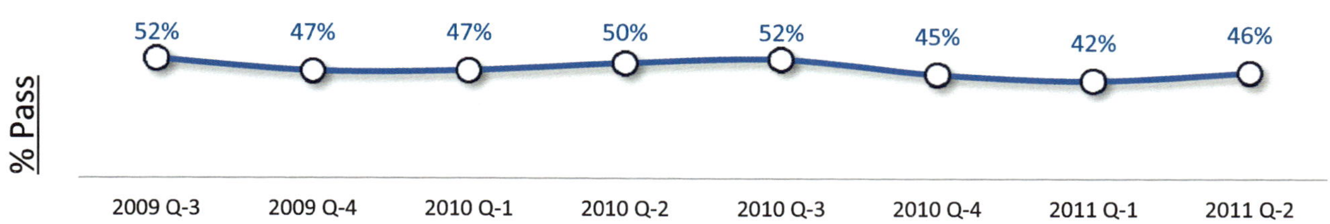

Data and Trends published by NASBA (www.nasba.org)
CPB@nasba.org

CPA Exam Performance: *All Jurisdictions*

Demographics

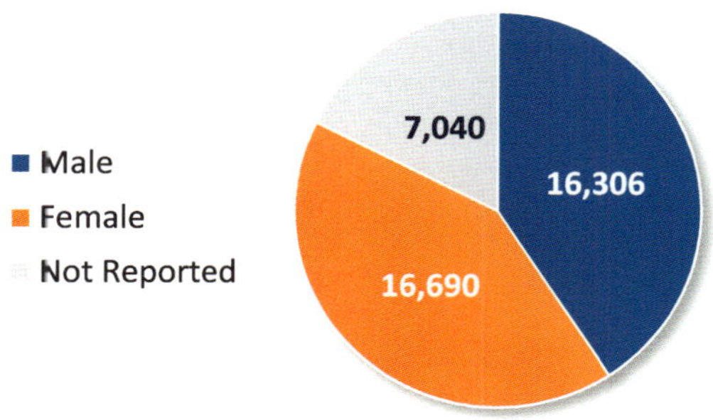

Residency

Candidate Count	
In-State Address	31,604
Out-of-State Address	5,675
Foreign Address	2,757

% of Candidates	
In-State Address	78.9%
Out-of-State Address	14.2%
Foreign Address	6.9%

Average Age

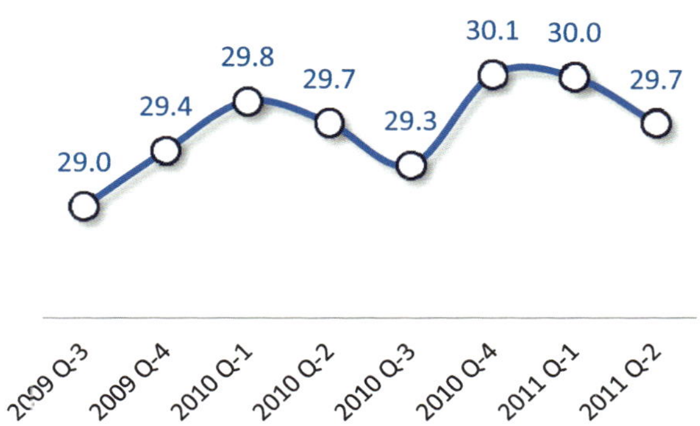

Degree Type

Candidate Count	
Bachelor's Degree	27,369
Advanced Degree	5,860
None/Other	7,040

% of Candidates	
Bachelor's Degree	68.4%
Advanced Degree	14.6%
None/Other	17.6%

New Candidates vs Candidates Passing 4th Section

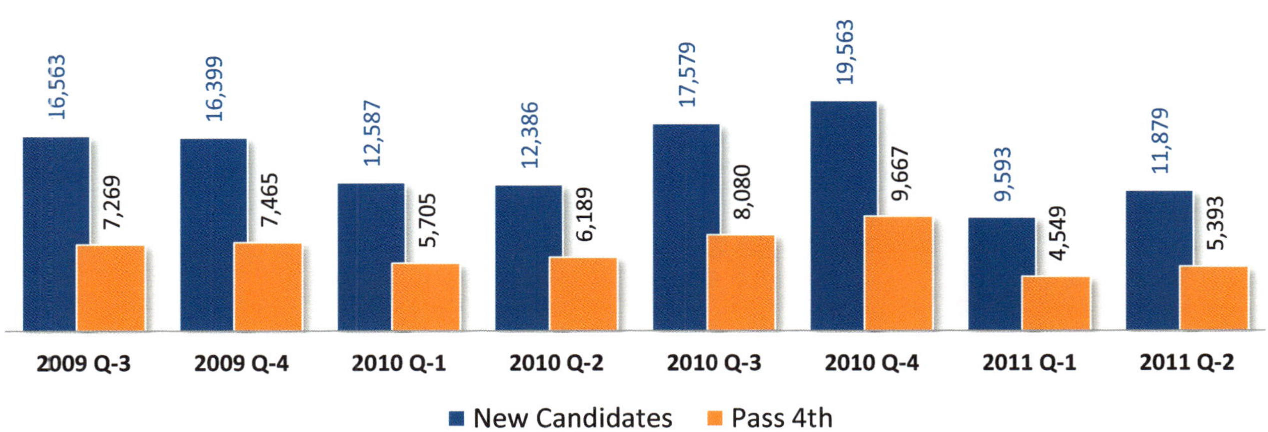

Notes about the Data

1. The data used to develop this report was pulled from NASBA's Gateway System, which houses the Uniform CPA Examination's Application and Performance information for all 55 jurisdictions.
2. The demographic data related to Age, Gender and Degree Type is provided by the individual candidates and may not be 100% accurate.

2011 Q-2

CPA Exam Performance: *All Jurisdictions*

2011 Q-3

Overall Performance

Unique Candidates	**47,914**
New Candidates	**16,190**
Total Sections	**70,371**
Passing 4th Section	**6,830**
Sections/Candidate	**1.47**
Pass Rate	**48.1%**
Average Score	**71.5**

Section Performance

	Sections	Score	% Pass
First-Time	**44,121**	**72.4**	**53.3%**
Re-Exam	**26,250**	**70.1**	**39.4%**
AUD	**18,719**	**72.3**	**47.0%**
BEC	**15,173**	**72.7**	**51.6%**
FAR	**18,113**	**70.8**	**49.5%**
REG	**18,366**	**70.6**	**45.1%**

Top 3 Jurisdictions

Most Candidates

1. California	**6,915**
2. New York	**4,304**
3. Texas	**2,945**

Highest Pass Rate

1. Missouri	**57.6%**
2. North Carolina	**56.7%**
3. Utah	**56.4%**

Exam Type by Percent

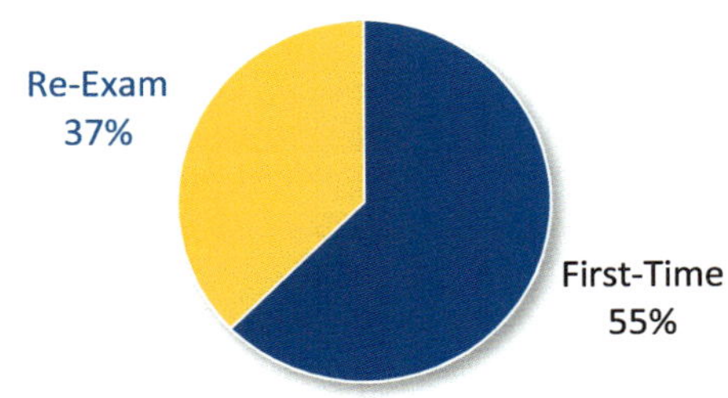

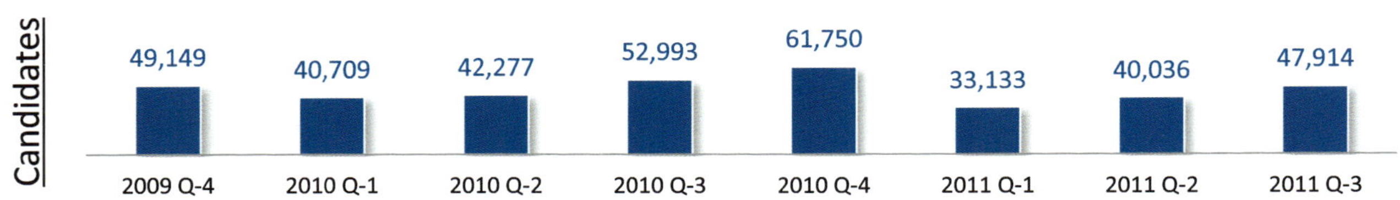

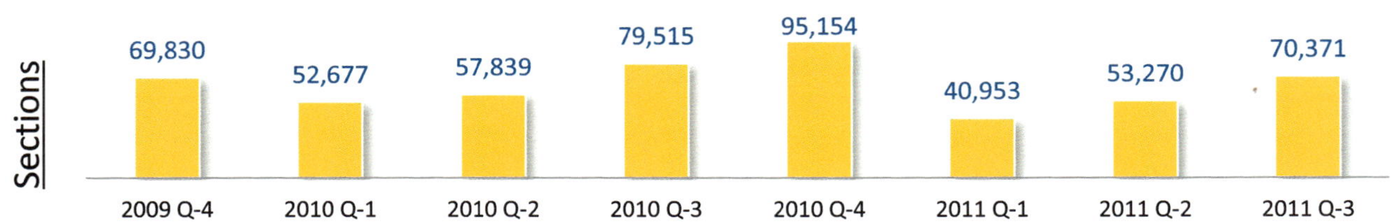

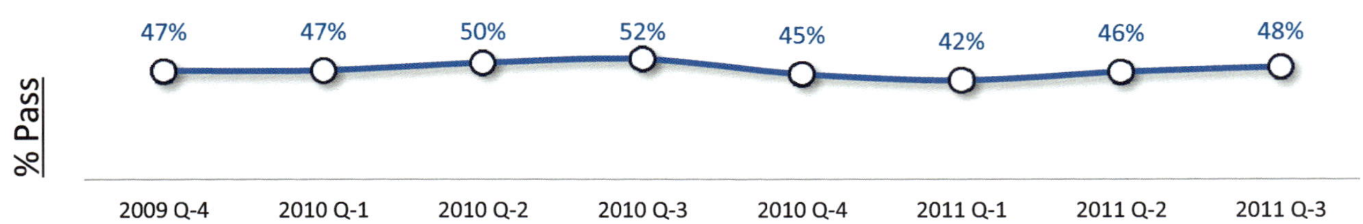

Data and Trends published by NASBA (www.nasba.org)
CPB@nasba.org

CPA Exam Performance: *All Jurisdictions*

Demographics

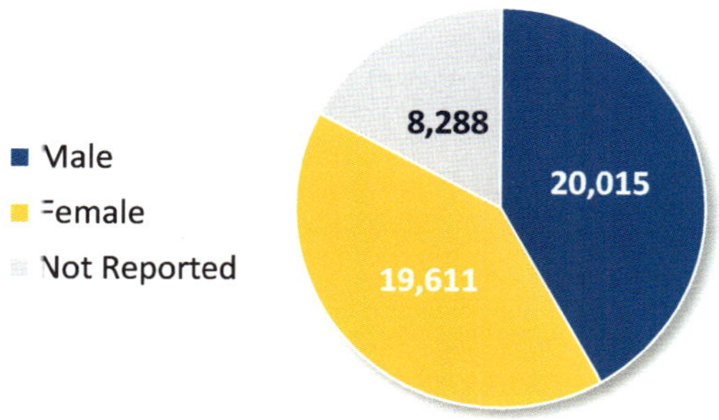

Residency

Candidate Count	
In-State Address	**37,705**
Out-of-State Address	**6,779**
Foreign Address	**3,430**
% of Candidates	
In-State Address	**78.7%**
Out-of-State Address	**14.1%**
Foreign Address	**7.2%**

Average Age

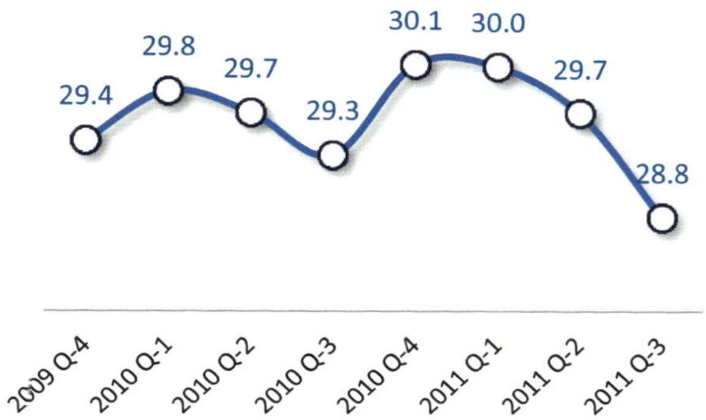

Degree Type

Candidate Count	
Bachelor's Degree	**33,550**
Advanced Degree	**6,532**
None/Other	**8,288**
% of Candidates	
Bachelor's Degree	**70.0%**
Advanced Degree	**13.6%**
None/Other	**17.3%**

New Candidates vs Candidates Passing 4th Section

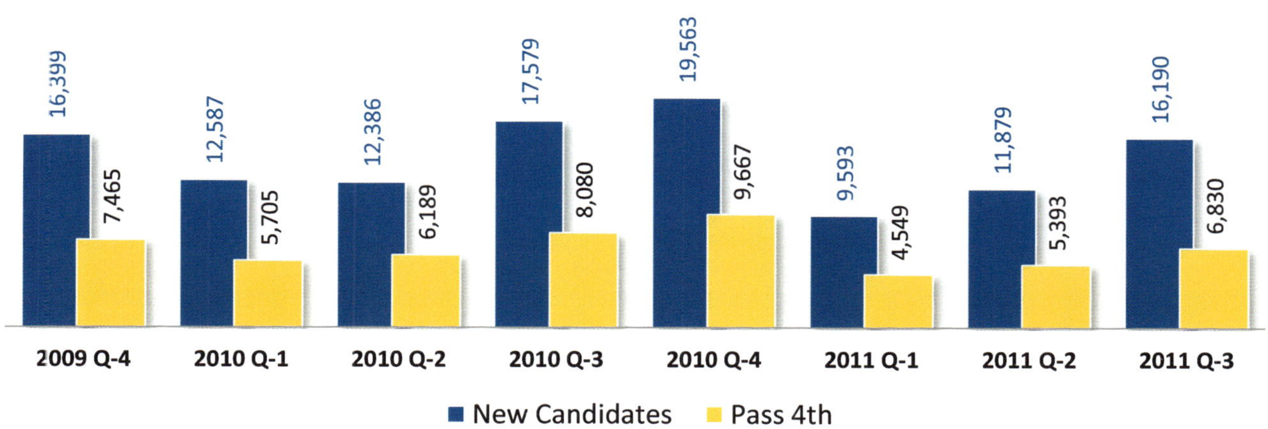

Notes about the Data

1. The data used to develop this report was pulled from NASBA's Gateway System, which houses the Uniform CPA Examination's Application and Performance information for all 55 jurisdictions.
2. The demographic data related to Age, Gender and Degree Type is provided by the individual candidates and may not be 100% accurate.

2011 Q-3

CPA Exam Performance: *All Jurisdictions*

2011 Q-4

Overall Performance

Unique Candidates	**48,278**
New Candidates	**14,593**
Total Sections	**65,970**
Passing 4th Section	**7,042**
Sections/Candidate	**1.37**
Pass Rate	**44.1%**
Average Score	**70.1**

Section Performance

	Sections	Score	% Pass
First-Time	**37,278**	**69.9**	**47.2%**
Re-Exam	**28,692**	**70.2**	**40.1%**
AUD	**17,886**	**70.9**	**43.1%**
BEC	**15,198**	**70.8**	**45.1%**
FAR	**15,743**	**68.6**	**44.2%**
REG	**17,143**	**69.8**	**44.2%**

Top 3 Jurisdictions

Most Candidates

1. California	**6,953**
2. New York	**4,752**
3. Pennsylvania	**3,301**

Highest Pass Rate

1. Utah	**59.5%**
2. North Dakota	**55.9%**
3. Oregon	**54.7%**

Exam Type by Percent

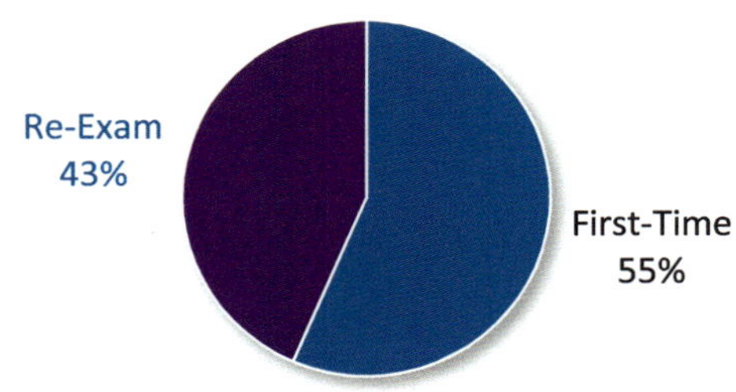

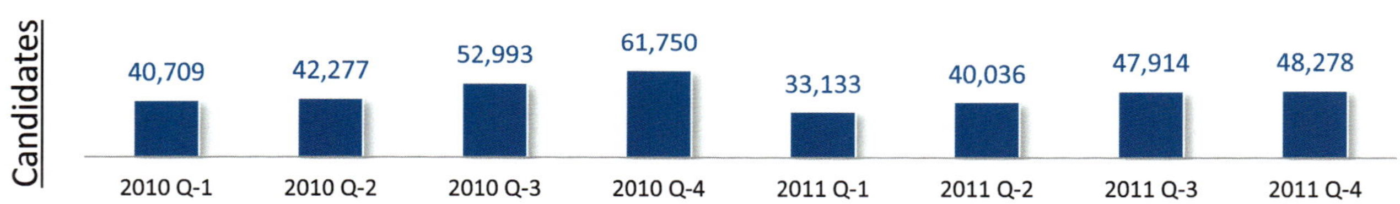

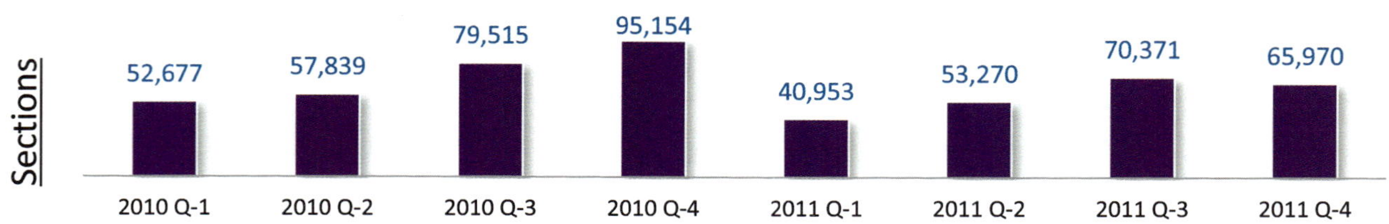

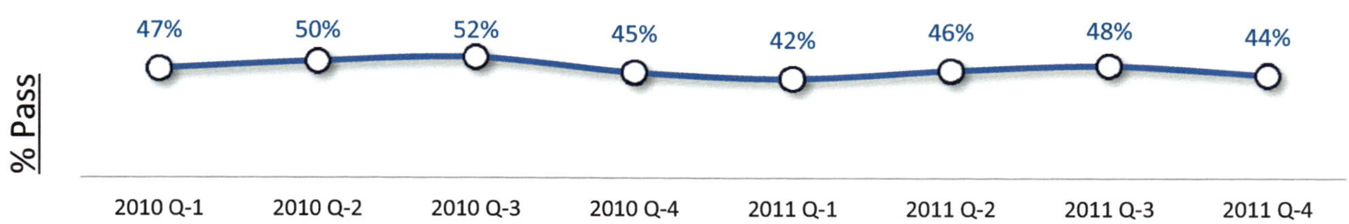

CPA Exam Performance: *All Jurisdictions*

Demographics

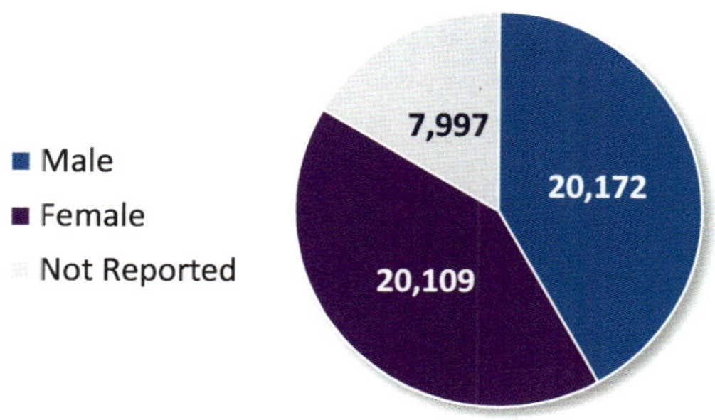

Residency

Candidate Count

In-State Address	**37,931**
Out-of-State Address	**6,472**
Foreign Address	**3,875**

% of Candidates

In-State Address	**78.6%**
Out-of-State Address	**13.4%**
Foreign Address	**8.0%**

Average Age

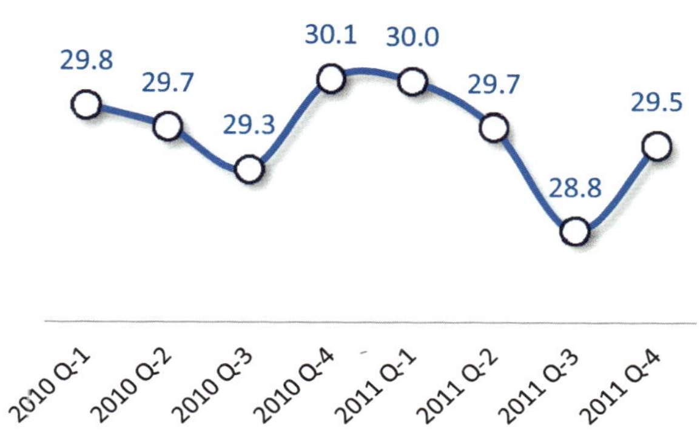

Degree Type

Candidate Count

Bachelor's Degree	**34,203**
Advanced Degree	**6,716**
None/Other	**7,997**

% of Candidates

Bachelor's Degree	**70.8%**
Advanced Degree	**13.9%**
None/Other	**16.6%**

New Candidates vs Candidates Passing 4th Section

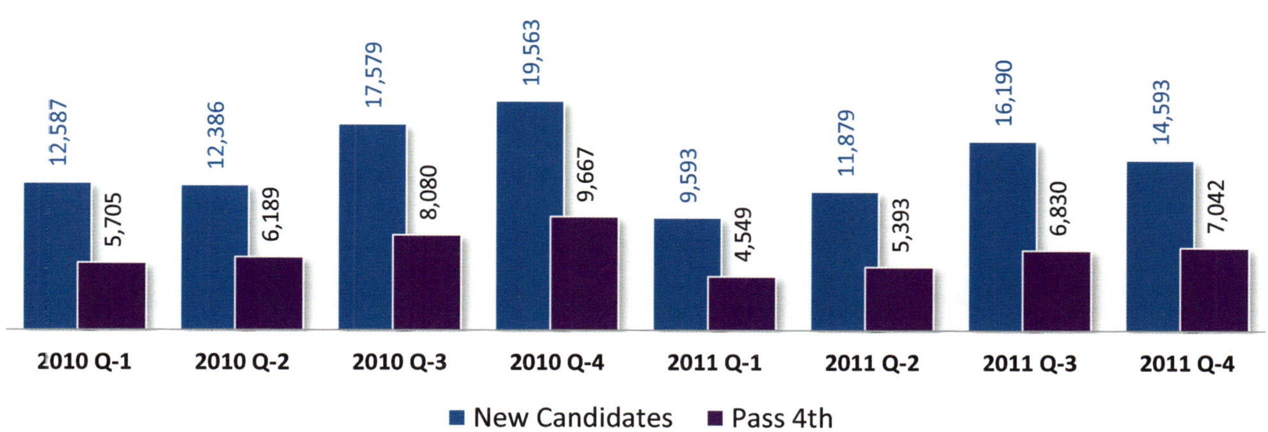

Notes about the Data

1. The data used to develop this report was pulled from NASBA's Gateway System, which houses the Uniform CPA Examination's Application and Performance information for all 55 jurisdictions.
2. The demographic data related to Age, Gender and Degree Type is provided by the individual candidates and may not be 100% accurate.

2011 Q-4

Jurisdiction Summary Statistics: All Testing Windows

Jurisdiction	Candidates Total	Sections Total	Sections First-Time	Sections Re-Exam	Percent Pass	Average Score	Average Age
Alabama	480	1,149	543	606	41.3%	70.0	30.6
Alaska	524	1,392	757	635	43.5%	69.5	30.3
Arizona	931	2,272	1,345	927	48.6%	71.5	31.5
Arkansas	409	1,087	614	473	41.9%	69.5	28.2
California	13,344	32,570	18,331	14,239	43.8%	69.8	30.5
Colorado	2,289	5,803	3,250	2,553	47.6%	71.7	30.9
Connecticut	1,054	2,545	1,497	1,048	45.0%	70.5	27.7
Delaware	1,297	3,253	1,463	1,790	35.2%	66.9	34.0
District of Columbia	155	377	223	154	44.0%	69.3	32.6
Florida	2,588	6,105	3,760	2,345	49.4%	72.4	31.2
Georgia	3,101	7,927	4,752	3,175	48.3%	71.6	29.6
Guam	581	1,538	712	826	35.0%	66.8	34.7
Hawaii	369	923	436	487	38.7%	68.8	31.0
Idaho	297	736	440	296	44.8%	70.6	30.9
Illinois	5,065	13,820	8,754	5,066	51.0%	72.5	28.5
Indiana	1,282	3,502	2,089	1,413	45.3%	70.6	28.3
Iowa	634	1,801	1,220	581	51.8%	72.7	27.0
Kansas	475	1,294	754	540	47.3%	71.4	28.5
Kentucky	812	2,065	1,187	878	45.7%	71.4	29.4
Louisiana	888	2,272	1,278	994	43.8%	70.3	28.7
Maine	2,448	6,351	3,704	2,647	39.9%	67.6	32.4
Maryland	1,495	3,727	2,070	1,657	43.2%	70.1	29.8
Massachusetts	2,709	6,902	4,309	2,593	49.9%	72.1	27.4
Michigan	1,868	4,962	3,084	1,878	52.1%	73.1	28.4
Minnesota	1,368	3,666	2,461	1,205	52.6%	72.9	27.5
Mississippi	374	900	479	421	33.9%	67.0	30.9
Missouri	1,272	3,669	2,410	1,259	54.8%	73.4	27.8
Montana	476	1,358	770	588	45.4%	70.7	28.4
Nebraska	311	859	521	338	48.1%	71.7	27.2
Nevada	324	842	458	384	45.0%	71.7	30.0
New Hampshire	2,641	6,462	3,666	2,796	41.3%	68.3	30.8
New Jersey	2,777	6,859	3,946	2,913	39.2%	67.9	28.7
New Mexico	354	852	450	402	37.4%	68.7	33.0
New York	8,366	20,468	11,029	9,439	42.7%	70.0	27.9
North Carolina	1,698	4,701	2,911	1,790	51.2%	72.7	28.9
North Dakota	261	664	422	242	55.1%	73.9	27.7
Ohio	2,490	6,725	4,204	2,521	48.6%	71.5	28.7
Oklahoma	706	1,679	857	822	44.7%	69.5	30.5
Oregon	685	1,680	1,019	661	53.3%	73.0	31.0
Pennsylvania	4,815	11,715	6,900	4,815	38.8%	68.2	27.4

Jurisdiction Summary Statistics: **All Testing Windows**

Jurisdiction	Candidates Total	Sections Total	Sections First-Time	Sections Re-Exam	Percent Pass	Average Score	Average Age
Puerto Rico	874	1,922	1,075	847	25.5%	59.3	28.6
Rhode Island	171	459	261	198	46.6%	69.8	28.2
South Carolina	586	1,552	951	601	51.4%	72.4	28.3
South Dakota	141	344	200	144	44.2%	71.6	28.7
Tennessee	1,538	4,118	2,441	1,677	44.2%	70.1	29.2
Texas	5,515	14,501	8,395	6,106	48.2%	71.9	29.9
Utah	523	1,310	885	425	57.4%	74.8	31.3
Vermont	602	1,737	1,015	722	39.1%	68.3	27.2
Virginia	2,954	7,443	4,427	3,016	48.4%	71.9	29.4
Washington	2,070	5,212	3,331	1,881	47.3%	70.7	30.9
West Virginia	302	752	397	355	37.6%	67.6	29.9
Wisconsin	1,267	3,513	2,246	1,267	50.9%	72.6	28.3
Wyoming	84	224	128	96	42.0%	69.9	29.0

Candidate Performance Summary: **International Exam**

Summary of Examination data for candidates sitting at an international location

Country of Exam	Candidates Total	Sections Total	Sections First-Time	Sections Re-Exam	Percent Pass	Average Score	Average Age
Bahrain	93	164	95	69	31.1%	65.6	29.5
2011 Q-3	39	58	30	28	37.9%	67.9	29.3
2011 Q-4	79	106	65	41	27.4%	64.4	29.6
Japan	898	1,749	824	925	35.1%	66.8	35.7
2011 Q-3	498	754	304	450	34.2%	67.0	35.7
2011 Q-4	681	995	520	475	35.7%	66.7	35.7
Kuwait	66	118	89	29	64.4%	75.4	31.4
2011 Q-3	33	46	32	14	60.9%	74.0	31.8
2011 Q-4	51	72	57	15	66.7%	76.4	31.2
Lebanon	176	333	247	86	52.0%	70.7	27.1
2011 Q-3	81	132	99	33	47.0%	68.7	27.1
2011 Q-4	141	201	148	53	55.2%	72.1	27.1
United Arab Emirates	371	705	453	252	43.3%	68.4	30.4
2011 Q-3	161	236	121	115	40.3%	68.1	31.0
2011 Q-4	307	469	332	137	44.8%	68.6	30.1

Ranking of top 30 Countries: **Number of Candidates**

Country classification based on a candidate's reported home address
International candidates using a U.S. address are not represented in the below figures

Rank	Country (Home)	Candidates	Sections	Percent Pass	Average Score	Average Age
1	Japan	2,336	6,365	34.1%	66.1	34.8
2	Korea, Republic of	1,661	4,843	39.0%	67.2	30.3
3	Canada	723	1,695	43.0%	70.4	34.2
4	China	380	973	49.3%	70.1	30.4
5	India	339	1,000	31.7%	64.6	29.2
6	United Arab Emirates	275	616	36.5%	66.9	32.3
7	Taiwan	231	608	43.6%	68.5	31.3
8	Egypt	217	430	40.5%	69.1	29.0
9	Hong Kong	187	477	39.0%	67.1	30.3
10	Saudi Arabia	151	309	39.8%	66.0	33.1
11	Bahamas	134	337	28.5%	65.8	29.1
12	Lebanon	112	239	54.4%	70.7	26.5
13	Bahrain	111	236	36.9%	66.4	27.9
14	Jordan	103	226	41.2%	68.4	27.2
15	Jamaica	101	219	26.5%	65.7	32.2
16	Kuwait	74	168	53.0%	71.5	32.1
17	Cayman Islands	60	168	41.1%	68.9	30.4
18	Germany	52	140	48.6%	72.4	34.4
19	Bermuda	51	107	36.5%	65.7	29.7
20	Qatar	49	108	50.0%	71.7	31.2
21	Russian Federation	39	92	37.0%	68.3	30.0
22	Macau	27	77	45.5%	69.7	26.0
23	Oman	24	43	25.6%	61.3	29.9
24	Singapore	21	44	34.1%	67.1	36.6
24	United Kingdom	21	38	42.1%	70.2	33.4
26	Australia	19	40	60.0%	72.2	28.4
26	Israel	19	42	45.2%	68.0	33.7
28	Kazakhstan	17	43	39.5%	70.2	35.0
28	Switzerland	17	34	64.7%	77.1	30.2
30	Palestinian Territory	16	52	42.3%	69.7	26.0

The Uniform CPA Examination continued its international presence. In 2011:

7,724 candidates from **95** countries outside the U.S. sat for **20,275** sections of those

43.1% were Women and **25.8%** had earned a Masters Degree

Demographic Trending: **Age and Gender Analysis**

Approximately 83% of candidates provided gender information in 2011

Exam Performance by Age Group: All

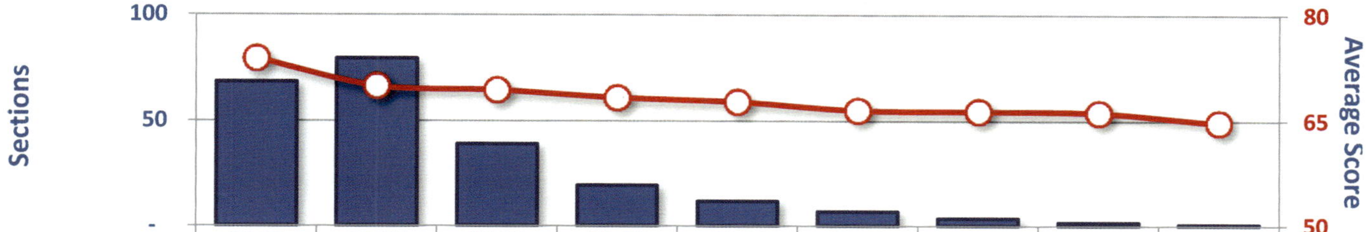

	20-24	25-29	30-34	35-39	40-44	45-49	50-54	55-59	60+
Sections	68,464	79,414	38,989	19,299	11,649	6,766	3,532	1,565	572
Average Score	73.8	69.9	69.4	68.3	67.7	66.5	66.4	66.1	64.7

Exam Performance by Age Group: Women

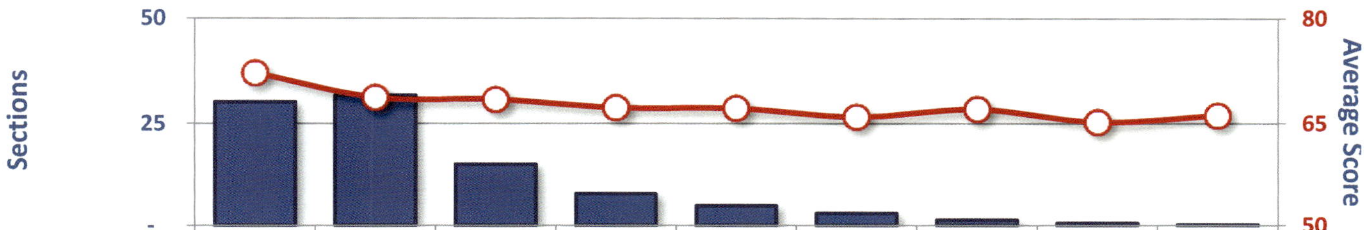

	20-24	25-29	30-34	35-39	40-44	45-49	50-54	55-59	60+
Sections	30,178	31,698	15,245	7,739	4,772	2,940	1,368	537	122
Average Score	72.2	68.8	68.5	67.3	67.2	66.0	67.0	65.2	66.2

Exam Performance by Age Group: Men

	20-24	25-29	30-34	35-39	40-44	45-49	50-54	55-59	60+
Sections	27,934	34,018	16,853	8,006	4,663	2,524	1,382	665	314
Average Score	74.7	70.8	70.0	69.4	68.3	67.0	65.7	66.6	64.9

	Candidates	Sections	Sections per Candidate	Average Score	Avg Pass Rate	Male	Female	Unknown
Advanced	8,509	22,460	2.64	72.9	51.5%	8,361	9,152	4,947
Bachelor's	42,615	111,969	2.63	69.7	41.0%	43,215	52,368	16,386
Other	11,123	29,475	2.65	70.6	43.8%	10,786	10,425	8,264

2011 JURISDICTION PERFORMANCE

This section contains a dashboard view of candidate performance for each jurisdiction. The format and content are similar to the quarterly dashboards that are published at the end of each testing window. Each jurisdiction independently provides data to NASBA, which may, at times, result in incomplete information.

CPA Exam Performance Summary: *2011*

Alabama

Overall Performance

Unique Candidates	**480**
New Candidates	**176**
Total Sections	**1,149**
Passing 4th Section	**132**
Sections/Candidate	**2.39**
Pass Rate	**41.3%**
Average Score	**70.0**

Section Performance

	Sections	Score	% Pass
First-Time	**543**	**69.3**	**39.6%**
Re-Exam	**606**	**70.6**	**42.9%**
AUD	**305**	**71.0**	**42.3%**
BEC	**289**	**69.5**	**35.6%**
FAR	**294**	**68.5**	**41.5%**
REG	**261**	**70.9**	**46.4%**

Jurisdiction Rankings (1 to 53)

Candidates	Sections
38	**39**
40	**34**
Pass Rate	Avg Score

Exam Type by Percent

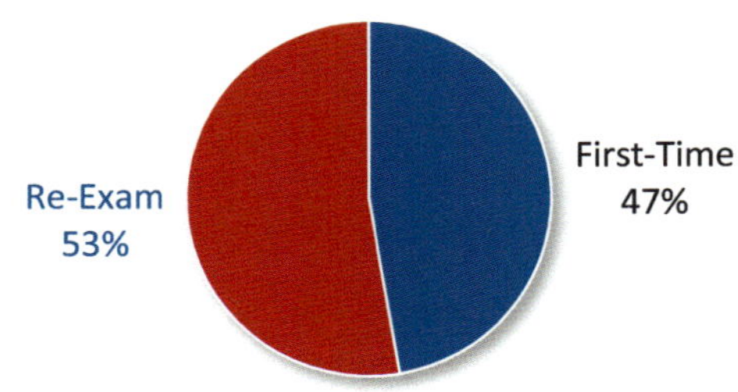

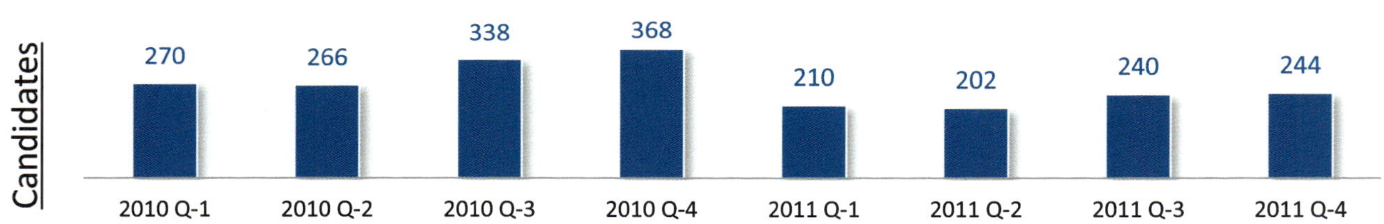

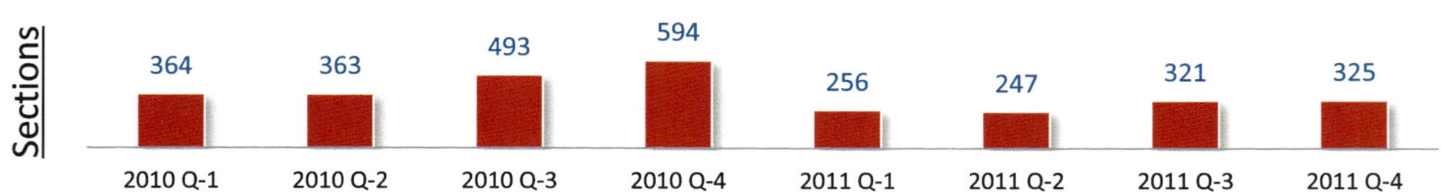

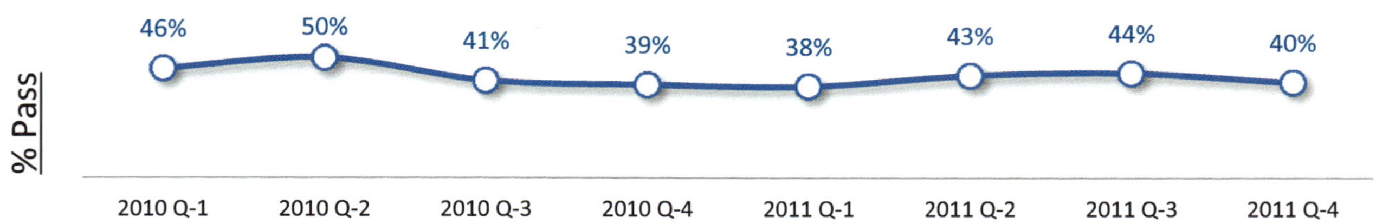

CPA Exam Performance Summary: *2011*

Demographics

Male Candidates	0	0.0%
Female Candidates	0	0.0%
Not Reported	480	100.0%

Average Age	**30.6**
Age Rank	**38**

Residency

Candidate Count	
In-State Address	**444**
Out-of-State Address	**36**
Foreign Address	**0**
% of Candidates	
In-State Address	**92.5%**
Out-of-State Address	**7.5%**
Foreign Address	**0.0%**

Degree Type

Candidate Count	
Bachelor's Degree	**480**
Advanced Degree	**0**
None/Other	**0**
% of Candidates	
Bachelor's Degree	**100.0%**
Advanced Degree	**0.0%**
None/Other	**0.0%**

New Candidates vs Candidates Passing 4th Section

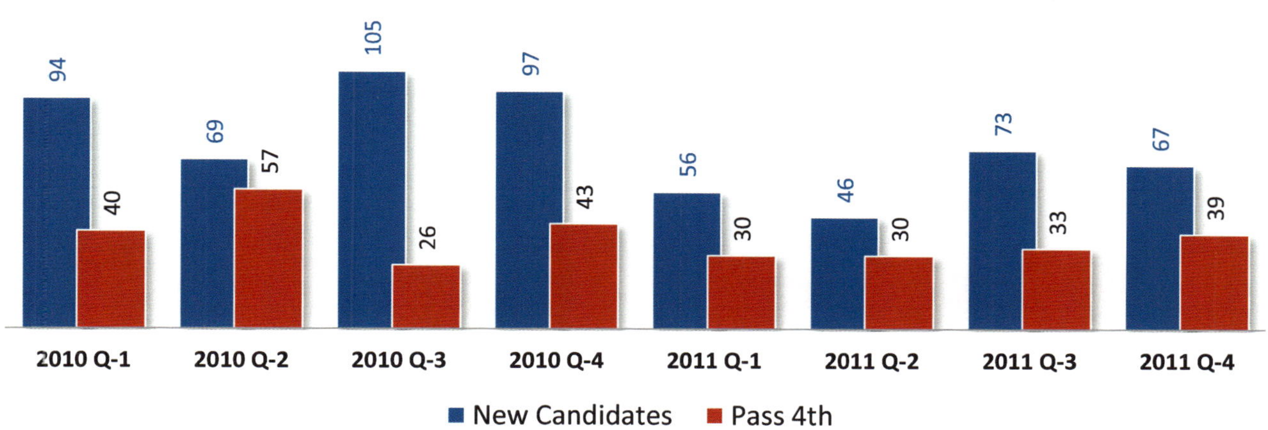

Notes about the Data

1. The data used to develop this report was pulled from NASBA's Gateway System, which houses the Uniform CPA Examination's Application and Performance information for all 55 jurisdictions.
2. The demographic data related to Age, Gender and Degree Type is provided by the individual candidates and may not be 100% accurate.

Alabama

CPA Exam Performance Summary: *2011*

Alaska

Overall Performance

Unique Candidates	524
New Candidates	218
Total Sections	1,392
Passing 4th Section	138
Sections/Candidate	2.66
Pass Rate	43.5%
Average Score	69.5

Section Performance

	Sections	Score	% Pass
First-Time	757	69.2	47.7%
Re-Exam	635	69.8	38.6%
AUD	372	71.4	48.4%
BEC	308	69.3	39.0%
FAR	348	69.0	46.0%
REG	364	68.2	40.1%

Jurisdiction Rankings (1 to 53)

Candidates	Sections
36	35
35	39
Pass Rate	Avg Score

Exam Type by Percent

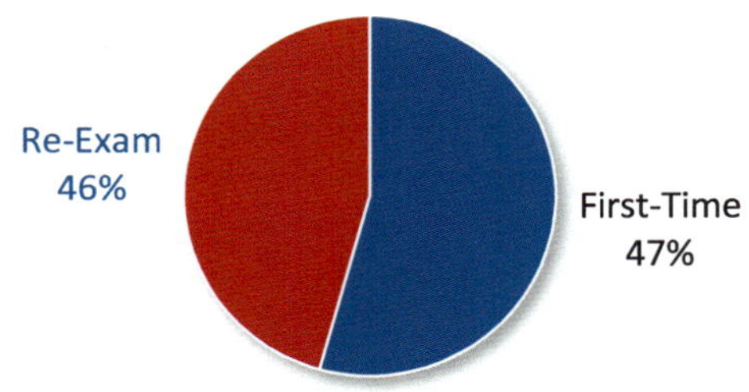

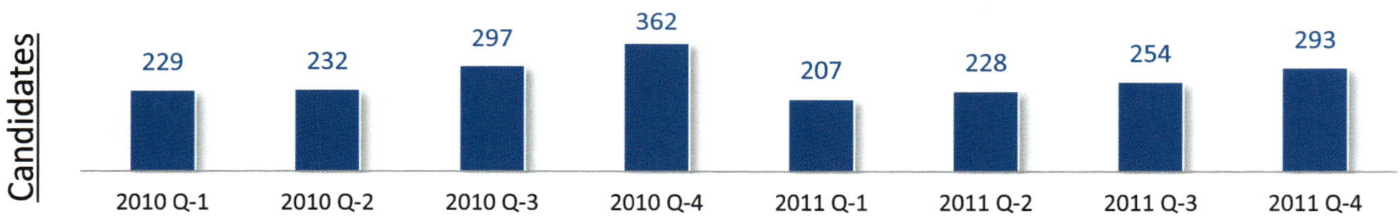

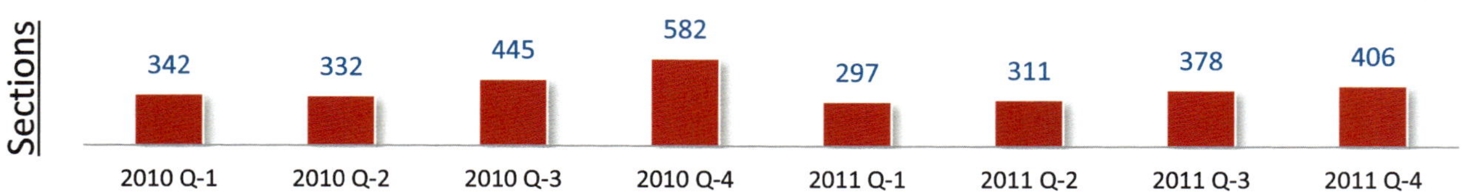

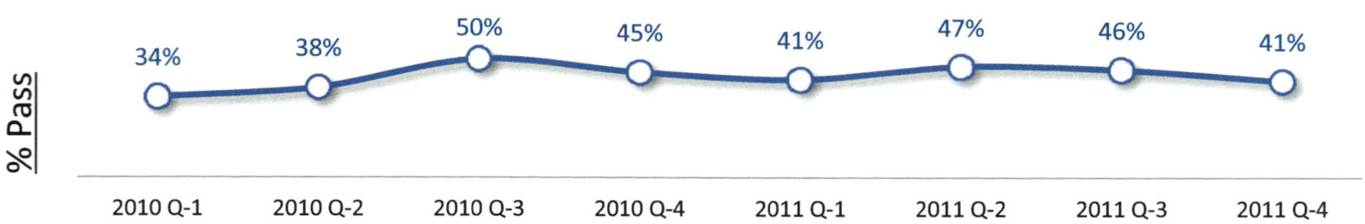

CPA Exam Performance Summary: *2011*

Demographics

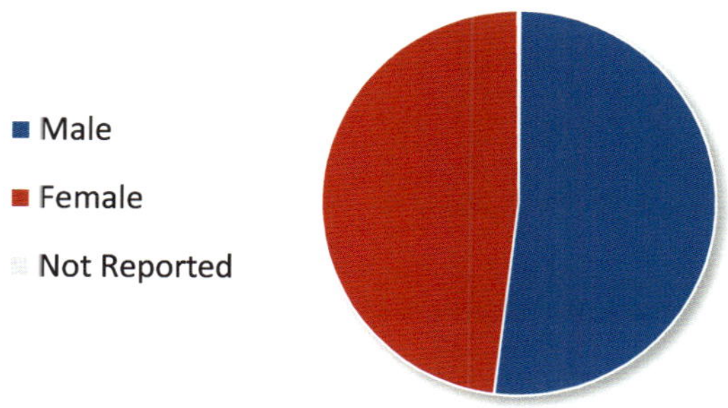

Male Candidates	272	51.9%
Female Candidates	251	47.9%
Not Reported	1	0.2%

Average Age	**30.3**
Age Rank	**35**

Residency

Candidate Count	
In-State Address	**144**
Out-of-State Address	**169**
Foreign Address	**211**
% of Candidates	
In-State Address	**27.5%**
Out-of-State Address	**32.3%**
Foreign Address	**40.3%**

Degree Type

Candidate Count	
Bachelor's Degree	**308**
Advanced Degree	**24**
None/Other	**192**
% of Candidates	
Bachelor's Degree	**58.8%**
Advanced Degree	**4.6%**
None/Other	**36.6%**

New Candidates vs Candidates Passing 4th Section

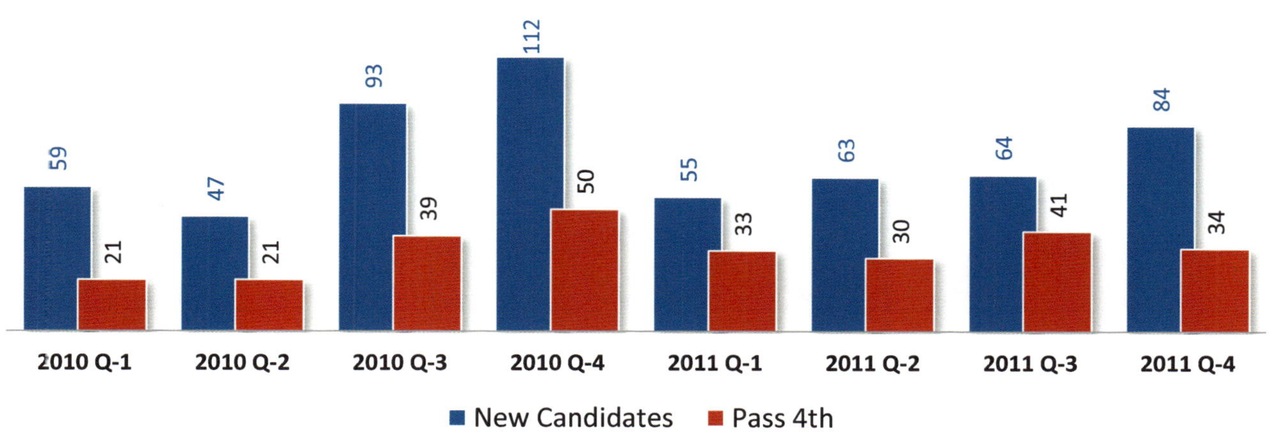

Notes about the Data

1. The data used to develop this report was pulled from NASBA's Gateway System, which houses the Uniform CPA Examination's Application and Performance information for all 55 jurisdictions.
2. The demographic data related to Age, Gender and Degree Type is provided by the individual candidates and may not be 100% accurate.

Alaska

CPA Exam Performance Summary: *2011*

Arizona

Overall Performance

Unique Candidates	**931**
New Candidates	**381**
Total Sections	**2,272**
Passing 4th Section	**274**
Sections/Candidate	**2.44**
Pass Rate	**48.6%**
Average Score	**71.5**

Section Performance

	Sections	Score	% Pass
First-Time	**1,345**	**72.1**	**53.2%**
Re-Exam	**927**	**70.7**	**42.0%**
AUD	**620**	**73.2**	**51.3%**
BEC	**478**	**72.3**	**51.3%**
FAR	**555**	**69.8**	**47.6%**
REG	**619**	**70.8**	**44.8%**

Jurisdiction Rankings (1 to 53)

Candidates	Sections
26	**26**
15	**22**
Pass Rate	Avg Score

Exam Type by Percent

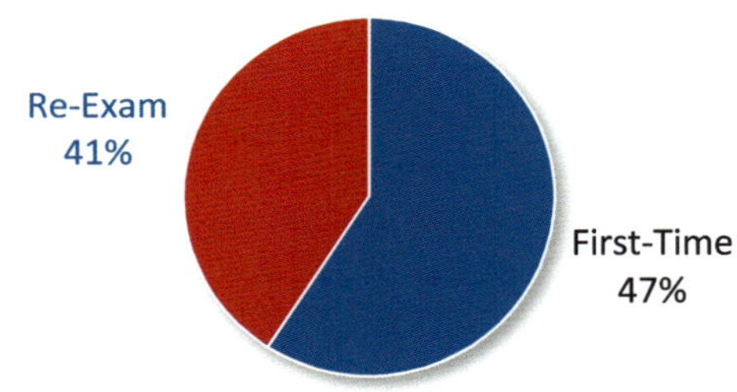

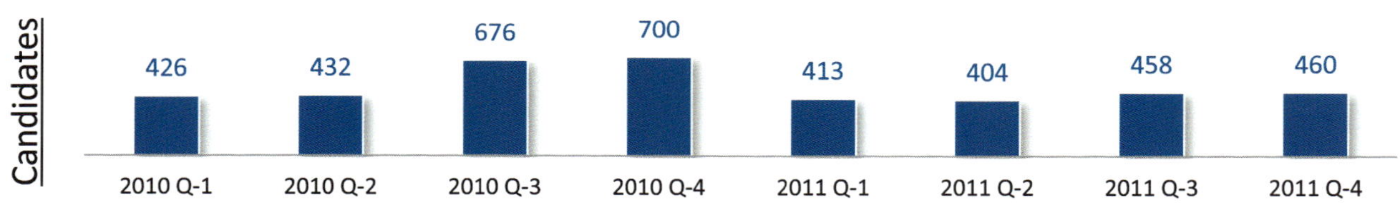

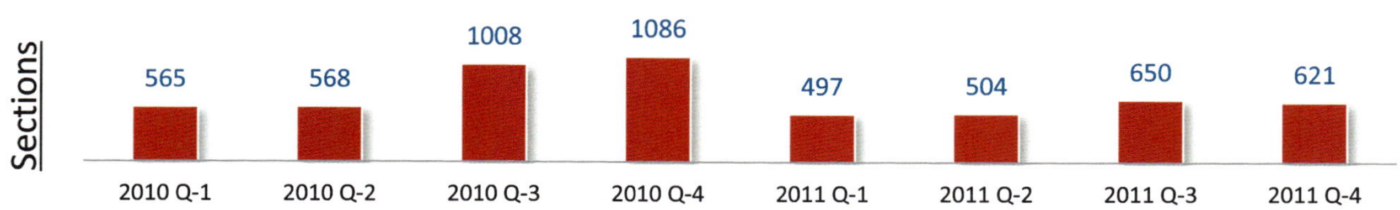

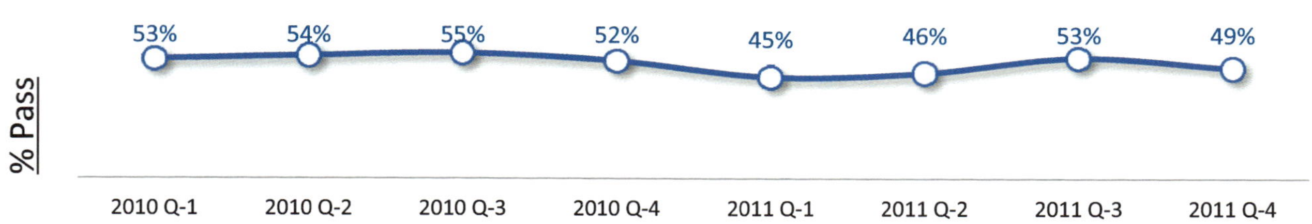

CPA Exam Performance Summary: *2011*

Demographics

Male Candidates	62	6.7%
Female Candidates	78	8.4%
Not Reported	791	85.0%

Average Age **31.5**

Age Rank **48**

Residency

Candidate Count

In-State Address	854
Out-of-State Address	71
Foreign Address	6

% of Candidates

In-State Address	91.7%
Out-of-State Address	7.6%
Foreign Address	0.6%

Degree Type

Candidate Count

Bachelor's Degree	855
Advanced Degree	75
None/Other	1

% of Candidates

Bachelor's Degree	91.8%
Advanced Degree	8.1%
None/Other	0.1%

New Candidates vs Candidates Passing 4th Section

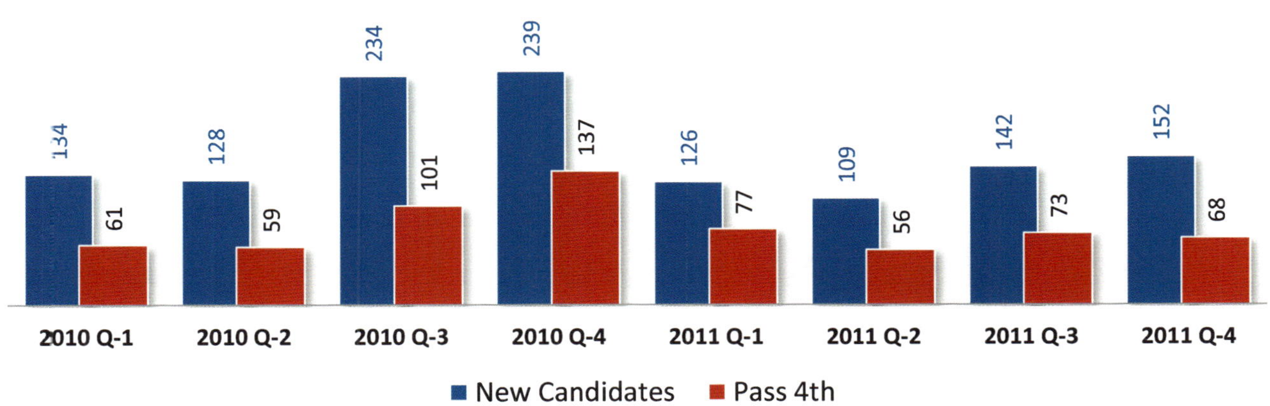

Nctes about the Data

1. The data used to develop this report was pulled from NASBA's Gateway System, which houses the Uniform CPA Examination's Application and Performance information for all 55 jurisdictions.
2. The demographic data related to Age, Gender and Degree Type is provided by the individual candidates and may not be 100% accurate.

Arizona

CPA Exam Performance Summary: *2011*

Arkansas

Overall Performance

Unique Candidates	**409**
New Candidates	**198**
Total Sections	**1,087**
Passing 4th Section	**109**
Sections/Candidate	**2.66**
Pass Rate	**41.9%**
Average Score	**69.5**

Section Performance

	Sections	Score	% Pass
First-Time	**614**	**69.7**	**46.1%**
Re-Exam	**473**	**69.2**	**36.4%**
AUD	**296**	**71.4**	**44.9%**
BEC	**239**	**69.7**	**41.8%**
FAR	**248**	**68.3**	**41.1%**
REG	**304**	**68.5**	**39.5%**

Jurisdiction Rankings (1 to 53)

Candidates	Sections
41	**40**
39	**40**
Pass Rate	Avg Score

Exam Type by Percent

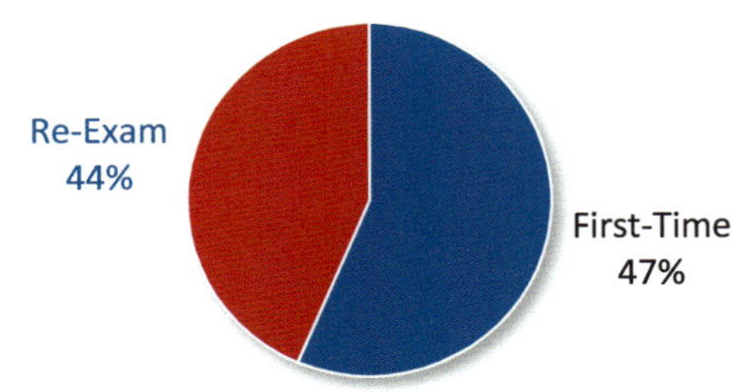

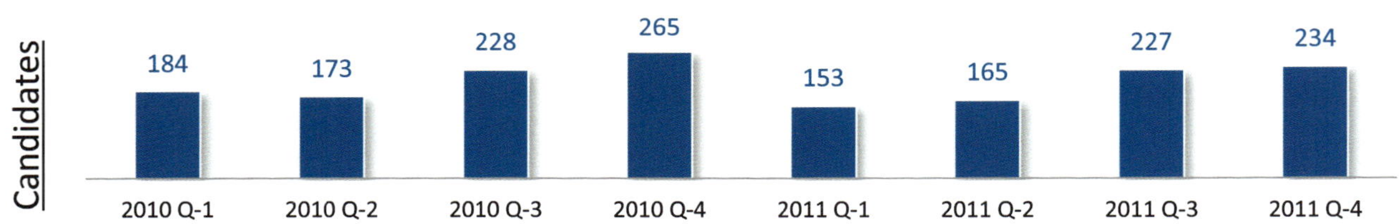

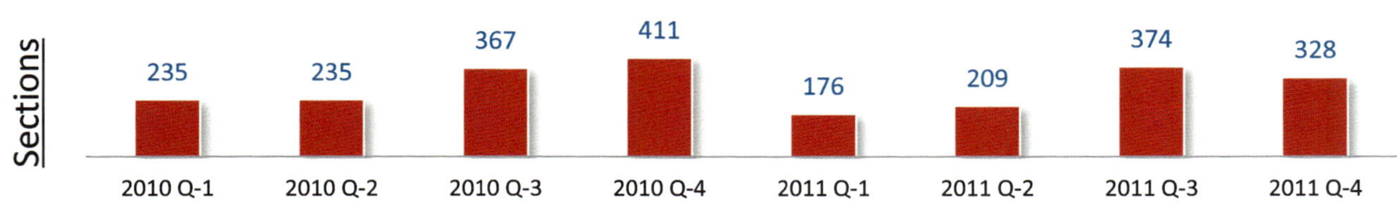

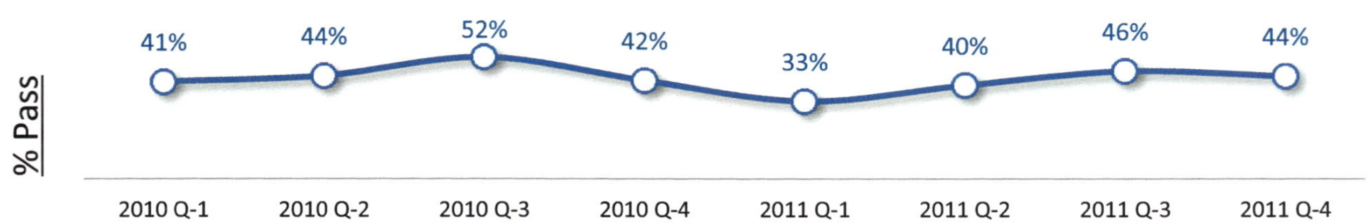

CPA Exam Performance Summary: *2011*

Demographics

Male Candidates	0	0.0%
Female Candidates	1	0.2%
Not Reported	408	99.8%

Average Age	**28.2**
Age Rank	**12**

Residency

Candidate Count	
In-State Address	**385**
Out-of-State Address	**24**
Foreign Address	**0**
% of Candidates	
In-State Address	**94.1%**
Out-of-State Address	**5.9%**
Foreign Address	**0.0%**

Degree Type

Candidate Count	
Bachelor's Degree	**309**
Advanced Degree	**90**
None/Other	**10**
% of Candidates	
Bachelor's Degree	**75.6%**
Advanced Degree	**22.0%**
None/Other	**2.4%**

New Candidates vs Candidates Passing 4th Section

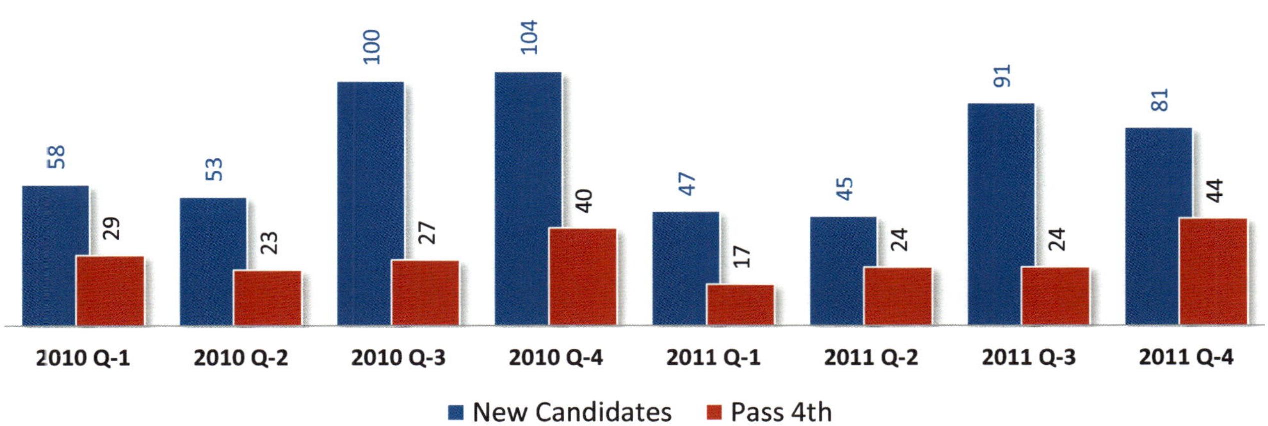

Notes about the Data

1. The data used to develop this report was pulled from NASBA's Gateway System, which houses the Uniform CPA Examination's Application and Performance information for all 55 jurisdictions.
2. The demographic data related to Age, Gender and Degree Type is provided by the individual candidates and may not be 100% accurate.

Arkansas

CPA Exam Performance Summary: *2011*

California

Overall Performance

Unique Candidates	13,344
New Candidates	5,012
Total Sections	32,570
Passing 4th Section	3,251
Sections/Candidate	2.44
Pass Rate	43.8%
Average Score	69.8

Section Performance

	Sections	Score	% Pass
First-Time	18,331	69.6	46.6%
Re-Exam	14,239	70.1	40.1%
AUD	8,977	70.8	44.1%
BEC	6,842	70.5	43.2%
FAR	7,799	68.7	44.7%
REG	8,952	69.3	43.0%

Jurisdiction Rankings (1 to 53)

Candidates	Sections
1	1
34	37
Pass Rate	Avg Score

Exam Type by Percent

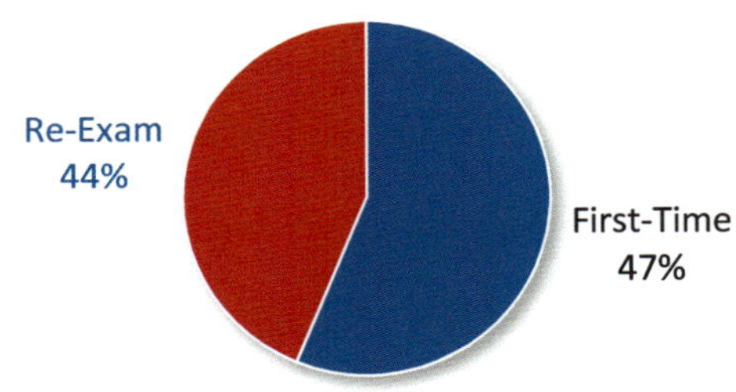

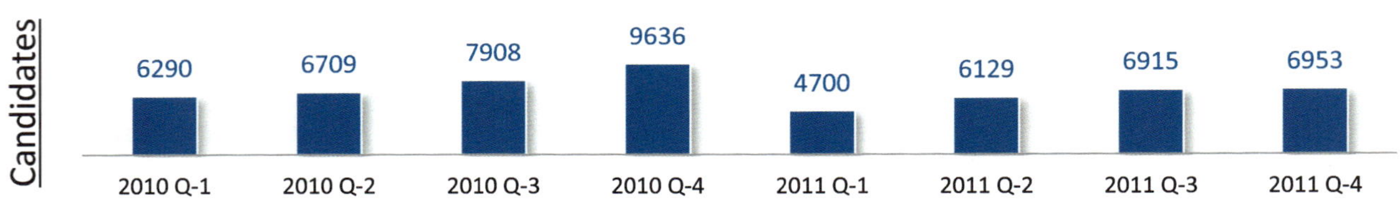

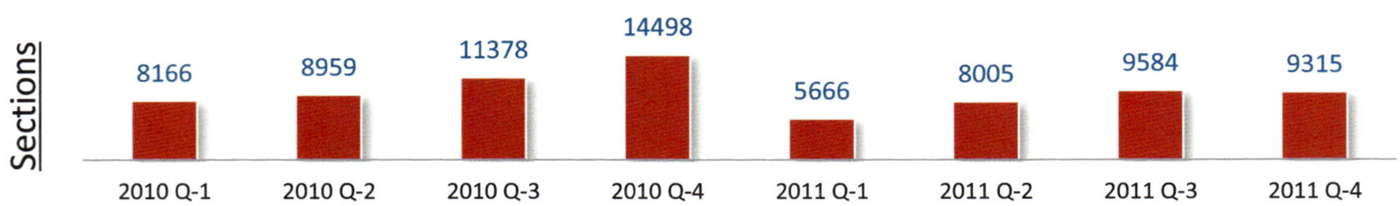

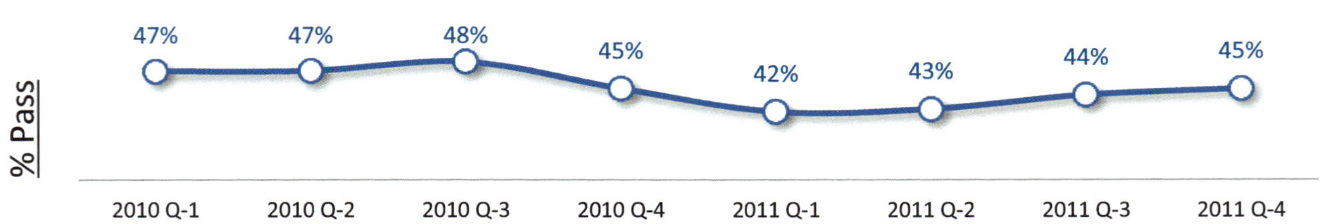

CPA Exam Performance Summary: *2011*

Demographics

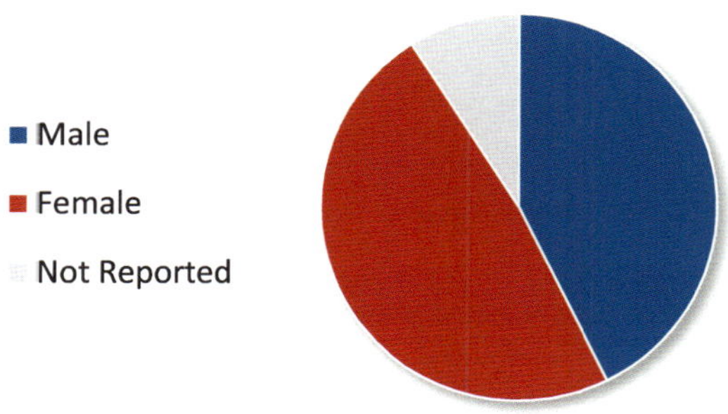

Male Candidates	5,682	42.6%
Female Candidates	6,445	48.3%
Not Reported	1,217	9.1%

Average Age **30.5**

Age Rank **36**

Residency

Candidate Count	
In-State Address	**11,219**
Out-of-State Address	**1,216**
Foreign Address	**909**
% of Candidates	
In-State Address	**84.1%**
Out-of-State Address	**9.1%**
Foreign Address	**6.8%**

Degree Type

Candidate Count	
Bachelor's Degree	**10,301**
Advanced Degree	**2,306**
None/Other	**737**
% of Candidates	
Bachelor's Degree	**77.2%**
Advanced Degree	**17.3%**
None/Other	**5.5%**

New Candidates vs Candidates Passing 4th Section

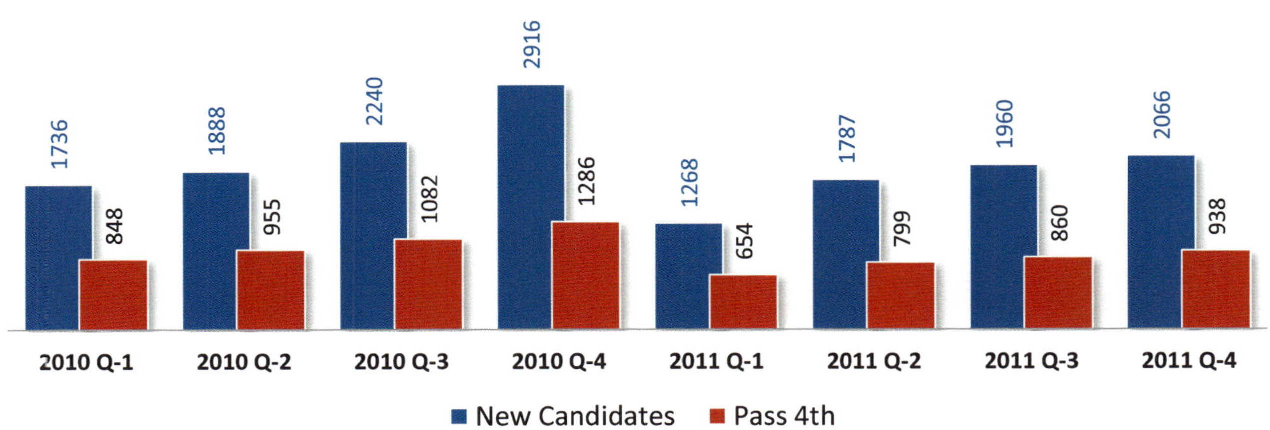

Notes about the Data

1. The data used to develop this report was pulled from NASBA's Gateway System, which houses the Uniform CPA Examination's Application and Performance information for all 55 jurisdictions.
2. The demographic data related to Age, Gender and Degree Type is provided by the individual candidates and may not be 100% accurate.

California

CPA Exam Performance Summary: *2011*

Colorado

Overall Performance

Unique Candidates	**2,289**
New Candidates	**983**
Total Sections	**5,803**
Passing 4th Section	**683**
Sections/Candidate	**2.54**
Pass Rate	**47.6%**
Average Score	**71.7**

Section Performance

	Sections	Score	% Pass
First-Time	**3,250**	**72.0**	**51.8%**
Re-Exam	**2,553**	**71.3**	**42.2%**
AUD	**1,543**	**72.3**	**46.3%**
BEC	**1,226**	**72.8**	**52.0%**
FAR	**1,415**	**70.7**	**47.7%**
REG	**1,619**	**71.1**	**45.4%**

Jurisdiction Rankings (1 to 53)

Candidates	Sections
14	**14**
20	**16**
Pass Rate	Avg Score

Exam Type by Percent

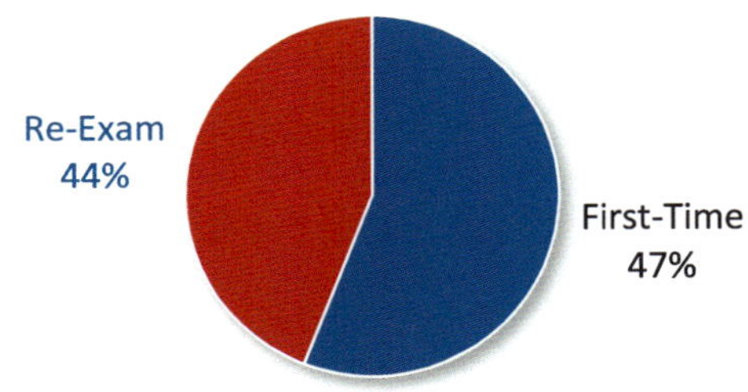

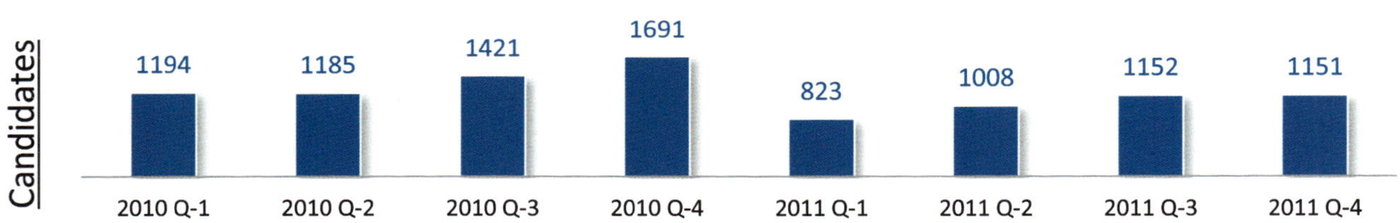

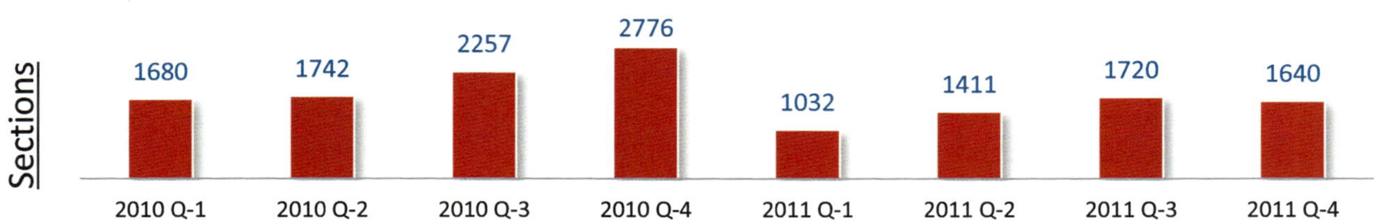

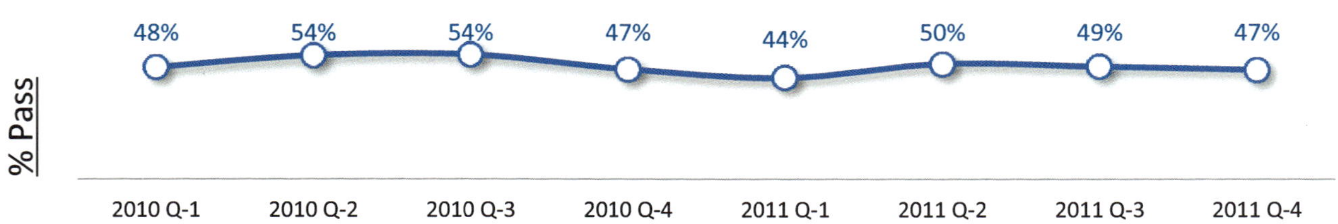

CPA Exam Performance Summary: *2011*

Demographics

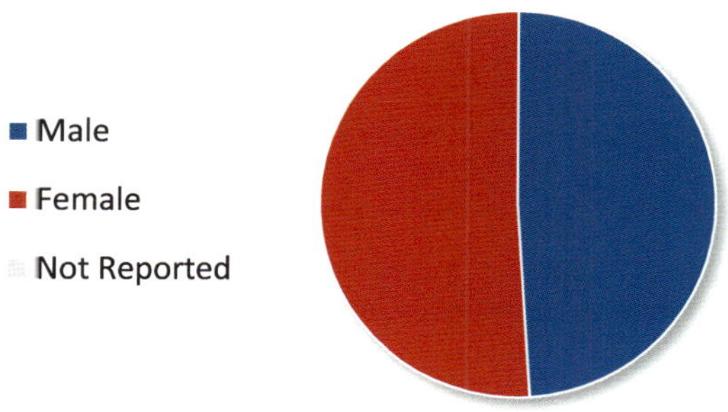

Male Candidates	1,121	49.0%
Female Candidates	1,168	51.0%
Not Reported	0	0.0%

Average Age	**30.9**
Age Rank	**42**

Residency

Candidate Count	
In-State Address	**1,315**
Out-of-State Address	**554**
Foreign Address	**420**

% of Candidates	
In-State Address	**57.4%**
Out-of-State Address	**24.2%**
Foreign Address	**18.3%**

Degree Type

Candidate Count	
Bachelor's Degree	**1,796**
Advanced Degree	**212**
None/Other	**281**

% of Candidates	
Bachelor's Degree	**78.5%**
Advanced Degree	**9.3%**
None/Other	**12.3%**

New Candidates vs Candidates Passing 4th Section

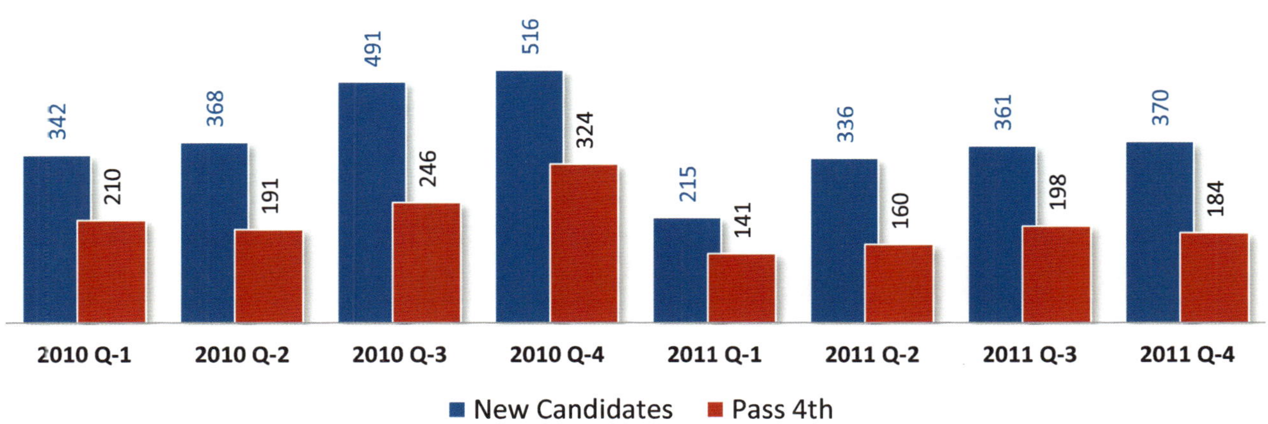

Notes about the Data

1. The data used to develop this report was pulled from NASBA's Gateway System, which houses the Uniform CPA Examination's Application and Performance information for all 55 jurisdictions.
2. The demographic data related to Age, Gender and Degree Type is provided by the individual candidates and may not be 100% accurate.

Colorado

CPA Exam Performance Summary: *2011*

Connecticut

Overall Performance

Unique Candidates	1,054
New Candidates	496
Total Sections	2,545
Passing 4th Section	249
Sections/Candidate	2.41
Pass Rate	45.0%
Average Score	70.5

Section Performance

	Sections	Score	% Pass
First-Time	1,497	70.6	48.0%
Re-Exam	1,048	70.4	40.8%
AUD	661	72.5	46.8%
BEC	543	72.1	51.0%
FAR	646	68.2	42.4%
REG	695	69.4	41.2%

Jurisdiction Rankings (1 to 53)

Candidates	Sections
25	25
27	29
Pass Rate	Avg Score

Exam Type by Percent

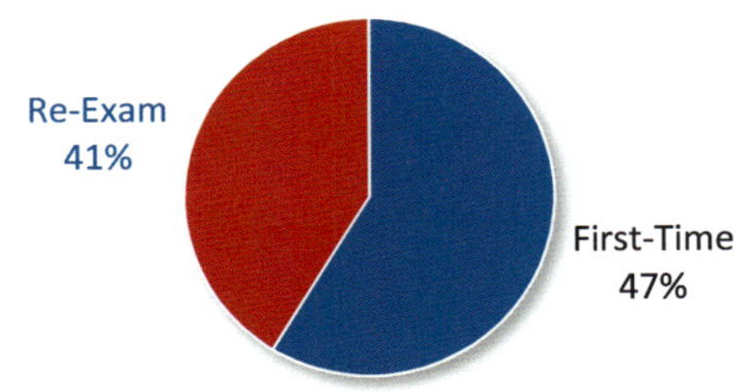

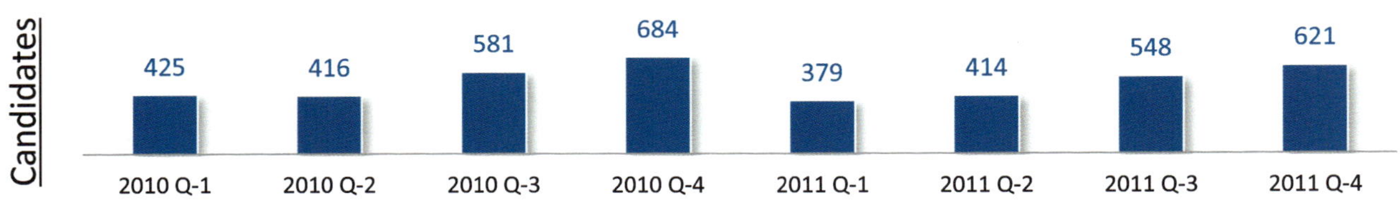

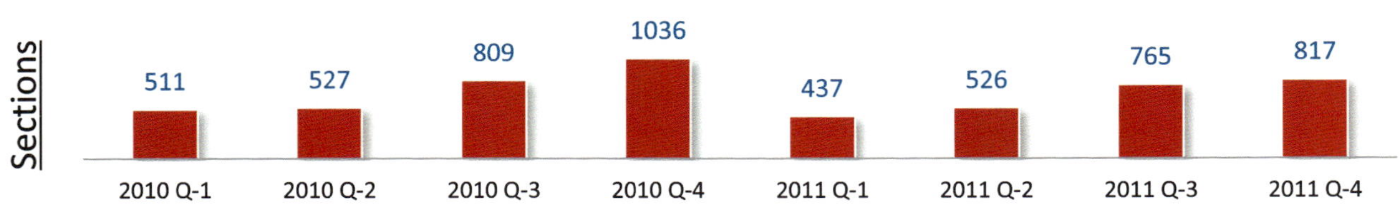

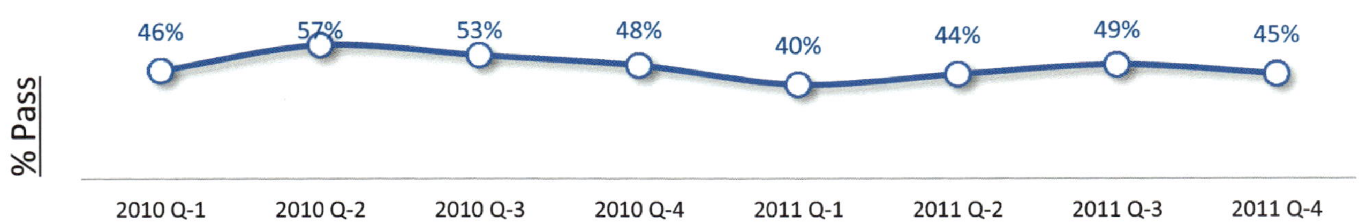

CPA Exam Performance Summary: *2011*

Demographics

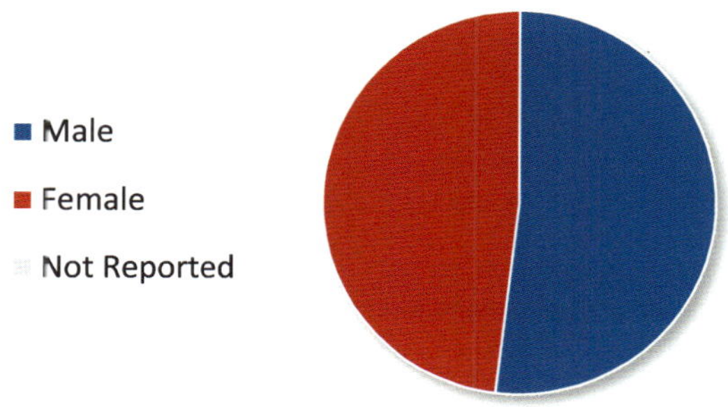

Male Candidates	547	51.9%
Female Candidates	507	48.1%
Not Reported	0	0.0%

Average Age	**27.7**
Age Rank	**7**

Residency

Candidate Count	
In-State Address	**846**
Out-of-State Address	**200**
Foreign Address	**8**

% of Candidates	
In-State Address	**80.3%**
Out-of-State Address	**19.0%**
Foreign Address	**0.8%**

Degree Type

Candidate Count	
Bachelor's Degree	**894**
Advanced Degree	**90**
None/Other	**70**

% of Candidates	
Bachelor's Degree	**84.8%**
Advanced Degree	**8.5%**
None/Other	**6.6%**

New Candidates vs Candidates Passing 4th Section

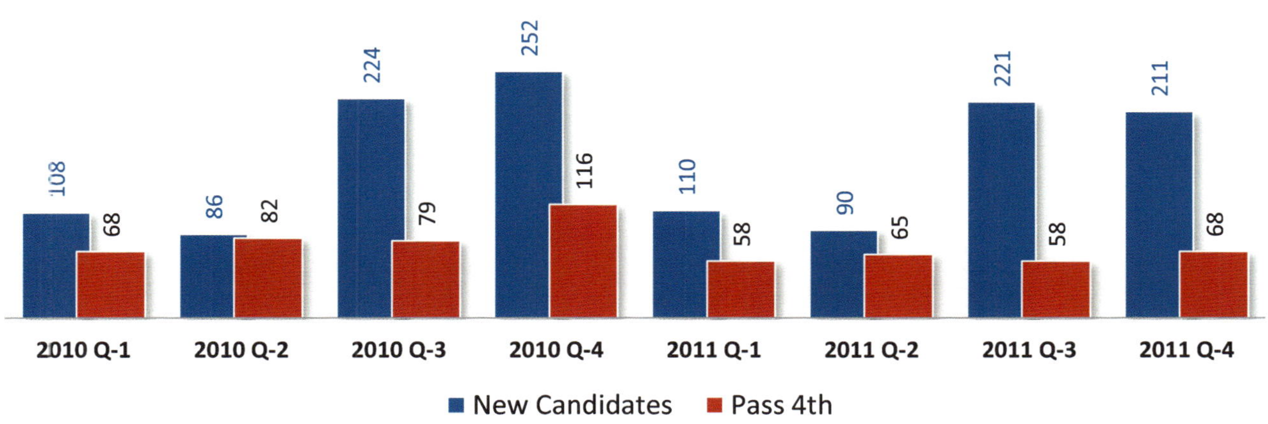

Notes about the Data

1. The data used to develop this report was pulled from NASBA's Gateway System, which houses the Uniform CPA Examination's Application and Performance information for all 55 jurisdictions.
2. The demographic data related to Age, Gender and Degree Type is provided by the individual candidates and may not be 100% accurate.

Connecticut

CPA Exam Performance Summary: *2011*

Delaware

Overall Performance

Unique Candidates	1,297
New Candidates	442
Total Sections	3,253
Passing 4th Section	282
Sections/Candidate	2.51
Pass Rate	35.2%
Average Score	66.9

Section Performance

	Sections	Score	% Pass
First-Time	1,463	65.6	36.3%
Re-Exam	1,790	67.9	34.3%
AUD	910	68.7	38.2%
BEC	711	65.1	27.9%
FAR	801	66.3	37.6%
REG	831	67.0	35.7%

Jurisdiction Rankings (1 to 53)

Candidates	Sections
21	24
49	51
Pass Rate	Avg Score

Exam Type by Percent

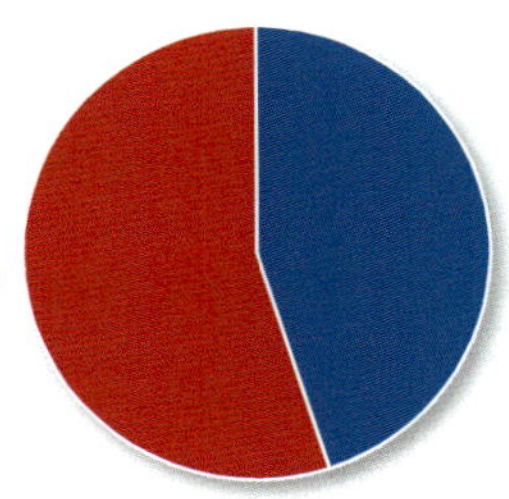

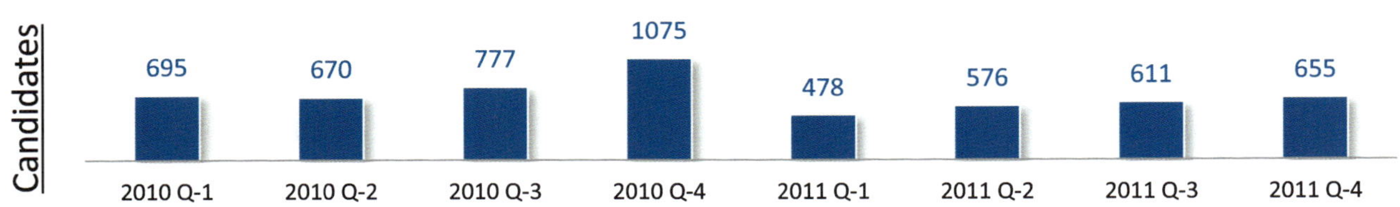

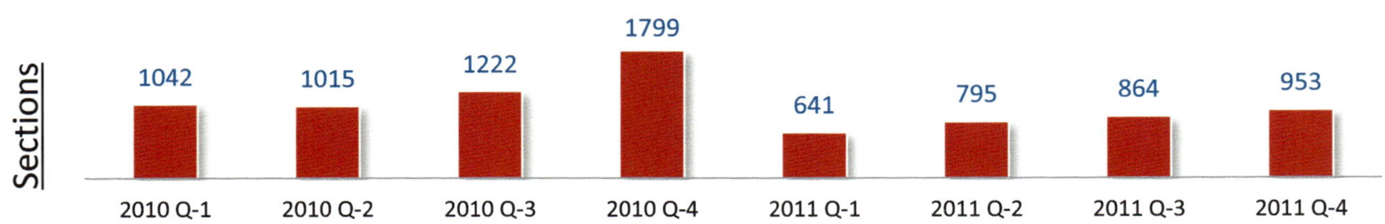

CPA Exam Performance Summary: *2011*

Demographics

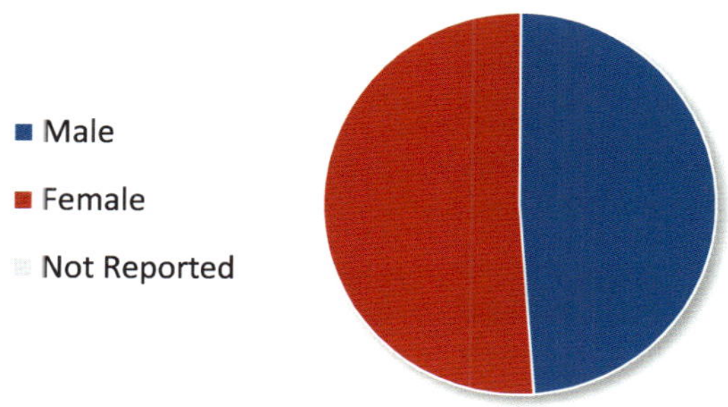

Male Candidates	632	48.7%
Female Candidates	665	51.3%
Not Reported	0	0.0%

Average Age	**34.0**
Age Rank	**52**

Residency

Candidate Count	
In-State Address	**152**
Out-of-State Address	**599**
Foreign Address	**546**
% of Candidates	
In-State Address	**11.7%**
Out-of-State Address	**46.2%**
Foreign Address	**42.1%**

Degree Type

Candidate Count	
Bachelor's Degree	**717**
Advanced Degree	**104**
None/Other	**476**
% of Candidates	
Bachelor's Degree	**55.3%**
Advanced Degree	**8.0%**
None/Other	**36.7%**

New Candidates vs Candidates Passing 4th Section

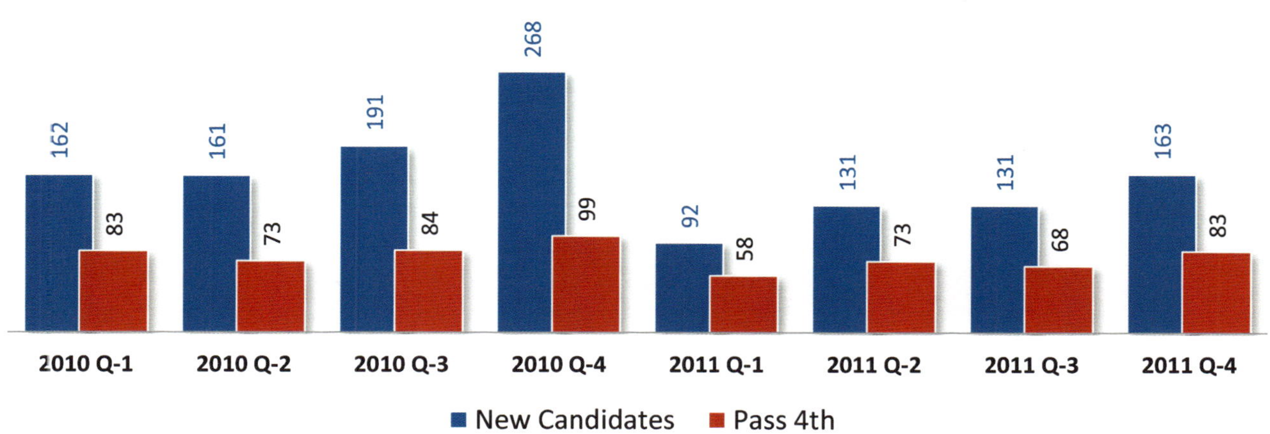

Notes about the Data

1. The data used to develop this report was pulled from NASBA's Gateway System, which houses the Uniform CPA Examination's Application and Performance information for all 55 jurisdictions.
2. The demographic data related to Age, Gender and Degree Type is provided by the individual candidates and may not be 100% accurate.

Delaware

CPA Exam Performance Summary: *2011*

District of Columbia

Overall Performance

Unique Candidates	**155**
New Candidates	**42**
Total Sections	**377**
Passing 4th Section	**48**
Sections/Candidate	**2.43**
Pass Rate	**44.0%**
Average Score	**69.3**

Section Performance

	Sections	Score	% Pass
First-Time	**223**	**69.0**	**45.7%**
Re-Exam	**154**	**69.9**	**41.6%**
AUD	**93**	**71.4**	**44.1%**
BEC	**77**	**70.3**	**49.4%**
FAR	**109**	**66.9**	**40.4%**
REG	**98**	**69.4**	**43.9%**

Jurisdiction Rankings (1 to 53)

Candidates	Sections
51	**50**
33	**41**
Pass Rate	Avg Score

Exam Type by Percent

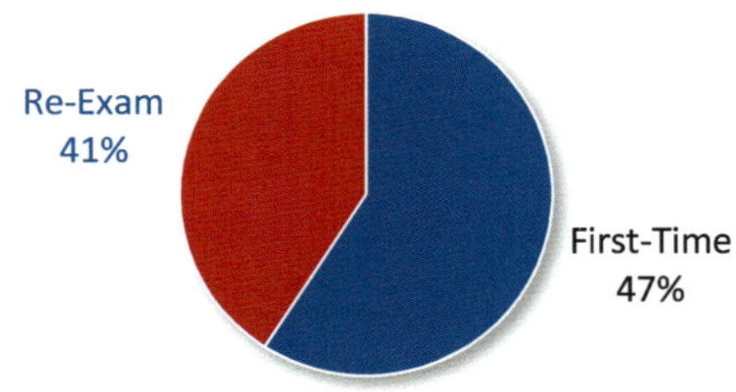

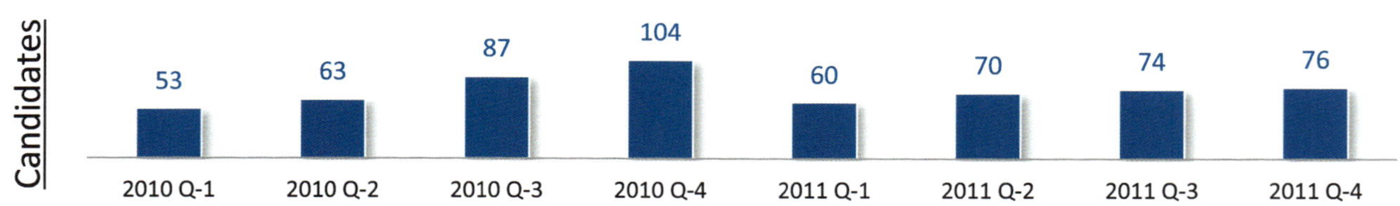

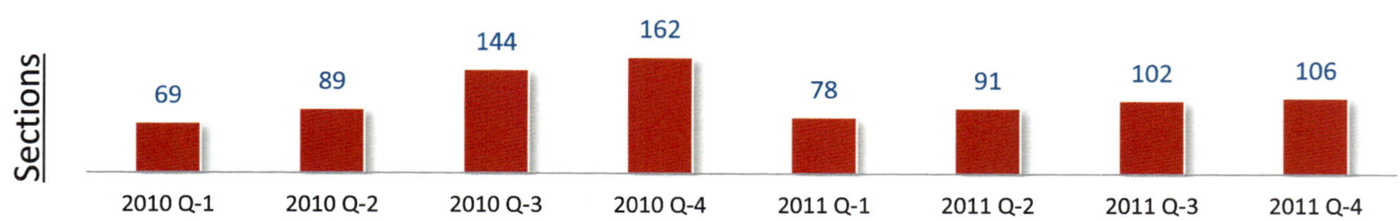

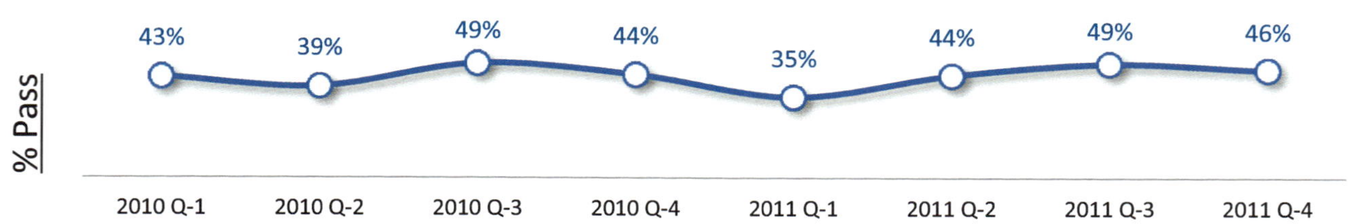

CPA Exam Performance Summary: *2011*

Demographics

Male Candidates	0	0.0%
Female Candidates	0	0.0%
Not Reported	155	100.0%

Average Age **32.6**

Age Rank **50**

Residency

Candidate Count	
In-State Address	51
Out-of-State Address	103
Foreign Address	1
% of Candidates	
In-State Address	32.9%
Out-of-State Address	66.5%
Foreign Address	0.6%

Degree Type

Candidate Count	
Bachelor's Degree	107
Advanced Degree	42
None/Other	6
% of Candidates	
Bachelor's Degree	69.0%
Advanced Degree	27.1%
None/Other	3.9%

New Candidates vs Candidates Passing 4th Section

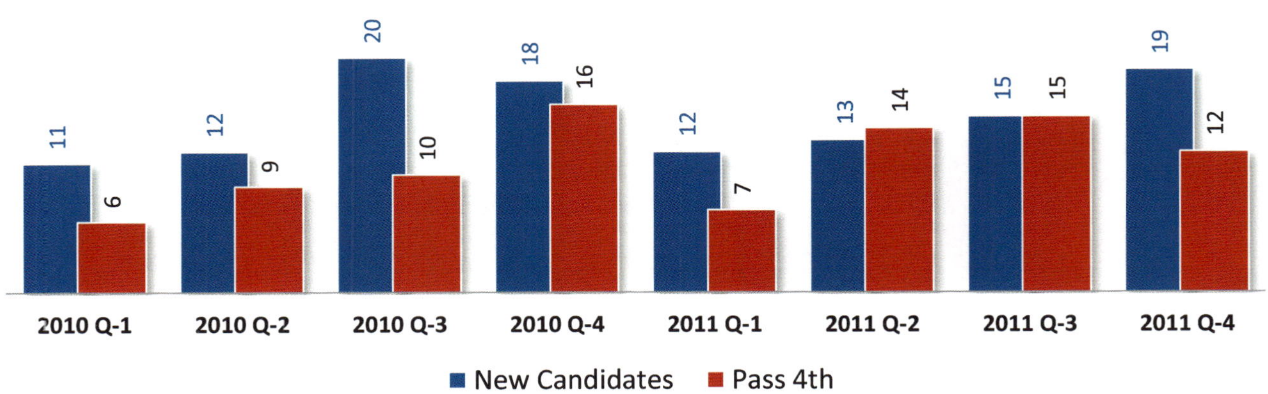

Notes about the Data

1. The data used to develop this report was pulled from NASBA's Gateway System, which houses the Uniform CPA Examination's Application and Performance information for all 55 jurisdictions.
2. The demographic data related to Age, Gender and Degree Type is provided by the individual candidates and may not be 100% accurate.

District of Columbia

CPA Exam Performance Summary: *2011*

Florida

Overall Performance

Unique Candidates	**2,588**
New Candidates	**1,111**
Total Sections	**6,105**
Passing 4th Section	**712**
Sections/Candidate	**2.36**
Pass Rate	**49.4%**
Average Score	**72.4**

Section Performance

	Sections	Score	% Pass
First-Time	**3,760**	**72.9**	**53.5%**
Re-Exam	**2,345**	**71.4**	**42.7%**
AUD	**1,669**	**73.6**	**49.8%**
BEC	**1,309**	**72.1**	**49.4%**
FAR	**1,471**	**70.8**	**46.7%**
REG	**1,656**	**72.7**	**51.2%**

Jurisdiction Rankings (1 to 53)

Candidates	Sections
11	**13**
13	**12**
Pass Rate	Avg Score

Exam Type by Percent

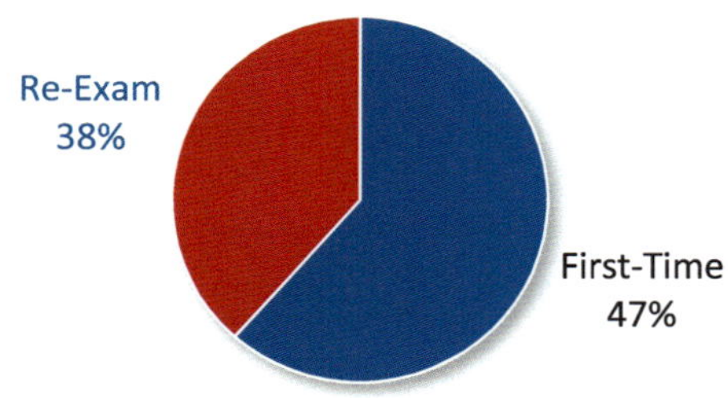

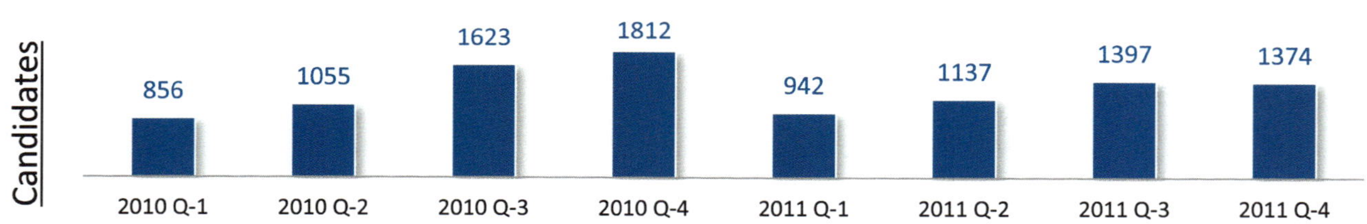

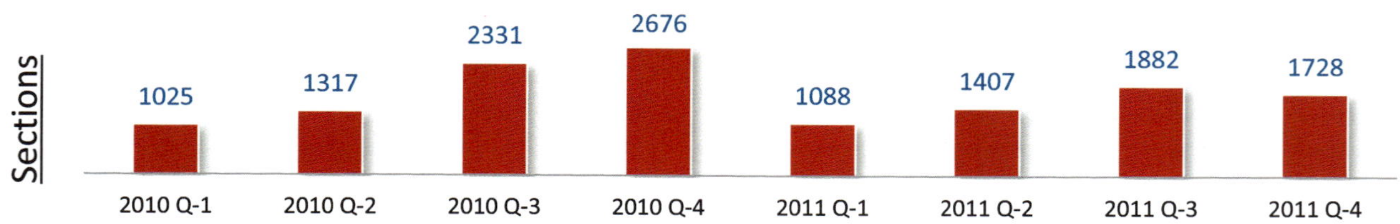

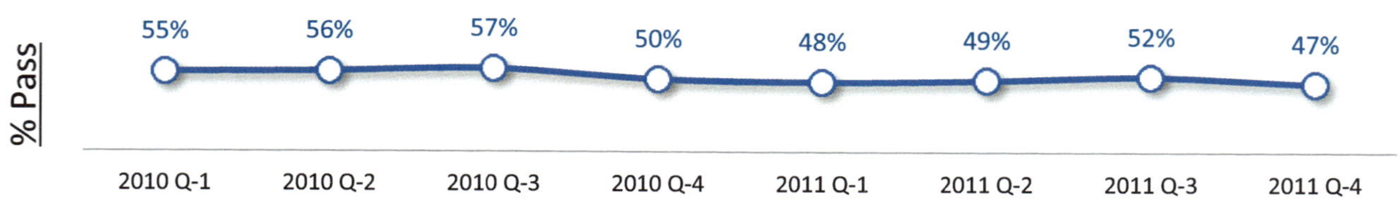

CPA Exam Performance Summary: *2011*

Demographics

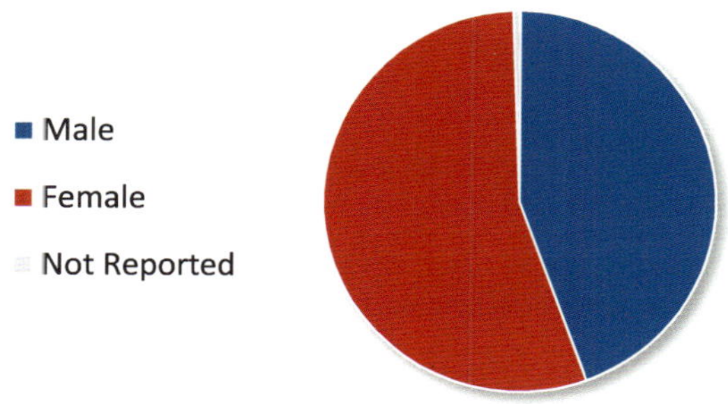

Male Candidates	1,149	44.4%
Female Candidates	1,424	55.0%
Not Reported	15	0.6%

Average Age	**31.2**
Age Rank	**46**

Residency

Candidate Count	
In-State Address	**2,493**
Out-of-State Address	**88**
Foreign Address	**7**
% of Candidates	
In-State Address	**96.3%**
Out-of-State Address	**3.4%**
Foreign Address	**0.3%**

Degree Type

Candidate Count	
Bachelor's Degree	**0**
Advanced Degree	**0**
None/Other	**2,588**
% of Candidates	
Bachelor's Degree	**0.0%**
Advanced Degree	**0.0%**
None/Other	**100.0%**

New Candidates vs Candidates Passing 4th Section

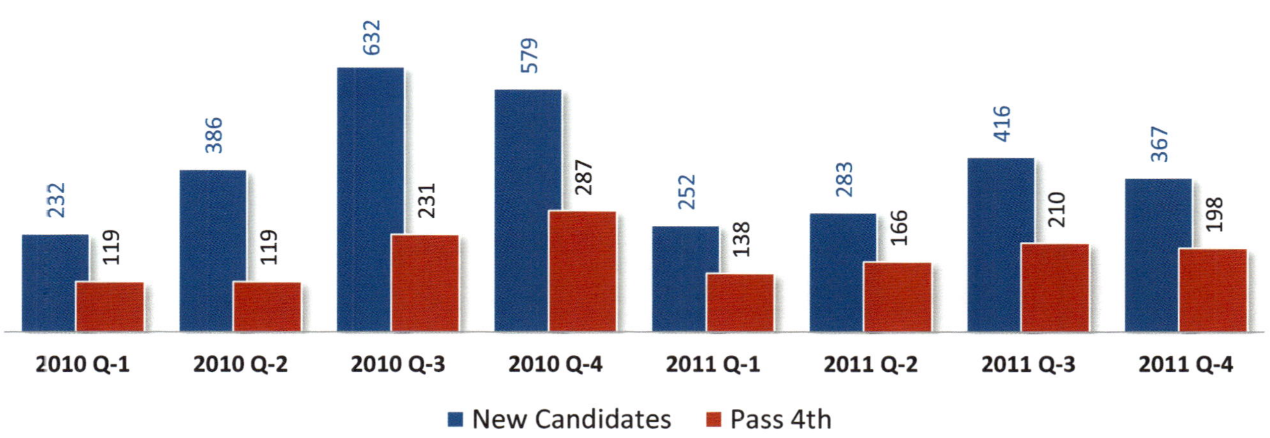

Notes about the Data

1. The data used to develop this report was pulled from NASBA's Gateway System, which houses the Uniform CPA Examination's Application and Performance information for all 55 jurisdictions.
2. The demographic data related to Age, Gender and Degree Type is provided by the individual candidates and may not be 100% accurate.

Florida

CPA Exam Performance Summary: *2011*

Georgia

Overall Performance

Unique Candidates	3,101
New Candidates	1,451
Total Sections	7,927
Passing 4th Section	861
Sections/Candidate	2.56
Pass Rate	48.3%
Average Score	71.6

Section Performance

	Sections	Score	% Pass
First-Time	4,752	72.0	53.5%
Re-Exam	3,175	70.9	40.5%
AUD	2,164	73.0	48.8%
BEC	1,786	72.0	49.5%
FAR	1,818	70.1	48.2%
REG	2,159	71.1	46.7%

Jurisdiction Rankings (1 to 53)

Candidates	Sections
6	6
17	20
Pass Rate	Avg Score

Exam Type by Percent

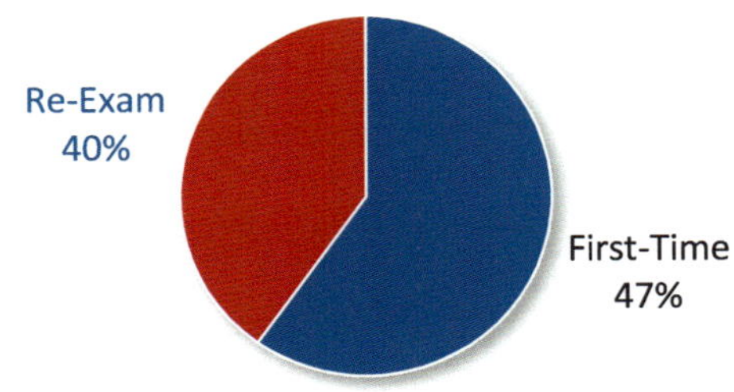

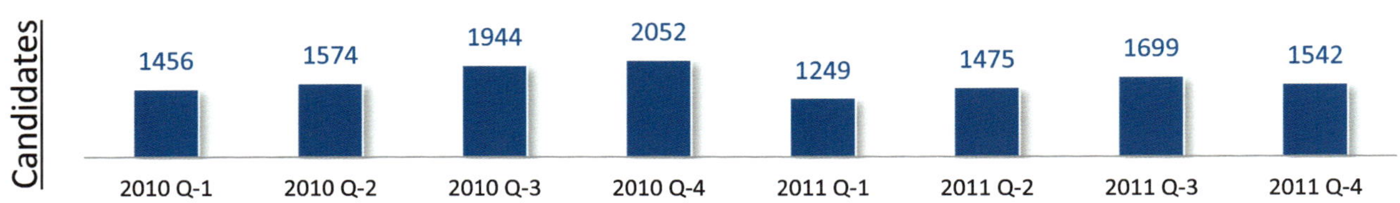

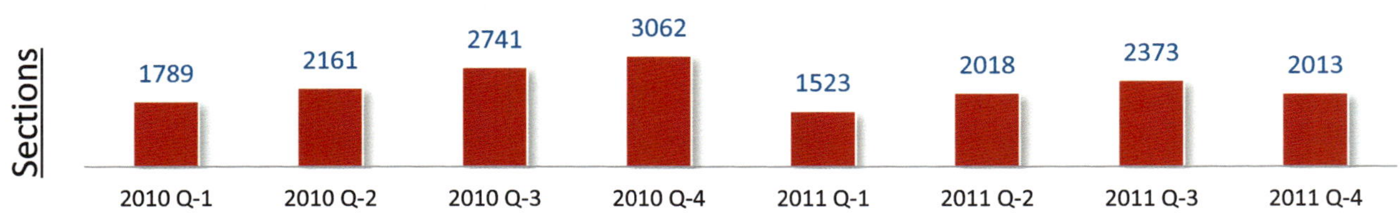

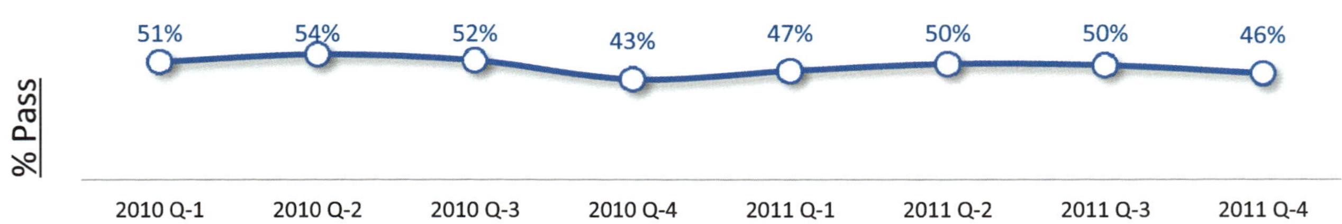

CPA Exam Performance Summary: *2011*

Demographics

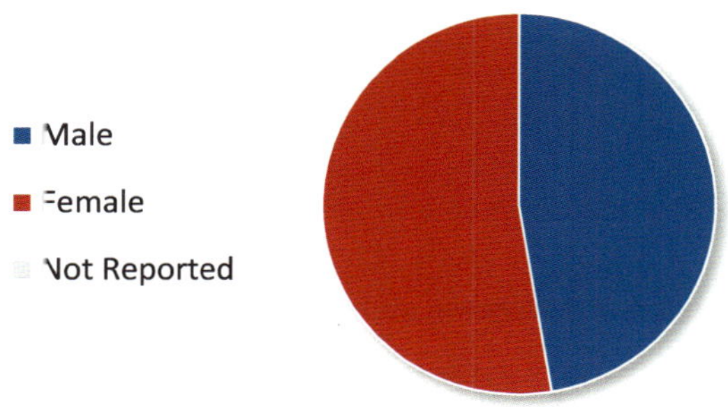

Male Candidates	1,467	47.3%
Female Candidates	1,634	52.7%
Not Reported	0	0.0%

Average Age	**29.6**
Age Rank	**30**

Residency

Candidate Count	
In-State Address	**2,171**
Out-of-State Address	**868**
Foreign Address	**62**
% of Candidates	
In-State Address	**70.0%**
Out-of-State Address	**28.0%**
Foreign Address	**2.0%**

Degree Type

Candidate Count	
Bachelor's Degree	**2,546**
Advanced Degree	**410**
None/Other	**145**
% of Candidates	
Bachelor's Degree	**82.1%**
Advanced Degree	**13.2%**
None/Other	**4.7%**

New Candidates vs Candidates Passing 4th Section

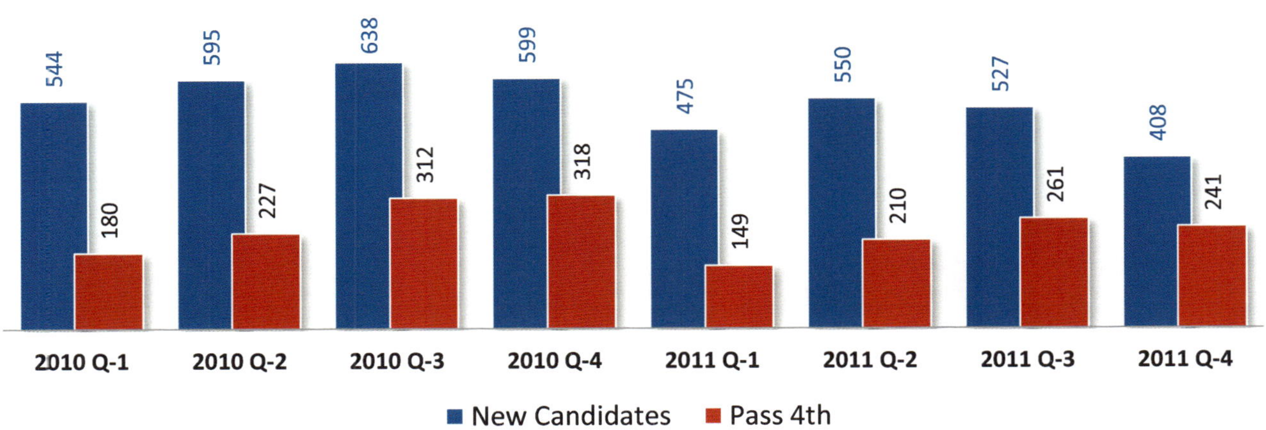

Notes about the Data

1. The data used to develop this report was pulled from NASBA's Gateway System, which houses the Uniform CPA Examination's Application and Performance information for all 55 jurisdictions.
2. The demographic data related to Age, Gender and Degree Type is provided by the individual candidates and may not be 100% accurate.

Georgia

CPA Exam Performance Summary: *2011*

Guam

Overall Performance

Unique Candidates	**581**
New Candidates	**161**
Total Sections	**1,538**
Passing 4th Section	**129**
Sections/Candidate	**2.65**
Pass Rate	**35.0%**
Average Score	**66.8**

Section Performance

	Sections	Score	% Pass
First-Time	**712**	**65.8**	**36.1%**
Re-Exam	**826**	**67.6**	**34.0%**
AUD	**432**	**67.9**	**37.3%**
BEC	**317**	**65.2**	**25.9%**
FAR	**368**	**68.8**	**48.6%**
REG	**421**	**65.1**	**27.6%**

Jurisdiction Rankings (1 to 53)

Candidates	Sections
35	**34**
50	**52**
Pass Rate	Avg Score

Exam Type by Percent

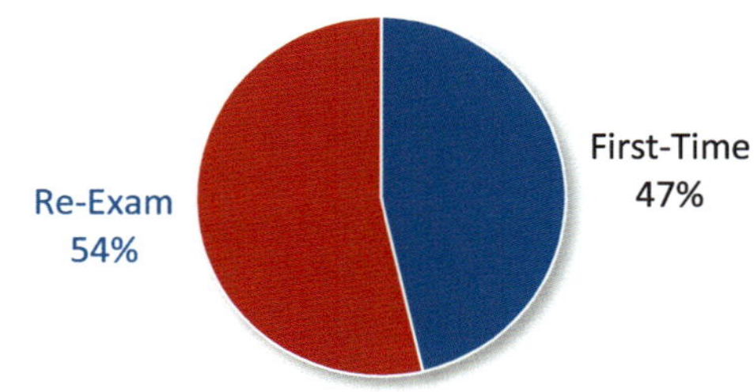

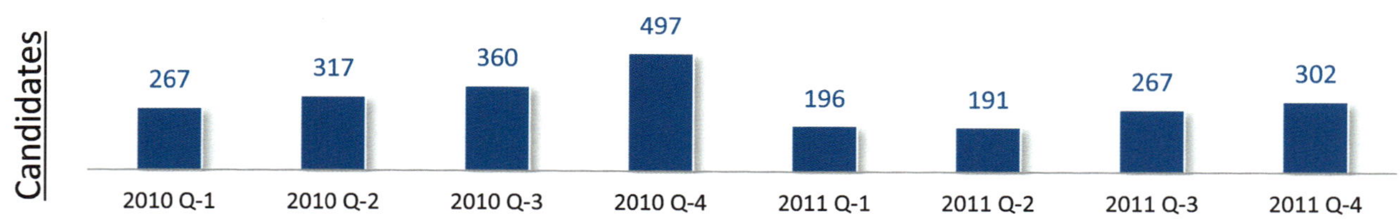

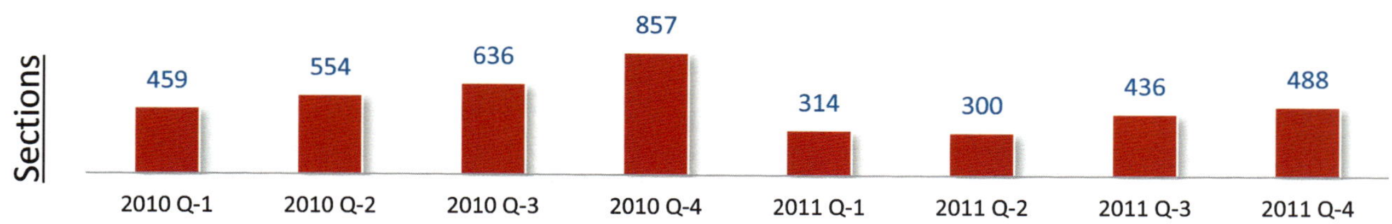

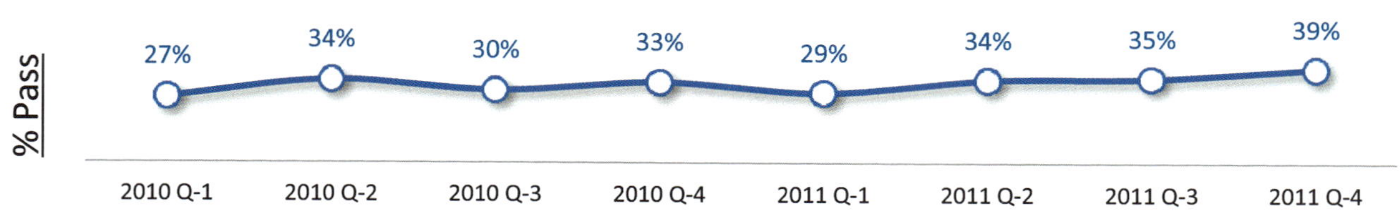

CPA Exam Performance Summary: *2011*

Demographics

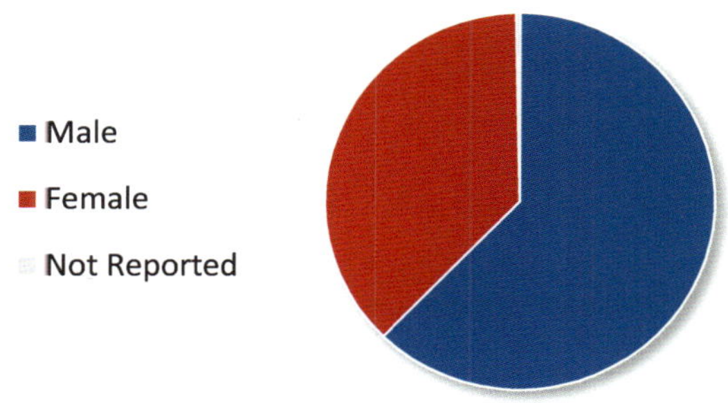

Male Candidates	362	62.3%
Female Candidates	217	37.3%
Not Reported	2	0.3%

Average Age	**34.7**
Age Rank	**53**

Residency

Candidate Count	
In-State Address	**16**
Out-of-State Address	**38**
Foreign Address	**527**

% of Candidates	
In-State Address	**2.8%**
Out-of-State Address	**6.5%**
Foreign Address	**90.7%**

Degree Type

Candidate Count	
Bachelor's Degree	**500**
Advanced Degree	**78**
None/Other	**3**

% of Candidates	
Bachelor's Degree	**86.1%**
Advanced Degree	**13.4%**
None/Other	**0.5%**

New Candidates vs Candidates Passing 4th Section

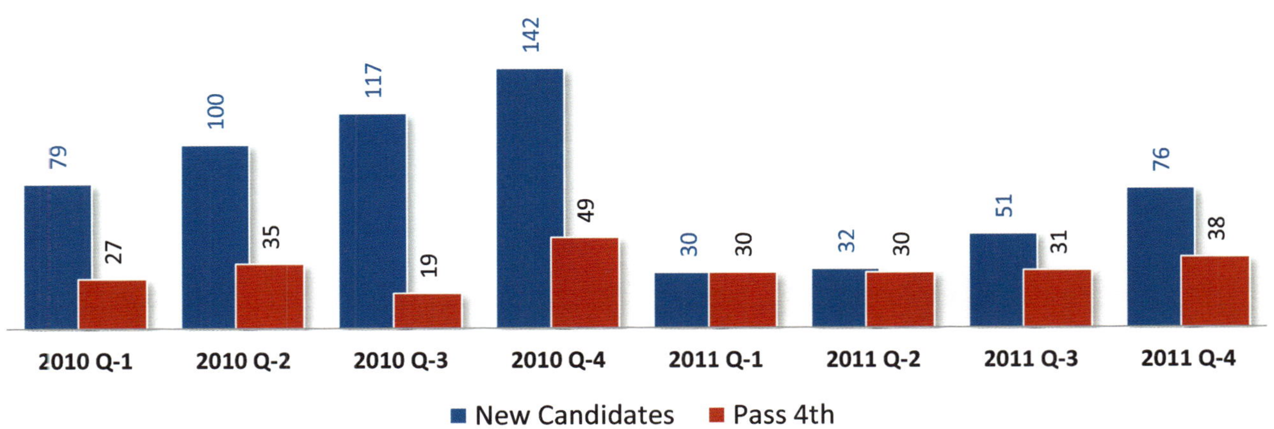

Notes about the Data

1. The data used to develop this report was pulled from NASBA's Gateway System, which houses the Uniform CPA Examination's Application and Performance information for all 55 jurisdictions.
2. The demographic data related to Age, Gender and Degree Type is provided by the individual candidates and may not be 100% accurate.

Guam

CPA Exam Performance Summary: *2011*

Hawaii

Overall Performance

Unique Candidates	**369**
New Candidates	**149**
Total Sections	**923**
Passing 4th Section	**90**
Sections/Candidate	**2.50**
Pass Rate	**38.7%**
Average Score	**68.8**

Section Performance

	Sections	Score	% Pass
First-Time	**436**	**67.8**	**42.7%**
Re-Exam	**487**	**69.7**	**35.1%**
AUD	**248**	**71.7**	**46.4%**
BEC	**198**	**67.3**	**30.3%**
FAR	**225**	**66.4**	**37.3%**
REG	**252**	**69.3**	**38.9%**

Jurisdiction Rankings (1 to 53)

Candidates	Sections
43	**41**
46	**42**
Pass Rate	Avg Score

Exam Type by Percent

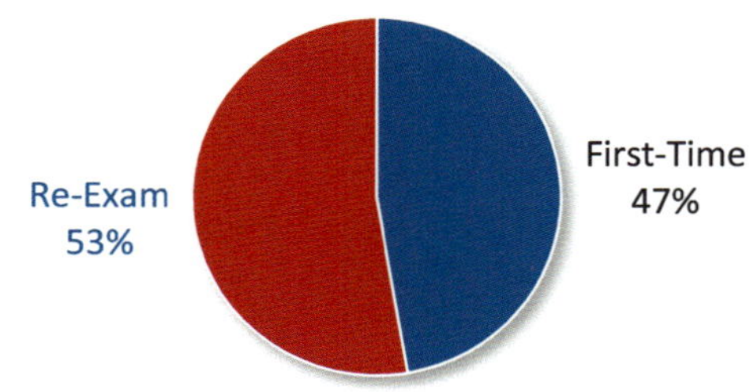

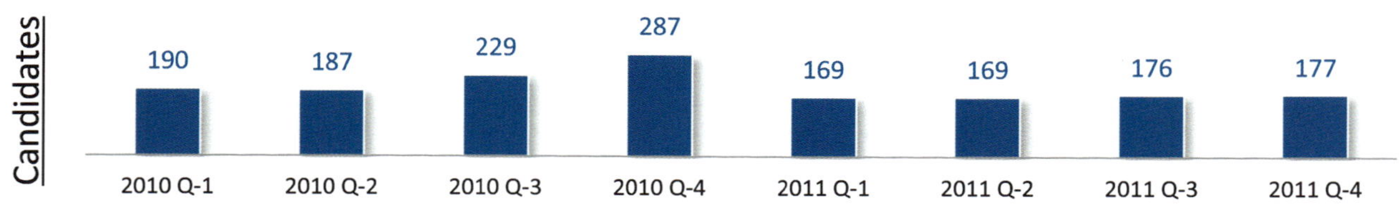

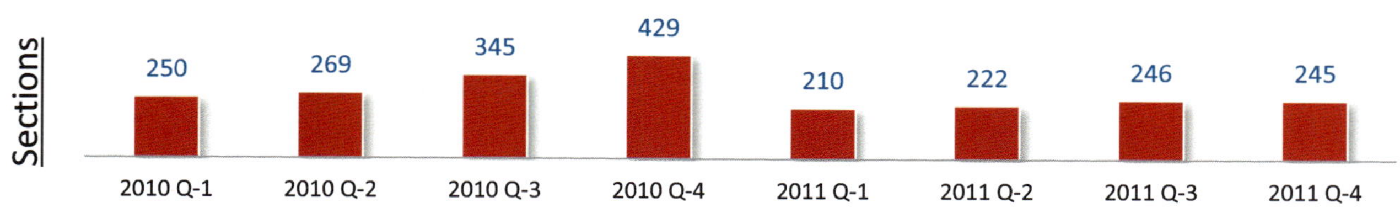

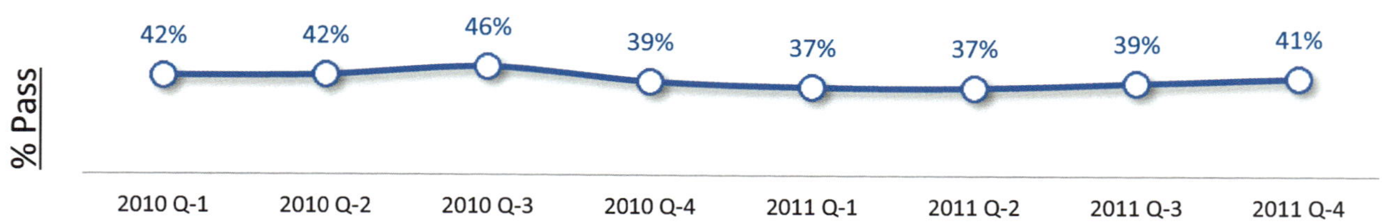

CPA Exam Performance Summary: *2011*

Demographics

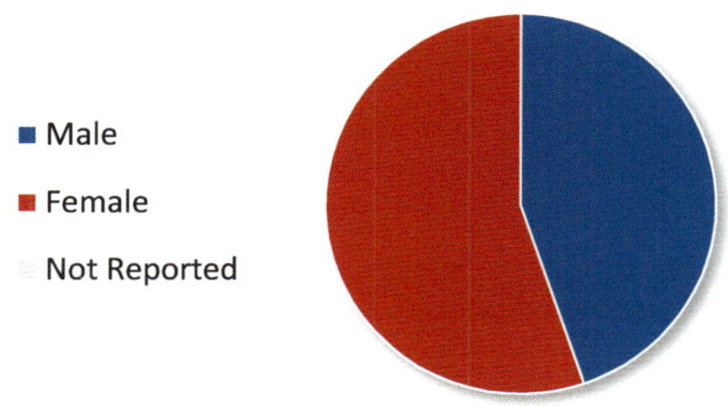

Male Candidates	165	44.7%
Female Candidates	204	55.3%
Not Reported	0	0.0%

Average Age **31.0**

Age Rank **44**

Residency

Candidate Count	
In-State Address	271
Out-of-State Address	36
Foreign Address	62

% of Candidates	
In-State Address	73.4%
Out-of-State Address	9.8%
Foreign Address	16.8%

Degree Type

Candidate Count	
Bachelor's Degree	287
Advanced Degree	36
None/Other	46

% of Candidates	
Bachelor's Degree	77.8%
Advanced Degree	9.8%
None/Other	12.5%

New Candidates vs Candidates Passing 4th Section

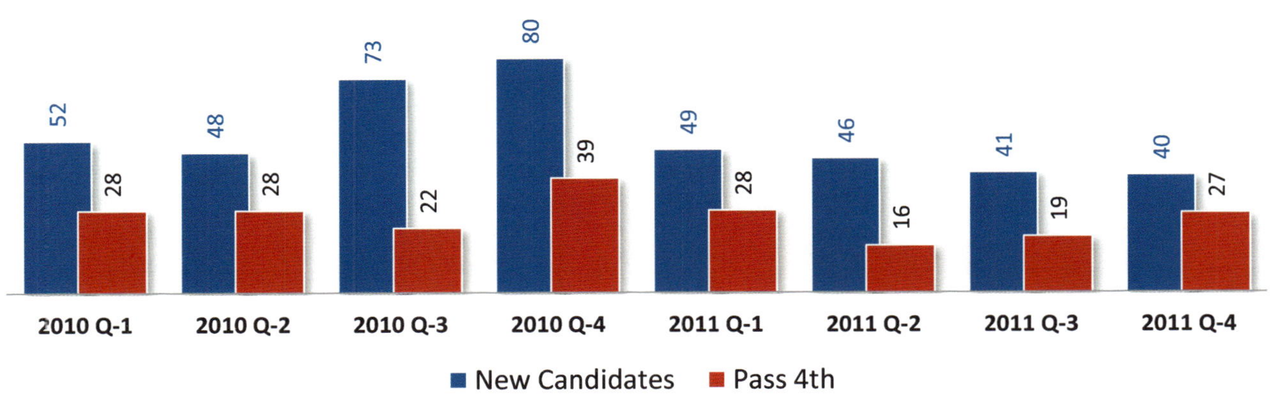

Notes about the Data

1. The data used to develop this report was pulled from NASBA's Gateway System, which houses the Uniform CPA Examination's Application and Performance information for all 55 jurisdictions.
2. The demographic data related to Age, Gender and Degree Type is provided by the individual candidates and may not be 100% accurate.

Hawaii

CPA Exam Performance Summary: *2011*

Idaho

Overall Performance

Unique Candidates	**297**
New Candidates	**118**
Total Sections	**736**
Passing 4th Section	**85**
Sections/Candidate	**2.48**
Pass Rate	**44.8%**
Average Score	**70.6**

Section Performance

	Sections	Score	% Pass
First-Time	**440**	**70.6**	**48.0%**
Re-Exam	**296**	**70.5**	**40.2%**
AUD	**207**	**70.7**	**44.4%**
BEC	**162**	**71.9**	**45.7%**
FAR	**171**	**70.2**	**46.8%**
REG	**196**	**69.6**	**42.9%**

Jurisdiction Rankings (1 to 53)

Candidates	Sections
48	**47**
29	**28**
Pass Rate	Avg Score

Exam Type by Percent

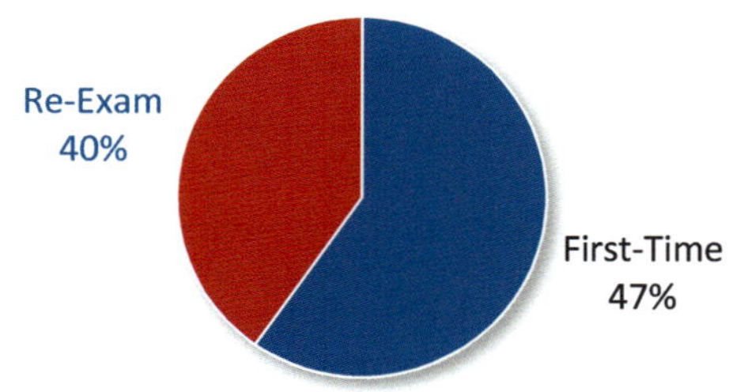

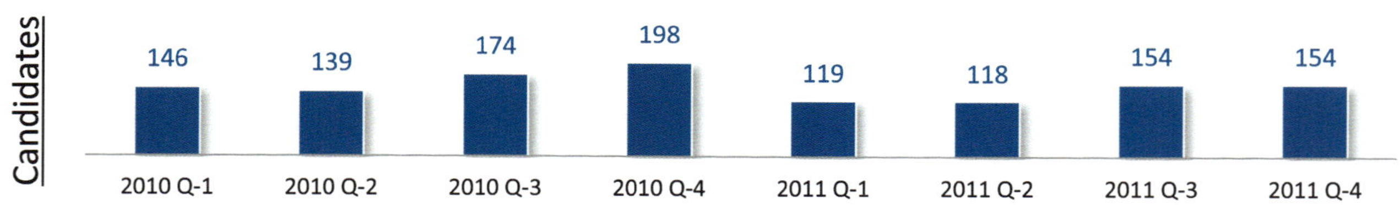

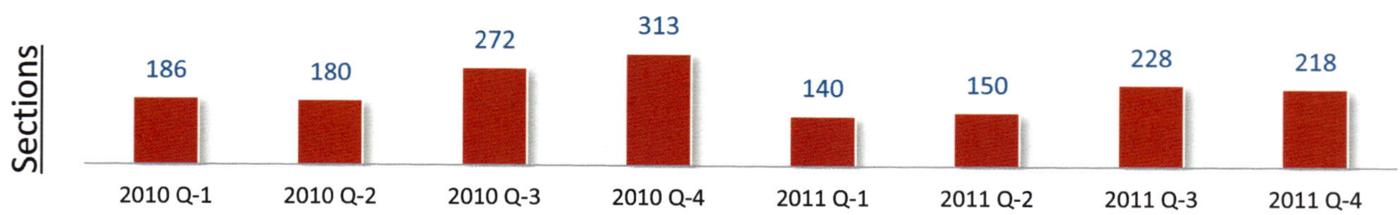

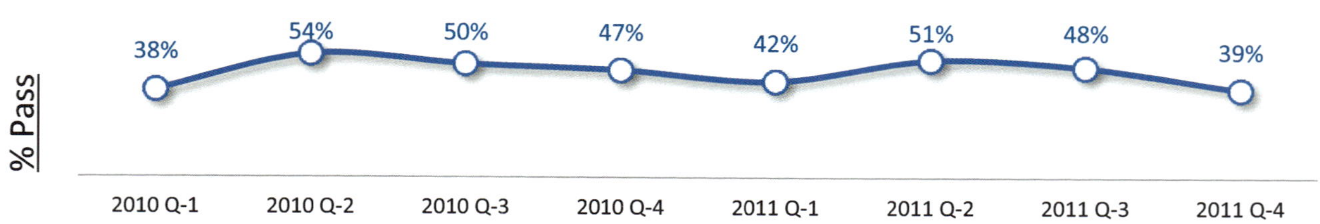

CPA Exam Performance Summary: *2011*

Demographics

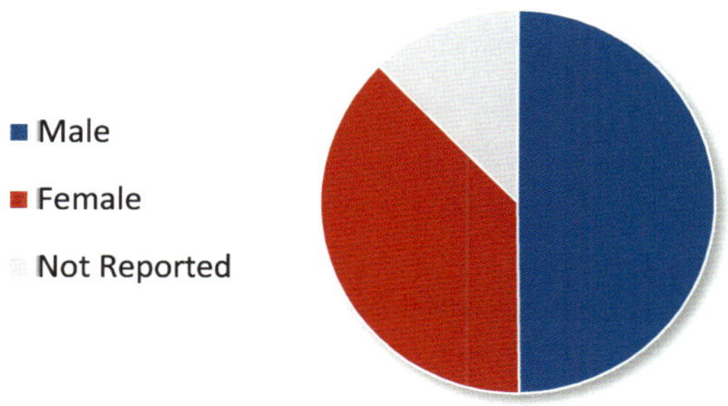

Male Candidates	148	49.8%
Female Candidates	112	37.7%
Not Reported	37	12.5%

Average Age	**30.9**
Age Rank	**41**

Residency

Candidate Count	
In-State Address	**273**
Out-of-State Address	**24**
Foreign Address	**0**

% of Candidates	
In-State Address	**91.9%**
Out-of-State Address	**8.1%**
Foreign Address	**0.0%**

Degree Type

Candidate Count	
Bachelor's Degree	**240**
Advanced Degree	**22**
None/Other	**35**

% of Candidates	
Bachelor's Degree	**80.8%**
Advanced Degree	**7.4%**
None/Other	**11.8%**

New Candidates vs Candidates Passing 4th Section

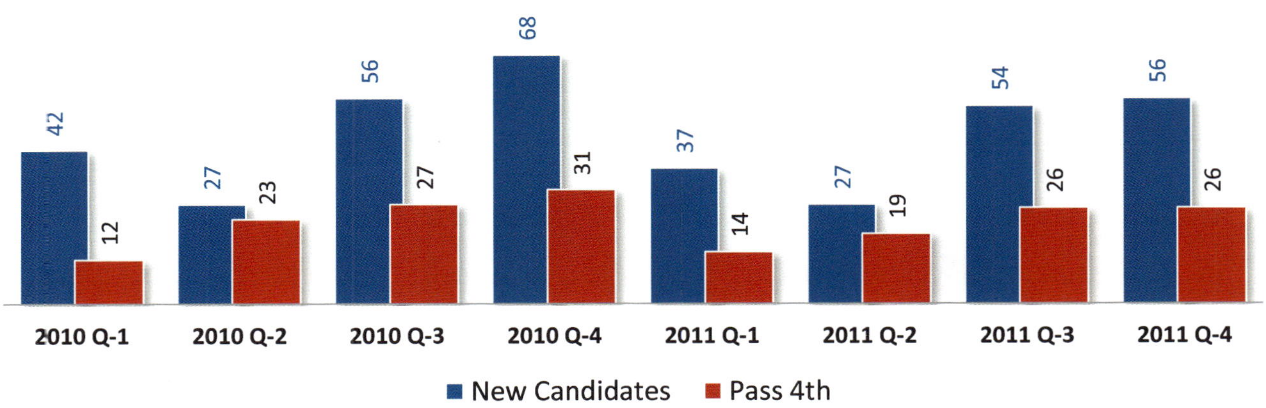

Nctes about the Data

1. The data used to develop this report was pulled from NASBA's Gateway System, which houses the Uniform CPA Examination's Application and Performance information for all 55 jurisdictions.
2. The demographic data related to Age, Gender and Degree Type is provided by the individual candidates and may not be 100% accurate.

Idaho

CPA Exam Performance Summary: *2011*

Illinois

Overall Performance

Unique Candidates	5,065
New Candidates	2,350
Total Sections	13,820
Passing 4th Section	1,574
Sections/Candidate	2.73
Pass Rate	51.0%
Average Score	72.5

Section Performance

	Sections	Score	% Pass
First-Time	8,754	73.4	56.5%
Re-Exam	5,066	70.9	41.5%
AUD	3,739	73.2	48.3%
BEC	2,948	74.5	58.9%
FAR	3,310	71.3	50.8%
REG	3,823	71.3	47.8%

Jurisdiction Rankings (1 to 53)

Candidates	Sections
4	4
10	10
Pass Rate	Avg Score

Exam Type by Percent

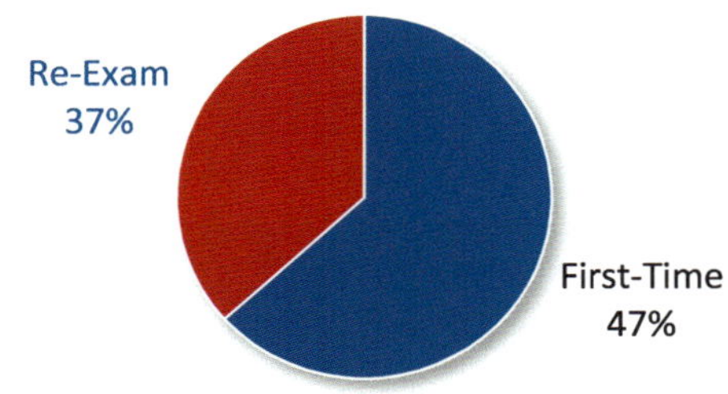

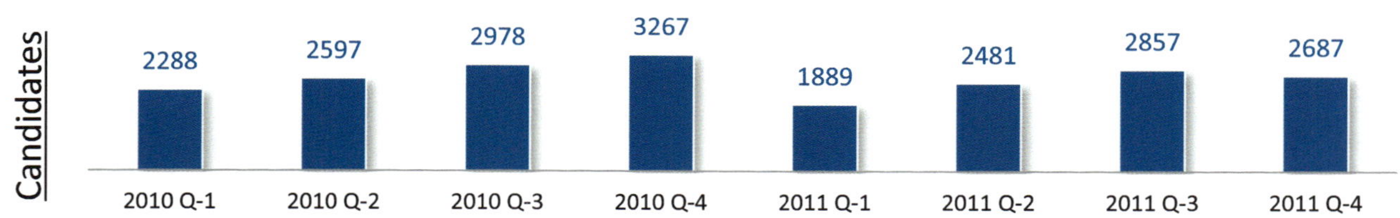

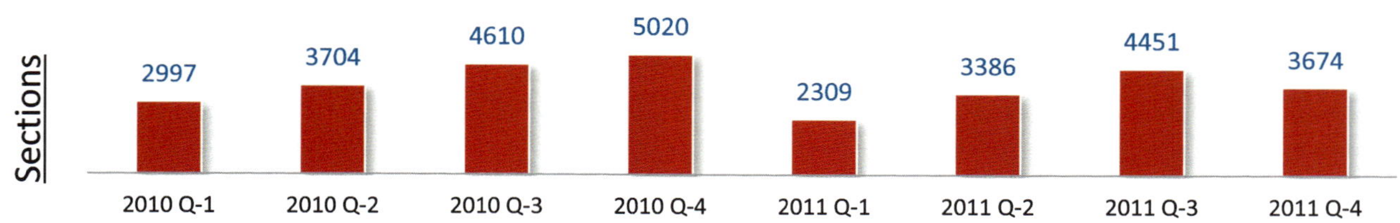

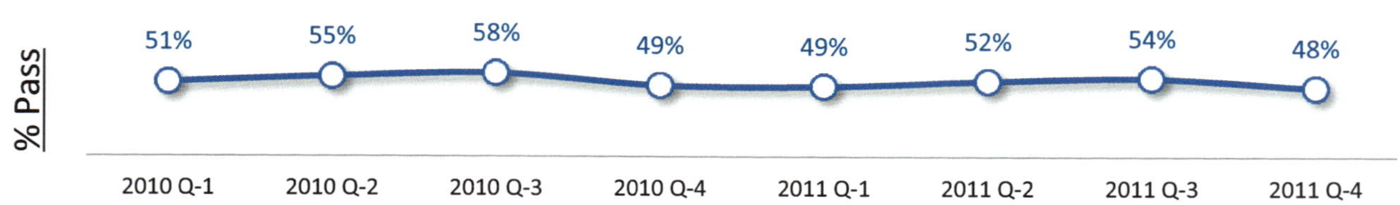

CPA Exam Performance Summary: *2011*

Demographics

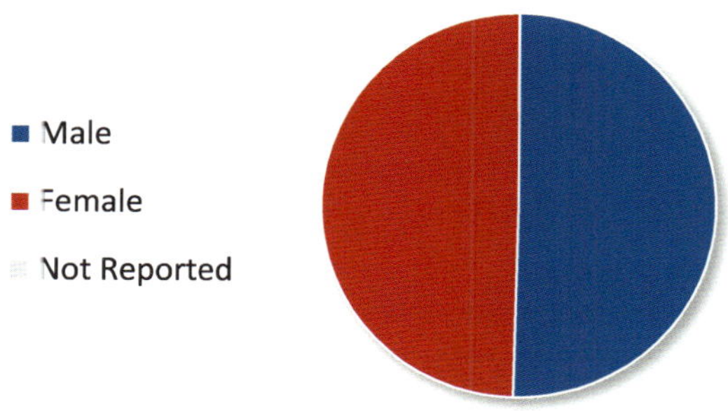

Male Candidates	2,550	50.3%
Female Candidates	2,514	49.6%
Not Reported	1	0.0%

Average Age	**28.5**
Age Rank	**18**

Residency

Candidate Count	
In-State Address	4,201
Out-of-State Address	679
Foreign Address	185
% of Candidates	
In-State Address	82.9%
Out-of-State Address	13.4%
Foreign Address	3.7%

Degree Type

Candidate Count	
Bachelor's Degree	4,144
Advanced Degree	914
None/Other	7
% of Candidates	
Bachelor's Degree	81.8%
Advanced Degree	18.0%
None/Other	0.1%

New Candidates vs Candidates Passing 4th Section

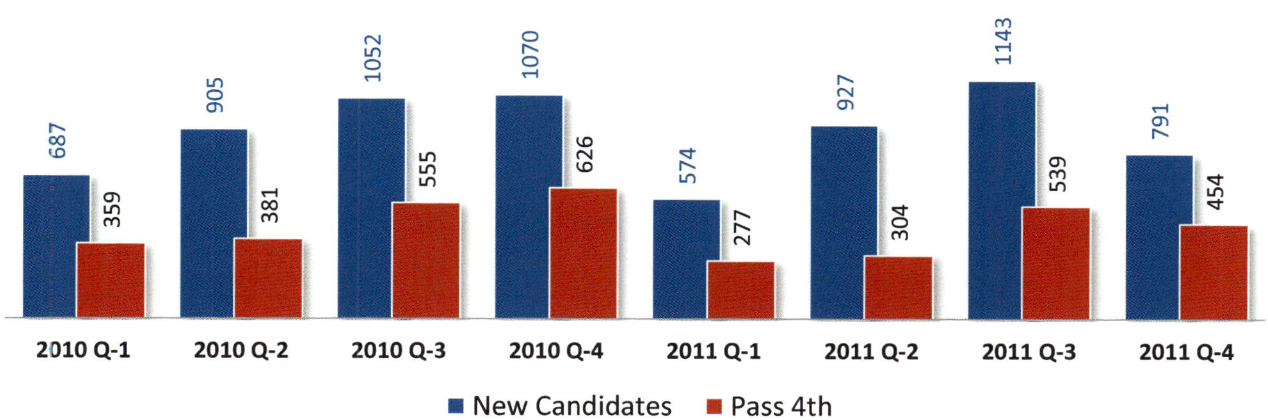

Notes about the Data

1. The data used to develop this report was pulled from NASBA's Gateway System, which houses the Uniform CPA Examination's Application and Performance information for all 55 jurisdictions.
2. The demographic data related to Age, Gender and Degree Type is provided by the individual candidates and may not be 100% accurate.

Illinois

CPA Exam Performance Summary: *2011*

Indiana

Overall Performance

Unique Candidates	1,282
New Candidates	624
Total Sections	3,502
Passing 4th Section	358
Sections/Candidate	2.73
Pass Rate	45.3%
Average Score	70.6

Section Performance

	Sections	Score	% Pass
First-Time	2,089	71.0	49.6%
Re-Exam	1,413	70.0	38.9%
AUD	953	71.5	44.4%
BEC	721	73.1	52.0%
FAR	864	68.7	43.2%
REG	964	69.6	43.0%

Jurisdiction Rankings (1 to 53)

Candidates	Sections
22	23
26	27
Pass Rate	Avg Score

Exam Type by Percent

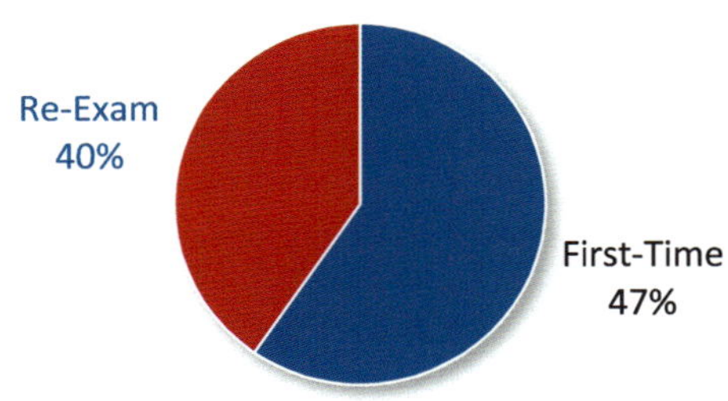

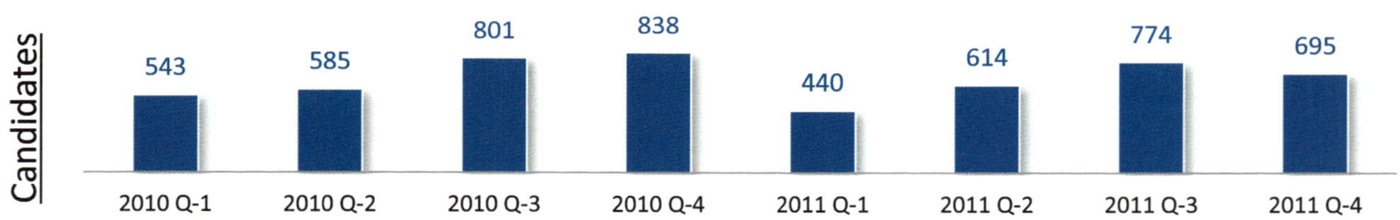

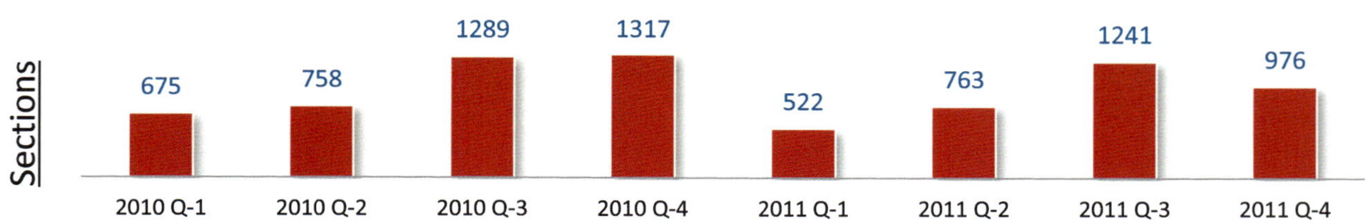

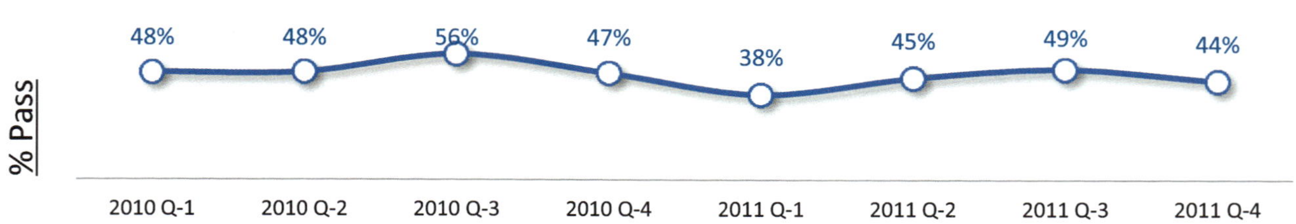

CPA Exam Performance Summary: *2011*

Demographics

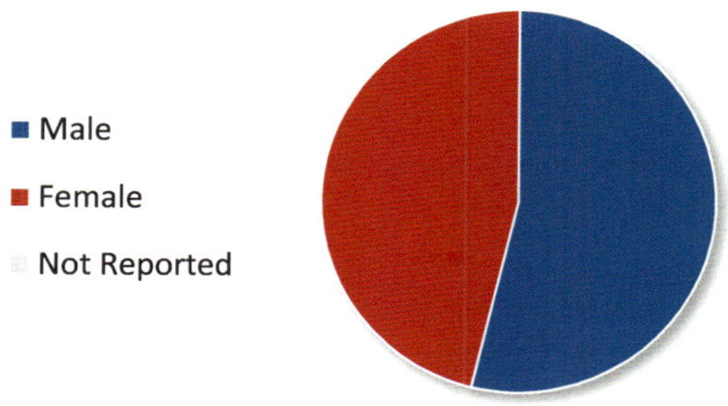

Male Candidates	689	53.7%
Female Candidates	593	46.3%
Not Reported	0	0.0%

Average Age	**28.3**
Age Rank	**15**

Residency

Candidate Count	
In-State Address	**1,167**
Out-of-State Address	**110**
Foreign Address	**5**

% of Candidates	
In-State Address	**91.0%**
Out-of-State Address	**8.6%**
Foreign Address	**0.4%**

Degree Type

Candidate Count	
Bachelor's Degree	**994**
Advanced Degree	**130**
None/Other	**158**

% of Candidates	
Bachelor's Degree	**77.5%**
Advanced Degree	**10.1%**
None/Other	**12.3%**

New Candidates vs Candidates Passing 4th Section

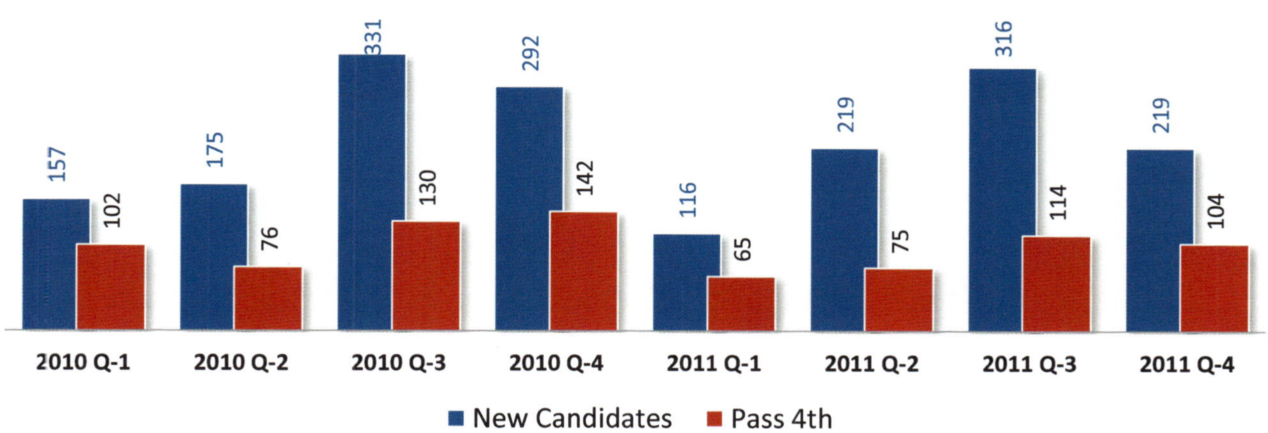

Notes about the Data

1. The data used to develop this report was pulled from NASBA's Gateway System, which houses the Uniform CPA Examination's Application and Performance information for all 55 jurisdictions.
2. The demographic data related to Age, Gender and Degree Type is provided by the individual candidates and may not be 100% accurate.

Indiana

CPA Exam Performance Summary: *2011*

Iowa

Overall Performance

Unique Candidates	**634**
New Candidates	**362**
Total Sections	**1,801**
Passing 4th Section	**213**
Sections/Candidate	**2.84**
Pass Rate	**51.8%**
Average Score	**72.7**

Section Performance

	Sections	Score	% Pass
First-Time	**1,220**	**73.6**	**55.4%**
Re-Exam	**581**	**71.0**	**44.1%**
AUD	**499**	**73.2**	**47.7%**
BEC	**383**	**74.2**	**56.1%**
FAR	**429**	**71.5**	**52.9%**
REG	**490**	**72.2**	**51.4%**

Jurisdiction Rankings (1 to 53)

Candidates	Sections
32	**29**
7	**7**
Pass Rate	Avg Score

Exam Type by Percent

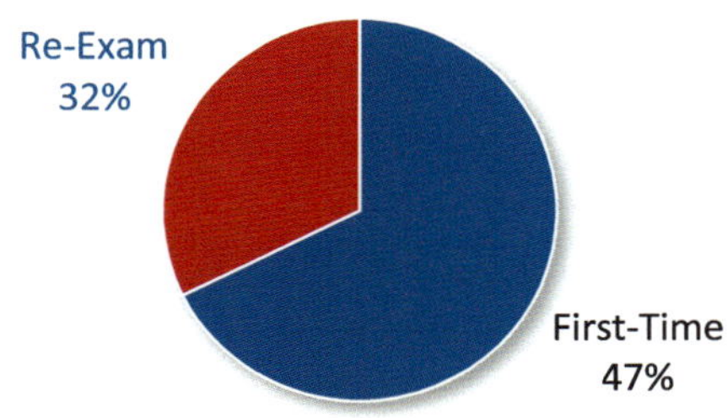

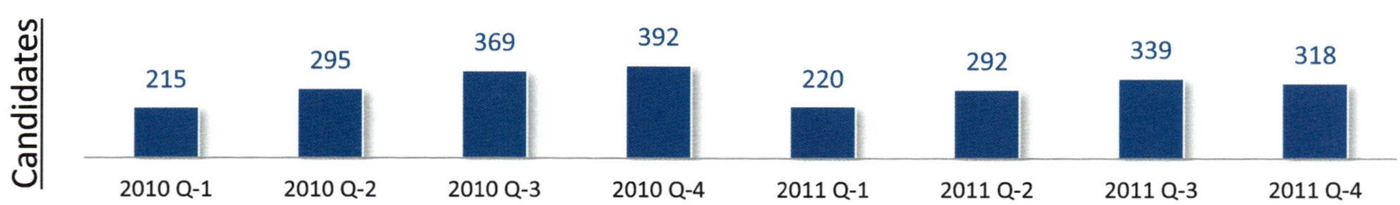

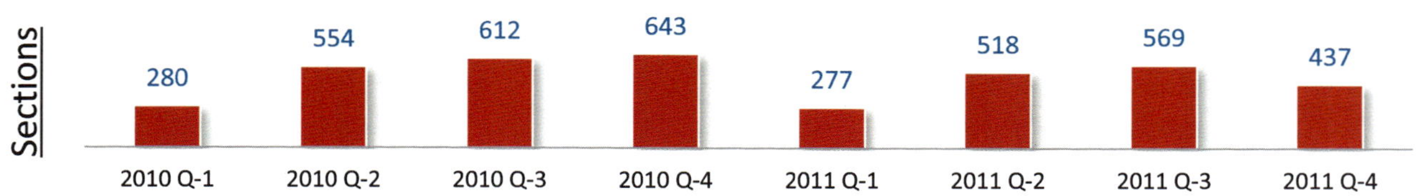

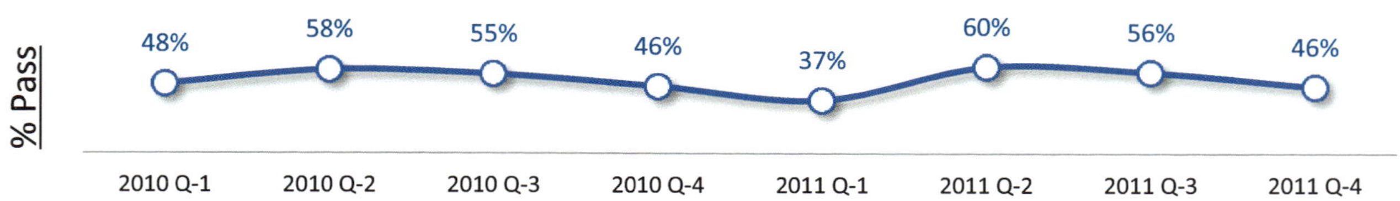

CPA Exam Performance Summary: *2011*

Demographics

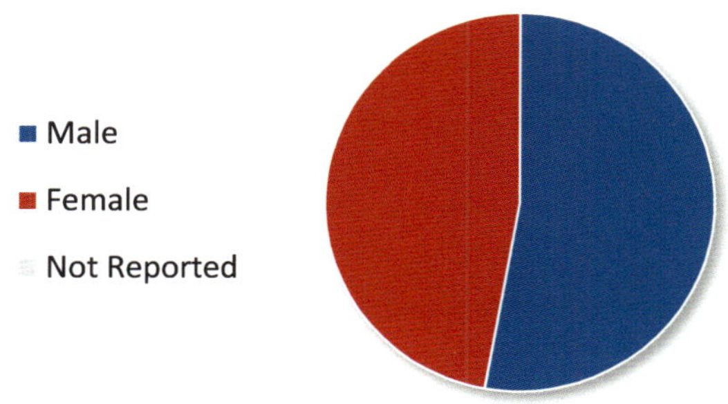

Male Candidates	335	52.8%
Female Candidates	299	47.2%
Not Reported	0	0.0%

Average Age	**27.0**
Age Rank	**1**

Residency

Candidate Count	
In-State Address	**541**
Out-of-State Address	**91**
Foreign Address	**2**
% of Candidates	
In-State Address	**85.3%**
Out-of-State Address	**14.4%**
Foreign Address	**0.3%**

Degree Type

Candidate Count	
Bachelor's Degree	**508**
Advanced Degree	**75**
None/Other	**51**
% of Candidates	
Bachelor's Degree	**80.1%**
Advanced Degree	**11.8%**
None/Other	**8.0%**

New Candidates vs Candidates Passing 4th Section

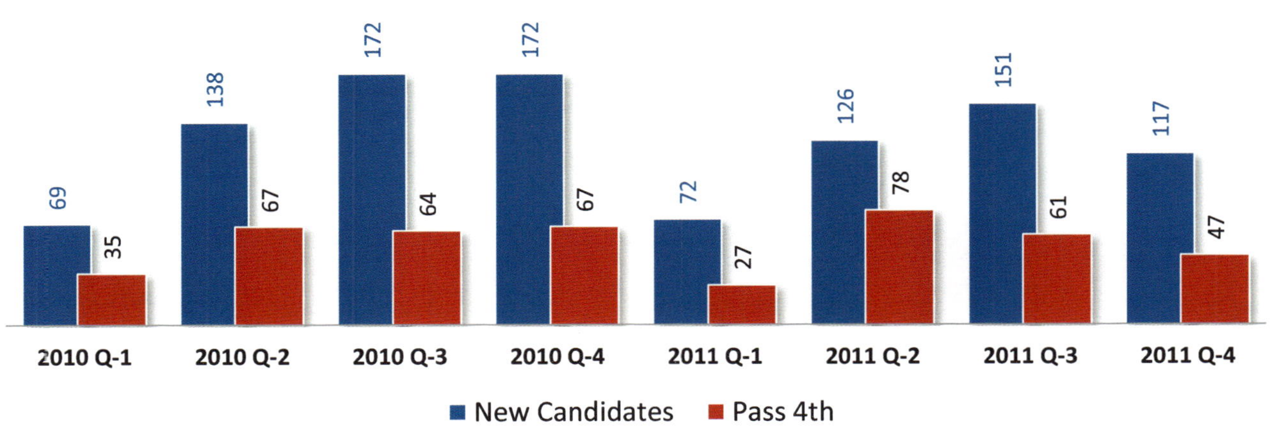

Notes about the Data

1. The data used to develop this report was pulled from NASBA's Gateway System, which houses the Uniform CPA Examination's Application and Performance information for all 55 jurisdictions.
2. The demographic data related to Age, Gender and Degree Type is provided by the individual candidates and may not be 100% accurate.

Iowa

CPA Exam Performance Summary: *2011*

Kansas

Overall Performance

Unique Candidates	475
New Candidates	240
Total Sections	1,294
Passing 4th Section	152
Sections/Candidate	2.72
Pass Rate	47.3%
Average Score	71.4

Section Performance

	Sections	Score	% Pass
First-Time	754	71.8	50.7%
Re-Exam	540	70.9	42.6%
AUD	357	72.3	46.2%
BEC	275	73.3	53.5%
FAR	303	69.5	41.6%
REG	359	70.9	48.5%

Jurisdiction Rankings (1 to 53)

Candidates	Sections
40	38
22	23
Pass Rate	Avg Score

Exam Type by Percent

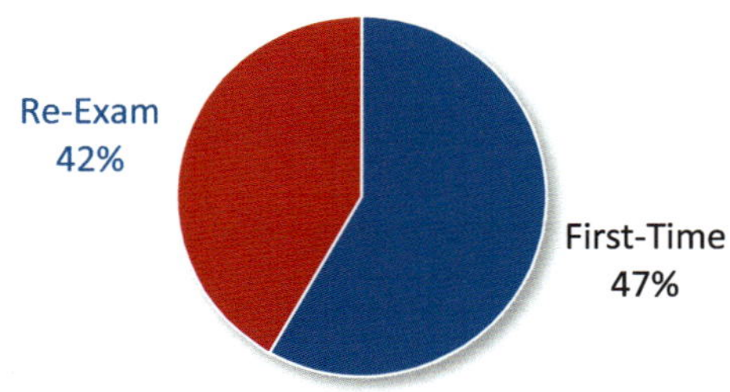

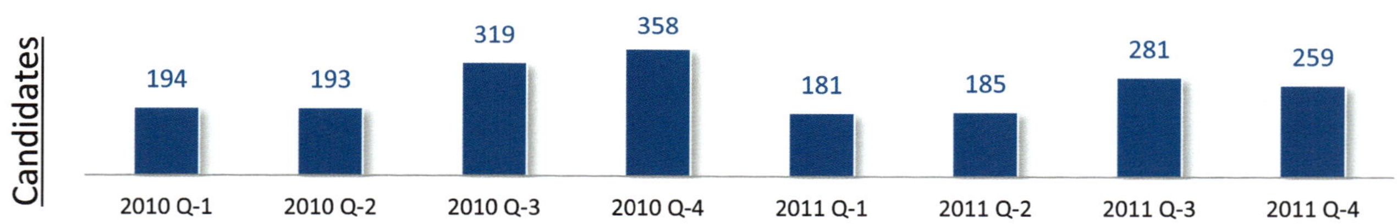

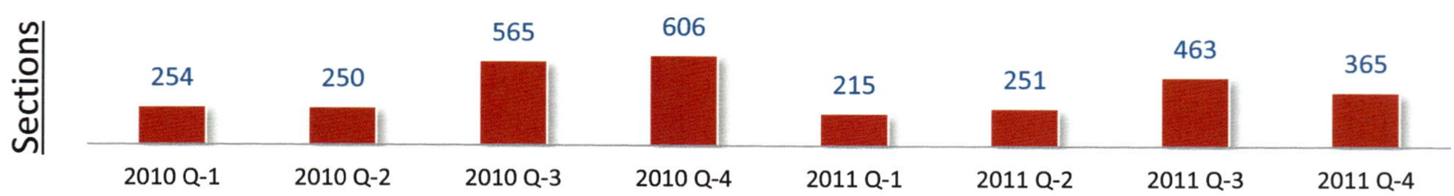

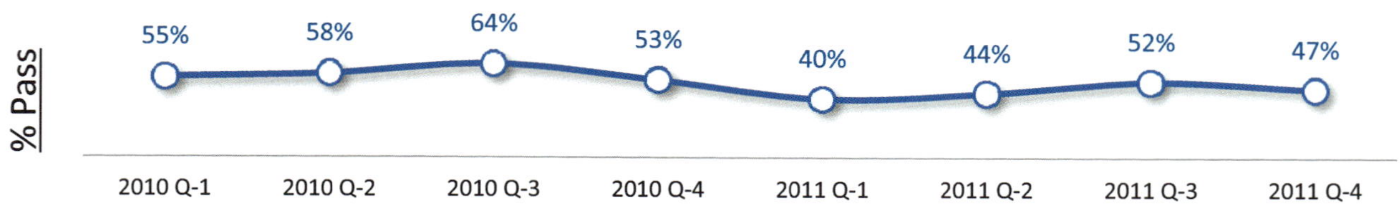

CPA Exam Performance Summary: *2011*

Demographics

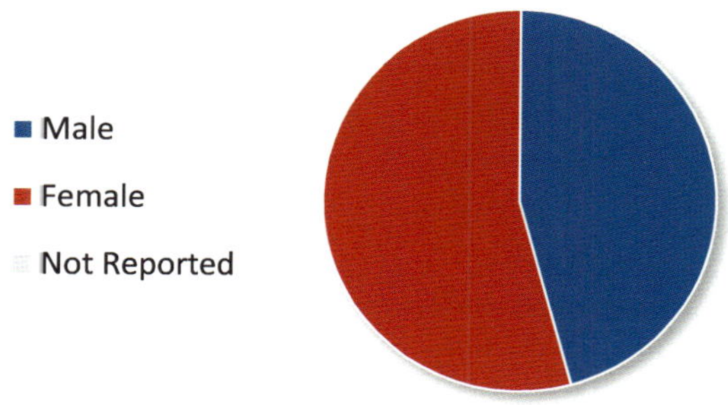

Male Candidates	217	45.7%
Female Candidates	258	54.3%
Not Reported	0	0.0%

Average Age	**28.5**
Age Rank	**19**

Residency

Candidate Count	
In-State Address	461
Out-of-State Address	14
Foreign Address	0
% of Candidates	
In-State Address	97.1%
Out-of-State Address	2.9%
Foreign Address	0.0%

Degree Type

Candidate Count	
Bachelor's Degree	366
Advanced Degree	71
None/Other	38
% of Candidates	
Bachelor's Degree	77.1%
Advanced Degree	14.9%
None/Other	8.0%

New Candidates vs Candidates Passing 4th Section

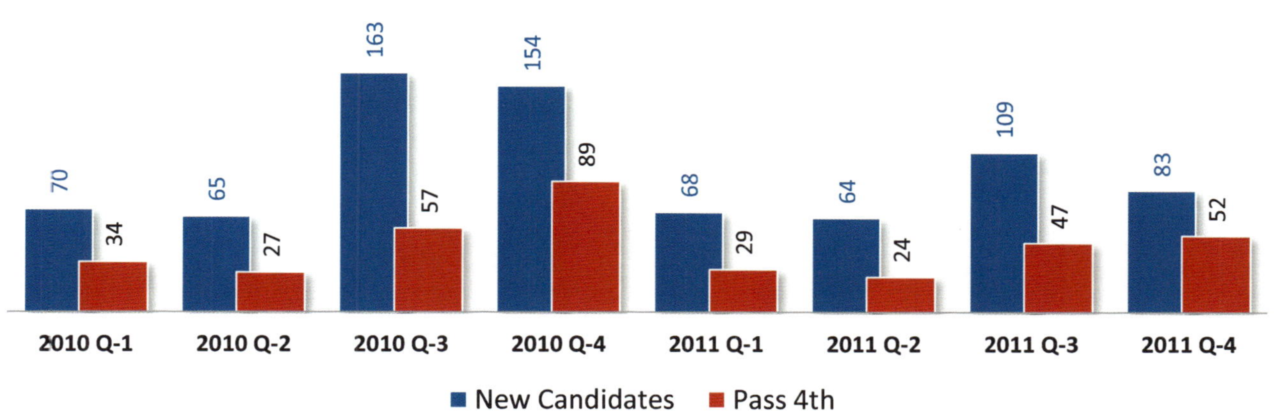

Notes about the Data

1. The data used to develop this report was pulled from NASBA's Gateway System, which houses the Uniform CPA Examination's Application and Performance information for all 55 jurisdictions.
2. The demographic data related to Age, Gender and Degree Type is provided by the individual candidates and may not be 100% accurate.

Kansas

CPA Exam Performance Summary: *2011*

Kentucky

Overall Performance

Unique Candidates	**812**
New Candidates	**314**
Total Sections	**2,065**
Passing 4th Section	**200**
Sections/Candidate	**2.54**
Pass Rate	**45.7%**
Average Score	**71.4**

Section Performance

	Sections	Score	% Pass
First-Time	**1,187**	**71.2**	**47.2%**
Re-Exam	**878**	**71.7**	**43.7%**
AUD	**596**	**72.6**	**44.5%**
BEC	**448**	**72.3**	**48.9%**
FAR	**493**	**68.6**	**43.2%**
REG	**528**	**71.7**	**46.8%**

Jurisdiction Rankings (1 to 53)

Candidates	Sections
29	**27**
24	**24**
Pass Rate	Avg Score

Exam Type by Percent

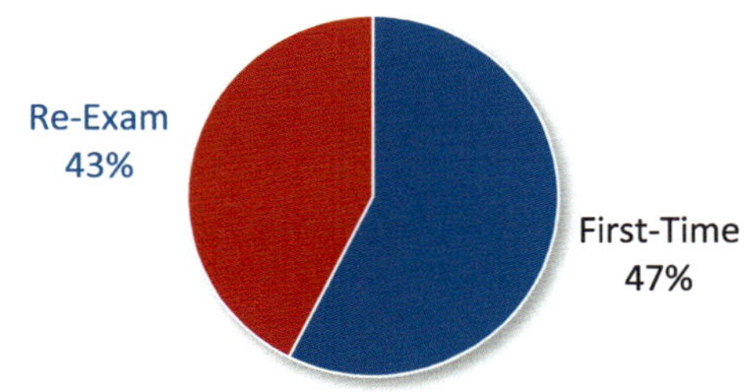

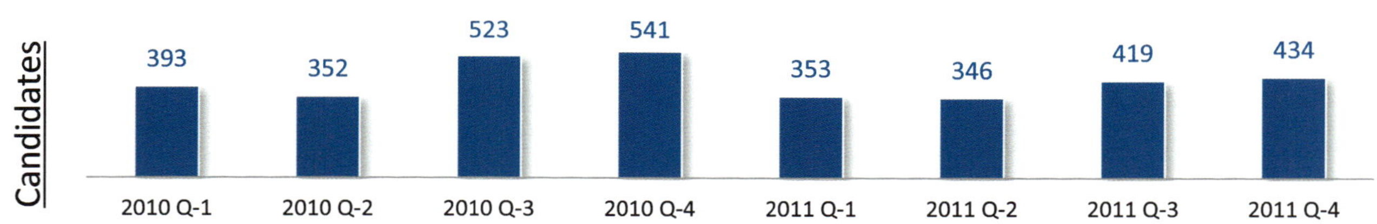

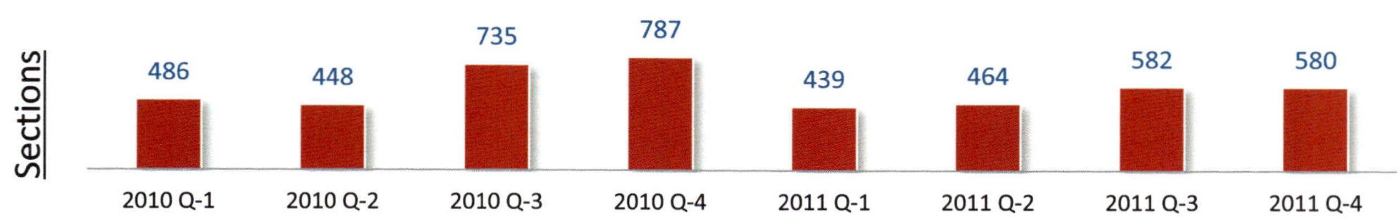

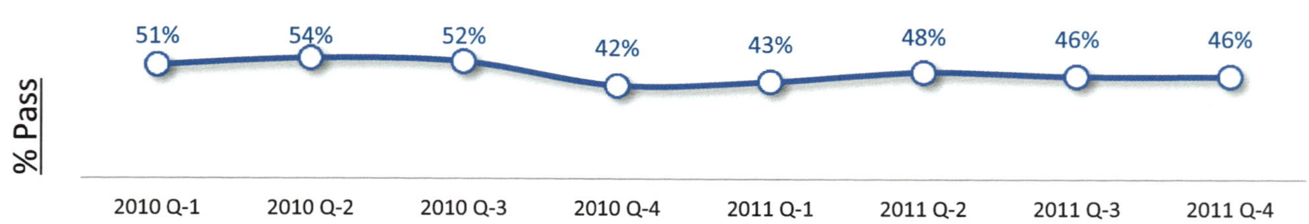

CPA Exam Performance Summary: *2011*

Demographics

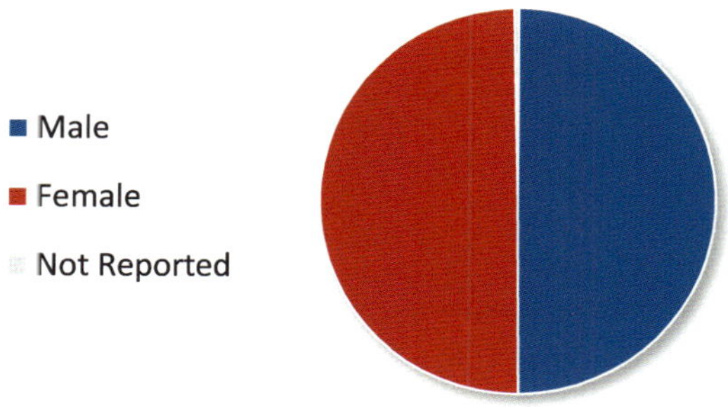

Male Candidates	405	49.9%
Female Candidates	404	49.8%
Not Reported	3	0.4%

Average Age	**29.4**
Age Rank	**29**

Residency

Candidate Count

In-State Address	**701**
Out-of-State Address	**109**
Foreign Address	**2**

% of Candidates

In-State Address	**86.3%**
Out-of-State Address	**13.4%**
Foreign Address	**0.2%**

Degree Type

Candidate Count

Bachelor's Degree	**805**
Advanced Degree	**7**
None/Other	**0**

% of Candidates

Bachelor's Degree	**99.1%**
Advanced Degree	**0.9%**
None/Other	**0.0%**

New Candidates vs Candidates Passing 4th Section

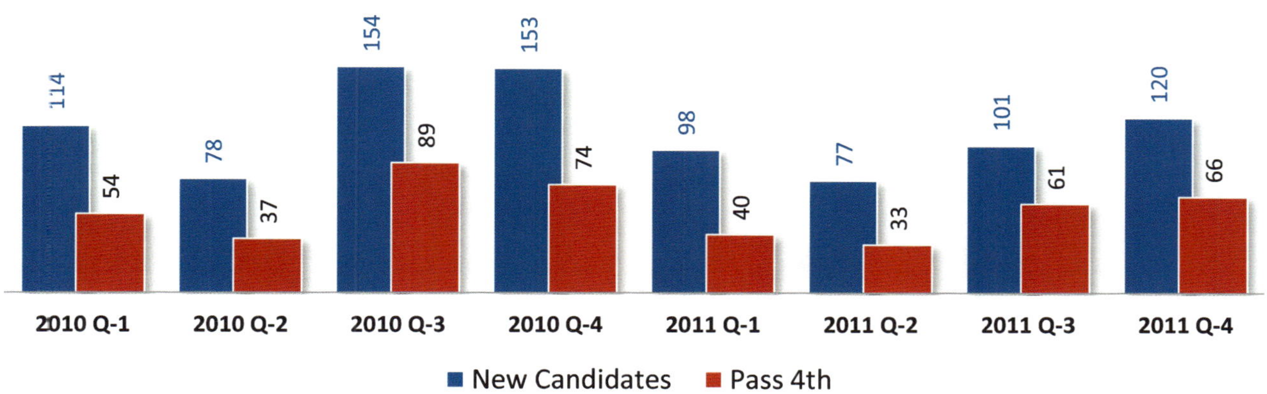

Notes about the Data

1. The data used to develop this report was pulled from NASBA's Gateway System, which houses the Uniform CPA Examination's Application and Performance information for all 55 jurisdictions.
2. The demographic data related to Age, Gender and Degree Type is provided by the individual candidates and may not be 100% accurate.

Kentucky

CPA Exam Performance Summary: *2011*

Louisiana

Overall Performance

Unique Candidates	**888**
New Candidates	**465**
Total Sections	**2,272**
Passing 4th Section	**232**
Sections/Candidate	**2.56**
Pass Rate	**43.8%**
Average Score	**70.3**

Section Performance

	Sections	Score	% Pass
First-Time	**1,278**	**69.6**	**45.2%**
Re-Exam	**994**	**71.1**	**42.0%**
AUD	**575**	**72.4**	**46.1%**
BEC	**529**	**69.7**	**40.8%**
FAR	**570**	**68.0**	**41.6%**
REG	**598**	**70.8**	**46.2%**

Jurisdiction Rankings (1 to 53)

Candidates	Sections
27	**26**
34	**30**
Pass Rate	Avg Score

Exam Type by Percent

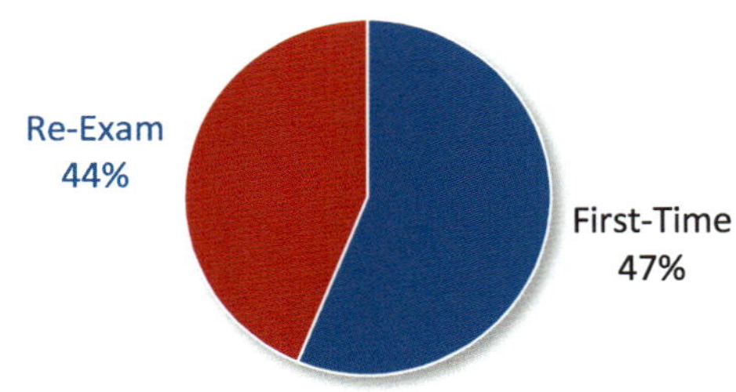

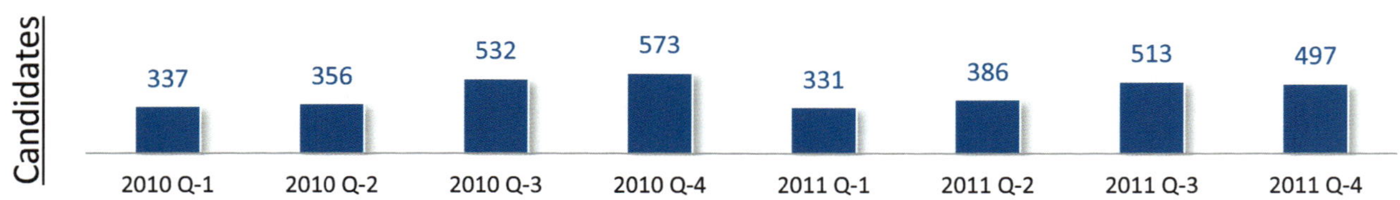

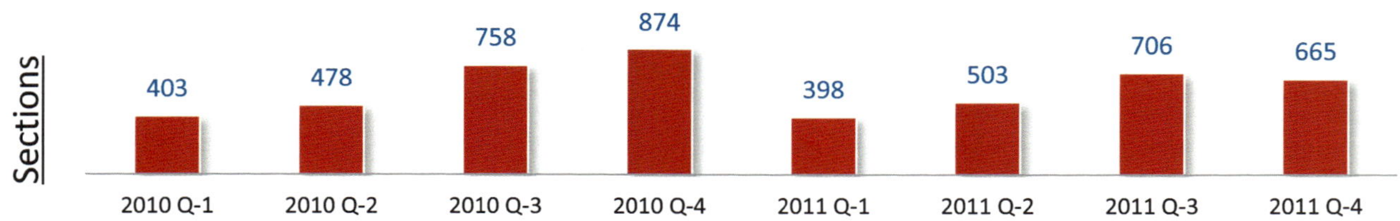

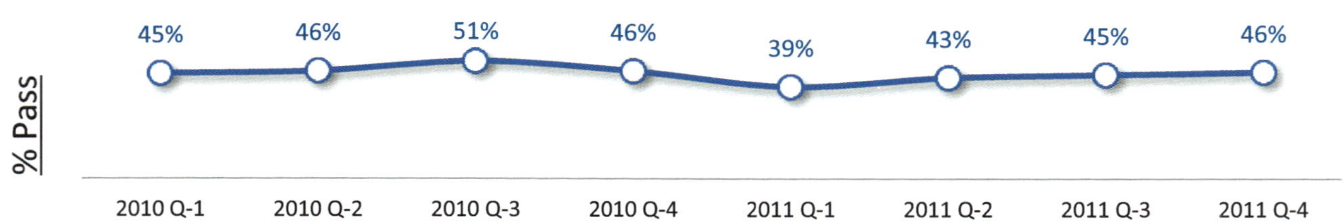

CPA Exam Performance Summary: *2011*

Demographics

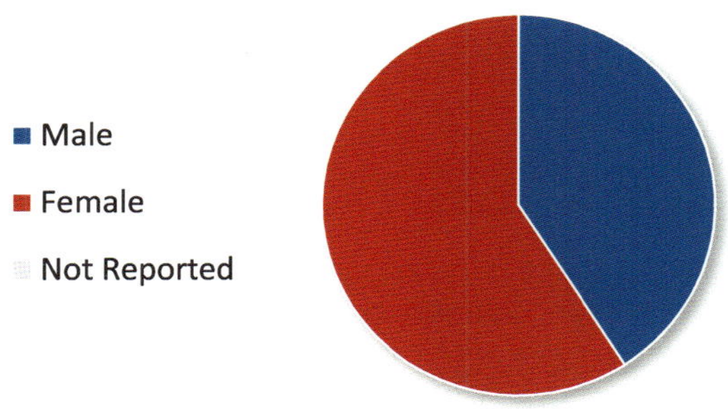

Male Candidates	363	40.9%
Female Candidates	525	59.1%
Not Reported	0	0.0%

Average Age **28.7**

Age Rank **22**

Residency

Candidate Count

In-State Address	866
Out-of-State Address	22
Foreign Address	0

% of Candidates

In-State Address	97.5%
Out-of-State Address	2.5%
Foreign Address	0.0%

Degree Type

Candidate Count

Bachelor's Degree	715
Advanced Degree	132
None/Other	41

% of Candidates

Bachelor's Degree	80.5%
Advanced Degree	14.9%
None/Other	4.6%

New Candidates vs Candidates Passing 4th Section

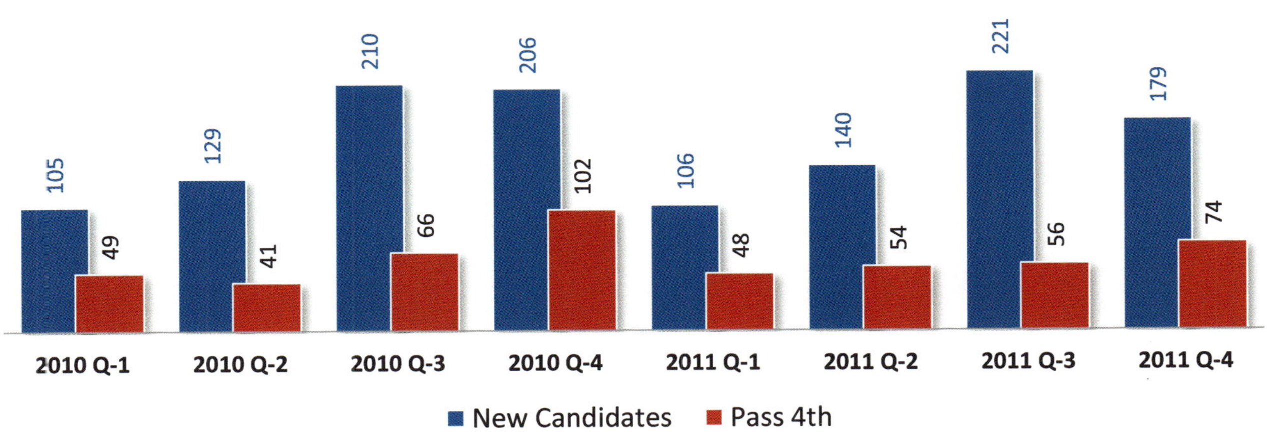

Notes about the Data

1. The data used to develop this report was pulled from NASBA's Gateway System, which houses the Uniform CPA Examination's Application and Performance information for all 55 jurisdictions.
2. The demographic data related to Age, Gender and Degree Type is provided by the individual candidates and may not be 100% accurate.

Louisiana

CPA Exam Performance Summary: *2011*

Maine

Overall Performance

Unique Candidates	2,448
New Candidates	1,039
Total Sections	6,351
Passing 4th Section	630
Sections/Candidate	2.59
Pass Rate	39.9%
Average Score	67.6

Section Performance

	Sections	Score	% Pass
First-Time	3,704	66.0	40.4%
Re-Exam	2,647	69.8	39.2%
AUD	1,712	69.5	43.9%
BEC	1,236	66.3	29.1%
FAR	1,612	67.7	44.7%
REG	1,791	66.5	39.3%

Jurisdiction Rankings (1 to 53)

Candidates	Sections
13	12
42	49
Pass Rate	Avg Score

Exam Type by Percent

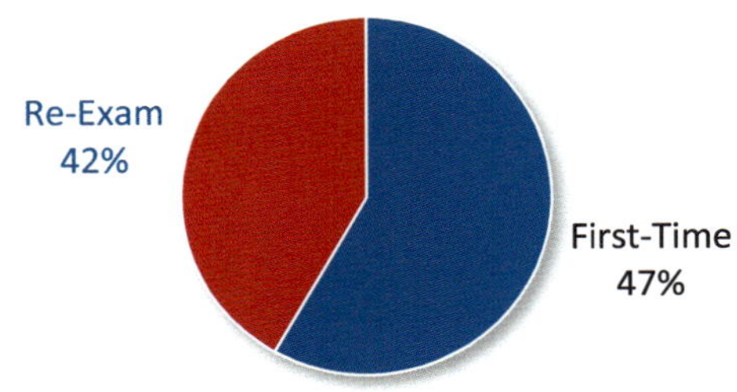

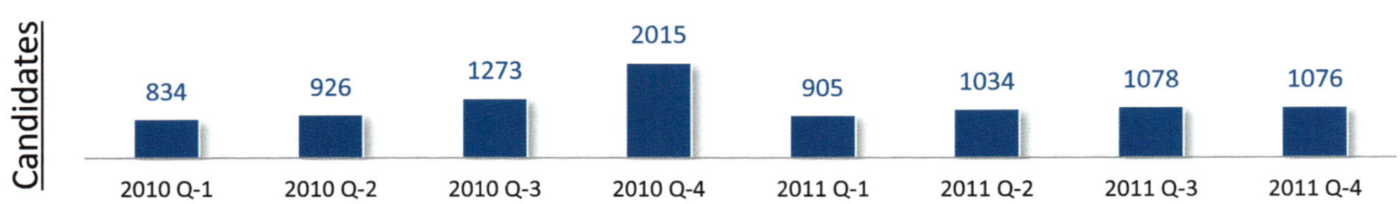

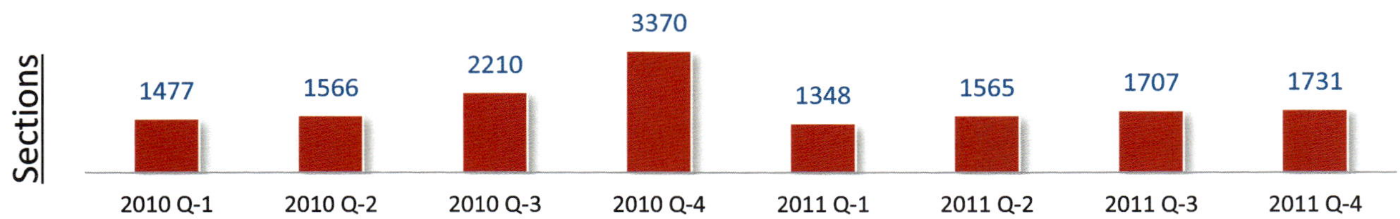

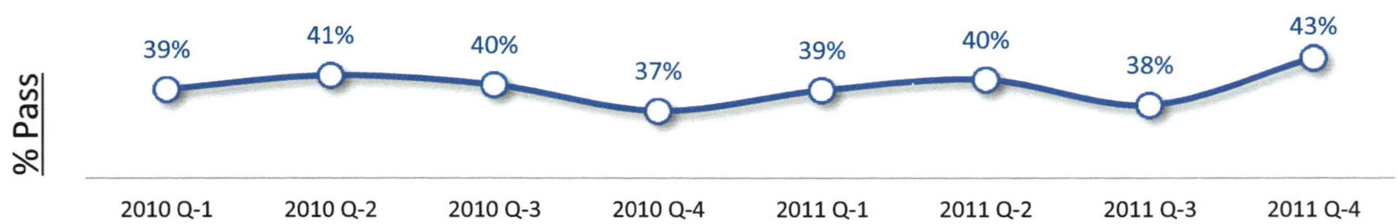

CPA Exam Performance Summary: *2011*

Demographics

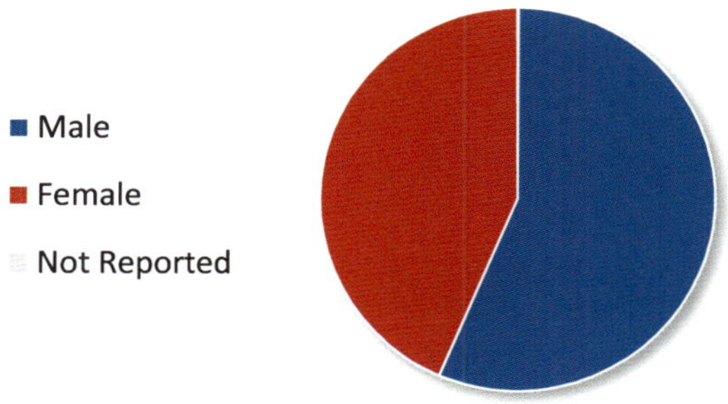

Male Candidates	1,381	56.4%
Female Candidates	1,065	43.5%
Not Reported	2	0.1%

Average Age	**32.4**
Age Rank	**49**

Residency

Candidate Count	
In-State Address	**125**
Out-of-State Address	**613**
Foreign Address	**1,710**

% of Candidates	
In-State Address	**5.1%**
Out-of-State Address	**25.0%**
Foreign Address	**69.9%**

Degree Type

Candidate Count	
Bachelor's Degree	**2,049**
Advanced Degree	**260**
None/Other	**139**

% of Candidates	
Bachelor's Degree	**83.7%**
Advanced Degree	**10.6%**
None/Other	**5.7%**

New Candidates vs Candidates Passing 4th Section

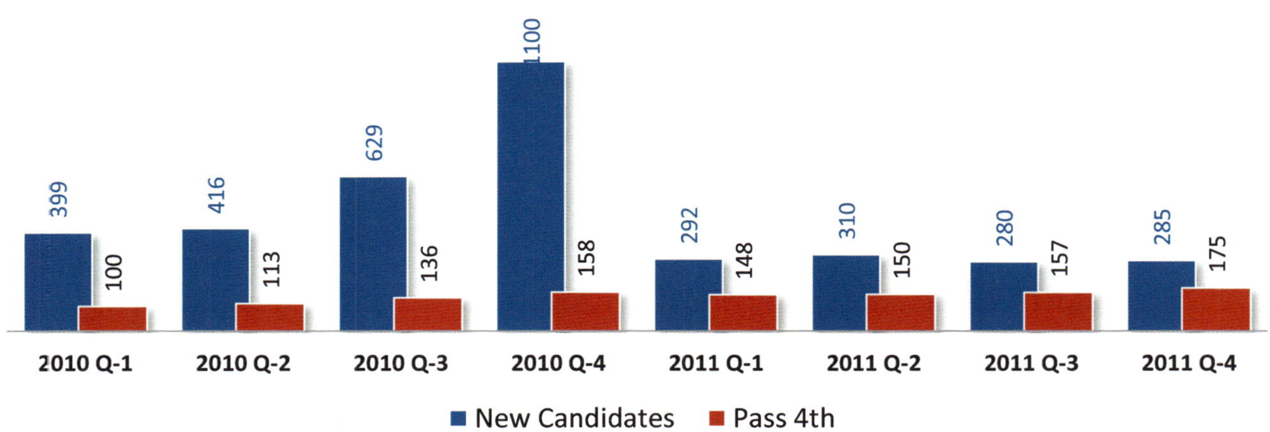

Notes about the Data

1. The data used to develop this report was pulled from NASBA's Gateway System, which houses the Uniform CPA Examination's Application and Performance information for all 55 jurisdictions.
2. The demographic data related to Age, Gender and Degree Type is provided by the individual candidates and may not be 100% accurate.

Maine

CPA Exam Performance Summary: *2011*

Maryland

Overall Performance

Unique Candidates	1,495
New Candidates	574
Total Sections	3,727
Passing 4th Section	363
Sections/Candidate	2.49
Pass Rate	43.2%
Average Score	70.1

Section Performance

	Sections	Score	% Pass
First-Time	2,070	70.3	47.4%
Re-Exam	1,657	69.8	37.9%
AUD	977	71.1	44.8%
BEC	826	70.4	43.1%
FAR	908	68.8	43.0%
REG	1,016	69.9	41.8%

Jurisdiction Rankings (1 to 53)

Candidates	Sections
19	19
36	32
Pass Rate	Avg Score

Exam Type by Percent

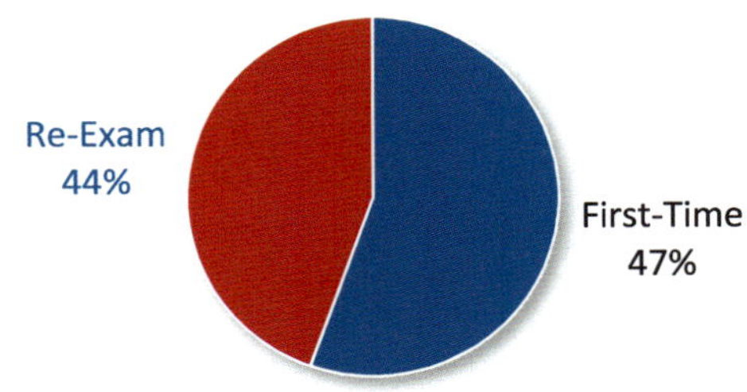

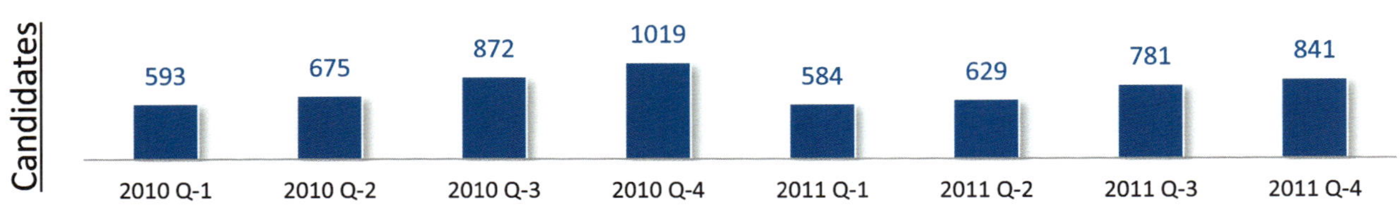

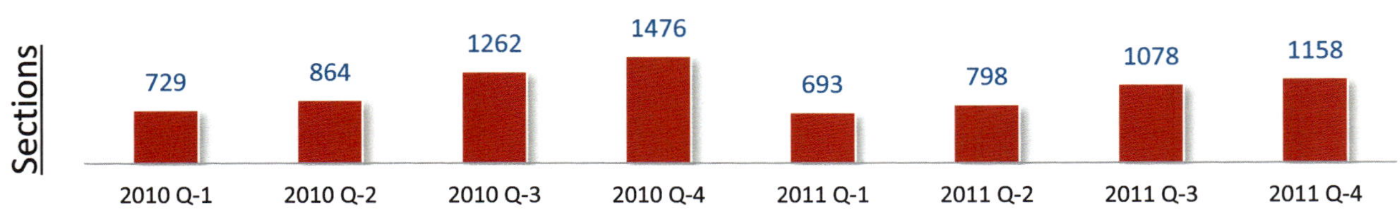

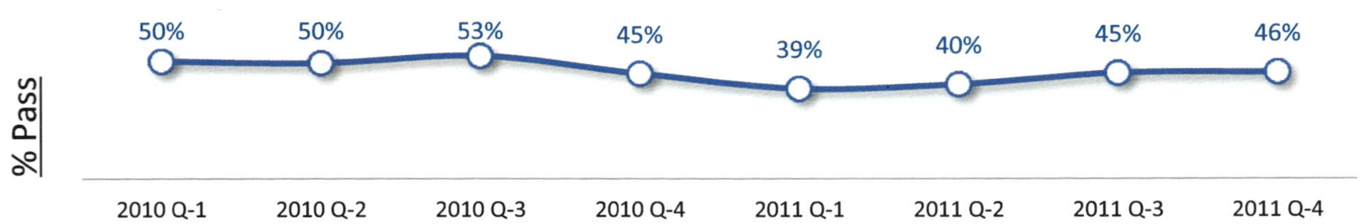

CPA Exam Performance Summary: *2011*

Demographics

Male Candidates	0	0.0%
Female Candidates	0	0.0%
Not Reported	1,495	100.0%

Average Age	**29.8**
Age Rank	**31**

Residency

Candidate Count	
In-State Address	**1,367**
Out-of-State Address	**126**
Foreign Address	**2**
% of Candidates	
In-State Address	**91.4%**
Out-of-State Address	**8.4%**
Foreign Address	**0.1%**

Degree Type

Candidate Count	
Bachelor's Degree	**0**
Advanced Degree	**0**
None/Other	**1,495**
% of Candidates	
Bachelor's Degree	**0.0%**
Advanced Degree	**0.0%**
None/Other	**100.0%**

New Candidates vs Candidates Passing 4th Section

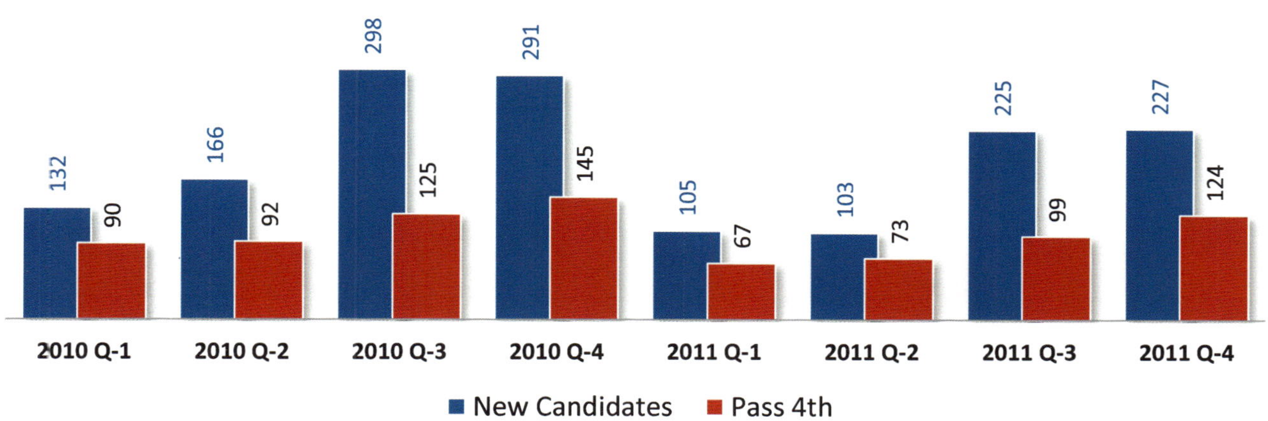

Nctes about the Data

1. The data used to develop this report was pulled from NASBA's Gateway System, which houses the Uniform CPA Examination's Application and Performance information for all 55 jurisdictions.
2. The demographic data related to Age, Gender and Degree Type is provided by the individual candidates and may not be 100% accurate.

Maryland

CPA Exam Performance Summary: *2011*

Massachusetts

Overall Performance

Unique Candidates	**2,709**
New Candidates	**1,418**
Total Sections	**6,902**
Passing 4th Section	**800**
Sections/Candidate	**2.55**
Pass Rate	**49.9%**
Average Score	**72.1**

Section Performance

	Sections	Score	% Pass
First-Time	**4,309**	**72.9**	**54.8%**
Re-Exam	**2,593**	**70.7**	**41.7%**
AUD	**1,835**	**73.5**	**50.6%**
BEC	**1,484**	**73.8**	**55.8%**
FAR	**1,704**	**70.8**	**48.7%**
REG	**1,879**	**70.5**	**45.6%**

Jurisdiction Rankings (1 to 53)

Candidates	Sections
9	**8**
12	**13**
Pass Rate	Avg Score

Exam Type by Percent

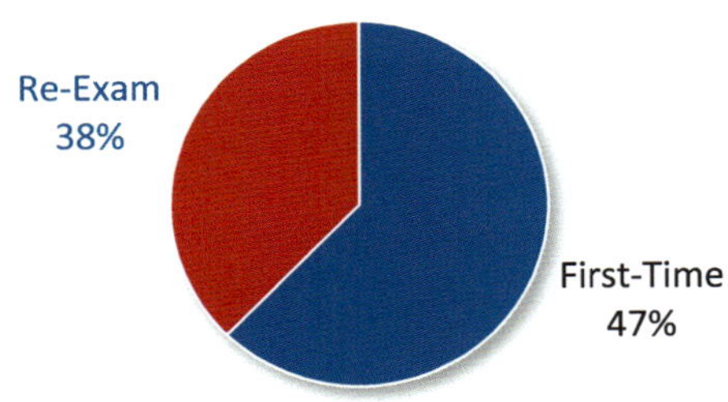

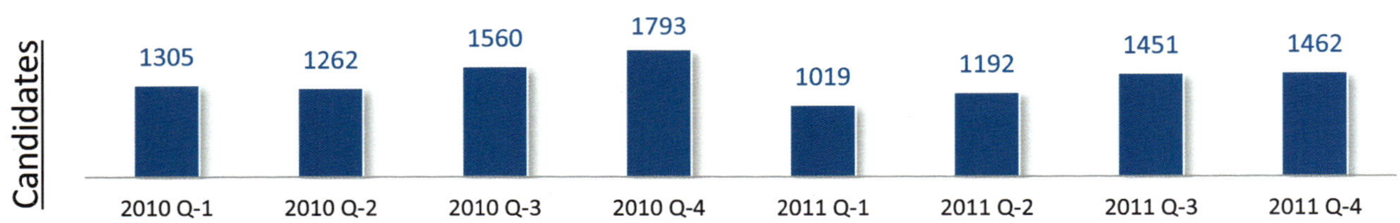

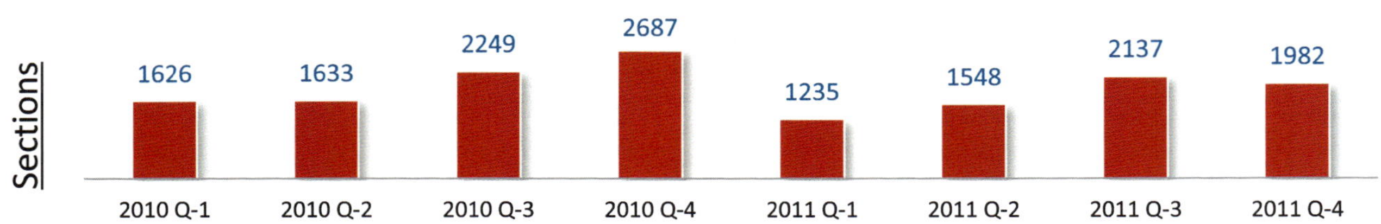

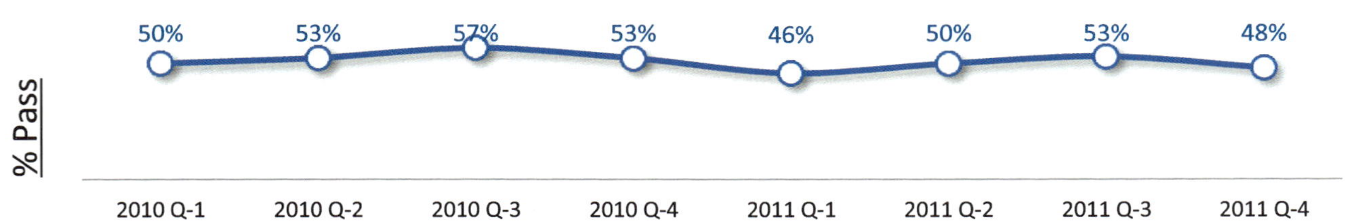

CPA Exam Performance Summary: *2011*

Demographics

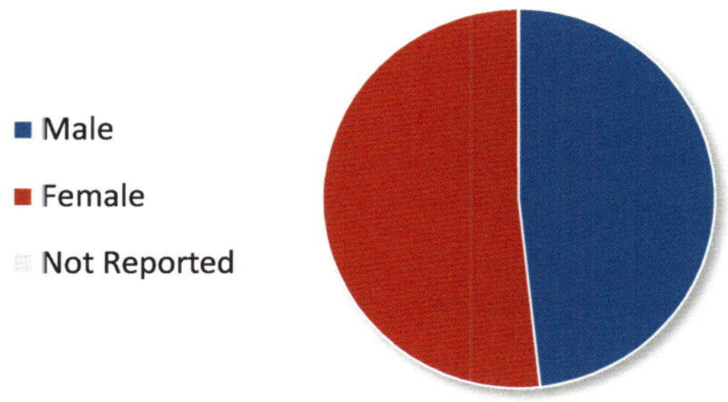

Male Candidates	1,307	48.2%
Female Candidates	1,400	51.7%
Not Reported	2	0.1%

Average Age	**27.4**
Age Rank	**5**

Residency

Candidate Count	
In-State Address	**2,216**
Out-of-State Address	**451**
Foreign Address	**42**
% of Candidates	
In-State Address	**81.8%**
Out-of-State Address	**16.6%**
Foreign Address	**1.6%**

Degree Type

Candidate Count	
Bachelor's Degree	**1,662**
Advanced Degree	**565**
None/Other	**482**
% of Candidates	
Bachelor's Degree	**61.4%**
Advanced Degree	**20.9%**
None/Other	**17.8%**

New Candidates vs Candidates Passing 4th Section

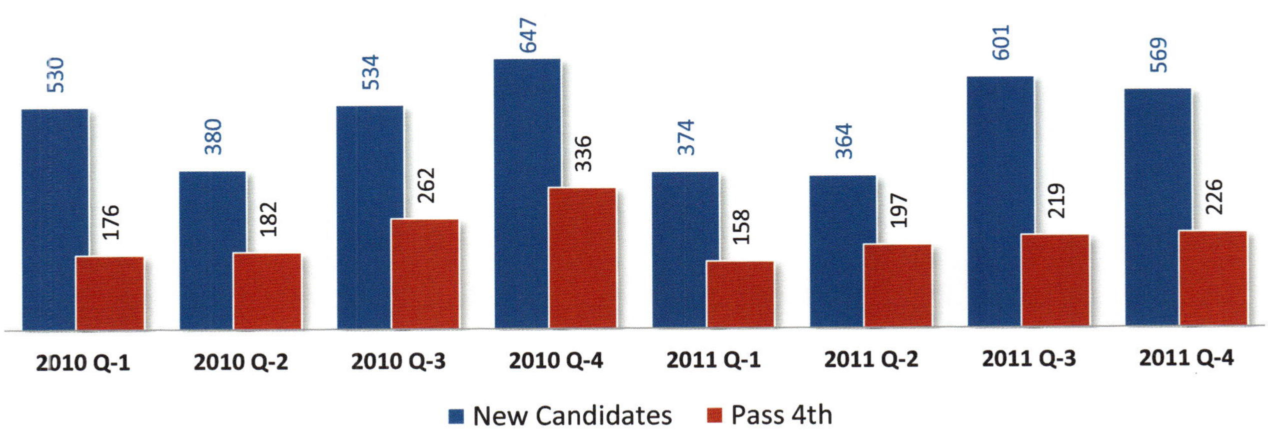

Notes about the Data

1. The data used to develop this report was pulled from NASBA's Gateway System, which houses the Uniform CPA Examination's Application and Performance information for all 55 jurisdictions.
2. The demographic data related to Age, Gender and Degree Type is provided by the individual candidates and may not be 100% accurate.

Massachusetts

CPA Exam Performance Summary: *2011*

Michigan

Overall Performance

Unique Candidates	**1,868**
New Candidates	**924**
Total Sections	**4,962**
Passing 4th Section	**596**
Sections/Candidate	**2.66**
Pass Rate	**52.1%**
Average Score	**73.1**

Section Performance

	Sections	Score	% Pass
First-Time	**3,084**	**74.0**	**57.8%**
Re-Exam	**1,878**	**71.7**	**42.8%**
AUD	**1,391**	**74.2**	**51.6%**
BEC	**1,063**	**74.2**	**56.3%**
FAR	**1,239**	**71.7**	**50.0%**
REG	**1,269**	**72.5**	**51.3%**

Jurisdiction Rankings (1 to 53)

Candidates	Sections
16	**16**
6	**4**
Pass Rate	Avg Score

Exam Type by Percent

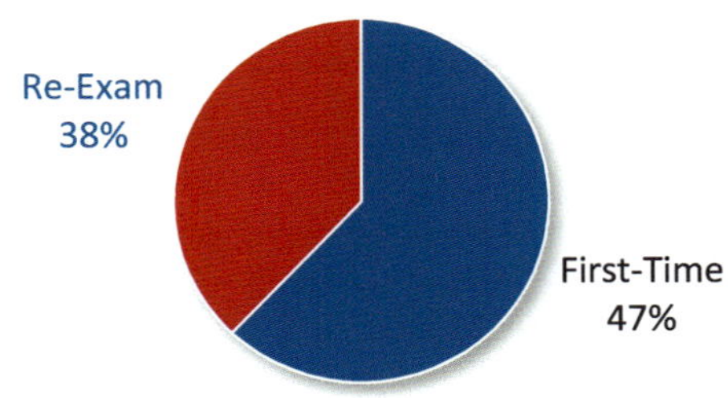

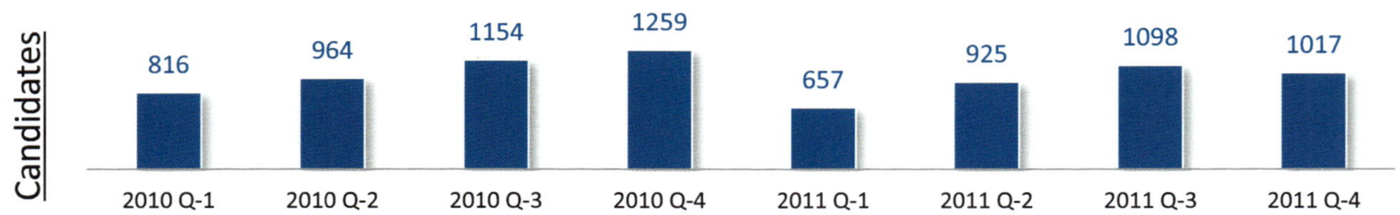

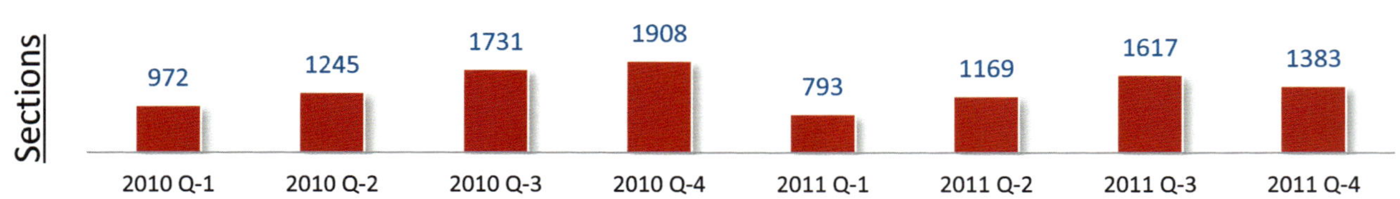

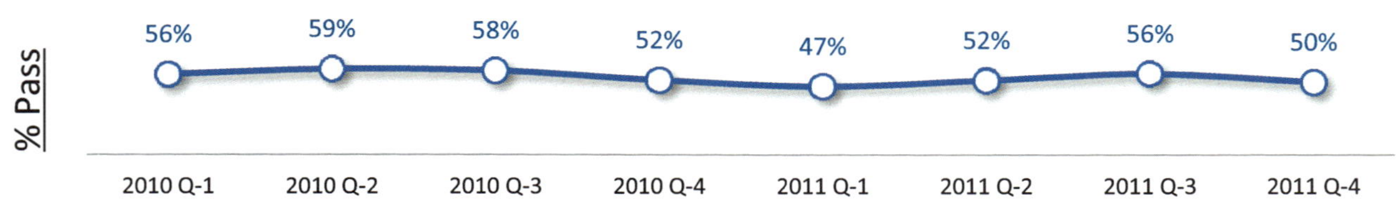

CPA Exam Performance Summary: *2011*

Demographics

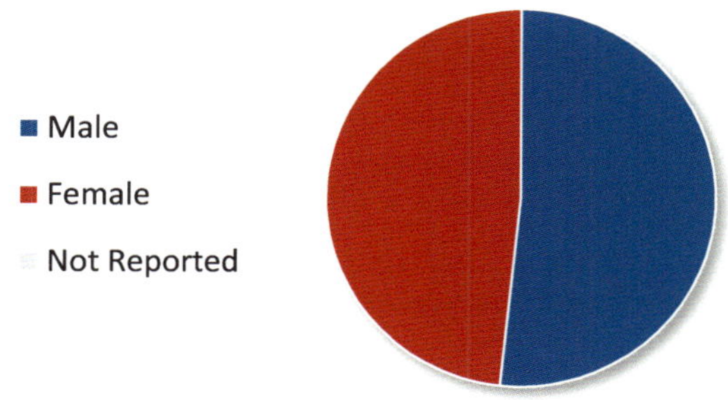

Male Candidates	965	51.7%
Female Candidates	903	48.3%
Not Reported	0	0.0%

Average Age	**28.4**
Age Rank	**17**

Residency

Candidate Count	
In-State Address	**1,650**
Out-of-State Address	**163**
Foreign Address	**55**

% of Candidates	
In-State Address	**88.3%**
Out-of-State Address	**8.7%**
Foreign Address	**2.9%**

Degree Type

Candidate Count	
Bachelor's Degree	**1,327**
Advanced Degree	**284**
None/Other	**257**

% of Candidates	
Bachelor's Degree	**71.0%**
Advanced Degree	**15.2%**
None/Other	**13.8%**

New Candidates vs Candidates Passing 4th Section

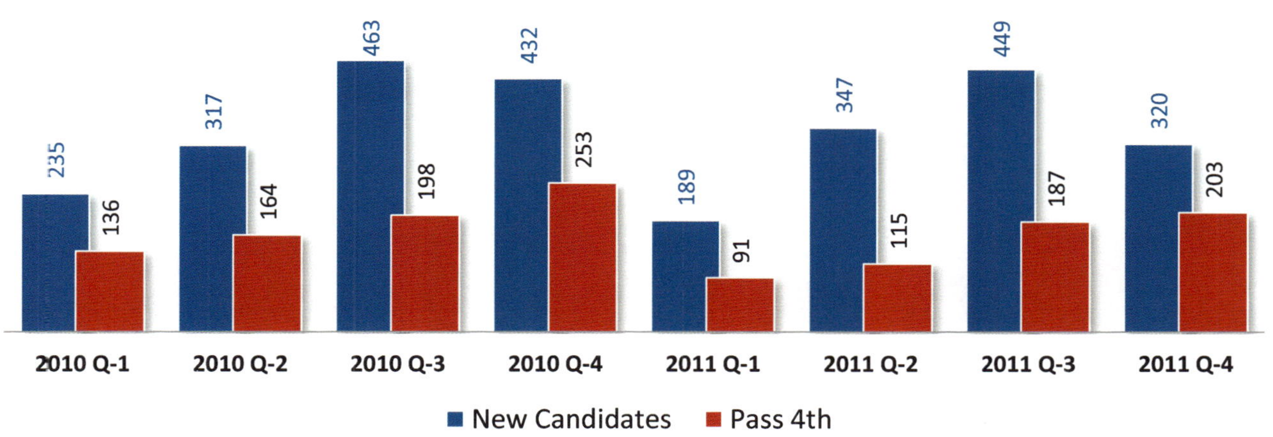

Nctes about the Data

1. The data used to develop this report was pulled from NASBA's Gateway System, which houses the Uniform CPA Examination's Application and Performance information for all 55 jurisdictions.
2. The demographic data related to Age, Gender and Degree Type is provided by the individual candidates and may not be 100% accurate.

Michigan

CPA Exam Performance Summary: *2011*

Minnesota

Overall Performance

Unique Candidates	**1,368**
New Candidates	**761**
Total Sections	**3,666**
Passing 4th Section	**465**
Sections/Candidate	**2.68**
Pass Rate	**52.6%**
Average Score	**72.9**

Section Performance

	Sections	Score	% Pass
First-Time	**2,461**	**73.6**	**56.7%**
Re-Exam	**1,205**	**71.4**	**44.2%**
AUD	**977**	**73.5**	**50.0%**
BEC	**804**	**75.0**	**60.8%**
FAR	**901**	**71.3**	**51.5%**
REG	**984**	**72.0**	**49.4%**

Jurisdiction Rankings (1 to 53)

Candidates	Sections
20	**21**
5	**6**
Pass Rate	Avg Score

Exam Type by Percent

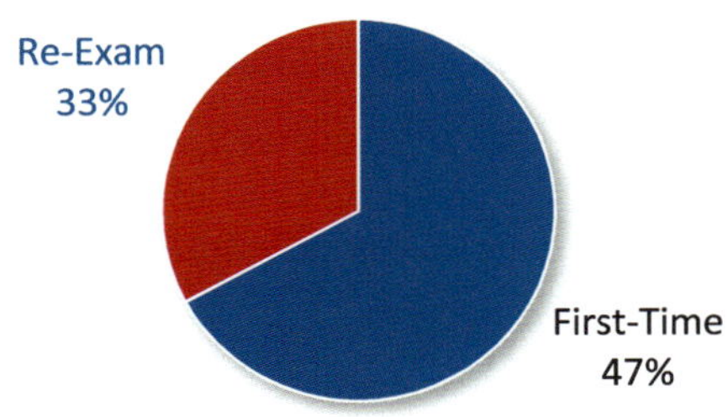

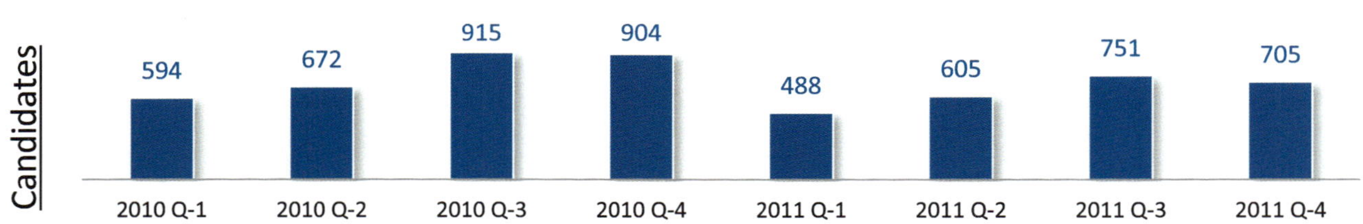

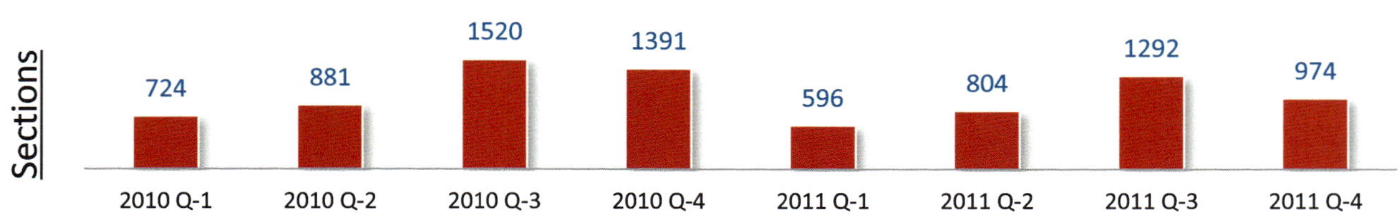

CPA Exam Performance Summary: *2011*

Demographics

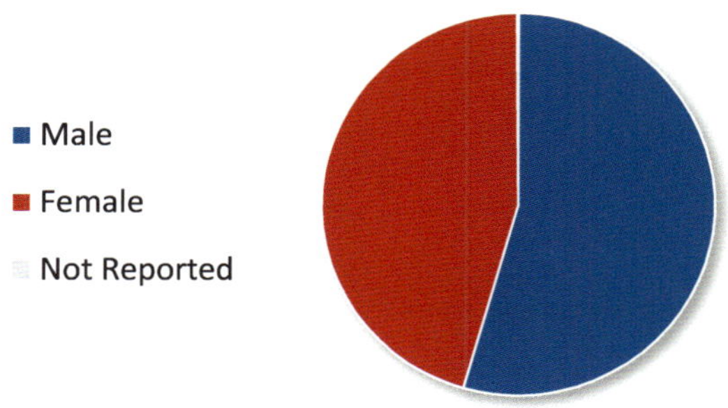

Male Candidates	745	54.5%
Female Candidates	621	45.4%
Not Reported	2	0.1%

Average Age	**27.5**
Age Rank	**6**

Residency

Candidate Count	
In-State Address	**1,290**
Out-of-State Address	**76**
Foreign Address	**2**

% of Candidates	
In-State Address	**94.3%**
Out-of-State Address	**5.6%**
Foreign Address	**0.1%**

Degree Type

Candidate Count	
Bachelor's Degree	**1,024**
Advanced Degree	**86**
None/Other	**258**

% of Candidates	
Bachelor's Degree	**74.9%**
Advanced Degree	**6.3%**
None/Other	**18.9%**

New Candidates vs Candidates Passing 4th Section

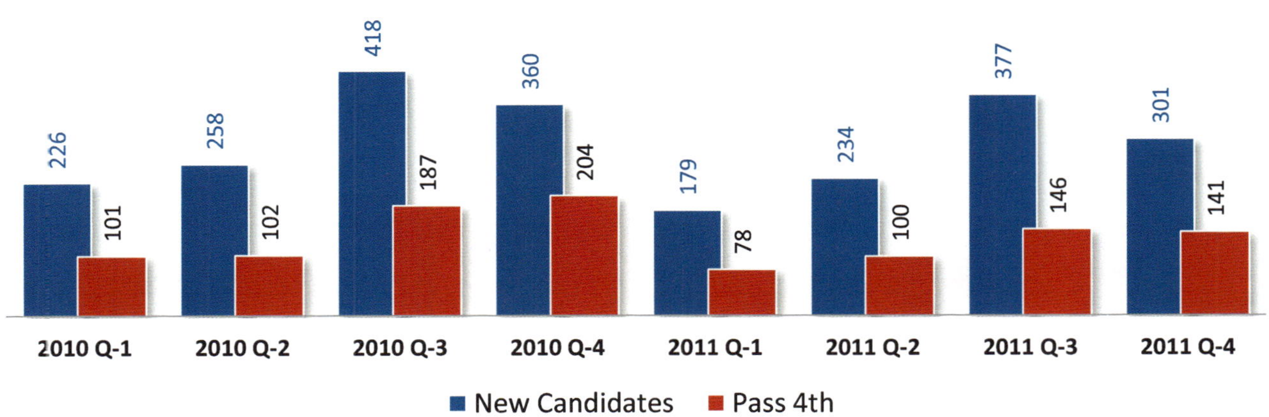

Notes about the Data

1. The data used to develop this report was pulled from NASBA's Gateway System, which houses the Uniform CPA Examination's Application and Performance information for all 55 jurisdictions.
2. The demographic data related to Age, Gender and Degree Type is provided by the individual candidates and may not be 100% accurate.

Minnesota

CPA Exam Performance Summary: *2011*

Mississippi

Overall Performance

Unique Candidates	**374**
New Candidates	**139**
Total Sections	**900**
Passing 4th Section	**73**
Sections/Candidate	**2.41**
Pass Rate	**33.9%**
Average Score	**67.0**

Section Performance

	Sections	Score	% Pass
First-Time	**479**	**66.6**	**37.2%**
Re-Exam	**421**	**67.5**	**30.2%**
AUD	**233**	**67.8**	**30.9%**
BEC	**221**	**67.4**	**33.9%**
FAR	**211**	**64.7**	**31.3%**
REG	**235**	**68.1**	**39.2%**

Jurisdiction Rankings (1 to 53)

Candidates	Sections
42	**42**
51	**50**
Pass Rate	Avg Score

Exam Type by Percent

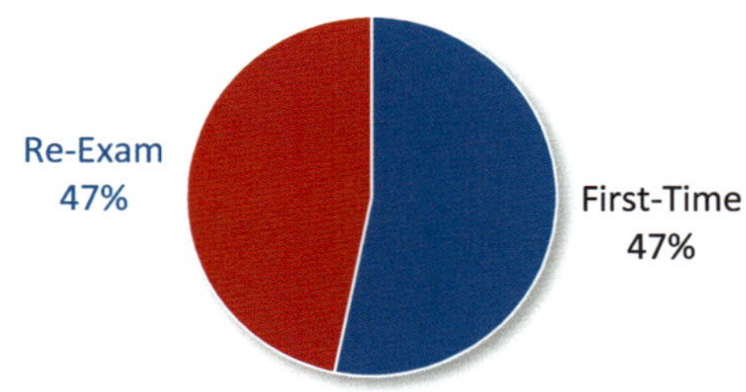

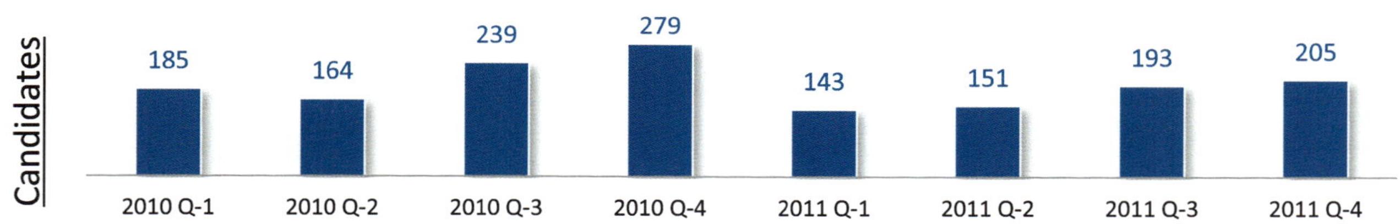

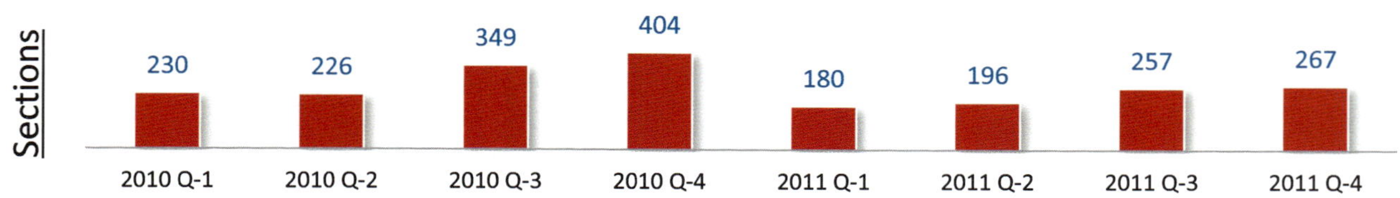

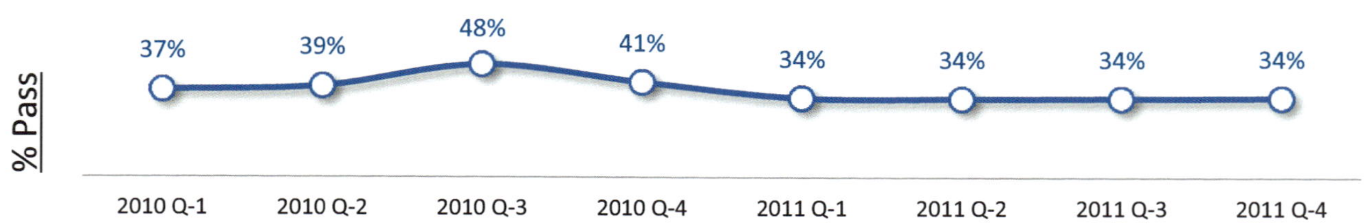

CPA Exam Performance Summary: *2011*

Demographics

Male Candidates	0	0.0%
Female Candidates	1	0.3%
Not Reported	373	99.7%

Average Age	**30.9**
Age Rank	**40**

Residency

Candidate Count	
In-State Address	**356**
Out-of-State Address	**18**
Foreign Address	**0**
% of Candidates	
In-State Address	**95.2%**
Out-of-State Address	**4.8%**
Foreign Address	**0.0%**

Degree Type

Candidate Count	
Bachelor's Degree	**325**
Advanced Degree	**49**
None/Other	**0**
% of Candidates	
Bachelor's Degree	**86.9%**
Advanced Degree	**13.1%**
None/Other	**0.0%**

New Candidates vs Candidates Passing 4th Section

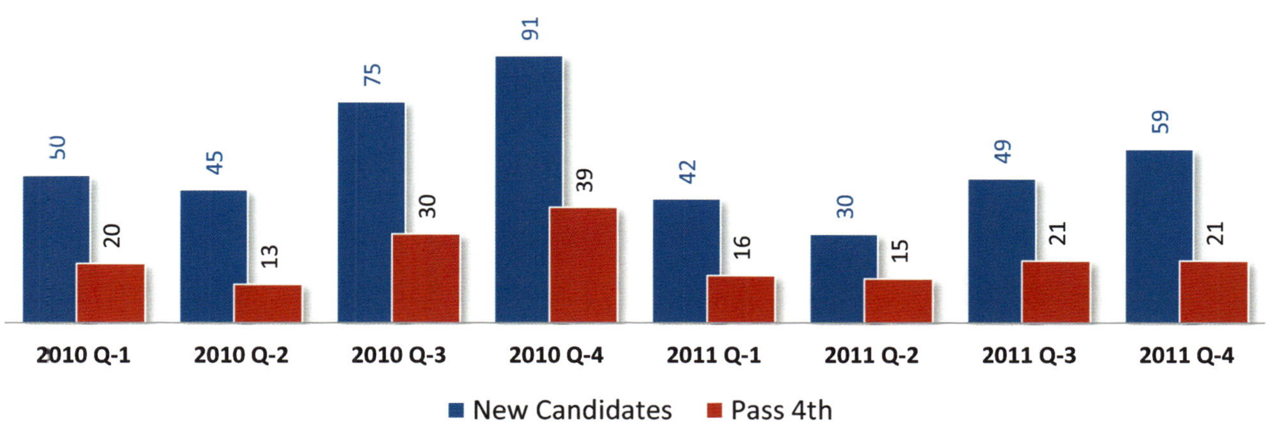

Nctes about the Data

1. The data used to develop this report was pulled from NASBA's Gateway System, which houses the Uniform CPA Examination's Application and Performance information for all 55 jurisdictions.
2. The demographic data related to Age, Gender and Degree Type is provided by the individual candidates and may not be 100% accurate.

Mississippi

CPA Exam Performance Summary: *2011*

Missouri

Overall Performance

Unique Candidates	**1,272**
New Candidates	**704**
Total Sections	**3,669**
Passing 4th Section	**472**
Sections/Candidate	**2.88**
Pass Rate	**54.8%**
Average Score	**73.4**

Section Performance

	Sections	Score	% Pass
First-Time	**2,410**	**74.3**	**59.5%**
Re-Exam	**1,259**	**71.8**	**45.8%**
AUD	**1,003**	**73.5**	**49.6%**
BEC	**787**	**75.7**	**62.9%**
FAR	**911**	**71.9**	**54.0%**
REG	**968**	**73.0**	**54.6%**

Jurisdiction Rankings (1 to 53)

Candidates	Sections
23	**20**
3	**3**
Pass Rate	Avg Score

Exam Type by Percent

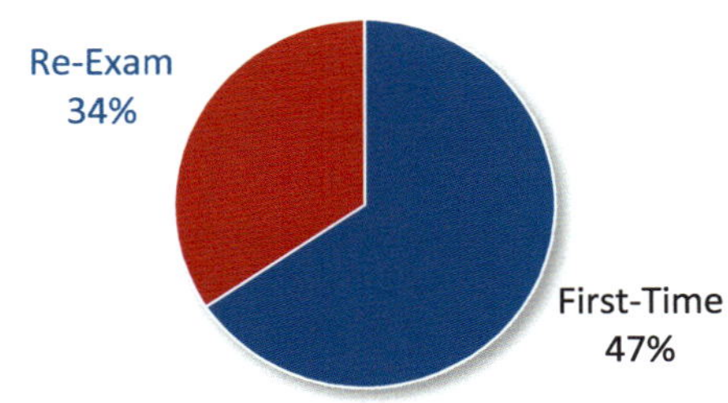

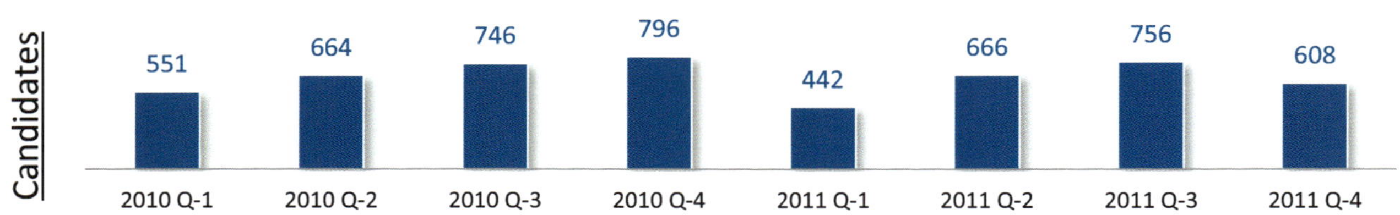

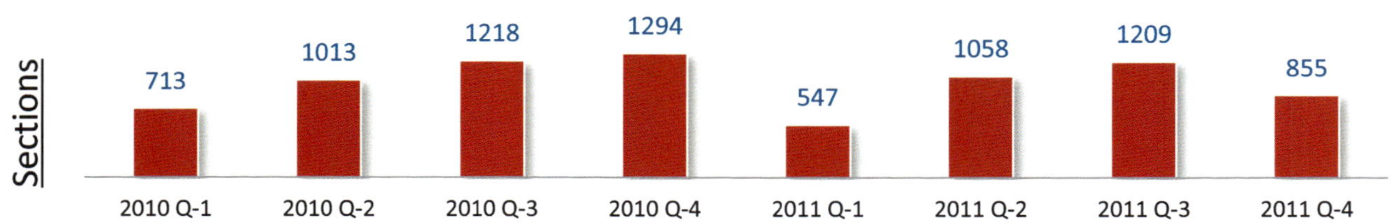

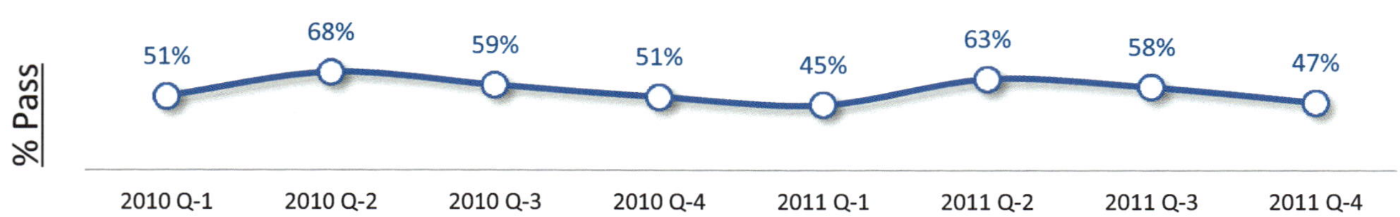

CPA Exam Performance Summary: *2011*

Demographics

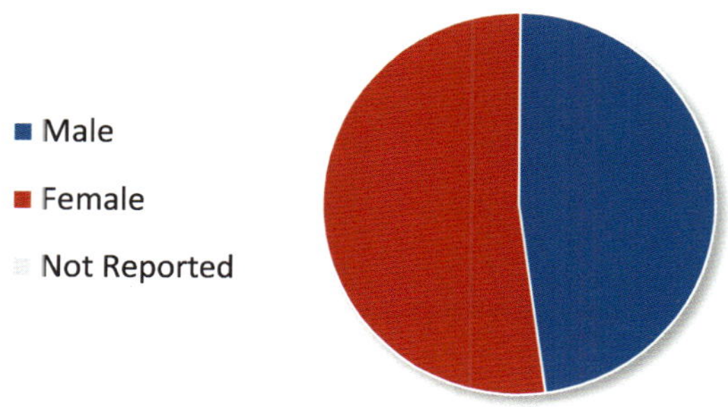

Male Candidates	607	47.7%
Female Candidates	665	52.3%
Not Reported	0	0.0%

Average Age	**27.8**
Age Rank	**9**

Residency

Candidate Count	
In-State Address	**1,104**
Out-of-State Address	**165**
Foreign Address	**3**

% of Candidates	
In-State Address	**86.8%**
Out-of-State Address	**13.0%**
Foreign Address	**0.2%**

Degree Type

Candidate Count	
Bachelor's Degree	**711**
Advanced Degree	**274**
None/Other	**287**

% of Candidates	
Bachelor's Degree	**55.9%**
Advanced Degree	**21.5%**
None/Other	**22.6%**

New Candidates vs Candidates Passing 4th Section

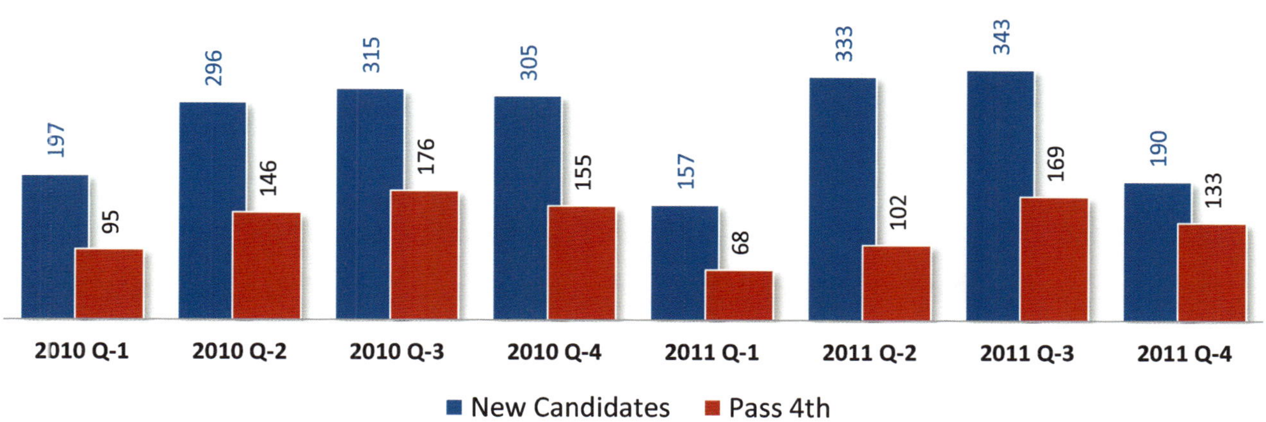

Notes about the Data

1. The data used to develop this report was pulled from NASBA's Gateway System, which houses the Uniform CPA Examination's Application and Performance information for all 55 jurisdictions.
2. The demographic data related to Age, Gender and Degree Type is provided by the individual candidates and may not be 100% accurate.

Missouri

CPA Exam Performance Summary: *2011*

Montana

Overall Performance

Unique Candidates	476
New Candidates	239
Total Sections	1,358
Passing 4th Section	143
Sections/Candidate	2.85
Pass Rate	45.4%
Average Score	70.7

Section Performance

	Sections	Score	% Pass
First-Time	770	70.9	49.6%
Re-Exam	588	70.4	40.0%
AUD	368	71.6	46.5%
BEC	293	70.6	40.6%
FAR	345	70.8	50.7%
REG	352	69.7	43.2%

Jurisdiction Rankings (1 to 53)

Candidates	Sections
39	36
25	26
Pass Rate	Avg Score

Exam Type by Percent

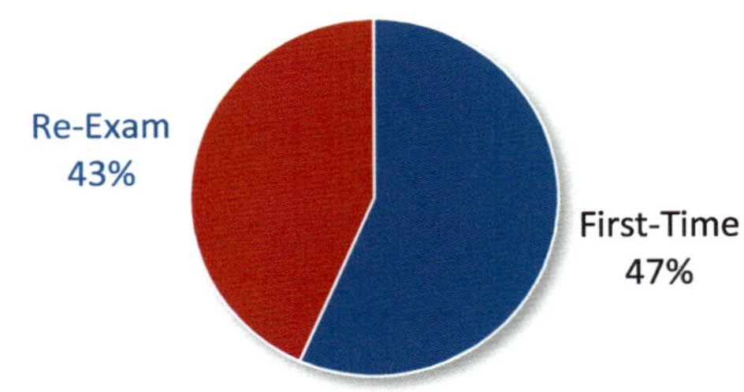

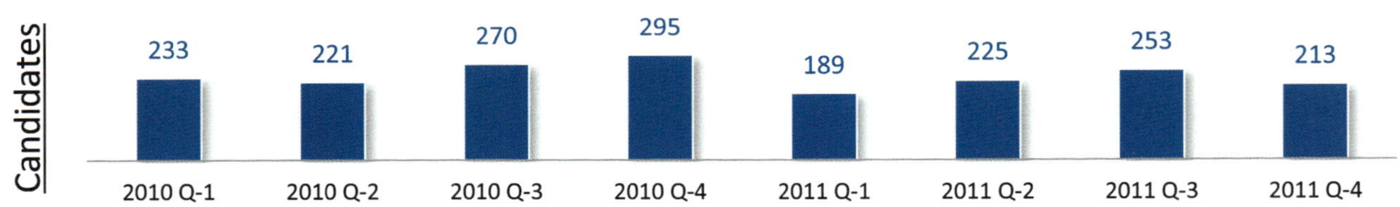

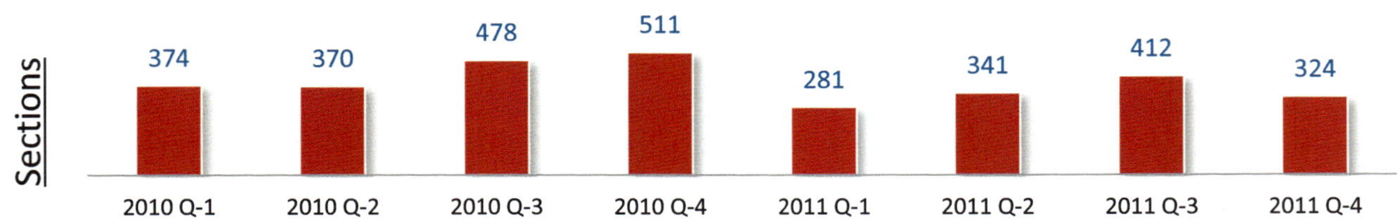

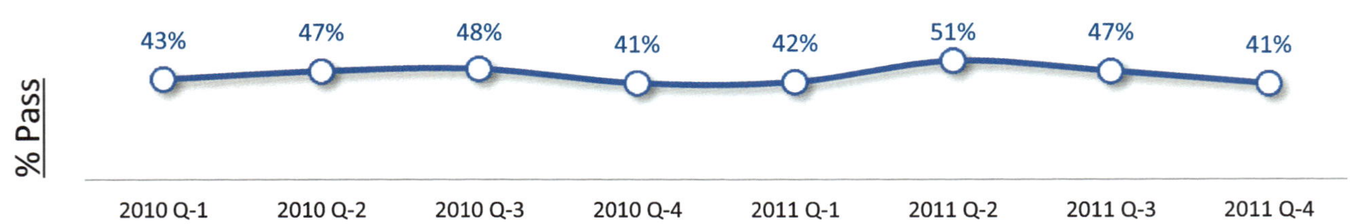

CPA Exam Performance Summary: *2011*

Demographics

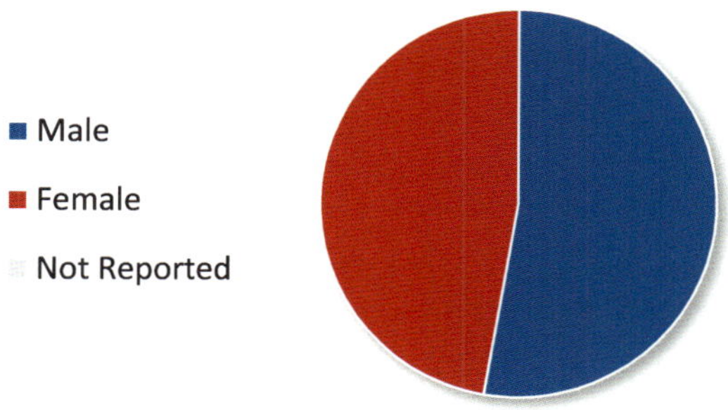

Male Candidates	251	52.7%
Female Candidates	225	47.3%
Not Reported	0	0.0%

Average Age	**28.4**
Age Rank	**16**

Residency

Candidate Count	
In-State Address	**190**
Out-of-State Address	**64**
Foreign Address	**222**
% of Candidates	
In-State Address	**39.9%**
Out-of-State Address	**13.4%**
Foreign Address	**46.6%**

Degree Type

Candidate Count	
Bachelor's Degree	**130**
Advanced Degree	**12**
None/Other	**334**
% of Candidates	
Bachelor's Degree	**27.3%**
Advanced Degree	**2.5%**
None/Other	**70.2%**

New Candidates vs Candidates Passing 4th Section

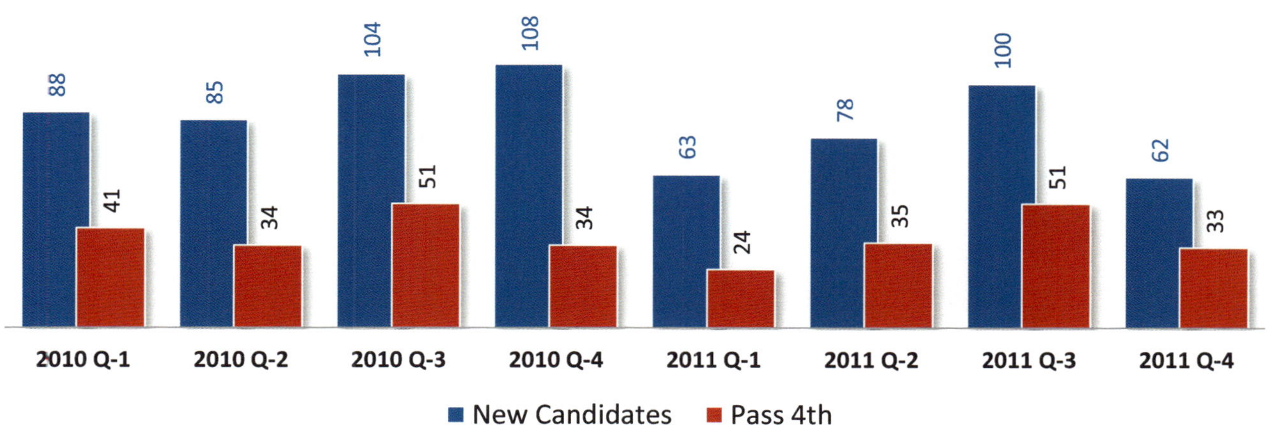

Notes about the Data

1. The data used to develop this report was pulled from NASBA's Gateway System, which houses the Uniform CPA Examination's Application and Performance information for all 55 jurisdictions.
2. The demographic data related to Age, Gender and Degree Type is provided by the individual candidates and may not be 100% accurate.

Montana

CPA Exam Performance Summary: *2011*

Nebraska

Overall Performance

Unique Candidates	311
New Candidates	166
Total Sections	859
Passing 4th Section	88
Sections/Candidate	2.76
Pass Rate	48.1%
Average Score	71.7

Section Performance

	Sections	Score	% Pass
First-Time	521	72.6	54.1%
Re-Exam	338	70.3	38.8%
AUD	233	72.5	44.6%
BEC	197	73.4	56.4%
FAR	220	70.9	47.7%
REG	209	70.0	44.5%

Jurisdiction Rankings (1 to 53)

Candidates	Sections
46	43
19	17
Pass Rate	Avg Score

Exam Type by Percent

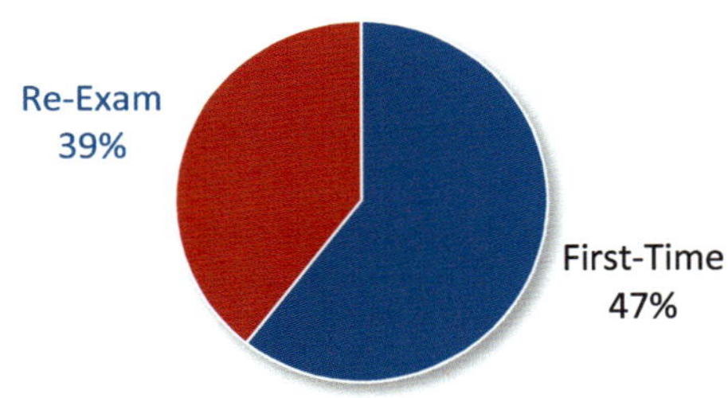

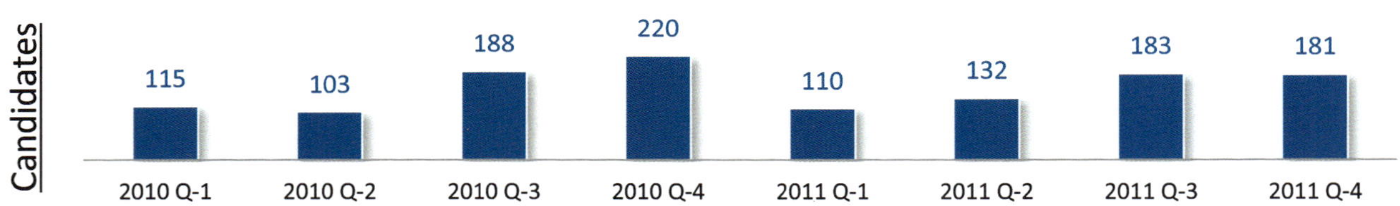

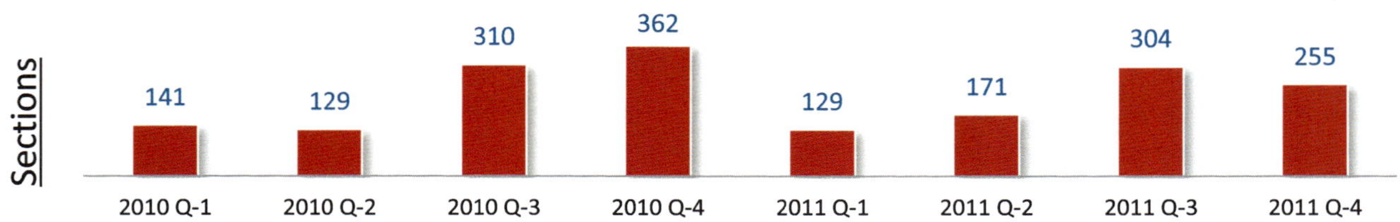

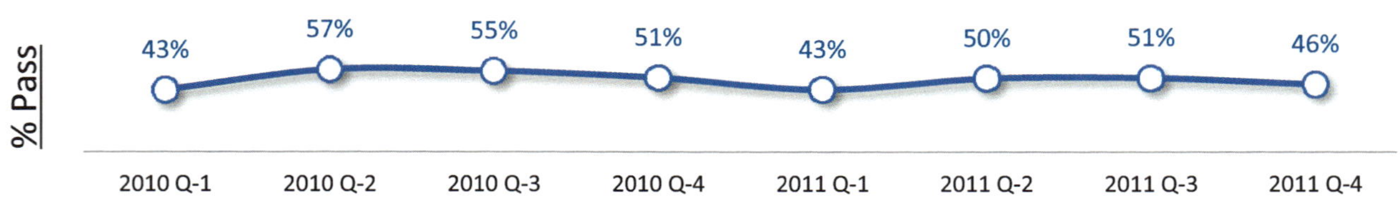

CPA Exam Performance Summary: *2011*

Demographics

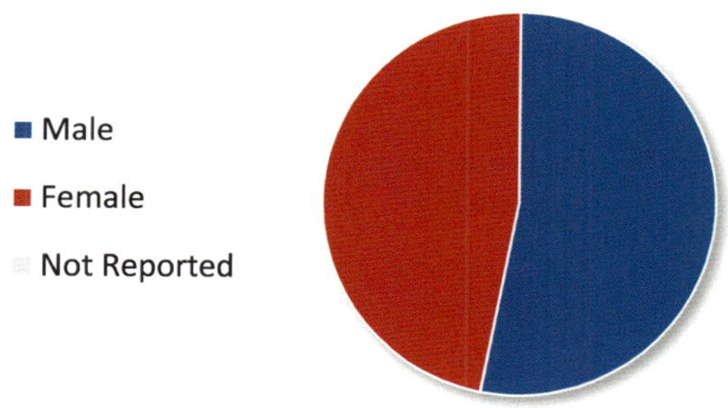

Male Candidates	165	53.1%
Female Candidates	146	46.9%
Not Reported	0	0.0%

Average Age	**27.2**
Age Rank	**2**

Residency

Candidate Count	
In-State Address	**296**
Out-of-State Address	**15**
Foreign Address	**0**
% of Candidates	
In-State Address	**95.2%**
Out-of-State Address	**4.8%**
Foreign Address	**0.0%**

Degree Type

Candidate Count	
Bachelor's Degree	**221**
Advanced Degree	**43**
None/Other	**47**
% of Candidates	
Bachelor's Degree	**71.1%**
Advanced Degree	**13.8%**
None/Other	**15.1%**

New Candidates vs Candidates Passing 4th Section

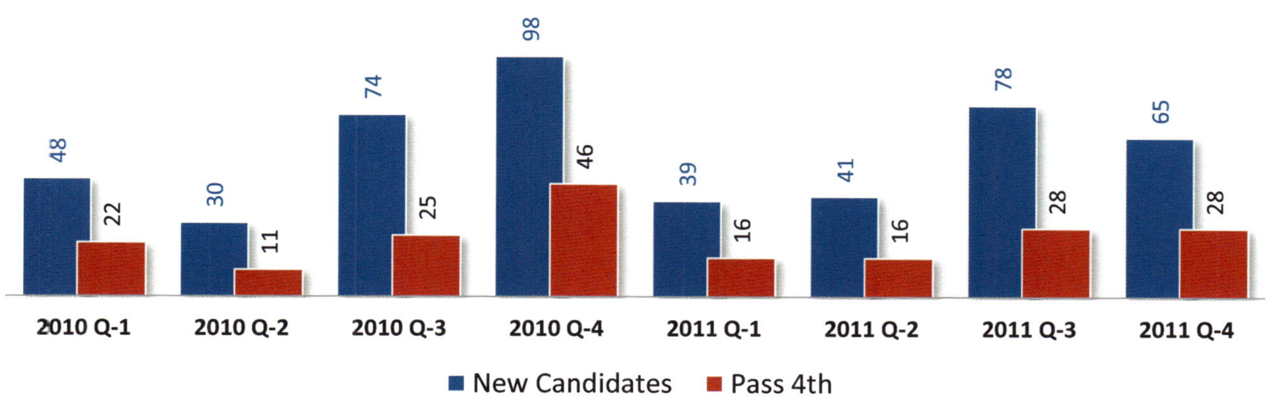

Notes about the Data

1. The data used to develop this report was pulled from NASBA's Gateway System, which houses the Uniform CPA Examination's Application and Performance information for all 55 jurisdictions.
2. The demographic data related to Age, Gender and Degree Type is provided by the individual candidates and may not be 100% accurate.

Nebraska

CPA Exam Performance Summary: *2011*

Nevada

Overall Performance

Unique Candidates	324
New Candidates	107
Total Sections	842
Passing 4th Section	86
Sections/Candidate	2.60
Pass Rate	45.0%
Average Score	71.7

Section Performance

	Sections	Score	% Pass
First-Time	**458**	**72.2**	**47.8%**
Re-Exam	**384**	**71.0**	**41.7%**
AUD	**232**	**73.4**	**45.3%**
BEC	**176**	**71.7**	**42.6%**
FAR	**202**	**69.6**	**43.6%**
REG	**232**	**71.7**	**47.8%**

Jurisdiction Rankings (1 to 53)

Candidates	Sections
45	**45**
28	**18**
Pass Rate	Avg Score

Exam Type by Percent

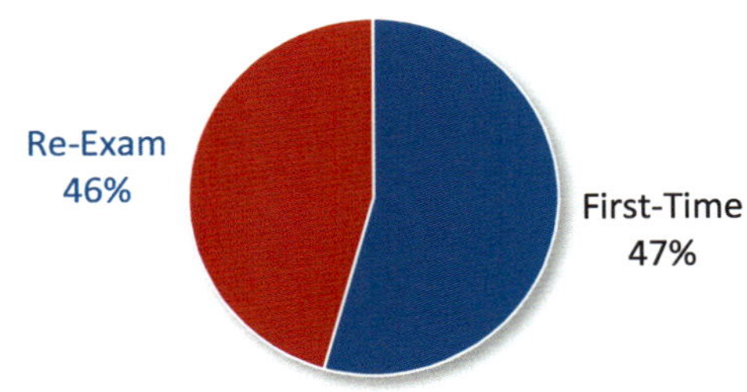

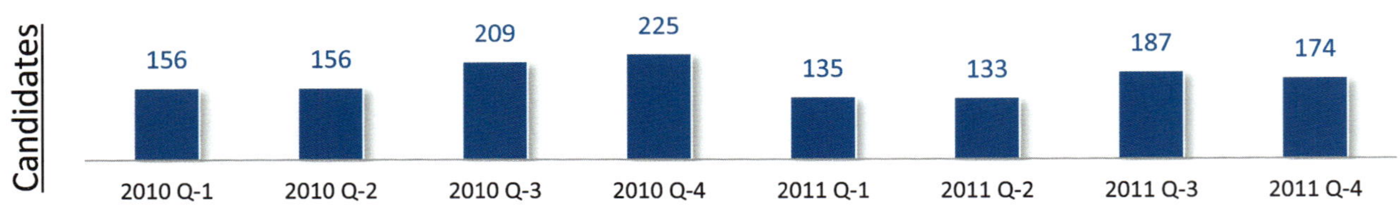

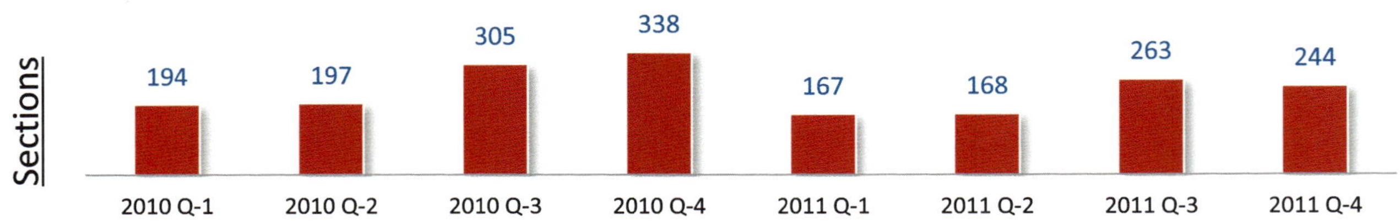

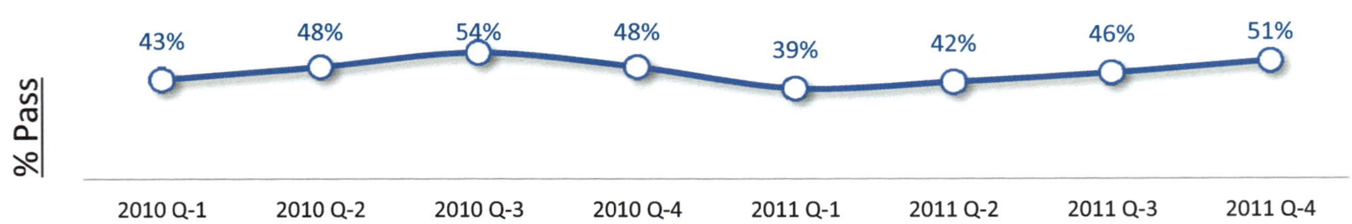

CPA Exam Performance Summary: *2011*

Demographics

Male Candidates	0	0.0%
Female Candidates	0	0.0%
Not Reported	324	100.0%

Average Age	**30.0**
Age Rank	**34**

Residency

Candidate Count

In-State Address	**295**
Out-of-State Address	**25**
Foreign Address	**4**

% of Candidates

In-State Address	**91.0%**
Out-of-State Address	**7.7%**
Foreign Address	**1.2%**

Degree Type

Candidate Count

Bachelor's Degree	**231**
Advanced Degree	**65**
None/Other	**28**

% of Candidates

Bachelor's Degree	**71.3%**
Advanced Degree	**20.1%**
None/Other	**8.6%**

New Candidates vs Candidates Passing 4th Section

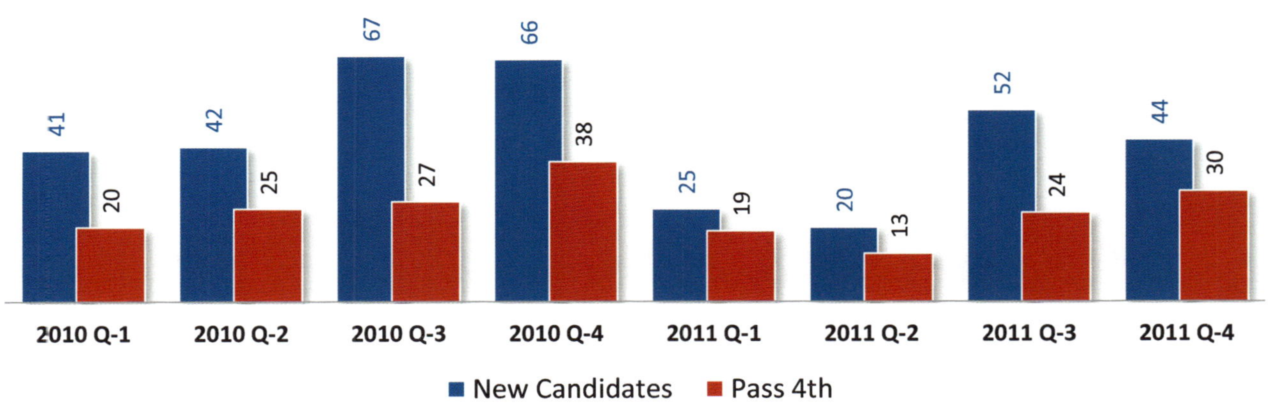

Notes about the Data

1. The data used to develop this report was pulled from NASBA's Gateway System, which houses the Uniform CPA Examination's Application and Performance information for all 55 jurisdictions.
2. The demographic data related to Age, Gender and Degree Type is provided by the individual candidates and may not be 100% accurate.

Nevada

CPA Exam Performance Summary: *2011*

New Hampshire

Overall Performance

Unique Candidates	**2,641**
New Candidates	**1,210**
Total Sections	**6,462**
Passing 4th Section	**587**
Sections/Candidate	**2.45**
Pass Rate	**41.3%**
Average Score	**68.3**

Section Performance

	Sections	Score	% Pass
First-Time	**3,666**	**67.6**	**43.7%**
Re-Exam	**2,796**	**69.3**	**38.2%**
AUD	**1,874**	**69.7**	**42.9%**
BEC	**1,336**	**67.7**	**36.9%**
FAR	**1,582**	**68.9**	**48.0%**
REG	**1,670**	**66.7**	**36.7%**

Jurisdiction Rankings (1 to 53)

Candidates	Sections
10	**11**
41	**45**
Pass Rate	Avg Score

Exam Type by Percent

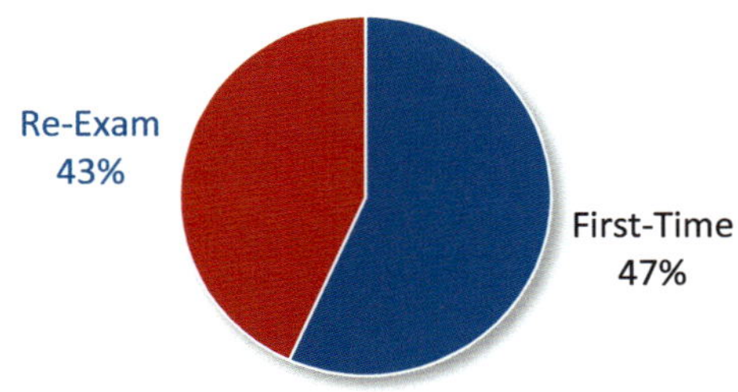

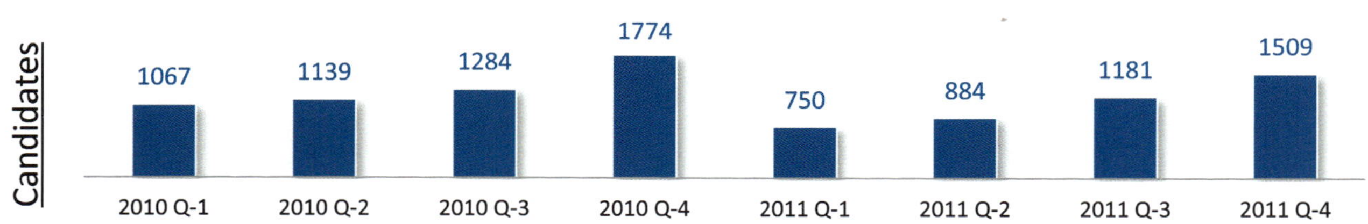

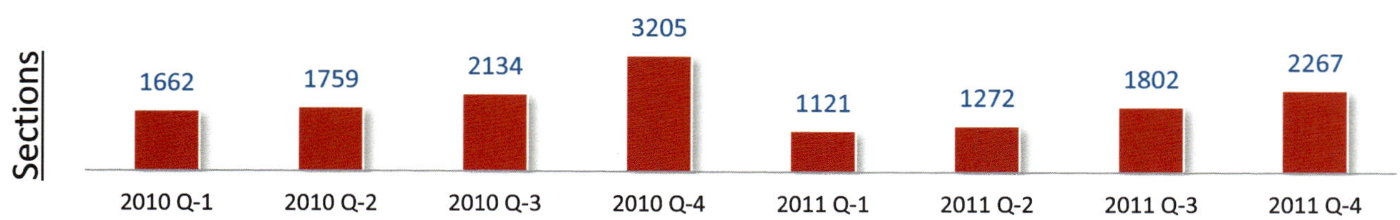

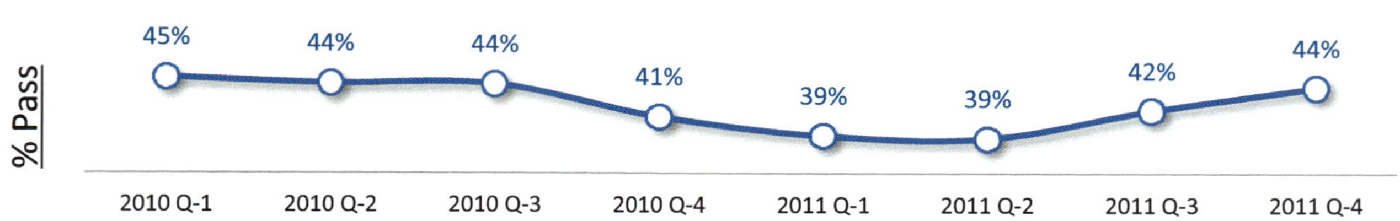

CPA Exam Performance Summary: *2011*

Demographics

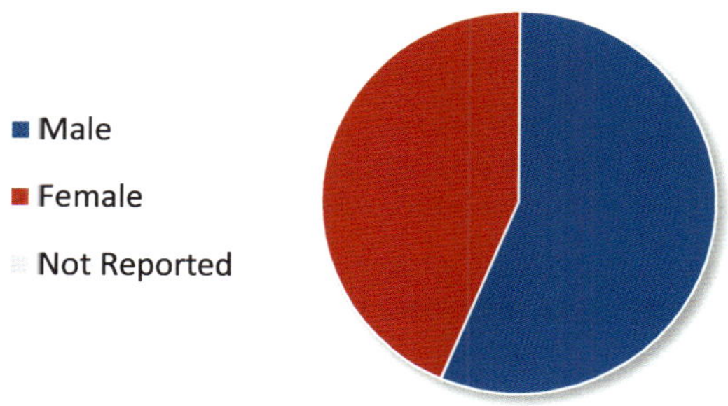

Male Candidates	**1,487**	**56.3%**
Female Candidates	**1,154**	**43.7%**
Not Reported	**0**	**0.0%**

Average Age	**30.8**
Age Rank	**39**

Residency

Candidate Count	
In-State Address	**120**
Out-of-State Address	**739**
Foreign Address	**1,782**
% of Candidates	
In-State Address	**4.5%**
Out-of-State Address	**28.0%**
Foreign Address	**67.5%**

Degree Type

Candidate Count	
Bachelor's Degree	**2,105**
Advanced Degree	**330**
None/Other	**206**
% of Candidates	
Bachelor's Degree	**79.7%**
Advanced Degree	**12.5%**
None/Other	**7.8%**

New Candidates vs Candidates Passing 4th Section

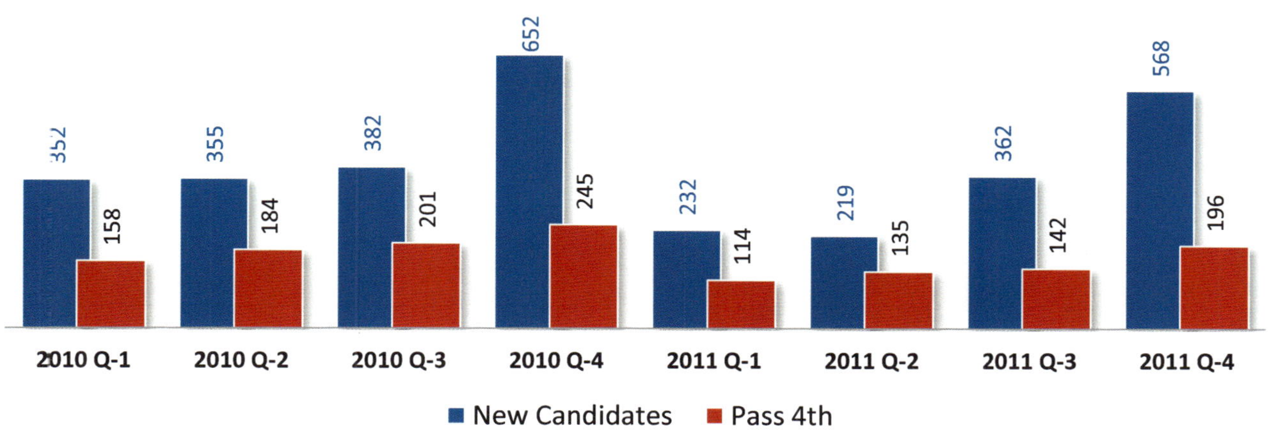

Notes about the Data

1. The data used to develop this report was pulled from NASBA's Gateway System, which houses the Uniform CPA Examination's Application and Performance information for all 55 jurisdictions.
2. The demographic data related to Age, Gender and Degree Type is provided by the individual candidates and may not be 100% accurate.

New Hampshire

CPA Exam Performance Summary: *2011*

New Jersey

Overall Performance

Unique Candidates	**2,777**
New Candidates	**1,264**
Total Sections	**6,859**
Passing 4th Section	**614**
Sections/Candidate	**2.47**
Pass Rate	**39.2%**
Average Score	**67.9**

Section Performance

	Sections	Score	% Pass
First-Time	**3,946**	**67.1**	**40.9%**
Re-Exam	**2,913**	**69.0**	**36.9%**
AUD	**1,835**	**69.2**	**39.4%**
BEC	**1,568**	**68.7**	**39.9%**
FAR	**1,654**	**66.2**	**38.0%**
REG	**1,802**	**67.5**	**39.4%**

Jurisdiction Rankings (1 to 53)

Candidates	Sections
8	**9**
43	**47**
Pass Rate	Avg Score

Exam Type by Percent

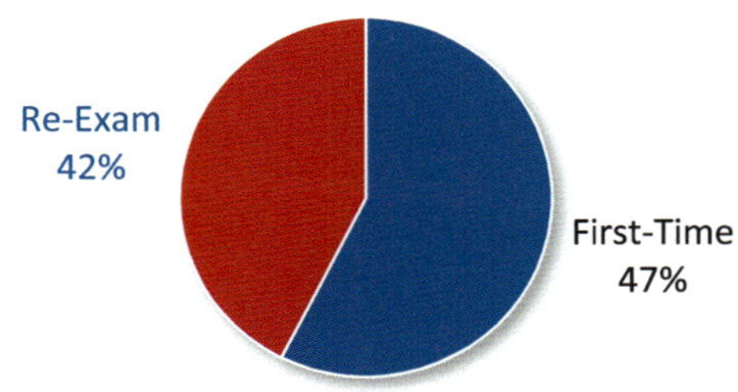

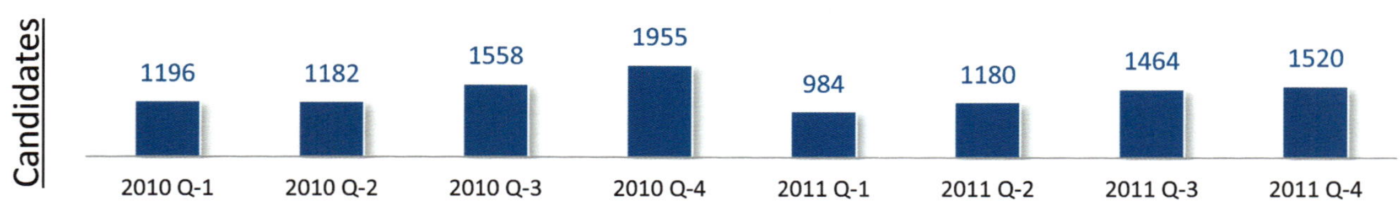

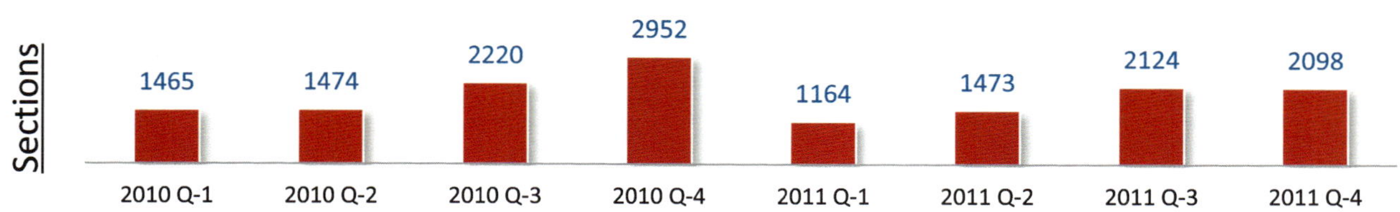

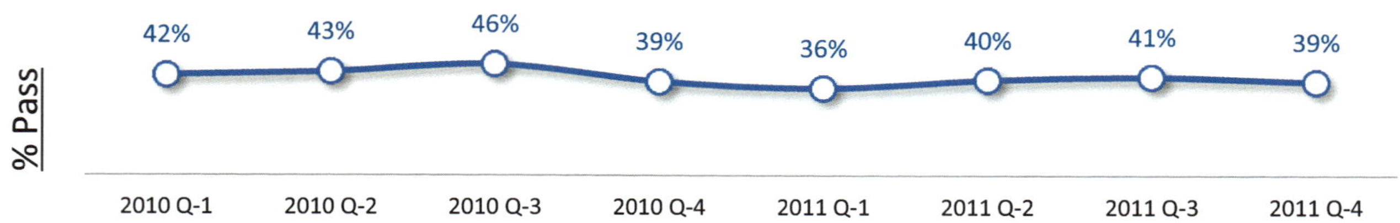

CPA Exam Performance Summary: *2011*

Demographics

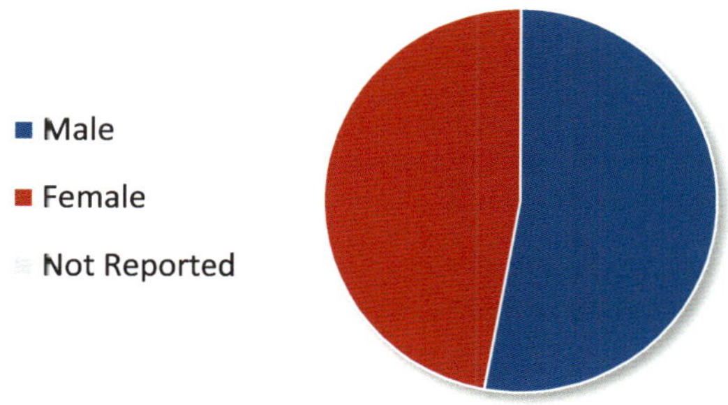

Male Candidates	1,469	52.9%
Female Candidates	1,308	47.1%
Not Reported	0	0.0%

Average Age **28.7**

Age Rank **23**

Residency

Candidate Count	
In-State Address	2,459
Out-of-State Address	260
Foreign Address	58

% of Candidates	
In-State Address	88.5%
Out-of-State Address	9.4%
Foreign Address	2.1%

Degree Type

Candidate Count	
Bachelor's Degree	1,985
Advanced Degree	419
None/Other	373

% of Candidates	
Bachelor's Degree	71.5%
Advanced Degree	15.1%
None/Other	13.4%

New Candidates vs Candidates Passing 4th Section

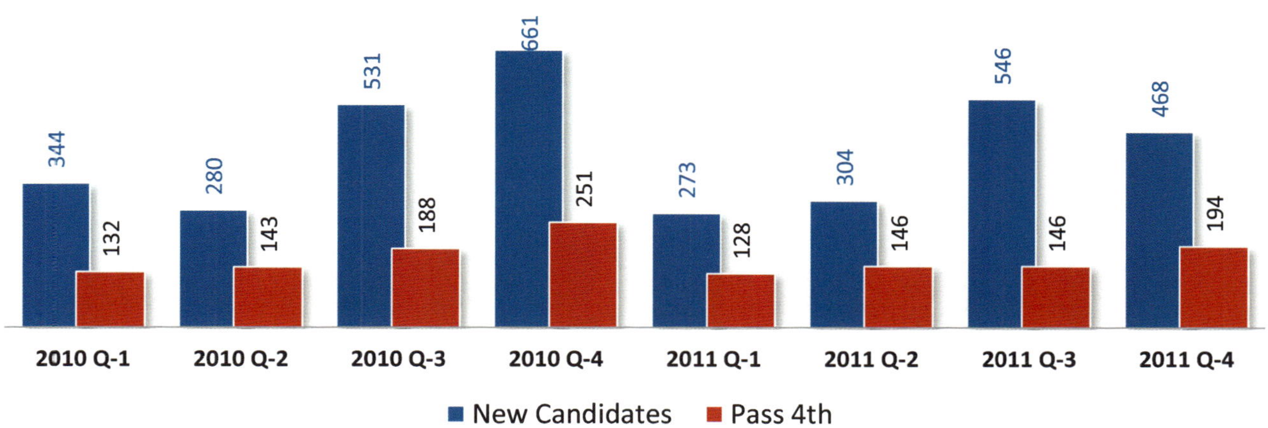

Notes about the Data

1. The data used to develop this report was pulled from NASBA's Gateway System, which houses the Uniform CPA Examination's Application and Performance information for all 55 jurisdictions.
2. The demographic data related to Age, Gender and Degree Type is provided by the individual candidates and may not be 100% accurate.

New Jersey

CPA Exam Performance Summary: *2011*

New Mexico

Overall Performance

Unique Candidates	**354**
New Candidates	**162**
Total Sections	**852**
Passing 4th Section	**73**
Sections/Candidate	**2.41**
Pass Rate	**37.4%**
Average Score	**68.7**

Section Performance

	Sections	Score	% Pass
First-Time	**450**	**67.4**	**37.6%**
Re-Exam	**402**	**70.1**	**37.3%**
AUD	**207**	**70.4**	**44.4%**
BEC	**191**	**70.1**	**37.2%**
FAR	**223**	**66.0**	**31.8%**
REG	**231**	**68.4**	**36.8%**

Jurisdiction Rankings (1 to 53)

Candidates	Sections
44	**44**
48	**43**
Pass Rate	Avg Score

Exam Type by Percent

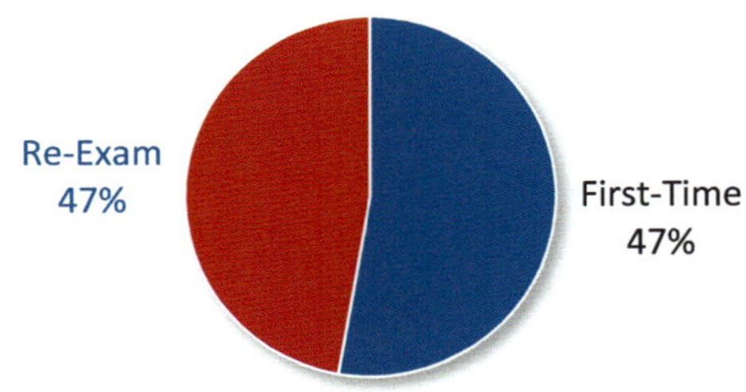

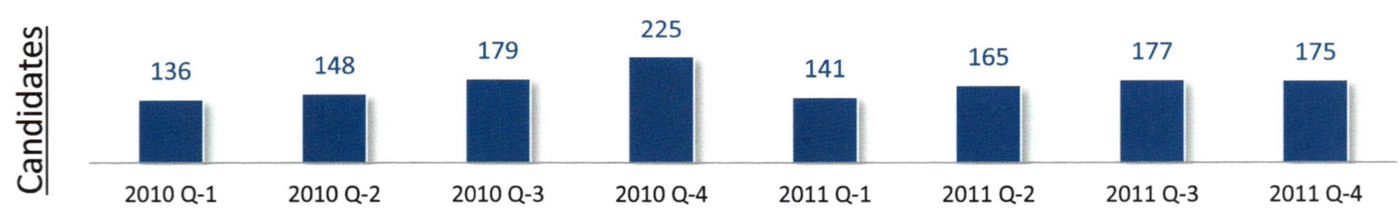

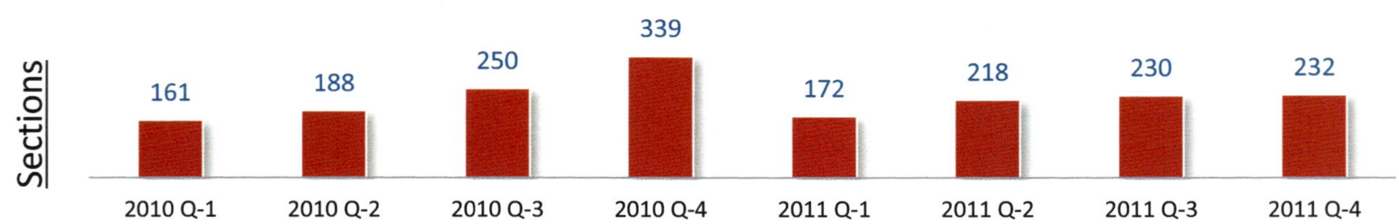

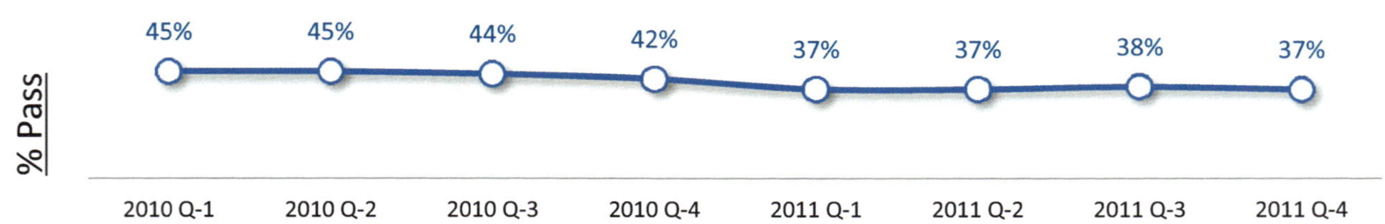

CPA Exam Performance Summary: *2011*

Demographics

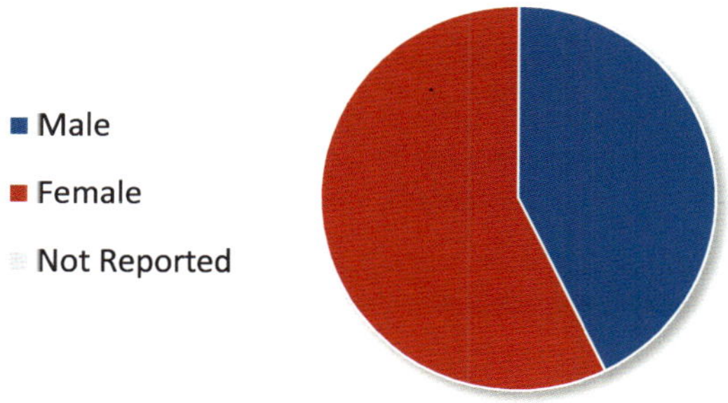

Male Candidates	151	42.7%
Female Candidates	203	57.3%
Not Reported	0	0.0%

Average Age	**33.0**
Age Rank	**51**

Residency

Candidate Count	
In-State Address	**281**
Out-of-State Address	**55**
Foreign Address	**18**
% of Candidates	
In-State Address	**79.4%**
Out-of-State Address	**15.5%**
Foreign Address	**5.1%**

Degree Type

Candidate Count	
Bachelor's Degree	**276**
Advanced Degree	**56**
None/Other	**22**
% of Candidates	
Bachelor's Degree	**78.0%**
Advanced Degree	**15.8%**
None/Other	**6.2%**

New Candidates vs Candidates Passing 4th Section

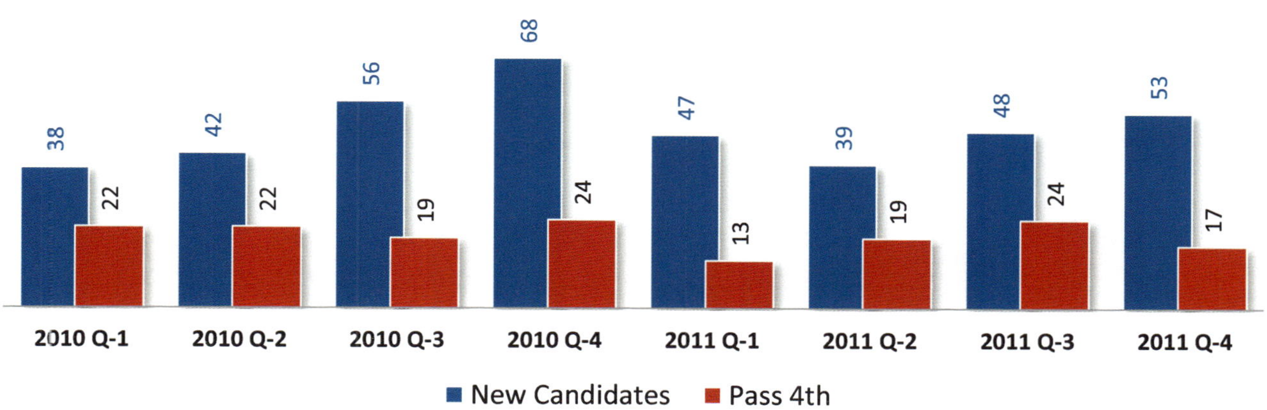

Notes about the Data

1. The data used to develop this report was pulled from NASBA's Gateway System, which houses the Uniform CPA Examination's Application and Performance information for all 55 jurisdictions.
2. The demographic data related to Age, Gender and Degree Type is provided by the individual candidates and may not be 100% accurate.

New Mexico

CPA Exam Performance Summary: *2011*

New York

Overall Performance

Unique Candidates	**8,366**
New Candidates	**3,372**
Total Sections	**20,468**
Passing 4th Section	**1,890**
Sections/Candidate	**2.45**
Pass Rate	**42.7%**
Average Score	**70.0**

Section Performance

	Sections	Score	% Pass
First-Time	**11,029**	**70.6**	**48.3%**
Re-Exam	**9,439**	**69.3**	**36.2%**
AUD	**5,528**	**71.6**	**44.1%**
BEC	**4,677**	**70.5**	**43.8%**
FAR	**4,966**	**68.2**	**41.1%**
REG	**5,297**	**69.7**	**41.7%**

Jurisdiction Rankings (1 to 53)

Candidates	Sections
2	**2**
37	**33**
Pass Rate	Avg Score

Exam Type by Percent

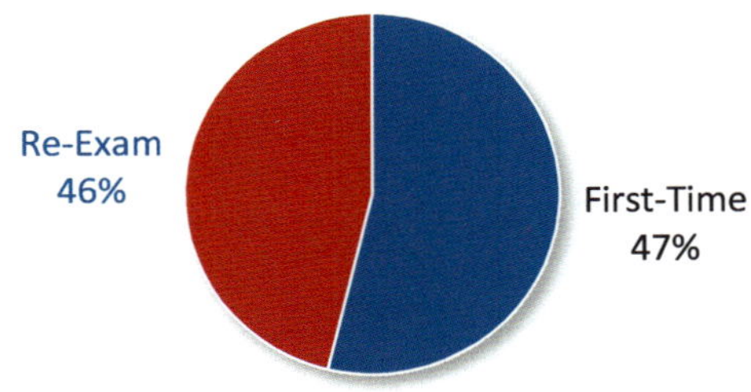

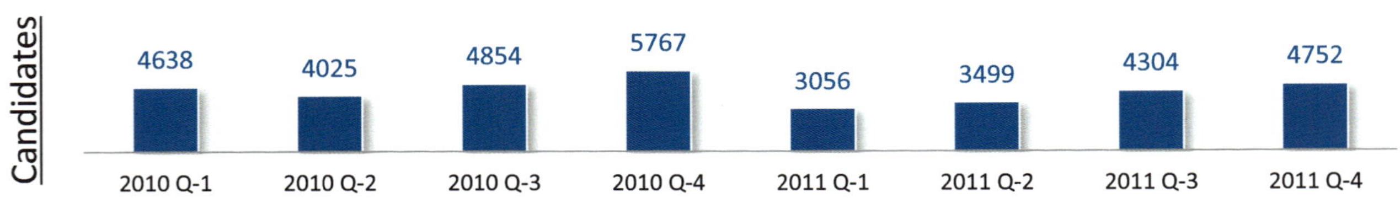

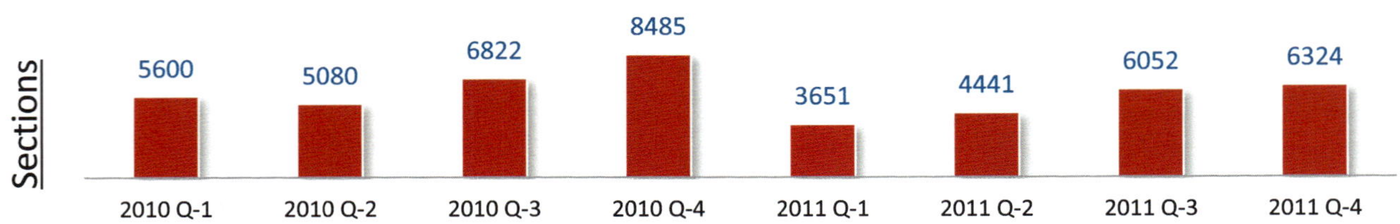

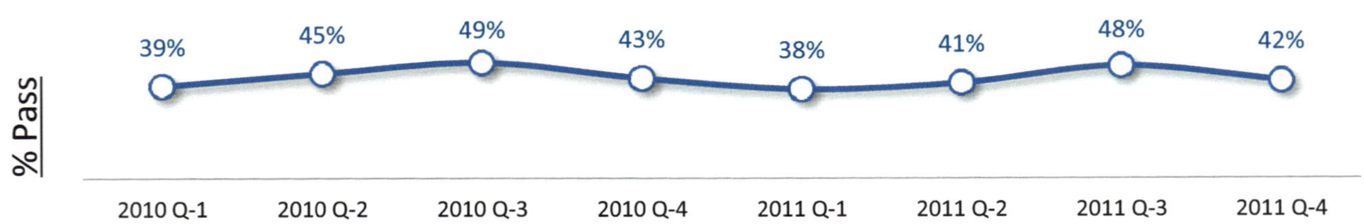

CPA Exam Performance Summary: *2011*

Demographics

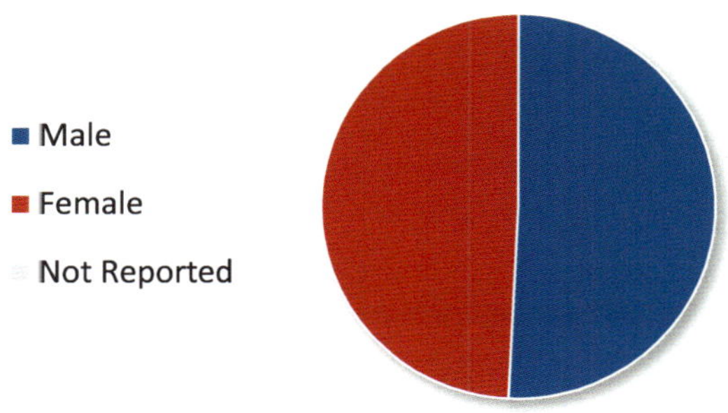

Male Candidates	4,247	50.8%
Female Candidates	4,118	49.2%
Not Reported	1	0.0%

Average Age	**27.9**
Age Rank	**10**

Residency

Candidate Count	
In-State Address	**6,676**
Out-of-State Address	**1,615**
Foreign Address	**75**

% of Candidates	
In-State Address	**79.8%**
Out-of-State Address	**19.3%**
Foreign Address	**0.9%**

Degree Type

Candidate Count	
Bachelor's Degree	**5,185**
Advanced Degree	**878**
None/Other	**2,303**

% of Candidates	
Bachelor's Degree	**62.0%**
Advanced Degree	**10.5%**
None/Other	**27.5%**

New Candidates vs Candidates Passing 4th Section

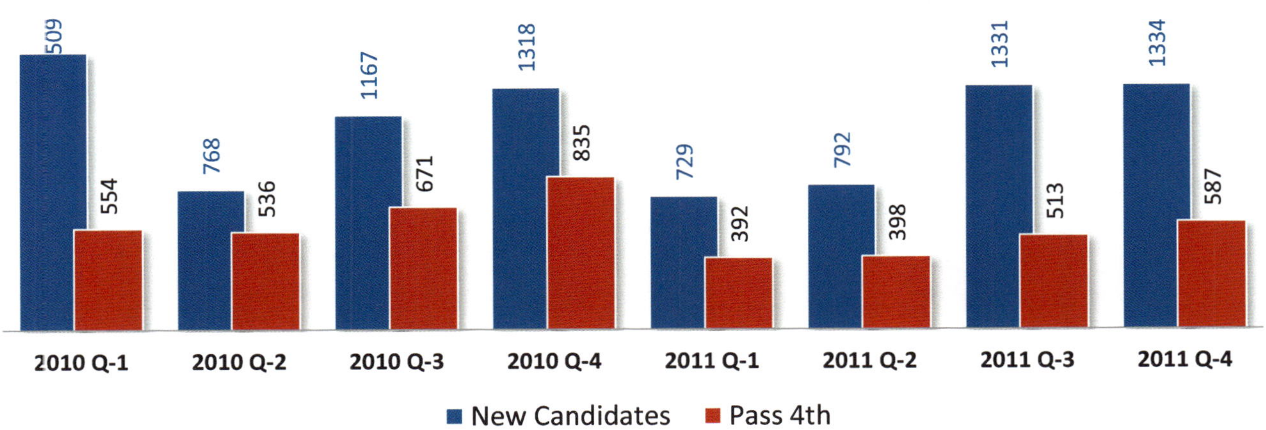

Notes about the Data

1. The data used to develop this report was pulled from NASBA's Gateway System, which houses the Uniform CPA Examination's Application and Performance information for all 55 jurisdictions.
2. The demographic data related to Age, Gender and Degree Type is provided by the individual candidates and may not be 100% accurate.

New York

CPA Exam Performance Summary: *2011*

North Carolina

Overall Performance

Unique Candidates	**1,698**
New Candidates	**719**
Total Sections	**4,701**
Passing 4th Section	**529**
Sections/Candidate	**2.77**
Pass Rate	**51.2%**
Average Score	**72.7**

Section Performance

	Sections	Score	% Pass
First-Time	**2,911**	**73.9**	**57.1%**
Re-Exam	**1,790**	**70.7**	**41.7%**
AUD	**1,257**	**73.7**	**50.0%**
BEC	**1,046**	**74.1**	**54.3%**
FAR	**1,160**	**71.3**	**50.1%**
REG	**1,238**	**71.9**	**50.9%**

Jurisdiction Rankings (1 to 53)

Candidates	Sections
17	**17**
9	**8**
Pass Rate	Avg Score

Exam Type by Percent

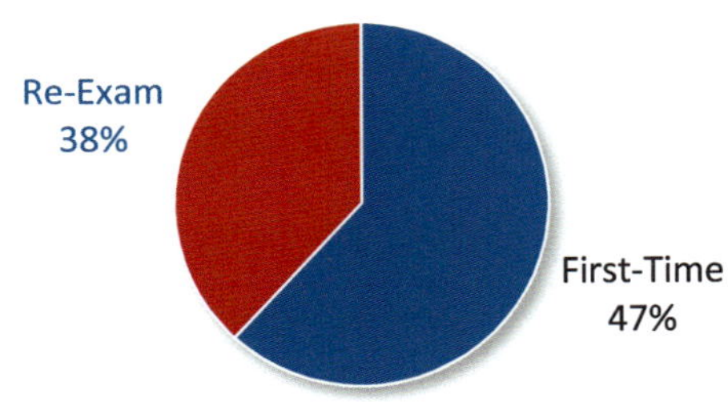

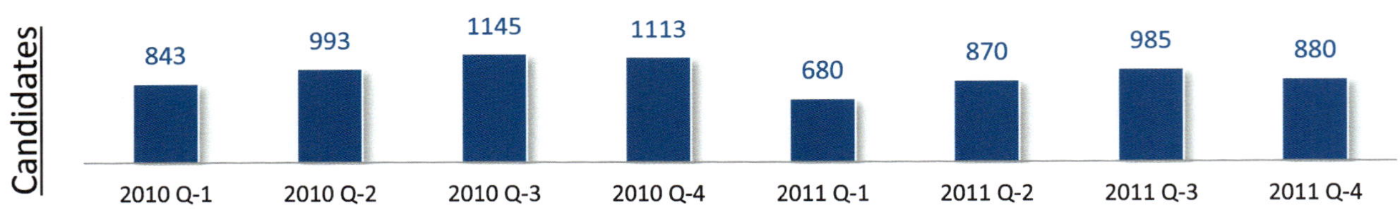

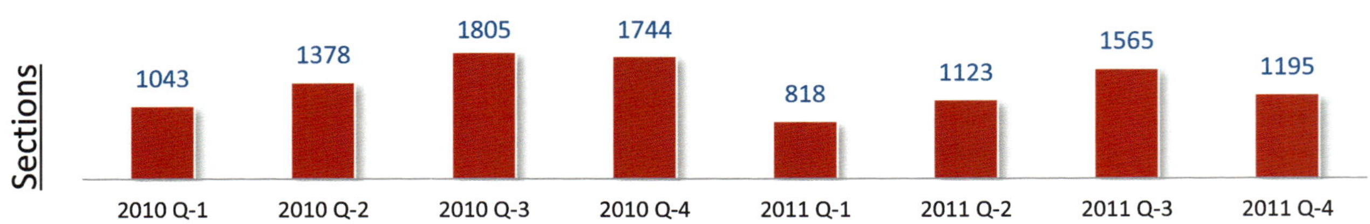

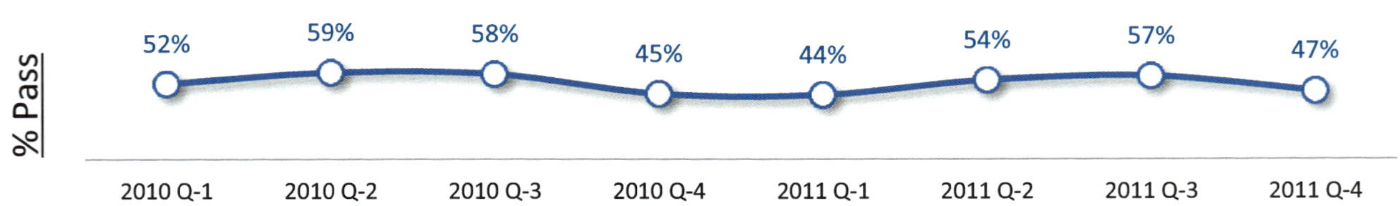

CPA Exam Performance Summary: *2011*

Demographics

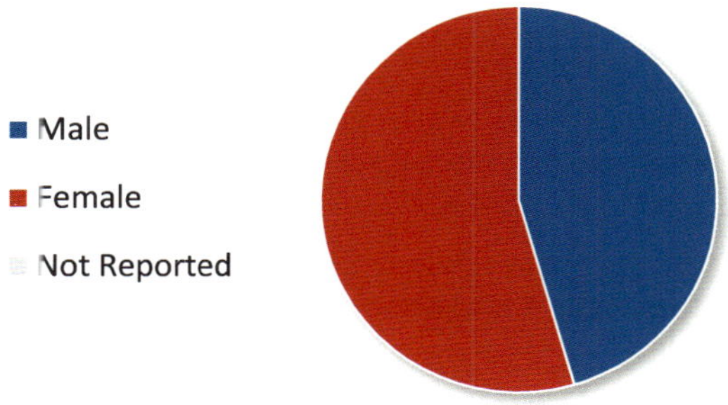

Male Candidates	772	45.5%
Female Candidates	926	54.5%
Not Reported	0	0.0%

Average Age	**28.9**
Age Rank	**25**

Residency

Candidate Count	
In-State Address	**1,518**
Out-of-State Address	**178**
Foreign Address	**2**

% of Candidates	
In-State Address	**89.4%**
Out-of-State Address	**10.5%**
Foreign Address	**0.1%**

Degree Type

Candidate Count	
Bachelor's Degree	**1,564**
Advanced Degree	**107**
None/Other	**27**

% of Candidates	
Bachelor's Degree	**92.1%**
Advanced Degree	**6.3%**
None/Other	**1.6%**

New Candidates vs Candidates Passing 4th Section

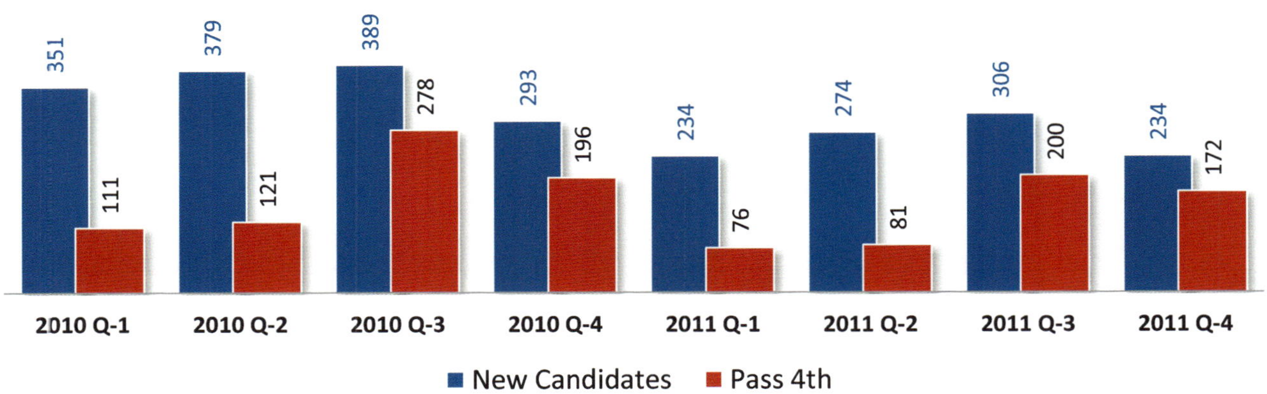

Notes about the Data

1. The data used to develop this report was pulled from NASBA's Gateway System, which houses the Uniform CPA Examination's Application and Performance information for all 55 jurisdictions.
2. The demographic data related to Age, Gender and Degree Type is provided by the individual candidates and may not be 100% accurate.

North Carolina

CPA Exam Performance Summary: *2011*

North Dakota

Overall Performance

Unique Candidates	**261**
New Candidates	**96**
Total Sections	**664**
Passing 4th Section	**89**
Sections/Candidate	**2.54**
Pass Rate	**55.1%**
Average Score	**73.9**

Section Performance

	Sections	Score	% Pass
First-Time	**422**	**74.7**	**60.4%**
Re-Exam	**242**	**72.4**	**45.9%**
AUD	**181**	**74.8**	**53.6%**
BEC	**134**	**73.9**	**53.7%**
FAR	**161**	**72.7**	**56.5%**
REG	**188**	**74.0**	**56.4%**

Jurisdiction Rankings (1 to 53)

Candidates	Sections
49	**48**
2	**2**
Pass Rate	Avg Score

Exam Type by Percent

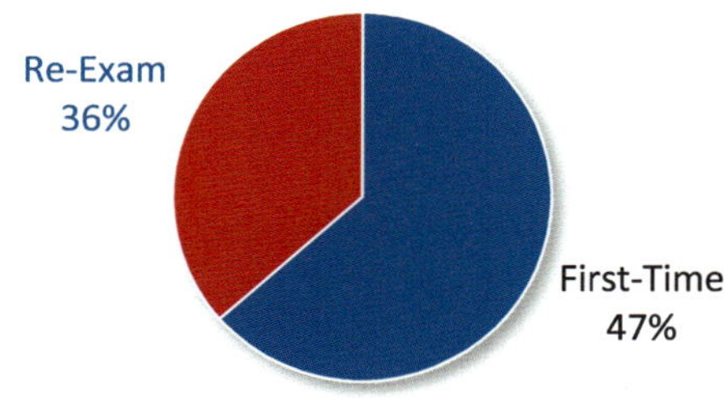

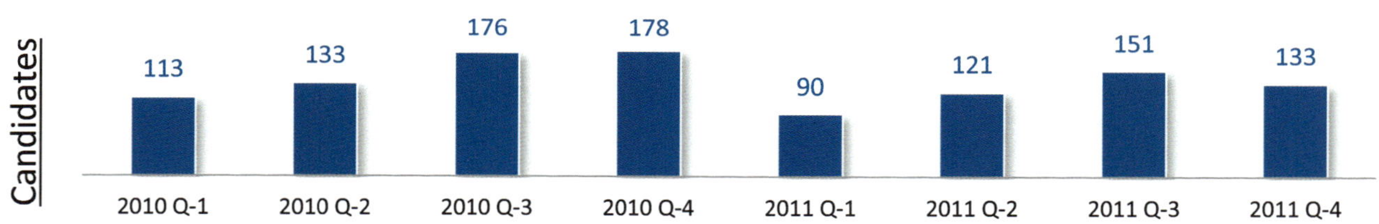

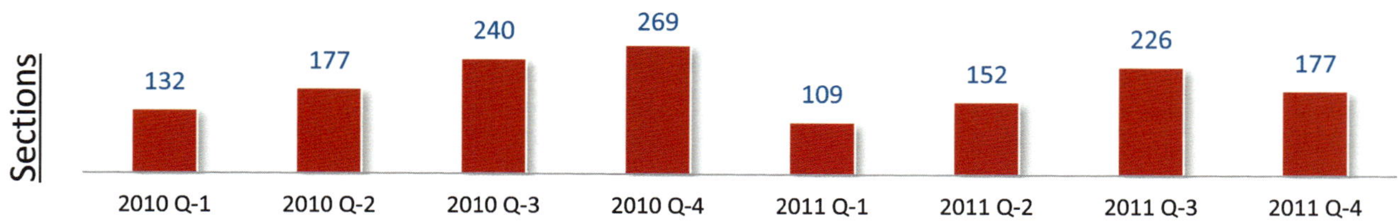

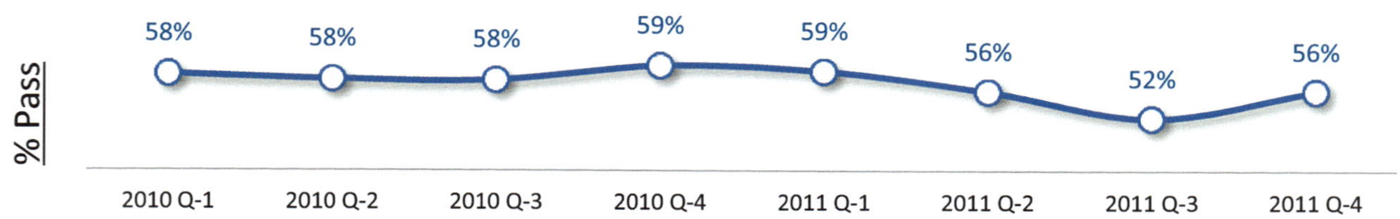

CPA Exam Performance Summary: *2011*

Demographics

Male Candidates	0	0.0%
Female Candidates	0	0.0%
Not Reported	261	100.0%

Average Age	**27.7**
Age Rank	**8**

Residency

Candidate Count	
In-State Address	199
Out-of-State Address	57
Foreign Address	5
% of Candidates	
In-State Address	76.2%
Out-of-State Address	21.8%
Foreign Address	1.9%

Degree Type

Candidate Count	
Bachelor's Degree	121
Advanced Degree	1
None/Other	139
% of Candidates	
Bachelor's Degree	46.4%
Advanced Degree	0.4%
None/Other	53.3%

New Candidates vs Candidates Passing 4th Section

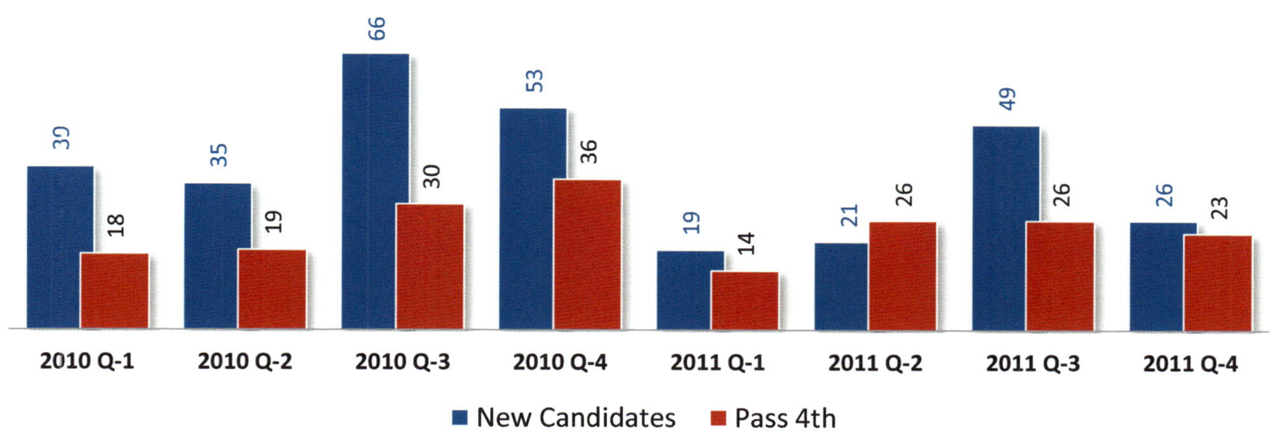

Notes about the Data

1. The data used to develop this report was pulled from NASBA's Gateway System, which houses the Uniform CPA Examination's Application and Performance information for all 55 jurisdictions.
2. The demographic data related to Age, Gender and Degree Type is provided by the individual candidates and may not be 100% accurate.

North Dakota

CPA Exam Performance Summary: *2011*

Ohio

Overall Performance

Unique Candidates	**2,490**
New Candidates	**1,243**
Total Sections	**6,725**
Passing 4th Section	**746**
Sections/Candidate	**2.70**
Pass Rate	**48.6%**
Average Score	**71.5**

Section Performance

	Sections	Score	% Pass
First-Time	**4,204**	**72.1**	**52.3%**
Re-Exam	**2,521**	**70.7**	**42.5%**
AUD	**1,855**	**72.4**	**47.3%**
BEC	**1,441**	**73.6**	**56.6%**
FAR	**1,658**	**70.0**	**47.3%**
REG	**1,771**	**70.4**	**44.8%**

Jurisdiction Rankings (1 to 53)

Candidates	Sections
12	**10**
14	**21**
Pass Rate	Avg Score

Exam Type by Percent

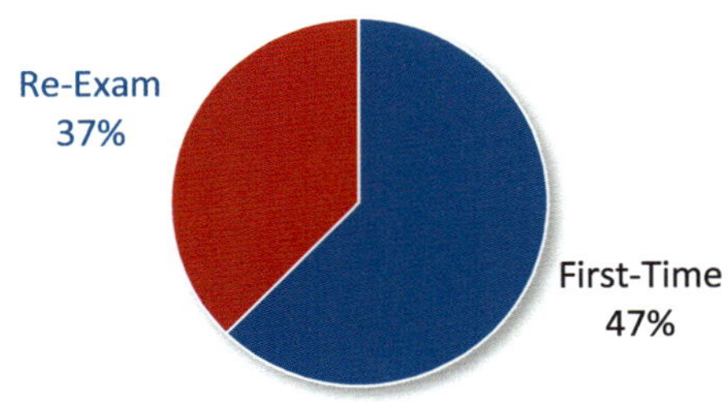

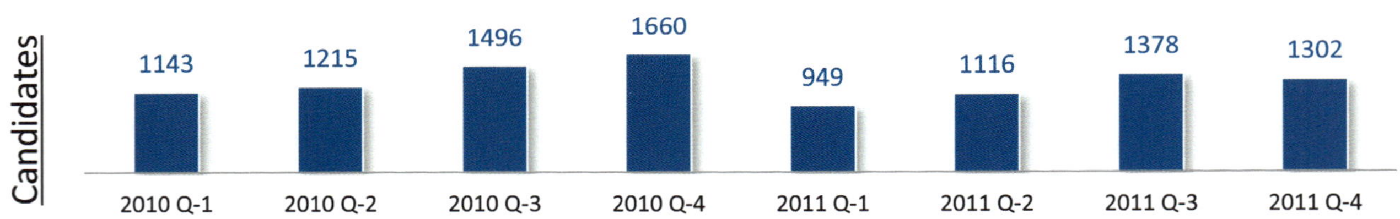

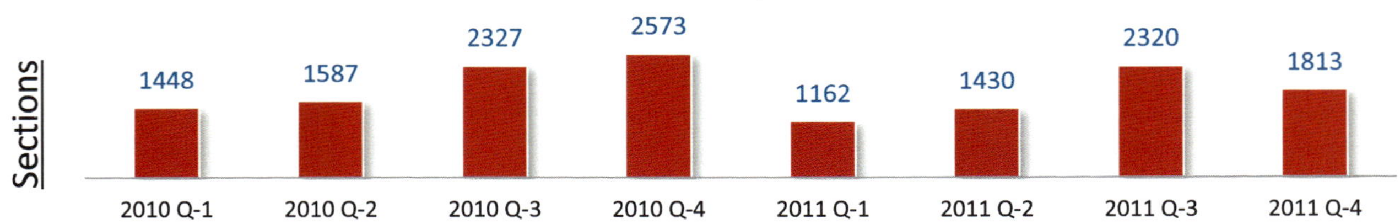

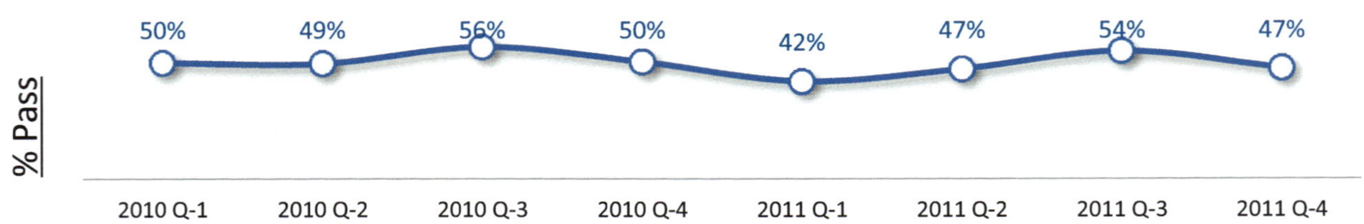

CPA Exam Performance Summary: *2011*

Demographics

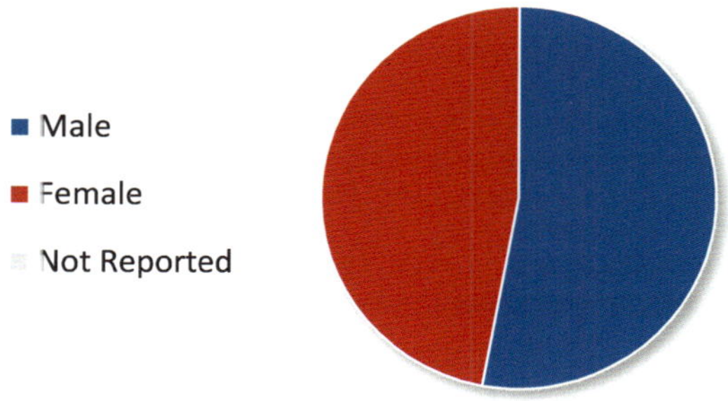

Male Candidates	1,317	52.9%
Female Candidates	1,173	47.1%
Not Reported	0	0.0%

Average Age	28.7
Age Rank	21

Residency

Candidate Count	
In-State Address	**2,299**
Out-of-State Address	**186**
Foreign Address	**5**
% of Candidates	
In-State Address	**92.3%**
Out-of-State Address	**7.5%**
Foreign Address	**0.2%**

Degree Type

Candidate Count	
Bachelor's Degree	**1,754**
Advanced Degree	**589**
None/Other	**147**
% of Candidates	
Bachelor's Degree	**70.4%**
Advanced Degree	**23.7%**
None/Other	**5.9%**

New Candidates vs Candidates Passing 4th Section

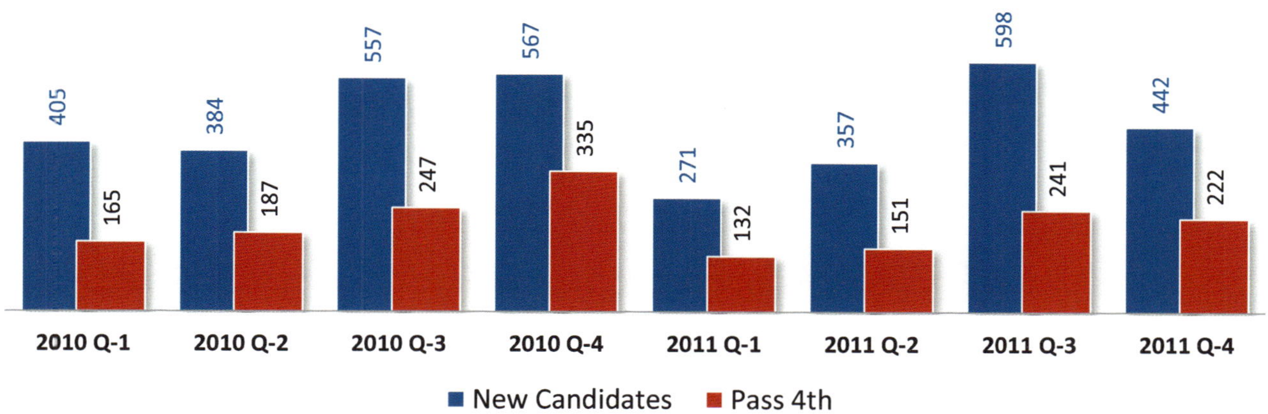

Notes about the Data

1. The data used to develop this report was pulled from NASBA's Gateway System, which houses the Uniform CPA Examination's Application and Performance information for all 55 jurisdictions.
2. The demographic data related to Age, Gender and Degree Type is provided by the individual candidates and may not be 100% accurate.

Ohio

CPA Exam Performance Summary: *2011*

Oklahoma

Overall Performance

Unique Candidates	706
New Candidates	242
Total Sections	1,679
Passing 4th Section	169
Sections/Candidate	2.38
Pass Rate	44.7%
Average Score	69.5

Section Performance

	Sections	Score	% Pass
First-Time	857	73.1	56.8%
Re-Exam	822	65.7	32.1%
AUD	472	71.1	45.1%
BEC	409	67.5	45.0%
FAR	362	68.6	45.9%
REG	436	70.4	43.1%

Jurisdiction Rankings (1 to 53)

Candidates	Sections
30	32
30	38
Pass Rate	Avg Score

Exam Type by Percent

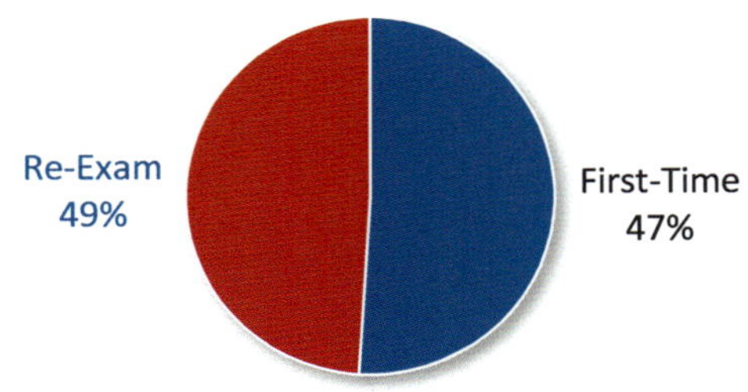

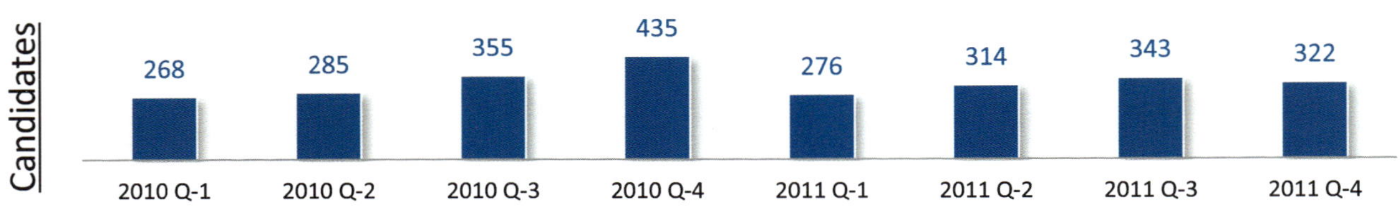

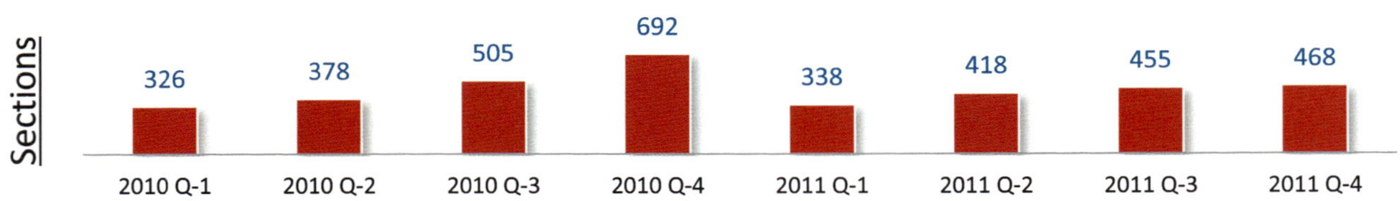

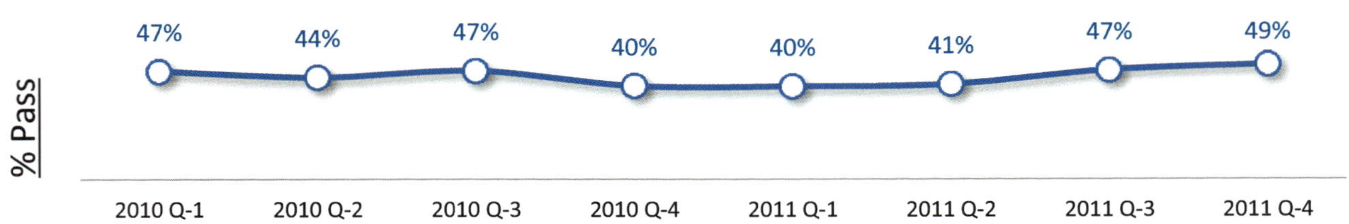

CPA Exam Performance Summary: *2011*

Demographics

Male Candidates	34	4.8%
Female Candidates	12	1.7%
Not Reported	660	93.5%

Average Age	**30.5**
Age Rank	**37**

Residency

Candidate Count	
In-State Address	678
Out-of-State Address	27
Foreign Address	1
% of Candidates	
In-State Address	96.0%
Out-of-State Address	3.8%
Foreign Address	0.1%

Degree Type

Candidate Count	
Bachelor's Degree	524
Advanced Degree	177
None/Other	5
% of Candidates	
Bachelor's Degree	74.2%
Advanced Degree	25.1%
None/Other	0.7%

New Candidates vs Candidates Passing 4th Section

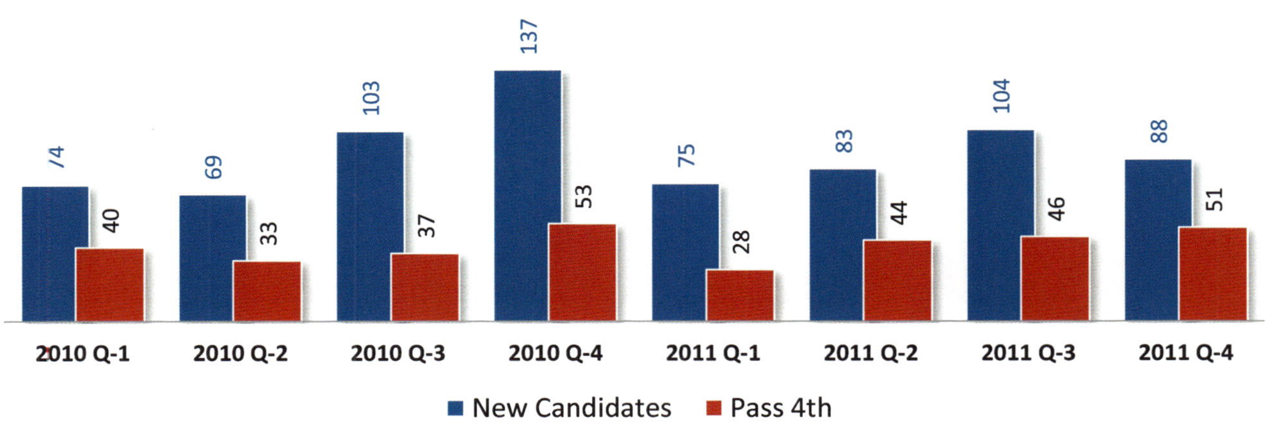

Notes about the Data

1. The data used to develop this report was pulled from NASBA's Gateway System, which houses the Uniform CPA Examination's Application and Performance information for all 55 jurisdictions.
2. The demographic data related to Age, Gender and Degree Type is provided by the individual candidates and may not be 100% accurate.

Oklahoma

CPA Exam Performance Summary: *2011*

Oregon

Overall Performance

Unique Candidates	**685**
New Candidates	**263**
Total Sections	**1,680**
Passing 4th Section	**212**
Sections/Candidate	**2.45**
Pass Rate	**53.3%**
Average Score	**73.0**

Section Performance

	Sections	Score	% Pass
First-Time	**1,019**	**74.2**	**58.7%**
Re-Exam	**661**	**71.0**	**44.9%**
AUD	**441**	**74.8**	**54.4%**
BEC	**363**	**73.5**	**56.2%**
FAR	**420**	**70.8**	**50.7%**
REG	**456**	**72.7**	**52.2%**

Jurisdiction Rankings (1 to 53)

Candidates	Sections
31	**31**
4	**5**
Pass Rate	Avg Score

Exam Type by Percent

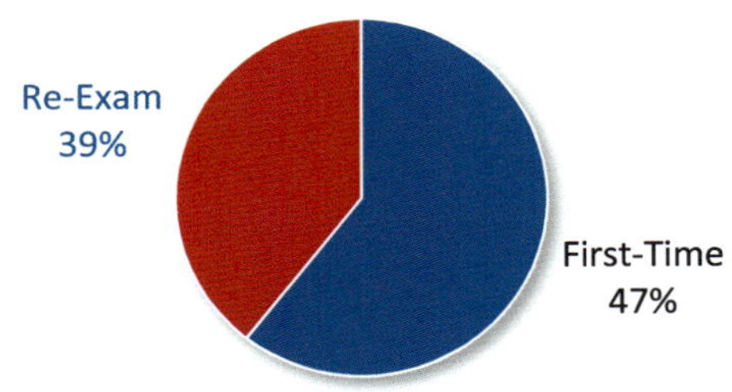

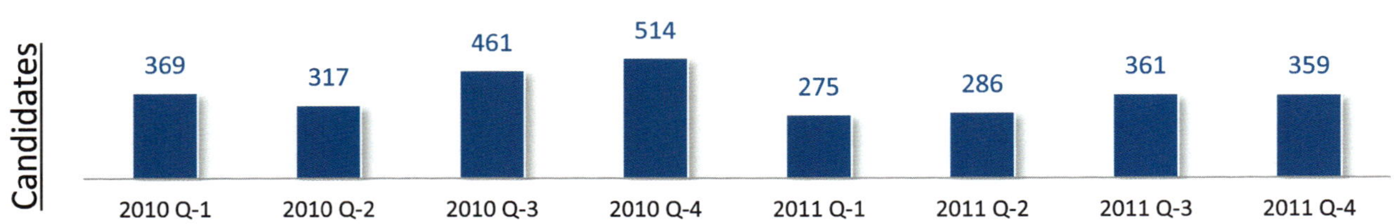

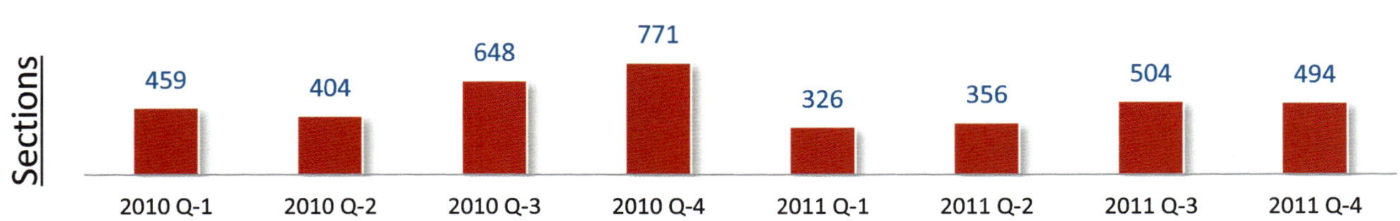

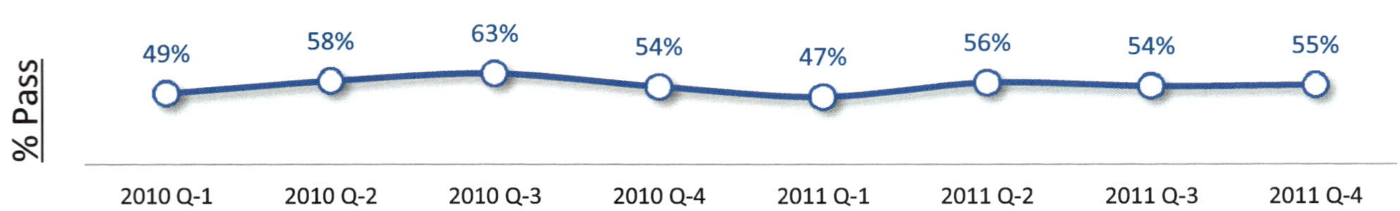

CPA Exam Performance Summary: *2011*

Demographics

Male Candidates	0	0.0%
Female Candidates	0	0.0%
Not Reported	685	100.0%

Average Age **31.0**

Age Rank **45**

Residency

Candidate Count	
In-State Address	613
Out-of-State Address	62
Foreign Address	10
% of Candidates	
In-State Address	89.5%
Out-of-State Address	9.1%
Foreign Address	1.5%

Degree Type

Candidate Count	
Bachelor's Degree	569
Advanced Degree	113
None/Other	3
% of Candidates	
Bachelor's Degree	83.1%
Advanced Degree	16.5%
None/Other	0.4%

New Candidates vs Candidates Passing 4th Section

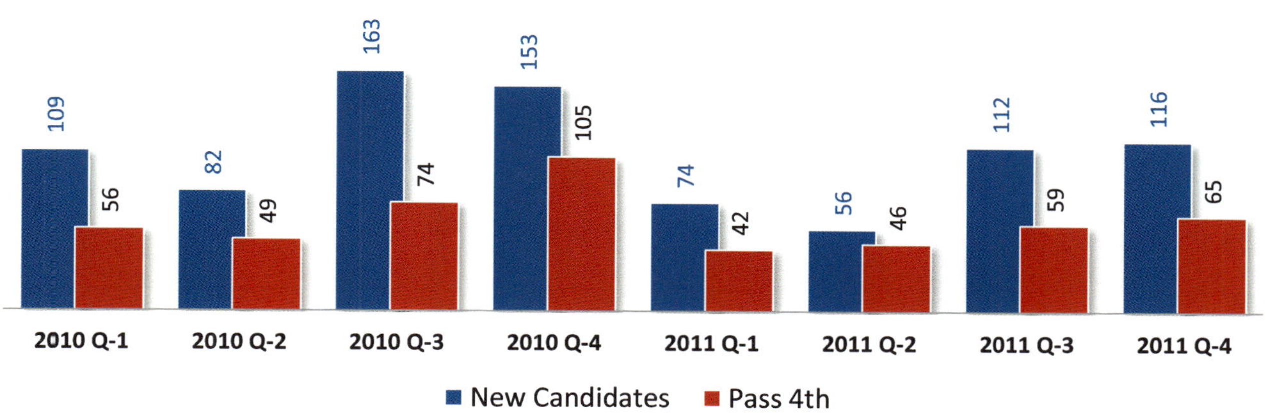

Notes about the Data

1. The data used to develop this report was pulled from NASBA's Gateway System, which houses the Uniform CPA Examination's Application and Performance information for all 55 jurisdictions.
2. The demographic data related to Age, Gender and Degree Type is provided by the individual candidates and may not be 100% accurate.

Oregon

CPA Exam Performance Summary: *2011*

Pennsylvania

Overall Performance

Unique Candidates	**4,815**
New Candidates	**2,525**
Total Sections	**11,715**
Passing 4th Section	**848**
Sections/Candidate	**2.43**
Pass Rate	**38.8%**
Average Score	**68.2**

Section Performance

	Sections	Score	% Pass
First-Time	**6,900**	**67.8**	**41.0%**
Re-Exam	**4,815**	**68.8**	**35.5%**
AUD	**3,301**	**69.5**	**39.5%**
BEC	**2,995**	**68.6**	**39.3%**
FAR	**2,415**	**67.1**	**39.8%**
REG	**3,004**	**67.2**	**36.6%**

Jurisdiction Rankings (1 to 53)

Candidates	Sections
5	**5**
45	**46**
Pass Rate	Avg Score

Exam Type by Percent

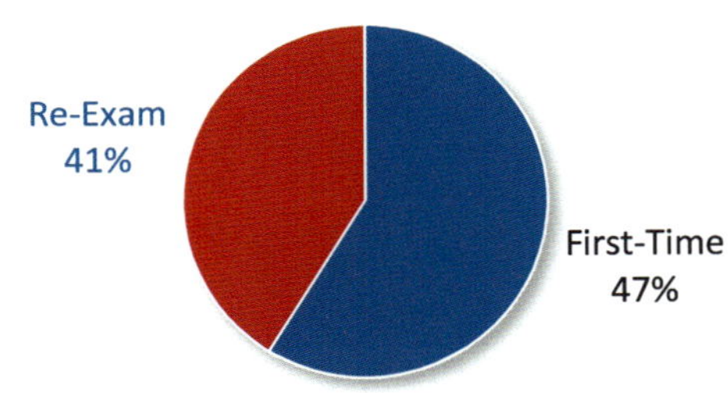

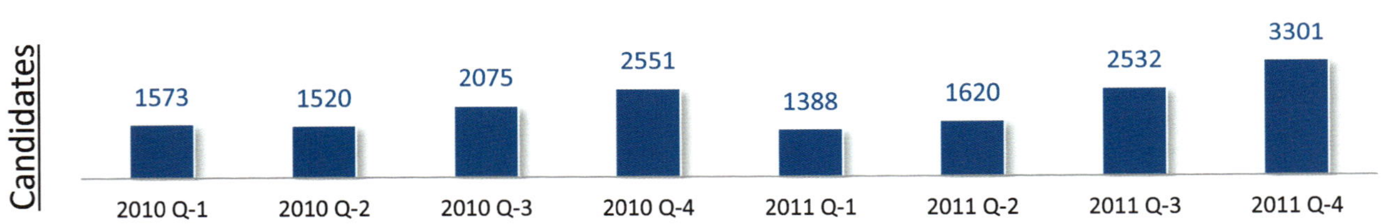

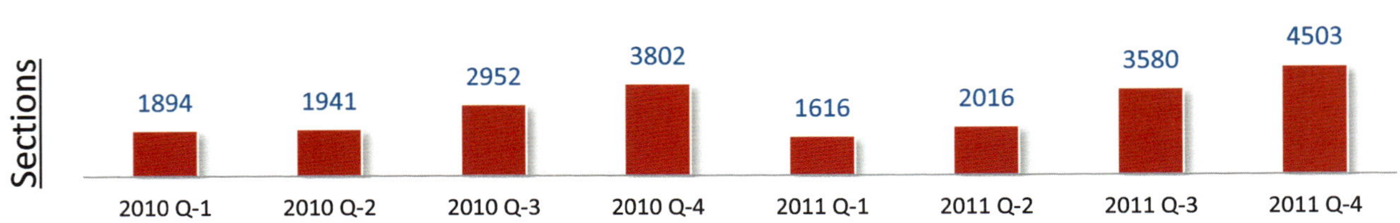

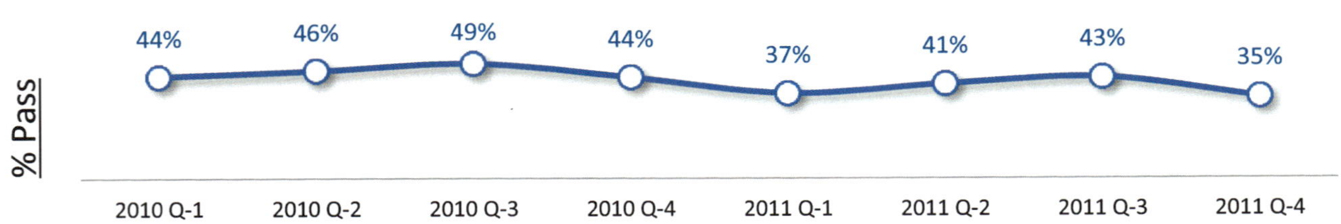

CPA Exam Performance Summary: *2011*

Demographics

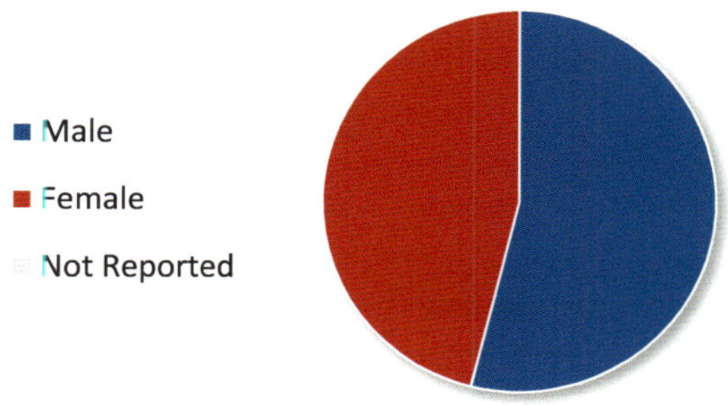

Male Candidates	**2,595**	**53.9%**
Female Candidates	**2,220**	**46.1%**
Not Reported	**0**	**0.0%**

Average Age	**27.4**
Age Rank	**4**

Residency

Candidate Count

In-State Address	**4,150**
Out-of-State Address	**655**
Foreign Address	**10**

% of Candidates

In-State Address	**86.2%**
Out-of-State Address	**13.6%**
Foreign Address	**0.2%**

Degree Type

Candidate Count

Bachelor's Degree	**4,453**
Advanced Degree	**263**
None/Other	**99**

% of Candidates

Bachelor's Degree	**92.5%**
Advanced Degree	**5.5%**
None/Other	**2.1%**

New Candidates vs Candidates Passing 4th Section

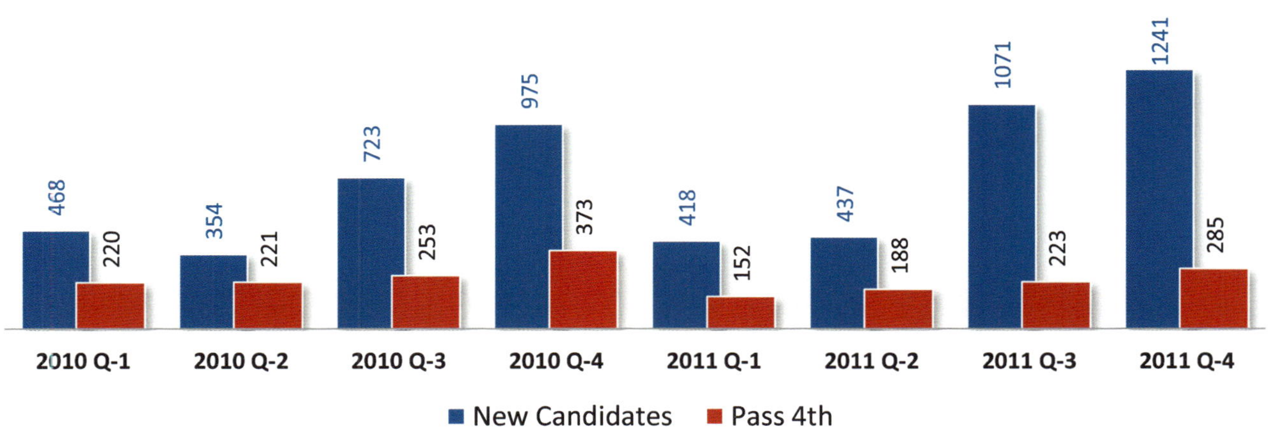

Notes about the Data

1. The data used to develop this report was pulled from NASBA's Gateway System, which houses the Uniform CPA Examination's Application and Performance information for all 55 jurisdictions.
2. The demographic data related to Age, Gender and Degree Type is provided by the individual candidates and may not be 100% accurate.

Pennsylvania

CPA Exam Performance Summary: *2011*

Puerto Rico

Overall Performance

Unique Candidates	**874**
New Candidates	**430**
Total Sections	**1,922**
Passing 4th Section	**117**
Sections/Candidate	**2.20**
Pass Rate	**25.5%**
Average Score	**59.3**

Section Performance

	Sections	Score	% Pass
First-Time	**1,075**	**52.4**	**18.9%**
Re-Exam	**847**	**68.0**	**33.9%**
AUD	**526**	**61.7**	**31.9%**
BEC	**453**	**57.1**	**16.6%**
FAR	**421**	**58.3**	**29.9%**
REG	**522**	**59.4**	**23.2%**

Jurisdiction Rankings (1 to 53)

Candidates	Sections
28	**28**
52	**53**
Pass Rate	Avg Score

Exam Type by Percent

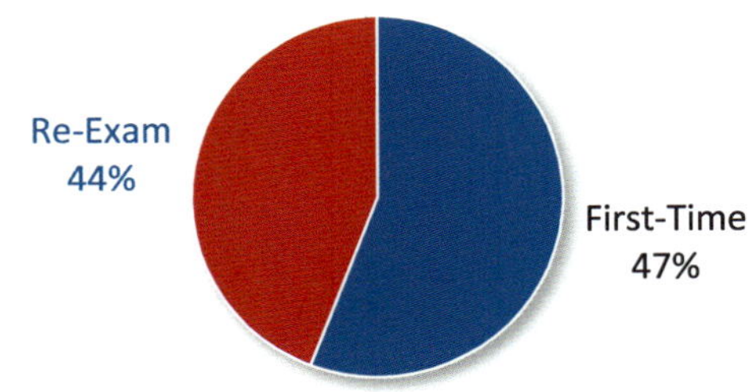

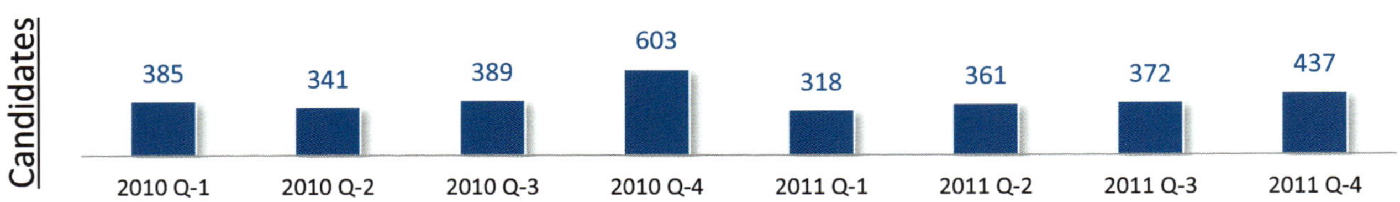

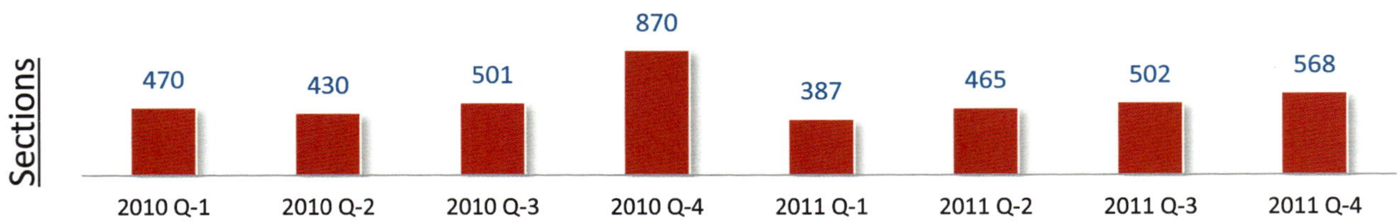

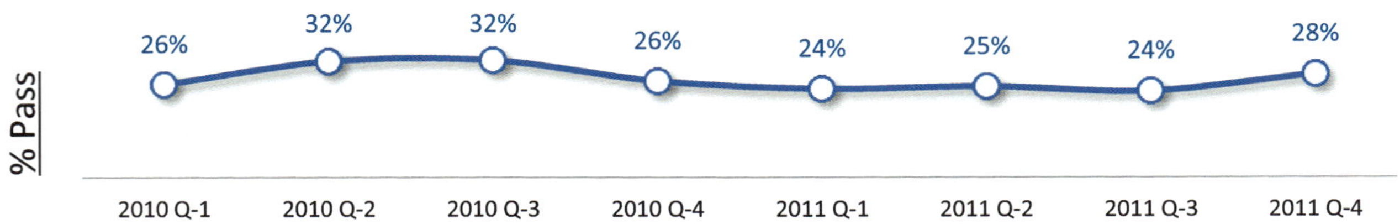

CPA Exam Performance Summary: *2011*

Demographics

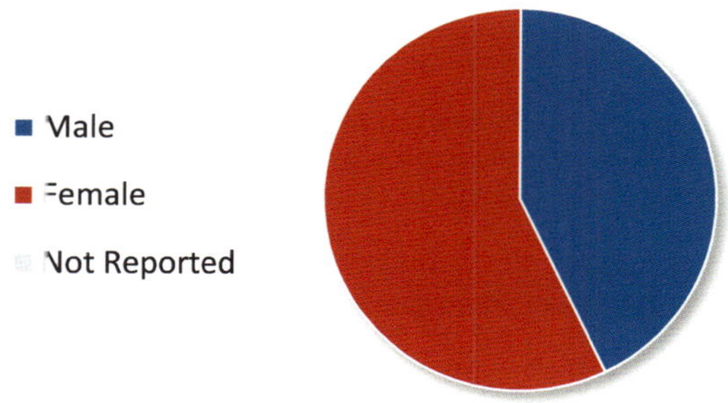

Male Candidates	374	42.8%
Female Candidates	500	57.2%
Not Reported	0	0.0%

Average Age	**28.6**
Age Rank	**20**

Residency

Candidate Count

In-State Address	**836**
Out-of-State Address	**8**
Foreign Address	**30**

% of Candidates

In-State Address	**95.7%**
Out-of-State Address	**0.9%**
Foreign Address	**3.4%**

Degree Type

Candidate Count

Bachelor's Degree	**699**
Advanced Degree	**48**
None/Other	**127**

% of Candidates

Bachelor's Degree	**80.0%**
Advanced Degree	**5.5%**
None/Other	**14.5%**

New Candidates vs Candidates Passing 4th Section

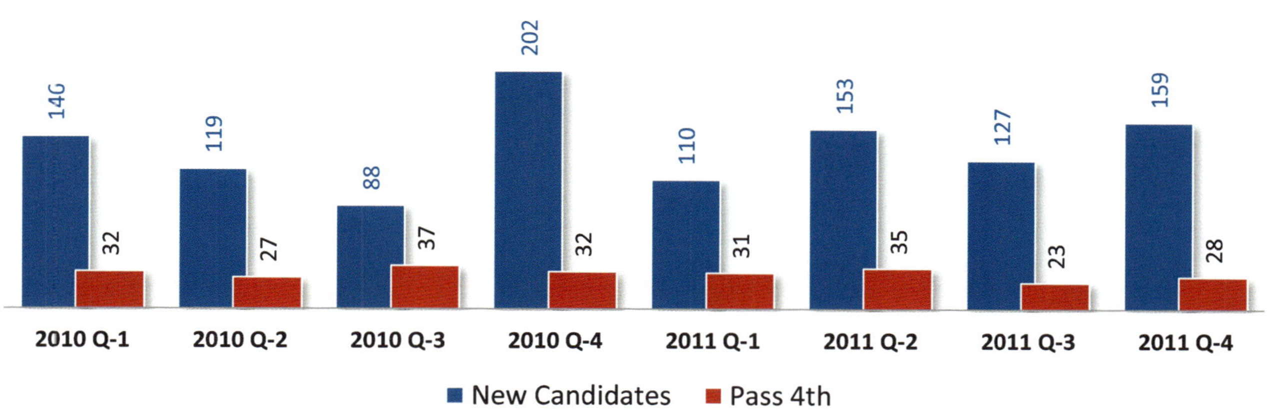

Notes about the Data

1. The data used to develop this report was pulled from NASBA's Gateway System, which houses the Uniform CPA Examination's Application and Performance information for all 55 jurisdictions.
2. The demographic data related to Age, Gender and Degree Type is provided by the individual candidates and may not be 100% accurate.

Puerto Rico

CPA Exam Performance Summary: *2011*

Rhode Island

Overall Performance

Unique Candidates	171
New Candidates	86
Total Sections	459
Passing 4th Section	51
Sections/Candidate	2.68
Pass Rate	46.6%
Average Score	69.8

Section Performance

	Sections	Score	% Pass
First-Time	261	69.9	49.8%
Re-Exam	198	69.8	42.4%
AUD	130	69.9	44.6%
BEC	82	71.2	53.7%
FAR	119	69.2	47.1%
REG	128	69.5	43.8%

Jurisdiction Rankings (1 to 53)

Candidates	Sections
50	49
23	36
Pass Rate	Avg Score

Exam Type by Percent

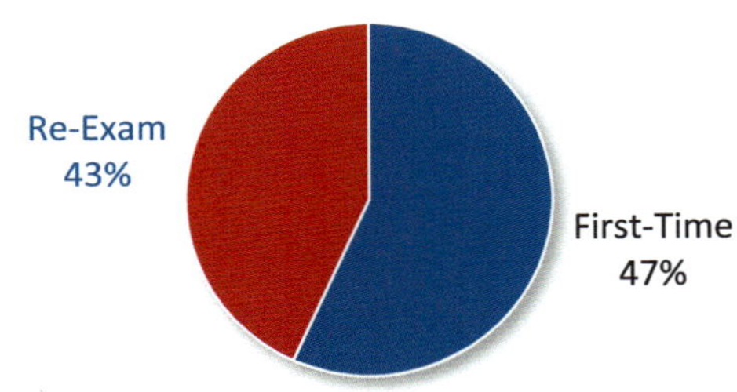

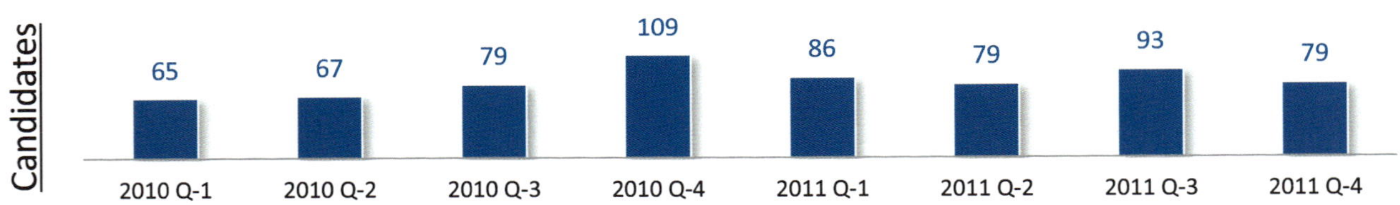

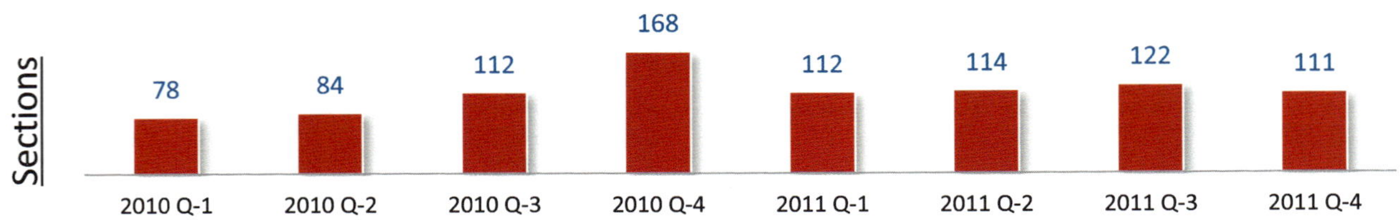

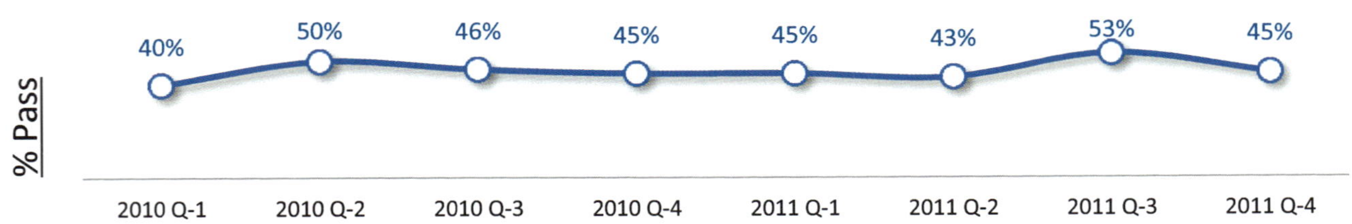

CPA Exam Performance Summary: *2011*

Demographics

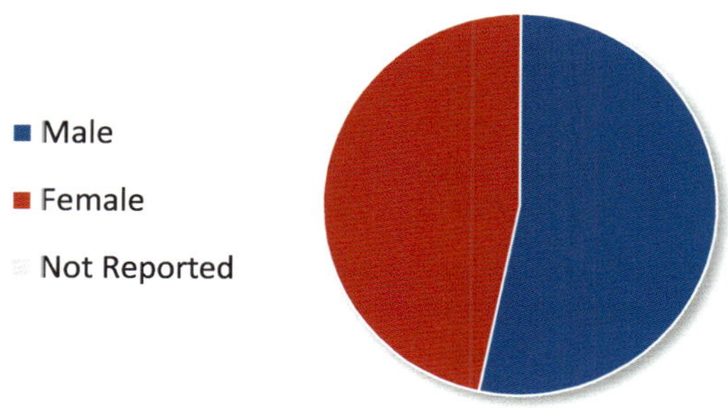

Male Candidates	91	53.2%
Female Candidates	80	46.8%
Not Reported	0	0.0%

Average Age	**28.2**
Age Rank	**11**

Residency

Candidate Count	
In-State Address	146
Out-of-State Address	25
Foreign Address	0

% of Candidates	
In-State Address	85.4%
Out-of-State Address	14.6%
Foreign Address	0.0%

Degree Type

Candidate Count	
Bachelor's Degree	120
Advanced Degree	31
None/Other	20

% of Candidates	
Bachelor's Degree	70.2%
Advanced Degree	18.1%
None/Other	11.7%

New Candidates vs Candidates Passing 4th Section

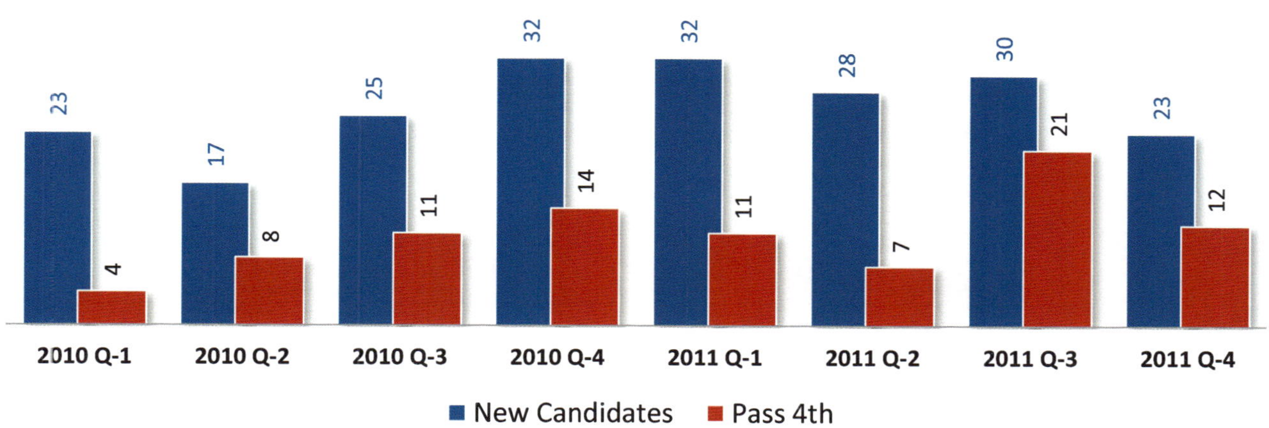

Notes about the Data

1. The data used to develop this report was pulled from NASBA's Gateway System, which houses the Uniform CPA Examination's Application and Performance information for all 55 jurisdictions.
2. The demographic data related to Age, Gender and Degree Type is provided by the individual candidates and may not be 100% accurate.

Rhode Island

CPA Exam Performance Summary: *2011*

South Carolina

Overall Performance

Unique Candidates	**586**
New Candidates	**272**
Total Sections	**1,552**
Passing 4th Section	**188**
Sections/Candidate	**2.65**
Pass Rate	**51.4%**
Average Score	**72.4**

Section Performance

	Sections	Score	% Pass
First-Time	**951**	**73.1**	**55.6%**
Re-Exam	**601**	**71.2**	**44.8%**
AUD	**447**	**73.8**	**49.4%**
BEC	**345**	**72.7**	**53.6%**
FAR	**353**	**70.8**	**50.7%**
REG	**407**	**71.8**	**52.3%**

Jurisdiction Rankings (1 to 53)

Candidates	Sections
34	**33**
8	**11**
Pass Rate	Avg Score

Exam Type by Percent

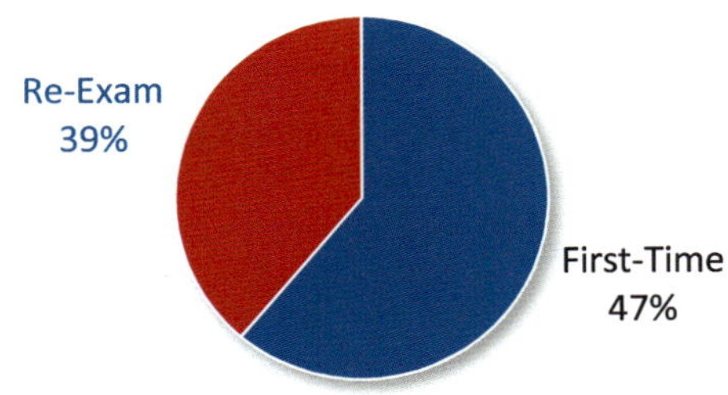

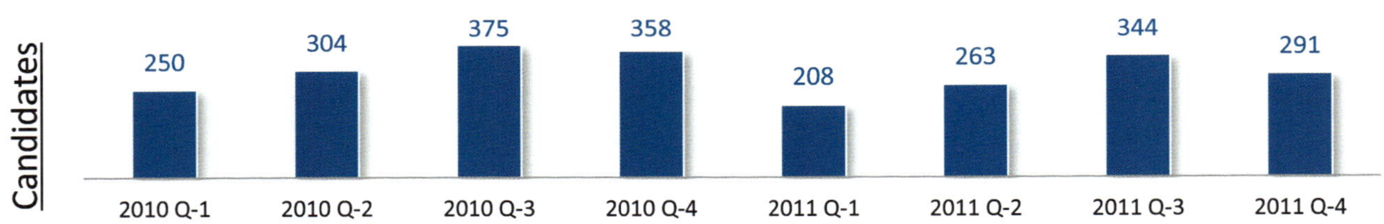

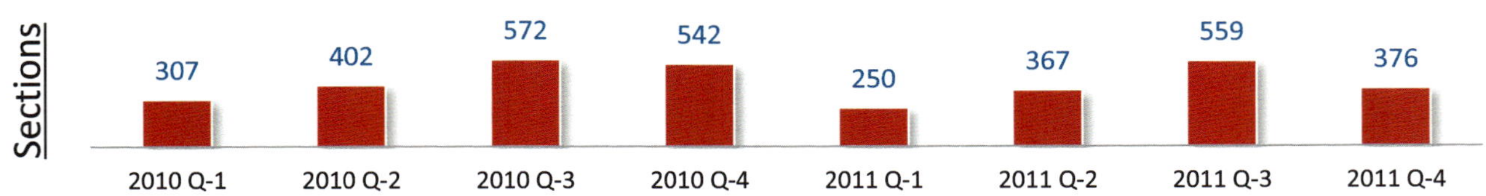

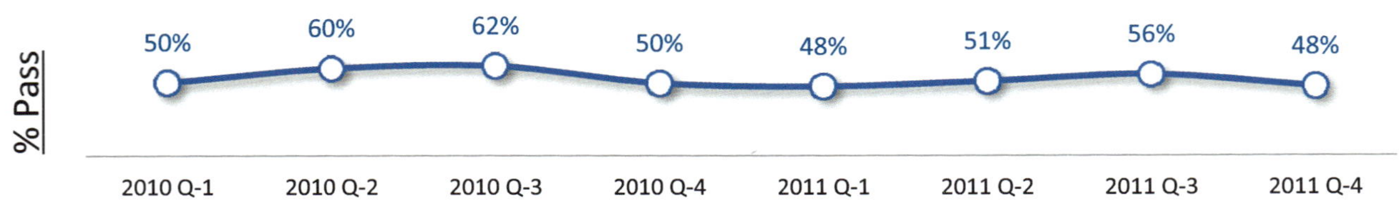

CPA Exam Performance Summary: *2011*

Demographics

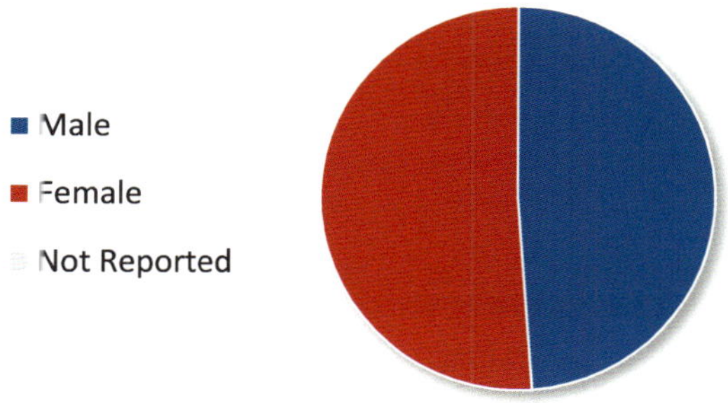

Male Candidates	286	48.8%
Female Candidates	300	51.2%
Not Reported	0	0.0%

Average Age	**28.3**
Age Rank	**14**

Residency

Candidate Count	
In-State Address	**470**
Out-of-State Address	**116**
Foreign Address	**0**
% of Candidates	
In-State Address	**80.2%**
Out-of-State Address	**19.8%**
Foreign Address	**0.0%**

Degree Type

Candidate Count	
Bachelor's Degree	**5**
Advanced Degree	**6**
None/Other	**575**
% of Candidates	
Bachelor's Degree	**0.9%**
Advanced Degree	**1.0%**
None/Other	**98.1%**

New Candidates vs Candidates Passing 4th Section

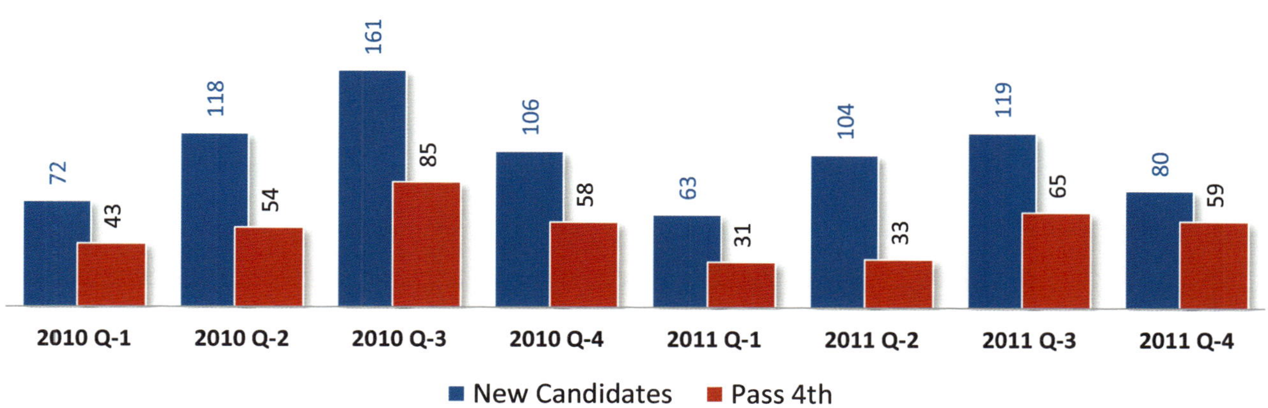

Notes about the Data

1. The data used to develop this report was pulled from NASBA's Gateway System, which houses the Uniform CPA Examination's Application and Performance information for all 55 jurisdictions.
2. The demographic data related to Age, Gender and Degree Type is provided by the individual candidates and may not be 100% accurate.

South Carolina

CPA Exam Performance Summary: *2011*

South Dakota

Overall Performance

Unique Candidates	141
New Candidates	48
Total Sections	344
Passing 4th Section	29
Sections/Candidate	2.44
Pass Rate	44.2%
Average Score	71.6

Section Performance

	Sections	Score	% Pass
First-Time	200	72.7	49.5%
Re-Exam	144	70.1	36.8%
AUD	103	73.1	43.7%
BEC	80	69.7	37.5%
FAR	67	70.1	43.3%
REG	94	72.8	51.1%

Jurisdiction Rankings (1 to 53)

Candidates	Sections
52	51
32	19
Pass Rate	Avg Score

Exam Type by Percent

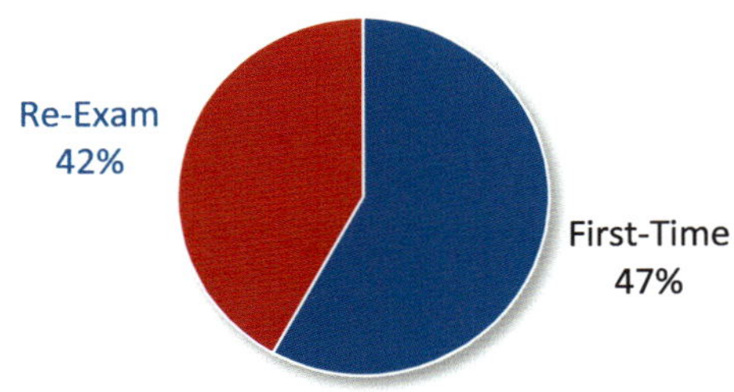

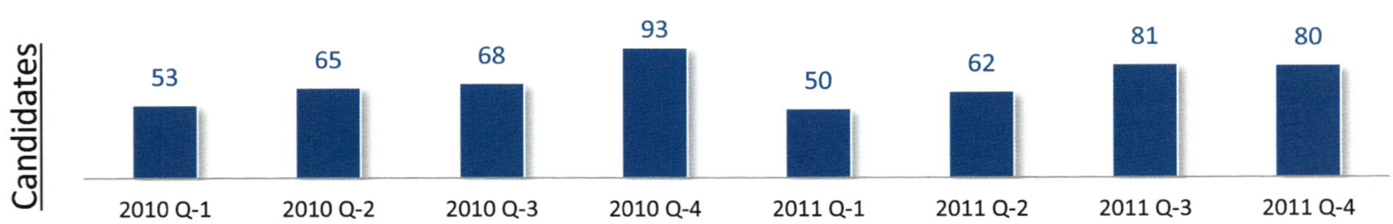

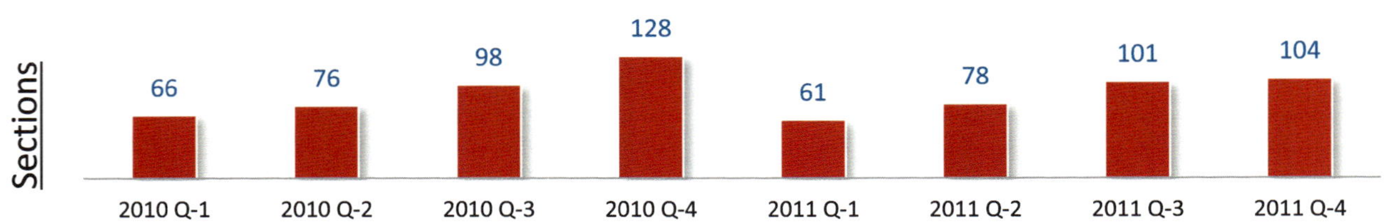

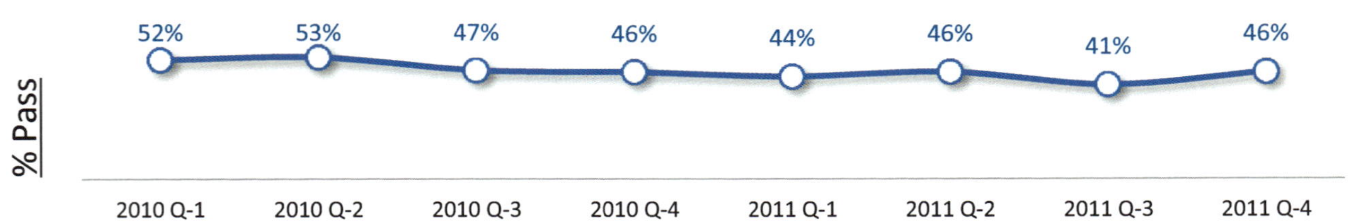

CPA Exam Performance Summary: *2011*

Demographics

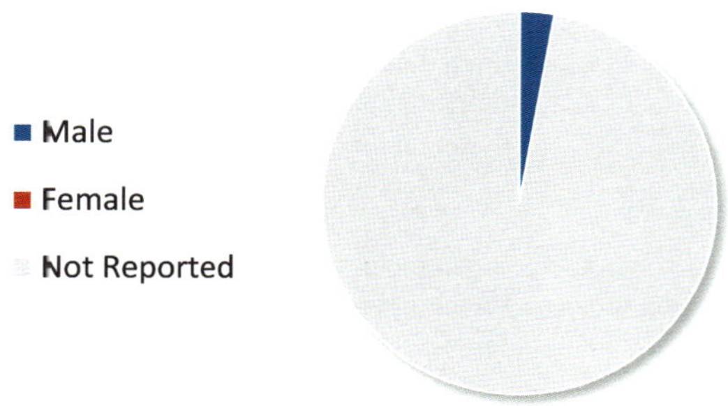

Male Candidates	4	2.8%
Female Candidates	0	0.0%
Not Reported	137	97.2%

Average Age	**28.7**
Age Rank	**24**

Residency

Candidate Count	
In-State Address	**124**
Out-of-State Address	**16**
Foreign Address	**1**
% of Candidates	
In-State Address	**87.9%**
Out-of-State Address	**11.3%**
Foreign Address	**0.7%**

Degree Type

Candidate Count	
Bachelor's Degree	**108**
Advanced Degree	**32**
None/Other	**1**
% of Candidates	
Bachelor's Degree	**76.6%**
Advanced Degree	**22.7%**
None/Other	**0.7%**

New Candidates vs Candidates Passing 4th Section

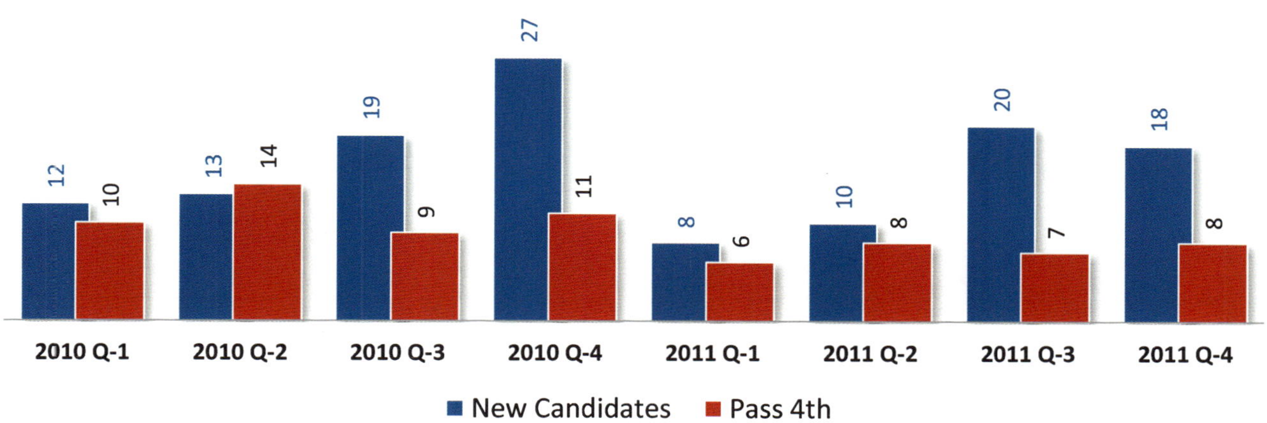

Notes about the Data

1. The data used to develop this report was pulled from NASBA's Gateway System, which houses the Uniform CPA Examination's Application and Performance information for all 55 jurisdictions.
2. The demographic data related to Age, Gender and Degree Type is provided by the individual candidates and may not be 100% accurate.

South Dakota

CPA Exam Performance Summary: *2011*

Tennessee

Overall Performance

Unique Candidates	**1,538**
New Candidates	**759**
Total Sections	**4,118**
Passing 4th Section	**385**
Sections/Candidate	**2.68**
Pass Rate	**44.2%**
Average Score	**70.1**

Section Performance

	Sections	Score	% Pass
First-Time	**2,441**	**70.4**	**48.6%**
Re-Exam	**1,677**	**69.8**	**37.8%**
AUD	**1,107**	**71.2**	**43.5%**
BEC	**934**	**71.5**	**47.0%**
FAR	**991**	**68.0**	**42.3%**
REG	**1,086**	**69.8**	**44.2%**

Jurisdiction Rankings (1 to 53)

Candidates	Sections
18	**18**
31	**31**
Pass Rate	Avg Score

Exam Type by Percent

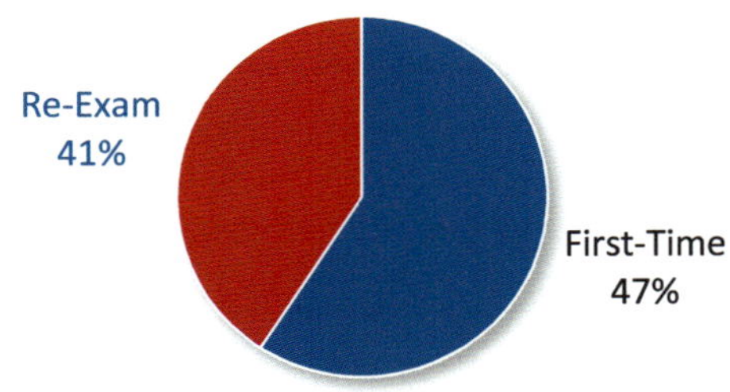

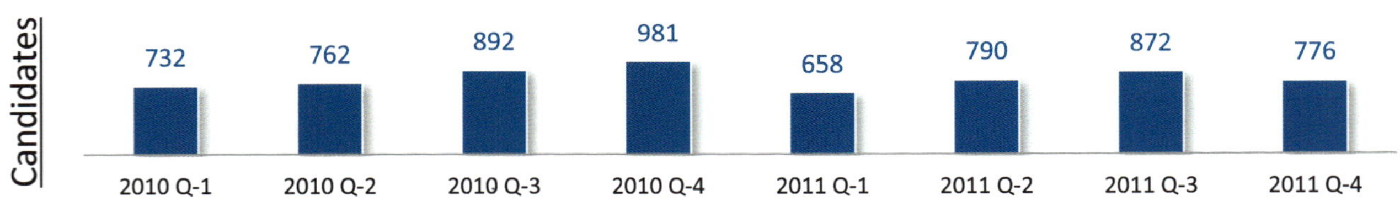

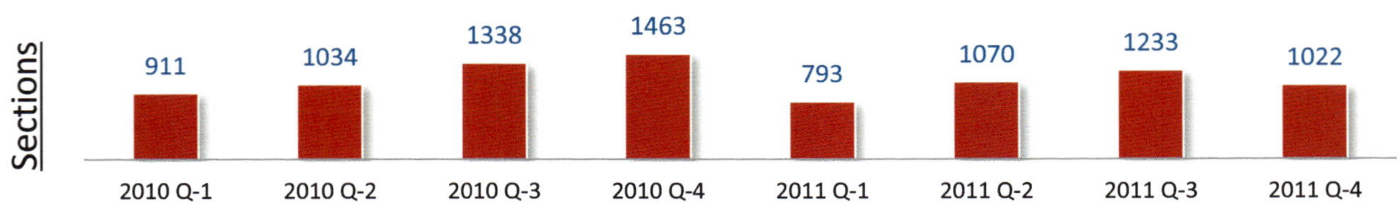

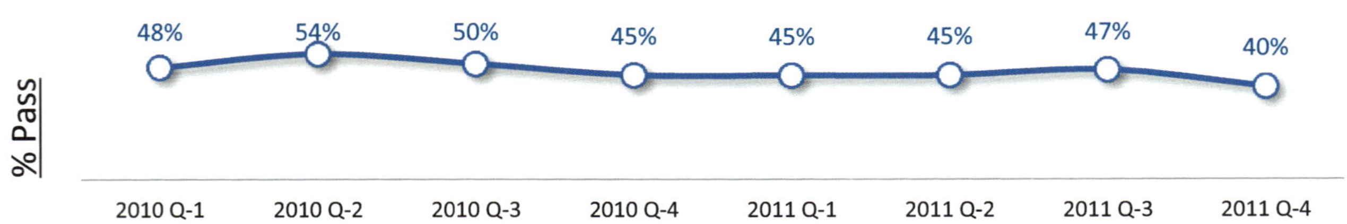

CPA Exam Performance Summary: *2011*

Demographics

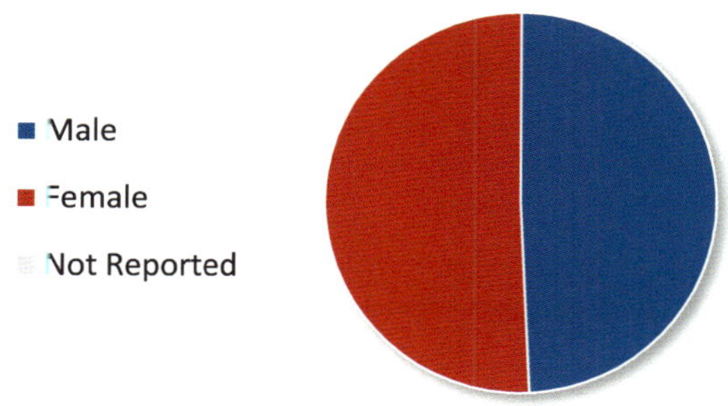

Male Candidates	757	49.2%
Female Candidates	781	50.8%
Not Reported	0	0.0%

Average Age	**29.2**
Age Rank	**27**

Residency

Candidate Count	
In-State Address	**1,231**
Out-of-State Address	**305**
Foreign Address	**2**
% of Candidates	
In-State Address	**80.0%**
Out-of-State Address	**19.8%**
Foreign Address	**0.1%**

Degree Type

Candidate Count	
Bachelor's Degree	**1,015**
Advanced Degree	**331**
None/Other	**192**
% of Candidates	
Bachelor's Degree	**66.0%**
Advanced Degree	**21.5%**
None/Other	**12.5%**

New Candidates vs Candidates Passing 4th Section

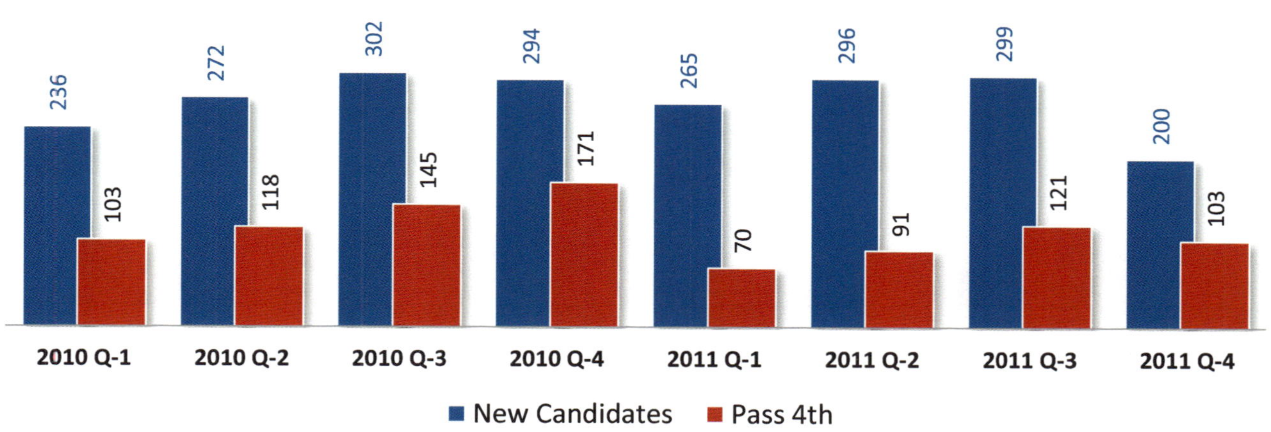

Notes about the Data

1. The data used to develop this report was pulled from NASBA's Gateway System, which houses the Uniform CPA Examination's Application and Performance information for all 55 jurisdictions.
2. The demographic data related to Age, Gender and Degree Type is provided by the individual candidates and may not be 100% accurate.

Tennessee

CPA Exam Performance Summary: *2011*

Texas

Overall Performance

Unique Candidates	5,515
New Candidates	2,023
Total Sections	14,501
Passing 4th Section	1,620
Sections/Candidate	2.63
Pass Rate	48.2%
Average Score	71.9

Section Performance

	Sections	Score	% Pass
First-Time	8,395	73.3	55.6%
Re-Exam	6,106	70.0	37.9%
AUD	3,962	73.1	47.5%
BEC	3,233	72.5	50.8%
FAR	3,415	70.6	48.2%
REG	3,891	71.3	46.7%

Jurisdiction Rankings (1 to 53)

Candidates	Sections
3	3
18	14
Pass Rate	Avg Score

Exam Type by Percent

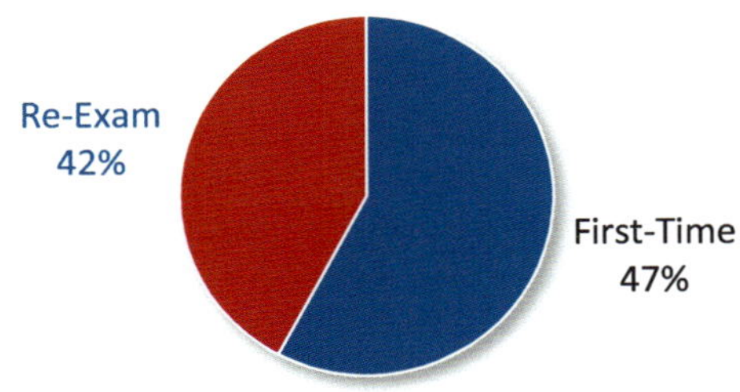

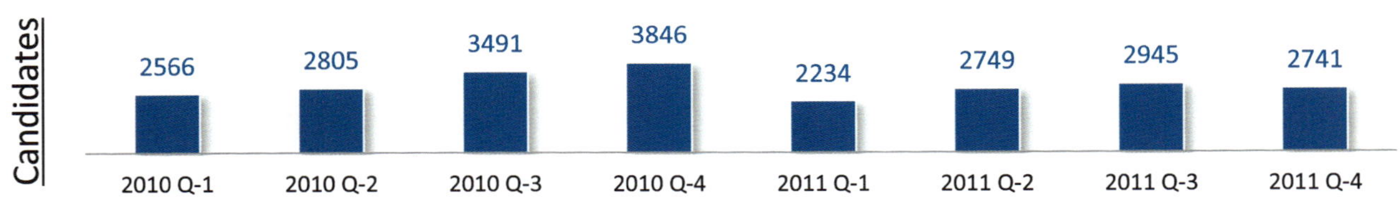

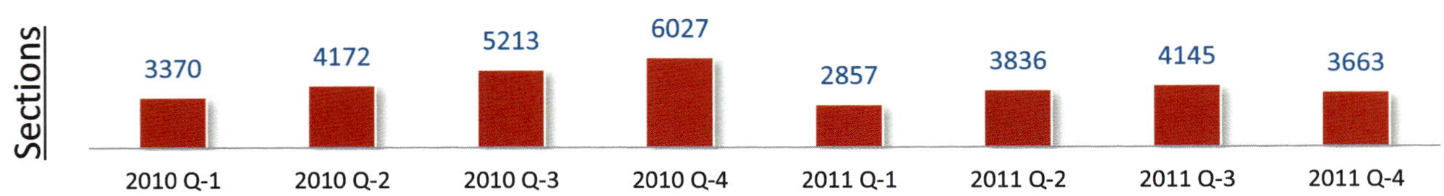

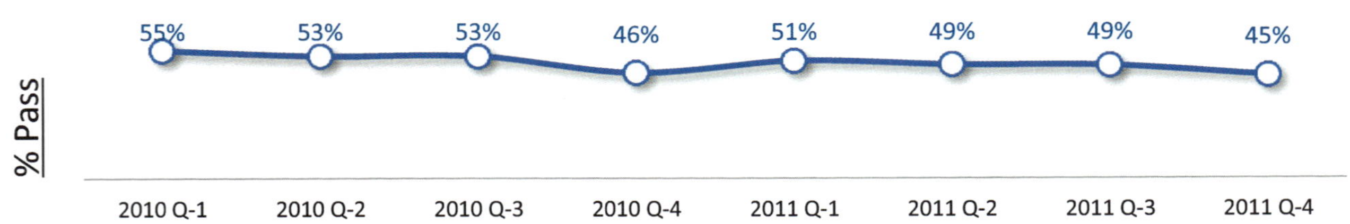

CPA Exam Performance Summary: *2011*

Demographics

Male Candidates	0	0.0%
Female Candidates	0	0.0%
Not Reported	5,515	100.0%

Average Age **29.9**

Age Rank **32**

Residency

Candidate Count

In-State Address	5,374
Out-of-State Address	136
Foreign Address	5

% of Candidates

In-State Address	97.4%
Out-of-State Address	2.5%
Foreign Address	0.1%

Degree Type

Candidate Count

Bachelor's Degree	2,945
Advanced Degree	1,665
None/Other	905

% of Candidates

Bachelor's Degree	53.4%
Advanced Degree	30.2%
None/Other	16.4%

New Candidates vs Candidates Passing 4th Section

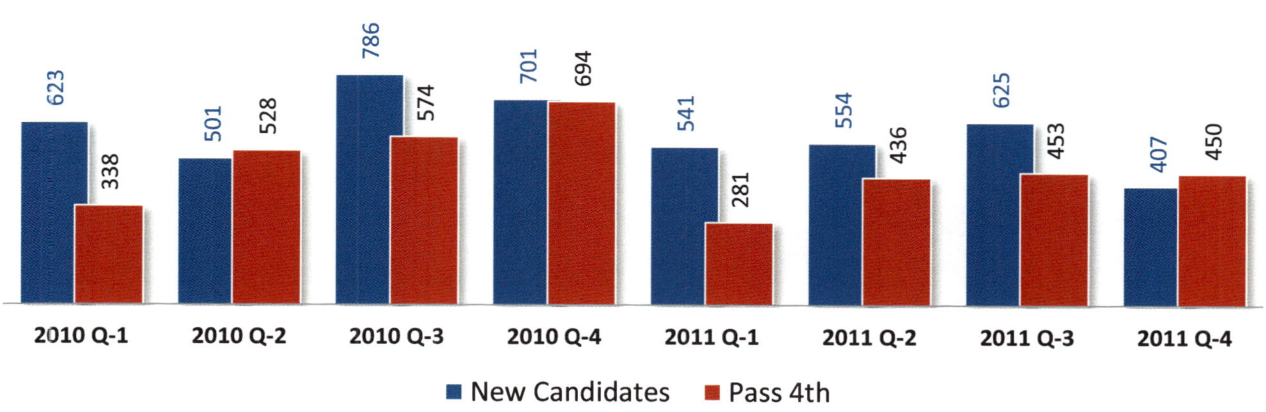

Notes about the Data

1. The data used to develop this report was pulled from NASBA's Gateway System, which houses the Uniform CPA Examination's Application and Performance information for all 55 jurisdictions.
2. The demographic data related to Age, Gender and Degree Type is provided by the individual candidates and may not be 100% accurate.

Texas

CPA Exam Performance Summary: *2011*

Utah

Overall Performance

Unique Candidates	**523**
New Candidates	**315**
Total Sections	**1,310**
Passing 4th Section	**175**
Sections/Candidate	**2.50**
Pass Rate	**57.4%**
Average Score	**74.8**

Section Performance

	Sections	Score	% Pass
First-Time	**885**	**75.8**	**62.9%**
Re-Exam	**425**	**72.8**	**45.9%**
AUD	**362**	**76.1**	**55.5%**
BEC	**272**	**76.5**	**63.6%**
FAR	**329**	**72.1**	**50.5%**
REG	**347**	**74.7**	**61.1%**

Jurisdiction Rankings (1 to 53)

Candidates	Sections
37	**37**
1	**1**
Pass Rate	Avg Score

Exam Type by Percent

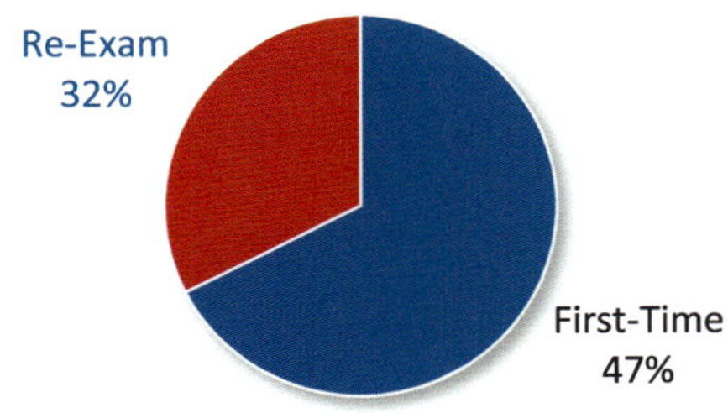

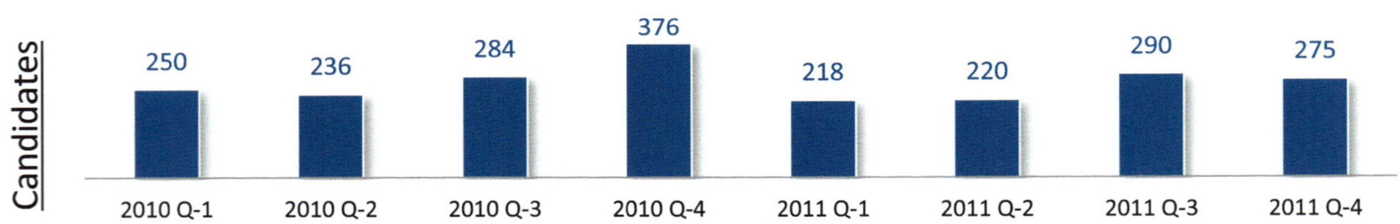

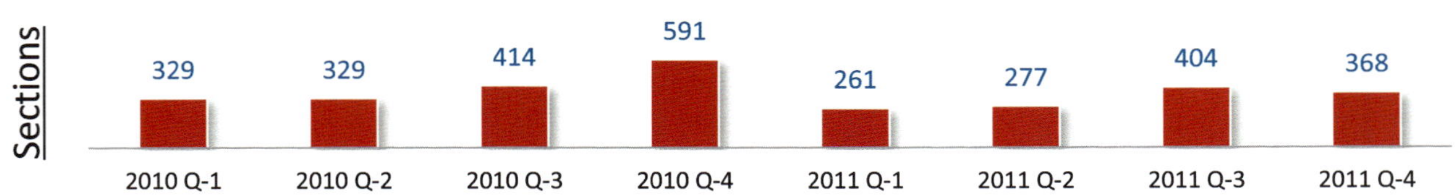

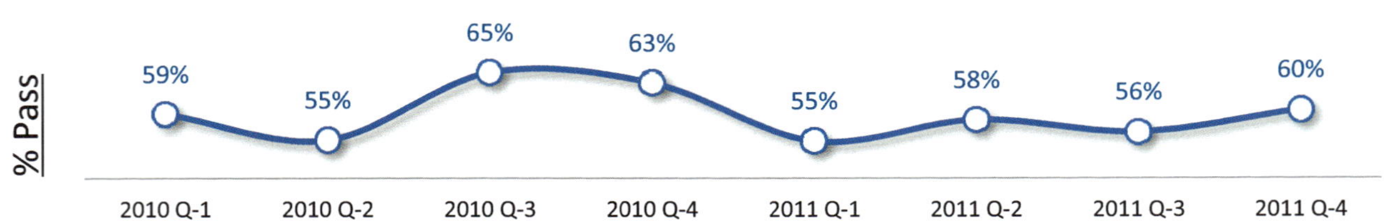

CPA Exam Performance Summary: *2011*

Demographics

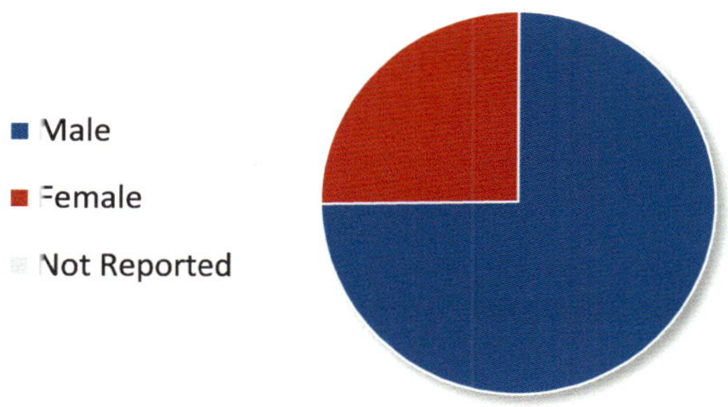

Male Candidates	391	74.8%
Female Candidates	132	25.2%
Not Reported	0	0.0%

Average Age	**31.3**
Age Rank	**47**

Residency

Candidate Count	
In-State Address	**509**
Out-of-State Address	**13**
Foreign Address	**1**
% of Candidates	
In-State Address	**97.3%**
Out-of-State Address	**2.5%**
Foreign Address	**0.2%**

Degree Type

Candidate Count	
Bachelor's Degree	**60**
Advanced Degree	**436**
None/Other	**27**
% of Candidates	
Bachelor's Degree	**11.5%**
Advanced Degree	**83.4%**
None/Other	**5.2%**

New Candidates vs Candidates Passing 4th Section

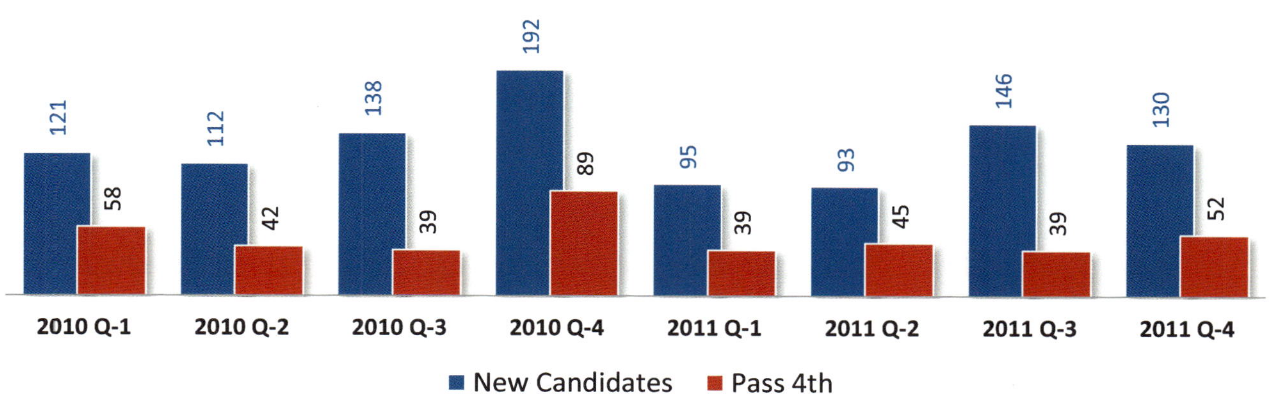

Notes about the Data

1. The data used to develop this report was pulled from NASBA's Gateway System, which houses the Uniform CPA Examination's Application and Performance information for all 55 jurisdictions.
2. The demographic data related to Age, Gender and Degree Type is provided by the individual candidates and may not be 100% accurate.

Utah

CPA Exam Performance Summary: *2011*

Vermont

Overall Performance

Unique Candidates	602
New Candidates	333
Total Sections	1,737
Passing 4th Section	159
Sections/Candidate	2.89
Pass Rate	39.1%
Average Score	68.3

Section Performance

	Sections	Score	% Pass
First-Time	1,015	66.8	39.0%
Re-Exam	722	70.6	39.2%
AUD	494	68.8	39.7%
BEC	335	68.3	31.3%
FAR	422	69.6	44.1%
REG	486	66.8	39.5%

Jurisdiction Rankings (1 to 53)

Candidates	Sections
33	30
44	44
Pass Rate	Avg Score

Exam Type by Percent

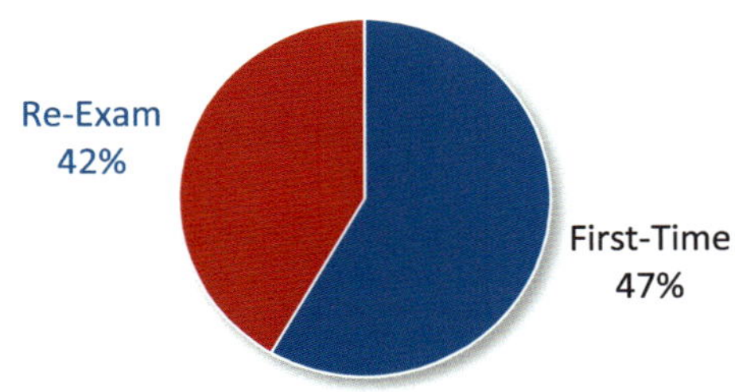

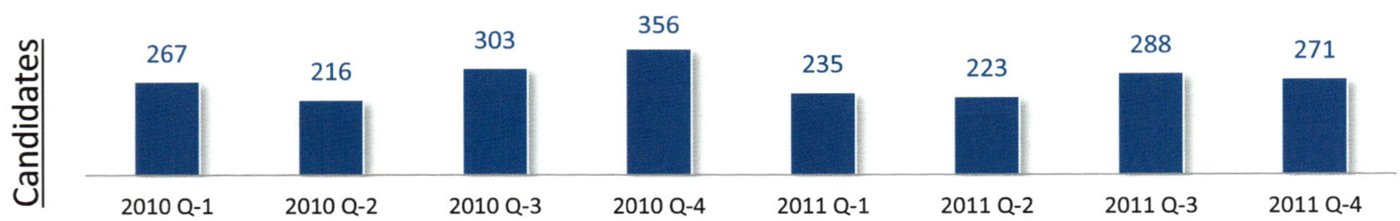

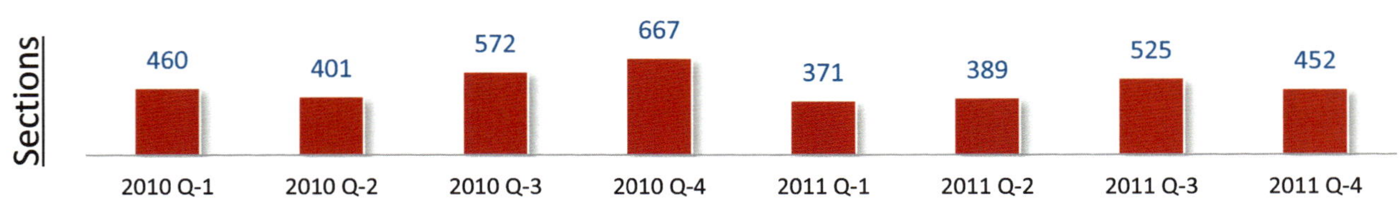

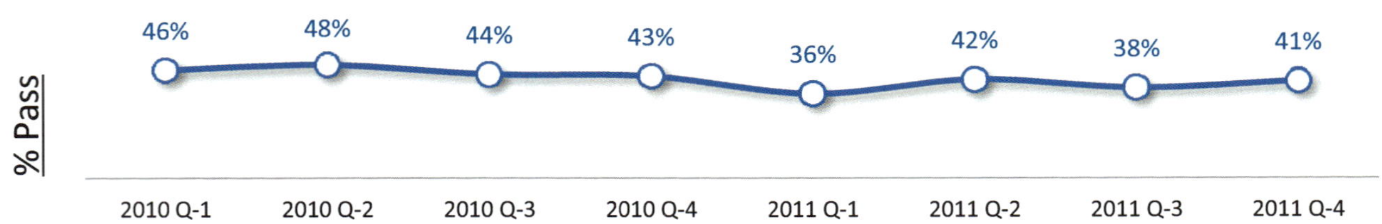

CPA Exam Performance Summary: *2011*

Demographics

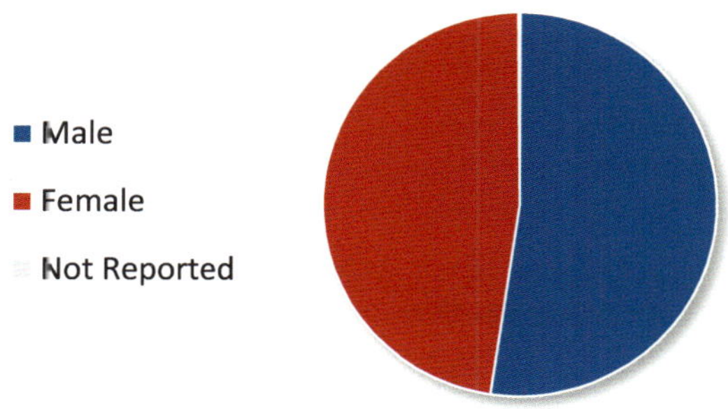

Male Candidates	315	52.3%
Female Candidates	286	47.5%
Not Reported	1	0.2%

Average Age	**27.2**
Age Rank	**3**

Residency

Candidate Count	
In-State Address	**86**
Out-of-State Address	**212**
Foreign Address	**304**
% of Candidates	
In-State Address	**14.3%**
Out-of-State Address	**35.2%**
Foreign Address	**50.5%**

Degree Type

Candidate Count	
Bachelor's Degree	**139**
Advanced Degree	**13**
None/Other	**450**
% of Candidates	
Bachelor's Degree	**23.1%**
Advanced Degree	**2.2%**
None/Other	**74.8%**

New Candidates vs Candidates Passing 4th Section

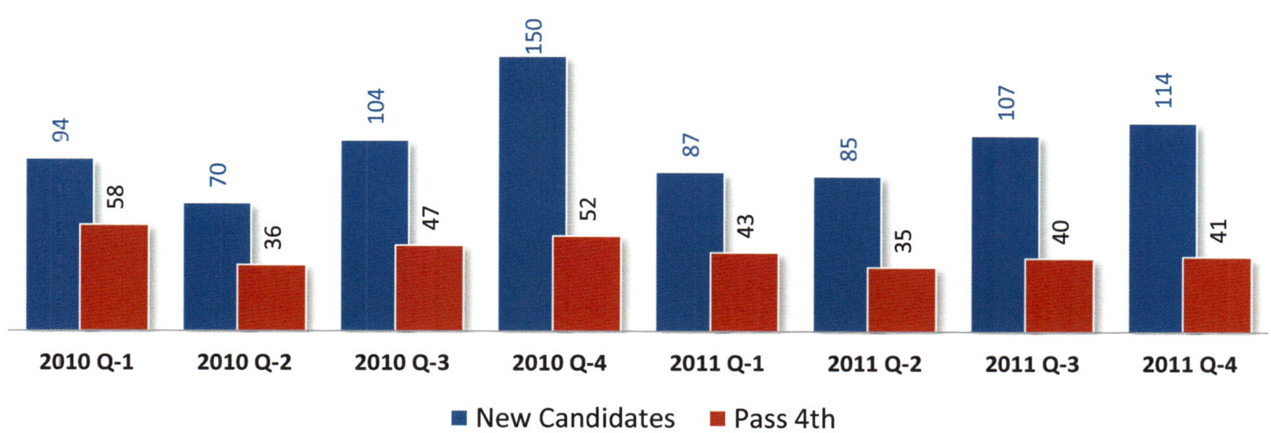

Notes about the Data

1. The data used to develop this report was pulled from NASBA's Gateway System, which houses the Uniform CPA Examination's Application and Performance information for all 55 jurisdictions.
2. The demographic data related to Age, Gender and Degree Type is provided by the individual candidates and may not be 100% accurate.

Vermont

CPA Exam Performance Summary: *2011*

Virginia

Overall Performance

Unique Candidates	**2,954**
New Candidates	**1,149**
Total Sections	**7,443**
Passing 4th Section	**817**
Sections/Candidate	**2.52**
Pass Rate	**48.4%**
Average Score	**71.9**

Section Performance

	Sections	Score	% Pass
First-Time	**4,427**	**72.7**	**53.9%**
Re-Exam	**3,016**	**70.7**	**40.3%**
AUD	**2,026**	**73.3**	**48.2%**
BEC	**1,614**	**72.6**	**50.4%**
FAR	**1,774**	**70.8**	**49.4%**
REG	**2,029**	**70.8**	**46.0%**

Jurisdiction Rankings (1 to 53)

Candidates	Sections
7	**7**
16	**15**
Pass Rate	Avg Score

Exam Type by Percent

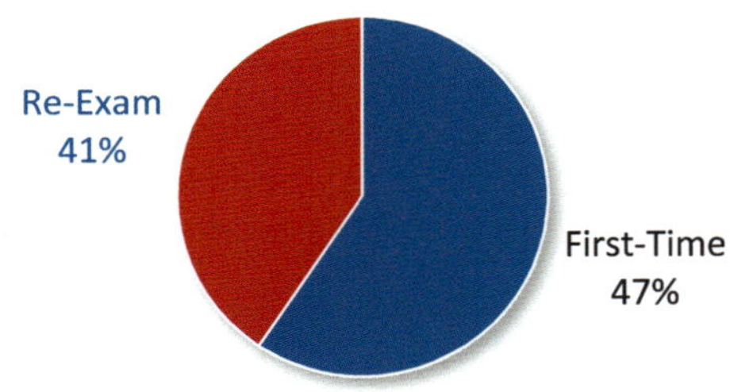

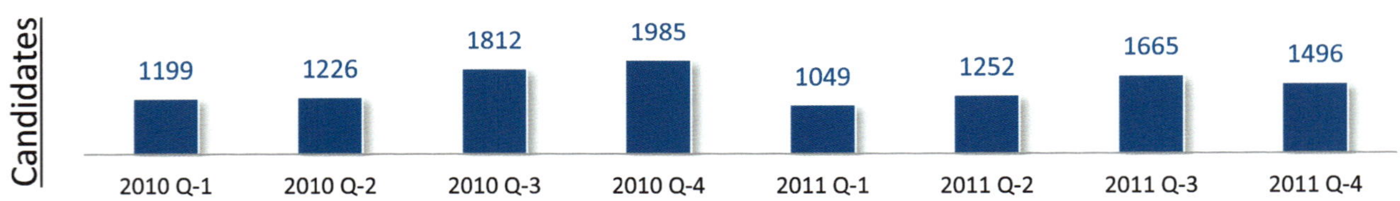

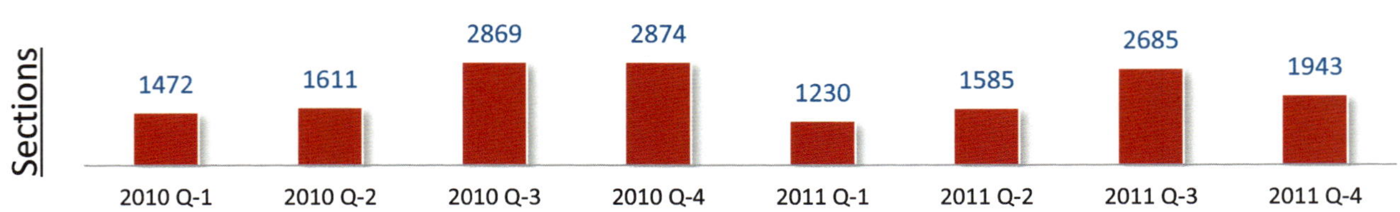

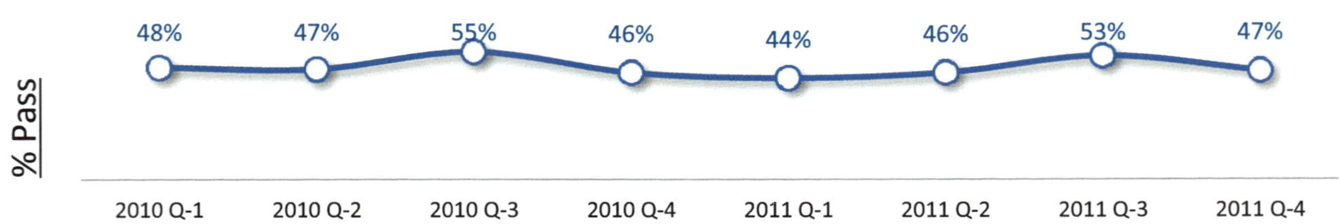

CPA Exam Performance Summary: *2011*

Demographics

Male Candidates	3	0.1%
Female Candidates	7	0.2%
Not Reported	2,944	99.7%

Average Age	**29.4**
Age Rank	**28**

Residency

Candidate Count	
In-State Address	**2,104**
Out-of-State Address	**835**
Foreign Address	**15**
% of Candidates	
In-State Address	**71.2%**
Out-of-State Address	**28.3%**
Foreign Address	**0.5%**

Degree Type

Candidate Count	
Bachelor's Degree	**2,531**
Advanced Degree	**398**
None/Other	**25**
% of Candidates	
Bachelor's Degree	**85.7%**
Advanced Degree	**13.5%**
None/Other	**0.8%**

New Candidates vs Candidates Passing 4th Section

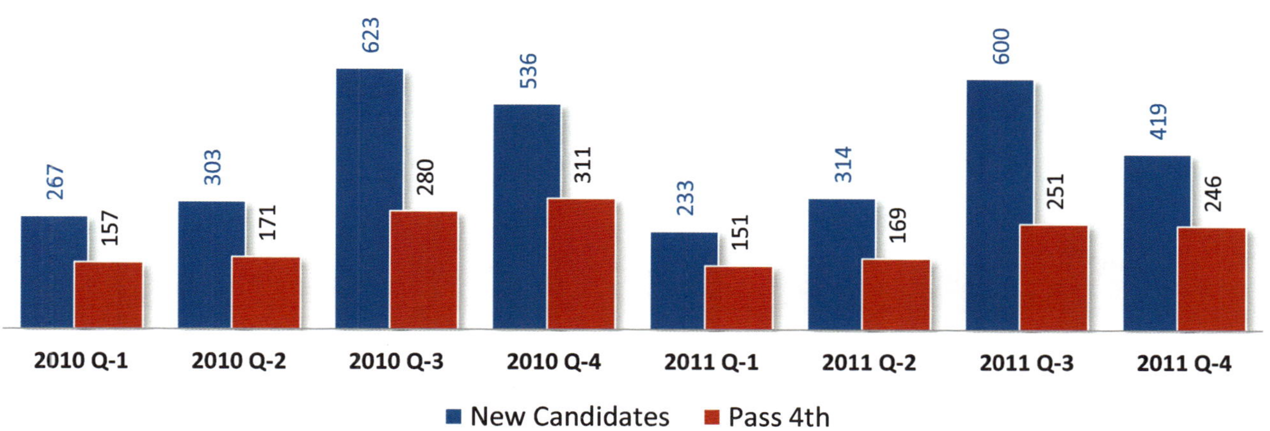

Notes about the Data

1. The data used to develop this report was pulled from NASBA's Gateway System, which houses the Uniform CPA Examination's Application and Performance information for all 55 jurisdictions.
2. The demographic data related to Age, Gender and Degree Type is provided by the individual candidates and may not be 100% accurate.

Virginia

CPA Exam Performance Summary: *2011*

Washington

Overall Performance

Unique Candidates	2,070
New Candidates	1,102
Total Sections	5,212
Passing 4th Section	530
Sections/Candidate	2.52
Pass Rate	47.3%
Average Score	70.7

Section Performance

	Sections	Score	% Pass
First-Time	3,331	71.2	51.7%
Re-Exam	1,881	69.9	39.6%
AUD	1,398	71.5	45.5%
BEC	1,089	72.1	50.0%
FAR	1,318	69.5	47.9%
REG	1,407	70.1	46.6%

Jurisdiction Rankings (1 to 53)

Candidates	Sections
15	15
21	25
Pass Rate	Avg Score

Exam Type by Percent

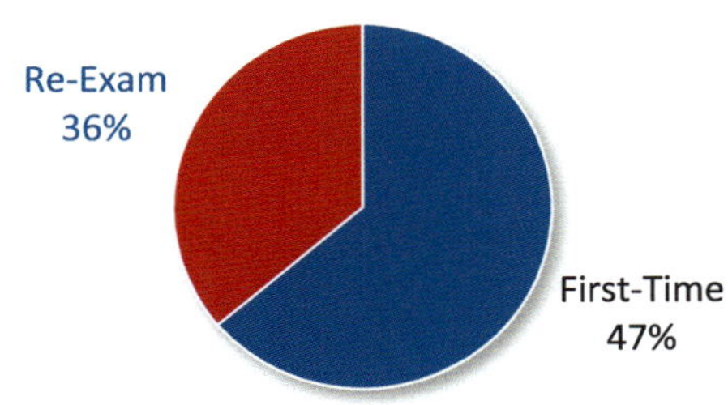

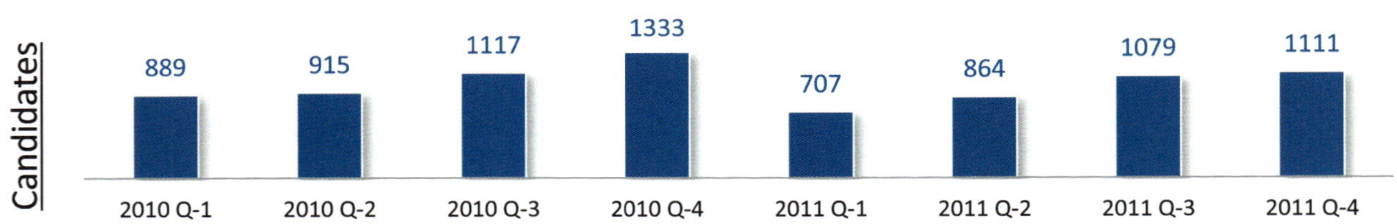

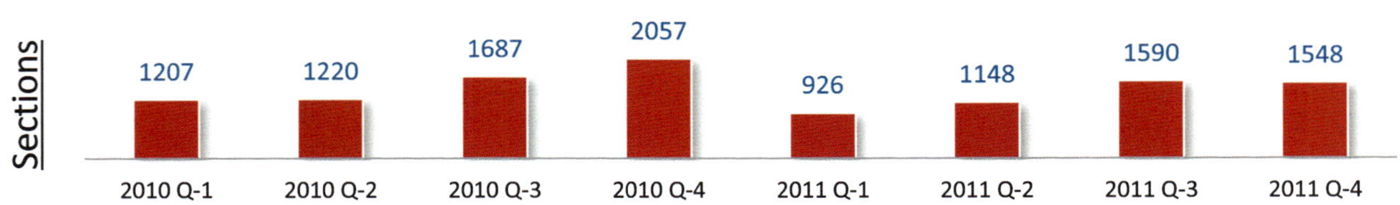

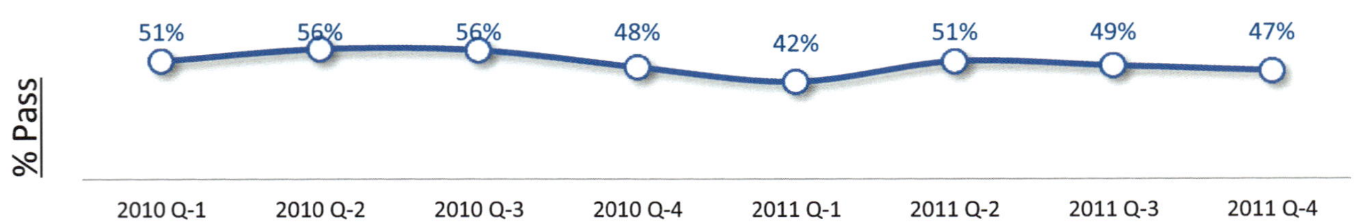

CPA Exam Performance Summary: *2011*

Demographics

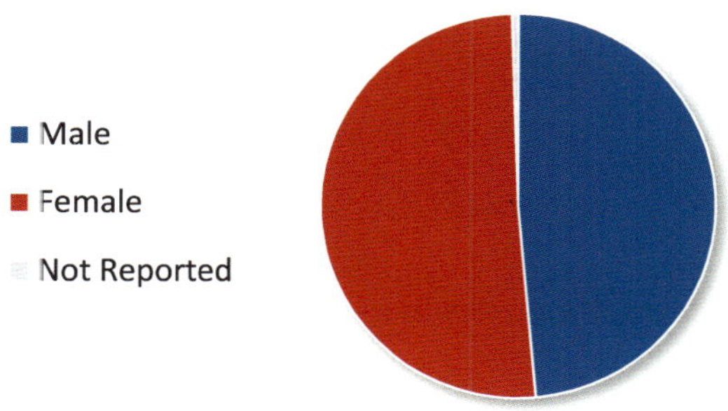

Male Candidates	1,005	48.6%
Female Candidates	1,054	50.9%
Not Reported	11	0.5%

Average Age	**30.9**
Age Rank	**43**

Residency

Candidate Count	
In-State Address	1,496
Out-of-State Address	170
Foreign Address	404
% of Candidates	
In-State Address	72.3%
Out-of-State Address	8.2%
Foreign Address	19.5%

Degree Type

Candidate Count	
Bachelor's Degree	1,059
Advanced Degree	157
None/Other	854
% of Candidates	
Bachelor's Degree	51.2%
Advanced Degree	7.6%
None/Other	41.3%

New Candidates vs Candidates Passing 4th Section

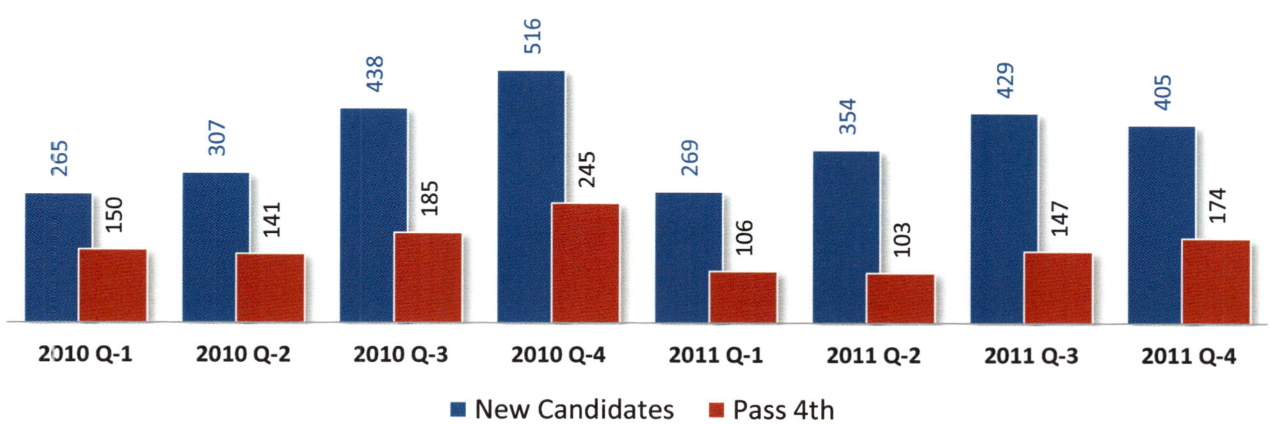

Notes about the Data

1. The data used to develop this report was pulled from NASBA's Gateway System, which houses the Uniform CPA Examination's Application and Performance information for all 55 jurisdictions.
2. The demographic data related to Age, Gender and Degree Type is provided by the individual candidates and may not be 100% accurate.

Washington

CPA Exam Performance Summary: *2011*

West Virginia

Overall Performance

Unique Candidates	**302**
New Candidates	**89**
Total Sections	**752**
Passing 4th Section	**68**
Sections/Candidate	**2.49**
Pass Rate	**37.6%**
Average Score	**67.6**

Section Performance

	Sections	Score	% Pass
First-Time	**397**	**66.9**	**36.5%**
Re-Exam	**355**	**68.5**	**38.9%**
AUD	**184**	**69.2**	**38.0%**
BEC	**187**	**67.3**	**36.4%**
FAR	**177**	**66.8**	**40.1%**
REG	**204**	**67.3**	**36.3%**

Jurisdiction Rankings (1 to 53)

Candidates	Sections
47	**46**
47	**48**
Pass Rate	Avg Score

Exam Type by Percent

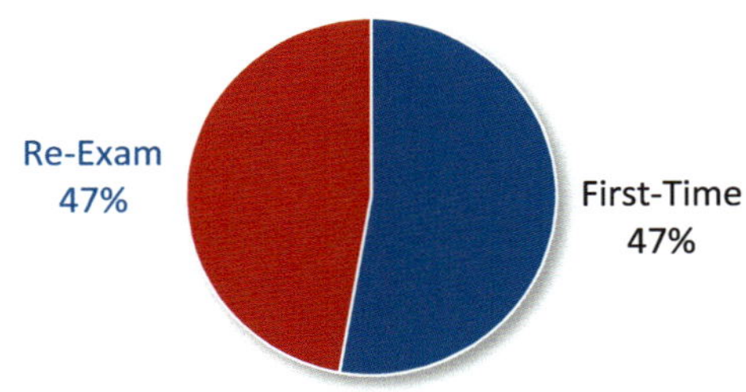

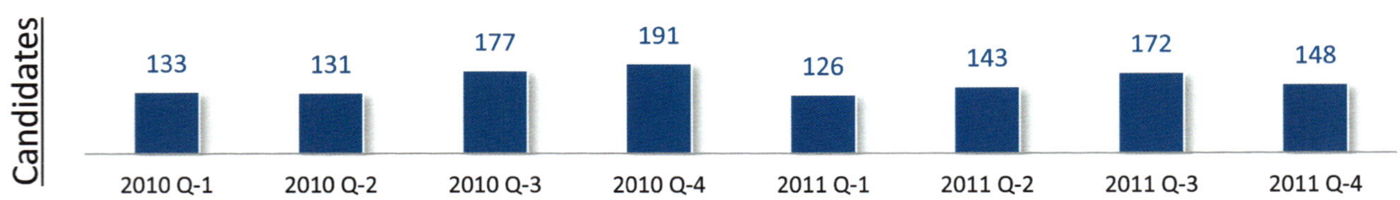

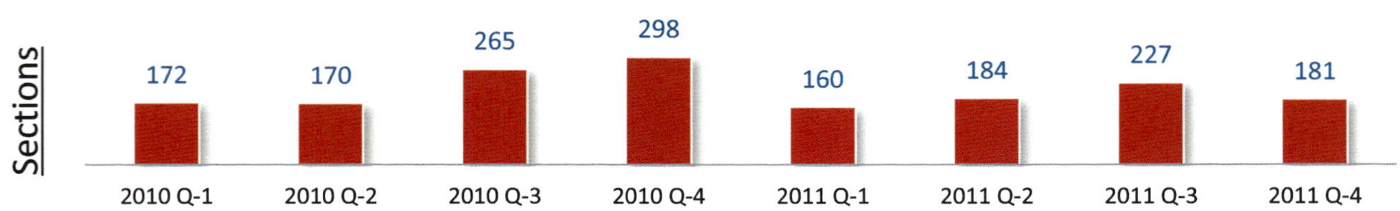

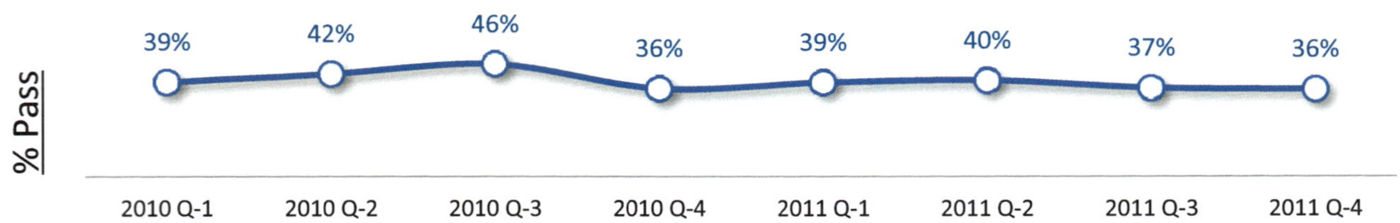

CPA Exam Performance Summary: *2011*

Demographics

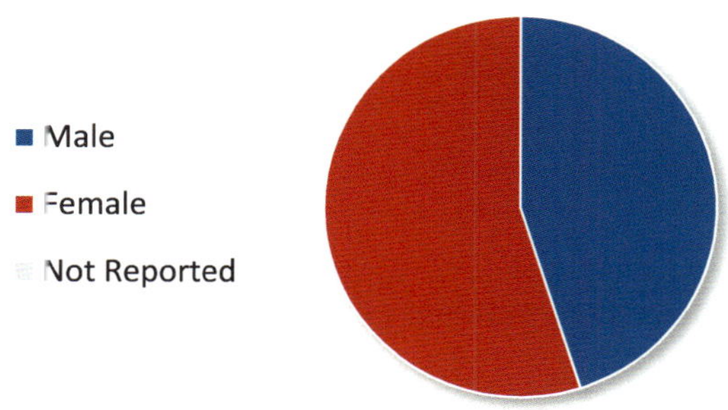

Male Candidates	136	45.0%
Female Candidates	166	55.0%
Not Reported	0	0.0%

Average Age	**29.9**
Age Rank	**33**

Residency

Candidate Count	
In-State Address	**283**
Out-of-State Address	**19**
Foreign Address	**0**

% of Candidates	
In-State Address	**93.7%**
Out-of-State Address	**6.3%**
Foreign Address	**0.0%**

Degree Type

Candidate Count	
Bachelor's Degree	**291**
Advanced Degree	**10**
None/Other	**1**

% of Candidates	
Bachelor's Degree	**96.4%**
Advanced Degree	**3.3%**
None/Other	**0.3%**

New Candidates vs Candidates Passing 4th Section

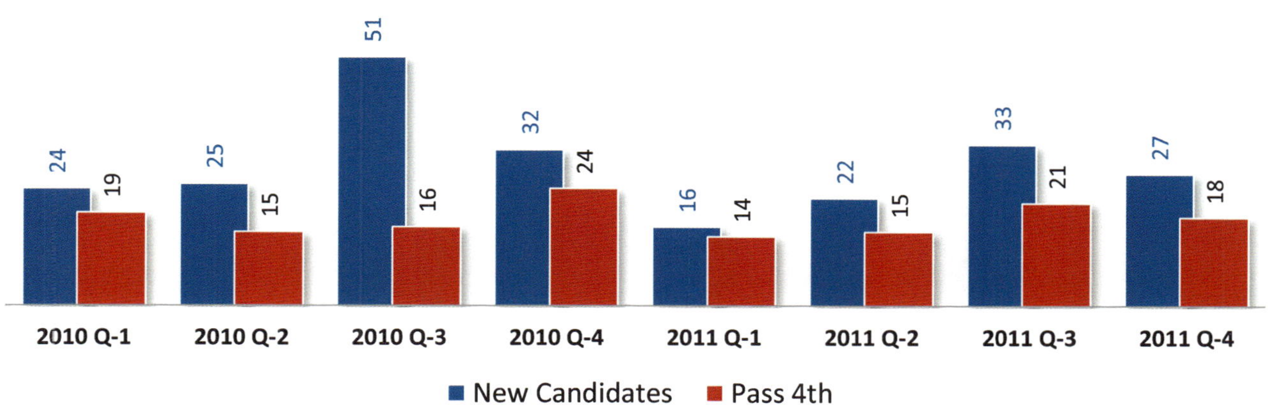

Notes about the Data

1. The data used to develop this report was pulled from NASBA's Gateway System, which houses the Uniform CPA Examination's Application and Performance information for all 55 jurisdictions.
2. The demographic data related to Age, Gender and Degree Type is provided by the individual candidates and may not be 100% accurate.

West Virginia

CPA Exam Performance Summary: *2011*

Wisconsin

Overall Performance

Unique Candidates	**1,267**
New Candidates	**701**
Total Sections	**3,513**
Passing 4th Section	**415**
Sections/Candidate	**2.77**
Pass Rate	**50.9%**
Average Score	**72.6**

Section Performance

	Sections	Score	% Pass
First-Time	**2,246**	**73.3**	**54.4%**
Re-Exam	**1,267**	**71.4**	**44.8%**
AUD	**1,015**	**72.7**	**46.1%**
BEC	**760**	**74.1**	**57.5%**
FAR	**807**	**72.1**	**51.7%**
REG	**931**	**71.9**	**50.1%**

Jurisdiction Rankings (1 to 53)

Candidates	Sections
24	**22**
11	**9**
Pass Rate	Avg Score

Exam Type by Percent

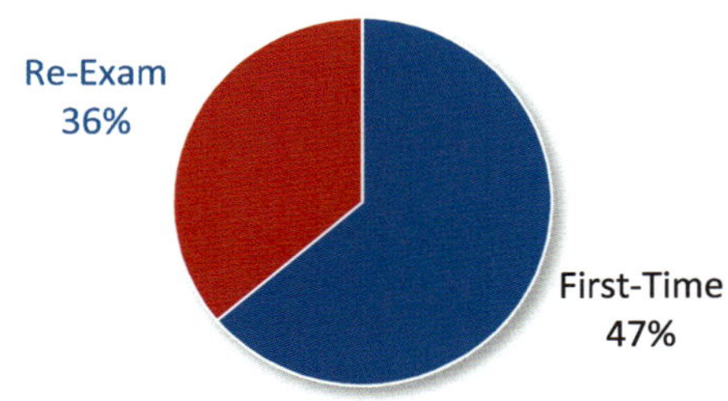

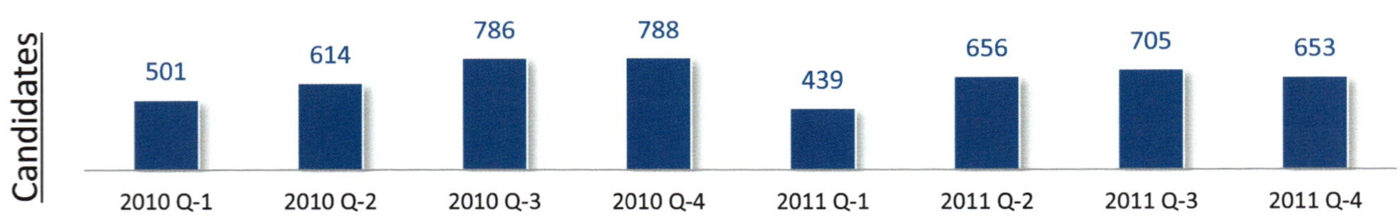

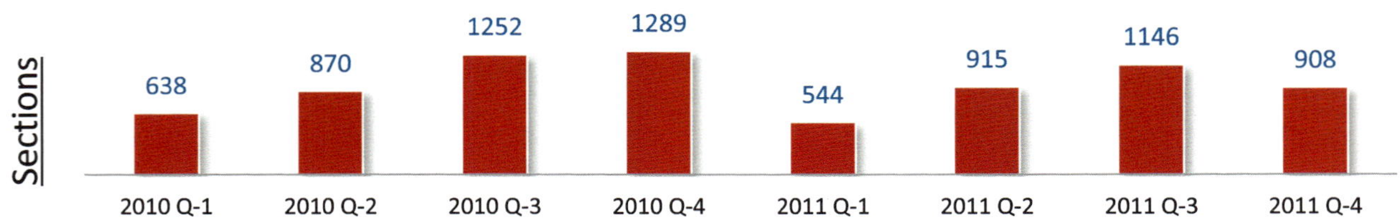

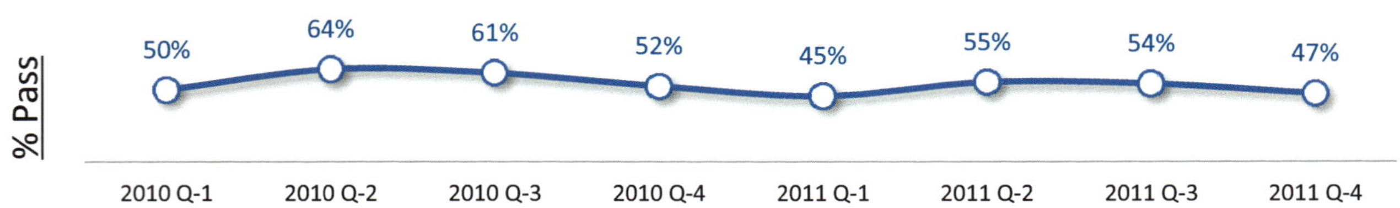

CPA Exam Performance Summary: *2011*

Demographics

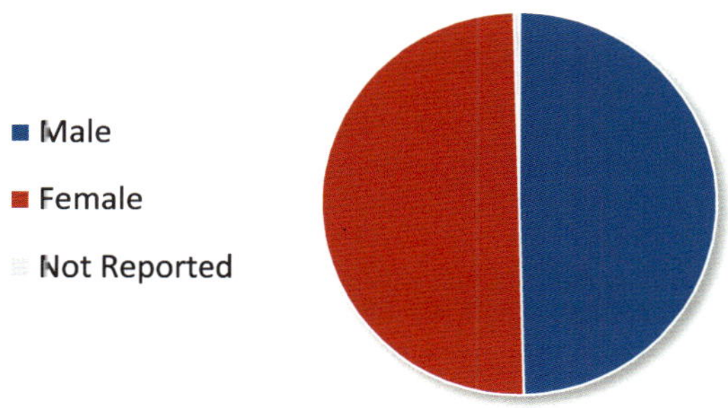

Male Candidates	628	49.6%
Female Candidates	633	50.0%
Not Reported	6	0.5%

Average Age	**28.3**
Age Rank	**13**

Residency

Candidate Count	
In-State Address	**1,217**
Out-of-State Address	**47**
Foreign Address	**3**
% of Candidates	
In-State Address	**96.1%**
Out-of-State Address	**3.7%**
Foreign Address	**0.2%**

Degree Type

Candidate Count	
Bachelor's Degree	**820**
Advanced Degree	**181**
None/Other	**266**
% of Candidates	
Bachelor's Degree	**64.7%**
Advanced Degree	**14.3%**
None/Other	**21.0%**

New Candidates vs Candidates Passing 4th Section

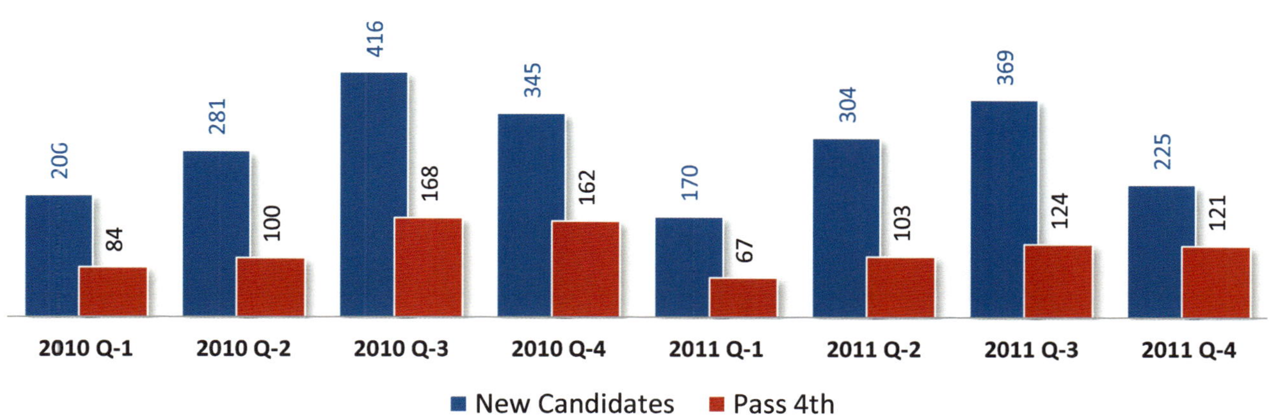

Notes about the Data

1. The data used to develop this report was pulled from NASBA's Gateway System, which houses the Uniform CPA Examination's Application and Performance information for all 55 jurisdictions.
2. The demographic data related to Age, Gender and Degree Type is provided by the individual candidates and may not be 100% accurate.

Wisconsin

CPA Exam Performance Summary: *2011*

Wyoming

Overall Performance

Unique Candidates	**84**
New Candidates	**36**
Total Sections	**224**
Passing 4th Section	**15**
Sections/Candidate	**2.67**
Pass Rate	**42.0%**
Average Score	**69.9**

Section Performance

	Sections	Score	% Pass
First-Time	**128**	**69.1**	**42.2%**
Re-Exam	**96**	**70.8**	**41.7%**
AUD	**51**	**69.5**	**39.2%**
BEC	**57**	**70.2**	**42.1%**
FAR	**54**	**68.3**	**40.7%**
REG	**62**	**71.1**	**45.2%**

Jurisdiction Rankings (1 to 53)

Candidates	Sections
53	**52**
38	**35**
Pass Rate	Avg Score

Exam Type by Percent

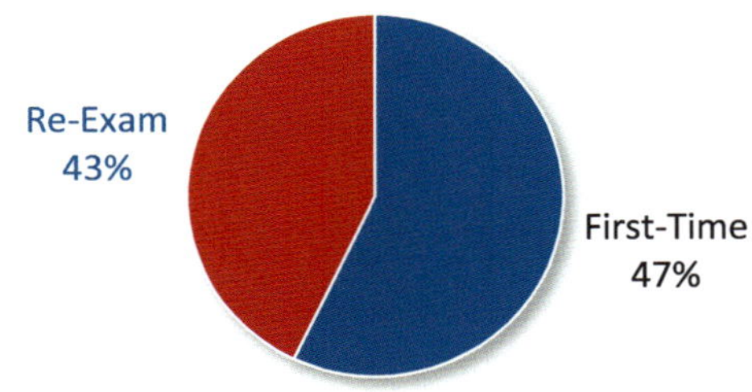

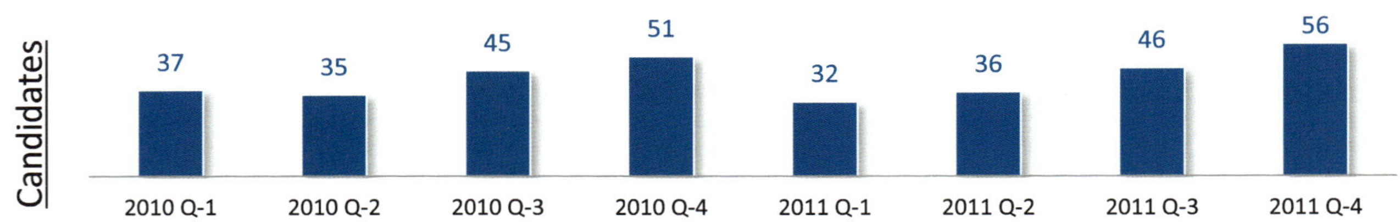

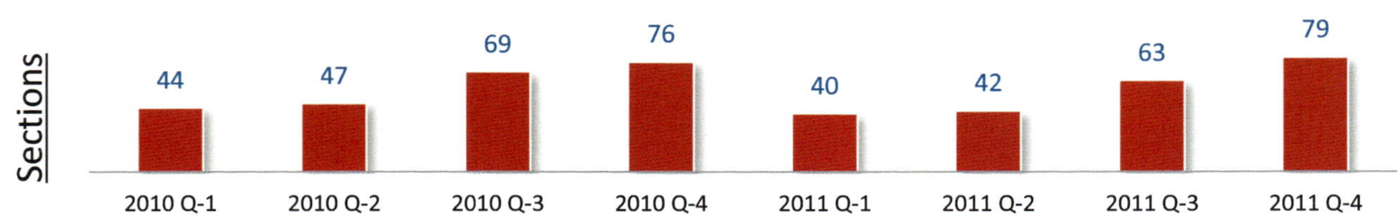

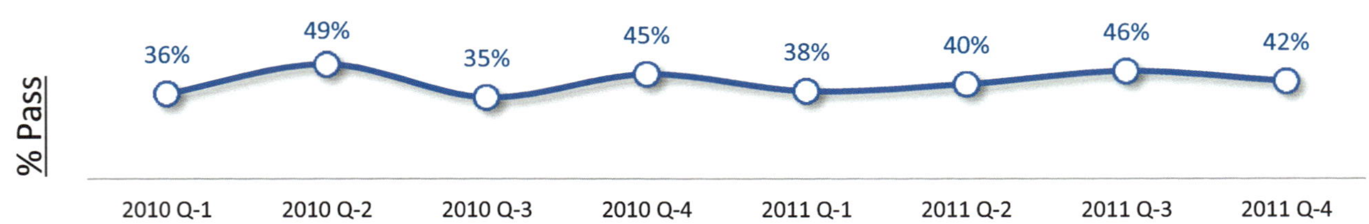

CPA Exam Performance Summary: *2011*

Demographics

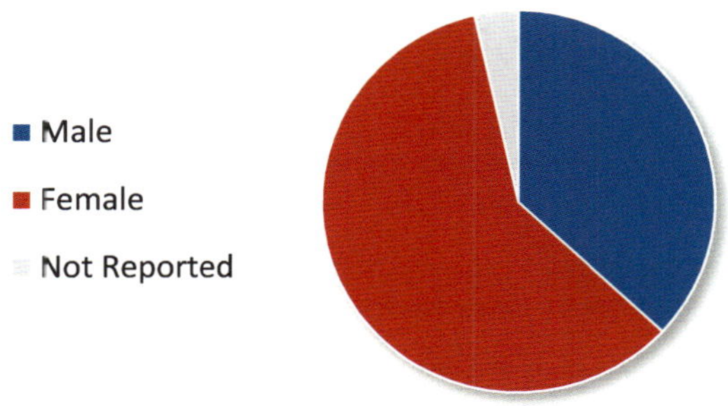

Male Candidates	31	36.9%
Female Candidates	50	59.5%
Not Reported	3	3.6%

Average Age **29.0**

Age Rank **26**

Residency

Candidate Count	
In-State Address	78
Out-of-State Address	6
Foreign Address	0

% of Candidates	
In-State Address	92.9%
Out-of-State Address	7.1%
Foreign Address	0.0%

Degree Type

Candidate Count	
Bachelor's Degree	57
Advanced Degree	21
None/Other	6

% of Candidates	
Bachelor's Degree	67.9%
Advanced Degree	25.0%
None/Other	7.1%

New Candidates vs Candidates Passing 4th Section

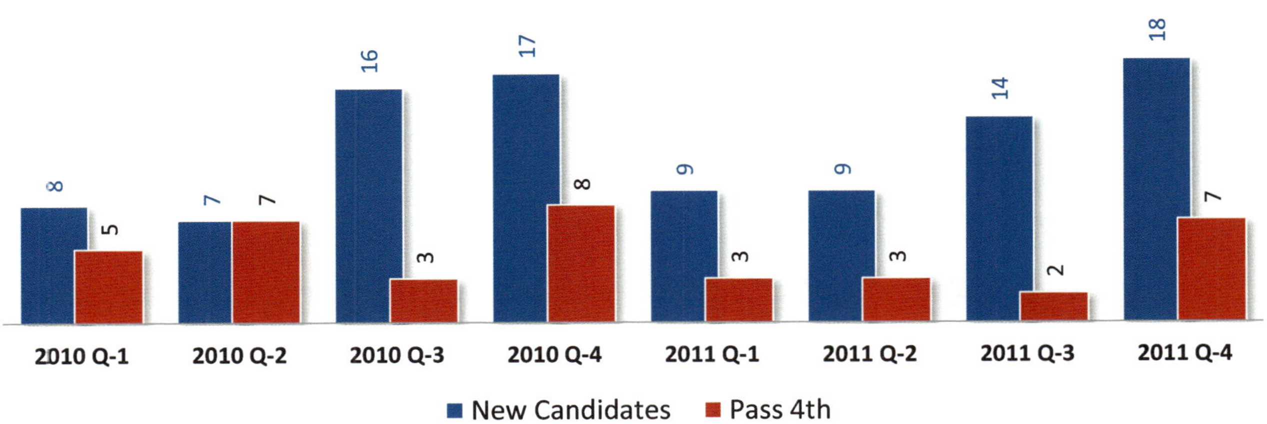

Notes about the Data

1. The data used to develop this report was pulled from NASBA's Gateway System, which houses the Uniform CPA Examination's Application and Performance information for all 55 jurisdictions.
2. The demographic data related to Age, Gender and Degree Type is provided by the individual candidates and may not be 100% accurate.

Wyoming

2011 RANKINGS

INSTITUTIONS

This section contains rankings of the top 40 educational institutions in the U.S. These rankings are calculated from the average pass rate for each institution. In addition to the overall rankings, the top 40 rankings for various program size groups are also provided.

Ranking of Institutions by Pass Rate: First-Time, All Programs

Includes 793 institutions with 10 or more reported candidates

Rank	State	Institution (FICE)	Candidates Total	Sections Total	Percent Pass	Average Score
1	NC	WAKE FOREST UNIV (2978)	63	216	88.4%	84.8
2	PA	UNIV PA (3378)	34	83	85.5%	82.6
3	MN	COLL OF SAINT BENEDICT (2341)	14	46	84.8%	82.2
4	VA	UNIV VA (3745)	127	339	84.7%	84.0
5	NC	DUKE UNIV (2920)	12	26	80.8%	82.8
6	MI	UNIV MI ANN ARBOR (2325)	109	307	80.1%	81.8
7	NY	COLUMBIA UNIV NY (2707)	14	34	79.4%	77.9
8	TN	VANDERBILT UNIV (3535)	41	143	79.0%	81.1
9	MO	TRUMAN ST UNIV (2495)	80	256	78.9%	80.4
10	IN	GRACE COLL & SEMINARY (1800)	10	23	78.3%	81.0
11	MO	WASHINGTON UNIV ST. LOUIS (2520)	47	109	77.1%	79.6
12	FL	UNIV FL (1535)	153	353	76.8%	79.9
13	MA	BOSTON COLL (2128)	206	489	76.7%	80.0
14	WI	UNIV WI MADISON (3895)	177	499	76.4%	80.5
15	TX	BAYLOR UNIV (3545)	132	339	76.1%	80.0
16	UT	BRIGHAM YOUNG UNIV (3670)	332	806	75.8%	79.9
17	TX	TX A&M UNIV (3632)	368	1,064	75.7%	80.1
18	MN	CONCORDIA COLL MOORHEAD (2346)	25	63	74.6%	77.2
19	GA	UNIV GA (1598)	227	595	74.1%	78.7
20	TX	UNIV TX AUSTIN (3658)	381	1,009	73.6%	79.5
21	MI	MI TECH UNIV (2292)	12	34	73.5%	77.9
22	MO	UNIV MO KANSAS CITY (2518)	57	123	73.2%	77.8
23	IN	TAYLOR UNIV (1838)	11	26	73.1%	78.8
24	NC	UNIV NC CHAPEL HILL (2974)	166	484	72.7%	78.6
25	IN	UNIV NOTRE DAME (1840)	240	633	72.7%	79.4
26	NY	CORNELL UNIV (2711)	52	113	72.6%	78.9
27	DC	GEORGETOWN UNIV (1445)	48	108	72.2%	79.9
28	IA	UNIV IA (1892)	180	456	71.7%	78.5
29	MA	COLL HOLY CROSS (2141)	34	81	71.6%	77.5
30	MO	UNIV MO COLUMBIA (2516)	147	461	71.6%	78.7
31	OH	CEDARVILLE UNIV (3025)	15	28	71.4%	76.9
32	WI	MARQUETTE UNIV (3863)	104	256	71.1%	78.3
33	GA	EMORY UNIV (1564)	56	131	71.0%	80.5
34	TX	RICE UNIV (3604)	16	31	71.0%	79.0
35	WA	GONZAGA UNIV (3778)	89	233	70.8%	78.7
36	MN	NORTHWESTERN COLL MN (2371)	11	27	70.4%	76.8
37	MI	GRAND VALLEY ST UNIV (2268)	122	279	70.3%	78.3
38	VA	JAMES MADISON UNIV (3721)	143	409	70.2%	78.9
39	LA	UNIV LA LAFAYETTE (2031)	69	150	70.0%	78.3
40	WA	WESTERN WA UNIV (3802)	47	101	69.3%	77.0

Ranking of Institutions by Pass Rate: First-Time, Large Programs

Includes 258 institutions with more than 60 reported candidates

Rank	State	Institution (FICE)	Candidates Total	Sections Total	Percent Pass	Average Score
1	NC	WAKE FOREST UNIV (2978)	63	216	88.4%	84.8
2	VA	UNIV VA (3745)	127	339	84.7%	84.0
3	MI	UNIV MI ANN ARBOR (2325)	109	307	80.1%	81.8
4	MO	TRUMAN ST UNIV (2495)	80	256	78.9%	80.4
5	FL	UNIV FL (1535)	153	353	76.8%	79.9
6	MA	BOSTON COLL (2128)	206	489	76.7%	80.0
7	WI	UNIV WI MADISON (3895)	177	499	76.4%	80.5
8	TX	BAYLOR UNIV (3545)	132	339	76.1%	80.0
9	UT	BRIGHAM YOUNG UNIV (3670)	332	806	75.8%	79.9
10	TX	TX A&M UNIV (3632)	368	1,064	75.7%	80.1
11	GA	UNIV GA (1598)	227	595	74.1%	78.7
12	TX	UNIV TX AUSTIN (3658)	381	1,009	73.6%	79.5
13	NC	UNIV NC CHAPEL HILL (2974)	166	484	72.7%	78.6
14	IN	UNIV NOTRE DAME (1840)	240	633	72.7%	79.4
15	IA	UNIV IA (1892)	180	456	71.7%	78.5
16	MO	UNIV MO COLUMBIA (2516)	147	461	71.6%	78.7
17	WI	MARQUETTE UNIV (3863)	104	256	71.1%	78.3
18	WA	GONZAGA UNIV (3778)	89	233	70.8%	78.7
19	MI	GRAND VALLEY ST UNIV (2268)	122	279	70.3%	78.3
20	VA	JAMES MADISON UNIV (3721)	143	409	70.2%	78.9
21	LA	UNIV LA LAFAYETTE (2031)	69	150	70.0%	78.3
22	PA	LEHIGH UNIV (3289)	128	296	69.3%	77.0
23	VA	UNIV RICHMOND (3744)	66	173	68.8%	78.3
23	TX	SOUTHERN METHODIST UNIV (3613)	105	282	68.8%	78.4
25	TX	TX CHRISTIAN UNIV (3636)	69	182	68.7%	78.1
26	TN	UNIV TN KNOXVILLE (3530)	148	378	68.3%	76.6
27	ND	UNIV ND (3005)	99	206	68.0%	77.8
28	AL	AUBURN UNIV (1009)	159	420	67.6%	77.4
29	MA	BOSTON UNIV (2130)	115	240	67.1%	76.9
30	UT	UNIV UT (3675)	165	358	66.8%	76.6
31	KS	KANSAS STATE UNIVERSITY (1928)	73	206	66.5%	76.8
31	MN	SAINT CLOUD ST UNIV (2377)	82	203	66.5%	76.9
33	UT	WEBER ST UNIV (3680)	63	118	66.1%	75.1
34	IA	UNIV NORTHERN IA (1890)	98	327	66.1%	77.3
35	MI	MI ST UNIV (2290)	348	777	66.0%	76.9
36	MT	UNIV MT (2536)	61	152	65.1%	78.2
37	FL	UNIV SOUTH FL (1537)	91	180	65.0%	75.7
38	IN	IN UNIV BLOOMINGTON (1809)	421	1,042	64.8%	75.9
39	OK	OK ST UNIV (3170)	150	388	64.7%	76.8
40	OH	JOHN CARROLL UNIV (3050)	74	163	64.4%	76.8

Ranking of Institutions by Pass Rate: First-Time, Medium Programs

Includes 270 institutions with 21 to 60 reported candidates

Rank	State	Institution (FICE)	Candidates Total	Sections Total	Percent Pass	Average Score
1	PA	UNIV PA (3378)	34	83	85.5%	82.6
2	TN	VANDERBILT UNIV (3535)	41	143	79.0%	81.1
3	MO	WASHINGTON UNIV ST. LOUIS (2520)	47	109	77.1%	79.6
4	MN	CONCORDIA COLL MOORHEAD (2346)	25	63	74.6%	77.2
5	MO	UNIV MO KANSAS CITY (2518)	57	123	73.2%	77.8
6	NY	CORNELL UNIV (2711)	52	113	72.6%	78.9
7	DC	GEORGETOWN UNIV (1445)	48	108	72.2%	79.9
8	MA	COLL HOLY CROSS (2141)	34	81	71.6%	77.5
9	GA	EMORY UNIV (1564)	56	131	71.0%	80.5
10	WA	WESTERN WA UNIV (3802)	47	101	69.3%	77.0
11	CA	CLAREMONT MCKENNA COLL (1170)	22	41	68.3%	79.3
12	AL	SAMFORD UNIV (1036)	21	44	68.2%	76.0
13	NY	CANISIUS COLL (2681)	38	103	68.0%	77.1
14	PA	BUCKNELL UNIV (3238)	49	112	67.9%	77.6
15	MI	CALVIN COLL (2241)	36	92	67.4%	76.0
16	ME	UNIV ME (2053)	30	49	67.4%	75.4
17	VA	WASHINGTON & LEE UNIV (3768)	32	81	66.7%	78.0
18	TX	TRINITY UNIV (3647)	40	83	66.3%	76.0
19	WI	SAINT NORBERT COLL (3892)	21	52	65.4%	74.0
20	MN	SAINT JOHN'S UNIV (2379)	45	115	65.2%	75.2
21	OH	CASE WESTERN RESERVE UNIV (3024)	45	106	64.2%	75.8
22	SC	FURMAN UNIV (3434)	21	60	63.3%	78.6
23	IL	IL WESLEYAN UNIV (1696)	40	116	62.9%	76.1
24	ND	ND ST UNIV (9265)	48	104	62.5%	76.1
25	VT	UNIV VT (3696)	28	58	62.1%	75.8
26	OK	OK CHRISTIAN UNIV (3165)	24	50	62.0%	74.0
27	IN	BUTLER UNIV (1788)	45	124	61.3%	74.8
28	NC	UNIV NC GREENSBORO (2976)	54	108	61.1%	75.0
29	GA	GA INST TECH (1569)	52	122	60.7%	76.8
30	NE	UNIV NE OMAHA (2554)	47	95	60.0%	75.8
31	SC	WINTHROP UNIV (3456)	22	37	59.5%	73.4
32	OH	XAVIER UNIV (3144)	52	120	59.2%	73.8
33	MT	MT ST UNIV BOZEMAN (2532)	54	122	59.0%	75.2
34	SD	UNIV SD (3474)	37	68	58.8%	77.0
35	KY	WESTERN KY UNIV (2002)	51	114	58.8%	75.4
36	TX	ABILENE CHRISTIAN UNIV (3537)	54	104	58.7%	74.7
37	IA	DRAKE UNIV (1860)	41	89	58.4%	71.2
38	PA	GROVE CITY COLL (3269)	37	84	58.3%	74.6
38	NY	ITHACA COLL (2739)	27	60	58.3%	75.1
40	OH	WRIGHT ST UNIV (3078)	54	112	58.0%	74.5

Ranking of Institutions by Pass Rate: First-Time, Small Programs

Includes 265 institutions with 10 to 20 reported candidates

Rank	State	Institution (FICE)	Candidates Total	Sections Total	Percent Pass	Average Score
1	MN	COLL OF SAINT BENEDICT (2341)	14	46	84.8%	82.2
2	NC	DUKE UNIV (2920)	12	26	80.8%	82.8
3	NY	COLUMBIA UNIV NY (2707)	14	34	79.4%	77.9
4	IN	GRACE COLL & SEMINARY (1800)	10	23	78.3%	81.0
5	MI	MI TECH UNIV (2292)	12	34	73.5%	77.9
6	IN	TAYLOR UNIV (1838)	11	26	73.1%	78.8
7	OH	CEDARVILLE UNIV (3025)	15	28	71.4%	76.9
8	TX	RICE UNIV (3604)	16	31	71.0%	79.0
9	MN	NORTHWESTERN COLL MN (2371)	11	27	70.4%	76.8
10	IN	GOSHEN COLL (1799)	20	48	68.8%	77.2
11	WA	WHITWORTH COLL (3804)	12	22	68.2%	77.6
12	IL	TRINITY CHRISTIAN COLL (1771)	11	21	66.7%	79.2
12	CO	WESTERN ST COLL (1372)	10	21	66.7%	75.0
12	NY	UNIV ROCHESTER (2894)	18	33	66.7%	76.8
12	NY	SUNY EMPIRE ST COLL (10286)	13	21	66.7%	73.2
16	SC	WOFFORD COLL (3457)	17	58	65.5%	76.5
17	MO	NORTHWEST MO ST UNIV (2496)	17	37	64.9%	75.0
18	NE	MIDLAND LUTHERAN COLL (2553)	16	31	64.5%	74.8
19	NY	NAZARETH COLL ROCHESTER (2779)	12	28	64.3%	79.7
20	MN	SOUTHWEST ST UNIV (2375)	12	27	63.0%	74.9
20	MA	CLARK UNIV (2139)	13	27	63.0%	73.6
20	MO	MO SOUTHERN ST UNIV (2488)	13	27	63.0%	72.6
23	NJ	THOMAS EDISON ST COLL (21922)	15	29	62.1%	78.3
24	TN	UNION UNIV (3528)	10	23	60.9%	73.6
24	IL	NORTHWESTERN UNIV (1739)	18	46	60.9%	75.8
26	IA	LORAS COLL (1873)	11	28	60.7%	74.9
26	MN	BEMIDJI ST UNIV (2336)	11	28	60.7%	73.4
28	OR	EASTERN OR UNIV (3193)	14	38	60.5%	72.8
29	MN	BETHEL COLL (MN) (9058)	20	53	60.4%	73.1
30	NC	GUILFORD COLL (2931)	10	20	60.0%	76.1
30	NY	SUNY FREDONIA (2844)	17	30	60.0%	73.4
30	TN	LEE UNIV (3500)	18	35	60.0%	72.9
30	IL	AUGUSTANA COLL (1633)	15	30	60.0%	71.9
30	WA	NORTH SEATTLE CC (9704)	11	20	60.0%	70.5
35	DC	SOUTHEASTERN UNIV (1456)	11	22	59.1%	71.6
36	SD	UNIV SIOUX FALLS (3469)	16	34	58.8%	75.1
37	ND	MINOT ST UNIV (2994)	13	24	58.3%	71.7
38	AZ	AZ ST UNIV WEST (66935)	10	16	56.3%	72.0
39	OK	ORAL ROBERTS UNIV (3985)	18	41	56.1%	73.1
40	NY	UTICA COLL (2883)	10	18	55.6%	74.1

Ranking of Institutions by Pass Rate: First-Time, Very Small

Includes 239 institutions with 5 to 9 reported candidates (Not included in overall ranking)

Rank	State	Institution (FICE)	Candidates Total	Sections Total	Percent Pass	Average Score
1	MA	MA INST TECH (2178)	6	16	93.8%	89.6
2	NE	PERU ST COLL (2559)	6	11	90.9%	84.1
3	OR	WILLAMETTE UNIV (3227)	5	12	83.3%	80.9
4	VT	CASTLETON ST COLL (3683)	8	17	82.4%	81.4
5	MA	TUFTS UNIV (2219)	5	16	81.3%	81.9
6	PA	FRANKLIN & MARSHALL COLL (3265)	6	15	80.0%	81.0
7	NE	NE WESLEYAN UNIV (2555)	9	24	79.2%	75.9
8	IA	WARTBURG COLL (1896)	6	14	78.6%	75.4
8	IL	IL INST TECH (1691)	7	14	78.6%	76.1
10	WA	UNIV PUGET SOUND (3797)	7	13	76.9%	76.8
10	CA	VANGUARD UNIV SOUTHERN CA (1293)	6	13	76.9%	78.1
12	NC	DAVIDSON COLL (2918)	7	25	76.0%	82.2
13	WV	BETHANY COLL (3808)	5	8	75.0%	76.0
14	IN	ANDERSON UNIV (1785)	8	19	73.7%	79.8
15	ME	UNIV ME AUGUSTA (6760)	6	11	72.7%	78.8
15	PA	PA ST ERIE (3333)	5	11	72.7%	76.0
15	TX	SOUTHWESTERN UNIV (3620)	8	22	72.7%	77.6
18	VA	EASTERN MENNONITE UNIV (3708)	5	18	72.2%	82.9
19	KY	UNIV OF CUMBERLANDS (1962)	5	7	71.4%	75.4
20	NC	MEREDITH COLL (2945)	6	17	70.6%	77.9
21	CO	CO COLL (1347)	6	10	70.0%	77.3
22	TN	TREVECCA NAZARENE UNIV (3526)	7	13	69.2%	75.1
22	NY	PACE UNIV WHITE PLAINS (2727)	5	13	69.2%	77.7
22	MN	SAINT CATHERINE UNIV (2342)	6	13	69.2%	73.4
25	MD	JOHNS HOPKINS UNIV (2077)	6	12	66.7%	73.6
25	MD	FROSTBURG ST UNIV (2072)	5	9	66.7%	71.3
25	IL	OLIVET NAZARENE UNIV (1741)	9	24	66.7%	78.3
25	IA	MORNINGSIDE COLL (1879)	5	9	66.7%	74.9
25	OH	MOUNT UNION COLL (3083)	9	18	66.7%	79.2
25	WA	WALLA WALLA UNIV (3799)	6	12	66.7%	78.3
31	IL	WHEATON COLL (1781)	9	17	64.7%	78.8
32	CA	GOLDEN WEST COLL (1206)	5	11	63.6%	70.2
32	FL	BARRY UNIV (1466)	7	11	63.6%	71.2
32	MA	BRANDEIS UNIV (2133)	5	11	63.6%	78.2
32	VA	FERRUM COLL (3711)	6	11	63.6%	74.5
32	VA	UNIV VA COL WISE (CLINCH VALLEY COLL) (3747)	7	11	63.6%	75.0
32	CA	AMERICAN RIVER COLL (1232)	7	11	63.6%	69.3
38	ME	COLBY COLL (2039)	5	8	62.5%	79.0
38	NY	HOUGHTON COLL (2734)	5	8	62.5%	71.3
38	PA	PEIRCE COLL (3309)	5	8	62.5%	67.5

Ranking of Institutions by Size: Most Candidates

Size measured by number of candidates sitting for a First-Time section during the year

Rank	State	Institution (FICE)	Candidates Total	Sections Total	Percent Pass	Average Score
1	NY	CUNY BARUCH (7273)	592	1,018	51.0%	70.6
2	CA	UNIV SOUTHERN CA (1328)	542	1,181	62.0%	75.4
3	PA	PA ST UNIV PARK (3329)	498	1,052	47.3%	70.3
4	CA	UNIV CA LOS ANGELES (1315)	455	935	63.9%	75.7
5	AZ	UNIV PHOENIX (20988)	435	777	30.4%	61.7
6	IN	IN UNIV BLOOMINGTON (1809)	421	1,042	64.8%	75.9
7	IL	UNIV IL URBANA CHAMPAIGN (1775)	410	1,010	60.0%	74.4
8	CA	UNIV CA SANTA BARBARA (1320)	401	750	51.7%	72.0
9	TX	UNIV TX AUSTIN (3658)	381	1,009	73.6%	79.5
10	TX	TX A&M UNIV (3632)	368	1,064	75.7%	80.1
11	CA	CA ST UNIV FULLERTON (1137)	366	697	37.7%	66.8
12	IL	UNIV IL CHICAGO (1776)	361	906	63.4%	75.5
13	IL	DE PAUL UNIV (1671)	356	670	41.0%	68.8
14	OH	OH ST UNIV (6883)	353	855	64.2%	76.6
15	PA	TEMPLE UNIV (3371)	350	659	31.9%	63.7
16	MI	MI ST UNIV (2290)	348	777	66.0%	76.9
17	TX	UNIV HOUSTON UNIV PARK (3652)	344	599	42.6%	68.8
18	UT	BRIGHAM YOUNG UNIV (3670)	332	806	75.8%	79.9
19	CA	SAN DIEGO ST UNIV (1151)	331	610	52.8%	72.1
20	WA	UNIV WA (3798)	327	798	64.2%	75.7
21	AZ	AZ ST UNIV (1081)	312	641	60.4%	74.9
22	MA	BENTLEY COLL (2124)	294	616	56.0%	73.6
23	NY	SUNY BINGHAMTON (2836)	289	545	49.5%	71.1
24	CA	CA ST UNIV NORTHRIDGE (1153)	285	532	46.1%	70.2
25	OH	MIAMI UNIV (3077)	281	708	63.7%	76.7
26	GA	GA ST UNIV (1574)	278	514	42.6%	69.0
27	PA	UNIV PITTSBURGH (3379)	263	522	54.4%	73.0
27	CA	SAN JOSE ST UNIV (1155)	263	501	46.5%	69.5
27	NJ	RUTGERS ST UNIV NEWARK (2631)	263	460	37.6%	66.3
30	CA	SANTA CLARA UNIV (1326)	261	469	45.8%	69.5
31	IL	NORTHERN IL UNIV (1737)	259	586	57.5%	74.5
32	CA	UNIV CA BERKELEY (1312)	252	535	62.4%	75.5
33	CT	UNIV CT (1417)	250	467	54.8%	74.2
34	IN	UNIV NOTRE DAME (1840)	240	633	72.7%	79.4
35	LA	LA ST UNIV AND A & M COLL (2010)	238	500	53.4%	73.7
35	VA	GEORGE MASON UNIV (3749)	238	425	46.1%	70.5
37	MA	NORTHEASTERN UNIV (2199)	234	472	52.5%	72.3
38	TX	UNIV TX DALLAS (9741)	232	515	41.9%	68.6
39	GA	UNIV GA (1598)	227	595	74.1%	78.7
40	VA	VA POLYTECHNIC INST & ST UNIV (3754)	226	518	61.2%	75.9

INSTITUTION ATTENDED

ALL TESTING EVENTS

APPENDIX A

SUMMARY PERFORMANCE

Appendix A: Summary Performance by Institution Attended - All Testing Events

	Candidates Total	Sections Total	Sections First-Time	Sections Re-Exam	Percent Pass	Average Score	Average Age
Alabama							
AL A&M UNIV (1002)	15	38	9	29	15.8%	58.9	33.6
AL ST UNIV (1005)	9	19	10	9	21.1%	65.9	35.4
ATHENS ST UNIV (1008)	23	42	15	27	26.2%	64.0	39.5
AUBURN UNIV (1009)	208	632	420	212	60.9%	75.6	26.8
AUBURN UNIV MONTGOMERY (8310)	38	92	33	59	30.4%	68.1	29.1
BIRMINGHAM SOUTHERN COLL (1012)	43	102	57	45	32.4%	66.9	27.2
HUNTINGDON COLL (1019)	10	25	18	7	48.0%	72.3	30.0
JACKSONVILLE ST UNIV (1020)	26	61	22	39	42.6%	68.3	29.9
OAKWOOD COLL (1033)	12	31	13	18	45.2%	68.8	29.8
SAMFORD UNIV (1036)	35	93	44	49	57.0%	74.5	25.8
SPRING HILL COLL (1041)	9	23	10	13	43.5%	70.4	28.5
TROY UNIV (1047)	96	220	126	94	34.6%	66.6	29.7
TUSKEGEE UNIV (1050)	7	19	8	11	21.1%	63.7	30.8
UNIV AL (1051)	263	782	468	314	50.4%	73.0	26.3
UNIV AL (8004)	8	17	4	13	52.9%	71.3	31.2
UNIV AL BIRMINGHAM (1052)	117	281	170	111	43.8%	71.2	30.1
UNIV AL HUNTSVILLE (1055)	27	60	34	26	30.0%	67.8	33.6
UNIV MONTEVALLO (1004)	15	32	20	12	50.0%	69.7	28.6
UNIV NORTH AL (1016)	28	63	40	23	57.1%	72.8	30.7
UNIV SOUTH AL (1057)	68	147	90	57	45.6%	71.6	31.3
UNIV WEST AL (1024)	7	16	9	7	25.0%	63.0	33.5
Alaska							
UNIV ALASKA ANCHORAGE (11462)	54	126	69	57	40.5%	67.2	29.7
UNIV ALASKA FAIRBANKS (1063)	17	36	28	8	44.4%	69.7	31.8
UNIV ALASKA SOUTHEAST (1065)	7	13	12	1	46.2%	68.3	34.4
Arizona							
AZ ST UNIV (1081)	410	982	641	341	55.6%	74.0	30.2
AZ ST UNIV WEST (66935)	18	43	16	27	55.8%	73.2	34.1
DEVRY UNIV PHOENIX (8322)	38	102	77	25	30.4%	64.1	35.5
GRAND CANYON UNIV (1074)	17	39	24	15	28.2%	62.5	33.7
NORTHERN AZ UNIV (1082)	83	199	114	85	41.2%	69.9	27.9
THUNDERBIRD SCHOOL OF GLOBAL MGMT (1070)	16	37	24	13	40.5%	69.5	40.4
UNIV AZ (1083)	247	673	393	280	51.7%	72.8	28.3
UNIV PHOENIX (20988)	595	1,350	777	573	30.9%	63.9	38.4
WESTERN INTL UNIV (21715)	13	24	19	5	54.2%	70.3	41.1
Arkansas							
AR ST UNIV (1090)	47	113	64	49	34.5%	66.5	28.1
AR TECH UNIV (1089)	25	77	59	18	48.1%	70.8	30.7
HARDING UNIV (1097)	76	205	101	104	37.1%	69.2	25.9
HENDERSON ST UNIV (1098)	20	54	36	18	24.1%	64.6	28.0
HENDRIX COLL (1099)	16	40	14	26	25.0%	64.7	26.4
OUACHITA BAPTIST UNIV (1102)	22	45	22	23	42.2%	69.8	26.9
SOUTHERN AR UNIV (1107)	18	44	21	23	40.9%	68.6	30.7
UNIV AR (1108)	121	370	232	138	51.6%	72.1	26.8
UNIV AR LITTLE ROCK (1101)	47	126	47	79	45.2%	68.1	32.9
UNIV AR MONTICELLO (1085)	9	18	14	4	27.8%	65.2	27.7
UNIV AR PINE BLUFF (1086)	5	13	8	5	0.0%	53.0	32.2
UNIV CENTRAL AR (1092)	86	229	108	121	34.9%	69.1	29.8

Appendix A: Summary Performance by Institution Attended - All Testing Events

	Candidates Total	Sections Total	Sections First-Time	Sections Re-Exam	Percent Pass	Average Score	Average Age
California							
ALLIANT INTL UNIV SAN DIEGO (1158)	5	14	8	6	28.6%	58.0	47.7
AMERICAN RIVER COLL (1232)	7	12	11	1	66.7%	71.6	32.5
AZUSA PACIFIC UNIV (1117)	25	63	34	29	30.2%	65.8	26.8
BIOLA UNIV (1122)	35	78	43	35	39.7%	70.0	26.0
CA BAPTIST UNIV (1125)	24	47	27	20	21.3%	61.3	30.2
CA LUTHERAN UNIV (1133)	36	101	39	62	37.6%	68.3	32.0
CA ST POLYTECH UNIV POMONA (1144)	176	413	223	190	29.1%	64.3	29.4
CA ST POLYTECH UNIV SAN LUIS OBISPO (1143)	305	712	411	301	50.7%	72.3	26.0
CA ST UNIV BAKERSFIELD (7993)	54	136	75	61	38.2%	68.7	29.7
CA ST UNIV CHICO (1146)	102	252	129	123	36.9%	70.4	30.8
CA ST UNIV DOMINGUEZ HILLS (1141)	64	162	62	100	22.2%	61.1	37.5
CA ST UNIV EAST BAY (1138)	305	771	362	409	36.6%	66.4	34.1
CA ST UNIV FRESNO (1147)	191	445	211	234	41.1%	70.3	30.6
CA ST UNIV FULLERTON (1137)	501	1,200	697	503	37.9%	68.0	30.2
CA ST UNIV LONG BEACH (1139)	278	669	368	301	38.0%	68.1	30.7
CA ST UNIV LOS ANGELES (1140)	295	770	362	408	32.3%	66.2	32.9
CA ST UNIV NORTHRIDGE (1153)	420	1,050	532	518	42.8%	70.4	32.2
CA ST UNIV SACRAMENTO (1150)	320	778	409	369	37.0%	68.1	30.8
CA ST UNIV SAN BERNARDINO (1142)	140	299	148	151	31.4%	67.3	31.5
CA ST UNIV SAN MARCOS (30113)	84	198	112	86	48.5%	72.8	30.7
CA ST UNIV STANISLAUS (1157)	64	148	55	93	32.4%	67.7	32.1
CHAPMAN UNIV (1164)	66	164	92	72	45.7%	72.3	28.3
CLAREMONT GRADUATE UNIV (1169)	5	7	7	0	14.3%	56.7	43.8
CLAREMONT MCKENNA COLL (1170)	33	82	41	41	50.0%	73.1	25.0
CONCORDIA UNIV (20705)	8	21	7	14	19.1%	68.7	28.4
DE ANZA COLL (4480)	20	46	24	22	45.7%	70.0	35.5
DEVRY UNIV LONG BEACH (666988)	29	78	37	41	20.5%	61.1	34.8
DEVRY UNIV POMONA (23329)	28	67	42	25	22.4%	58.9	34.2
DIABLO VALLEY COLL (1191)	5	9	7	2	22.2%	60.7	29.5
FOOTHILL COLL (1199)	14	38	21	17	47.4%	70.8	32.7
FRESNO PACIFIC UNIV (1253)	15	42	18	24	50.0%	71.1	26.1
FULLERTON COLL (1201)	5	8	2	6	50.0%	72.0	33.8
GLENDALE CC (1203)	14	32	18	14	34.4%	66.7	31.2
GOLDEN GATE UNIV (1205)	199	470	242	228	38.7%	68.0	35.6
GOLDEN WEST COLL (1206)	5	11	11	0	63.6%	70.2	36.6
HUMBOLDT ST UNIV (1149)	22	50	25	25	40.0%	69.6	32.7
IRVINE VALLEY COLL (25395)	6	21	6	15	19.1%	68.9	36.4
LA SIERRA UNIV (1215)	16	38	19	19	18.4%	58.9	29.7
LOYOLA MARYMOUNT UNIV (11649)	112	287	169	118	48.4%	72.6	25.8
MASTERS COLL & SEMINARY (1220)	14	32	26	6	50.0%	71.5	24.2
MENLO COLL (1236)	6	12	9	3	25.0%	59.2	29.0
MOUNT SAINT MARYS COLL (1243)	15	44	20	24	27.3%	67.0	34.9
NATIONAL UNIV (11460)	73	178	89	89	36.5%	67.5	38.4
ORANGE COAST COLL (1250)	7	22	9	13	45.5%	74.8	35.3
PACIFIC ST UNIV (31633)	22	66	19	47	18.2%	61.4	39.0
PACIFIC UNION COLL (1258)	11	26	17	9	50.0%	71.7	26.9
PEPPERDINE (1264)	62	168	95	73	43.5%	70.9	33.2
POINT LOMA NAZARENE UNIV (1262)	21	41	28	13	51.2%	73.9	25.0
SAINT MARYS COLL CA (1302)	52	123	69	54	32.5%	65.3	27.5
SAN DIEGO ST UNIV (1151)	427	1,032	610	422	48.9%	71.9	28.9

Appendix A: Summary Performance by Institution Attended - All Testing Events

	Candidates Total	Sections Total	Sections First-Time	Sections Re-Exam	Percent Pass	Average Score	Average Age
SAN FRANCISCO ST UNIV (1154)	304	734	375	359	37.2%	67.5	31.5
SAN JOSE ST UNIV (1155)	377	904	501	403	43.7%	69.7	31.1
SANTA CLARA UNIV (1326)	334	788	469	319	44.3%	70.5	27.0
SANTA MONICA COLL (1286)	30	72	34	38	33.3%	64.3	35.3
SIMPSON UNIV (1291)	8	24	19	5	29.2%	61.5	25.4
SONOMA ST UNIV (1156)	128	293	158	135	28.7%	66.7	30.3
STANFORD UNIV (1305)	8	23	12	11	56.5%	76.7	39.6
UNIV CA BERKELEY (1312)	329	843	535	308	55.4%	73.5	27.4
UNIV CA DAVIS (1313)	131	311	186	125	50.2%	71.3	28.5
UNIV CA IRVINE (1314)	207	485	299	186	46.4%	69.8	27.4
UNIV CA LOS ANGELES (1315)	585	1,470	935	535	58.6%	74.3	27.8
UNIV CA RIVERSIDE (1316)	233	570	308	262	31.6%	66.4	27.5
UNIV CA SAN DIEGO (1317)	131	326	183	143	46.0%	71.0	29.8
UNIV CA SANTA BARBARA (1320)	563	1,360	750	610	51.0%	72.5	26.5
UNIV CA SANTA CRUZ (1321)	168	400	220	180	36.8%	69.1	26.4
UNIV LA VERNE (1216)	36	89	51	38	38.2%	66.4	33.1
UNIV PACIFIC (1329)	44	109	58	51	46.8%	72.3	27.4
UNIV REDLANDS (1322)	34	79	44	35	26.6%	64.1	30.7
UNIV SAN DIEGO (10395)	175	421	273	148	50.4%	73.2	25.8
UNIV SAN FRANCISCO (1325)	98	229	127	102	33.2%	64.8	28.0
UNIV SOUTHERN CA (1328)	701	1,814	1,181	633	56.2%	74.1	26.9
VANGUARD UNIV SOUTHERN CA (1293)	7	22	13	9	59.1%	71.4	30.2
WOODBURY UNIV (1343)	16	45	16	29	22.2%	66.6	36.3
Colorado							
ADAMS ST COLL (1345)	13	25	6	19	40.0%	68.6	29.9
CHARTERED ACCT (199999)	121	307	184	123	55.4%	74.0	35.4
CO CHRISTIAN UNIV (9401)	5	10	5	5	0.0%	70.1	30.3
CO COLL (1347)	6	14	10	4	64.3%	75.6	42.6
CO ST UNIV (1350)	168	450	278	172	53.3%	73.4	28.7
FORT LEWIS COLL (1353)	46	109	51	58	34.9%	67.4	28.9
MESA ST COLL (1358)	25	75	51	24	48.0%	74.6	30.0
METRO ST COLL DENVER (1360)	118	297	174	123	33.0%	67.1	34.3
REGIS UNIV (1363)	105	250	141	109	44.0%	69.8	36.1
UNIV CO BOULDER (1370)	190	520	333	187	56.5%	75.2	27.7
UNIV CO COLORADO SPRINGS (4509)	50	119	64	55	42.0%	70.1	30.8
UNIV CO DENVER (6740)	110	243	145	98	43.2%	69.1	30.3
UNIV DENVER (1371)	114	276	157	119	53.3%	73.0	27.0
UNIV NORTHERN CO (1349)	82	223	115	108	43.5%	70.8	27.4
UNIV SOUTHERN CO (1365)	24	59	39	20	44.1%	69.9	33.5
WESTERN ST COLL (1372)	18	46	21	25	41.3%	70.4	30.9
Connecticut							
ALBERTUS MAGNUS COLL (1374)	8	12	7	5	8.3%	53.4	34.0
BRIARWOOD COLL (9407)	6	8	4	4	25.0%	59.0	29.1
CENTRAL CT ST UNIV (1378)	60	132	70	62	44.7%	70.1	31.2
EASTERN CT ST UNIV (1425)	29	44	34	10	45.5%	69.2	31.6
FAIRFIELD UNIV (1385)	149	379	214	165	50.7%	72.6	25.0
QUINNIPIAC UNIV (1402)	91	265	141	124	38.1%	68.2	25.1
SACRED HEART UNIV (1403)	62	122	67	55	29.5%	64.2	27.9
SOUTHERN CT ST UNIV (1406)	33	75	48	27	40.0%	69.9	30.3
TEIKYO POST UNIV (1401)	13	29	17	12	31.0%	62.0	28.0
UNIV BRIDGEPORT (1416)	18	48	19	29	22.9%	64.5	35.3

Appendix A: Summary Performance by Institution Attended - All Testing Events

	Candidates Total	Sections Total	Sections First-Time	Sections Re-Exam	Percent Pass	Average Score	Average Age
UNIV CT (1417)	341	837	467	370	51.1%	73.4	25.7
UNIV HARTFORD (1422)	37	87	55	32	39.1%	66.1	29.1
UNIV NEW HAVEN (1397)	20	55	26	29	27.3%	64.8	31.3
WESTERN CT ST UNIV (1380)	22	58	37	21	46.6%	70.9	32.9
Delaware							
DE ST UNIV (1428)	13	39	11	28	15.4%	65.8	33.7
DE TECH & CC OWENS (7053)	6	15	6	9	53.3%	73.6	36.4
GOLDEY BEACOM COLL (1429)	38	82	39	43	26.8%	63.8	34.2
UNIV DE (1431)	234	627	407	220	52.6%	73.3	25.3
WESLEY COLL (1433)	6	13	5	8	38.5%	63.1	28.4
WILMINGTON COLL (7948)	29	64	46	18	35.9%	66.8	36.6
District of Columbia							
AMERICAN UNIV (1434)	92	221	142	79	51.1%	73.5	27.2
CATHOLIC UNIV OF AMERICA (1437)	8	18	8	10	33.3%	65.4	26.1
GEORGE WASHINGTON UNIV (1444)	125	318	198	120	55.0%	73.5	29.9
GEORGETOWN UNIV (1445)	54	144	108	36	67.4%	78.8	30.0
HOWARD UNIV (1443)	77	166	70	96	21.1%	62.5	31.0
SOUTHEASTERN UNIV (1456)	20	43	22	21	39.5%	70.4	32.0
STRAYER COLL (1459)	145	288	154	134	24.0%	60.7	36.8
UNIV DC (1441)	16	39	18	21	18.0%	57.8	41.3
Florida							
BARRY UNIV (1466)	8	13	11	2	53.9%	70.5	31.8
BETHUNE COOKMAN COLL (1467)	8	13	3	10	23.1%	62.7	30.3
FL A&M UNIV (1480)	45	100	36	64	33.0%	66.5	28.5
FL ATLANTIC UNIV (1481)	82	205	105	100	39.5%	68.5	32.9
FL GULF COAST UNIV (32553)	12	30	20	10	40.0%	69.3	29.7
FL INST TECH (1469)	5	12	4	8	41.7%	75.1	44.6
FL INTL UNIV (9635)	135	322	138	184	43.8%	71.9	31.2
FL MEMORIAL UNIV (1486)	6	11	6	5	18.2%	55.4	38.0
FL SOUTHERN COLL (1488)	6	18	3	15	27.8%	71.3	35.7
FL ST UNIV (1489)	116	300	183	117	50.7%	73.4	29.7
FLAGLER COLL (7893)	9	20	9	11	40.0%	69.0	32.1
JACKSONVILLE UNIV (1495)	5	11	9	2	54.6%	73.7	34.4
LYNN UNIV (1505)	5	15	5	10	33.3%	70.3	31.5
NOVA SOUTHEASTERN UNIV (1509)	38	73	26	47	19.2%	59.8	33.8
NOVA SOUTHEASTERN UNIV (150909)	6	17	6	11	35.3%	67.0	34.8
PENSACOLA CHRISTIAN COLL (99998)	10	24	20	4	50.0%	70.7	27.2
SAINT LEO UNIV (1526)	31	68	42	26	45.6%	70.0	37.0
STETSON UNIV (1531)	15	33	20	13	42.4%	70.9	27.4
UNIV CENTRAL FL (3954)	108	275	168	107	50.9%	73.4	28.8
UNIV FL (1535)	177	486	353	133	68.9%	78.2	26.5
UNIV MIAMI (1536)	110	319	185	134	54.6%	74.3	26.6
UNIV NORTH FL (9841)	33	91	54	37	50.6%	73.9	31.0
UNIV SOUTH FL (1537)	124	296	180	116	55.4%	74.2	30.1
UNIV TAMPA (1538)	37	101	62	39	54.5%	72.6	26.6
UNIV WEST FL (3955)	14	28	16	12	39.3%	72.7	34.3
Georgia							
ALBANY ST UNIV (1544)	14	29	13	16	34.5%	65.4	33.5
AMERICAN INTERCONT GA (21136)	14	34	9	25	29.4%	64.8	35.7
AUGUSTA ST UNIV (1552)	29	70	34	36	45.7%	70.7	32.7
BERRY COLL (1554)	15	48	26	22	43.8%	72.1	26.1

Appendix A: Summary Performance by Institution Attended - All Testing Events

	Candidates Total	Sections Total	Sections First-Time	Sections Re-Exam	Percent Pass	Average Score	Average Age
BRENAU UNIV (1556)	12	25	16	9	32.0%	62.6	29.4
CLARK ATLANTA UNIV (1559)	24	52	22	30	19.2%	61.2	29.6
CLAYTON ST UNIV (8976)	34	92	53	39	41.3%	68.8	33.8
COLUMBUS ST UNIV (1561)	18	40	15	25	32.5%	65.3	35.8
DEVRY UNIV ALPHARETTA (666989)	7	13	10	3	0.0%	55.1	36.4
DEVRY UNIV DECATUR (9224)	19	32	19	13	15.6%	60.4	37.0
EMORY UNIV (1564)	75	205	131	74	62.0%	77.2	24.8
GA COLL & ST UNIV (1602)	52	112	64	48	36.6%	68.9	29.9
GA INST TECH (1569)	79	205	122	83	56.6%	75.6	27.3
GA SOUTHERN UNIV (1572)	149	373	214	159	44.0%	70.3	27.1
GA SOUTHWESTERN ST UNIV (1573)	21	47	26	21	42.6%	66.1	32.9
GA ST UNIV (1574)	381	900	514	386	41.3%	69.8	30.6
KENNESAW ST UNIV (1577)	202	448	237	211	44.0%	69.5	32.8
LAGRANGE COLL (1578)	7	11	9	2	36.4%	61.7	26.2
MACON ST COLL (7728)	21	52	35	17	46.2%	70.8	30.5
MERCER UNIV ATLANTA (8419)	10	22	13	9	27.3%	64.8	31.5
MERCER UNIV MACON (1580)	28	79	39	40	43.0%	71.5	31.8
MOREHOUSE COLL (1582)	17	44	20	24	36.4%	68.2	27.1
NORTH GA COLL & ST UNIV (1585)	46	116	66	50	46.6%	72.8	29.7
OGLETHORPE UNIV (1586)	26	57	33	24	52.6%	72.5	27.5
SAVANNAH ST UNIV (1590)	5	12	4	8	0.0%	50.6	38.7
SHORTER COLL (1591)	13	34	21	13	35.3%	65.3	30.1
SOUTHERN POLYTECHNIC ST UNIV (1570)	5	14	11	3	42.9%	64.4	28.4
SPELMAN COLL (1594)	5	11	6	5	36.4%	71.1	29.8
UNIV GA (1598)	276	814	595	219	67.8%	77.6	26.6
UNIV WEST GA (1601)	38	98	56	42	27.6%	64.8	29.0
VALDOSTA ST UNIV (1599)	67	160	92	68	41.9%	69.3	30.7
Guam							
UNIV GU (3935)	30	61	27	34	31.2%	62.9	32.5
Hawaii							
BRIGHAM YOUNG UNIV HI (1606)	38	95	69	26	45.3%	70.0	30.0
CHAMINADE UNIV HONOLULU (1605)	5	8	8	0	25.0%	60.0	26.7
HI PACIFIC UNIV (7279)	44	118	57	61	32.2%	66.8	34.2
UNIV HI HILO (1611)	12	22	15	7	40.9%	68.5	29.9
UNIV HI MANOA (1610)	188	473	226	247	39.8%	68.7	29.3
UNIV HI WEST OAHU (21078)	12	25	12	13	36.0%	68.4	35.5
Idaho							
ALBERTSON COLL (1617)	8	23	19	4	39.1%	68.4	27.4
BOISE ST UNIV (1616)	111	267	153	114	43.8%	71.4	32.2
BRIGHAM YOUNG UNIV ID (1625)	91	203	139	64	49.8%	72.2	28.3
ID ST UNIV (1620)	44	98	53	45	46.9%	72.3	31.2
LEWIS CLARK ST COLL (1621)	18	47	29	18	36.2%	70.4	34.7
UNIV ID (1626)	68	178	103	75	43.8%	70.9	27.2
Illinois							
AMERICAN INTERCONT IL (666723)	11	30	22	8	6.7%	47.7	34.7
AUGUSTANA COLL (1633)	20	48	30	18	58.3%	73.3	26.5
AURORA UNIV (1634)	15	42	21	21	38.1%	68.5	31.0
BENEDICTINE UNIV (1767)	34	71	43	28	33.8%	63.6	32.0
BRADLEY UNIV (1641)	92	250	185	65	58.4%	75.4	26.8
CHICAGO ST UNIV (1694)	27	56	25	31	21.4%	65.0	38.0
DE PAUL UNIV (1671)	465	1,158	670	488	38.5%	69.0	28.8

Appendix A: Summary Performance by Institution Attended - All Testing Events

	Candidates Total	Sections Total	Sections First-Time	Sections Re-Exam	Percent Pass	Average Score	Average Age
DEVRY UNIV ADDISON (22966)	39	101	82	19	33.7%	61.7	32.2
DEVRY UNIV OAK BROOK TERRACE (1672)	34	82	41	41	13.4%	59.0	35.5
DOMINCAN UNIV (1750)	24	71	33	38	25.4%	64.9	31.4
EASTERN IL UNIV (1674)	65	157	106	51	46.5%	69.6	28.7
ELMHURST COLL (1576)	31	91	57	34	40.7%	70.0	27.8
GOVERNORS ST UNIV (9145)	40	107	58	49	36.5%	68.4	37.5
IL COLL (1688)	8	21	8	13	33.3%	70.0	28.5
IL INST TECH (1691)	10	20	14	6	70.0%	73.2	31.2
IL ST UNIV (1692)	187	567	373	194	54.7%	74.0	26.9
IL WESLEYAN UNIV (1696)	59	201	116	85	59.2%	74.9	23.7
KELLER GRAD SCHOOL DEVRY (20754)	223	466	320	146	31.1%	62.8	35.9
LEWIS UNIV (1707)	22	61	33	28	44.3%	71.6	31.1
LOYOLA UNIV CHICAGO (1710)	213	546	326	220	45.4%	70.9	27.0
MCKENDREE UNIVERSITY (1722)	18	41	30	11	43.9%	68.5	28.4
MILLIKIN UNIV (1724)	25	72	42	30	37.5%	68.2	29.5
MONMOUTH COLL (1725)	7	21	13	8	42.9%	70.1	28.3
NATIONAL LOUIS UNIV (1733)	7	8	7	1	12.5%	48.0	38.7
NORTH CENTRAL COLL (1734)	38	96	59	37	46.9%	73.3	28.6
NORTH PARK UNIV (1735)	11	31	15	16	51.6%	72.4	30.4
NORTHEASTERN IL UNIV (1693)	77	171	92	79	38.0%	67.2	35.3
NORTHERN IL UNIV (1737)	335	929	586	343	52.4%	73.3	28.1
NORTHWESTERN UNIV (1739)	23	66	46	20	60.6%	75.7	36.6
OLIVET NAZARENE UNIV (1741)	12	33	24	9	66.7%	78.1	24.5
QUINCY UNIV (1745)	11	18	12	6	50.0%	75.1	27.9
ROBERT MORRIS COLL (1746)	30	66	32	34	31.8%	66.9	32.1
ROCKFORD COLL (1748)	12	34	15	19	50.0%	72.7	32.5
ROOSEVELT UNIV (1749)	74	173	106	67	35.8%	67.5	34.6
SAINT XAVIER UNIV (1768)	16	36	24	12	50.0%	71.0	28.3
SOUTHERN IL UNIV CARBONDALE (1758)	104	259	145	114	39.8%	69.2	28.4
SOUTHERN IL UNIV EDWARDSVILLE (1759)	89	211	153	58	52.6%	71.6	28.2
TRINITY CHRISTIAN COLL (1771)	14	29	21	8	62.1%	77.8	24.8
UNIV CHICAGO (1774)	29	63	38	25	52.4%	75.1	38.9
UNIV IL CHICAGO (1776)	479	1,395	906	489	56.8%	74.3	26.4
UNIV IL SPRINGFIELD (9333)	50	121	62	59	32.2%	68.0	32.6
UNIV IL URBANA CHAMPAIGN (1775)	556	1,561	1,010	551	54.2%	73.1	26.8
UNIV SAINT FRANCIS (1664)	6	16	13	3	50.0%	68.1	26.8
WESTERN IL UNIV (1780)	48	103	64	39	39.8%	69.7	29.6
WHEATON COLL (1781)	10	26	17	9	61.5%	77.2	32.3
Indiana							
ANDERSON UNIV (1785)	9	26	19	7	69.2%	78.2	25.3
BALL ST UNIV (1786)	126	347	169	178	38.6%	69.0	27.9
BETHEL COLL (IN) (1787)	12	32	19	13	50.0%	71.8	25.5
BUTLER UNIV (1788)	60	187	124	63	55.6%	73.6	26.2
FRANKLIN COLL IN (1798)	16	47	30	17	29.8%	69.2	25.1
GOSHEN COLL (1799)	22	52	48	4	69.2%	77.2	24.5
GRACE COLL & SEMINARY (1800)	15	42	23	19	59.5%	77.3	25.9
HUNTINGTON COLL (1803)	6	14	9	5	14.3%	58.8	26.7
IN INST TECH (1805)	11	28	17	11	28.6%	65.9	35.1
IN ST UNIV (1807)	37	79	52	27	29.1%	64.1	29.0
IN UNIV BLOOMINGTON (1809)	537	1,490	1,042	448	60.1%	75.1	26.3
IN UNIV EAST (1811)	7	11	5	6	9.1%	63.3	28.5

Appendix A: Summary Performance by Institution Attended - All Testing Events

	Candidates Total	Sections Total	Sections First-Time	Sections Re-Exam	Percent Pass	Average Score	Average Age
IN UNIV KOKOMO (1814)	8	24	8	16	54.2%	76.3	32.6
IN UNIV NORTHWEST (1815)	13	33	20	13	39.4%	63.6	31.5
IN UNIV- PURDUE UNIV - FORT WAYNE (1812)	8	21	3	18	38.1%	71.0	29.4
IN UNIV PURDUE UNIV FORT WAYNE (1828)	26	75	44	31	49.3%	72.7	28.3
IN UNIV PURDUE UNIV INDIANAPOLIS (1813)	175	425	254	171	44.9%	70.8	31.4
IN UNIV SOUTH BEND (1816)	31	88	57	31	42.1%	65.8	30.3
IN UNIV SOUTHEAST (1817)	25	70	40	30	35.7%	68.8	31.3
IN WESLEYAN UNIV (1822)	53	119	79	40	42.9%	67.9	32.6
MANCHESTER COLL (1820)	43	114	67	47	47.4%	71.1	25.0
MARIAN COLL (1821)	14	45	24	21	26.7%	66.5	28.9
OAKLAND CITY UNIV (1824)	6	21	9	12	38.1%	66.7	27.2
PURDUE UNIV (1825)	281	843	476	367	39.0%	68.7	27.0
PURDUE UNIV CALUMET (1827)	7	14	7	7	42.9%	72.1	31.2
SAINT JOSEPHS COLL (1833)	10	25	14	11	44.0%	66.5	27.3
SAINT MARYS COLL (1836)	33	100	44	56	30.0%	68.4	25.0
TAYLOR UNIV (1838)	13	36	26	10	63.9%	75.5	23.6
TRINE UNIV (1839)	10	23	8	15	43.5%	71.4	30.3
UNIV EVANSVILLE (1795)	20	52	27	25	32.7%	68.2	26.0
UNIV INDIANAPOLIS (1804)	27	86	35	51	34.9%	68.5	28.5
UNIV NOTRE DAME (1840)	293	852	633	219	70.0%	78.4	24.7
UNIV SOUTHERN IN (1808)	47	116	74	42	42.2%	71.2	27.7
UNIV ST FRANCIS (1832)	8	26	11	15	30.8%	71.0	26.8
VALPARAISO UNIV (1842)	25	66	38	28	39.4%	69.7	25.9
Iowa							
AIB COLL BUSINESS (3963)	13	27	19	8	29.6%	60.8	27.8
BRIAR CLIFF UNIV (1846)	9	19	17	2	52.6%	68.3	29.6
BUENA VISTA UNIV (1847)	23	54	31	23	27.8%	65.5	30.7
CLARKE COLL (1852)	8	13	7	6	46.2%	69.6	31.1
COE COLL (1854)	13	29	19	10	44.8%	70.5	26.0
DORDT COLL (1859)	10	25	19	6	64.0%	76.9	23.7
DRAKE UNIV (1860)	53	133	89	44	54.1%	71.1	27.5
GRACELAND UNIV (1866)	5	16	1	15	25.0%	63.3	32.0
GRAND VIEW UNIV (1867)	6	14	11	3	42.9%	68.8	30.7
IA ST UNIV (1869)	152	440	291	149	52.1%	72.6	27.9
IA WESLEYAN COLL (1871)	9	16	9	7	43.8%	74.1	28.3
KAPLAN UNIV (4586)	21	54	39	15	24.1%	60.4	39.6
LORAS COLL (1873)	17	48	28	20	52.1%	72.6	24.2
LUTHER COLL (1874)	24	77	58	19	48.1%	73.2	25.7
MAHARISHI UNIV MANAGEMENT (11113)	8	17	9	8	47.1%	67.9	33.3
MORNINGSIDE COLL (1879)	8	22	9	13	45.5%	68.2	35.8
MOUNT MERCY COLL (1880)	6	14	7	7	50.0%	75.6	29.9
MOUNT SAINT CLARE COLL (1881)	8	16	13	3	25.0%	63.4	31.6
NORTHWESTERN COLL IA (1883)	20	44	29	15	45.5%	69.6	25.5
SAINT AMBROSE UNIV (1889)	29	75	37	38	42.7%	69.6	26.5
SIMPSON COLL (1887)	19	49	31	18	40.8%	67.9	26.0
UNIV DUBUQUE (1891)	19	63	32	31	27.0%	65.2	26.2
UNIV IA (1892)	219	622	456	166	64.5%	76.6	26.9
UNIV NORTHERN IA (1890)	129	454	327	127	59.3%	75.6	25.5
UPPER IA UNIV (1893)	43	95	41	54	29.5%	64.0	35.2
WARTBURG COLL (1896)	7	22	14	8	59.1%	74.3	23.7

Appendix A: Summary Performance by Institution Attended - All Testing Events

	Candidates Total	Sections Total	Sections First-Time	Sections Re-Exam	Percent Pass	Average Score	Average Age
Kansas							
BAKER UNIV (1903)	14	38	21	17	18.4%	63.7	28.0
BENEDICTINE COLL (10256)	13	34	26	8	32.4%	67.2	27.5
EMPORIA ST UNIV (1927)	39	101	36	65	32.7%	70.2	28.7
FORT HAYS ST UNIV (1915)	51	120	72	48	31.7%	66.4	27.9
FRIENDS UNIV (1918)	5	21	14	7	38.1%	66.7	26.1
KANSAS STATE UNIVERSITY (1928)	107	317	206	111	59.0%	74.9	27.2
NEWMAN UNIV (1939)	10	24	14	10	29.2%	63.2	29.6
OTTAWA UNIV (1937)	12	29	19	10	34.5%	64.3	33.6
PITTSBURG ST UNIV (1926)	32	82	41	41	34.2%	67.7	27.6
SOUTHWESTERN COLL (1940)	5	11	6	5	45.5%	72.7	38.9
UNIV KS (1948)	229	713	460	253	57.1%	74.4	26.2
WASHBURN UNIV (1949)	49	137	73	64	45.3%	70.6	29.5
WICHITA ST UNIV (1950)	67	174	114	60	48.9%	72.0	30.7
Kentucky							
ASBURY COLL (1952)	6	18	13	5	44.4%	71.7	27.8
BELLARMINE UNIV (1954)	45	111	76	35	53.2%	73.5	25.7
BEREA COLL (1955)	9	19	12	7	57.9%	73.7	26.8
BRESCIA UNIV (1958)	11	27	10	17	25.9%	67.7	27.4
EASTERN KY UNIV (1963)	37	71	47	24	46.5%	70.0	30.5
GEORGETOWN COLL (1964)	10	24	9	15	29.2%	64.0	26.6
KY ST UNIV (1968)	8	24	11	13	4.2%	61.4	30.8
KY WESLEYAN COLL (1969)	8	23	17	6	47.8%	70.3	23.9
LINDSEY WILSON COLL (1972)	9	28	15	13	35.7%	67.3	32.8
MOREHEAD ST UNIV (1976)	17	53	23	30	43.4%	68.4	30.4
MURRAY ST UNIV (1977)	60	145	75	70	43.5%	71.9	29.2
NORTHERN KY UNIV (9275)	78	196	116	80	41.8%	71.3	28.6
PIKEVILLE COLL (1980)	7	10	4	6	60.0%	68.0	29.4
SPALDING UNIV (1960)	8	19	13	6	42.1%	67.3	37.0
SULLIVAN UNIV (4619)	16	44	23	21	25.0%	61.6	38.2
THOMAS MORE COLL (2001)	17	43	16	27	27.9%	68.1	29.2
TRANSYLVANIA UNIV (1987)	28	72	48	24	51.4%	73.2	24.5
UNIV KY (1989)	216	602	350	252	51.0%	72.9	27.5
UNIV LOUISVILLE (1999)	114	292	147	145	41.4%	69.6	31.8
UNIV OF CUMBERLANDS (1962)	5	9	7	2	55.6%	73.1	31.6
WESTERN KY UNIV (2002)	70	182	114	68	56.0%	74.6	28.8
Louisiana							
CENTENARY COLL LA (2003)	9	27	9	18	40.7%	73.6	32.6
DILLARD UNIV (2004)	10	24	9	15	8.3%	54.8	29.3
GRAMBLING ST UNIV (2006)	17	43	19	24	23.3%	60.6	30.1
LA COLL (2007)	5	7	5	2	57.1%	72.6	26.0
LA ST UNIV AND A & M COLL (2010)	314	818	500	318	50.6%	73.3	27.0
LA ST UNIV IN SHREVEPORT (2013)	32	67	31	36	41.8%	70.2	34.7
LA TECH UNIV (2008)	60	181	93	88	45.3%	71.6	28.0
LOYOLA UNIV NEW ORLEANS (2016)	35	92	61	31	53.3%	71.6	27.7
MCNEESE ST UNIV (2017)	48	133	71	62	40.6%	69.5	30.9
NICHOLLS ST UNIV (2005)	36	84	51	33	44.1%	71.3	30.7
NORTHWESTERN ST UNIV (2021)	25	61	32	29	37.7%	69.4	30.2
OUR LADY HOLY CROSS COLL (2023)	12	28	18	10	3.6%	42.9	36.4
SOUTHEASTERN LA UNIV (2024)	130	334	162	172	33.2%	68.0	29.7
SOUTHERN UNIV A&M BATON ROUGE (9636)	22	64	14	50	25.0%	68.3	34.7

Appendix A: Summary Performance by Institution Attended - All Testing Events

	Candidates Total	Sections Total	Sections First-Time	Sections Re-Exam	Percent Pass	Average Score	Average Age
SOUTHERN UNIV NEW ORLEANS (2026)	6	10	3	7	10.0%	52.1	37.0
TULANE UNIV LA (2029)	101	264	157	107	57.2%	72.3	27.3
UNIV LA LAFAYETTE (2031)	102	252	150	102	53.6%	74.8	28.4
UNIV LA MONROE (2020)	42	118	70	48	34.8%	67.8	27.7
UNIV NEW ORLEANS (2015)	134	334	170	164	39.2%	69.5	31.4
XAVIER UNIV LA (2032)	7	9	5	4	11.1%	40.8	33.9
Maine							
COLBY COLL (2039)	7	14	8	6	50.0%	73.3	37.2
HUSSON UNIV (2043)	31	69	36	33	24.6%	63.7	28.5
SAINT JOSEPHS COLL (2051)	7	13	7	6	38.5%	67.9	24.8
THOMAS COLL (2052)	16	39	19	20	46.2%	72.4	29.0
UNIV ME (2053)	36	81	49	32	59.3%	74.6	26.3
UNIV ME AUGUSTA (6760)	6	12	11	1	66.7%	77.8	33.9
UNIV SOUTHERN ME (2054)	34	77	47	30	50.7%	74.2	31.9
Maryland							
BOWIE ST UNIV (2062)	21	38	18	20	7.9%	59.4	34.4
FROSTBURG ST UNIV (2072)	9	20	9	11	40.0%	67.8	34.0
JOHNS HOPKINS UNIV (2077)	12	36	12	24	36.1%	69.0	39.1
LOYOLA UNIVERSITY MD (2078)	70	190	121	69	47.9%	73.1	24.4
MORGAN ST UNIV (2083)	12	21	10	11	19.1%	62.3	32.2
MOUNT SAINT MARYS UNIV (2086)	9	15	8	7	46.7%	69.3	30.3
SALISBURY UNIV (2091)	21	44	22	22	47.7%	73.0	28.2
TOWSON UNIV (2099)	44	126	49	77	47.6%	71.8	30.0
UNIV BALTIMORE (2102)	22	50	28	22	34.0%	68.6	38.0
UNIV MD BALTIMORE COUNTY (2105)	15	44	23	21	22.7%	63.3	29.9
UNIV MD COLL PARK (2103)	235	558	363	195	50.2%	72.7	27.9
UNIV MD EASTERN SHORE (2106)	6	12	7	5	25.0%	70.8	28.1
UNIV MD UNIV COLL (11644)	120	301	192	109	37.2%	68.1	32.6
Massachusetts							
AMERICAN INTL COLL (2114)	9	22	17	5	54.6%	72.2	30.6
ASSUMPTION COLL (2118)	67	165	94	71	39.4%	68.4	26.3
BABSON COLL (2121)	99	283	162	121	48.8%	73.1	26.1
BENTLEY COLL (2124)	392	1,074	616	458	50.0%	72.6	26.6
BOSTON COLL (2128)	245	652	489	163	69.0%	78.0	24.9
BOSTON UNIV (2130)	152	354	240	114	60.2%	75.2	25.1
BRANDEIS UNIV (2133)	6	14	11	3	71.4%	78.4	28.5
BRIDGEWATER ST COLL (2183)	25	64	30	34	42.2%	70.6	32.9
CLARK UNIV (2139)	20	50	27	23	60.0%	72.9	29.3
COLL HOLY CROSS (2141)	40	111	81	30	64.0%	76.2	23.5
COLL OUR LADY OF THE ELMS (2140)	6	15	5	10	6.7%	61.7	25.6
CURRY COLL (2143)	5	15	9	6	46.7%	61.4	31.6
FITCHBURG ST COLL (2184)	7	19	5	14	15.8%	65.8	29.5
GORDON COLL (2153)	11	28	13	15	28.6%	63.5	26.1
LASELL COLL (2158)	8	14	7	7	14.3%	59.1	27.6
MA INST TECH (2178)	7	17	16	1	94.1%	88.8	38.5
MERRIMACK COLL (2120)	41	95	46	49	32.6%	65.8	27.8
NICHOLS COLL (2197)	19	44	28	16	27.3%	65.6	29.2
NORTHEASTERN UNIV (2199)	309	817	472	345	47.1%	71.5	27.7
SALEM ST UNIV (2188)	42	88	46	42	28.4%	62.0	29.4
STONEHILL COLL (2217)	57	122	86	36	52.5%	72.5	24.8
SUFFOLK UNIV (2218)	130	324	184	140	37.4%	66.3	29.0

Appendix A: Summary Performance by Institution Attended - All Testing Events

	Candidates Total	Sections Total	Sections First-Time	Sections Re-Exam	Percent Pass	Average Score	Average Age
TUFTS UNIV (2219)	5	21	16	5	76.2%	80.4	32.8
UNIV MA AMHERST (2221)	267	655	419	236	46.0%	70.4	25.6
UNIV MA BOSTON (2222)	102	235	134	101	36.6%	67.4	32.2
UNIV MA DARTMOUTH (2210)	56	135	70	65	40.0%	66.4	29.0
UNIV MA LOWELL (2161)	40	102	59	43	50.0%	71.7	28.3
WESTERN NEW ENGLAND COLL (2226)	45	121	61	60	40.5%	70.5	28.2
WESTFIELD ST COLL (2189)	14	31	24	7	45.2%	69.6	27.8
WORCESTER ST COLL (2190)	19	37	17	20	21.6%	60.5	31.7
Michigan							
ALBION COLL (2235)	23	65	32	33	46.2%	71.5	24.4
ALMA COLL (2236)	12	32	17	15	46.9%	70.8	24.2
ANDREWS UNIV (2238)	17	38	23	15	34.2%	65.9	29.7
AQUINAS COLL (2239)	19	51	23	28	33.3%	66.5	26.4
BAKER COLL FLINT (4673)	28	54	34	20	38.9%	65.4	35.9
CALVIN COLL (2241)	46	138	92	46	59.4%	75.5	24.6
CENTRAL MI UNIV (2243)	138	380	212	168	49.7%	72.4	27.6
DAVENPORT UNIV (2249)	61	134	87	47	41.0%	68.1	31.1
EASTERN MI UNIV (2259)	113	292	170	122	43.5%	70.6	30.8
FERRIS ST UNIV (2260)	36	101	56	45	53.5%	71.0	27.0
GRAND VALLEY ST UNIV (2268)	150	418	279	139	64.8%	77.0	26.9
HILLSDALE COLL (2272)	22	56	31	25	37.5%	69.5	24.1
HOPE COLL (2273)	28	76	53	23	40.8%	68.5	23.8
LAKE SUPERIOR ST UNIV (2293)	19	55	28	27	40.0%	71.3	29.3
MI ST UNIV (2290)	434	1,143	777	366	60.7%	75.8	26.6
MI TECH UNIV (2292)	18	50	34	16	64.0%	76.9	26.8
NORTHERN MI UNIV (2301)	27	68	33	35	29.4%	67.3	28.2
NORTHWOOD UNIV (4072)	64	171	92	79	40.9%	68.3	28.7
OAKLAND UNIV (2307)	93	269	154	115	52.0%	74.0	28.8
SAGINAW VALLEY ST UNIV (2314)	47	129	70	59	34.1%	67.8	28.7
SIENA HEIGHTS UNIV (2316)	12	38	26	12	39.5%	67.4	28.8
SPRING ARBOR UNIV (2318)	8	23	8	15	26.1%	67.2	29.5
UNIV DETROIT MERCY (2323)	7	11	7	4	18.2%	62.0	38.8
UNIV MI ANN ARBOR (2325)	137	421	307	114	72.5%	79.6	27.1
UNIV MI DEARBORN (2326)	87	225	144	81	55.1%	73.5	30.1
UNIV MI FLINT (2327)	31	66	41	25	33.3%	68.9	31.0
WALSH COLL (4071)	150	366	229	137	50.3%	72.7	33.1
WAYNE ST UNIV (2329)	103	274	153	121	46.4%	70.4	32.0
WESTERN MI UNIV (2330)	154	424	225	199	40.6%	70.2	27.6
Minnesota							
AUGSBURG COLL (2334)	35	93	55	38	40.9%	70.8	29.8
BEMIDJI ST UNIV (2336)	18	50	28	22	44.0%	69.2	28.0
BETHEL COLL (MN) (9058)	23	66	53	13	59.1%	73.6	25.5
COLL OF SAINT BENEDICT (2341)	17	51	46	5	82.4%	81.3	23.3
COLL OF SAINT SCHOLASTICA (2343)	15	43	20	23	46.5%	70.3	28.0
CONCORDIA COLL MOORHEAD (2346)	36	104	63	41	64.4%	76.0	24.3
CONCORDIA UNIV MN (2347)	8	16	11	5	31.3%	59.0	31.2
GUSTAVUS ADOLPHUS COLL (2353)	21	54	33	21	46.3%	70.7	24.4
HAMLINE UNIV (2354)	7	21	11	10	52.4%	73.9	30.9
METROPOLITAN ST UNIV (10374)	77	184	113	71	39.1%	68.0	35.4
MN SCHOOL OF BUSINESS (4646)	9	21	13	8	38.1%	68.1	31.7
MN ST UNIV MANKATO (2360)	103	263	177	86	45.6%	70.3	27.6

Appendix A: Summary Performance by Institution Attended - All Testing Events

	Candidates Total	Sections Total	Sections First-Time	Sections Re-Exam	Percent Pass	Average Score	Average Age
MN ST UNIV MOORHEAD (2367)	39	101	60	41	40.6%	71.7	29.3
NORTHWESTERN COLL MN (2371)	16	40	27	13	57.5%	74.8	24.0
SAINT CATHERINE UNIV (2342)	9	22	13	9	54.6%	71.3	29.7
SAINT CLOUD ST UNIV (2377)	117	307	203	104	59.9%	75.5	27.5
SAINT JOHN'S UNIV (2379)	62	186	115	71	54.8%	73.4	24.8
SAINT MARY'S UNIV OF MN (2380)	23	59	36	23	37.3%	66.0	30.3
SOUTHWEST ST UNIV (2375)	13	35	27	8	60.0%	74.6	27.7
UNIV MN DULUTH (2388)	97	257	160	97	47.1%	71.1	26.2
UNIV MN TWIN CITIES (3969)	228	624	470	154	61.1%	76.2	27.6
UNIV ST THOMAS (2345)	139	389	258	131	48.3%	72.5	28.0
WINONA ST UNIV (2394)	54	148	85	63	32.4%	67.4	28.2
Mississippi							
ALCORN ST UNIV (2396)	5	8	8	0	25.0%	51.3	42.3
BELHAVEN COLL (2397)	19	43	25	18	32.6%	70.2	37.6
DELTA ST UNIV (2403)	17	48	22	26	29.2%	65.1	28.3
JACKSON ST UNIV (2410)	45	109	38	71	16.5%	58.7	32.0
MILLSAPS COLL (2414)	37	96	59	37	50.0%	72.2	29.1
MS COLL (2415)	40	107	57	50	33.6%	65.4	31.5
MS ST UNIV (2423)	136	391	232	159	43.2%	69.6	28.1
MS UNIV FOR WOMEN (2422)	9	25	9	16	32.0%	68.2	31.7
UNIV MS (2440)	193	586	378	208	52.2%	73.0	26.7
UNIV SOUTHERN MS (2441)	95	211	112	99	34.6%	67.7	31.5
Missouri							
AVILA UNIV (2449)	9	29	22	7	44.8%	71.6	29.1
CENTRAL METHODIST UNIV (2453)	13	31	15	16	32.3%	66.8	27.8
COLL OF OZARKS (2500)	8	19	9	10	26.3%	70.1	24.9
COLUMBIA COLL (2456)	32	70	54	16	37.1%	64.6	35.3
CULVER STOCKTON COLL (2460)	8	29	24	5	58.6%	69.5	28.6
DEVRY UNIV KANSAS CITY (2455)	21	39	21	18	18.0%	64.2	31.6
DRURY UNIV (2461)	37	115	65	50	40.0%	69.7	26.3
EVANGEL UNIV (2463)	7	21	8	13	66.7%	72.8	27.9
FONTBONNE UNIV (2464)	14	34	17	17	26.5%	62.9	31.6
LINCOLN UNIV (2479)	10	37	10	27	10.8%	66.6	34.9
LINDENWOOD UNIV (2480)	30	80	47	33	35.0%	66.7	30.5
MARYVILLE UNIV ST. LOUIS (2482)	34	92	37	55	38.0%	69.4	29.5
MO BAPTIST UNIV (7540)	6	16	11	5	25.0%	65.9	30.9
MO SOUTHERN ST UNIV (2488)	18	42	27	15	54.8%	72.3	31.2
MO ST UNIV (2503)	131	346	206	140	50.6%	73.2	28.3
MO VALLEY COLL (2489)	6	16	13	3	50.0%	73.2	26.5
MO WESTERN ST UNIV (2490)	11	38	18	20	15.8%	58.8	41.5
NORTHWEST MO ST UNIV (2496)	25	62	37	25	62.9%	75.2	28.2
PARK UNIV (2498)	33	77	34	43	35.1%	68.7	37.7
ROCKHURST UNIV (2499)	23	76	45	31	43.4%	71.2	25.2
SOUTHEAST MO ST UNIV (2501)	40	104	68	36	43.3%	68.7	30.7
SOUTHWEST BAPTIST UNIV (2502)	20	72	33	39	38.9%	69.6	24.9
ST. LOUIS UNIV (2506)	125	358	240	118	53.4%	71.9	26.4
TRUMAN ST UNIV (2495)	96	337	256	81	70.9%	78.6	25.3
UNIV CENTRAL MO (2454)	53	158	91	67	44.9%	71.5	31.1
UNIV MO COLUMBIA (2516)	184	626	461	165	65.2%	77.1	25.0
UNIV MO KANSAS CITY (2518)	69	176	123	53	62.5%	74.8	30.0
UNIV MO ST. LOUIS (2519)	110	278	180	98	47.8%	71.0	31.7

Appendix A: Summary Performance by Institution Attended - All Testing Events

	Candidates Total	Sections Total	Sections First-Time	Sections Re-Exam	Percent Pass	Average Score	Average Age
WASHINGTON UNIV ST. LOUIS (2520)	57	153	109	44	71.2%	78.0	26.8
WEBSTER UNIV (2521)	45	99	61	38	26.3%	63.3	33.9
WESTMINSTER COLL (2523)	12	39	12	27	25.6%	67.7	25.1
WILLIAM WOODS UNIV (2525)	6	10	8	2	30.0%	63.5	34.6
Montana							
CARROLL COLL (MT) (2526)	19	60	22	38	30.0%	65.6	26.1
MT ST UNIV BILLINGS (2530)	33	98	56	42	31.6%	67.0	33.1
MT ST UNIV BOZEMAN (2532)	75	204	122	82	53.4%	74.5	26.1
MT TECH UNIV (2531)	8	16	13	3	37.5%	74.4	26.5
ROCKY MOUNTAIN COLL (2534)	6	14	3	11	64.3%	76.1	27.6
UNIV MT (2536)	79	234	152	82	57.7%	75.7	28.3
Nebraska							
BELLEVUE UNIV (9743)	24	61	34	27	37.7%	69.5	33.1
CHADRON ST COLL (2539)	6	14	7	7	42.9%	69.6	30.0
CREIGHTON UNIV (2542)	59	168	115	53	48.8%	70.9	25.0
DOANE COLL (2544)	19	57	25	32	40.4%	69.2	28.4
HASTINGS COLL (2548)	17	47	23	24	34.0%	66.9	26.7
MIDLAND LUTHERAN COLL (2553)	24	64	31	33	42.2%	71.0	27.6
NE WESLEYAN UNIV (2555)	16	43	24	19	65.1%	73.4	25.2
PERU ST COLL (2559)	8	20	11	9	60.0%	77.7	32.2
UNION COLL (2563)	5	15	8	7	40.0%	67.8	25.6
UNIV NE KEARNEY (2551)	30	74	38	36	40.5%	69.4	28.7
UNIV NE LINCOLN (2565)	104	291	172	119	52.2%	73.6	27.8
UNIV NE OMAHA (2554)	62	147	95	52	57.1%	74.9	28.4
WAYNE ST COLL (2566)	16	38	21	17	44.7%	69.9	28.0
YORK COLL (2567)	11	24	11	13	29.2%	65.5	32.5
Nevada							
UNIV NV LAS VEGAS (2569)	192	494	259	235	43.7%	69.9	30.2
UNIV NV RENO (2568)	89	243	141	102	38.7%	69.0	30.3
New Hampshire							
NEW ENGLAND COLL (2579)	5	13	6	7	46.2%	72.0	29.3
PLYMOUTH ST UNIV (2591)	19	35	23	12	45.7%	71.1	31.0
SAINT ANSELM COLL (2587)	16	45	30	15	37.8%	69.8	25.9
SOUTHERN NH UNIV (2580)	51	128	79	49	37.5%	67.9	35.2
UNIV NH (2589)	79	213	149	64	54.9%	74.3	25.8
New Jersey							
BERKELEY COLL (7502)	19	26	18	8	11.5%	56.7	29.1
BETH MEDRASH GOVOHA (7947)	21	55	29	26	43.6%	72.0	31.6
BLOOMFIELD COLL (2597)	8	15	6	9	33.3%	61.1	31.7
CALDWELL COLL (2598)	18	35	15	20	37.1%	68.7	30.1
CENTENARY COLL (2599)	13	31	22	9	25.8%	62.5	29.0
COLL NJ (2642)	127	327	224	103	59.3%	75.3	25.2
FAIRLEIGH DICKINSON UNIV (2607)	98	217	158	59	43.3%	68.2	28.9
FAIRLEIGH DICKINSON UNIV MADISON (4738)	26	66	34	32	40.9%	71.5	34.1
FAIRLEIGH DICKINSON UNIV RUTHERFORD (2604)	33	79	37	42	38.0%	70.3	31.6
FELICIAN COLL (2610)	7	20	19	1	5.0%	53.2	30.4
GEORGIAN COURT UNIV (2608)	22	51	31	20	31.4%	62.0	33.0
KEAN UNIV (2622)	100	225	114	111	28.0%	63.2	32.5
MONMOUTH UNIV (2616)	97	251	146	105	30.3%	63.9	27.1
MONTCLAIR ST UNIV (2617)	206	525	282	243	33.9%	66.5	28.9
NJ CITY UNIV (2613)	46	95	51	44	26.3%	62.3	37.6

Appendix A: Summary Performance by Institution Attended - All Testing Events

	Candidates Total	Sections Total	Sections First-Time	Sections Re-Exam	Percent Pass	Average Score	Average Age
NJ INST TECH (2621)	6	7	5	2	28.6%	67.4	37.4
QUALIFYING CERTIFICATE (88822)	6	15	9	6	33.3%	62.6	44.3
RAMAPO COLL NJ (9344)	98	275	153	122	38.2%	68.4	26.4
RICHARD STOCKTON COLL NJ (9345)	69	171	114	57	42.1%	70.0	28.6
RIDER UNIV (2628)	129	355	192	163	27.3%	65.2	28.5
ROWAN UNIV (2609)	98	243	144	99	42.4%	67.7	27.3
RUTGERS ST UNIV CAMDEN (4741)	98	263	144	119	38.0%	68.7	28.2
RUTGERS ST UNIV NEW BRUNSWICK (6964)	242	615	358	257	39.7%	68.3	27.6
RUTGERS ST UNIV NEWARK (2631)	368	826	460	366	38.3%	67.7	27.7
SAINT PETERS COLL (2638)	44	103	43	60	27.2%	63.2	30.3
SETON HALL UNIV (2632)	98	257	117	140	31.9%	66.8	27.6
THOMAS EDISON ST COLL (21922)	19	44	29	15	54.6%	74.5	34.6
WILLIAM PATERSON UNIV NJ (2625)	79	161	85	76	28.6%	66.5	29.3
New Mexico							
COLL SANTA FE (2649)	6	13	10	3	0.0%	47.4	35.8
EASTERN NM UNIV (2651)	15	33	21	12	39.4%	67.2	28.8
NM HIGHLANDS UNIV (2653)	8	18	8	10	38.9%	66.9	39.1
NM ST UNIV (2657)	70	172	79	93	33.7%	68.7	30.8
SAINT JOHNS COLL (2093)	6	13	11	2	38.5%	70.5	26.1
UNIV NM (2663)	121	333	157	176	40.2%	69.9	31.6
WESTERN NM UNIV (2664)	11	31	13	18	22.6%	65.2	28.9
New York							
ADELPHI UNIV (2666)	50	125	56	69	28.0%	65.1	27.5
ALFRED UNIV (2668)	16	24	18	6	33.3%	67.4	24.7
AMERICAN UNIV IN CAIRO (5034)	5	10	4	6	20.0%	72.1	24.4
BARNARD COLL (2708)	5	9	6	3	44.4%	67.6	30.0
BERKELEY COLL NY (7394)	23	49	19	30	18.4%	58.8	31.1
CANISIUS COLL (2681)	50	164	103	61	60.4%	75.0	25.7
CLARKSON UNIV (2699)	7	19	14	5	52.6%	72.5	36.5
COLGATE UNIV (2701)	5	9	9	0	55.6%	73.6	30.3
COLL SAINT ROSE (2705)	22	62	29	33	37.1%	68.3	28.2
COLUMBIA UNIV NY (2707)	17	42	34	8	78.6%	77.2	32.8
CONCORDIA COLL (2709)	5	10	3	7	30.0%	66.0	29.4
CORNELL UNIV (2711)	58	147	113	34	71.4%	78.6	27.4
CUNY BARUCH (7273)	873	2,026	1,018	1,008	43.2%	70.0	30.2
CUNY BROOKLYN (2687)	222	495	311	184	36.6%	67.3	29.1
CUNY HERBERT H LEHMAN (7022)	69	127	73	54	21.3%	61.0	33.8
CUNY HUNTER (2689)	159	343	166	177	29.7%	65.3	29.6
CUNY MEDGAR EVERS (10097)	19	54	9	45	11.1%	57.6	37.0
CUNY QUEENS (2690)	326	693	320	373	31.5%	65.2	30.4
CUNY STATEN ISLAND (2698)	8	15	4	11	40.0%	68.6	31.5
CUNY STATEN ISLAND (29040)	69	141	77	64	29.8%	65.6	30.3
CUNY YORK COLL (4759)	24	50	19	31	16.0%	62.9	35.8
DAEMEN COLL (2808)	16	53	20	33	39.6%	68.0	28.3
DOWLING COLL (2667)	24	51	21	30	25.5%	65.6	33.5
ELMIRA COLL (2718)	10	25	15	10	68.0%	78.8	27.2
EXCELSIOR COLL (2834)	48	102	69	33	45.1%	69.1	33.0
FORDHAM UNIV (2722)	218	537	275	262	41.9%	70.9	25.9
HARTWICK COLL (2729)	19	40	22	18	32.5%	69.8	28.6
HOFSTRA UNIV (2732)	219	537	283	254	36.7%	68.4	27.0
HOUGHTON COLL (2734)	5	10	8	2	70.0%	73.6	30.0

Appendix A: Summary Performance by Institution Attended - All Testing Events

	Candidates Total	Sections Total	Sections First-Time	Sections Re-Exam	Percent Pass	Average Score	Average Age
IONA COLL (2737)	45	129	53	76	29.5%	67.2	28.2
ITHACA COLL (2739)	39	108	60	48	46.3%	72.7	25.8
LE MOYNE COLL (2748)	57	148	79	69	35.8%	69.1	27.3
LONG ISLAND UNIV BROOKLYN CENTER (4779)	25	55	22	33	20.0%	63.0	30.9
LONG ISLAND UNIV CW POST (2754)	103	239	110	129	35.2%	68.0	30.1
MANHATTAN COLL (2758)	57	141	74	67	24.1%	61.2	26.6
MARIST COLL (2765)	58	154	82	72	41.6%	70.9	26.3
MERCY COLL (2772)	21	53	17	36	34.0%	68.2	36.6
MOLLOY COLL (2775)	17	41	20	21	22.0%	61.7	27.1
MONROE COLL (4799)	35	73	25	48	6.9%	55.9	35.4
MOUNT SAINT MARY COLL (2778)	9	19	16	3	5.3%	56.8	28.2
NAZARETH COLL ROCHESTER (2779)	14	40	28	12	65.0%	78.6	25.1
NIAGARA UNIV (2788)	48	125	58	67	31.2%	66.9	27.3
NY INST TECH MANHATTAN (2782)	25	58	35	23	24.1%	62.0	32.8
NY INST TECH OLD WESTBURY (4804)	14	26	13	13	23.1%	59.1	25.2
NY UNIV (2785)	205	545	373	172	58.0%	74.9	26.5
NYACK COLL (2790)	6	14	8	6	42.9%	67.8	27.3
PACE UNIV NY (2791)	235	602	264	338	34.1%	68.0	29.6
PACE UNIV PLEASANTVILLE (2792)	68	171	87	84	34.5%	67.2	27.8
PACE UNIV WHITE PLAINS (2727)	10	27	13	14	48.2%	74.3	39.2
POLYTECH UNIV (2796)	5	11	6	5	45.5%	56.5	31.6
ROBERTS WESLEYAN COLL (2805)	5	11	1	10	27.3%	69.2	27.4
ROCHESTER INST TECH (2806)	34	99	51	48	36.4%	69.6	30.8
SAINT BONAVENTURE UNIV (2817)	57	154	88	66	40.9%	70.1	26.9
SAINT FRANCIS COLL (2820)	28	63	35	28	38.1%	68.7	29.2
SAINT JOHN FISHER COLL (2821)	44	126	68	58	45.2%	72.2	25.7
SAINT JOHNS UNIV NEW YORK (2823)	316	732	387	345	31.2%	65.0	27.2
SAINT JOSEPHS COLL NY (2825)	15	28	25	3	42.9%	68.7	26.8
SAINT JOSEPHS COLL SUFFOLK (29081)	20	45	23	22	33.3%	68.2	29.1
SAINT THOMAS AQUINAS COLL (2832)	12	34	13	21	20.6%	65.8	27.4
SIENA COLL (2816)	103	244	128	116	41.0%	69.5	26.6
SKIDMORE COLL (2814)	7	19	10	9	42.1%	75.7	28.5
SUNY OLD WESTBURY (7109)	94	208	113	95	34.1%	64.9	32.5
SUNY ALBANY (2835)	267	614	353	261	42.4%	70.6	26.2
SUNY BINGHAMTON (2836)	363	918	545	373	46.2%	70.5	25.6
SUNY BROCKPORT (2841)	54	131	69	62	44.3%	71.9	28.8
SUNY BUFFALO (2837)	228	597	364	233	54.3%	74.0	26.9
SUNY BUFFALO (2842)	11	29	16	13	58.6%	75.0	30.0
SUNY EMPIRE ST COLL (10286)	13	35	21	14	54.3%	72.0	39.5
SUNY FREDONIA (2844)	23	47	30	17	57.5%	73.0	28.7
SUNY GENESEO (2845)	96	240	154	86	53.8%	74.4	25.1
SUNY INST TECH UTICA ROME (11678)	10	25	18	7	16.0%	61.7	32.4
SUNY NEW PALTZ (2846)	55	130	69	61	51.5%	73.8	28.8
SUNY ONEONTA (2847)	28	67	26	41	43.3%	70.1	26.1
SUNY OSWEGO (2848)	67	182	101	81	35.7%	67.3	26.2
SUNY PLATTSBURGH (2849)	46	124	53	71	26.6%	66.2	27.3
SUNY STONY BROOK (2838)	51	132	88	44	42.4%	69.6	28.2
SUNY UTICA-ROME (6792)	5	10	1	9	60.0%	76.1	31.5
SYRACUSE UNIV (2882)	213	547	281	266	40.6%	69.7	26.0
TOURO COLL (10142)	125	306	184	122	51.0%	73.2	26.1
UNION COLL (2889)	6	11	5	6	63.6%	77.0	29.7

Appendix A: Summary Performance by Institution Attended - All Testing Events

	Candidates Total	Sections Total	Sections First-Time	Sections Re-Exam	Percent Pass	Average Score	Average Age
UNIV ROCHESTER (2894)	22	47	33	14	63.8%	76.4	30.3
UTICA COLL (2883)	16	45	18	27	44.4%	71.8	32.7
VASSAR COLL (2895)	5	11	9	2	72.7%	77.5	27.2
WAGNER COLL (2899)	49	105	61	44	31.4%	64.8	27.3
YESHIVA UNIV (2903)	122	293	154	139	41.3%	70.5	24.8
North Carolina							
APPALACHIAN ST UNIV (2906)	123	351	191	160	53.0%	74.2	27.4
BARTON COLL (2908)	9	21	10	11	28.6%	59.3	34.2
BELMONT ABBEY COLL (2910)	7	14	11	3	14.3%	65.3	34.6
CAMPBELL UNIV (2913)	44	115	54	61	44.4%	71.6	31.2
CATAWBA COLL (2914)	10	22	13	9	40.9%	62.6	29.7
DAVIDSON COLL (2918)	8	29	25	4	79.3%	82.8	24.9
DUKE UNIV (2920)	15	36	26	10	63.9%	77.6	31.7
EAST CAROLINA UNIV (2923)	145	416	245	171	42.6%	70.5	28.0
ELIZABETH CITY ST UNIV (2926)	7	14	10	4	0.0%	46.2	40.2
ELON UNIV (2927)	99	257	138	119	42.8%	69.8	24.8
FAYETTEVILLE ST UNIV (2928)	9	14	6	8	14.3%	58.3	36.8
GARDNER WEBB UNIV (2929)	21	48	37	11	41.7%	67.8	34.3
GREENSBORO COLL (2930)	10	24	7	17	37.5%	68.7	32.6
GUILFORD COLL (2931)	13	30	20	10	50.0%	75.0	36.1
HIGH POINT UNIV (2933)	26	67	20	47	34.3%	66.4	34.5
LENOIR RHYNE COLL (2941)	13	32	5	27	37.5%	71.0	29.5
MEREDITH COLL (2945)	10	31	17	14	45.2%	73.3	27.1
METHODIST UNIV (2946)	8	14	8	6	21.4%	64.9	35.7
MOUNT OLIVE COLL (2949)	7	15	12	3	6.7%	47.1	28.3
NC AGRICULTURAL & TECH ST UNIV (2905)	41	117	46	71	32.5%	67.7	28.7
NC CENTRAL UNIV (2950)	18	39	17	22	23.1%	58.6	32.5
NC ST UNIV RALEIGH (2972)	226	638	397	241	55.5%	74.8	27.2
NC WESLEYAN COLL (2951)	9	26	17	9	38.5%	57.7	40.5
PFEIFFER UNIV (2955)	8	29	13	16	24.1%	63.2	31.7
QUEENS UNIV CHARLOTTE (2957)	5	12	9	3	83.3%	78.7	29.6
UNIV NC ASHEVILLE (2907)	22	55	38	17	40.0%	72.1	35.1
UNIV NC CHAPEL HILL (2974)	207	646	484	162	67.0%	77.2	26.5
UNIV NC CHARLOTTE (2975)	106	277	159	118	49.1%	72.5	29.6
UNIV NC GREENSBORO (2976)	75	195	108	87	49.2%	72.1	29.3
UNIV NC PEMBROKE (2954)	10	22	13	9	45.5%	69.5	32.2
UNIV NC WILMINGTON (2984)	159	452	274	178	47.6%	72.5	27.1
WAKE FOREST UNIV (2978)	69	247	216	31	84.6%	83.6	25.0
WESTERN CAROLINA UNIV (2981)	23	58	45	13	41.4%	67.0	32.3
WINGATE UNIV (2985)	12	28	20	8	25.0%	66.2	25.5
WINSTON SALEM ST UNIV (2986)	15	48	17	31	20.8%	66.3	32.6
North Dakota							
DICKINSON ST UNIV (2989)	41	95	53	42	35.8%	65.2	27.5
JAMESTOWN COLL (2990)	5	13	7	6	38.5%	69.6	25.7
MINOT ST UNIV (2994)	14	34	24	10	58.8%	72.1	26.3
ND ST UNIV (9265)	66	185	104	81	53.5%	74.3	27.7
UNIV MARY (2992)	21	66	35	31	42.4%	69.9	30.1
UNIV ND (3005)	113	282	206	76	63.1%	76.7	26.0
Ohio							
ASHLAND UNIV (3012)	22	63	42	21	42.9%	72.4	31.1
BALDWIN WALLACE COLL (3014)	62	156	90	66	47.4%	70.7	30.7

Appendix A: Summary Performance by Institution Attended - All Testing Events

	Candidates Total	Sections Total	Sections First-Time	Sections Re-Exam	Percent Pass	Average Score	Average Age
BOWLING GREEN ST UNIV (3018)	124	339	210	129	46.0%	71.7	28.5
CAPITAL UNIV (3023)	28	91	63	28	40.7%	67.5	26.2
CASE WESTERN RESERVE UNIV (3024)	50	148	106	42	61.5%	74.3	29.1
CEDARVILLE UNIV (3025)	24	67	28	39	55.2%	74.2	26.5
CENTRAL ST UNIV (3026)	5	12	5	7	25.0%	57.6	40.9
Chancellor University (3043)	9	26	8	18	26.9%	67.6	44.7
CLEVELAND ST UNIV (3032)	127	315	193	122	47.9%	71.0	31.8
COLUMBUS ST CC (6867)	7	12	12	0	41.7%	70.0	28.9
DEFIANCE COLL (3041)	7	19	17	2	47.4%	70.1	26.6
DEVRY UNIV COLUMBUS (3099)	22	45	29	16	35.6%	62.0	38.4
FRANCISCAN UNIV STEUBENVILLE (3036)	8	18	13	5	38.9%	66.3	33.4
FRANKLIN UNIV (3046)	124	271	156	115	29.9%	62.8	35.7
HEIDELBERG COLL (3048)	12	34	11	23	20.6%	69.0	29.7
HIRAM COLL (3049)	13	44	18	26	34.1%	66.4	26.8
JOHN CARROLL UNIV (3050)	97	272	163	109	55.9%	75.0	26.3
KENT ST UNIV (3051)	127	330	191	139	52.4%	72.4	28.8
LAKE ERIE COLL (3066)	5	14	12	2	35.7%	65.7	31.5
MALONE COLL (3072)	6	20	14	6	50.0%	73.2	25.9
MARIETTA COLL (3073)	11	26	11	15	34.6%	67.7	28.6
MIAMI UNIV (3077)	350	985	708	277	59.2%	75.5	25.0
MOUNT UNION COLL (3083)	15	38	18	20	57.9%	75.6	25.9
MOUNT VERNON NAZARENE UNIV (7085)	13	34	26	8	32.4%	65.3	32.2
MUSKINGUM COLL (3084)	7	18	10	8	44.4%	66.7	29.9
NOTRE DAME COLL OH (3085)	11	29	21	8	13.8%	56.6	24.9
OH DOMINICAN UNIV (3035)	16	52	34	18	26.9%	65.0	27.5
OH NORTHERN UNIV (3089)	24	75	49	26	32.0%	67.3	25.2
OH ST UNIV (6883)	460	1,267	855	412	59.0%	75.1	26.6
OH UNIV (3100)	176	488	309	179	45.3%	70.8	25.6
OH WESLEYAN UNIV (3109)	15	34	21	13	44.1%	72.9	25.5
OTTERBEIN UNIV (3110)	13	32	21	11	50.0%	70.0	32.4
TIFFIN UNIV (3121)	7	18	9	9	22.2%	61.3	29.5
UNIV AKRON (3123)	133	378	243	135	53.7%	72.9	29.8
UNIV CINCINNATI (3125)	129	326	199	127	46.6%	71.1	30.2
UNIV DAYTON (3127)	129	349	212	137	47.0%	71.4	25.5
UNIV FINDLAY (3045)	19	62	31	31	41.9%	70.1	29.9
UNIV NORTHWESTERN OH (4861)	5	11	10	1	18.2%	62.9	32.1
UNIV TOLEDO (3131)	96	248	168	80	48.8%	70.5	28.8
WALSH UNIV (3135)	19	50	19	31	20.0%	65.8	28.5
WILMINGTON COLL (3142)	7	13	9	4	30.8%	61.6	34.3
WITTENBERG UNIV (3143)	6	18	14	4	44.4%	70.5	28.7
WRIGHT ST UNIV (3078)	69	182	112	70	52.2%	72.8	29.4
XAVIER UNIV (3144)	76	199	120	79	55.8%	72.6	26.0
YOUNGSTOWN ST UNIV (3145)	66	168	99	69	44.6%	69.0	29.4
Oklahoma							
CAMERON UNIV (3150)	18	31	20	11	25.8%	59.4	35.2
EAST CENTRAL UNIV (3154)	23	46	11	35	34.8%	68.0	37.5
LANGSTON UNIV (3157)	21	32	4	28	15.6%	54.0	40.9
NORTHEASTERN ST UNIV (3161)	45	95	48	47	30.5%	63.9	31.7
NORTHWESTERN OK ST UNIV (3163)	8	17	11	6	41.2%	71.6	29.8
OK BAPTIST UNIV (3164)	7	19	11	8	47.4%	70.3	33.6
OK CHRISTIAN UNIV (3165)	34	87	50	37	50.6%	71.1	26.7

Appendix A: Summary Performance by Institution Attended - All Testing Events

	Candidates Total	Sections Total	Sections First-Time	Sections Re-Exam	Percent Pass	Average Score	Average Age
OK ST UNIV (3170)	205	578	388	190	56.8%	74.7	27.7
OK ST UNIV OK CITY (9647)	6	9	4	5	33.3%	64.7	37.5
OKLAHOMA CITY UNIV (3166)	29	63	27	36	38.1%	68.2	32.5
ORAL ROBERTS UNIV (3985)	28	74	41	33	56.8%	73.8	28.7
SOUTHEASTERN OK ST UNIV (3179)	9	28	9	19	35.7%	66.6	34.6
SOUTHERN NAZARENE UNIV (3149)	14	33	5	28	30.3%	65.2	31.7
SOUTHWESTERN OK ST UNIV (3181)	37	87	34	53	32.2%	64.7	30.0
UNIV CENTRAL OK (3152)	142	313	147	166	37.7%	66.7	32.0
UNIV OK NORMAN (3184)	166	432	255	177	55.6%	73.3	27.9
UNIV TULSA (3185)	40	92	41	51	39.1%	70.5	30.2
Oregon							
CONCORDIA UNIV (3191)	5	12	8	4	8.3%	56.1	26.1
EASTERN OR UNIV (3193)	26	76	38	38	48.7%	71.7	31.8
GEORGE FOX UNIV (3194)	22	54	24	30	40.7%	69.8	25.6
LINFIELD COLL (3198)	50	140	83	57	40.0%	70.7	32.8
OR ST UNIV (3210)	106	245	159	86	55.5%	73.7	30.5
PACIFIC UNIV (3212)	12	27	13	14	48.2%	68.3	27.2
PORTLAND ST UNIV (3216)	139	322	191	131	55.0%	72.0	32.7
SOUTHERN OR UNIV (3219)	32	80	45	35	47.5%	72.6	31.4
UNIV OR (3223)	196	498	300	198	54.2%	73.0	28.8
UNIV PORTLAND (3224)	32	89	62	27	41.6%	69.3	26.7
WESTERN OR UNIV (3209)	5	21	14	7	23.8%	63.0	30.8
WILLAMETTE UNIV (3227)	6	18	12	6	83.3%	79.9	28.7
Pennsylvania							
ALBRIGHT COLL (3229)	36	67	46	21	23.9%	65.7	32.4
ALVERNIA COLL (3233)	19	46	21	25	30.4%	67.7	33.0
ARCADIA UNIV (3235)	17	57	29	28	35.1%	65.7	25.5
BLOOMSBURG UNIV PA (3315)	115	296	158	138	48.0%	72.2	26.8
BUCKNELL UNIV (3238)	69	190	112	78	58.4%	75.6	25.2
CA UNIV PA (3316)	26	59	33	26	28.8%	64.2	33.2
CABRINI COLL (3241)	23	60	26	34	25.0%	58.2	28.7
CARLOW UNIV (3303)	9	17	11	6	41.2%	64.9	28.4
CARNEGIE MELLON UNIV (3242)	16	42	22	20	45.2%	72.6	32.4
CEDAR CREST COLL (3243)	5	11	3	8	36.4%	65.6	29.2
CHATHAM UNIV (3244)	7	20	16	4	30.0%	63.4	29.8
CHESTNUT HILL COLL (3245)	11	21	10	11	38.1%	64.7	30.6
CHEYNEY UNIV PA (3317)	5	8	5	3	0.0%	47.9	28.3
CLARION UNIV PA (9235)	32	71	29	42	46.5%	70.4	27.8
COLL MISERICORDIA (3247)	10	25	10	15	12.0%	59.2	30.8
DE VALLEY COLL (3252)	15	42	21	21	33.3%	65.8	26.2
DESALES UNIV (3986)	46	128	65	63	31.3%	66.4	28.3
DREXEL UNIV (3256)	249	598	323	275	38.0%	67.8	27.0
DUQUESNE UNIV (3258)	140	346	209	137	44.2%	70.5	25.7
EAST STROUDSBURG UNIV PA (3320)	21	42	22	20	42.9%	67.8	32.7
EASTERN UNIV (3259)	16	42	24	18	45.2%	73.2	28.2
EDINBORO UNIV PA (3321)	12	32	16	16	21.9%	64.5	29.6
ELIZABETHTOWN COLL (3262)	36	101	55	46	26.7%	65.1	27.8
FRANKLIN & MARSHALL COLL (3265)	8	21	15	6	76.2%	79.1	30.2
GANNON UNIV (3266)	20	47	20	27	23.4%	60.7	35.2
GENEVA COLL (3267)	18	44	23	21	34.1%	68.4	27.7
GETTYSBURG COLL (3268)	6	12	6	6	33.3%	67.2	28.9

Appendix A: Summary Performance by Institution Attended - All Testing Events

	Candidates Total	Sections Total	Sections First-Time	Sections Re-Exam	Percent Pass	Average Score	Average Age
GROVE CITY COLL (3269)	43	108	84	24	54.6%	74.1	25.8
GWYNEDD MERCY COLL (3270)	16	41	27	14	31.7%	63.3	28.5
HOLY FAMILY COLL (3275)	16	26	22	4	15.4%	62.2	28.7
IMMACULATA UNIV (3276)	7	16	10	6	37.5%	63.9	27.1
IN UNIV OF PA (8810)	5	14	7	7	7.1%	64.0	38.4
INDIANA UNIV PA (3277)	91	248	133	115	32.3%	65.6	27.8
JUNIATA COLL (3279)	19	37	17	20	35.1%	65.8	27.0
KEYSTONE COLL (3280)	11	22	15	7	13.6%	60.4	26.3
KINGS COLL (3282)	75	159	88	71	31.5%	65.1	26.1
KUTZTOWN UNIV PA (3322)	77	189	129	60	39.2%	69.0	26.2
LA ROCHE COLL (3987)	26	59	24	35	17.0%	57.5	27.5
LA SALLE UNIV (3287)	160	395	206	189	30.6%	65.5	27.3
LAFAYETTE COLL (3284)	10	26	19	7	30.8%	62.9	29.2
LEBANON VALLEY COLL (3288)	35	92	63	29	40.2%	72.6	27.8
LEHIGH UNIV (3289)	166	436	296	140	62.4%	75.3	24.5
LINCOLN UNIV (3290)	11	27	10	17	25.9%	60.3	25.9
LOCK HAVEN UNIV PA (3323)	18	47	27	20	31.9%	58.9	28.6
LYCOMING COLL (3293)	14	39	22	17	41.0%	70.6	27.7
MARYWOOD UNIV (3296)	12	33	17	16	30.3%	67.3	35.6
MERCYHURST COLL (3297)	33	74	46	28	29.7%	63.0	25.9
MESSIAH COLL (3298)	42	120	85	35	55.0%	72.1	24.2
MILLERSVILLE UNIV PA (3325)	39	94	53	41	39.4%	66.6	28.1
MORAVIAN COLL (3301)	35	87	48	39	34.5%	67.2	26.2
MOUNT ALOYSIUS COLL (3302)	10	16	9	7	43.8%	71.4	28.1
MUHLENBERG COLL (3304)	56	158	90	68	44.3%	70.9	25.7
NEUMANN UNIV (3988)	13	29	18	11	34.5%	64.1	30.4
PA COLL TECH (3395)	6	11	8	3	18.2%	62.0	31.2
PA ST ERIE (3333)	6	14	11	3	71.4%	75.4	32.4
PA ST HARRISBURG (6814)	5	14	8	6	50.0%	75.0	30.4
PA ST UNIV PARK (3329)	616	1,601	1,052	549	45.3%	70.2	25.7
PA ST UNIV PARK (6965)	63	184	32	152	30.4%	69.5	30.3
PEIRCE COLL (3309)	5	9	8	1	66.7%	69.8	34.6
PHILADELPHIA UNIV (3354)	38	107	41	66	29.0%	62.8	30.1
POINT PARK UNIV (3357)	12	25	18	7	20.0%	63.9	31.0
ROBERT MORRIS UNIV (3359)	108	236	126	110	33.9%	65.7	27.4
SAINT FRANCIS UNIV (3366)	41	94	49	45	26.6%	62.6	28.2
SAINT JOSEPHS UNIV (3367)	170	465	248	217	38.3%	68.8	25.6
SAINT VINCENT COLL (3368)	38	94	62	32	38.3%	69.6	25.0
SETON HILL UNIV (3362)	11	22	13	9	36.4%	65.9	27.0
SHIPPENSBURG UNIV PA (3326)	94	223	133	90	47.5%	71.1	26.9
SLIPPERY ROCK UNIV PA (3327)	44	98	61	37	24.5%	61.6	25.3
SUSQUEHANNA UNIV (3369)	29	76	49	27	40.8%	68.9	26.6
TEMPLE UNIV (3371)	452	1,063	659	404	32.4%	64.9	28.3
THIEL COLL (3376)	16	49	28	21	24.5%	61.8	25.3
UNIV PA (3378)	41	112	83	29	73.2%	78.3	31.5
UNIV PITTSBURGH (3379)	319	786	522	264	48.0%	71.9	26.3
UNIV PITTSBURGH JOHNSTOWN (3382)	9	21	6	15	23.8%	62.9	29.4
UNIV SCRANTON (3384)	85	182	103	79	42.9%	68.8	26.3
URSINUS COLL (3385)	11	24	10	14	25.0%	69.5	32.5
VILLANOVA UNIV (3388)	284	796	479	317	55.9%	74.5	25.1
WASHINGTON & JEFFERSON COLL (3389)	51	116	72	44	40.5%	70.6	25.4

Appendix A: Summary Performance by Institution Attended - All Testing Events

	Candidates Total	Sections Total	Sections First-Time	Sections Re-Exam	Percent Pass	Average Score	Average Age
WAYNESBURG COLL (3391)	14	26	13	13	15.4%	60.7	28.2
WEST CHESTER UNIV PA (3328)	212	506	280	226	37.4%	68.2	26.4
WESTMINSTER COLL (3392)	27	60	38	22	23.3%	60.6	26.0
WIDENER UNIV PA (3313)	91	219	117	102	26.9%	63.3	26.3
WILKES UNIV (3394)	38	91	54	37	30.8%	63.3	28.4
YORK COLL PA (3399)	45	100	62	38	48.0%	71.5	27.5
Puerto Rico							
INTER AMERICAN UNIV PR (8242)	32	48	30	18	14.6%	46.3	33.9
INTER AMERICAN UNIV PR AGUADILLA (3939)	5	8	5	3	37.5%	62.9	35.1
INTER AMERICAN UNIV PR BARRANQUITAS (5027)	9	14	13	1	0.0%	34.8	31.0
INTER AMERICAN UNIV PR BAYAMON (5028)	13	25	18	7	8.0%	47.7	30.7
INTER AMERICAN UNIV PR METROPOLITAN (3940)	53	100	65	35	19.0%	56.6	31.4
INTER AMERICAN UNIV PR PONCE (5029)	17	36	29	7	0.0%	29.8	32.9
INTER AMERICAN UNIV PR SAN GERMAN (3938)	18	35	21	14	17.1%	58.9	32.7
PONTIFICAL CATHOLIC UNIV PR (3936)	44	97	69	28	17.5%	47.8	30.8
UNIV ESTE (3941)	11	24	21	3	8.3%	36.8	40.9
UNIV METROPOLITANA (25875)	16	28	23	5	17.9%	38.6	37.3
UNIV POLITECNICA DE PR (21000)	6	16	6	10	25.0%	67.6	34.6
UNIV PR AGUADILLA (12123)	17	26	20	6	3.9%	44.8	31.2
UNIV PR ARECIBO (7228)	29	55	35	20	14.6%	55.5	28.7
UNIV PR BAYAMON (10975)	79	166	87	79	21.7%	59.2	27.6
UNIV PR CAROLINA (30160)	12	25	18	7	12.0%	54.8	28.8
UNIV PR CAYEY (7206)	62	146	60	86	15.8%	57.2	28.2
UNIV PR HUMACAO (3943)	50	105	53	52	21.9%	58.1	27.1
UNIV PR MAYAGUEZ (3944)	64	137	72	65	31.4%	66.9	27.4
UNIV PR PONCE (9652)	28	77	47	30	18.2%	51.4	26.6
UNIV PR RIO PIEDRAS (7108)	274	682	341	341	37.8%	68.1	26.7
UNIV SACRED HEART (3937)	15	30	17	13	50.0%	71.9	28.5
UNIV TURABO GURABO (11719)	14	33	22	11	6.1%	46.3	29.8
Rhode Island							
BRYANT UNIV (3402)	220	539	329	210	48.8%	72.7	25.7
JOHNSON & WALES UNIV (3404)	62	151	118	33	33.1%	61.9	28.2
PROVIDENCE COLL (3406)	72	191	117	74	50.8%	73.9	25.6
RI COLL (3407)	19	50	33	17	30.0%	61.7	29.8
ROGER WILLIAMS UNIV (3410)	24	65	37	28	29.2%	65.4	23.3
SALVE REGINA UNIV (3411)	32	83	33	50	25.3%	64.6	26.5
UNIV RI (3414)	104	279	170	109	52.7%	72.9	26.9
South Carolina							
BOB JONES UNIV (3421)	29	68	47	21	48.5%	71.1	24.9
CITADEL MILITARY COLL SC (3423)	22	61	40	21	27.9%	63.8	27.0
CLEMSON UNIV (3425)	89	249	189	60	62.3%	75.4	26.2
COASTAL CAROLINA UNIV (3451)	24	56	31	25	46.4%	70.3	26.6
COLL CHARLESTON (3428)	57	178	127	51	53.4%	73.7	27.0
FRANCIS MARION UNIV (9226)	8	13	7	6	46.2%	64.8	31.7
FURMAN UNIV (3434)	26	87	60	27	62.1%	77.9	24.6
LANDER UNIV (3435)	5	9	3	6	44.4%	73.6	31.7
PRESBYTERIAN COLL (3445)	5	14	8	6	92.9%	83.7	25.7
UNIV SC COLUMBIA (3448)	157	437	326	111	51.3%	74.5	27.4
WINTHROP UNIV (3456)	36	75	37	38	45.3%	71.7	33.0
WOFFORD COLL (3457)	19	71	58	13	62.0%	75.9	26.0

Appendix A: Summary Performance by Institution Attended - All Testing Events

	Candidates Total	Sections Total	Sections First-Time	Sections Re-Exam	Percent Pass	Average Score	Average Age
South Dakota							
AUGUSTANA COLL (3458)	34	96	65	31	47.9%	72.9	25.9
BLACK HILLS ST UNIV (3459)	14	32	21	11	37.5%	70.3	29.8
CO TECHNICAL UNIV (666731)	13	26	17	9	34.6%	60.5	37.9
NATIONAL AMERICAN UNIV (4057)	11	22	14	8	27.3%	60.8	35.6
NORTHERN ST UNIV (3466)	14	40	19	21	22.5%	63.9	30.3
SD ST UNIV (3471)	15	32	23	9	40.6%	73.3	27.3
UNIV SD (3474)	49	128	68	60	53.9%	75.0	28.4
UNIV SIOUX FALLS (3469)	18	42	34	8	54.8%	74.9	27.5
Tennessee							
AUSTIN PEAY ST UNIV (3478)	33	84	45	39	33.3%	64.5	29.2
BELMONT UNIV (3479)	67	170	104	66	44.7%	70.8	28.2
CARSON NEWMAN COLL (3481)	13	30	11	19	40.0%	68.7	33.4
CHRISTIAN BROTHERS UNIV (3482)	20	60	19	41	28.3%	67.4	28.7
COVENANT COLL (3484)	5	12	10	2	75.0%	76.3	23.3
CUMBERLAND UNIV (3485)	7	17	9	8	5.9%	54.4	27.7
EAST TN ST UNIV (3487)	78	190	120	70	39.0%	68.2	30.6
FISK UNIV (3490)	6	12	9	3	41.7%	68.0	25.3
FREED HARDEMAN UNIV (3492)	16	40	18	22	37.5%	67.3	29.7
LAMBUTH UNIV (3498)	6	18	8	10	22.2%	63.7	28.2
LEE UNIV (3500)	23	60	35	25	50.0%	69.2	29.0
LINCOLN MEMORIAL UNIV (3502)	8	26	6	20	38.5%	69.5	30.4
LIPSCOMB UNIV (3486)	71	188	120	68	32.5%	66.7	29.4
MIDDLE TN ST UNIV (3510)	144	394	244	150	45.7%	71.2	29.6
MILLIGAN COLL (3511)	5	13	5	8	30.8%	73.2	31.7
RHODES COLL (3519)	30	70	51	19	55.7%	74.4	24.5
SOUTHERN ADVENTIST UNIV (3518)	13	39	24	15	41.0%	70.0	25.9
TN ST UNIV (3522)	34	67	40	27	29.9%	63.8	33.9
TN TECH UNIV (3523)	73	183	116	67	32.8%	66.9	29.8
TN WESLEYAN COLL (3525)	11	24	11	13	45.8%	64.7	36.1
TREVECCA NAZARENE UNIV (3526)	8	30	13	17	50.0%	73.6	26.6
TUSCULUM COLL (3527)	8	14	9	5	35.7%	69.2	30.4
UNION UNIV (3528)	14	32	23	9	50.0%	71.9	28.7
UNIV MEMPHIS (3509)	90	215	127	88	32.1%	65.8	30.5
UNIV TN CHATTANOOGA (3529)	95	227	132	95	42.3%	69.6	30.3
UNIV TN KNOXVILLE (3530)	206	624	378	246	57.4%	74.2	27.5
UNIV TN MARTIN (3531)	40	106	49	57	32.1%	64.0	29.2
VANDERBILT UNIV (3535)	48	175	143	32	75.4%	80.1	26.1
Texas							
ABILENE CHRISTIAN UNIV (3537)	77	203	104	99	50.3%	73.2	26.1
AMBERTON UNIV (22594)	11	19	6	13	31.6%	61.8	45.3
ANGELO ST UNIV (3541)	41	125	67	58	48.0%	71.3	31.1
BAYLOR UNIV (3545)	169	487	339	148	66.9%	77.9	25.8
BAYLOR UNIV (6967)	15	45	31	14	53.3%	72.9	28.7
DALLAS BAPTIST UNIV (3560)	31	87	40	47	27.6%	65.1	32.4
DEVRY UNIV IRVING (10139)	19	41	24	17	14.6%	56.0	34.9
EAST TX BAPTIST UNIV (3564)	5	12	6	6	41.7%	62.6	30.1
HARDIN SIMMONS UNIV (3571)	7	14	10	4	42.9%	71.1	26.5
HOUSTON BAPTIST UNIV (3576)	35	75	37	38	38.7%	68.8	29.5
LAMAR COLL (3581)	43	141	48	93	32.6%	68.4	30.6
LETOURNEAU UNIV (3584)	16	34	25	9	20.6%	66.3	35.7

Appendix A: Summary Performance by Institution Attended - All Testing Events

	Candidates Total	Sections Total	Sections First-Time	Sections Re-Exam	Percent Pass	Average Score	Average Age
LUBBOCK CHRISTIAN UNIV (3586)	8	23	11	12	39.1%	72.4	31.3
MIDWESTERN ST UNIV (3592)	35	83	48	35	49.4%	72.2	32.7
OUR LADY THE LAKE UNIV (3598)	12	27	18	9	33.3%	67.0	37.7
PRAIRIE VIEW A & M UNIV (3630)	11	27	13	14	29.6%	64.3	28.4
RICE UNIV (3604)	20	43	31	12	62.8%	76.5	32.4
SAINT EDWARDS UNIV (3621)	34	103	50	53	42.7%	72.1	34.3
SAINT MARYS UNIV (3623)	25	57	30	27	35.1%	68.6	32.0
SAM HOUSTON ST UNIV (3606)	130	350	158	192	38.6%	69.3	31.1
SCHREINER UNIV (3610)	8	22	9	13	27.3%	67.2	27.9
SOUTHERN METHODIST UNIV (3613)	152	431	282	149	60.6%	76.3	26.3
SOUTHWESTERN ASSEMBLIES OF GOD UNIV (3616)	6	11	5	6	27.3%	67.3	33.4
SOUTHWESTERN UNIV (3620)	10	26	22	4	73.1%	77.7	29.7
STEPHEN F AUSTIN ST UNIV (3624)	93	238	125	113	45.0%	70.2	28.2
TARLETON ST UNIV (3631)	31	67	38	29	35.8%	67.5	32.7
TRINITY UNIV (3647)	59	156	83	73	53.9%	73.4	26.1
TX A&M INTL UNIV (9651)	20	41	24	17	22.0%	59.0	31.6
TX A&M UNIV (3632)	440	1,446	1,064	382	68.4%	78.2	25.6
TX A&M UNIV COMMERCE (3565)	42	105	54	51	35.2%	67.5	33.5
TX A&M UNIV CORPUS CHRISTI (11161)	53	126	72	54	38.9%	68.5	30.8
TX A&M UNIV KINGSVILLE (3639)	13	22	10	12	22.7%	63.4	34.9
TX A&M UNIV TEXARKANA (31703)	6	13	4	9	53.9%	73.8	33.6
TX CHRISTIAN UNIV (3636)	88	238	182	56	65.6%	77.5	25.8
TX LUTHERAN UNIV (3641)	32	62	30	32	45.2%	70.0	26.8
TX SOUTHERN UNIV (3642)	22	47	17	30	8.5%	55.3	38.2
TX ST UNIV SAN MARCOS (3615)	182	481	222	259	43.5%	71.4	30.5
TX TECH UNIV (3644)	209	587	382	205	54.0%	73.0	27.4
TX WESLEYAN UNIV (3645)	17	47	26	21	34.0%	67.2	33.0
TX WOMANS UNIV (3646)	23	62	32	30	37.1%	67.0	30.0
UNIV DALLAS (3651)	39	102	43	59	35.3%	68.9	35.7
UNIV HOUSTON (12826)	7	17	9	8	23.5%	66.2	33.7
UNIV HOUSTON CLEAR LAKE (11711)	134	297	165	132	37.4%	66.9	33.5
UNIV HOUSTON DOWNTOWN (3612)	163	325	185	140	28.0%	63.0	32.2
UNIV HOUSTON UNIV PARK (3652)	505	1,207	599	608	38.4%	68.7	30.5
UNIV HOUSTON VICTORIA (13231)	30	83	36	47	38.6%	69.6	34.0
UNIV INCARNATE WORD (3578)	27	59	27	32	13.6%	57.3	32.0
UNIV MARY HARDIN BAYLOR (3588)	22	54	40	14	46.3%	70.4	27.9
UNIV NORTH TX (3594)	189	477	263	214	40.0%	70.2	31.7
UNIV SAINT THOMAS (3654)	77	167	97	70	43.1%	69.1	30.2
UNIV TX ARLINGTON (3656)	213	551	291	260	45.6%	71.5	32.4
UNIV TX AUSTIN (3658)	469	1,393	1,009	384	66.8%	77.7	26.7
UNIV TX BROWNSVILLE (30646)	15	32	19	13	40.6%	68.6	30.1
UNIV TX DALLAS (9741)	336	900	515	385	39.7%	68.8	31.2
UNIV TX EL PASO (3661)	47	104	49	55	43.3%	69.9	30.9
UNIV TX PAN AMERICAN (3599)	41	77	41	36	40.3%	67.0	30.1
UNIV TX PERMIAN BASIN (9930)	32	73	42	31	45.2%	70.2	33.6
UNIV TX SAN ANTONIO (10115)	164	397	201	196	39.8%	68.7	32.8
UNIV TX TYLER (11163)	46	109	64	45	42.2%	68.8	29.6
WAYLAND BAPTIST UNIV (3663)	8	22	16	6	45.5%	70.0	35.6
WEST TX A & M UNIV (3665)	55	146	60	86	30.8%	68.3	29.3

Appendix A: Summary Performance by Institution Attended - All Testing Events

	Candidates Total	Sections Total	Sections First-Time	Sections Re-Exam	Percent Pass	Average Score	Average Age
Utah							
BRIGHAM YOUNG UNIV (3670)	381	1,006	806	200	71.6%	78.9	27.8
SOUTHERN UT UNIV (3678)	72	191	110	81	49.2%	73.2	29.0
UNIV UT (3675)	203	539	358	181	60.1%	75.3	30.8
UT ST UNIV (3677)	110	279	185	94	54.1%	73.9	30.4
UT VALLEY ST COLL (4027)	27	63	41	22	44.4%	71.0	32.1
WEBER ST UNIV (3680)	87	207	118	89	50.7%	73.3	31.9
Western Governors Univ (33394)	9	17	14	3	35.3%	67.2	34.2
WESTMINSTER COLL (3681)	41	87	47	40	34.5%	67.6	32.7
Vermont							
CASTLETON ST COLL (3683)	9	29	17	12	65.5%	77.7	34.1
CHAMPLAIN COLL (3684)	27	75	48	27	24.0%	67.0	28.5
SAINT MICHAELS COLL (3694)	34	84	50	34	42.9%	71.1	25.8
UNIV VT (3696)	35	97	58	39	55.7%	74.8	29.2
VERMONT 60 (88803)	7	19	2	17	10.5%	62.6	39.6
Virgin Islands							
UNIV VI (3946)	10	15	10	5	33.3%	67.6	28.4
Virginia							
AVERETT UNIV (3702)	8	26	8	18	30.8%	67.6	35.5
BRIDGEWATER COLL (3704)	15	51	22	29	31.4%	65.7	24.9
CHRISTOPHER NEWPORT UNIV (3706)	23	54	32	22	35.2%	71.4	27.6
COLL WILLIAM & MARY (3705)	119	361	260	101	63.4%	76.2	25.6
EASTERN MENNONITE UNIV (3708)	5	19	18	1	68.4%	82.4	29.5
EMORY & HENRY COLL (3709)	10	22	6	16	45.5%	67.9	28.3
FERRUM COLL (3711)	8	15	11	4	60.0%	72.3	26.7
GEORGE MASON UNIV (3749)	313	724	425	299	43.8%	71.0	30.0
HAMPDEN SYDNEY COLL (3713)	5	11	8	3	63.6%	75.9	27.1
HAMPTON UNIV (3714)	46	125	51	74	20.0%	64.9	27.9
JAMES MADISON UNIV (3721)	187	564	409	155	61.9%	76.5	25.5
LIBERTY UNIV (20530)	69	153	93	60	45.8%	71.9	30.8
LONGWOOD UNIV (3719)	22	52	30	22	46.2%	68.4	25.9
LYNCHBURG COLL (3720)	8	22	13	9	54.6%	75.0	25.8
MARYMOUNT UNIV (3724)	6	19	10	9	57.9%	74.8	31.5
NORFOLK ST UNIV (3765)	16	32	10	22	37.5%	67.7	37.2
NORTHERN VA CC (3727)	24	52	32	20	51.9%	71.4	32.0
OLD DOMINION UNIV (3728)	90	199	131	68	45.2%	69.5	31.0
RADFORD UNIV (3732)	40	97	38	59	40.2%	69.5	27.5
RANDOLPH MACON COLL (3733)	20	57	33	24	43.9%	69.7	27.4
ROANOKE COLL (3736)	13	36	19	17	50.0%	73.1	26.2
TIDEWATER CC (3712)	6	12	9	3	33.3%	64.0	31.2
UNIV MARY WASHINGTON (3746)	19	40	31	9	45.0%	69.2	28.3
UNIV RICHMOND (3744)	96	280	173	107	63.2%	76.5	25.3
UNIV VA (3745)	150	426	339	87	79.3%	81.9	26.0
UNIV VA COL WISE (CLINCH VALLEY COLL) (3747)	11	22	11	11	50.0%	74.4	29.7
VA COMMONWEALTH UNIV (3735)	125	313	160	153	36.1%	68.0	29.3
VA MILITARY INST (3753)	5	15	7	8	53.3%	74.1	31.7
VA POLYTECHNIC INST & ST UNIV (3754)	289	800	518	282	56.1%	75.1	26.5
VA WESLEYAN COLL (3767)	6	18	7	11	38.9%	66.9	31.1
WASHINGTON & LEE UNIV (3768)	33	104	81	23	59.6%	76.1	24.9

Appendix A: Summary Performance by Institution Attended - All Testing Events

	Candidates Total	Sections Total	Sections First-Time	Sections Re-Exam	Percent Pass	Average Score	Average Age
Washington							
BELLEVUE CC (3769)	7	9	7	2	33.3%	69.8	28.8
CENTRAL WA UNIV (3771)	128	338	247	91	45.9%	70.1	30.3
CITY UNIV SEATTLE (13022)	20	53	44	9	30.2%	62.3	40.5
EASTERN WA UNIV (3775)	68	167	115	52	35.3%	65.8	31.4
EDMONDS CC (5001)	5	11	10	1	9.1%	54.9	28.2
GONZAGA UNIV (3778)	97	291	233	58	67.7%	78.0	25.3
NORTH SEATTLE CC (9704)	11	20	20	0	60.0%	70.5	30.2
PACIFIC LUTHERAN UNIV (3785)	19	56	40	16	23.2%	61.9	24.7
SAINT MARTINS COLL (3794)	10	25	22	3	28.0%	61.5	33.6
SEATTLE PACIFIC UNIV (3788)	31	80	58	22	43.8%	71.4	24.7
SEATTLE UNIV (3790)	53	138	100	38	42.0%	70.0	28.1
UNIV PUGET SOUND (3797)	7	14	13	1	78.6%	77.1	33.4
UNIV WA (3798)	354	957	798	159	61.8%	75.3	27.6
WA ST UNIV (3800)	136	346	265	81	49.1%	72.2	27.4
WALLA WALLA UNIV (3799)	8	18	12	6	61.1%	76.8	27.0
WESTERN WA UNIV (3802)	52	132	101	31	66.7%	76.8	28.3
WHITWORTH COLL (3804)	13	31	22	9	61.3%	76.1	27.1
West Virginia							
BETHANY COLL (3808)	6	11	8	3	72.7%	73.5	28.7
BLUEFIELD ST COLL (3809)	7	21	8	13	57.1%	75.2	34.6
CONCORD UNIV (3810)	17	35	14	21	31.4%	67.4	26.8
FAIRMONT ST COLL (3812)	12	30	12	18	40.0%	61.3	34.4
GLENVILLE ST COLL (3813)	5	8	6	2	12.5%	60.1	25.7
MARSHALL UNIV (3815)	82	205	99	106	42.0%	69.5	30.7
MOUNTAIN ST UNIV (3807)	5	8	3	5	12.5%	55.6	32.8
SALEM INTL UNIV (3820)	8	24	12	12	41.7%	71.3	36.6
SHEPHERD UNIV (3822)	13	40	16	24	60.0%	73.3	31.3
UNIV CHARLESTON (3818)	14	35	25	10	25.7%	61.1	26.8
WEST LIBERTY ST COLL (3823)	23	57	24	33	33.3%	66.5	28.7
WHEELING JESUIT UNIV (3831)	23	50	24	26	32.0%	66.3	28.3
WV INST TECH (3825)	13	33	15	18	15.2%	58.6	38.2
WV ST UNIV (3826)	33	78	33	45	25.6%	61.6	33.5
WV UNIV (3827)	199	502	300	202	48.0%	71.0	27.7
WV UNIV PARKERSBURG (3828)	10	21	16	5	42.9%	68.3	28.6
WV WESLEYAN COLL (3830)	12	33	22	11	48.5%	68.9	24.8
Wisconsin							
BELOIT COLL (3835)	5	11	8	3	45.5%	70.6	28.9
CARDINAL STRITCH UNIV (3837)	17	39	23	16	33.3%	65.7	36.3
CARROLL UNIV (WI) (3838)	25	65	41	24	52.3%	72.6	28.0
CARTHAGE COLL (3839)	20	57	28	29	19.3%	60.8	25.5
CONCORDIA UNIV WI (3842)	15	37	27	10	37.8%	65.8	27.9
EDGEWOOD COLL (3848)	21	58	30	28	32.8%	65.5	31.8
LAKELAND COLL (3854)	64	166	99	67	38.6%	69.7	36.6
Marion University (3861)	6	20	8	12	35.0%	67.6	25.4
MARQUETTE UNIV (3863)	127	366	256	110	63.1%	76.4	25.6
MOUNT MARY COLL (3869)	7	15	13	2	26.7%	61.5	39.3
SAINT NORBERT COLL (3892)	27	71	52	19	62.0%	72.8	24.4
UNIV WI EAU CLAIRE (3917)	105	250	152	98	55.2%	73.8	26.1
UNIV WI GREEN BAY (3899)	57	132	81	51	39.4%	70.7	27.2
UNIV WI LA CROSSE (3919)	104	280	190	90	52.5%	73.5	25.1

Appendix A: Summary Performance by Institution Attended - All Testing Events

	Candidates Total	Sections Total	Sections First-Time	Sections Re-Exam	Percent Pass	Average Score	Average Age
UNIV WI MADISON (3895)	208	651	499	152	73.0%	78.8	25.9
UNIV WI MILWAUKEE (3896)	218	650	429	221	53.5%	73.5	28.6
UNIV WI OSHKOSH (3920)	78	204	149	55	55.9%	73.5	26.6
UNIV WI PARKSIDE (5015)	23	41	26	15	14.6%	62.0	30.2
UNIV WI PLATTEVILLE (3921)	22	63	28	35	41.3%	71.1	28.5
UNIV WI RIVER FALLS (3923)	34	94	56	38	52.1%	72.3	28.5
UNIV WI STEVENS POINT (3924)	20	61	31	30	49.2%	74.0	29.8
UNIV WI SUPERIOR (3925)	14	43	29	14	37.2%	68.5	28.1
UNIV WI WHITEWATER (3926)	226	670	414	256	54.6%	74.2	26.7
VITERBO UNIV (3911)	6	15	6	9	20.0%	64.5	29.7
Wyoming							
UNIV WY (3932)	75	199	130	69	51.8%	73.8	28.4

INSTITUTION ATTENDED
ALL TESTING EVENTS

APPENDIX B

SECTION PERFORMANCE

Appendix B: Section Performance by Institution Attended - All Testing Events

	Total Events per Section				Percent Pass			
	AUD	BEC	FAR	REG	AUD	BEC	FAR	REG
Alabama								
AL A&M UNIV (1002)	10	13	7	8	10%	8%	14%	38%
AL ST UNIV (1005)	4	6	5	4	25%	0%	40%	25%
ATHENS ST UNIV (1008)	13	12	10	7	15%	42%	30%	14%
AUBURN UNIV (1009)	153	144	167	168	60%	63%	57%	63%
AUBURN UNIV MONTGOMERY (8310)	37	13	24	18	30%	23%	29%	39%
BIRMINGHAM SOUTHERN COLL (1012)	27	26	29	20	26%	38%	28%	40%
HUNTINGDON COLL (1019)	6	5	8	6	50%	60%	25%	67%
JACKSONVILLE ST UNIV (1020)	18	17	12	14	44%	35%	58%	36%
OAKWOOD COLL (1033)	7	9	3	12	57%	44%	100%	25%
SAMFORD UNIV (1036)	24	18	26	25	58%	67%	42%	64%
SPRING HILL COLL (1041)	5	6	6	6	40%	33%	67%	33%
TROY UNIV (1047)	62	52	47	59	34%	29%	43%	34%
TUSKEGEE UNIV (1050)	2	5	7	5	0%	0%	43%	20%
UNIV AL (1051)	217	179	200	186	48%	56%	47%	51%
UNIV AL (8004)	4	4	2	7	75%	50%	100%	29%
UNIV AL BIRMINGHAM (1052)	85	61	70	65	49%	48%	37%	40%
UNIV AL HUNTSVILLE (1055)	16	16	10	18	31%	19%	20%	44%
UNIV MONTEVALLO (1004)	8	8	9	7	63%	50%	56%	29%
UNIV NORTH AL (1016)	13	22	15	13	69%	50%	47%	69%
UNIV SOUTH AL (1057)	39	38	36	34	41%	47%	44%	50%
UNIV WEST AL (1024)	6	6	3	1	33%	0%	33%	100%
Alaska								
UNIV ALASKA ANCHORAGE (11462)	35	23	40	28	46%	30%	38%	46%
UNIV ALASKA FAIRBANKS (1063)	9	10	8	9	56%	30%	50%	44%
UNIV ALASKA SOUTHEAST (1065)	4	3	3	3	25%	67%	67%	33%
Arizona								
AZ ST UNIV (1081)	282	195	244	261	57%	62%	52%	52%
AZ ST UNIV WEST (66935)	11	8	10	14	73%	50%	50%	50%
DEVRY UNIV PHOENIX (8322)	25	28	21	28	24%	25%	33%	39%
GRAND CANYON UNIV (1074)	7	11	13	8	29%	18%	23%	50%
NORTHERN AZ UNIV (1082)	51	42	48	58	41%	50%	42%	34%
THUNDERBIRD SCHOOL OF GLOBAL MGMT (1070)	8	5	11	13	63%	60%	18%	38%
UNIV AZ (1083)	168	132	169	204	55%	60%	56%	41%
UNIV PHOENIX (20988)	347	350	331	322	33%	25%	32%	34%
WESTERN INTL UNIV (21715)	7	6	4	7	57%	50%	50%	57%
Arkansas								
AR ST UNIV (1090)	33	28	25	27	36%	36%	36%	30%
AR TECH UNIV (1089)	18	18	21	20	39%	56%	43%	55%
HARDING UNIV (1097)	49	52	46	58	51%	31%	35%	33%
HENDERSON ST UNIV (1098)	15	12	15	12	13%	42%	20%	25%
HENDRIX COLL (1099)	9	7	8	16	33%	29%	13%	25%
OUACHITA BAPTIST UNIV (1102)	13	13	8	11	54%	23%	50%	45%
SOUTHERN AR UNIV (1107)	12	9	13	10	58%	33%	31%	40%
UNIV AR (1108)	96	76	95	103	57%	61%	48%	43%
UNIV AR LITTLE ROCK (1101)	32	24	32	38	50%	46%	34%	50%
UNIV AR MONTICELLO (1085)	6	5	4	3	17%	20%	50%	33%
UNIV AR PINE BLUFF (1086)	2	3	4	4	0%	0%	0%	0%
UNIV CENTRAL AR (1092)	74	52	44	59	32%	23%	45%	41%

Appendix B: Section Performance by Institution Attended - All Testing Events

	Total Events per Section				Percent Pass			
	AUD	BEC	FAR	REG	AUD	BEC	FAR	REG
California								
ALLIANT INTL UNIV SAN DIEGO (1158)	3	2	6	3	33%	50%	17%	33%
AMERICAN RIVER COLL (1232)	3	2	4	3	33%	100%	75%	67%
AZUSA PACIFIC UNIV (1117)	15	15	18	15	27%	33%	28%	33%
BIOLA UNIV (1122)	18	20	14	26	50%	30%	50%	35%
CA BAPTIST UNIV (1125)	13	15	10	9	38%	20%	10%	11%
CA LUTHERAN UNIV (1133)	28	22	24	27	25%	45%	38%	44%
CA ST POLYTECH UNIV POMONA (1144)	97	97	109	110	31%	24%	33%	28%
CA ST POLYTECH UNIV SAN LUIS OBISPO (1143)	202	153	158	199	51%	48%	47%	54%
CA ST UNIV BAKERSFIELD (7993)	50	30	30	26	38%	43%	33%	38%
CA ST UNIV CHICO (1146)	65	60	58	69	43%	35%	38%	32%
CA ST UNIV DOMINGUEZ HILLS (1141)	42	33	49	38	19%	12%	29%	26%
CA ST UNIV EAST BAY (1138)	209	185	168	209	39%	32%	40%	35%
CA ST UNIV FRESNO (1147)	113	107	124	101	45%	38%	41%	40%
CA ST UNIV FULLERTON (1137)	319	278	276	327	36%	37%	40%	38%
CA ST UNIV LONG BEACH (1139)	175	153	153	188	42%	28%	37%	43%
CA ST UNIV LOS ANGELES (1140)	221	160	183	206	33%	26%	35%	34%
CA ST UNIV NORTHRIDGE (1153)	318	214	252	266	42%	37%	43%	48%
CA ST UNIV SACRAMENTO (1150)	207	188	174	209	39%	38%	36%	35%
CA ST UNIV SAN BERNARDINO (1142)	91	60	70	78	36%	23%	29%	35%
CA ST UNIV SAN MARCOS (30113)	55	44	44	55	51%	55%	48%	42%
CA ST UNIV STANISLAUS (1157)	43	36	33	36	30%	31%	36%	33%
CHAPMAN UNIV (1164)	37	40	44	43	49%	33%	50%	51%
CLAREMONT GRADUATE UNIV (1169)	0	1	3	3	0%	0%	0%	33%
CLAREMONT MCKENNA COLL (1170)	27	12	20	23	44%	83%	50%	39%
CONCORDIA UNIV (20705)	3	1	10	7	33%	0%	20%	14%
DE ANZA COLL (4480)	13	9	9	15	23%	67%	44%	53%
DEVRY UNIV LONG BEACH (666988)	20	15	20	23	25%	0%	30%	22%
DEVRY UNIV POMONA (23329)	19	11	15	22	37%	9%	13%	23%
DIABLO VALLEY COLL (1191)	3	2	2	2	0%	50%	0%	50%
FOOTHILL COLL (1199)	9	8	11	10	33%	63%	55%	40%
FRESNO PACIFIC UNIV (1253)	13	10	8	11	62%	30%	63%	45%
FULLERTON COLL (1201)	0	1	5	2	0%	0%	60%	50%
GLENDALE CC (1203)	11	4	8	9	36%	25%	25%	44%
GOLDEN GATE UNIV (1205)	135	101	117	117	35%	36%	38%	46%
GOLDEN WEST COLL (1206)	4	3	3	1	50%	67%	67%	100%
HUMBOLDT ST UNIV (1149)	13	15	9	13	46%	13%	44%	62%
IRVINE VALLEY COLL (25395)	5	5	6	5	40%	20%	17%	0%
LA SIERRA UNIV (1215)	10	9	9	10	20%	44%	0%	10%
LOYOLA MARYMOUNT UNIV (11649)	77	67	65	78	47%	51%	55%	42%
MASTERS COLL & SEMINARY (1220)	7	8	7	10	57%	75%	43%	30%
MENLO COLL (1236)	3	3	3	3	33%	33%	33%	0%
MOUNT SAINT MARYS COLL (1243)	14	15	9	6	21%	33%	22%	33%
NATIONAL UNIV (11460)	47	33	48	50	36%	48%	44%	22%
ORANGE COAST COLL (1250)	4	2	8	8	75%	0%	38%	50%
PACIFIC ST UNIV (31633)	21	9	17	19	19%	11%	24%	16%
PACIFIC UNION COLL (1258)	6	5	7	8	33%	60%	57%	50%
PEPPERDINE (1264)	52	35	27	54	44%	49%	44%	39%
POINT LOMA NAZARENE UNIV (1262)	14	8	9	10	50%	63%	56%	40%
SAINT MARYS COLL CA (1302)	33	30	27	33	30%	37%	30%	33%
SAN DIEGO ST UNIV (1151)	268	227	245	292	50%	44%	50%	51%

Appendix B: Section Performance by Institution Attended - All Testing Events

	Total Events per Section				Percent Pass			
	AUD	BEC	FAR	REG	AUD	BEC	FAR	REG
SAN FRANCISCO ST UNIV (1154)	199	160	174	201	40%	33%	39%	37%
SAN JOSE ST UNIV (1155)	255	196	214	239	45%	43%	42%	45%
SANTA CLARA UNIV (1326)	198	165	184	241	48%	57%	39%	37%
SANTA MONICA COLL (1286)	19	18	19	16	21%	39%	42%	31%
SIMPSON UNIV (1291)	7	5	8	4	29%	40%	25%	25%
SONOMA ST UNIV (1156)	81	61	77	74	30%	26%	27%	31%
STANFORD UNIV (1305)	8	3	8	4	63%	67%	38%	75%
UNIV CA BERKELEY (1312)	241	166	199	237	51%	68%	54%	52%
UNIV CA DAVIS (1313)	84	71	70	86	45%	55%	51%	50%
UNIV CA IRVINE (1314)	135	102	116	132	44%	52%	41%	49%
UNIV CA LOS ANGELES (1315)	390	300	356	424	58%	63%	60%	55%
UNIV CA RIVERSIDE (1316)	154	136	121	159	32%	29%	31%	33%
UNIV CA SAN DIEGO (1317)	95	55	84	92	51%	49%	43%	42%
UNIV CA SANTA BARBARA (1320)	354	284	339	383	58%	51%	51%	44%
UNIV CA SANTA CRUZ (1321)	104	89	97	110	37%	40%	34%	36%
UNIV LA VERNE (1216)	23	16	20	30	39%	44%	50%	27%
UNIV PACIFIC (1329)	32	23	24	30	53%	48%	54%	33%
UNIV REDLANDS (1322)	24	17	19	19	29%	29%	26%	21%
UNIV SAN DIEGO (10395)	106	85	105	125	50%	61%	44%	49%
UNIV SAN FRANCISCO (1325)	66	45	56	62	35%	33%	32%	32%
UNIV SOUTHERN CA (1328)	493	342	438	541	54%	71%	56%	49%
VANGUARD UNIV SOUTHERN CA (1293)	7	4	6	5	43%	75%	67%	60%
WOODBURY UNIV (1343)	11	12	13	9	27%	25%	15%	22%
Colorado								
ADAMS ST COLL (1345)	3	10	4	8	33%	10%	75%	63%
CHARTERED ACCT (199999)	80	61	70	96	50%	75%	60%	44%
CO CHRISTIAN UNIV (9401)	1	3	2	4	0%	0%	0%	0%
CO COLL (1347)	4	1	6	3	75%	100%	50%	67%
CO ST UNIV (1350)	113	94	115	128	58%	59%	50%	49%
FORT LEWIS COLL (1353)	20	30	31	28	40%	40%	35%	25%
MESA ST COLL (1358)	20	15	20	20	45%	60%	50%	40%
METRO ST COLL DENVER (1360)	67	62	90	78	31%	29%	33%	37%
REGIS UNIV (1363)	68	59	57	66	49%	39%	33%	53%
UNIV CO BOULDER (1370)	116	121	130	153	57%	64%	58%	49%
UNIV CO COLORADO SPRINGS (4509)	36	16	33	34	39%	56%	39%	41%
UNIV CO DENVER (6740)	52	52	67	72	50%	42%	42%	40%
UNIV DENVER (1371)	78	59	63	76	41%	73%	54%	50%
UNIV NORTHERN CO (1349)	54	57	55	57	41%	47%	44%	42%
UNIV SOUTHERN CO (1365)	13	15	18	13	38%	40%	56%	38%
WESTERN ST COLL (1372)	10	13	10	13	60%	23%	50%	38%
Connecticut								
ALBERTUS MAGNUS COLL (1374)	3	3	3	3	0%	0%	33%	0%
BRIARWOOD COLL (9407)	1	2	2	3	0%	0%	50%	33%
CENTRAL CT ST UNIV (1378)	35	37	31	29	46%	35%	48%	52%
EASTERN CT ST UNIV (1425)	10	10	14	10	20%	80%	43%	40%
FAIRFIELD UNIV (1385)	92	79	110	98	46%	65%	46%	49%
QUINNIPIAC UNIV (1402)	83	54	47	81	37%	44%	38%	35%
SACRED HEART UNIV (1403)	34	22	30	36	35%	27%	20%	33%
SOUTHERN CT ST UNIV (1406)	15	14	26	20	27%	43%	42%	45%
TEIKYO POST UNIV (1401)	7	7	8	7	29%	43%	25%	29%
UNIV BRIDGEPORT (1416)	16	11	12	9	25%	18%	25%	22%

Appendix B: Section Performance by Institution Attended - All Testing Events

	Total Events per Section				Percent Pass			
	AUD	BEC	FAR	REG	AUD	BEC	FAR	REG
UNIV CT (1417)	221	175	222	219	54%	57%	46%	48%
UNIV HARTFORD (1422)	23	24	20	20	35%	42%	35%	45%
UNIV NEW HAVEN (1397)	13	16	15	11	46%	13%	27%	27%
WESTERN CT ST UNIV (1380)	18	13	11	16	61%	46%	36%	38%
Delaware								
DE ST UNIV (1428)	6	14	7	12	17%	14%	14%	17%
DE TECH & CC OWENS (7053)	4	7	1	3	75%	43%	100%	33%
GOLDEY BEACOM COLL (1429)	26	14	22	20	31%	21%	27%	25%
UNIV DE (1431)	181	141	145	160	50%	60%	56%	46%
WESLEY COLL (1433)	5	4	1	3	20%	25%	100%	67%
WILMINGTON COLL (7948)	21	17	11	15	48%	41%	36%	13%
District of Columbia								
AMERICAN UNIV (1434)	53	47	59	62	47%	62%	51%	47%
CATHOLIC UNIV OF AMERICA (1437)	6	5	3	4	17%	40%	33%	50%
GEORGE WASHINGTON UNIV (1444)	89	67	86	76	53%	64%	52%	53%
GEORGETOWN UNIV (1445)	33	34	28	49	67%	79%	71%	57%
HOWARD UNIV (1448)	37	44	37	48	32%	18%	14%	21%
SOUTHEASTERN UNIV (1456)	15	7	10	11	27%	43%	40%	55%
STRAYER COLL (1459)	76	72	60	80	26%	19%	20%	29%
UNIV DC (1441)	11	6	13	9	9%	17%	23%	22%
Florida								
BARRY UNIV (1466)	5	3	2	3	60%	67%	50%	33%
BETHUNE COOKMAN COLL (1467)	5	4	3	1	20%	0%	33%	100%
FL A&M UNIV (1480)	26	24	22	28	46%	25%	32%	29%
FL ATLANTIC UNIV (1481)	53	49	48	55	51%	29%	40%	38%
FL GULF COAST UNIV (32553)	8	6	7	9	50%	33%	43%	33%
FL INST TECH (1469)	3	3	4	2	67%	33%	50%	0%
FL INTL UNIV (9635)	78	71	66	107	45%	45%	48%	39%
FL MEMORIAL UNIV (1486)	4	2	3	2	25%	0%	33%	0%
FL SOUTHERN COLL (1488)	8	4	2	4	25%	25%	50%	25%
FL ST UNIV (1489)	89	54	70	87	55%	52%	49%	47%
FLAGLER COLL (7893)	6	2	8	4	17%	0%	38%	100%
JACKSONVILLE UNIV (1495)	2	3	4	2	50%	33%	50%	100%
LYNN UNIV (1505)	2	5	0	8	100%	20%	0%	25%
NOVA SOUTHEASTERN UNIV (1509)	22	17	13	21	9%	18%	23%	29%
NOVA SOUTHEASTERN UNIV (150909)	4	1	2	10	25%	100%	50%	30%
PENSACOLA CHRISTIAN COLL (99998)	7	7	6	4	71%	57%	33%	25%
SAINT LEO UNIV (1526)	16	16	17	19	44%	44%	41%	53%
STETSON UNIV (1531)	11	2	10	10	45%	50%	30%	50%
UNIV CENTRAL FL (3954)	72	58	63	82	54%	64%	38%	49%
UNIV FL (1535)	152	107	108	119	62%	74%	77%	66%
UNIV MIAMI (1536)	93	63	84	79	51%	68%	51%	52%
UNIV NORTH FL (9841)	24	24	20	23	54%	54%	45%	48%
UNIV SOUTH FL (1537)	88	63	76	69	56%	56%	51%	59%
UNIV TAMPA (1538)	30	15	32	24	57%	73%	50%	46%
UNIV WEST FL (3955)	7	9	8	4	29%	44%	38%	50%
Georgia								
ALBANY ST UNIV (1544)	7	6	6	10	29%	50%	50%	20%
AMERICAN INTERCONT GA (21136)	6	13	7	8	17%	38%	43%	13%
AUGUSTA ST UNIV (1552)	22	17	9	22	45%	53%	44%	41%
BERRY COLL (1554)	13	7	14	14	54%	43%	29%	50%

Appendix B: Section Performance by Institution Attended - All Testing Events

	Total Events per Section				Percent Pass			
	AUD	BEC	FAR	REG	AUD	BEC	FAR	REG
BRENAU UNIV (1556)	6	7	6	6	0%	29%	33%	67%
CLARK ATLANTA UNIV (1559)	13	12	11	16	38%	17%	0%	19%
CLAYTON ST UNIV (8976)	24	20	21	27	50%	40%	33%	41%
COLUMBUS ST UNIV (1561)	11	8	11	10	45%	38%	18%	30%
DEVRY UNIV ALPHARETTA (666989)	4	6	0	3	0%	0%	0%	0%
DEVRY UNIV DECATUR (9224)	11	9	7	5	27%	11%	0%	20%
EMORY UNIV (1564)	69	40	47	49	51%	78%	62%	65%
GA COLL & ST UNIV (1602)	26	33	21	32	35%	27%	43%	44%
GA INST TECH (1569)	54	42	55	54	54%	67%	64%	44%
GA SOUTHERN UNIV (1572)	88	88	89	108	51%	45%	43%	38%
GA SOUTHWESTERN ST UNIV (1573)	12	11	11	13	50%	36%	18%	62%
GA ST UNIV (1574)	253	184	203	260	39%	42%	41%	43%
KENNESAW ST UNIV (1577)	102	107	115	124	50%	37%	42%	47%
LAGRANGE COLL (1578)	3	4	1	3	0%	50%	0%	67%
MACON ST COLL (7728)	15	11	10	16	40%	55%	70%	31%
MERCER UNIV ATLANTA (8419)	4	5	6	7	0%	60%	33%	14%
MERCER UNIV MACON (1580)	18	17	16	28	44%	35%	44%	46%
MOREHOUSE COLL (1582)	10	10	14	10	40%	30%	36%	40%
NORTH GA COLL & ST UNIV (1585)	21	24	33	38	81%	42%	45%	32%
OGLETHORPE UNIV (1586)	14	9	17	17	71%	44%	47%	47%
SAVANNAH ST UNIV (1590)	2	5	2	3	0%	0%	0%	0%
SHORTER COLL (1591)	12	6	7	9	33%	33%	43%	33%
SOUTHERN POLYTECHNIC ST UNIV (1570)	4	2	4	4	25%	50%	50%	50%
SPELMAN COLL (1594)	4	1	4	2	25%	0%	50%	50%
UNIV GA (1598)	236	171	171	236	65%	79%	68%	62%
UNIV WEST GA (1601)	28	18	21	31	32%	39%	24%	19%
VALDOSTA ST UNIV (1599)	43	46	34	37	47%	35%	35%	51%
Guam								
UNIV GU (3935)	13	15	17	16	38%	27%	35%	25%
Hawaii								
BRIGHAM YOUNG UNIV HI (1606)	26	22	17	30	42%	55%	47%	40%
CHAMINADE UNIV HONOLULU (1605)	3	0	4	1	33%	0%	25%	0%
HI PACIFIC UNIV (7279)	34	25	28	31	35%	24%	36%	32%
UNIV HI HILO (1611)	4	8	6	4	50%	13%	50%	75%
UNIV HI MANOA (1610)	133	102	116	122	46%	32%	34%	44%
UNIV HI WEST OAHU (21078)	4	9	6	6	50%	11%	50%	50%
Idaho								
ALBERTSON COLL (1617)	7	5	6	5	29%	40%	33%	60%
BOISE ST UNIV (1616)	75	69	56	67	44%	41%	45%	46%
BRIGHAM YOUNG UNIV ID (1625)	58	43	51	51	45%	58%	49%	49%
ID ST UNIV (1620)	22	18	27	31	41%	56%	52%	42%
LEWIS CLARK ST COLL (1621)	14	16	9	8	36%	38%	44%	25%
UNIV ID (1626)	48	40	37	53	38%	53%	49%	40%
Illinois								
AMERICAN INTERCONT IL (666723)	9	11	4	6	11%	9%	0%	0%
AUGUSTANA COLL (1633)	14	8	15	11	57%	63%	60%	55%
AURORA UNIV (1634)	9	10	11	12	33%	30%	45%	42%
BENEDICTINE UNIV (1767)	16	17	19	19	31%	29%	32%	42%
BRADLEY UNIV (1641)	64	59	65	62	61%	61%	51%	61%
CHICAGO ST UNIV (1694)	15	9	15	17	20%	22%	27%	18%
DE PAUL UNIV (1671)	333	263	260	302	36%	40%	40%	39%

Appendix B: Section Performance by Institution Attended - All Testing Events

	Total Events per Section				Percent Pass			
	AUD	BEC	FAR	REG	AUD	BEC	FAR	REG
DEVRY UNIV ADDISON (22966)	26	19	25	31	23%	37%	44%	32%
DEVRY UNIV OAK BROOK TERRACE (1672)	25	16	18	23	12%	6%	11%	22%
DOMINCAN UNIV (1750)	21	17	16	17	24%	29%	13%	35%
EASTERN IL UNIV (1674)	37	41	37	42	49%	44%	51%	43%
ELMHURST COLL (1676)	22	22	21	26	45%	36%	33%	46%
GOVERNORS ST UNIV (9145)	28	22	24	33	32%	36%	38%	39%
IL COLL (1688)	6	4	6	5	33%	50%	17%	40%
IL INST TECH (1691)	5	3	9	3	80%	100%	44%	100%
IL ST UNIV (1692)	149	121	141	156	55%	64%	52%	49%
IL WESLEYAN UNIV (1696)	53	44	50	54	60%	77%	54%	48%
KELLER GRAD SCHOOL DEVRY (20754)	129	108	101	128	31%	25%	34%	34%
LEWIS UNIV (1707)	17	12	16	16	53%	33%	31%	56%
LOYOLA UNIV CHICAGO (1710)	155	99	141	151	45%	52%	39%	48%
MCKENDREE UNIVERSITY (1722)	10	9	10	12	50%	56%	40%	33%
MILLIKIN UNIV (1724)	17	17	14	24	29%	35%	57%	33%
MONMOUTH COLL (1725)	4	6	3	8	50%	67%	67%	13%
NATIONAL LOUIS UNIV (1733)	4	2	0	2	25%	0%	0%	0%
NORTH CENTRAL COLL (1734)	24	19	23	30	33%	74%	57%	33%
NORTH PARK UNIV (1735)	4	11	3	13	75%	55%	100%	31%
NORTHEASTERN IL UNIV (1693)	46	45	36	44	37%	31%	39%	45%
NORTHERN IL UNIV (1737)	232	228	208	261	50%	59%	55%	46%
NORTHWESTERN UNIV (1739)	19	15	16	16	53%	80%	56%	56%
OLIVET NAZARENE UNIV (1741)	9	7	10	7	78%	100%	50%	43%
QUINCY UNIV (1745)	5	2	5	6	40%	50%	60%	50%
ROBERT MORRIS COLL (1746)	23	12	12	19	35%	25%	42%	26%
ROCKFORD COLL (1748)	8	7	6	13	50%	86%	17%	46%
ROOSEVELT UNIV (1749)	43	38	51	41	44%	37%	33%	29%
SAINT XAVIER UNIV (1768)	11	6	9	10	36%	50%	44%	70%
SOUTHERN IL UNIV CARBONDALE (1758)	66	45	74	74	36%	51%	34%	42%
SOUTHERN IL UNIV EDWARDSVILLE (1759)	55	46	46	64	55%	59%	52%	47%
TRINITY CHRISTIAN COLL (1771)	9	7	3	10	56%	57%	67%	70%
UNIV CHICAGO (1774)	20	13	13	17	40%	77%	38%	59%
UNIV IL CHICAGO (1776)	369	283	352	391	54%	67%	55%	54%
UNIV IL SPRINGFIELD (9333)	41	19	33	28	29%	26%	30%	43%
UNIV IL URBANA CHAMPAIGN (1775)	416	333	411	401	51%	67%	51%	50%
UNIV SAINT FRANCIS (1664)	5	3	4	4	60%	33%	50%	50%
WESTERN IL UNIV (1780)	29	29	16	29	48%	45%	31%	31%
WHEATON COLL (1781)	6	8	4	8	67%	75%	75%	38%
Indiana								
ANDERSON UNIV (1785)	8	3	9	6	75%	67%	56%	83%
BALL ST UNIV (1786)	98	70	77	102	42%	40%	36%	36%
BETHEL COLL (IN) (1787)	12	5	5	10	42%	60%	80%	40%
BUTLER UNIV (1788)	46	45	47	49	59%	62%	45%	57%
FRANKLIN COLL IN (1798)	14	8	14	11	29%	25%	29%	36%
GOSHEN COLL (1799)	12	10	16	14	58%	100%	75%	50%
GRACE COLL & SEMINARY (1800)	18	5	9	10	39%	80%	67%	80%
HUNTINGTON COLL (1803)	2	4	3	5	50%	0%	33%	0%
IN INST TECH (1805)	8	6	8	6	25%	17%	25%	50%
IN ST UNIV (1807)	18	21	17	23	33%	38%	24%	22%
IN UNIV BLOOMINGTON (1809)	428	296	349	417	57%	75%	62%	51%
IN UNIV EAST (1811)	3	2	4	2	0%	0%	25%	0%

Appendix B: Section Performance by Institution Attended - All Testing Events

	Total Events per Section				Percent Pass			
	AUD	BEC	FAR	REG	AUD	BEC	FAR	REG
IN UNIV KOKOMO (1814)	6	3	8	7	33%	67%	50%	71%
IN UNIV NORTHWEST (1815)	9	7	10	7	44%	71%	20%	29%
IN UNIV- PURDUE UNIV - FORT WAYNE (1812)	7	5	8	1	43%	40%	38%	0%
IN UNIV PURDUE UNIV FORT WAYNE (1828)	24	9	20	22	42%	67%	55%	45%
IN UNIV PURDUE UNIV INDIANAPOLIS (1813)	111	95	111	108	43%	54%	41%	43%
IN UNIV SOUTH BEND (1816)	22	19	17	30	55%	47%	35%	33%
IN UNIV SOUTHEAST (1817)	22	14	20	14	36%	43%	30%	36%
IN WESLEYAN UNIV (1822)	31	26	31	31	45%	35%	32%	58%
MANCHESTER COLL (1820)	30	22	24	38	47%	50%	54%	42%
MARIAN COLL (1821)	10	13	9	13	40%	15%	33%	23%
OAKLAND CITY UNIV (1824)	4	5	5	7	50%	40%	40%	29%
PURDUE UNIV (1825)	263	159	192	229	34%	52%	39%	36%
PURDUE UNIV CALUMET (1827)	3	1	1	9	33%	100%	0%	44%
SAINT JOSEPHS COLL (1833)	7	8	4	6	57%	38%	50%	33%
SAINT MARYS COLL (1836)	31	19	21	29	32%	32%	33%	24%
TAYLOR UNIV (1838)	9	9	8	10	89%	67%	50%	50%
TRINE UNIV (1839)	2	6	7	8	0%	33%	71%	38%
UNIV EVANSVILLE (1795)	12	11	15	14	42%	45%	13%	36%
UNIV INDIANAPOLIS (1804)	19	18	29	20	37%	39%	28%	40%
UNIV NOTRE DAME (1840)	223	172	202	255	73%	83%	67%	60%
UNIV SOUTHERN IN (1808)	34	22	30	30	44%	41%	40%	43%
UNIV ST FRANCIS (1832)	8	9	3	6	25%	33%	0%	50%
VALPARAISO UNIV (1842)	13	17	19	17	38%	53%	37%	29%
Iowa								
AIB COLL BUSINESS (3963)	9	6	6	6	22%	33%	33%	33%
BRIAR CLIFF UNIV (1846)	3	6	6	4	67%	50%	33%	75%
BUENA VISTA UNIV (1847)	17	13	15	9	41%	0%	27%	44%
CLARKE COLL (1852)	3	2	4	4	33%	100%	50%	25%
COE COLL (1854)	8	8	7	6	38%	50%	43%	50%
DORDT COLL (1859)	7	4	6	8	71%	75%	50%	63%
DRAKE UNIV (1860)	38	27	26	42	53%	70%	50%	48%
GRACELAND UNIV (1866)	5	2	4	5	40%	0%	0%	40%
GRAND VIEW UNIV (1867)	4	2	2	6	50%	100%	0%	33%
IA ST UNIV (1869)	132	96	100	112	42%	65%	57%	49%
IA WESLEYAN COLL (1871)	5	5	4	2	20%	40%	50%	100%
KAPLAN UNIV (4586)	12	16	13	13	17%	19%	31%	31%
LORAS COLL (1873)	12	10	8	18	42%	70%	63%	44%
LUTHER COLL (1874)	25	16	17	19	32%	81%	47%	42%
MAHARISHI UNIV MANAGEMENT (11113)	6	4	3	4	33%	50%	67%	50%
MORNINGSIDE COLL (1879)	4	3	8	7	50%	33%	63%	29%
MOUNT MERCY COLL (1880)	5	3	5	1	40%	33%	60%	100%
MOUNT SAINT CLARE COLL (1881)	3	3	6	4	67%	33%	0%	25%
NORTHWESTERN COLL IA (1883)	7	9	11	17	43%	56%	36%	47%
SAINT AMBROSE UNIV (1889)	25	13	17	20	28%	38%	53%	55%
SIMPSON COLL (1887)	16	11	10	12	44%	36%	50%	33%
UNIV DUBUQUE (1891)	19	12	15	17	26%	33%	20%	29%
UNIV IA (1892)	177	124	159	162	55%	74%	64%	68%
UNIV NORTHERN IA (1890)	113	108	110	123	62%	58%	60%	57%
UPPER IA UNIV (1893)	19	33	21	22	26%	36%	19%	32%
WARTBURG COLL (1896)	4	7	4	7	75%	71%	50%	43%

Appendix B: Section Performance by Institution Attended - All Testing Events

	Total Events per Section				Percent Pass			
	AUD	BEC	FAR	REG	AUD	BEC	FAR	REG
Kansas								
BAKER UNIV (1903)	7	13	9	9	14%	31%	11%	11%
BENEDICTINE COLL (10256)	10	8	9	7	10%	50%	33%	43%
EMPORIA ST UNIV (1927)	29	23	22	27	41%	30%	27%	30%
FORT HAYS ST UNIV (1915)	29	30	27	34	31%	37%	19%	38%
FRIENDS UNIV (1918)	5	3	6	7	20%	33%	33%	57%
KANSAS STATE UNIVERSITY (1928)	82	75	69	91	61%	64%	64%	49%
NEWMAN UNIV (1939)	8	6	3	7	38%	33%	0%	29%
OTTAWA UNIV (1937)	10	5	4	10	40%	20%	25%	40%
PITTSBURG ST UNIV (1926)	25	15	24	18	44%	40%	33%	17%
SOUTHWESTERN COLL (1940)	2	4	1	4	100%	0%	100%	50%
UNIV KS (1948)	227	135	164	187	48%	71%	55%	59%
WASHBURN UNIV (1949)	26	24	40	47	38%	67%	35%	47%
WICHITA ST UNIV (1950)	46	45	38	45	48%	44%	50%	53%
Kentucky								
ASBURY COLL (1952)	6	4	4	4	17%	100%	25%	50%
BELLARMINE UNIV (1954)	37	24	22	28	51%	63%	50%	50%
BEREA COLL (1955)	4	6	2	7	25%	83%	100%	43%
BRESCIA UNIV (1958)	5	10	8	4	0%	10%	63%	25%
EASTERN KY UNIV (1963)	24	14	16	17	50%	50%	44%	41%
GEORGETOWN COLL (1964)	6	5	6	7	33%	40%	33%	14%
KY ST UNIV (1968)	9	4	7	4	11%	0%	0%	0%
KY WESLEYAN COLL (1969)	7	10	3	3	43%	50%	33%	67%
LINDSEY WILSON COLL (1972)	5	8	5	10	40%	38%	60%	20%
MOREHEAD ST UNIV (1976)	14	11	15	13	43%	45%	40%	46%
MURRAY ST UNIV (1977)	41	27	37	40	37%	44%	46%	48%
NORTHERN KY UNIV (9275)	54	47	53	42	31%	51%	47%	38%
PIKEVILLE COLL (1980)	0	4	1	5	0%	50%	100%	60%
SPALDING UNIV (1960)	4	6	3	6	50%	33%	33%	50%
SULLIVAN UNIV (4619)	12	10	12	10	25%	20%	33%	20%
THOMAS MORE COLL (2001)	14	13	9	7	29%	15%	44%	29%
TRANSYLVANIA UNIV (1987)	21	15	23	13	67%	53%	35%	54%
UNIV KY (1989)	170	130	136	166	49%	52%	50%	54%
UNIV LOUISVILLE (1999)	81	63	76	72	42%	49%	30%	46%
UNIV OF CUMBERLANDS (1962)	5	2	0	2	60%	50%	0%	50%
WESTERN KY UNIV (2002)	48	41	40	53	48%	56%	58%	62%
Louisiana								
CENTENARY COLL LA (2003)	11	6	7	3	27%	50%	57%	33%
DILLARD UNIV (2004)	7	7	6	4	29%	0%	0%	0%
GRAMBLING ST UNIV (2006)	10	13	11	9	40%	8%	27%	22%
LA COLL (2007)	2	1	2	2	50%	100%	50%	50%
LA ST UNIV AND A & M COLL (2010)	211	178	186	243	57%	54%	46%	46%
LA ST UNIV IN SHREVEPORT (2013)	18	18	17	14	33%	39%	24%	79%
LA TECH UNIV (2008)	46	41	44	50	46%	46%	45%	44%
LOYOLA UNIV NEW ORLEANS (2016)	20	20	27	25	55%	55%	56%	48%
MCNEESE ST UNIV (2017)	34	36	37	26	41%	39%	38%	46%
NICHOLLS ST UNIV (2005)	20	14	24	26	40%	36%	50%	46%
NORTHWESTERN ST UNIV (2021)	17	15	11	18	41%	40%	18%	44%
OUR LADY HOLY CROSS COLL (2023)	8	5	8	7	0%	0%	0%	14%
SOUTHEASTERN LA UNIV (2024)	89	78	83	84	36%	29%	30%	37%
SOUTHERN UNIV A&M BATON ROUGE (9636)	18	23	11	12	50%	9%	27%	17%

Appendix B: Section Performance by Institution Attended - All Testing Events

	Total Events per Section				Percent Pass			
	AUD	BEC	FAR	REG	AUD	BEC	FAR	REG
SOUTHERN UNIV NEW ORLEANS (2026)	3	5	0	2	0%	0%	0%	50%
TULANE UNIV LA (2029)	63	45	73	83	59%	67%	58%	51%
UNIV LA LAFAYETTE (2031)	58	68	58	68	57%	41%	55%	62%
UNIV LA MONROE (2020)	30	34	22	32	43%	32%	45%	22%
UNIV NEW ORLEANS (2015)	78	75	99	82	44%	36%	36%	41%
XAVIER UNIV LA (2032)	3	1	5	0	0%	100%	0%	0%
Maine								
COLBY COLL (2039)	5	4	1	4	60%	50%	0%	50%
HUSSON UNIV (2043)	20	11	17	21	25%	27%	24%	24%
SAINT JOSEPHS COLL (2051)	5	2	2	4	20%	100%	50%	25%
THOMAS COLL (2052)	10	7	11	11	70%	43%	18%	55%
UNIV ME (2053)	20	12	22	27	60%	75%	55%	56%
UNIV ME AUGUSTA (6760)	3	2	4	3	67%	50%	75%	67%
UNIV SOUTHERN ME (2054)	16	27	14	20	56%	44%	43%	60%
Maryland								
BOWIE ST UNIV (2062)	16	8	10	4	0%	13%	10%	25%
FROSTBURG ST UNIV (2072)	8	6	3	3	38%	17%	33%	100%
JOHNS HOPKINS UNIV (2077)	11	8	10	7	45%	25%	30%	43%
LOYOLA UNIVERSITY MD (2078)	51	42	39	58	51%	55%	51%	38%
MORGAN ST UNIV (2083)	4	8	5	4	50%	0%	0%	50%
MOUNT SAINT MARYS UNIV (2086)	3	7	2	3	67%	43%	50%	33%
SALISBURY UNIV (2091)	11	11	7	15	55%	45%	29%	53%
TOWSON UNIV (2099)	31	32	35	28	58%	50%	40%	43%
UNIV BALTIMORE (2102)	10	11	13	16	40%	18%	46%	31%
UNIV MD BALTIMORE COUNTY (2105)	16	8	8	12	25%	25%	38%	8%
UNIV MD COLL PARK (2103)	164	105	129	160	49%	63%	48%	45%
UNIV MD EASTERN SHORE (2106)	5	4	0	3	40%	25%	0%	0%
UNIV MD UNIV COLL (11644)	83	74	69	75	42%	34%	38%	35%
Massachusetts								
AMERICAN INTL COLL (2114)	6	5	7	4	67%	60%	43%	50%
ASSUMPTION COLL (2118)	44	43	36	42	41%	40%	39%	38%
BABSON COLL (2121)	68	54	64	97	50%	65%	50%	38%
BENTLEY COLL (2124)	304	230	271	269	46%	60%	47%	49%
BOSTON COLL (2128)	178	141	159	174	63%	83%	68%	65%
BOSTON UNIV (2130)	94	75	79	106	59%	68%	66%	52%
BRANDEIS UNIV (2133)	6	4	3	1	67%	75%	67%	100%
BRIDGEWATER ST COLL (2183)	17	14	14	19	53%	29%	43%	42%
CLARK UNIV (2139)	12	11	13	14	58%	73%	46%	64%
COLL HOLY CROSS (2141)	33	23	27	28	61%	83%	63%	54%
COLL OUR LADY OF THE ELMS (2140)	6	4	0	5	0%	25%	0%	0%
CURRY COLL (2143)	5	3	4	3	40%	67%	50%	33%
FITCHBURG ST COLL (2184)	8	4	2	5	38%	0%	0%	0%
GORDON COLL (2153)	8	6	3	11	25%	50%	33%	18%
LASELL COLL (2158)	4	4	3	3	0%	0%	33%	33%
MA INST TECH (2178)	5	4	3	5	100%	100%	100%	80%
MERRIMACK COLL (2120)	21	22	26	26	43%	14%	35%	38%
NICHOLS COLL (2197)	10	13	9	12	40%	23%	22%	25%
NORTHEASTERN UNIV (2199)	211	186	201	219	51%	49%	42%	47%
SALEM ST UNIV (2188)	29	16	22	21	31%	31%	32%	19%
STONEHILL COLL (2217)	33	26	33	30	58%	65%	45%	43%
SUFFOLK UNIV (2218)	89	65	75	95	35%	45%	32%	39%

Appendix B: Section Performance by Institution Attended - All Testing Events

	Total Events per Section				Percent Pass			
	AUD	BEC	FAR	REG	AUD	BEC	FAR	REG
TUFTS UNIV (2219)	8	4	3	6	63%	100%	100%	67%
UNIV MA AMHERST (2221)	161	143	163	188	50%	55%	44%	38%
UNIV MA BOSTON (2222)	61	51	61	62	44%	31%	36%	34%
UNIV MA DARTMOUTH (2210)	33	34	28	40	36%	32%	50%	43%
UNIV MA LOWELL (2161)	25	23	24	30	56%	61%	50%	37%
WESTERN NEW ENGLAND COLL (2226)	28	31	42	20	54%	32%	36%	45%
WESTFIELD ST COLL (2189)	7	7	7	10	43%	57%	43%	40%
WORCESTER ST COLL (2190)	10	8	9	10	30%	0%	22%	30%
Michigan								
ALBION COLL (2235)	17	15	17	16	47%	60%	41%	38%
ALMA COLL (2236)	9	10	6	7	44%	50%	50%	43%
ANDREWS UNIV (2238)	8	9	12	9	25%	56%	33%	22%
AQUINAS COLL (2239)	16	12	10	13	31%	42%	10%	46%
BAKER COLL FLINT (4673)	17	10	15	12	24%	40%	47%	50%
CALVIN COLL (2241)	38	26	35	39	61%	62%	60%	56%
CENTRAL MI UNIV (2243)	110	80	93	97	50%	51%	47%	51%
DAVENPORT UNIV (2249)	33	32	34	35	42%	41%	47%	34%
EASTERN MI UNIV (2259)	93	69	67	63	42%	46%	42%	44%
FERRIS ST UNIV (2260)	25	27	24	25	56%	56%	58%	44%
GRAND VALLEY ST UNIV (2268)	123	88	104	103	59%	78%	60%	65%
HILLSDALE COLL (2272)	14	12	16	14	36%	58%	19%	43%
HOPE COLL (2273)	19	20	17	20	42%	35%	47%	40%
LAKE SUPERIOR ST UNIV (2293)	11	14	18	12	45%	36%	33%	50%
MI ST UNIV (2290)	315	241	290	297	58%	68%	58%	60%
MI TECH UNIV (2292)	15	12	11	12	53%	67%	82%	58%
NORTHERN MI UNIV (2301)	22	12	15	19	18%	25%	20%	53%
NORTHWOOD UNIV (4072)	46	40	48	37	37%	48%	44%	35%
OAKLAND UNIV (2307)	75	61	65	68	49%	56%	54%	50%
SAGINAW VALLEY ST UNIV (2314)	33	27	36	33	36%	30%	36%	33%
SIENA HEIGHTS UNIV (2316)	11	9	11	7	36%	44%	45%	29%
SPRING ARBOR UNIV (2318)	3	5	5	10	33%	20%	40%	20%
UNIV DETROIT MERCY (2323)	2	1	5	3	50%	0%	0%	33%
UNIV MI ANN ARBOR (2325)	120	76	105	120	68%	84%	74%	68%
UNIV MI DEARBORN (2326)	61	48	59	57	56%	54%	56%	54%
UNIV MI FLINT (2327)	17	15	20	14	53%	20%	35%	21%
WALSH COLL (4071)	112	68	91	95	51%	53%	49%	48%
WAYNE ST UNIV (2329)	74	64	62	74	57%	44%	44%	41%
WESTERN MI UNIV (2330)	121	90	112	101	46%	44%	32%	40%
Minnesota								
AUGSBURG COLL (2334)	27	22	22	22	37%	50%	23%	55%
BEMIDJI ST UNIV (2336)	11	14	12	13	36%	29%	58%	54%
BETHEL COLL (MN) (9058)	16	17	16	17	56%	71%	63%	47%
COLL OF SAINT BENEDICT (2341)	15	11	11	14	67%	100%	91%	79%
COLL OF SAINT SCHOLASTICA (2343)	13	7	12	11	62%	29%	42%	45%
CONCORDIA COLL MOORHEAD (2346)	29	22	23	30	62%	73%	74%	53%
CONCORDIA UNIV MN (2347)	4	4	6	2	50%	25%	17%	50%
GUSTAVUS ADOLPHUS COLL (2353)	11	16	15	12	64%	44%	53%	25%
HAMLINE UNIV (2354)	7	3	5	6	43%	100%	40%	50%
METROPOLITAN ST UNIV (10374)	44	40	45	55	36%	45%	40%	36%
MN SCHOOL OF BUSINESS (4646)	5	6	4	6	40%	50%	25%	33%
MN ST UNIV MANKATO (2360)	71	52	70	70	46%	50%	47%	40%

Appendix B: Section Performance by Institution Attended - All Testing Events

	Total Events per Section				Percent Pass			
	AUD	BEC	FAR	REG	AUD	BEC	FAR	REG
MN ST UNIV MOORHEAD (2367)	28	24	26	23	43%	54%	31%	35%
NORTHWESTERN COLL MN (2371)	8	8	11	13	50%	63%	73%	46%
SAINT CATHERINE UNIV (2342)	6	4	6	6	67%	75%	50%	33%
SAINT CLOUD ST UNIV (2377)	76	81	75	75	63%	53%	63%	61%
SAINT JOHN'S UNIV (2379)	53	35	47	51	53%	71%	51%	49%
SAINT MARY'S UNIV OF MN (2380)	14	12	15	18	50%	33%	40%	28%
SOUTHWEST ST UNIV (2375)	11	6	10	8	45%	67%	50%	88%
UNIV MN DULUTH (2388)	62	59	63	73	40%	56%	46%	47%
UNIV MN TWIN CITIES (3969)	165	119	167	173	61%	75%	57%	55%
UNIV ST THOMAS (2345)	114	91	79	105	42%	60%	52%	42%
WINONA ST UNIV (2394)	35	38	44	31	40%	34%	30%	26%
Mississippi								
ALCORN ST UNIV (2396)	4	2	1	1	25%	50%	0%	0%
BELHAVEN COLL (2397)	11	7	10	15	36%	29%	40%	27%
DELTA ST UNIV (2403)	12	16	12	8	33%	19%	25%	50%
JACKSON ST UNIV (2410)	33	29	28	19	18%	21%	14%	11%
MILLSAPS COLL (2414)	23	21	24	28	57%	48%	42%	54%
MS COLL (2415)	32	28	22	25	25%	32%	41%	40%
MS ST UNIV (2423)	89	95	101	106	44%	44%	41%	44%
MS UNIV FOR WOMEN (2422)	10	4	6	5	50%	50%	17%	0%
UNIV MS (2440)	167	135	122	162	45%	59%	52%	54%
UNIV SOUTHERN MS (2441)	59	49	49	54	39%	27%	35%	37%
Missouri								
AVILA UNIV (2449)	9	8	7	5	33%	38%	43%	80%
CENTRAL METHODIST UNIV (2453)	8	6	5	12	38%	17%	20%	42%
COLL OF OZARKS (2500)	4	1	7	7	50%	0%	14%	29%
COLUMBIA COLL (2456)	21	13	17	19	33%	31%	47%	37%
CULVER STOCKTON COLL (2460)	9	7	7	6	56%	71%	43%	67%
DEVRY UNIV KANSAS CITY (2455)	9	9	10	11	22%	11%	30%	9%
DRURY UNIV (2461)	35	27	25	28	31%	52%	44%	36%
EVANGEL UNIV (2463)	6	6	5	4	67%	67%	60%	75%
FONTBONNE UNIV (2464)	8	9	6	11	13%	33%	33%	27%
LINCOLN UNIV (2479)	10	9	10	8	0%	22%	10%	13%
LINDENWOOD UNIV (2480)	27	21	14	18	22%	52%	36%	33%
MARYVILLE UNIV ST. LOUIS (2482)	26	22	24	20	35%	45%	42%	30%
MO BAPTIST UNIV (7540)	5	3	4	4	20%	33%	50%	0%
MO SOUTHERN ST UNIV (2488)	10	12	9	11	60%	58%	56%	45%
MO ST UNIV (2503)	95	74	91	86	43%	50%	51%	59%
MO VALLEY COLL (2489)	3	5	4	4	100%	40%	50%	25%
MO WESTERN ST UNIV (2490)	12	9	8	9	25%	11%	0%	22%
NORTHWEST MO ST UNIV (2496)	13	14	13	22	62%	50%	92%	55%
PARK UNIV (2498)	26	15	17	19	38%	40%	29%	32%
ROCKHURST UNIV (2499)	18	16	19	23	50%	44%	53%	30%
SOUTHEAST MO ST UNIV (2501)	32	12	30	30	44%	58%	37%	43%
SOUTHWEST BAPTIST UNIV (2502)	21	17	15	19	48%	41%	40%	26%
ST. LOUIS UNIV (2506)	90	88	88	92	50%	61%	51%	51%
TRUMAN ST UNIV (2495)	94	74	79	90	59%	91%	71%	68%
UNIV CENTRAL MO (2454)	48	30	45	35	38%	63%	38%	49%
UNIV MO COLUMBIA (2516)	169	130	156	171	58%	80%	67%	60%
UNIV MO KANSAS CITY (2518)	51	37	37	51	69%	59%	57%	63%
UNIV MO ST. LOUIS (2519)	82	55	71	70	40%	44%	45%	63%

Appendix B: Section Performance by Institution Attended - All Testing Events

	Total Events per Section				Percent Pass			
	AUD	BEC	FAR	REG	AUD	BEC	FAR	REG
WASHINGTON UNIV ST. LOUIS (2520)	45	29	35	44	78%	83%	69%	59%
WEBSTER UNIV (2521)	28	18	23	30	18%	28%	30%	30%
WESTMINSTER COLL (2523)	9	6	14	10	11%	50%	36%	10%
WILLIAM WOODS UNIV (2525)	2	3	2	3	0%	33%	0%	67%
Montana								
CARROLL COLL (MT) (2526)	15	18	15	12	40%	22%	40%	17%
MT ST UNIV BILLINGS (2530)	21	29	24	24	33%	24%	29%	42%
MT ST UNIV BOZEMAN (2532)	56	41	44	63	54%	49%	66%	48%
MT TECH UNIV (2531)	7	4	4	1	43%	25%	50%	0%
ROCKY MOUNTAIN COLL (2534)	3	4	2	5	100%	50%	50%	60%
UNIV MT (2536)	63	53	53	65	52%	60%	64%	55%
Nebraska								
BELLEVUE UNIV (9743)	16	10	15	20	50%	40%	33%	30%
CHADRON ST COLL (2539)	4	5	3	2	50%	40%	33%	50%
CREIGHTON UNIV (2542)	45	37	41	45	40%	65%	49%	44%
DOANE COLL (2544)	18	11	13	15	33%	36%	54%	40%
HASTINGS COLL (2548)	13	11	12	11	54%	27%	25%	27%
MIDLAND LUTHERAN COLL (2553)	13	18	17	16	38%	44%	47%	38%
NE WESLEYAN UNIV (2555)	8	9	13	13	63%	78%	62%	62%
PERU ST COLL (2559)	8	3	7	2	63%	100%	29%	100%
UNION COLL (2563)	6	3	3	3	33%	33%	67%	33%
UNIV NE KEARNEY (2551)	25	20	18	11	48%	30%	39%	45%
UNIV NE LINCOLN (2565)	71	68	77	75	46%	65%	52%	47%
UNIV NE OMAHA (2554)	42	24	47	34	50%	63%	62%	56%
WAYNE ST COLL (2566)	11	6	12	9	45%	50%	33%	56%
YORK COLL (2567)	8	3	8	5	25%	67%	25%	20%
Nevada								
UNIV NV LAS VEGAS (2569)	136	99	124	135	46%	38%	37%	51%
UNIV NV RENO (2568)	70	54	60	59	41%	35%	33%	44%
New Hampshire								
NEW ENGLAND COLL (2579)	3	4	5	1	100%	50%	20%	0%
PLYMOUTH ST UNIV (2591)	7	9	12	7	29%	67%	33%	57%
SAINT ANSELM COLL (2587)	18	6	11	10	44%	67%	27%	20%
SOUTHERN NH UNIV (2580)	37	29	31	31	41%	38%	32%	39%
UNIV NH (2589)	68	36	49	60	54%	72%	55%	45%
New Jersey								
BERKELEY COLL (7502)	6	6	8	6	17%	0%	13%	17%
BETH MEDRASH GOVOHA (7947)	17	15	13	10	47%	40%	31%	60%
BLOOMFIELD COLL (2597)	2	3	4	6	0%	33%	50%	33%
CALDWELL COLL (2598)	8	11	8	8	38%	18%	38%	63%
CENTENARY COLL (2599)	10	5	8	8	20%	20%	25%	38%
COLL NJ (2642)	85	65	75	102	58%	65%	65%	53%
FAIRLEIGH DICKINSON UNIV (2607)	52	51	52	62	38%	47%	37%	50%
FAIRLEIGH DICKINSON UNIV MADISON (4738)	13	21	14	18	54%	43%	36%	33%
FAIRLEIGH DICKINSON UNIV RUTHERFORD (2604)	21	19	16	23	52%	21%	38%	39%
FELICIAN COLL (2610)	7	4	4	5	14%	0%	0%	0%
GEORGIAN COURT UNIV (2608)	18	9	13	11	39%	22%	38%	18%
KEAN UNIV (2622)	54	59	44	68	28%	20%	30%	34%
MONMOUTH UNIV (2616)	68	72	54	57	24%	36%	22%	39%
MONTCLAIR ST UNIV (2617)	148	127	110	140	38%	32%	36%	30%
NJ CITY UNIV (2613)	24	23	23	25	33%	13%	22%	36%

Appendix B: Section Performance by Institution Attended - All Testing Events

	Total Events per Section				Percent Pass			
	AUD	BEC	FAR	REG	AUD	BEC	FAR	REG
NJ INST TECH (2621)	1	2	3	1	100%	0%	0%	100%
QUALIFYING CERTIFICATE (88822)	6	2	2	5	33%	0%	50%	40%
RAMAPO COLL NJ (9344)	69	65	66	75	39%	42%	33%	39%
RICHARD STOCKTON COLL NJ (9345)	48	46	34	43	38%	41%	47%	44%
RIDER UNIV (2628)	98	89	86	82	29%	26%	20%	35%
ROWAN UNIV (2609)	65	62	58	58	46%	34%	48%	41%
RUTGERS ST UNIV CAMDEN (4741)	58	56	78	71	40%	38%	37%	38%
RUTGERS ST UNIV NEW BRUNSWICK (6964)	172	142	155	146	42%	37%	39%	40%
RUTGERS ST UNIV NEWARK (2631)	208	178	221	219	41%	38%	36%	38%
SAINT PETERS COLL (2638)	24	26	25	28	17%	27%	28%	36%
SETON HALL UNIV (2632)	60	60	66	71	40%	33%	27%	28%
THOMAS EDISON ST COLL (21922)	15	12	10	7	53%	50%	50%	71%
WILLIAM PATERSON UNIV NJ (2625)	42	42	43	34	26%	21%	28%	41%
New Mexico								
COLL SANTA FE (2649)	5	2	3	3	0%	0%	0%	0%
EASTERN NM UNIV (2651)	9	7	9	8	44%	29%	22%	63%
NM HIGHLANDS UNIV (2653)	3	4	4	7	33%	50%	25%	43%
NM ST UNIV (2657)	36	38	49	49	44%	37%	24%	33%
SAINT JOHNS COLL (2093)	3	1	4	5	33%	100%	50%	20%
UNIV NM (2663)	81	75	88	89	48%	41%	31%	42%
WESTERN NM UNIV (2664)	8	6	9	8	50%	17%	11%	13%
New York								
ADELPHI UNIV (2666)	26	35	27	37	27%	31%	19%	32%
ALFRED UNIV (2668)	7	2	10	5	29%	50%	30%	40%
AMERICAN UNIV IN CAIRO (5034)	4	1	3	2	25%	0%	33%	0%
BARNARD COLL (2708)	2	2	3	2	0%	0%	67%	100%
BERKELEY COLL NY (7394)	12	13	9	15	25%	0%	22%	27%
CANISIUS COLL (2681)	49	37	31	47	57%	68%	65%	55%
CLARKSON UNIV (2699)	9	3	3	4	56%	33%	67%	50%
COLGATE UNIV (2701)	5	1	2	1	40%	100%	50%	100%
COLL SAINT ROSE (2705)	17	14	20	11	53%	36%	15%	55%
COLUMBIA UNIV NY (2707)	15	11	8	8	60%	100%	88%	75%
CONCORDIA COLL (2709)	2	1	5	2	50%	0%	40%	0%
CORNELL UNIV (2711)	43	31	33	40	77%	84%	52%	73%
CUNY BARUCH (7273)	573	417	520	516	43%	41%	42%	47%
CUNY BROOKLYN (2687)	140	122	108	125	39%	30%	42%	36%
CUNY HERBERT H LEHMAN (7022)	31	37	30	29	26%	8%	23%	31%
CUNY HUNTER (2689)	99	79	77	88	29%	20%	32%	36%
CUNY MEDGAR EVERS (10097)	15	12	16	11	20%	0%	6%	18%
CUNY QUEENS (2690)	205	170	147	171	38%	24%	32%	32%
CUNY STATEN ISLAND (2698)	5	4	1	5	40%	25%	0%	60%
CUNY STATEN ISLAND (29040)	43	38	29	31	28%	32%	31%	29%
CUNY YORK COLL (4759)	12	15	9	14	33%	7%	11%	14%
DAEMEN COLL (2808)	17	10	13	13	41%	50%	15%	54%
DOWLING COLL (2667)	10	17	9	15	20%	18%	33%	33%
ELMIRA COLL (2718)	9	5	5	6	67%	80%	60%	67%
EXCELSIOR COLL (2834)	29	21	33	19	41%	43%	45%	53%
FORDHAM UNIV (2722)	142	128	140	127	44%	45%	39%	39%
HARTWICK COLL (2729)	9	12	6	13	33%	42%	17%	31%
HOFSTRA UNIV (2732)	148	132	127	130	39%	32%	30%	46%
HOUGHTON COLL (2734)	3	2	2	3	100%	50%	100%	33%

Appendix B: Section Performance by Institution Attended - All Testing Events

	Total Events per Section				Percent Pass			
	AUD	BEC	FAR	REG	AUD	BEC	FAR	REG
IONA COLL (2737)	30	37	35	27	43%	30%	17%	30%
ITHACA COLL (2739)	29	25	29	25	52%	60%	38%	36%
LE MOYNE COLL (2748)	35	40	38	35	34%	33%	42%	34%
LONG ISLAND UNIV BROOKLYN CENTER (4779)	14	19	9	13	7%	11%	33%	38%
LONG ISLAND UNIV CW POST (2754)	70	58	46	65	36%	31%	35%	38%
MANHATTAN COLL (2758)	31	35	40	35	35%	31%	20%	11%
MARIST COLL (2765)	37	36	39	42	46%	42%	38%	40%
MERCY COLL (2772)	14	13	13	13	29%	23%	38%	46%
MOLLOY COLL (2775)	7	13	8	13	14%	15%	13%	38%
MONROE COLL (4799)	20	19	15	19	10%	0%	7%	11%
MOUNT SAINT MARY COLL (2778)	7	3	4	5	0%	0%	0%	20%
NAZARETH COLL ROCHESTER (2779)	6	7	12	15	83%	71%	75%	47%
NIAGARA UNIV (2788)	29	31	28	37	34%	32%	29%	30%
NY INST TECH MANHATTAN (2782)	24	11	13	10	8%	27%	31%	50%
NY INST TECH OLD WESTBURY (4804)	4	9	6	7	0%	11%	17%	57%
NY UNIV (2785)	146	98	135	166	57%	81%	59%	45%
NYACK COLL (2790)	3	3	5	3	67%	33%	20%	67%
PACE UNIV NY (2791)	147	129	162	164	35%	40%	29%	34%
PACE UNIV PLEASANTVILLE (2792)	45	41	36	49	38%	41%	33%	27%
PACE UNIV WHITE PLAINS (2727)	6	8	3	10	83%	63%	33%	20%
POLYTECH UNIV (2796)	3	2	2	4	67%	50%	50%	25%
ROBERTS WESLEYAN COLL (2805)	5	3	3	0	40%	33%	0%	0%
ROCHESTER INST TECH (2806)	28	18	30	23	32%	50%	40%	26%
SAINT BONAVENTURE UNIV (2817)	42	30	38	44	43%	57%	26%	41%
SAINT FRANCIS COLL (2820)	21	13	12	17	48%	15%	58%	29%
SAINT JOHN FISHER COLL (2821)	30	34	29	33	53%	44%	41%	42%
SAINT JOHNS UNIV NEW YORK (2823)	209	189	175	159	27%	31%	33%	36%
SAINT JOSEPHS COLL NY (2825)	8	10	4	6	63%	30%	25%	50%
SAINT JOSEPHS COLL SUFFOLK (29081)	14	11	10	10	21%	36%	30%	50%
SAINT THOMAS AQUINAS COLL (2832)	8	7	12	7	38%	29%	17%	0%
SIENA COLL (2816)	69	59	57	59	43%	46%	33%	41%
SKIDMORE COLL (2814)	5	6	5	3	20%	50%	60%	33%
SUNY OLD WESTBURY (7109)	60	40	51	57	28%	35%	27%	46%
SUNY ALBANY (2835)	183	127	150	154	38%	48%	42%	44%
SUNY BINGHAMTON (2836)	256	168	236	258	46%	54%	44%	43%
SUNY BROCKPORT (2841)	27	37	37	30	48%	43%	41%	47%
SUNY BUFFALO (2837)	149	128	167	153	59%	59%	47%	53%
SUNY BUFFALO (2842)	9	6	8	6	67%	33%	63%	67%
SUNY EMPIRE ST COLL (10286)	10	9	9	7	50%	56%	56%	57%
SUNY FREDONIA (2844)	13	9	10	15	46%	67%	60%	60%
SUNY GENESEO (2845)	54	53	69	64	52%	60%	54%	50%
SUNY INST TECH UTICA ROME (11678)	8	5	7	5	0%	20%	29%	20%
SUNY NEW PALTZ (2846)	28	32	33	37	54%	53%	52%	49%
SUNY ONEONTA (2847)	20	18	17	12	50%	33%	24%	75%
SUNY OSWEGO (2848)	45	50	41	46	40%	38%	32%	33%
SUNY PLATTSBURGH (2849)	40	24	28	32	23%	38%	18%	31%
SUNY STONY BROOK (2838)	33	27	35	37	39%	56%	34%	43%
SUNY UTICA-ROME (6792)	2	2	4	2	100%	50%	50%	50%
SYRACUSE UNIV (2882)	142	121	112	172	41%	48%	42%	34%
TOURO COLL (10142)	87	77	68	74	51%	45%	56%	53%
UNION COLL (2889)	3	3	3	2	33%	67%	67%	100%

Appendix B: Section Performance by Institution Attended - All Testing Events

	Total Events per Section				Percent Pass			
	AUD	BEC	FAR	REG	AUD	BEC	FAR	REG
UNIV ROCHESTER (2894)	14	9	13	11	71%	78%	54%	55%
UTICA COLL (2883)	12	11	9	13	42%	45%	56%	38%
VASSAR COLL (2895)	2	1	4	4	50%	100%	100%	50%
WAGNER COLL (2899)	33	26	28	18	27%	38%	29%	33%
YESHIVA UNIV (2903)	72	60	80	81	43%	47%	39%	38%
North Carolina								
APPALACHIAN ST UNIV (2906)	85	91	91	84	60%	55%	48%	49%
BARTON COLL (2908)	5	3	8	5	40%	0%	38%	20%
BELMONT ABBEY COLL (2910)	4	5	3	2	50%	0%	0%	0%
CAMPBELL UNIV (2913)	32	20	30	33	50%	40%	50%	36%
CATAWBA COLL (2914)	4	7	6	5	25%	43%	33%	60%
DAVIDSON COLL (2918)	8	6	9	6	88%	83%	67%	83%
DUKE UNIV (2920)	10	5	7	14	70%	100%	71%	43%
EAST CAROLINA UNIV (2923)	118	84	96	118	45%	50%	42%	36%
ELIZABETH CITY ST UNIV (2926)	6	2	3	3	0%	0%	0%	0%
ELON UNIV (2927)	62	50	72	73	42%	60%	33%	41%
FAYETTEVILLE ST UNIV (2928)	5	2	3	4	40%	0%	0%	0%
GARDNER WEBB UNIV (2929)	13	9	10	16	31%	22%	60%	50%
GREENSBORO COLL (2930)	6	5	7	6	50%	40%	29%	33%
GUILFORD COLL (2931)	8	9	8	5	50%	44%	63%	40%
HIGH POINT UNIV (2933)	18	11	23	15	44%	27%	30%	33%
LENOIR RHYNE COLL (2941)	11	9	7	5	27%	44%	57%	20%
MEREDITH COLL (2945)	8	8	8	7	13%	50%	50%	71%
METHODIST UNIV (2946)	3	4	5	2	33%	0%	40%	0%
MOUNT OLIVE COLL (2949)	4	3	4	4	0%	33%	0%	0%
NC AGRICULTURAL & TECH ST UNIV (2905)	23	31	26	37	43%	32%	23%	32%
NC CENTRAL UNIV (2950)	12	14	7	6	8%	21%	29%	50%
NC ST UNIV RALEIGH (2972)	177	121	173	167	52%	60%	57%	54%
NC WESLEYAN COLL (2951)	5	7	6	8	40%	29%	50%	38%
PFEIFFER UNIV (2955)	5	10	4	10	40%	30%	25%	10%
QUEENS UNIV CHARLOTTE (2957)	2	4	3	3	100%	75%	100%	67%
UNIV NC ASHEVILLE (2907)	13	14	15	13	31%	36%	40%	54%
UNIV NC CHAPEL HILL (2974)	174	135	166	171	62%	83%	62%	64%
UNIV NC CHARLOTTE (2975)	69	71	72	65	42%	56%	39%	60%
UNIV NC GREENSBORO (2976)	48	40	55	52	54%	53%	47%	44%
UNIV NC PEMBROKE (2954)	6	5	6	5	33%	60%	50%	40%
UNIV NC WILMINGTON (2984)	128	113	100	111	48%	50%	47%	44%
WAKE FOREST UNIV (2978)	63	56	61	67	81%	89%	85%	84%
WESTERN CAROLINA UNIV (2981)	15	12	17	14	33%	33%	59%	36%
WINGATE UNIV (2985)	6	7	7	8	17%	14%	29%	38%
WINSTON SALEM ST UNIV (2986)	10	9	12	17	40%	33%	8%	12%
North Dakota								
DICKINSON ST UNIV (2989)	32	14	26	23	31%	43%	35%	39%
JAMESTOWN COLL (2990)	4	3	3	3	25%	67%	33%	33%
MINOT ST UNIV (2994)	8	7	9	10	38%	57%	89%	50%
ND ST UNIV (9265)	50	39	47	49	48%	51%	53%	61%
UNIV MARY (2992)	18	16	17	15	44%	38%	35%	53%
UNIV ND (3005)	75	58	61	88	64%	66%	66%	59%
Ohio								
ASHLAND UNIV (3012)	14	16	19	14	43%	56%	32%	43%
BALDWIN WALLACE COLL (3014)	35	33	41	47	49%	52%	46%	45%

Appendix B: Section Performance by Institution Attended - All Testing Events

	Total Events per Section				Percent Pass			
	AUD	BEC	FAR	REG	AUD	BEC	FAR	REG
BOWLING GREEN ST UNIV (3018)	97	70	68	104	48%	54%	41%	41%
CAPITAL UNIV (3023)	27	21	22	21	44%	43%	36%	38%
CASE WESTERN RESERVE UNIV (3024)	38	35	30	45	63%	83%	53%	49%
CEDARVILLE UNIV (3025)	18	10	17	22	56%	50%	53%	59%
CENTRAL ST UNIV (3026)	3	2	3	4	67%	0%	33%	0%
Chancellor University (3043)	8	7	7	4	38%	14%	29%	25%
CLEVELAND ST UNIV (3032)	89	67	78	81	48%	48%	47%	48%
COLUMBUS ST CC (6867)	5	2	3	2	40%	50%	33%	50%
DEFIANCE COLL (3041)	8	3	4	4	38%	67%	50%	50%
DEVRY UNIV COLUMBUS (3099)	14	8	9	14	36%	50%	44%	21%
FRANCISCAN UNIV STEUBENVILLE (3036)	3	8	2	5	33%	25%	0%	80%
FRANKLIN UNIV (3046)	80	70	65	56	29%	29%	29%	34%
HEIDELBERG COLL (3048)	8	8	12	6	0%	50%	8%	33%
HIRAM COLL (3049)	8	13	8	15	63%	23%	38%	27%
JOHN CARROLL UNIV (3050)	77	54	69	72	57%	63%	58%	47%
KENT ST UNIV (3051)	88	72	85	85	57%	54%	47%	52%
LAKE ERIE COLL (3066)	4	4	3	3	25%	25%	33%	67%
MALONE COLL (3072)	5	4	5	6	40%	100%	20%	50%
MARIETTA COLL (3073)	8	6	6	6	38%	33%	33%	33%
MIAMI UNIV (3077)	279	215	228	263	57%	73%	56%	52%
MOUNT UNION COLL (3083)	8	12	8	10	38%	42%	88%	70%
MOUNT VERNON NAZARENE UNIV (7085)	12	8	6	8	25%	50%	33%	25%
MUSKINGUM COLL (3084)	5	4	3	6	60%	25%	33%	50%
NOTRE DAME COLL OH (3085)	7	7	6	9	0%	29%	33%	0%
OH DOMINICAN UNIV (3035)	10	12	18	12	20%	50%	17%	25%
OH NORTHERN UNIV (3089)	24	18	15	18	29%	50%	33%	17%
OH ST UNIV (6883)	359	240	302	366	55%	76%	57%	54%
OH UNIV (3100)	140	87	122	139	41%	60%	49%	37%
OH WESLEYAN UNIV (3109)	11	9	4	10	55%	67%	25%	20%
OTTERBEIN UNIV (3110)	9	8	7	8	44%	50%	57%	50%
TIFFIN UNIV (3121)	3	4	6	5	33%	50%	0%	20%
UNIV AKRON (3123)	97	88	97	96	55%	59%	54%	48%
UNIV CINCINNATI (3125)	94	73	78	81	48%	49%	40%	49%
UNIV DAYTON (3127)	101	65	87	96	49%	69%	44%	33%
UNIV FINDLAY (3045)	16	15	8	23	56%	47%	63%	22%
UNIV NORTHWESTERN OH (4861)	4	3	1	3	50%	0%	0%	0%
UNIV TOLEDO (3131)	68	47	66	67	47%	57%	47%	46%
WALSH UNIV (3135)	13	10	15	12	23%	20%	27%	8%
WILMINGTON COLL (3142)	4	2	4	3	50%	0%	25%	33%
WITTENBERG UNIV (3143)	5	6	4	3	20%	67%	50%	33%
WRIGHT ST UNIV (3078)	48	40	51	43	56%	55%	51%	47%
XAVIER UNIV (3144)	49	47	54	49	63%	66%	48%	47%
YOUNGSTOWN ST UNIV (3145)	45	38	43	42	44%	45%	47%	43%
Oklahoma								
CAMERON UNIV (3150)	7	7	11	6	43%	14%	27%	17%
EAST CENTRAL UNIV (3154)	12	11	9	14	58%	18%	33%	29%
LANGSTON UNIV (3157)	9	10	3	10	11%	0%	33%	30%
NORTHEASTERN ST UNIV (3161)	28	20	22	25	29%	35%	36%	24%
NORTHWESTERN OK ST UNIV (3163)	3	7	3	4	67%	14%	67%	50%
OK BAPTIST UNIV (3164)	6	5	2	6	33%	60%	50%	50%
OK CHRISTIAN UNIV (3165)	20	22	25	20	55%	50%	48%	50%

Appendix B: Section Performance by Institution Attended - All Testing Events

	Total Events per Section				Percent Pass			
	AUD	BEC	FAR	REG	AUD	BEC	FAR	REG
OK ST UNIV (3170)	163	134	130	151	56%	60%	55%	56%
OK ST UNIV OK CITY (9647)	3	1	2	3	67%	0%	0%	33%
OKLAHOMA CITY UNIV (3166)	17	12	17	17	29%	58%	35%	35%
ORAL ROBERTS UNIV (3985)	25	17	21	11	40%	59%	71%	64%
SOUTHEASTERN OK ST UNIV (3179)	10	7	4	7	40%	43%	0%	43%
SOUTHERN NAZARENE UNIV (3149)	12	5	8	8	25%	20%	50%	25%
SOUTHWESTERN OK ST UNIV (3181)	30	15	19	23	30%	33%	42%	26%
UNIV CENTRAL OK (3152)	87	77	63	86	40%	32%	37%	41%
UNIV OK NORMAN (3184)	121	89	100	122	55%	61%	58%	51%
UNIV TULSA (3185)	25	20	19	28	48%	40%	37%	32%
Oregon								
CONCORDIA UNIV (3191)	2	5	3	2	50%	0%	0%	0%
EASTERN OR UNIV (3193)	21	16	21	18	62%	44%	38%	50%
GEORGE FOX UNIV (3194)	17	9	12	16	41%	44%	33%	44%
LINFIELD COLL (3198)	39	33	28	40	38%	52%	39%	33%
OR ST UNIV (3210)	57	49	61	78	63%	59%	56%	47%
PACIFIC UNIV (3212)	7	4	10	6	57%	25%	40%	67%
PORTLAND ST UNIV (3216)	87	73	77	85	53%	56%	49%	61%
SOUTHERN OR UNIV (3219)	26	18	18	18	54%	44%	33%	56%
UNIV OR (3223)	141	108	121	128	52%	64%	55%	47%
UNIV PORTLAND (3224)	21	17	26	25	48%	59%	35%	32%
WESTERN OR UNIV (3209)	5	6	4	6	20%	33%	25%	17%
WILLAMETTE UNIV (3227)	4	4	3	7	100%	75%	100%	71%
Pennsylvania								
ALBRIGHT COLL (3229)	18	22	10	17	39%	9%	20%	29%
ALVERNIA COLL (3233)	13	12	9	12	31%	33%	22%	33%
ARCADIA UNIV (3235)	17	17	9	14	35%	41%	33%	29%
BLOOMSBURG UNIV PA (3315)	90	63	65	78	53%	52%	48%	38%
BUCKNELL UNIV (3238)	48	42	39	61	65%	71%	64%	41%
CA UNIV PA (3316)	12	19	14	14	17%	32%	29%	36%
CABRINI COLL (3241)	11	19	12	18	18%	37%	25%	17%
CARLOW UNIV (3303)	5	6	3	3	60%	33%	33%	33%
CARNEGIE MELLON UNIV (3242)	10	5	12	15	30%	80%	42%	47%
CEDAR CREST COLL (3243)	2	3	2	4	0%	0%	100%	50%
CHATHAM UNIV (3244)	6	5	4	5	17%	40%	50%	20%
CHESTNUT HILL COLL (3245)	5	6	4	6	20%	50%	50%	33%
CHEYNEY UNIV PA (3317)	1	4	0	3	0%	0%	0%	0%
CLARION UNIV PA (9235)	16	18	13	24	50%	33%	46%	54%
COLL MISERICORDIA (3247)	6	6	3	10	0%	0%	67%	10%
DE VALLEY COLL (3252)	12	8	10	12	42%	38%	20%	33%
DESALES UNIV (3986)	33	32	23	40	30%	28%	17%	43%
DREXEL UNIV (3256)	163	158	132	145	37%	36%	34%	45%
DUQUESNE UNIV (3258)	116	74	61	95	42%	51%	46%	40%
EAST STROUDSBURG UNIV PA (3320)	15	8	9	10	53%	13%	44%	50%
EASTERN UNIV (3259)	6	14	13	9	50%	36%	38%	67%
EDINBORO UNIV PA (3321)	12	4	5	11	33%	0%	40%	9%
ELIZABETHTOWN COLL (3262)	36	24	17	24	31%	33%	18%	21%
FRANKLIN & MARSHALL COLL (3265)	9	3	4	5	67%	100%	75%	80%
GANNON UNIV (3266)	11	15	14	7	18%	20%	29%	29%
GENEVA COLL (3267)	13	9	8	14	38%	33%	25%	36%
GETTYSBURG COLL (3268)	7	1	2	2	29%	100%	50%	0%

Appendix B: Section Performance by Institution Attended - All Testing Events

	Total Events per Section				Percent Pass			
	AUD	BEC	FAR	REG	AUD	BEC	FAR	REG
GROVE CITY COLL (3269)	33	24	26	25	45%	58%	58%	60%
GWYNEDD MERCY COLL (3270)	13	6	8	14	31%	17%	50%	29%
HOLY FAMILY COLL (3275)	7	5	5	9	14%	20%	20%	11%
IMMACULATA UNIV (3276)	6	5	3	2	33%	40%	67%	0%
IN UNIV OF PA (8810)	2	5	0	7	0%	20%	0%	0%
INDIANA UNIV PA (3277)	69	68	44	67	39%	32%	23%	31%
JUNIATA COLL (3279)	12	7	7	11	50%	29%	29%	27%
KEYSTONE COLL (3280)	7	7	3	5	14%	0%	33%	20%
KINGS COLL (3282)	42	50	32	35	31%	30%	44%	23%
KUTZTOWN UNIV PA (3322)	48	47	36	58	38%	45%	36%	38%
LA ROCHE COLL (3987)	12	17	13	17	17%	12%	23%	18%
LA SALLE UNIV (3287)	120	115	65	95	32%	33%	29%	27%
LAFAYETTE COLL (3284)	7	4	10	5	29%	75%	30%	0%
LEBANON VALLEY COLL (3288)	18	25	20	29	50%	44%	40%	31%
LEHIGH UNIV (3289)	110	87	103	136	64%	77%	61%	53%
LINCOLN UNIV (3290)	11	7	4	5	18%	29%	25%	40%
LOCK HAVEN UNIV PA (3323)	15	10	9	13	20%	40%	22%	46%
LYCOMING COLL (3293)	9	10	11	9	33%	40%	45%	44%
MARYWOOD UNIV (3296)	11	6	8	8	18%	33%	38%	38%
MERCYHURST COLL (3297)	22	18	15	19	27%	28%	33%	32%
MESSIAH COLL (3298)	30	27	28	35	57%	63%	54%	49%
MILLERSVILLE UNIV PA (3325)	28	21	20	25	46%	33%	40%	36%
MORAVIAN COLL (3301)	33	22	15	17	30%	41%	33%	35%
MOUNT ALOYSIUS COLL (3302)	3	9	1	3	67%	33%	0%	67%
MUHLENBERG COLL (3304)	42	38	39	39	50%	58%	44%	26%
NEUMANN UNIV (3988)	5	5	10	9	40%	40%	30%	33%
PA COLL TECH (3395)	3	4	2	2	0%	0%	50%	50%
PA ST ERIE (3333)	3	3	3	5	67%	100%	67%	60%
PA ST HARRISBURG (6814)	5	3	3	3	60%	33%	67%	33%
PA ST UNIV PARK (3329)	424	411	355	411	48%	48%	42%	42%
PA ST UNIV PARK (6965)	44	42	44	54	34%	31%	30%	28%
PEIRCE COLL (3309)	3	2	2	2	100%	50%	50%	50%
PHILADELPHIA UNIV (3354)	18	34	30	25	28%	24%	30%	36%
POINT PARK UNIV (3357)	6	7	5	7	0%	29%	40%	14%
ROBERT MORRIS UNIV (3359)	67	60	52	57	36%	30%	35%	35%
SAINT FRANCIS UNIV (3366)	28	20	19	27	32%	30%	26%	19%
SAINT JOSEPHS UNIV (3367)	136	100	99	130	34%	53%	39%	31%
SAINT VINCENT COLL (3368)	26	28	15	25	35%	54%	33%	28%
SETON HILL UNIV (3362)	7	4	4	7	43%	25%	50%	29%
SHIPPENSBURG UNIV PA (3326)	62	58	49	54	60%	45%	49%	35%
SLIPPERY ROCK UNIV PA (3327)	34	23	16	25	24%	26%	25%	24%
SUSQUEHANNA UNIV (3369)	15	22	23	16	53%	45%	35%	31%
TEMPLE UNIV (3371)	304	258	227	274	33%	35%	31%	30%
THIEL COLL (3376)	12	12	11	14	8%	17%	27%	43%
UNIV PA (3378)	27	23	34	28	85%	87%	59%	68%
UNIV PITTSBURGH (3379)	228	198	167	193	46%	52%	49%	46%
UNIV PITTSBURGH JOHNSTOWN (3382)	5	5	7	4	40%	20%	0%	50%
UNIV SCRANTON (3384)	49	58	42	33	53%	34%	50%	33%
URSINUS COLL (3385)	8	8	4	4	25%	0%	50%	50%
VILLANOVA UNIV (3388)	185	178	195	238	62%	66%	54%	45%
WASHINGTON & JEFFERSON COLL (3389)	33	27	24	32	36%	44%	46%	38%

Appendix B: Section Performance by Institution Attended - All Testing Events

	Total Events per Section				Percent Pass			
	AUD	BEC	FAR	REG	AUD	BEC	FAR	REG
WAYNESBURG COLL (3391)	5	10	6	5	20%	10%	33%	0%
WEST CHESTER UNIV PA (3328)	137	142	101	126	35%	32%	42%	43%
WESTMINSTER COLL (3392)	23	13	10	14	13%	23%	30%	36%
WIDENER UNIV PA (3313)	63	56	45	55	29%	25%	36%	20%
WILKES UNIV (3394)	24	29	15	23	33%	24%	40%	30%
YORK COLL PA (3399)	21	27	22	30	67%	41%	36%	50%
Puerto Rico								
INTER AMERICAN UNIV PR (8242)	10	15	14	9	20%	13%	14%	11%
INTER AMERICAN UNIV PR AGUADILLA (3939)	2	0	4	2	50%	0%	25%	50%
INTER AMERICAN UNIV PR BARRANQUITAS (5027)	3	2	3	6	0%	0%	0%	0%
INTER AMERICAN UNIV PR BAYAMON (5028)	5	4	10	6	0%	0%	10%	17%
INTER AMERICAN UNIV PR METROPOLITAN (3940)	37	15	26	22	22%	20%	15%	18%
INTER AMERICAN UNIV PR PONCE (5029)	9	12	5	10	0%	0%	0%	0%
INTER AMERICAN UNIV PR SAN GERMAN (3938)	9	4	12	10	22%	0%	17%	20%
PONTIFICAL CATHOLIC UNIV PR (3936)	26	27	15	29	27%	7%	13%	21%
UNIV ESTE (3941)	5	8	8	3	0%	13%	13%	0%
UNIV METROPOLITANA (25875)	5	7	7	9	40%	0%	14%	22%
UNIV POLITECNICA DE PR (21000)	5	6	4	1	20%	0%	50%	100%
UNIV PR AGUADILLA (12123)	5	5	9	7	0%	0%	11%	0%
UNIV PR ARECIBO (7228)	16	12	12	15	19%	17%	0%	20%
UNIV PR BAYAMON (10975)	46	38	40	42	24%	21%	23%	19%
UNIV PR CAROLINA (30160)	9	6	5	5	22%	0%	20%	0%
UNIV PR CAYEY (7206)	31	47	27	41	26%	9%	19%	15%
UNIV PR HUMACAO (3943)	27	20	19	39	22%	5%	37%	23%
UNIV PR MAYAGUEZ (3944)	39	30	29	39	46%	23%	34%	21%
UNIV PR PONCE (9652)	21	16	22	18	19%	6%	18%	28%
UNIV PR RIO PIEDRAS (7108)	198	157	132	195	43%	26%	52%	32%
UNIV SACRED HEART (3937)	10	7	7	6	70%	43%	43%	33%
UNIV TURABO GURABO (11719)	11	8	8	6	9%	0%	0%	17%
Rhode Island								
BRYANT UNIV (3402)	151	99	143	146	47%	53%	46%	51%
JOHNSON & WALES UNIV (3404)	50	35	30	36	34%	26%	37%	36%
PROVIDENCE COLL (3406)	54	43	41	53	54%	67%	41%	42%
RI COLL (3407)	15	12	11	12	20%	25%	36%	42%
ROGER WILLIAMS UNIV (3410)	17	17	15	16	18%	24%	40%	38%
SALVE REGINA UNIV (3411)	17	28	19	19	35%	21%	21%	26%
UNIV RI (3414)	77	57	64	81	58%	65%	47%	43%
South Carolina								
BOB JONES UNIV (3421)	19	18	17	14	42%	56%	35%	64%
CITADEL MILITARY COLL SC (3423)	18	22	8	13	22%	27%	38%	31%
CLEMSON UNIV (3425)	72	48	56	73	63%	65%	63%	60%
COASTAL CAROLINA UNIV (3451)	18	13	16	9	33%	38%	50%	78%
COLL CHARLESTON (3428)	56	42	33	47	41%	64%	55%	57%
FRANCIS MARION UNIV (9226)	3	3	4	3	67%	67%	50%	0%
FURMAN UNIV (3434)	21	24	21	21	62%	63%	67%	57%
LANDER UNIV (3435)	3	0	2	4	67%	0%	50%	25%
PRESBYTERIAN COLL (3445)	3	4	4	3	67%	100%	100%	100%
UNIV SC COLUMBIA (3448)	135	93	93	116	50%	63%	52%	43%
WINTHROP UNIV (3456)	21	17	14	23	52%	35%	50%	43%
WOFFORD COLL (3457)	19	20	16	16	47%	55%	69%	81%

Appendix B: Section Performance by Institution Attended - All Testing Events

	Total Events per Section				Percent Pass			
	AUD	BEC	FAR	REG	AUD	BEC	FAR	REG
South Dakota								
AUGUSTANA COLL (3458)	30	25	21	20	43%	56%	43%	50%
BLACK HILLS ST UNIV (3459)	8	10	5	9	38%	20%	40%	56%
CO TECHNICAL UNIV (666731)	5	6	10	5	60%	33%	20%	40%
NATIONAL AMERICAN UNIV (4057)	3	6	6	7	33%	17%	33%	29%
NORTHERN ST UNIV (3466)	9	8	10	13	22%	25%	20%	23%
SD ST UNIV (3471)	9	9	6	8	44%	33%	33%	50%
UNIV SD (3474)	34	26	32	36	53%	50%	59%	53%
UNIV SIOUX FALLS (3469)	12	13	8	9	50%	38%	63%	78%
Tennessee								
AUSTIN PEAY ST UNIV (3478)	24	21	18	21	21%	33%	39%	43%
BELMONT UNIV (3479)	41	33	39	57	51%	42%	46%	40%
CARSON NEWMAN COLL (3481)	6	8	10	6	33%	38%	40%	50%
CHRISTIAN BROTHERS UNIV (3482)	10	9	25	16	50%	44%	8%	38%
COVENANT COLL (3484)	2	1	5	4	100%	100%	60%	75%
CUMBERLAND UNIV (3485)	6	6	2	3	0%	0%	0%	33%
EAST TN ST UNIV (3487)	48	41	50	51	46%	39%	28%	43%
FISK UNIV (3490)	1	4	2	5	100%	25%	50%	40%
FREED HARDEMAN UNIV (3492)	12	10	9	9	17%	40%	56%	44%
LAMBUTH UNIV (3498)	7	2	2	7	14%	50%	0%	29%
LEE UNIV (3500)	17	14	18	11	65%	36%	50%	45%
LINCOLN MEMORIAL UNIV (3502)	7	11	1	7	43%	45%	0%	29%
LIPSCOMB UNIV (3486)	50	45	48	45	30%	38%	25%	38%
MIDDLE TN ST UNIV (3510)	107	95	89	103	46%	47%	49%	41%
MILLIGAN COLL (3511)	6	2	2	3	50%	0%	50%	0%
RHODES COLL (3519)	19	13	19	19	63%	62%	58%	42%
SOUTHERN ADVENTIST UNIV (3518)	9	8	10	12	33%	75%	30%	33%
TN ST UNIV (3522)	17	14	15	21	29%	43%	20%	29%
TN TECH UNIV (3523)	49	46	45	43	33%	39%	24%	35%
TN WESLEYAN COLL (3525)	5	7	5	7	80%	29%	40%	43%
TREVECCA NAZARENE UNIV (3526)	9	7	4	10	67%	43%	75%	30%
TUSCULUM COLL (3527)	4	5	3	2	25%	20%	67%	50%
UNION UNIV (3528)	7	8	11	6	43%	50%	55%	50%
UNIV MEMPHIS (3509)	53	50	56	56	30%	24%	41%	32%
UNIV TN CHATTANOOGA (3529)	62	54	53	58	47%	44%	36%	41%
UNIV TN KNOXVILLE (3530)	175	137	139	173	59%	57%	59%	54%
UNIV TN MARTIN (3531)	39	18	28	21	28%	33%	25%	48%
VANDERBILT UNIV (3535)	44	40	41	50	70%	95%	68%	70%
Texas								
ABILENE CHRISTIAN UNIV (3537)	42	48	47	66	64%	56%	43%	42%
AMBERTON UNIV (22594)	5	7	3	4	20%	29%	67%	25%
ANGELO ST UNIV (3541)	40	32	20	33	38%	50%	55%	55%
BAYLOR UNIV (3545)	135	99	113	140	61%	78%	69%	64%
BAYLOR UNIV (6967)	13	11	8	13	38%	82%	50%	46%
DALLAS BAPTIST UNIV (3560)	19	24	20	24	26%	21%	30%	33%
DEVRY UNIV IRVING (10139)	12	3	14	12	25%	0%	21%	0%
EAST TX BAPTIST UNIV (3564)	1	4	4	3	100%	0%	25%	100%
HARDIN SIMMONS UNIV (3571)	5	5	2	2	40%	60%	0%	50%
HOUSTON BAPTIST UNIV (3576)	19	18	15	23	42%	28%	53%	35%
LAMAR COLL (3581)	48	29	32	32	31%	31%	38%	31%
LETOURNEAU UNIV (3584)	12	8	7	7	8%	38%	14%	29%

Appendix B: Section Performance by Institution Attended - All Testing Events

	Total Events per Section				Percent Pass			
	AUD	BEC	FAR	REG	AUD	BEC	FAR	REG
LUBBOCK CHRISTIAN UNIV (3586)	6	6	5	6	50%	17%	40%	50%
MIDWESTERN ST UNIV (3592)	21	24	13	25	38%	38%	69%	60%
OUR LADY THE LAKE UNIV (3598)	8	8	6	5	50%	63%	0%	0%
PRAIRIE VIEW A & M UNIV (3630)	10	6	5	6	30%	17%	40%	33%
RICE UNIV (3604)	12	8	9	14	67%	75%	56%	57%
SAINT EDWARDS UNIV (3621)	27	31	18	27	48%	32%	56%	41%
SAINT MARYS UNIV (3623)	19	16	10	12	37%	31%	20%	50%
SAM HOUSTON ST UNIV (3606)	80	76	91	103	48%	47%	31%	32%
SCHREINER UNIV (3610)	9	3	5	5	33%	0%	20%	40%
SOUTHERN METHODIST UNIV (3613)	111	90	119	111	63%	68%	61%	52%
SOUTHWESTERN ASSEMBLIES OF GOD UNIV (3616)	3	1	3	4	67%	0%	33%	0%
SOUTHWESTERN UNIV (3620)	6	8	8	4	67%	75%	75%	75%
STEPHEN F AUSTIN ST UNIV (3624)	56	60	60	62	57%	40%	53%	31%
TARLETON ST UNIV (3631)	13	19	18	17	38%	26%	33%	47%
TRINITY UNIV (3647)	35	31	47	43	60%	71%	45%	47%
TX A&M INTL UNIV (9651)	13	11	8	9	31%	9%	25%	22%
TX A&M UNIV (3632)	432	294	332	388	59%	81%	73%	65%
TX A&M UNIV COMMERCE (3565)	22	26	22	35	36%	42%	36%	29%
TX A&M UNIV CORPUS CHRISTI (11161)	37	28	29	32	30%	50%	34%	44%
TX A&M UNIV KINGSVILLE (3639)	3	7	7	5	33%	14%	14%	40%
TX A&M UNIV TEXARKANA (31703)	5	1	3	4	40%	100%	33%	75%
TX CHRISTIAN UNIV (3636)	69	48	59	62	59%	75%	68%	63%
TX LUTHERAN UNIV (3641)	22	15	13	12	45%	27%	62%	50%
TX SOUTHERN UNIV (3642)	9	14	12	12	11%	7%	8%	8%
TX ST UNIV SAN MARCOS (3615)	122	100	119	140	48%	48%	44%	36%
TX TECH UNIV (3644)	162	120	152	153	48%	62%	53%	56%
TX WESLEYAN UNIV (3645)	13	12	11	11	46%	25%	27%	36%
TX WOMANS UNIV (3646)	16	14	20	12	31%	36%	35%	50%
UNIV DALLAS (3651)	22	18	25	37	45%	33%	36%	30%
UNIV HOUSTON (12826)	2	6	3	6	0%	17%	33%	33%
UNIV HOUSTON CLEAR LAKE (11711)	80	70	78	69	40%	30%	36%	43%
UNIV HOUSTON DOWNTOWN (3612)	80	88	81	76	35%	22%	27%	29%
UNIV HOUSTON UNIV PARK (3652)	355	294	244	314	38%	39%	36%	39%
UNIV HOUSTON VICTORIA (13231)	18	13	26	26	44%	62%	38%	23%
UNIV INCARNATE WORD (3578)	19	17	12	11	21%	6%	17%	9%
UNIV MARY HARDIN BAYLOR (3588)	13	14	11	16	38%	50%	55%	44%
UNIV NORTH TX (3594)	120	104	123	130	40%	48%	33%	41%
UNIV SAINT THOMAS (3654)	45	43	32	47	51%	33%	50%	40%
UNIV TX ARLINGTON (3656)	136	117	151	147	50%	49%	40%	44%
UNIV TX AUSTIN (3658)	389	291	332	381	60%	78%	69%	64%
UNIV TX BROWNSVILLE (30646)	9	10	4	9	67%	30%	50%	22%
UNIV TX DALLAS (9741)	268	178	224	230	40%	45%	39%	37%
UNIV TX EL PASO (3661)	31	29	14	30	39%	38%	50%	50%
UNIV TX PAN AMERICAN (3599)	22	16	20	19	36%	38%	40%	47%
UNIV TX PERMIAN BASIN (9930)	18	18	13	24	33%	33%	38%	67%
UNIV TX SAN ANTONIO (10115)	118	83	105	91	44%	34%	38%	42%
UNIV TX TYLER (11163)	23	36	24	26	35%	39%	46%	50%
WAYLAND BAPTIST UNIV (3663)	6	4	7	5	67%	50%	29%	40%
WEST TX A & M UNIV (3665)	37	44	37	28	35%	32%	24%	32%

Appendix B: Section Performance by Institution Attended - All Testing Events

	Total Events per Section				Percent Pass			
	AUD	BEC	FAR	REG	AUD	BEC	FAR	REG
Utah								
BRIGHAM YOUNG UNIV (3670)	277	201	244	284	68%	89%	71%	64%
SOUTHERN UT UNIV (3678)	55	44	46	46	45%	43%	52%	57%
UNIV UT (3675)	148	101	130	160	57%	68%	58%	59%
UT ST UNIV (3677)	84	43	68	84	50%	72%	49%	54%
UT VALLEY ST COLL (4027)	16	17	16	14	44%	41%	44%	50%
WEBER ST UNIV (3680)	55	37	57	58	45%	59%	39%	62%
Western Governors Univ (33394)	4	4	5	4	0%	50%	60%	25%
WESTMINSTER COLL (3681)	20	23	24	20	40%	48%	25%	25%
Vermont								
CASTLETON ST COLL (3683)	8	9	9	3	63%	67%	56%	100%
CHAMPLAIN COLL (3684)	19	16	22	18	32%	19%	18%	28%
SAINT MICHAELS COLL (3694)	25	19	22	18	48%	42%	45%	33%
UNIV VT (3696)	34	12	20	31	53%	75%	45%	58%
VERMONT 60 (88803)	4	3	6	6	0%	0%	17%	17%
Virgin Islands								
UNIV VI (3946)	5	1	1	8	40%	0%	100%	25%
Virginia								
AVERETT UNIV (3702)	7	6	5	8	43%	33%	0%	38%
BRIDGEWATER COLL (3704)	12	15	13	11	25%	27%	15%	64%
CHRISTOPHER NEWPORT UNIV (3706)	20	10	6	18	20%	30%	83%	39%
COLL WILLIAM & MARY (3705)	100	87	82	92	59%	71%	63%	61%
EASTERN MENNONITE UNIV (3708)	6	4	4	5	50%	100%	75%	60%
EMORY & HENRY COLL (3709)	3	6	8	5	67%	33%	50%	40%
FERRUM COLL (3711)	5	3	3	4	60%	33%	100%	50%
GEORGE MASON UNIV (3749)	202	156	168	198	41%	44%	52%	40%
HAMPDEN SYDNEY COLL (3713)	4	3	1	3	75%	67%	0%	67%
HAMPTON UNIV (3714)	36	27	26	36	25%	19%	19%	17%
JAMES MADISON UNIV (3721)	140	128	137	159	64%	69%	66%	51%
LIBERTY UNIV (20530)	40	35	44	34	58%	37%	32%	59%
LONGWOOD UNIV (3719)	14	12	12	14	43%	58%	50%	36%
LYNCHBURG COLL (3720)	5	6	5	6	60%	50%	100%	17%
MARYMOUNT UNIV (3724)	7	3	3	6	43%	67%	67%	67%
NORFOLK ST UNIV (3765)	7	10	7	8	43%	20%	43%	50%
NORTHERN VA CC (3727)	12	10	14	16	50%	50%	64%	44%
OLD DOMINION UNIV (3728)	50	39	58	52	48%	44%	50%	38%
RADFORD UNIV (3732)	31	29	19	18	35%	38%	37%	56%
RANDOLPH MACON COLL (3733)	13	16	15	13	31%	50%	33%	62%
ROANOKE COLL (3736)	6	7	10	13	33%	100%	50%	31%
TIDEWATER CC (3712)	2	3	0	7	0%	33%	0%	43%
UNIV MARY WASHINGTON (3746)	14	9	8	9	50%	44%	38%	44%
UNIV RICHMOND (3744)	76	51	62	91	70%	82%	65%	46%
UNIV VA (3745)	110	90	99	127	75%	88%	83%	75%
UNIV VA COL WISE (CLINCH VALLEY COLL) (3747)	5	7	4	6	40%	57%	25%	67%
VA COMMONWEALTH UNIV (3735)	89	62	91	71	39%	26%	36%	41%
VA MILITARY INST (3753)	4	3	3	5	75%	67%	0%	60%
VA POLYTECHNIC INST & ST UNIV (3754)	209	175	192	224	55%	66%	56%	50%
VA WESLEYAN COLL (3767)	3	5	5	5	33%	40%	40%	40%
WASHINGTON & LEE UNIV (3768)	27	18	24	35	59%	83%	71%	40%

Appendix B: Section Performance by Institution Attended - All Testing Events

	Total Events per Section				Percent Pass			
	AUD	BEC	FAR	REG	AUD	BEC	FAR	REG
Washington								
BELLEVUE CC (3769)	1	4	1	3	0%	75%	0%	0%
CENTRAL WA UNIV (3771)	80	87	85	86	45%	55%	44%	40%
CITY UNIV SEATTLE (13022)	13	13	13	14	31%	31%	31%	29%
EASTERN WA UNIV (3775)	49	38	42	38	41%	42%	26%	32%
EDMONDS CC (5001)	4	1	3	3	0%	0%	0%	33%
GONZAGA UNIV (3778)	82	65	69	75	60%	75%	75%	63%
NORTH SEATTLE CC (9704)	5	3	7	5	60%	33%	71%	60%
PACIFIC LUTHERAN UNIV (3785)	13	11	18	14	8%	45%	17%	29%
SAINT MARTINS COLL (3794)	4	6	9	6	0%	33%	33%	33%
SEATTLE PACIFIC UNIV (3788)	22	22	14	22	45%	45%	36%	45%
SEATTLE UNIV (3790)	39	26	32	41	51%	46%	34%	37%
UNIV PUGET SOUND (3797)	4	3	5	2	50%	100%	100%	50%
UNIV WA (3798)	249	200	238	270	59%	74%	58%	59%
WA ST UNIV (3800)	82	85	91	88	49%	49%	47%	51%
WALLA WALLA UNIV (3799)	5	4	3	6	100%	25%	67%	50%
WESTERN WA UNIV (3802)	38	29	34	31	63%	62%	68%	74%
WHITWORTH COLL (3804)	10	7	7	7	50%	71%	57%	71%
West Virginia								
BETHANY COLL (3808)	4	1	2	4	75%	100%	50%	75%
BLUEFIELD ST COLL (3809)	5	6	4	6	60%	33%	75%	67%
CONCORD UNIV (3810)	5	9	7	14	20%	33%	43%	29%
FAIRMONT ST COLL (3812)	10	7	6	7	30%	43%	33%	57%
GLENVILLE ST COLL (3813)	4	2	2	0	25%	0%	0%	0%
MARSHALL UNIV (3815)	56	44	49	56	43%	43%	45%	38%
MOUNTAIN ST UNIV (3807)	1	2	2	3	0%	0%	50%	0%
SALEM INTL UNIV (3820)	6	7	7	4	50%	43%	29%	50%
SHEPHERD UNIV (3822)	11	12	7	10	45%	58%	57%	80%
UNIV CHARLESTON (3818)	8	14	8	5	13%	21%	38%	40%
WEST LIBERTY ST COLL (3823)	14	12	18	13	21%	50%	33%	31%
WHEELING JESUIT UNIV (3831)	13	11	13	13	54%	36%	31%	8%
WV INST TECH (3825)	7	8	7	11	14%	13%	14%	18%
WV ST UNIV (3826)	14	25	16	23	36%	24%	19%	26%
WV UNIV (3827)	122	126	118	136	54%	43%	49%	46%
WV UNIV PARKERSBURG (3828)	5	5	6	5	60%	20%	50%	40%
WV WESLEYAN COLL (3830)	11	7	5	10	27%	71%	40%	60%
Wisconsin								
BELOIT COLL (3835)	3	3	1	4	67%	67%	0%	25%
CARDINAL STRITCH UNIV (3837)	10	10	9	10	20%	40%	33%	40%
CARROLL UNIV (WI) (3838)	22	16	11	16	41%	56%	55%	63%
CARTHAGE COLL (3839)	18	12	16	11	28%	25%	13%	9%
CONCORDIA UNIV WI (3842)	11	8	10	8	36%	25%	60%	25%
EDGEWOOD COLL (3848)	13	16	14	15	31%	31%	36%	33%
LAKELAND COLL (3854)	43	36	39	48	40%	39%	46%	31%
Marion University (3861)	5	5	4	6	20%	40%	25%	50%
MARQUETTE UNIV (3863)	99	80	73	114	66%	71%	70%	51%
MOUNT MARY COLL (3869)	6	3	4	2	17%	67%	0%	50%
SAINT NORBERT COLL (3892)	15	19	21	16	67%	68%	52%	63%
UNIV WI EAU CLAIRE (3917)	70	50	56	74	50%	62%	57%	54%
UNIV WI GREEN BAY (3899)	39	32	28	33	41%	31%	46%	39%
UNIV WI LA CROSSE (3919)	90	53	66	71	46%	64%	48%	56%

Appendix B: Section Performance by Institution Attended - All Testing Events

	Total Events per Section				Percent Pass			
	AUD	BEC	FAR	REG	AUD	BEC	FAR	REG
UNIV WI MADISON (3895)	196	130	150	175	65%	90%	75%	68%
UNIV WI MILWAUKEE (3896)	186	137	147	180	46%	61%	56%	54%
UNIV WI OSHKOSH (3920)	61	48	43	52	48%	69%	56%	54%
UNIV WI PARKSIDE (5015)	8	9	11	13	13%	33%	0%	15%
UNIV WI PLATTEVILLE (3921)	18	15	14	16	33%	47%	50%	38%
UNIV WI RIVER FALLS (3923)	24	22	18	30	33%	73%	56%	50%
UNIV WI STEVENS POINT (3924)	21	12	12	16	38%	58%	50%	56%
UNIV WI SUPERIOR (3925)	10	10	9	14	40%	40%	33%	36%
UNIV WI WHITEWATER (3926)	200	145	158	167	46%	63%	59%	53%
VITERBO UNIV (3911)	5	4	2	4	40%	0%	0%	25%
Wyoming								
UNIV WY (3932)	52	48	40	59	46%	65%	60%	41%

INSTITUTION ATTENDED FIRST-TIME TESTING EVENTS

APPENDIX C

SUMMARY PERFORMANCE

Appendix C: Summary Performance by Institution Attended - First-Time Testing Events

	Candidates Total	Sections Total	Percent Pass	Average Score	Average Age
Alabama					
AL A&M UNIV (1002)	5	9	11.1%	48.2	41.0
AL ST UNIV (1005)	8	10	20.0%	60.9	29.7
ATHENS ST UNIV (1008)	12	15	20.0%	58.8	40.4
AUBURN UNIV (1009)	159	420	67.6%	77.4	25.7
AUBURN UNIV MONTGOMERY (8310)	21	33	12.1%	63.1	28.9
BIRMINGHAM SOUTHERN COLL (1012)	29	57	29.8%	65.1	26.0
HUNTINGDON COLL (1019)	9	18	55.6%	72.9	29.5
JACKSONVILLE ST UNIV (1020)	12	22	50.0%	67.2	27.1
OAKWOOD COLL (1033)	8	13	38.5%	65.8	25.6
SAMFORD UNIV (1036)	21	44	68.2%	76.0	24.7
TROY UNIV (1047)	68	126	30.2%	64.8	30.0
UNIV AL (1051)	190	468	57.7%	74.3	25.1
UNIV AL BIRMINGHAM (1052)	81	170	45.3%	71.6	29.4
UNIV AL HUNTSVILLE (1055)	21	34	41.2%	69.7	33.7
UNIV MONTEVALLO (1004)	11	20	50.0%	69.1	29.0
UNIV NORTH AL (1016)	19	40	50.0%	70.4	31.2
UNIV SOUTH AL (1057)	48	90	41.1%	70.8	30.8
Alaska					
UNIV ALASKA ANCHORAGE (11462)	42	69	36.2%	65.8	30.1
UNIV ALASKA FAIRBANKS (1063)	14	28	50.0%	70.9	31.9
UNIV ALASKA SOUTHEAST (1065)	7	12	41.7%	67.7	33.4
Arizona					
AZ ST UNIV (1081)	312	641	60.4%	74.9	29.3
AZ ST UNIV WEST (66935)	10	16	56.3%	72.0	33.3
DEVRY UNIV PHOENIX (8322)	33	77	29.9%	62.0	34.2
GRAND CANYON UNIV (1074)	11	24	29.2%	56.8	33.8
NORTHERN AZ UNIV (1082)	62	114	44.7%	70.0	27.7
THUNDERBIRD SCHOOL OF GLOBAL MGMT (1070)	12	24	37.5%	69.3	40.9
UNIV AZ (1083)	184	393	54.5%	73.2	28.1
UNIV PHOENIX (20988)	435	777	30.4%	61.7	37.4
WESTERN INTL UNIV (21715)	11	19	52.6%	68.9	41.4
Arkansas					
AR ST UNIV (1090)	32	64	28.1%	64.3	27.5
AR TECH UNIV (1089)	23	59	54.2%	71.1	28.4
HARDING UNIV (1097)	47	101	41.6%	70.4	25.0
HENDERSON ST UNIV (1098)	15	36	25.0%	65.5	27.1
HENDRIX COLL (1099)	8	14	14.3%	56.6	26.0
OUACHITA BAPTIST UNIV (1102)	14	22	45.5%	69.6	25.0
SOUTHERN AR UNIV (1107)	13	21	19.1%	61.5	30.4
UNIV AR (1108)	89	232	56.0%	73.0	26.1
UNIV AR LITTLE ROCK (1101)	28	47	48.9%	68.0	36.1
UNIV AR MONTICELLO (1085)	9	14	35.7%	64.9	27.0
UNIV CENTRAL AR (1092)	55	108	40.7%	70.0	29.9
California					
AMERICAN RIVER COLL (1232)	7	11	63.6%	69.3	33.0
AZUSA PACIFIC UNIV (1117)	20	34	23.5%	62.4	25.0
BIOLA UNIV (1122)	25	43	32.6%	66.8	25.9
CA BAPTIST UNIV (1125)	18	27	18.5%	59.0	29.9
CA LUTHERAN UNIV (1133)	20	39	28.2%	64.5	29.7
CA ST POLYTECH UNIV POMONA (1144)	129	223	27.8%	62.1	28.6
CA ST POLYTECH UNIV SAN LUIS OBISPO (1143)	225	411	50.4%	72.1	25.3

Appendix C: Summary Performance by Institution Attended - First-Time Testing Events

	Candidates Total	Sections Total	Percent Pass	Average Score	Average Age
CA ST UNIV BAKERSFIELD (7993)	38	75	42.7%	66.6	30.5
CA ST UNIV CHICO (1146)	73	129	40.3%	69.3	29.7
CA ST UNIV DOMINGUEZ HILLS (1141)	38	62	25.8%	60.0	37.1
CA ST UNIV EAST BAY (1138)	195	362	37.6%	65.4	33.1
CA ST UNIV FRESNO (1147)	127	211	40.8%	69.1	29.9
CA ST UNIV FULLERTON (1137)	366	697	37.7%	66.8	29.6
CA ST UNIV LONG BEACH (1139)	204	368	40.2%	67.5	30.3
CA ST UNIV LOS ANGELES (1140)	200	362	29.3%	63.0	32.3
CA ST UNIV NORTHRIDGE (1153)	285	532	46.1%	70.2	31.2
CA ST UNIV SACRAMENTO (1150)	221	409	38.1%	66.4	30.3
CA ST UNIV SAN BERNARDINO (1142)	93	148	25.7%	64.8	30.9
CA ST UNIV SAN MARCOS (30113)	62	112	54.5%	72.8	29.1
CA ST UNIV STANISLAUS (1157)	37	55	29.1%	65.2	31.5
CHAPMAN UNIV (1164)	49	92	54.4%	73.7	27.6
CLAREMONT GRADUATE UNIV (1169)	5	7	14.3%	56.7	43.8
CLAREMONT MCKENNA COLL (1170)	22	41	68.3%	79.3	24.0
CONCORDIA UNIV (20705)	5	7	28.6%	69.6	32.3
DE ANZA COLL (4480)	14	24	37.5%	68.2	32.5
DEVRY UNIV LONG BEACH (666988)	21	37	8.1%	53.4	33.7
DEVRY UNIV POMONA (23329)	20	42	19.1%	54.5	34.1
FOOTHILL COLL (1199)	8	21	57.1%	75.1	31.4
FRESNO PACIFIC UNIV (1253)	11	18	44.4%	66.6	26.4
GLENDALE CC (1203)	9	18	27.8%	63.9	29.5
GOLDEN GATE UNIV (1205)	132	242	42.2%	66.8	34.1
GOLDEN WEST COLL (1206)	5	11	63.6%	70.2	36.6
HUMBOLDT ST UNIV (1149)	15	25	36.0%	65.9	31.3
LA SIERRA UNIV (1215)	14	19	5.3%	55.1	30.7
LOYOLA MARYMOUNT UNIV (11649)	79	169	53.3%	73.6	24.9
MASTERS COLL & SEMINARY (1220)	12	26	46.2%	70.5	23.8
MENLO COLL (1236)	5	9	11.1%	55.6	28.4
MOUNT SAINT MARYS COLL (1243)	10	20	40.0%	69.2	26.1
NATIONAL UNIV (11460)	49	89	40.5%	66.6	39.7
PACIFIC ST UNIV (31633)	11	19	15.8%	53.9	38.4
PACIFIC UNION COLL (1258)	8	17	58.8%	72.6	25.0
PEPPERDINE (1264)	50	95	43.2%	70.5	32.3
POINT LOMA NAZARENE UNIV (1262)	17	28	53.6%	74.4	23.8
SAINT MARYS COLL CA (1302)	38	69	30.4%	64.9	27.5
SAN DIEGO ST UNIV (1151)	331	610	52.8%	72.1	28.3
SAN FRANCISCO ST UNIV (1154)	213	375	41.6%	67.1	30.6
SAN JOSE ST UNIV (1155)	263	501	46.5%	69.5	29.8
SANTA CLARA UNIV (1326)	261	469	45.8%	69.5	26.9
SANTA MONICA COLL (1286)	17	34	23.5%	56.7	37.3
SIMPSON UNIV (1291)	7	19	31.6%	63.0	25.5
SONOMA ST UNIV (1156)	94	158	26.0%	65.2	28.8
STANFORD UNIV (1305)	6	12	50.0%	73.8	41.5
UNIV CA BERKELEY (1312)	252	535	62.4%	75.5	27.0
UNIV CA DAVIS (1313)	97	186	54.3%	72.4	28.4
UNIV CA IRVINE (1314)	163	299	47.2%	69.0	26.8
UNIV CA LOS ANGELES (1315)	455	935	63.9%	75.7	26.9
UNIV CA RIVERSIDE (1316)	158	308	32.5%	66.0	27.3
UNIV CA SAN DIEGO (1317)	99	183	49.7%	70.4	29.6
UNIV CA SANTA BARBARA (1320)	401	750	51.7%	72.0	25.7

Appendix C: Summary Performance by Institution Attended - First-Time Testing Events

	Candidates Total	Sections Total	Percent Pass	Average Score	Average Age
UNIV CA SANTA CRUZ (1321)	129	220	38.6%	68.4	26.1
UNIV LA VERNE (1216)	29	51	31.4%	61.0	33.7
UNIV PACIFIC (1329)	30	58	55.2%	73.3	27.1
UNIV REDLANDS (1322)	26	44	25.0%	60.3	30.7
UNIV SAN DIEGO (10395)	135	273	52.8%	73.5	25.1
UNIV SAN FRANCISCO (1325)	64	127	30.7%	62.0	27.9
UNIV SOUTHERN CA (1328)	542	1,181	62.0%	75.4	26.2
VANGUARD UNIV SOUTHERN CA (1293)	6	13	76.9%	78.1	30.0
WOODBURY UNIV (1343)	8	16	31.3%	63.5	31.8
Colorado					
ADAMS ST COLL (1345)	5	6	33.3%	67.0	31.4
CHARTERED ACCT (199999)	88	184	60.9%	74.9	34.0
CO COLL (1347)	6	10	70.0%	77.3	42.2
CO ST UNIV (1350)	129	278	64.4%	75.2	27.9
FORT LEWIS COLL (1353)	31	51	31.4%	64.4	29.4
JONES INTL UNIV (35343)	5	8	37.5%	68.8	35.0
MESA ST COLL (1358)	23	51	49.0%	73.7	29.6
METRO ST COLL DENVER (1360)	90	174	33.9%	66.1	34.9
REGIS UNIV (1363)	69	141	46.1%	68.5	36.6
UNIV CO BOULDER (1370)	135	333	63.4%	77.0	26.7
UNIV CO COLORADO SPRINGS (4509)	37	64	46.9%	68.5	31.6
UNIV CO DENVER (6740)	88	145	35.9%	66.0	29.7
UNIV DENVER (1371)	80	157	55.4%	72.7	26.0
UNIV NORTHERN CO (1349)	55	115	45.2%	71.1	26.9
UNIV SOUTHERN CO (1365)	20	39	46.2%	72.9	30.8
WESTERN ST COLL (1372)	10	21	66.7%	75.0	30.4
Connecticut					
ALBERTUS MAGNUS COLL (1374)	6	7	0.0%	47.9	32.6
CENTRAL CT ST UNIV (1378)	39	70	44.3%	67.7	31.6
EASTERN CT ST UNIV (1425)	23	34	41.2%	67.5	31.2
FAIRFIELD UNIV (1385)	112	214	53.7%	73.5	24.1
QUINNIPIAC UNIV (1402)	66	141	41.8%	69.3	24.3
SACRED HEART UNIV (1403)	43	67	23.9%	62.5	26.3
SOUTHERN CT ST UNIV (1406)	28	48	35.4%	68.4	28.1
TEIKYO POST UNIV (1401)	10	17	35.3%	60.0	25.3
UNIV BRIDGEPORT (1416)	12	19	21.1%	60.4	29.9
UNIV CT (1417)	250	467	54.8%	74.2	24.6
UNIV HARTFORD (1422)	27	55	38.2%	64.1	29.5
UNIV NEW HAVEN (1397)	16	26	23.1%	63.0	28.7
WESTERN CT ST UNIV (1380)	20	37	51.4%	71.4	32.3
Delaware					
DE ST UNIV (1428)	8	11	18.2%	66.1	27.4
GOLDEY BEACOM COLL (1429)	24	39	23.1%	59.2	32.7
UNIV DE (1431)	193	407	56.3%	73.6	24.9
WILMINGTON COLL (7948)	22	46	30.4%	64.1	37.0
District of Columbia					
AMERICAN UNIV (1434)	69	142	54.9%	74.6	25.8
CATHOLIC UNIV OF AMERICA (1437)	5	8	12.5%	53.5	25.0
GEORGE WASHINGTON UNIV (1444)	94	198	62.6%	75.4	29.1
GEORGETOWN UNIV (1445)	48	108	72.2%	79.9	28.4
HOWARD UNIV (1448)	40	70	17.1%	60.4	29.3
SOUTHEASTERN UNIV (1456)	11	22	59.1%	71.6	27.8

Appendix C: Summary Performance by Institution Attended - First-Time Testing Events

	Candidates Total	Sections Total	Percent Pass	Average Score	Average Age
STRAYER COLL (1459)	105	154	18.8%	54.7	36.1
UNIV DC (1441)	10	18	0.0%	49.2	41.0
Florida					
BARRY UNIV (1466)	7	11	63.6%	71.2	31.9
FL A&M UNIV (1480)	23	36	16.7%	62.6	26.3
FL ATLANTIC UNIV (1481)	60	105	39.1%	67.1	33.3
FL GULF COAST UNIV (32553)	10	20	40.0%	69.8	28.0
FL INTL UNIV (9635)	87	138	47.8%	72.3	31.2
FL ST UNIV (1489)	91	183	54.1%	74.0	29.3
FLAGLER COLL (7893)	5	9	44.4%	65.2	32.0
NOVA SOUTHEASTERN UNIV (1509)	21	26	26.9%	56.4	33.8
PENSACOLA CHRISTIAN COLL (99998)	9	20	45.0%	68.5	26.6
SAINT LEO UNIV (1526)	24	42	33.3%	66.0	35.5
STETSON UNIV (1531)	13	20	35.0%	68.8	28.5
UNIV CENTRAL FL (3954)	85	168	53.0%	73.6	28.8
UNIV FL (1535)	153	353	76.8%	79.9	26.1
UNIV MIAMI (1536)	79	185	61.1%	75.4	25.0
UNIV NORTH FL (9841)	25	54	50.0%	73.9	30.0
UNIV SOUTH FL (1537)	91	180	65.0%	75.7	28.9
UNIV TAMPA (1538)	30	62	53.2%	72.3	25.9
UNIV WEST FL (3955)	9	16	43.8%	74.3	32.8
Georgia					
ALBANY ST UNIV (1544)	7	13	46.2%	62.9	32.5
AMERICAN INTERCONT GA (21136)	6	9	22.2%	58.3	36.8
AUGUSTA ST UNIV (1552)	19	34	47.1%	69.6	31.0
BERRY COLL (1554)	11	26	46.2%	73.8	26.0
BRENAU UNIV (1556)	9	16	37.5%	61.7	29.2
CLARK ATLANTA UNIV (1559)	12	22	13.6%	52.0	29.3
CLAYTON ST UNIV (8976)	27	53	43.4%	68.9	33.5
COLUMBUS ST UNIV (1561)	9	15	33.3%	61.3	36.5
DEVRY UNIV ALPHARETTA (666989)	6	10	0.0%	50.8	36.5
DEVRY UNIV DECATUR (9224)	14	19	21.1%	55.4	37.0
EMORY UNIV (1564)	56	131	71.0%	80.5	23.9
GA COLL & ST UNIV (1602)	37	64	37.5%	67.3	29.1
GA INST TECH (1569)	52	122	60.7%	76.8	26.9
GA SOUTHERN UNIV (1572)	98	214	46.3%	70.0	26.3
GA SOUTHWESTERN ST UNIV (1573)	16	26	38.5%	61.7	32.0
GA ST UNIV (1574)	278	514	42.6%	69.0	29.4
KENNESAW ST UNIV (1577)	142	237	44.3%	67.9	32.5
LAGRANGE COLL (1578)	6	9	44.4%	62.9	26.8
MACON ST COLL (7728)	18	35	45.7%	68.3	29.9
MERCER UNIV ATLANTA (8419)	9	13	46.2%	67.7	28.7
MERCER UNIV MACON (1580)	20	39	51.3%	71.2	29.9
MOREHOUSE COLL (1582)	10	20	55.0%	71.6	26.1
NORTH GA COLL & ST UNIV (1585)	33	66	56.1%	73.9	29.8
OGLETHORPE UNIV (1586)	16	33	51.5%	71.0	25.3
SHORTER COLL (1591)	10	21	23.8%	60.1	30.1
UNIV GA (1598)	227	595	74.1%	78.7	25.8
UNIV WEST GA (1601)	29	56	21.4%	60.9	27.9
VALDOSTA ST UNIV (1599)	55	92	43.5%	67.8	29.0
Guam					
UNIV GU (3935)	19	27	33.3%	56.2	33.0

Appendix C: Summary Performance by Institution Attended - First-Time Testing Events

	Candidates Total	Sections Total	Percent Pass	Average Score	Average Age
Hawaii					
BRIGHAM YOUNG UNIV HI (1606)	31	69	46.4%	69.6	28.9
CHAMINADE UNIV HONOLULU (1605)	5	8	25.0%	60.0	26.7
HI PACIFIC UNIV (7279)	33	57	36.8%	65.6	32.7
UNIV HI HILO (1611)	8	15	33.3%	65.3	26.9
UNIV HI MANOA (1610)	123	226	40.7%	66.9	28.5
UNIV HI WEST OAHU (21078)	8	12	33.3%	65.8	38.0
Idaho					
ALBERTSON COLL (1617)	8	19	31.6%	66.8	27.2
BOISE ST UNIV (1616)	74	153	45.1%	71.3	30.6
BRIGHAM YOUNG UNIV ID (1625)	71	139	56.1%	74.0	27.8
ID ST UNIV (1620)	28	53	49.1%	71.6	30.3
LEWIS CLARK ST COLL (1621)	13	29	41.4%	70.7	30.9
UNIV ID (1626)	51	103	48.5%	71.5	27.0
Illinois					
AMERICAN INTERCONT IL (666723)	11	22	0.0%	43.6	35.6
AUGUSTANA COLL (1633)	15	30	60.0%	71.9	25.7
AURORA UNIV (1634)	10	21	23.8%	65.9	34.2
BENEDICTINE UNIV (1767)	24	43	30.2%	60.2	29.4
BRADLEY UNIV (1641)	78	185	60.5%	75.8	25.7
CHICAGO ST UNIV (1694)	18	25	16.0%	62.0	36.6
DE PAUL UNIV (1671)	356	670	41.0%	68.8	27.6
DEVRY UNIV ADDISON (22966)	35	82	35.4%	62.0	32.1
DEVRY UNIV OAK BROOK TERRACE (1672)	21	41	7.3%	53.2	35.3
DOMINCAN UNIV (1750)	16	33	18.2%	60.9	29.2
EASTERN IL UNIV (1674)	50	106	50.0%	69.2	27.8
ELMHURST COLL (1676)	26	57	43.9%	69.9	26.6
GOVERNORS ST UNIV (9145)	28	58	22.4%	64.7	34.7
IL INST TECH (1691)	7	14	78.6%	76.1	29.4
IL ST UNIV (1692)	138	373	62.7%	75.5	26.1
IL WESLEYAN UNIV (1696)	40	116	62.9%	76.1	22.9
KELLER GRAD SCHOOL DEVRY (20754)	178	320	30.6%	62.1	35.2
LEWIS UNIV (1707)	19	33	42.4%	70.7	29.9
LOYOLA UNIV CHICAGO (1710)	161	326	48.8%	71.4	26.3
MCKENDREE UNIVERSITY (1722)	15	30	43.3%	67.4	28.0
MILLIKIN UNIV (1724)	21	42	33.3%	65.3	30.0
MONMOUTH COLL (1725)	6	13	53.9%	72.4	26.6
NATIONAL LOUIS UNIV (1733)	6	7	14.3%	46.4	38.8
NORTH CENTRAL COLL (1734)	31	59	49.2%	73.4	26.5
NORTH PARK UNIV (1735)	6	15	53.3%	73.5	25.4
NORTHEASTERN IL UNIV (1693)	53	92	47.8%	68.3	33.4
NORTHERN IL UNIV (1737)	259	586	57.5%	74.5	27.5
NORTHWESTERN UNIV (1739)	18	46	60.9%	75.8	36.7
OLIVET NAZARENE UNIV (1741)	9	24	66.7%	78.3	23.7
QUINCY UNIV (1745)	8	12	58.3%	76.8	28.4
ROBERT MORRIS COLL (1746)	22	32	21.9%	61.6	30.1
ROCKFORD COLL (1748)	9	15	53.3%	73.3	29.3
ROOSEVELT UNIV (1749)	54	106	39.6%	67.3	32.6
SAINT XAVIER UNIV (1768)	12	24	50.0%	68.9	27.5
SOUTHERN IL UNIV CARBONDALE (1758)	77	145	41.4%	67.8	27.1
SOUTHERN IL UNIV EDWARDSVILLE (1759)	69	153	53.6%	71.9	27.9
TRINITY CHRISTIAN COLL (1771)	11	21	66.7%	79.2	24.7

Appendix C: Summary Performance by Institution Attended - First-Time Testing Events

	Candidates Total	Sections Total	Percent Pass	Average Score	Average Age
UNIV CHICAGO (1774)	21	38	55.3%	76.7	40.1
UNIV IL CHICAGO (1776)	361	906	63.4%	75.5	25.8
UNIV IL SPRINGFIELD (9333)	32	62	24.2%	63.2	30.1
UNIV IL URBANA CHAMPAIGN (1775)	410	1,010	60.0%	74.4	25.8
UNIV SAINT FRANCIS (1664)	6	13	46.2%	66.1	25.6
WESTERN IL UNIV (1780)	34	64	42.2%	69.9	29.0
WHEATON COLL (1781)	9	17	64.7%	78.8	34.5
Indiana					
ANDERSON UNIV (1785)	8	19	73.7%	79.8	24.6
BALL ST UNIV (1786)	79	169	46.2%	69.5	27.1
BETHEL COLL (IN) (1787)	7	19	57.9%	73.9	24.3
BUTLER UNIV (1788)	45	124	61.3%	74.8	26.2
FRANKLIN COLL IN (1798)	14	30	26.7%	69.4	24.8
GOSHEN COLL (1799)	20	48	68.8%	77.2	24.5
GRACE COLL & SEMINARY (1800)	10	23	78.3%	81.0	23.8
HUNTINGTON COLL (1803)	5	9	22.2%	55.4	28.1
IN INST TECH (1805)	9	17	35.3%	63.9	34.1
IN ST UNIV (1807)	29	52	26.9%	62.9	28.4
IN UNIV BLOOMINGTON (1809)	421	1,042	64.8%	75.9	25.8
IN UNIV NORTHWEST (1815)	9	20	50.0%	69.9	30.0
IN UNIV PURDUE UNIV FORT WAYNE (1828)	21	44	47.7%	72.2	28.1
IN UNIV PURDUE UNIV INDIANAPOLIS (1813)	125	254	50.4%	72.1	30.9
IN UNIV SOUTH BEND (1816)	23	57	47.4%	64.7	29.8
IN UNIV SOUTHEAST (1817)	19	40	40.0%	68.9	30.0
IN WESLEYAN UNIV (1822)	44	79	39.2%	65.7	31.9
MANCHESTER COLL (1820)	30	67	46.3%	69.6	24.3
MARIAN COLL (1821)	13	24	25.0%	66.0	30.2
PURDUE UNIV (1825)	202	476	42.4%	68.1	26.8
SAINT JOSEPHS COLL (1833)	5	14	35.7%	63.4	26.8
SAINT MARYS COLL (1836)	22	44	34.1%	69.5	23.8
TAYLOR UNIV (1838)	11	26	73.1%	78.8	23.0
TRINE UNIV (1839)	7	8	37.5%	69.8	30.9
UNIV EVANSVILLE (1795)	15	27	37.0%	70.2	25.5
UNIV INDIANAPOLIS (1804)	16	35	37.1%	69.6	28.8
UNIV NOTRE DAME (1840)	240	633	72.7%	79.4	24.0
UNIV SOUTHERN IN (1808)	35	74	47.3%	71.6	27.0
UNIV ST FRANCIS (1832)	6	11	18.2%	66.5	28.7
VALPARAISO UNIV (1842)	17	38	47.4%	69.5	25.1
Iowa					
AIB COLL BUSINESS (3963)	10	19	10.5%	54.1	26.3
BRIAR CLIFF UNIV (1846)	8	17	52.9%	69.5	29.6
BUENA VISTA UNIV (1847)	15	31	16.1%	64.1	30.0
CLARKE COLL (1852)	6	7	42.9%	67.1	34.8
COE COLL (1854)	9	19	47.4%	71.2	25.4
DORDT COLL (1859)	8	19	57.9%	76.1	23.5
DRAKE UNIV (1860)	41	89	58.4%	71.2	26.8
GRAND VIEW UNIV (1867)	6	11	36.4%	67.1	31.1
IA ST UNIV (1869)	120	291	53.6%	72.9	26.7
KAPLAN UNIV (4586)	17	39	30.8%	59.5	39.6
LORAS COLL (1873)	11	28	60.7%	74.9	24.2
LUTHER COLL (1874)	23	58	53.5%	74.3	25.6
MAHARISHI UNIV MANAGEMENT (11113)	6	9	33.3%	64.1	35.3

Appendix C: Summary Performance by Institution Attended - First-Time Testing Events

	Candidates Total	Sections Total	Percent Pass	Average Score	Average Age
MORNINGSIDE COLL (1879)	5	9	66.7%	74.9	38.4
MOUNT SAINT CLARE COLL (1881)	6	13	30.8%	64.9	31.5
NORTHWESTERN COLL IA (1883)	16	29	55.2%	75.0	25.7
SAINT AMBROSE UNIV (1889)	19	37	40.5%	68.4	25.6
SIMPSON COLL (1887)	16	31	41.9%	67.3	25.3
UNIV DUBUQUE (1891)	11	32	25.0%	62.6	26.6
UNIV IA (1892)	180	456	71.7%	78.5	26.6
UNIV NORTHERN IA (1890)	98	327	66.1%	77.3	24.6
UPPER IA UNIV (1893)	28	41	29.3%	62.0	34.3
WARTBURG COLL (1896)	6	14	78.6%	75.4	23.5
Kansas					
BAKER UNIV (1903)	10	21	14.3%	59.2	28.9
BENEDICTINE COLL (10256)	11	26	34.6%	67.0	26.8
EMPORIA ST UNIV (1927)	23	36	19.4%	65.9	28.0
FORT HAYS ST UNIV (1915)	38	72	27.8%	66.2	27.3
FRIENDS UNIV (1918)	5	14	28.6%	62.5	25.6
KANSAS STATE UNIVERSITY (1928)	73	206	66.5%	76.8	26.0
NEWMAN UNIV (1939)	7	14	21.4%	62.7	29.7
OTTAWA UNIV (1937)	9	19	26.3%	59.6	34.4
PITTSBURG ST UNIV (1926)	24	41	19.5%	64.1	26.7
UNIV KS (1948)	168	460	61.5%	75.3	25.8
WASHBURN UNIV (1949)	33	73	32.9%	68.0	30.6
WICHITA ST UNIV (1950)	55	114	57.9%	73.1	29.2
Kentucky					
ASBURY COLL (1952)	5	13	46.2%	70.9	28.1
BELLARMINE UNIV (1954)	35	76	51.3%	72.4	25.0
BEREA COLL (1955)	6	12	50.0%	72.3	25.0
BRESCIA UNIV (1958)	7	10	30.0%	67.3	26.6
EASTERN KY UNIV (1963)	30	47	44.7%	70.4	29.4
GEORGETOWN COLL (1964)	5	9	22.2%	55.6	26.4
KY ST UNIV (1968)	6	11	9.1%	57.0	28.2
KY WESLEYAN COLL (1969)	7	17	52.9%	70.2	24.0
LINDSEY WILSON COLL (1972)	8	15	20.0%	61.7	34.0
MOREHEAD ST UNIV (1976)	9	23	56.5%	73.3	27.1
MURRAY ST UNIV (1977)	47	75	41.3%	71.0	27.7
NORTHERN KY UNIV (9275)	53	116	40.5%	70.8	28.5
SPALDING UNIV (1960)	6	13	23.1%	62.8	39.8
SULLIVAN UNIV (4619)	13	23	17.4%	55.4	38.0
THOMAS MORE COLL (2001)	8	16	43.8%	68.8	26.0
TRANSYLVANIA UNIV (1987)	23	48	45.8%	72.1	23.9
UNIV KY (1989)	160	350	54.9%	73.8	26.4
UNIV LOUISVILLE (1999)	84	147	39.5%	66.8	31.5
UNIV OF CUMBERLANDS (1962)	5	7	71.4%	75.4	28.1
WESTERN KY UNIV (2002)	51	114	58.8%	75.4	28.9
Louisiana					
DILLARD UNIV (2004)	5	9	0.0%	50.2	27.1
GRAMBLING ST UNIV (2006)	13	19	10.5%	55.3	28.6
LA ST UNIV AND A & M COLL (2010)	238	500	53.4%	73.7	26.1
LA ST UNIV IN SHREVEPORT (2013)	19	31	45.2%	67.8	36.2
LA TECH UNIV (2008)	45	93	43.0%	71.6	28.1
LOYOLA UNIV NEW ORLEANS (2016)	28	61	55.7%	71.3	27.9
MCNEESE ST UNIV (2017)	37	71	42.3%	68.3	29.8

Appendix C: Summary Performance by Institution Attended - First-Time Testing Events

	Candidates Total	Sections Total	Percent Pass	Average Score	Average Age
NICHOLLS ST UNIV (2005)	27	51	51.0%	72.3	29.7
NORTHWESTERN ST UNIV (2021)	19	32	31.3%	65.3	28.0
OUR LADY HOLY CROSS COLL (2023)	9	18	0.0%	38.9	34.6
SOUTHEASTERN LA UNIV (2024)	91	162	29.0%	65.4	29.0
SOUTHERN UNIV A&M BATON ROUGE (9636)	11	14	14.3%	59.4	37.7
TULANE UNIV LA (2029)	75	157	63.7%	73.4	26.7
UNIV LA LAFAYETTE (2031)	69	150	70.0%	78.3	27.4
UNIV LA MONROE (2020)	32	70	35.7%	66.1	27.2
UNIV NEW ORLEANS (2015)	94	170	38.8%	67.4	30.7
XAVIER UNIV LA (2032)	5	5	20.0%	39.8	29.8
Maine					
COLBY COLL (2039)	5	8	62.5%	79.0	32.3
HUSSON UNIV (2043)	21	36	27.8%	61.7	28.3
THOMAS COLL (2052)	9	19	57.9%	72.9	27.5
UNIV ME (2053)	30	49	67.4%	75.4	26.6
UNIV ME AUGUSTA (6760)	6	11	72.7%	78.8	34.0
UNIV SOUTHERN ME (2054)	27	47	57.5%	76.9	32.2
Maryland					
BOWIE ST UNIV (2062)	12	18	0.0%	58.9	35.7
FROSTBURG ST UNIV (2072)	5	9	66.7%	71.3	31.7
JOHNS HOPKINS UNIV (2077)	6	12	66.7%	73.6	37.4
LOYOLA UNIVERSITY MD (2078)	54	121	57.0%	74.5	23.6
MORGAN ST UNIV (2083)	8	10	10.0%	54.4	32.3
MOUNT SAINT MARYS UNIV (2086)	6	8	25.0%	61.3	30.5
SALISBURY UNIV (2091)	12	22	50.0%	73.5	25.5
TOWSON UNIV (2099)	27	49	49.0%	69.8	30.6
UNIV BALTIMORE (2102)	18	28	42.9%	69.9	35.2
UNIV MD BALTIMORE COUNTY (2105)	12	23	17.4%	61.1	29.4
UNIV MD COLL PARK (2103)	184	363	54.3%	72.9	27.4
UNIV MD EASTERN SHORE (2106)	5	7	14.3%	69.4	27.8
UNIV MD UNIV COLL (11644)	91	192	42.2%	68.1	30.1
Massachusetts					
AMERICAN INTL COLL (2114)	9	17	52.9%	71.5	30.8
ASSUMPTION COLL (2118)	49	94	42.6%	67.1	25.5
BABSON COLL (2121)	76	162	53.7%	74.6	24.9
BENTLEY COLL (2124)	294	616	56.0%	73.6	26.0
BOSTON COLL (2128)	206	489	76.7%	80.0	24.5
BOSTON UNIV (2130)	115	240	67.1%	76.9	24.8
BRANDEIS UNIV (2133)	5	11	63.6%	78.2	28.9
BRIDGEWATER ST COLL (2183)	15	30	53.3%	70.9	32.1
CLARK UNIV (2139)	13	27	63.0%	73.6	26.9
COLL HOLY CROSS (2141)	34	81	71.6%	77.5	23.3
COLL OUR LADY OF THE ELMS (2140)	5	5	0.0%	53.2	24.3
GORDON COLL (2153)	7	13	23.1%	56.2	26.5
LASELL COLL (2158)	5	7	14.3%	60.4	25.4
MA INST TECH (2178)	6	16	93.8%	89.6	38.4
MERRIMACK COLL (2120)	28	46	28.3%	63.4	27.6
NICHOLS COLL (2197)	14	28	25.0%	64.3	28.9
NORTHEASTERN UNIV (2199)	234	472	52.5%	72.3	26.9
SALEM ST UNIV (2188)	27	46	28.3%	61.1	28.7
STONEHILL COLL (2217)	46	86	54.7%	72.8	24.3
SUFFOLK UNIV (2218)	93	184	42.4%	66.8	28.4

Appendix C: Summary Performance by Institution Attended - First-Time Testing Events

	Candidates Total	Sections Total	Percent Pass	Average Score	Average Age
TUFTS UNIV (2219)	5	16	81.3%	81.9	33.4
UNIV MA AMHERST (2221)	201	419	45.8%	70.1	25.2
UNIV MA BOSTON (2222)	70	134	35.1%	65.0	31.1
UNIV MA DARTMOUTH (2210)	37	70	32.9%	62.4	28.4
UNIV MA LOWELL (2161)	34	59	49.2%	72.1	27.6
WESTERN NEW ENGLAND COLL (2226)	32	61	44.3%	71.8	27.4
WESTFIELD ST COLL (2189)	12	24	41.7%	70.0	27.2
WORCESTER ST COLL (2190)	12	17	23.5%	59.8	29.5
Michigan					
ALBION COLL (2235)	18	32	53.1%	72.6	23.8
ALMA COLL (2236)	7	17	58.8%	72.0	23.7
ANDREWS UNIV (2238)	13	23	34.8%	63.7	31.0
AQUINAS COLL (2239)	11	23	34.8%	66.5	27.3
BAKER COLL FLINT (4673)	20	34	41.2%	63.7	35.4
CALVIN COLL (2241)	36	92	67.4%	76.0	23.9
CENTRAL MI UNIV (2243)	100	212	53.3%	72.2	26.8
DAVENPORT UNIV (2249)	40	87	36.8%	66.1	30.5
EASTERN MI UNIV (2259)	87	170	43.5%	71.0	30.1
FERRIS ST UNIV (2260)	25	56	55.4%	69.6	25.0
GRAND VALLEY ST UNIV (2268)	122	279	70.3%	78.3	26.4
HILLSDALE COLL (2272)	15	31	45.2%	69.9	24.0
HOPE COLL (2273)	21	53	50.9%	69.1	23.2
LAKE SUPERIOR ST UNIV (2293)	14	28	42.9%	71.1	28.4
MI ST UNIV (2290)	348	777	66.0%	76.9	25.6
MI TECH UNIV (2292)	12	34	73.5%	77.9	26.2
NORTHERN MI UNIV (2301)	16	33	27.3%	66.2	26.7
NORTHWOOD UNIV (4072)	42	92	41.3%	68.0	28.6
OAKLAND UNIV (2307)	65	154	61.7%	76.2	27.8
SAGINAW VALLEY ST UNIV (2314)	36	70	27.1%	64.9	27.8
SIENA HEIGHTS UNIV (2316)	10	26	42.3%	66.1	28.7
SPRING ARBOR UNIV (2318)	7	8	25.0%	65.9	25.2
UNIV DETROIT MERCY (2323)	5	7	28.6%	60.9	37.0
UNIV MI ANN ARBOR (2325)	109	307	80.1%	81.8	26.3
UNIV MI DEARBORN (2326)	69	144	60.4%	74.5	29.0
UNIV MI FLINT (2327)	22	41	26.8%	68.0	30.8
WALSH COLL (4071)	118	229	54.6%	72.8	32.4
WAYNE ST UNIV (2329)	83	153	47.1%	69.0	31.0
WESTERN MI UNIV (2330)	108	225	46.2%	71.1	27.1
Minnesota					
AUGSBURG COLL (2334)	28	55	32.7%	68.3	30.3
BEMIDJI ST UNIV (2336)	11	28	60.7%	73.4	27.1
BETHEL COLL (MN) (9058)	20	53	60.4%	73.1	25.7
COLL OF SAINT BENEDICT (2341)	14	46	84.8%	82.2	22.6
COLL OF SAINT SCHOLASTICA (2343)	12	20	40.0%	64.6	27.3
CONCORDIA COLL MOORHEAD (2346)	25	63	74.6%	77.2	23.4
CONCORDIA UNIV MN (2347)	5	11	36.4%	60.3	33.3
GUSTAVUS ADOLPHUS COLL (2353)	14	33	48.5%	69.8	23.7
HAMLINE UNIV (2354)	5	11	45.5%	70.8	29.9
METROPOLITAN ST UNIV (10374)	58	113	38.9%	66.6	34.9
MN SCHOOL OF BUSINESS (4646)	7	13	30.8%	65.5	27.2
MN ST UNIV MANKATO (2360)	83	177	44.6%	69.0	27.3
MN ST UNIV MOORHEAD (2367)	33	60	36.7%	70.8	29.4

Appendix C: Summary Performance by Institution Attended - First-Time Testing Events

	Candidates Total	Sections Total	Percent Pass	Average Score	Average Age
NORTHWESTERN COLL MN (2371)	11	27	70.4%	76.8	23.8
SAINT CATHERINE UNIV (2342)	6	13	69.2%	73.4	29.4
SAINT CLOUD ST UNIV (2377)	82	203	66.5%	76.9	26.5
SAINT JOHN'S UNIV (2379)	45	115	65.2%	75.2	23.7
SAINT MARY'S UNIV OF MN (2380)	16	36	27.8%	62.5	31.3
SOUTHWEST ST UNIV (2375)	12	27	63.0%	74.9	28.1
UNIV MN DULUTH (2388)	70	160	46.3%	70.1	25.0
UNIV MN TWIN CITIES (3969)	190	470	64.3%	77.2	26.8
UNIV ST THOMAS (2345)	103	258	50.4%	73.5	27.5
WINONA ST UNIV (2394)	40	85	27.1%	64.5	27.4
Mississippi					
ALCORN ST UNIV (2396)	5	8	25.0%	51.3	42.3
BELHAVEN COLL (2397)	15	25	36.0%	69.4	34.5
DELTA ST UNIV (2403)	12	22	40.9%	65.5	27.1
JACKSON ST UNIV (2410)	23	38	15.8%	51.2	29.4
MILLSAPS COLL (2414)	25	59	47.5%	71.6	27.5
MS COLL (2415)	28	57	35.1%	63.2	30.6
MS ST UNIV (2423)	97	232	47.0%	70.0	26.8
MS UNIV FOR WOMEN (2422)	5	9	33.3%	65.3	26.8
UNIV MS (2440)	141	378	57.1%	74.0	25.5
UNIV SOUTHERN MS (2441)	66	112	40.2%	68.9	31.7
Missouri					
AVILA UNIV (2449)	8	22	59.1%	72.2	29.4
CENTRAL METHODIST UNIV (2453)	11	15	20.0%	58.5	26.6
COLL OF OZARKS (2500)	6	9	22.2%	70.3	23.8
COLUMBIA COLL (2456)	28	54	27.8%	61.3	36.5
CULVER STOCKTON COLL (2460)	8	24	58.3%	69.9	28.9
DEVRY UNIV KANSAS CITY (2455)	16	21	23.8%	61.5	32.8
DRURY UNIV (2461)	25	65	41.5%	68.8	26.1
FONTBONNE UNIV (2464)	10	17	23.5%	55.8	33.5
LINCOLN UNIV (2479)	6	10	30.0%	64.6	31.5
LINDENWOOD UNIV (2480)	26	47	29.8%	64.6	28.3
MARYVILLE UNIV ST. LOUIS (2482)	20	37	24.3%	64.4	30.6
MO BAPTIST UNIV (7540)	5	11	18.2%	64.9	31.8
MO SOUTHERN ST UNIV (2488)	13	27	63.0%	72.6	31.7
MO ST UNIV (2503)	92	206	52.9%	73.0	26.9
MO VALLEY COLL (2489)	6	13	46.2%	72.7	26.2
MO WESTERN ST UNIV (2490)	8	18	22.2%	58.6	37.2
NORTHWEST MO ST UNIV (2496)	17	37	64.9%	75.0	27.3
PARK UNIV (2498)	18	34	29.4%	63.8	39.5
ROCKHURST UNIV (2499)	19	45	37.8%	70.5	24.9
SOUTHEAST MO ST UNIV (2501)	31	68	50.0%	70.1	28.9
SOUTHWEST BAPTIST UNIV (2502)	15	33	24.2%	64.0	23.9
ST. LOUIS UNIV (2506)	99	240	56.3%	73.3	25.6
TRUMAN ST UNIV (2495)	80	256	78.9%	80.4	24.3
UNIV CENTRAL MO (2454)	36	91	45.1%	71.6	30.7
UNIV MO COLUMBIA (2516)	147	461	71.6%	78.7	24.5
UNIV MO KANSAS CITY (2518)	57	123	73.2%	77.8	28.9
UNIV MO ST. LOUIS (2519)	84	180	51.7%	71.6	29.6
WASHINGTON UNIV ST. LOUIS (2520)	47	109	77.1%	79.6	26.6
WEBSTER UNIV (2521)	33	61	26.2%	60.3	34.1
WESTMINSTER COLL (2523)	6	12	33.3%	68.9	23.7

Appendix C: Summary Performance by Institution Attended - First-Time Testing Events

	Candidates Total	Sections Total	Percent Pass	Average Score	Average Age
WILLIAM WOODS UNIV (2525)	5	8	37.5%	64.5	33.1
Montana					
CARROLL COLL (MT) (2526)	10	22	18.2%	63.5	23.9
MT ST UNIV BILLINGS (2530)	21	56	30.4%	65.3	30.3
MT ST UNIV BOZEMAN (2532)	54	122	59.0%	75.2	25.5
MT TECH UNIV (2531)	6	13	38.5%	75.0	26.4
UNIV MT (2536)	61	152	65.1%	78.2	28.2
Nebraska					
BELLEVUE UNIV (9743)	17	34	41.2%	70.3	31.3
CREIGHTON UNIV (2542)	46	115	53.9%	71.6	24.3
DOANE COLL (2544)	12	25	48.0%	66.3	28.5
HASTINGS COLL (2548)	10	23	39.1%	64.0	25.3
MIDLAND LUTHERAN COLL (2553)	16	31	64.5%	74.8	25.2
NE WESLEYAN UNIV (2555)	9	24	79.2%	75.9	24.2
PERU ST COLL (2559)	6	11	90.9%	84.1	35.1
UNIV NE KEARNEY (2551)	19	38	42.1%	68.1	27.1
UNIV NE LINCOLN (2565)	78	172	58.7%	75.2	26.7
UNIV NE OMAHA (2554)	47	95	60.0%	75.8	27.8
WAYNE ST COLL (2566)	9	21	33.3%	64.8	25.8
YORK COLL (2567)	7	11	45.5%	69.6	28.3
Nevada					
UNIV NV LAS VEGAS (2569)	137	259	46.3%	69.9	29.6
UNIV NV RENO (2568)	68	141	41.1%	70.0	29.2
New Hampshire					
PLYMOUTH ST UNIV (2591)	14	23	30.4%	68.3	31.0
SAINT ANSELM COLL (2587)	14	30	36.7%	69.3	25.4
SOUTHERN NH UNIV (2580)	40	79	40.5%	66.1	35.7
UNIV NH (2589)	68	149	57.7%	74.3	25.0
New Jersey					
BERKELEY COLL (7502)	13	18	5.6%	53.4	28.9
BETH MEDRASH GOVOHA (7947)	18	29	48.3%	72.9	32.4
CALDWELL COLL (2598)	12	15	40.0%	67.9	28.5
CENTENARY COLL (2599)	12	22	31.8%	64.3	30.2
COLL NJ (2642)	103	224	62.1%	76.2	24.7
FAIRLEIGH DICKINSON UNIV (2607)	84	158	45.6%	67.6	28.6
FAIRLEIGH DICKINSON UNIV MADISON (4738)	18	34	38.2%	69.5	35.6
FAIRLEIGH DICKINSON UNIV RUTHERFORD (2604)	16	37	37.8%	71.9	31.7
FELICIAN COLL (2610)	7	19	5.3%	52.4	30.0
GEORGIAN COURT UNIV (2608)	14	31	16.1%	55.5	31.3
KEAN UNIV (2622)	67	114	26.3%	60.0	32.8
MONMOUTH UNIV (2616)	67	146	34.9%	62.7	25.8
MONTCLAIR ST UNIV (2617)	144	282	33.0%	63.9	27.4
NJ CITY UNIV (2613)	31	51	25.5%	58.1	37.1
NJ INST TECH (2621)	5	5	0.0%	61.0	38.8
QUALIFYING CERTIFICATE (88822)	5	9	22.2%	53.9	43.7
RAMAPO COLL NJ (9344)	76	153	40.5%	68.0	25.4
RICHARD STOCKTON COLL NJ (9345)	53	114	39.5%	69.0	28.6
RIDER UNIV (2628)	87	192	27.6%	63.8	27.3
ROWAN UNIV (2609)	73	144	44.4%	66.8	26.1
RUTGERS ST UNIV CAMDEN (4741)	64	144	42.4%	69.7	28.6
RUTGERS ST UNIV NEW BRUNSWICK (6964)	187	358	40.2%	67.5	26.8
RUTGERS ST UNIV NEWARK (2631)	263	460	37.6%	66.3	26.9

Appendix C: Summary Performance by Institution Attended - First-Time Testing Events

	Candidates Total	Sections Total	Percent Pass	Average Score	Average Age
SAINT PETERS COLL (2638)	27	43	23.3%	59.4	29.9
SETON HALL UNIV (2632)	68	117	27.4%	64.2	26.1
THOMAS EDISON ST COLL (21922)	15	29	62.1%	78.3	32.8
WILLIAM PATERSON UNIV NJ (2625)	56	85	28.2%	65.3	28.0
New Mexico					
COLL SANTA FE (2649)	5	10	0.0%	48.4	36.8
EASTERN NM UNIV (2651)	13	21	42.9%	65.6	27.1
NM HIGHLANDS UNIV (2653)	5	8	37.5%	62.9	43.2
NM ST UNIV (2657)	45	79	38.0%	68.7	30.1
SAINT JOHNS COLL (2093)	5	11	45.5%	71.9	25.9
UNIV NM (2663)	93	157	37.6%	68.0	31.5
WESTERN NM UNIV (2664)	8	13	15.4%	59.7	26.7
New York					
ADELPHI UNIV (2666)	34	56	30.4%	62.2	27.8
ALFRED UNIV (2668)	12	18	33.3%	66.4	23.7
BERKELEY COLL NY (7394)	11	19	5.3%	43.9	29.8
CANISIUS COLL (2681)	38	103	68.0%	77.1	24.8
CLARKSON UNIV (2699)	7	14	42.9%	70.1	36.0
COLGATE UNIV (2701)	5	9	55.6%	73.6	30.3
COLL SAINT ROSE (2705)	14	29	24.1%	64.9	28.3
COLUMBIA UNIV NY (2707)	14	34	79.4%	77.9	32.8
CORNELL UNIV (2711)	52	113	72.6%	78.9	26.5
CUNY BARUCH (7273)	592	1,018	51.0%	70.6	29.4
CUNY BROOKLYN (2687)	177	311	38.6%	66.7	28.5
CUNY HERBERT H LEHMAN (7022)	50	73	19.2%	57.6	31.7
CUNY HUNTER (2689)	111	166	25.9%	62.4	29.3
CUNY MEDGAR EVERS (10097)	8	9	0.0%	55.1	37.1
CUNY QUEENS (2690)	213	320	31.3%	63.2	29.5
CUNY STATEN ISLAND (29040)	50	77	23.4%	60.5	30.6
CUNY YORK COLL (4759)	16	19	15.8%	59.4	33.1
DAEMEN COLL (2808)	7	20	45.0%	67.6	24.0
DOWLING COLL (2667)	14	21	14.3%	61.3	33.1
ELMIRA COLL (2718)	6	15	60.0%	79.0	23.4
EXCELSIOR COLL (2834)	40	69	49.3%	69.9	32.6
FORDHAM UNIV (2722)	148	275	45.1%	70.4	24.7
HARTWICK COLL (2729)	15	22	27.3%	66.8	28.8
HOFSTRA UNIV (2732)	159	283	38.9%	68.1	26.5
HOUGHTON COLL (2734)	5	8	62.5%	71.3	28.2
IONA COLL (2737)	26	53	41.5%	65.6	25.3
ITHACA COLL (2739)	27	60	58.3%	75.1	23.9
LE MOYNE COLL (2748)	40	79	38.0%	69.1	25.6
LONG ISLAND UNIV BROOKLYN CENTER (4779)	16	22	18.2%	60.7	31.3
LONG ISLAND UNIV CW POST (2754)	66	110	35.5%	65.9	29.6
MANHATTAN COLL (2758)	41	74	18.9%	56.8	25.9
MARIST COLL (2765)	45	82	41.5%	70.5	25.6
MERCY COLL (2772)	10	17	29.4%	66.8	39.8
MOLLOY COLL (2775)	12	20	20.0%	56.3	25.6
MONROE COLL (4799)	19	25	4.0%	45.8	34.4
MOUNT SAINT MARY COLL (2778)	8	16	6.3%	57.3	28.2
NAZARETH COLL ROCHESTER (2779)	12	28	64.3%	79.7	24.7
NIAGARA UNIV (2788)	26	58	31.0%	66.0	25.8
NY INST TECH MANHATTAN (2782)	20	35	20.0%	57.5	31.1

Appendix C: Summary Performance by Institution Attended - First-Time Testing Events

	Candidates Total	Sections Total	Percent Pass	Average Score	Average Age
NY INST TECH OLD WESTBURY (4804)	9	13	15.4%	56.4	25.5
NY UNIV (2785)	168	373	62.2%	75.9	26.0
NYACK COLL (2790)	5	8	25.0%	65.0	26.3
PACE UNIV NY (2791)	160	264	37.5%	67.7	29.3
PACE UNIV PLEASANTVILLE (2792)	48	87	37.9%	66.2	26.4
PACE UNIV WHITE PLAINS (2727)	5	13	69.2%	77.7	39.1
ROCHESTER INST TECH (2806)	23	51	43.1%	69.3	30.9
SAINT BONAVENTURE UNIV (2817)	40	88	40.9%	69.5	26.1
SAINT FRANCIS COLL (2820)	24	35	31.4%	64.2	25.8
SAINT JOHN FISHER COLL (2821)	31	68	47.1%	72.8	25.8
SAINT JOHNS UNIV NEW YORK (2823)	226	387	35.1%	64.3	26.2
SAINT JOSEPHS COLL NY (2825)	15	25	36.0%	67.2	26.9
SAINT JOSEPHS COLL SUFFOLK (29081)	12	23	47.8%	72.7	27.9
SAINT THOMAS AQUINAS COLL (2832)	7	13	23.1%	61.8	24.9
SIENA COLL (2816)	73	128	47.7%	70.9	25.8
SUNY OLD WESTBURY (7109)	70	113	33.6%	62.0	32.7
SUNY ALBANY (2835)	198	353	47.0%	71.1	26.0
SUNY BINGHAMTON (2836)	289	545	49.5%	71.1	24.7
SUNY BROCKPORT (2841)	37	69	42.0%	71.1	28.2
SUNY BUFFALO (2837)	162	364	58.8%	75.1	26.1
SUNY BUFFALO (2842)	7	16	62.5%	75.3	27.8
SUNY EMPIRE ST COLL (10286)	13	21	66.7%	73.2	36.6
SUNY FREDONIA (2844)	17	30	60.0%	73.4	28.3
SUNY GENESEO (2845)	77	154	61.7%	76.2	23.9
SUNY INST TECH UTICA ROME (11678)	8	18	16.7%	62.7	30.8
SUNY NEW PALTZ (2846)	38	69	55.1%	75.7	27.7
SUNY ONEONTA (2847)	16	26	34.6%	64.1	25.3
SUNY OSWEGO (2848)	52	101	36.6%	66.6	25.7
SUNY PLATTSBURGH (2849)	31	53	30.2%	65.9	27.3
SUNY STONY BROOK (2838)	43	88	39.8%	68.1	27.9
SYRACUSE UNIV (2882)	147	281	42.7%	69.1	25.0
TOURO COLL (10142)	106	184	57.1%	74.3	25.7
UNIV ROCHESTER (2894)	18	33	66.7%	76.8	31.3
UTICA COLL (2883)	10	18	55.6%	74.1	32.0
WAGNER COLL (2899)	37	61	24.6%	62.3	25.8
YESHIVA UNIV (2903)	92	154	39.0%	68.4	24.5
North Carolina					
APPALACHIAN ST UNIV (2906)	81	191	64.4%	76.1	26.5
BARTON COLL (2908)	6	10	30.0%	55.4	35.6
BELMONT ABBEY COLL (2910)	5	11	18.2%	65.0	31.8
CAMPBELL UNIV (2913)	27	54	44.4%	70.9	27.8
CATAWBA COLL (2914)	5	13	38.5%	56.8	30.1
DAVIDSON COLL (2918)	7	25	76.0%	82.2	24.4
DUKE UNIV (2920)	12	26	80.8%	82.8	29.5
EAST CAROLINA UNIV (2923)	100	245	39.2%	69.1	27.3
ELIZABETH CITY ST UNIV (2926)	5	10	0.0%	40.2	40.5
ELON UNIV (2927)	65	138	44.9%	70.5	24.3
FAYETTEVILLE ST UNIV (2928)	5	6	0.0%	39.7	39.8
GARDNER WEBB UNIV (2929)	17	37	40.5%	67.3	34.6
GUILFORD COLL (2931)	10	20	60.0%	76.1	37.2
HIGH POINT UNIV (2933)	11	20	40.0%	65.4	36.7
LENOIR RHYNE COLL (2941)	5	5	20.0%	67.2	33.4

Appendix C: Summary Performance by Institution Attended - First-Time Testing Events

	Candidates Total	Sections Total	Percent Pass	Average Score	Average Age
MEREDITH COLL (2945)	6	17	70.6%	77.9	24.5
METHODIST UNIV (2946)	5	8	12.5%	61.6	35.1
MOUNT OLIVE COLL (2949)	5	12	0.0%	43.8	27.6
NC AGRICULTURAL & TECH ST UNIV (2905)	24	46	23.9%	66.1	28.7
NC CENTRAL UNIV (2950)	10	17	23.5%	50.8	31.7
NC ST UNIV RALEIGH (2972)	158	397	62.7%	76.6	26.3
NC WESLEYAN COLL (2951)	7	17	29.4%	48.8	35.7
PFEIFFER UNIV (2955)	6	13	15.4%	55.2	28.8
UNIV NC ASHEVILLE (2907)	18	38	34.2%	71.2	35.5
UNIV NC CHAPEL HILL (2974)	166	484	72.7%	78.6	26.1
UNIV NC CHARLOTTE (2975)	73	159	58.5%	75.1	30.1
UNIV NC GREENSBORO (2976)	54	108	61.1%	75.0	29.0
UNIV NC PEMBROKE (2954)	6	13	53.9%	70.5	31.1
UNIV NC WILMINGTON (2984)	112	274	49.6%	72.7	25.8
WAKE FOREST UNIV (2978)	63	216	88.4%	84.8	24.8
WESTERN CAROLINA UNIV (2981)	21	45	46.7%	67.2	30.6
WINGATE UNIV (2985)	9	20	20.0%	64.9	25.0
WINSTON SALEM ST UNIV (2986)	9	17	35.3%	65.0	32.4
North Dakota					
DICKINSON ST UNIV (2989)	28	53	37.7%	63.3	25.8
MINOT ST UNIV (2994)	13	24	58.3%	71.7	26.2
ND ST UNIV (9255)	48	104	62.5%	76.1	27.6
UNIV MARY (2992)	17	35	51.4%	71.3	30.1
UNIV ND (3005)	99	206	68.0%	77.8	25.5
Ohio					
ASHLAND UNIV (3012)	18	42	52.4%	72.6	32.6
BALDWIN WALLACE COLL (3014)	44	90	48.9%	69.5	30.1
BOWLING GREEN ST UNIV (3018)	100	210	49.5%	72.2	28.0
CAPITAL UNIV (3023)	23	63	44.4%	66.4	26.3
CASE WESTERN RESERVE UNIV (3024)	45	106	64.2%	75.8	28.0
CEDARVILLE UNIV (3025)	15	28	71.4%	76.9	24.8
CLEVELAND ST UNIV (3032)	94	193	52.9%	71.1	31.2
COLUMBUS ST CC (6867)	7	12	41.7%	70.0	28.9
DEFIANCE COLL (3041)	7	17	47.1%	69.6	26.5
DEVRY UNIV COLUMBUS (3099)	17	29	41.4%	62.1	38.3
FRANCISCAN UNIV STEUBENVILLE (3036)	6	13	46.2%	64.6	32.1
FRANKLIN UNIV (3046)	86	156	26.9%	61.8	35.4
HEIDELBERG COLL (3048)	6	11	9.1%	68.4	28.0
HIRAM COLL (3049)	8	18	38.9%	67.2	25.5
JOHN CARROLL UNIV (3050)	74	163	64.4%	76.8	25.7
KENT ST UNIV (3051)	88	191	57.1%	73.5	28.0
MALONE COLL (3072)	5	14	50.0%	73.1	25.2
MARIETTA COLL (3073)	6	11	45.5%	69.8	28.8
MIAMI UNIV (3077)	281	708	63.7%	76.7	24.4
MOUNT UNION COLL (3083)	9	18	66.7%	79.2	25.3
MOUNT VERNON NAZARENE UNIV (7085)	11	26	34.6%	65.1	32.6
MUSKINGUM COLL (3084)	6	10	60.0%	73.2	26.3
NOTRE DAME COLL OH (3085)	9	21	19.1%	60.4	25.0
OH DOMINICAN UNIV (3035)	13	34	23.5%	63.0	28.2
OH NORTHERN UNIV (3089)	19	49	28.6%	65.2	24.8
OH ST UNIV (6883)	353	855	64.2%	76.6	25.7
OH UNIV (3100)	134	309	46.0%	70.5	25.2

Appendix C: Summary Performance by Institution Attended - First-Time Testing Events

	Candidates Total	Sections Total	Percent Pass	Average Score	Average Age
OH WESLEYAN UNIV (3109)	12	21	52.4%	74.6	24.9
OTTERBEIN UNIV (3110)	9	21	52.4%	68.3	29.1
UNIV AKRON (3123)	97	243	53.1%	73.1	28.8
UNIV CINCINNATI (3125)	94	199	46.2%	69.8	29.1
UNIV DAYTON (3127)	90	212	52.4%	72.9	24.9
UNIV FINDLAY (3045)	14	31	41.9%	68.7	27.7
UNIV NORTHWESTERN OH (4861)	5	10	20.0%	63.2	32.0
UNIV TOLEDO (3131)	75	168	50.6%	69.9	28.1
WALSH UNIV (3135)	8	19	15.8%	64.5	29.8
WILMINGTON COLL (3142)	5	9	33.3%	69.2	31.2
WITTENBERG UNIV (3143)	6	14	42.9%	69.9	29.2
WRIGHT ST UNIV (3078)	54	112	58.0%	74.5	28.2
XAVIER UNIV (3144)	52	120	59.2%	73.8	26.1
YOUNGSTOWN ST UNIV (3145)	50	99	37.4%	66.3	29.0
Oklahoma					
CAMERON UNIV (3150)	14	20	30.0%	59.8	34.5
EAST CENTRAL UNIV (3154)	5	11	54.6%	73.7	30.0
NORTHEASTERN ST UNIV (3161)	30	48	22.9%	59.1	31.5
NORTHWESTERN OK ST UNIV (3163)	6	11	54.6%	75.7	28.1
OK BAPTIST UNIV (3164)	6	11	45.5%	71.7	35.4
OK CHRISTIAN UNIV (3165)	24	50	62.0%	74.0	25.7
OK ST UNIV (3170)	150	388	64.7%	76.8	26.6
OKLAHOMA CITY UNIV (3166)	19	27	40.7%	68.4	30.8
ORAL ROBERTS UNIV (3985)	18	41	56.1%	73.1	26.9
SOUTHEASTERN OK ST UNIV (3179)	5	9	44.4%	66.8	34.4
SOUTHWESTERN OK ST UNIV (3181)	16	34	50.0%	66.6	26.3
UNIV CENTRAL OK (3152)	83	147	45.6%	70.0	30.8
UNIV OK NORMAN (3184)	115	255	60.8%	74.9	26.4
UNIV TULSA (3185)	24	41	53.7%	73.1	30.1
Oregon					
CONCORDIA UNIV (3191)	5	8	12.5%	59.0	25.7
EASTERN OR UNIV (3193)	14	38	60.5%	72.8	29.5
GEORGE FOX UNIV (3194)	14	24	33.3%	69.6	24.2
LINFIELD COLL (3198)	40	83	42.2%	70.3	34.1
OR ST UNIV (3210)	84	159	61.0%	74.9	29.3
PACIFIC UNIV (3212)	8	13	38.5%	64.6	25.3
PORTLAND ST UNIV (3216)	93	191	60.7%	73.6	31.4
SOUTHERN OR UNIV (3219)	23	45	53.3%	73.9	32.5
UNIV OR (3223)	146	300	60.7%	74.8	27.1
UNIV PORTLAND (3224)	28	62	43.6%	69.5	24.7
WESTERN OR UNIV (3209)	5	14	28.6%	63.1	30.0
WILLAMETTE UNIV (3227)	5	12	83.3%	80.9	25.6
Pennsylvania					
ALBRIGHT COLL (3229)	32	46	17.4%	62.3	32.3
ALVERNIA COLL (3233)	15	21	28.6%	65.1	32.2
ARCADIA UNIV (3235)	11	29	37.9%	64.2	24.0
BLOOMSBURG UNIV PA (3315)	88	158	50.6%	72.3	26.2
BUCKNELL UNIV (3238)	49	112	67.9%	77.6	24.4
CA UNIV PA (3316)	19	33	30.3%	60.9	32.6
CABRINI COLL (3241)	13	26	30.8%	62.3	24.6
CARLOW UNIV (3303)	6	11	36.4%	59.0	28.4
CARNEGIE MELLON UNIV (3242)	12	22	50.0%	71.0	32.8

Appendix C: Summary Performance by Institution Attended - First-Time Testing Events

	Candidates Total	Sections Total	Percent Pass	Average Score	Average Age
CHATHAM UNIV (3244)	7	16	31.3%	62.3	30.3
CHESTNUT HILL COLL (3245)	6	10	30.0%	55.7	34.6
CLARION UNIV PA (9235)	19	29	51.7%	71.0	27.7
COLL MISERICORDIA (3247)	8	10	0.0%	50.1	29.2
DE VALLEY COLL (3252)	12	21	23.8%	58.5	26.3
DESALES UNIV (3986)	35	65	32.3%	64.0	27.1
DREXEL UNIV (3256)	185	323	40.6%	67.0	26.2
DUQUESNE UNIV (3258)	111	209	48.3%	71.5	25.5
EAST STROUDSBURG UNIV PA (3320)	14	22	31.8%	62.4	29.8
EASTERN UNIV (3259)	11	24	54.2%	74.2	29.6
EDINBORO UNIV PA (3321)	10	16	18.8%	58.8	29.9
ELIZABETHTOWN COLL (3262)	32	55	30.9%	63.7	25.9
FRANKLIN & MARSHALL COLL (3265)	6	15	80.0%	81.0	29.1
GANNON UNIV (3266)	14	20	20.0%	56.7	33.3
GENEVA COLL (3267)	14	23	30.4%	65.5	27.8
GROVE CITY COLL (3269)	37	84	58.3%	74.6	25.9
GWYNEDD MERCY COLL (3270)	13	27	22.2%	57.8	28.6
HOLY FAMILY COLL (3275)	15	22	18.2%	63.5	28.2
IMMACULATA UNIV (3276)	6	10	30.0%	57.6	27.1
INDIANA UNIV PA (3277)	71	133	33.1%	63.5	28.0
JUNIATA COLL (3279)	12	17	52.9%	64.9	25.8
KEYSTONE COLL (3280)	10	15	0.0%	55.4	24.8
KINGS COLL (3282)	53	88	34.1%	65.0	25.3
KUTZTOWN UNIV PA (3322)	65	129	37.2%	67.9	25.9
LA ROCHE COLL (3987)	17	24	4.2%	47.0	24.5
LA SALLE UNIV (3287)	104	206	27.7%	62.9	26.2
LAFAYETTE COLL (3284)	8	19	36.8%	63.5	27.2
LEBANON VALLEY COLL (3288)	29	63	41.3%	72.5	26.8
LEHIGH UNIV (3289)	128	296	69.3%	77.0	23.6
LINCOLN UNIV (3290)	6	10	20.0%	54.8	24.7
LOCK HAVEN UNIV PA (3323)	13	27	33.3%	55.3	27.5
LYCOMING COLL (3293)	9	22	40.9%	70.1	25.6
MARYWOOD UNIV (3296)	10	17	17.7%	62.1	28.8
MERCYHURST COLL (3297)	24	46	30.4%	62.4	25.3
MESSIAH COLL (3298)	37	85	54.1%	71.6	23.8
MILLERSVILLE UNIV PA (3325)	31	53	37.7%	66.0	26.9
MORAVIAN COLL (3301)	26	48	25.0%	62.8	24.8
MOUNT ALOYSIUS COLL (3302)	7	9	55.6%	73.8	29.4
MUHLENBERG COLL (3304)	42	90	47.8%	71.1	24.9
NEUMANN UNIV (3988)	9	18	38.9%	65.7	33.6
PA ST ERIE (3333)	5	11	72.7%	76.0	34.2
PA ST UNIV PARK (3329)	498	1,052	47.3%	70.3	25.4
PA ST UNIV PARK (6965)	20	32	46.9%	72.8	30.0
PEIRCE COLL (3309)	5	8	62.5%	67.5	35.1
PHILADELPHIA UNIV (3354)	18	41	19.5%	55.8	29.5
POINT PARK UNIV (3357)	9	18	22.2%	63.1	32.5
ROBERT MORRIS UNIV (3359)	78	126	32.5%	63.5	27.7
SAINT FRANCIS UNIV (3366)	31	49	28.6%	62.4	27.2
SAINT JOSEPHS UNIV (3367)	119	248	40.3%	68.7	25.1
SAINT VINCENT COLL (3368)	28	62	41.9%	71.1	24.8
SETON HILL UNIV (3362)	8	13	46.2%	66.5	26.5
SHIPPENSBURG UNIV PA (3326)	67	133	54.9%	71.7	26.2

Appendix C: Summary Performance by Institution Attended - First-Time Testing Events

	Candidates Total	Sections Total	Percent Pass	Average Score	Average Age
SLIPPERY ROCK UNIV PA (3327)	35	61	24.6%	60.2	24.7
SUSQUEHANNA UNIV (3369)	25	49	44.9%	68.5	26.7
TEMPLE UNIV (3371)	350	659	31.9%	63.7	27.6
THIEL COLL (3376)	11	28	25.0%	60.1	23.7
UNIV PA (3378)	34	83	85.5%	82.6	32.5
UNIV PITTSBURGH (3379)	263	522	54.4%	73.0	25.5
UNIV PITTSBURGH JOHNSTOWN (3382)	5	6	50.0%	62.2	30.6
UNIV SCRANTON (3384)	60	103	48.5%	69.9	25.8
URSINUS COLL (3385)	8	10	20.0%	67.2	32.4
VILLANOVA UNIV (3388)	208	479	64.1%	76.3	24.2
WASHINGTON & JEFFERSON COLL (3389)	41	72	45.8%	71.7	24.8
WAYNESBURG COLL (3391)	10	13	0.0%	52.4	29.8
WEST CHESTER UNIV PA (3328)	148	280	35.4%	66.9	26.0
WESTMINSTER COLL (3392)	21	38	29.0%	61.3	25.7
WIDENER UNIV PA (3313)	67	117	26.5%	61.7	25.6
WILKES UNIV (3394)	32	54	22.2%	62.8	28.1
YORK COLL PA (3399)	33	62	46.8%	71.1	25.6
Puerto Rico					
INTER AMERICAN UNIV PR (8242)	22	30	6.7%	37.0	37.1
INTER AMERICAN UNIV PR BARRANQUITAS (5027)	8	13	0.0%	32.6	31.6
INTER AMERICAN UNIV PR BAYAMON (5028)	9	18	0.0%	40.3	30.2
INTER AMERICAN UNIV PR METROPOLITAN (3940)	42	65	9.2%	49.7	31.6
INTER AMERICAN UNIV PR PONCE (5029)	14	29	0.0%	25.6	33.2
INTER AMERICAN UNIV PR SAN GERMAN (3938)	14	21	19.1%	61.0	32.9
PONTIFICAL CATHOLIC UNIV PR (3936)	37	69	10.1%	38.3	31.3
UNIV ESTE (3941)	11	21	9.5%	32.9	40.3
UNIV METROPOLITANA (25875)	14	23	17.4%	37.0	38.0
UNIV PR AGUADILLA (12123)	14	20	5.0%	40.6	30.7
UNIV PR ARECIBO (7228)	23	35	20.0%	53.7	27.8
UNIV PR BAYAMON (10975)	54	87	9.2%	51.3	27.2
UNIV PR CAROLINA (30160)	10	18	11.1%	53.1	29.2
UNIV PR CAYEY (7206)	39	60	6.7%	46.5	27.3
UNIV PR HUMACAO (3943)	31	53	15.1%	50.8	26.4
UNIV PR MAYAGUEZ (3944)	45	72	18.1%	61.0	27.0
UNIV PR PONCE (9652)	20	47	10.6%	43.7	26.4
UNIV PR RIO PIEDRAS (7108)	183	341	37.5%	65.9	25.7
UNIV SACRED HEART (3937)	10	17	35.3%	69.6	27.8
UNIV TURABO GURABO (11719)	12	22	0.0%	41.5	30.1
Rhode Island					
BRYANT UNIV (3402)	168	329	54.7%	73.4	24.9
JOHNSON & WALES UNIV (3404)	55	118	33.9%	61.6	28.1
PROVIDENCE COLL (3406)	55	117	54.7%	75.2	24.6
RI COLL (3407)	14	33	27.3%	60.1	28.0
ROGER WILLIAMS UNIV (3410)	20	37	29.7%	63.4	23.3
SALVE REGINA UNIV (3411)	19	33	27.3%	64.0	26.4
UNIV RI (3414)	82	170	60.0%	73.5	25.9
South Carolina					
BOB JONES UNIV (3421)	22	47	55.3%	72.6	23.8
CITADEL MILITARY COLL SC (3423)	17	40	22.5%	61.7	27.0
CLEMSON UNIV (3425)	74	189	64.0%	76.5	25.4
COASTAL CAROLINA UNIV (3451)	19	31	41.9%	67.5	25.9
COLL CHARLESTON (3428)	47	127	50.4%	73.6	26.6

Appendix C: Summary Performance by Institution Attended - First-Time Testing Events

	Candidates Total	Sections Total	Percent Pass	Average Score	Average Age
FRANCIS MARION UNIV (9226)	5	7	42.9%	66.6	30.9
FURMAN UNIV (3434)	21	60	63.3%	78.6	24.3
UNIV SC COLUMBIA (3448)	138	326	56.8%	75.3	26.4
WINTHROP UNIV (3456)	22	37	59.5%	73.4	29.7
WOFFORD COLL (3457)	17	58	65.5%	76.5	25.3
South Dakota					
AUGUSTANA COLL (3458)	27	65	52.3%	74.4	25.6
BLACK HILLS ST UNIV (3459)	11	21	47.6%	72.0	31.3
CO TECHNICAL UNIV (666731)	10	17	41.2%	60.9	32.0
NATIONAL AMERICAN UNIV (4057)	7	14	42.9%	63.4	36.2
NORTHERN ST UNIV (3466)	10	19	15.8%	59.9	29.7
SD ST UNIV (3471)	12	23	47.8%	75.0	26.4
UNIV SD (3474)	37	68	58.8%	77.0	27.7
UNIV SIOUX FALLS (3469)	16	34	58.8%	75.1	27.2
Tennessee					
AUSTIN PEAY ST UNIV (3478)	21	45	37.8%	63.3	28.3
BELMONT UNIV (3479)	51	104	53.9%	72.4	26.9
CARSON NEWMAN COLL (3481)	9	11	45.5%	66.7	27.5
CHRISTIAN BROTHERS UNIV (3482)	10	19	21.1%	63.6	27.2
CUMBERLAND UNIV (3485)	5	9	11.1%	54.3	27.8
EAST TN ST UNIV (3487)	58	120	43.3%	69.2	30.3
FISK UNIV (3490)	5	9	44.4%	68.3	23.5
FREED HARDEMAN UNIV (3492)	11	18	33.3%	65.6	27.8
LEE UNIV (3500)	18	35	60.0%	72.9	27.4
LIPSCOMB UNIV (3486)	59	120	31.7%	65.6	29.1
MIDDLE TN ST UNIV (3510)	111	244	47.5%	71.0	28.9
RHODES COLL (3519)	26	51	54.9%	74.6	24.1
SOUTHERN ADVENTIST UNIV (3518)	10	24	45.8%	70.0	25.0
TN ST UNIV (3522)	25	40	37.5%	64.5	33.1
TN TECH UNIV (3523)	59	116	32.8%	65.7	28.8
TN WESLEYAN COLL (3525)	7	11	54.6%	58.5	34.5
TREVECCA NAZARENE UNIV (3526)	7	13	69.2%	75.1	26.8
TUSCULUM COLL (3527)	7	9	22.2%	64.9	30.3
UNION UNIV (3528)	10	23	60.9%	73.6	27.8
UNIV MEMPHIS (3509)	63	127	34.7%	64.0	29.8
UNIV TN CHATTANOOGA (3529)	69	132	40.2%	68.3	28.7
UNIV TN KNOXVILLE (3530)	148	378	68.3%	76.6	26.3
UNIV TN MARTIN (3531)	26	49	26.5%	57.0	29.2
VANDERBILT UNIV (3535)	41	143	79.0%	81.1	25.4
Texas					
ABILENE CHRISTIAN UNIV (3537)	54	104	58.7%	74.7	25.4
AMBERTON UNIV (22594)	5	6	33.3%	58.3	42.9
ANGELO ST UNIV (3541)	30	67	52.2%	73.2	30.8
BAYLOR UNIV (3545)	132	339	76.1%	80.0	24.9
BAYLOR UNIV (6967)	14	31	48.4%	71.1	28.2
DALLAS BAPTIST UNIV (3560)	21	40	25.0%	63.3	32.1
DEVRY UNIV IRVING (10139)	12	24	16.7%	54.0	32.6
HARDIN SIMMONS UNIV (3571)	7	10	40.0%	70.2	26.0
HOUSTON BAPTIST UNIV (3576)	23	37	37.8%	68.5	31.8
LAMAR COLL (3581)	24	48	45.8%	72.4	28.8
LETOURNEAU UNIV (3584)	15	25	24.0%	67.0	35.8
LUBBOCK CHRISTIAN UNIV (3586)	5	11	54.6%	77.4	32.3

Appendix C: Summary Performance by Institution Attended - First-Time Testing Events

	Candidates Total	Sections Total	Percent Pass	Average Score	Average Age
MIDWESTERN ST UNIV (3592)	27	48	50.0%	72.6	32.3
OUR LADY THE LAKE UNIV (3598)	12	18	22.2%	63.6	37.2
PRAIRIE VIEW A & M UNIV (3630)	6	13	7.7%	57.5	27.7
RICE UNIV (3604)	16	31	71.0%	79.0	32.3
SAINT EDWARDS UNIV (3621)	24	50	42.0%	70.8	34.6
SAINT MARYS UNIV (3623)	18	30	40.0%	69.4	35.3
SAM HOUSTON ST UNIV (3606)	89	158	46.8%	69.9	29.5
SCHREINER UNIV (3610)	7	9	11.1%	61.4	28.3
SOUTHERN METHODIST UNIV (3613)	105	282	68.8%	78.4	25.4
SOUTHWESTERN UNIV (3620)	8	22	72.7%	77.6	29.4
STEPHEN F AUSTIN ST UNIV (3624)	64	125	44.8%	68.9	28.3
TARLETON ST UNIV (3631)	20	38	39.5%	66.8	32.5
TRINITY UNIV (3647)	40	83	66.3%	76.0	25.4
TX A&M INTL UNIV (9651)	15	24	20.8%	57.3	31.8
TX A&M UNIV (3632)	368	1,064	75.7%	80.1	24.8
TX A&M UNIV COMMERCE (3565)	27	54	40.7%	65.7	31.5
TX A&M UNIV CORPUS CHRISTI (11161)	43	72	38.9%	67.0	29.9
TX A&M UNIV KINGSVILLE (3639)	8	10	10.0%	58.3	32.2
TX CHRISTIAN UNIV (3636)	69	182	68.7%	78.1	25.5
TX LUTHERAN UNIV (3641)	19	30	53.3%	71.3	25.8
TX SOUTHERN UNIV (3642)	12	17	0.0%	42.4	39.5
TX ST UNIV SAN MARCOS (3615)	121	222	51.4%	71.8	29.7
TX TECH UNIV (3644)	168	382	60.5%	73.9	26.9
TX WESLEYAN UNIV (3645)	13	26	23.1%	63.5	31.9
TX WOMANS UNIV (3646)	17	32	37.5%	65.2	29.8
UNIV DALLAS (3651)	25	43	48.8%	71.3	35.8
UNIV HOUSTON (12826)	5	9	22.2%	64.9	34.5
UNIV HOUSTON CLEAR LAKE (11711)	101	165	35.2%	64.8	33.1
UNIV HOUSTON DOWNTOWN (3612)	121	185	29.7%	62.0	32.6
UNIV HOUSTON UNIV PARK (3652)	344	599	42.6%	68.8	30.0
UNIV HOUSTON VICTORIA (13231)	19	36	27.8%	68.3	33.2
UNIV INCARNATE WORD (3578)	19	27	3.7%	47.6	32.3
UNIV MARY HARDIN BAYLOR (3588)	19	40	50.0%	70.6	27.2
UNIV NORTH TX (3594)	143	263	44.1%	70.2	30.7
UNIV SAINT THOMAS (3654)	55	97	45.4%	69.8	29.7
UNIV TX ARLINGTON (3656)	163	291	46.4%	71.4	32.0
UNIV TX AUSTIN (3658)	381	1,009	73.6%	79.5	26.0
UNIV TX BROWNSVILLE (30646)	11	19	42.1%	67.8	29.2
UNIV TX DALLAS (9741)	232	515	41.9%	68.6	30.1
UNIV TX EL PASO (3661)	30	49	53.1%	71.8	31.7
UNIV TX PAN AMERICAN (3599)	28	41	41.5%	65.5	29.4
UNIV TX PERMIAN BASIN (9930)	26	42	42.9%	70.0	32.7
UNIV TX SAN ANTONIO (10115)	120	201	48.3%	70.1	31.5
UNIV TX TYLER (11163)	34	64	50.0%	70.6	29.0
WAYLAND BAPTIST UNIV (3663)	7	16	43.8%	69.4	37.2
WEST TX A & M UNIV (3665)	38	60	26.7%	66.5	30.0
Utah					
BRIGHAM YOUNG UNIV (3670)	332	806	75.8%	79.9	27.3
SOUTHERN UT UNIV (3678)	55	110	50.9%	73.0	27.8
UNIV UT (3675)	165	358	66.8%	76.6	29.7
UT ST UNIV (3677)	86	185	54.6%	73.8	30.2
UT VALLEY ST COLL (4027)	21	41	46.3%	72.2	31.4

Appendix C: Summary Performance by Institution Attended - First-Time Testing Events

	Candidates Total	Sections Total	Percent Pass	Average Score	Average Age
WEBER ST UNIV (3680)	63	118	66.1%	75.1	30.6
Western Governors Univ (33394)	7	14	28.6%	65.6	33.8
WESTMINSTER COLL (3681)	27	47	34.0%	64.9	32.3
Vermont					
CASTLETON ST COLL (3683)	8	17	82.4%	81.4	28.2
CHAMPLAIN COLL (3684)	26	48	31.3%	67.6	27.8
SAINT MICHAELS COLL (3694)	26	50	56.0%	73.1	25.4
UNIV VT (3696)	28	58	62.1%	75.8	30.1
Virgin Islands					
UNIV VI (3946)	7	10	30.0%	66.9	28.7
Virginia					
AVERETT UNIV (3702)	5	8	25.0%	66.6	34.2
BRIDGEWATER COLL (3704)	10	22	27.3%	61.2	24.0
CHRISTOPHER NEWPORT UNIV (3706)	16	32	50.0%	73.4	26.1
COLL WILLIAM & MARY (3705)	100	260	64.2%	76.6	24.9
EASTERN MENNONITE UNIV (3708)	5	18	72.2%	82.9	29.8
FERRUM COLL (3711)	6	11	63.6%	74.5	26.0
GEORGE MASON UNIV (3749)	238	425	46.1%	70.5	29.0
HAMPDEN SYDNEY COLL (3713)	5	8	50.0%	75.9	27.0
HAMPTON UNIV (3714)	30	51	15.7%	61.4	29.0
JAMES MADISON UNIV (3721)	143	409	70.2%	78.9	24.7
LIBERTY UNIV (20530)	54	93	46.2%	71.0	31.6
LONGWOOD UNIV (3719)	17	30	43.3%	67.2	25.5
LYNCHBURG COLL (3720)	7	13	61.5%	75.8	25.3
MARYMOUNT UNIV (3724)	5	10	60.0%	75.6	32.3
NORFOLK ST UNIV (3765)	7	10	40.0%	60.0	33.2
NORTHERN VA CC (3727)	18	32	50.0%	70.8	31.6
OLD DOMINION UNIV (3728)	67	131	49.6%	70.0	30.4
RADFORD UNIV (3732)	24	38	44.7%	69.3	26.2
RANDOLPH MACON COLL (3733)	15	33	45.5%	69.6	26.9
ROANOKE COLL (3736)	11	19	36.8%	69.9	25.8
TIDEWATER CC (3712)	6	9	33.3%	63.6	32.4
UNIV MARY WASHINGTON (3746)	16	31	48.4%	72.0	28.2
UNIV RICHMOND (3744)	66	173	68.8%	78.3	24.8
UNIV VA (3745)	127	339	84.7%	84.0	25.1
UNIV VA COL WISE (CLINCH VALLEY COLL) (3747)	7	11	63.6%	75.0	28.6
VA COMMONWEALTH UNIV (3735)	92	160	38.1%	66.9	28.5
VA POLYTECHNIC INST & ST UNIV (3754)	226	518	61.2%	75.9	25.7
WASHINGTON & LEE UNIV (3768)	32	81	66.7%	78.0	24.6
Washington					
BELLEVUE CC (3769)	6	7	42.9%	71.0	26.4
CENTRAL WA UNIV (3771)	114	247	43.7%	69.1	30.5
CITY UNIV SEATTLE (13022)	21	44	27.3%	61.2	40.3
EASTERN WA UNIV (3775)	57	115	37.4%	66.3	30.9
GONZAGA UNIV (3778)	89	233	70.8%	78.7	25.3
NORTH SEATTLE CC (9704)	11	20	60.0%	70.5	30.2
PACIFIC LUTHERAN UNIV (3785)	17	40	15.0%	58.4	24.8
SAINT MARTINS COLL (3794)	11	22	31.8%	62.1	32.8
SEATTLE PACIFIC UNIV (3788)	26	58	50.0%	72.3	24.3
SEATTLE UNIV (3790)	46	100	43.0%	69.1	28.1
UNIV PUGET SOUND (3797)	7	13	76.9%	76.8	33.3
UNIV WA (3798)	327	798	64.2%	75.7	27.4

Appendix C: Summary Performance by Institution Attended - First-Time Testing Events

	Candidates Total	Sections Total	Percent Pass	Average Score	Average Age
WA ST UNIV (3800)	125	265	49.1%	71.8	27.1
WALLA WALLA UNIV (3799)	6	12	66.7%	78.3	27.1
WESTERN WA UNIV (3802)	47	101	69.3%	77.0	27.4
WHITWORTH COLL (3804)	12	22	68.2%	77.6	28.2
West Virginia					
BETHANY COLL (3808)	5	8	75.0%	76.0	29.3
CONCORD UNIV (3810)	9	14	28.6%	68.1	26.6
FAIRMONT ST COLL (3812)	5	12	41.7%	62.6	31.4
GLENVILLE ST COLL (3813)	5	6	16.7%	59.5	26.1
MARSHALL UNIV (3815)	58	99	40.4%	67.9	27.4
SALEM INTL UNIV (3820)	5	12	41.7%	67.2	37.9
SHEPHERD UNIV (3822)	7	16	50.0%	68.1	26.4
UNIV CHARLESTON (3818)	11	25	28.0%	60.6	23.5
WEST LIBERTY ST COLL (3823)	12	24	20.8%	64.7	29.4
WHEELING JESUIT UNIV (3831)	15	24	37.5%	63.7	29.8
WV INST TECH (3825)	7	15	13.3%	54.9	40.1
WV ST UNIV (3826)	22	33	18.2%	57.3	29.0
WV UNIV (3827)	145	300	50.7%	71.5	26.8
WV UNIV PARKERSBURG (3828)	9	16	31.3%	64.8	28.5
WV WESLEYAN COLL (3830)	11	22	54.6%	68.9	24.4
Wisconsin					
CARDINAL STRITCH UNIV (3837)	12	23	34.8%	61.0	38.3
CARROLL UNIV (WI) (3838)	16	41	51.2%	70.4	26.8
CARTHAGE COLL (3839)	13	28	7.1%	54.0	25.5
CONCORDIA UNIV WI (3842)	13	27	33.3%	63.0	28.9
EDGEWOOD COLL (3848)	14	30	30.0%	62.9	31.7
LAKELAND COLL (3854)	44	99	41.4%	70.0	38.6
MARQUETTE UNIV (3863)	104	256	71.1%	78.3	24.9
MOUNT MARY COLL (3869)	6	13	23.1%	60.0	41.2
SAINT NORBERT COLL (3892)	21	52	65.4%	74.0	24.2
UNIV WI EAU CLAIRE (3917)	71	152	57.9%	74.5	25.9
UNIV WI GREEN BAY (3899)	35	81	33.3%	70.2	26.6
UNIV WI LA CROSSE (3919)	80	190	55.3%	74.0	24.9
UNIV WI MADISON (3895)	177	499	76.4%	80.5	25.2
UNIV WI MILWAUKEE (3896)	164	429	56.4%	74.4	28.1
UNIV WI OSHKOSH (3920)	62	149	55.0%	73.2	26.2
UNIV WI PARKSIDE (5015)	17	26	11.5%	59.3	29.7
UNIV WI PLATTEVILLE (3921)	13	28	53.6%	71.8	29.1
UNIV WI RIVER FALLS (3923)	25	56	57.1%	73.4	28.1
UNIV WI STEVENS POINT (3924)	15	31	54.8%	75.2	29.1
UNIV WI SUPERIOR (3925)	12	29	37.9%	66.9	28.6
UNIV WI WHITEWATER (3926)	157	414	58.7%	75.0	26.0
Wyoming					
UNIV WY (3932)	63	130	53.1%	74.1	27.4

INSTITUTION ATTENDED FIRST-TIME TESTING EVENTS

APPENDIX D

SECTION PERFORMANCE

Appendix D: Section Performance by Institution Attended - First-Time Testing Events

	Total Events per Section				Percent Pass			
	AUD	BEC	FAR	REG	AUD	BEC	FAR	REG
Alabama								
AL A&M UNIV (1002)	3	1	3	2	0%	0%	0%	50%
AL ST UNIV (1005)	2	4	3	1	50%	0%	33%	0%
ATHENS ST UNIV (1008)	5	4	5	1	0%	50%	20%	0%
AUBURN UNIV (1009)	104	92	101	123	64%	74%	65%	67%
AUBURN UNIV MONTGOMERY (8310)	13	1	9	10	15%	0%	11%	10%
BIRMINGHAM SOUTHERN COLL (1012)	15	13	16	13	13%	46%	31%	31%
HUNTINGDON COLL (1019)	5	5	3	5	60%	60%	33%	60%
JACKSONVILLE ST UNIV (1020)	9	4	5	4	44%	50%	60%	50%
OAKWOOD COLL (1033)	2	5	2	4	50%	20%	100%	25%
SAMFORD UNIV (1036)	10	11	7	16	70%	64%	57%	75%
TROY UNIV (1047)	36	26	29	35	19%	31%	38%	34%
UNIV AL (1051)	137	109	106	116	51%	68%	55%	59%
UNIV AL BIRMINGHAM (1052)	51	39	40	40	49%	56%	40%	35%
UNIV AL HUNTSVILLE (1055)	10	8	6	10	40%	38%	33%	50%
UNIV MONTEVALLO (1004)	5	5	6	4	60%	60%	50%	25%
UNIV NORTH AL (1016)	7	13	11	9	57%	46%	27%	78%
UNIV SOUTH AL (1057)	26	21	22	21	46%	38%	36%	43%
Alaska								
UNIV ALASKA ANCHORAGE (11462)	17	14	22	16	53%	29%	27%	38%
UNIV ALASKA FAIRBANKS (1063)	7	6	8	7	57%	50%	50%	43%
UNIV ALASKA SOUTHEAST (1065)	4	3	2	3	25%	67%	50%	33%
Arizona								
AZ ST UNIV (1081)	180	136	155	170	58%	70%	59%	56%
AZ ST UNIV WEST (66935)	5	2	4	5	80%	100%	50%	20%
DEVRY UNIV PHOENIX (8322)	17	22	15	23	18%	27%	33%	39%
GRAND CANYON UNIV (1074)	5	5	7	7	20%	20%	29%	43%
NORTHERN AZ UNIV (1082)	27	26	30	31	33%	54%	47%	45%
THUNDERBIRD SCHOOL OF GLOBAL MGMT (1070)	4	5	6	9	75%	60%	0%	33%
UNIV AZ (1083)	100	80	107	106	53%	66%	59%	42%
UNIV PHOENIX (20988)	185	186	207	199	29%	26%	30%	35%
WESTERN INTL UNIV (21715)	5	4	4	6	60%	50%	50%	50%
Arkansas								
AR ST UNIV (1090)	16	14	17	17	31%	43%	24%	18%
AR TECH UNIV (1089)	12	14	17	16	58%	50%	47%	63%
HARDING UNIV (1097)	26	21	24	30	54%	38%	33%	40%
HENDERSON ST UNIV (1098)	11	7	11	7	18%	43%	27%	14%
HENDRIX COLL (1099)	4	3	3	4	0%	33%	33%	0%
OUACHITA BAPTIST UNIV (1102)	6	5	5	6	33%	40%	40%	67%
SOUTHERN AR UNIV (1107)	5	5	6	5	20%	0%	17%	40%
UNIV AR (1108)	59	49	64	60	61%	76%	50%	42%
UNIV AR LITTLE ROCK (1101)	14	7	11	15	43%	57%	36%	60%
UNIV AR MONTICELLO (1085)	4	4	4	2	25%	25%	50%	50%
UNIV CENTRAL AR (1092)	34	18	27	29	35%	39%	48%	41%
California								
AMERICAN RIVER COLL (1232)	3	2	4	2	33%	100%	75%	50%
AZUSA PACIFIC UNIV (1117)	9	6	11	8	22%	17%	18%	38%
BIOLA UNIV (1122)	10	14	8	11	30%	29%	38%	36%
CA BAPTIST UNIV (1125)	7	7	6	7	29%	14%	17%	14%
CA LUTHERAN UNIV (1133)	11	7	10	11	9%	43%	30%	36%
CA ST POLYTECH UNIV POMONA (1144)	53	49	58	63	26%	22%	36%	25%
CA ST POLYTECH UNIV SAN LUIS OBISPO (1143)	124	76	101	110	54%	45%	46%	55%
CA ST UNIV BAKERSFIELD (7993)	24	16	15	20	46%	50%	20%	50%
CA ST UNIV CHICO (1146)	30	30	31	38	37%	43%	48%	34%
CA ST UNIV DOMINGUEZ HILLS (1141)	18	13	17	14	22%	23%	24%	36%
CA ST UNIV EAST BAY (1138)	95	72	88	107	38%	46%	33%	36%
CA ST UNIV FRESNO (1147)	50	44	56	61	46%	48%	38%	34%

Appendix D: Section Performance by Institution Attended - First-Time Testing Events

	Total Events per Section				Percent Pass			
	AUD	BEC	FAR	REG	AUD	BEC	FAR	REG
CA ST UNIV FULLERTON (1137)	179	142	171	205	35%	42%	37%	37%
CA ST UNIV LONG BEACH (1139)	106	74	84	104	41%	35%	40%	43%
CA ST UNIV LOS ANGELES (1140)	100	70	89	103	24%	36%	27%	32%
CA ST UNIV NORTHRIDGE (1153)	149	100	128	155	40%	48%	47%	50%
CA ST UNIV SACRAMENTO (1150)	105	95	96	113	37%	47%	33%	35%
CA ST UNIV SAN BERNARDINO (1142)	44	32	35	37	30%	19%	20%	32%
CA ST UNIV SAN MARCOS (30113)	29	27	25	31	62%	59%	48%	48%
CA ST UNIV STANISLAUS (1157)	17	10	13	15	24%	40%	23%	33%
CHAPMAN UNIV (1164)	22	21	24	25	64%	48%	46%	60%
CLAREMONT GRADUATE UNIV (1169)	0	1	3	3	0%	0%	0%	33%
CLAREMONT MCKENNA COLL (1170)	13	9	9	10	62%	100%	67%	50%
CONCORDIA UNIV (20705)	0	0	3	4	0%	0%	33%	25%
DE ANZA COLL (4480)	5	5	5	9	0%	60%	20%	56%
DEVRY UNIV LONG BEACH (666988)	11	7	7	12	9%	0%	14%	8%
DEVRY UNIV POMONA (23329)	10	8	13	11	30%	0%	15%	27%
FOOTHILL COLL (1199)	5	6	6	4	40%	83%	33%	75%
FRESNO PACIFIC UNIV (1253)	6	5	5	2	67%	20%	40%	50%
GLENDALE CC (1203)	5	2	5	6	20%	50%	20%	33%
GOLDEN GATE UNIV (1205)	66	42	67	67	36%	40%	42%	49%
GOLDEN WEST COLL (1206)	4	3	3	1	50%	67%	67%	100%
HUMBOLDT ST UNIV (1149)	7	7	4	7	43%	14%	50%	43%
LA SIERRA UNIV (1215)	6	1	5	7	0%	0%	0%	14%
LOYOLA MARYMOUNT UNIV (11649)	43	38	43	45	56%	53%	58%	47%
MASTERS COLL & SEMINARY (1220)	6	5	6	9	50%	80%	50%	22%
MENLO COLL (1236)	2	1	3	3	0%	0%	33%	0%
MOUNT SAINT MARYS COLL (1243)	4	8	2	6	50%	50%	0%	33%
NATIONAL UNIV (11460)	26	22	21	20	38%	50%	38%	35%
PACIFIC ST UNIV (31633)	6	1	3	9	0%	0%	67%	11%
PACIFIC UNION COLL (1258)	4	3	5	5	50%	67%	60%	60%
PEPPERDINE (1264)	26	19	16	34	46%	53%	44%	35%
POINT LOMA NAZARENE UNIV (1262)	11	4	6	7	36%	75%	67%	57%
SAINT MARYS COLL CA (1302)	17	13	19	20	24%	38%	26%	35%
SAN DIEGO ST UNIV (1151)	150	128	152	180	49%	52%	53%	56%
SAN FRANCISCO ST UNIV (1154)	97	66	98	114	40%	47%	41%	40%
SAN JOSE ST UNIV (1155)	138	101	123	139	46%	51%	45%	46%
SANTA CLARA UNIV (1326)	118	107	108	136	47%	64%	38%	37%
SANTA MONICA COLL (1286)	11	7	10	6	18%	29%	30%	17%
SIMPSON UNIV (1291)	6	5	5	3	33%	40%	20%	33%
SONOMA ST UNIV (1156)	37	30	49	42	19%	27%	27%	31%
STANFORD UNIV (1305)	3	2	4	3	67%	50%	25%	67%
UNIV CA BERKELEY (1312)	145	113	128	149	54%	78%	59%	61%
UNIV CA DAVIS (1313)	45	47	46	48	42%	60%	57%	58%
UNIV CA IRVINE (1314)	79	54	79	87	43%	57%	41%	51%
UNIV CA LOS ANGELES (1315)	239	192	224	280	59%	74%	68%	58%
UNIV CA RIVERSIDE (1316)	75	70	73	90	33%	33%	29%	34%
UNIV CA SAN DIEGO (1317)	54	36	45	48	57%	50%	49%	42%
UNIV CA SANTA BARBARA (1320)	195	148	208	199	55%	61%	48%	46%
UNIV CA SANTA CRUZ (1321)	64	41	59	56	36%	54%	31%	39%
UNIV LA VERNE (1216)	13	10	10	18	31%	40%	60%	11%
UNIV PACIFIC (1329)	19	12	10	17	58%	67%	60%	41%
UNIV REDLANDS (1322)	13	7	12	12	23%	29%	25%	25%
UNIV SAN DIEGO (10395)	74	61	64	74	49%	66%	44%	54%
UNIV SAN FRANCISCO (1325)	43	23	31	30	26%	39%	32%	30%
UNIV SOUTHERN CA (1328)	309	245	303	324	56%	82%	61%	53%
VANGUARD UNIV SOUTHERN CA (1293)	3	2	4	4	67%	100%	75%	75%
WOODBURY UNIV (1343)	5	4	5	2	40%	25%	20%	50%
Colorado								
ADAMS ST COLL (1345)	1	2	1	2	0%	0%	100%	50%
CHARTERED ACCT (199999)	43	47	44	50	58%	79%	59%	48%
CO COLL (1347)	3	1	3	3	67%	100%	67%	67%
CO ST UNIV (1350)	76	60	64	78	63%	72%	63%	62%

Appendix D: Section Performance by Institution Attended - First-Time Testing Events

	Total Events per Section				Percent Pass			
	AUD	BEC	FAR	REG	AUD	BEC	FAR	REG
FORT LEWIS COLL (1353)	9	16	13	13	33%	38%	38%	15%
JONES INTL UNIV (35343)	3	0	2	3	0%	0%	50%	67%
MESA ST COLL (1358)	13	13	12	13	38%	62%	50%	46%
METRO ST COLL DENVER (1360)	39	39	50	46	36%	31%	30%	39%
REGIS UNIV (1363)	39	37	32	33	51%	49%	31%	52%
UNIV CO BOULDER (1370)	84	78	86	85	58%	76%	63%	58%
UNIV CO COLORADO SPRINGS (4509)	24	11	15	14	46%	55%	33%	57%
UNIV CO DENVER (6740)	31	36	42	36	39%	39%	33%	33%
UNIV DENVER (1371)	42	36	38	41	40%	83%	53%	49%
UNIV NORTHERN CO (1349)	28	31	26	30	46%	48%	50%	37%
UNIV SOUTHERN CO (1365)	9	9	13	8	33%	44%	62%	38%
WESTERN ST COLL (1372)	5	4	5	7	60%	75%	80%	57%
Connecticut								
ALBERTUS MAGNUS COLL (1374)	2	2	2	1	0%	0%	0%	0%
CENTRAL CT ST UNIV (1378)	19	18	16	17	42%	39%	56%	41%
EASTERN CT ST UNIV (1425)	6	9	12	7	17%	78%	33%	29%
FAIRFIELD UNIV (1385)	54	45	57	58	48%	67%	51%	52%
QUINNIPIAC UNIV (1402)	42	28	26	45	43%	54%	42%	33%
SACRED HEART UNIV (1403)	20	9	18	20	25%	33%	22%	20%
SOUTHERN CT ST UNIV (1406)	10	9	15	14	20%	33%	40%	43%
TEIKYO POST UNIV (1401)	2	6	5	4	50%	33%	20%	50%
UNIV BRIDGEPORT (1416)	5	4	5	5	20%	0%	40%	20%
UNIV CT (1417)	125	91	117	134	53%	74%	48%	50%
UNIV HARTFORD (1422)	16	13	13	13	25%	54%	31%	46%
UNIV NEW HAVEN (1397)	6	7	6	7	33%	14%	17%	29%
WESTERN CT ST UNIV (1380)	11	10	7	9	73%	50%	29%	44%
Delaware								
DE ST UNIV (1428)	2	5	2	2	0%	20%	0%	50%
GOLDEY BEACOM COLL (1429)	10	8	12	9	20%	13%	25%	33%
UNIV DE (1431)	112	85	99	111	49%	69%	61%	50%
WILMINGTON COLL (7948)	17	12	9	8	35%	33%	33%	13%
District of Columbia								
AMERICAN UNIV (1434)	33	29	40	40	58%	72%	53%	43%
CATHOLIC UNIV OF AMERICA (1437)	4	2	0	2	0%	0%	0%	50%
GEORGE WASHINGTON UNIV (1444)	56	45	50	47	54%	80%	58%	62%
GEORGETOWN UNIV (1445)	25	28	24	31	72%	89%	71%	58%
HOWARD UNIV (1448)	20	15	17	18	15%	27%	12%	17%
SOUTHEASTERN UNIV (1456)	6	5	5	6	50%	60%	60%	67%
STRAYER COLL (1459)	35	37	35	47	23%	8%	14%	28%
UNIV DC (1441)	5	4	6	3	0%	0%	0%	0%
Florida								
BARRY UNIV (1466)	3	3	2	3	100%	67%	50%	33%
FL A&M UNIV (1480)	8	12	8	8	25%	8%	25%	13%
FL ATLANTIC UNIV (1481)	25	25	28	27	44%	32%	43%	37%
FL GULF COAST UNIV (32553)	7	3	6	4	43%	67%	33%	25%
FL INTL UNIV (9635)	34	29	27	48	38%	59%	52%	46%
FL ST UNIV (1489)	52	34	42	55	56%	68%	45%	51%
FLAGLER COLL (7893)	1	2	3	3	100%	0%	0%	100%
NOVA SOUTHEASTERN UNIV (1509)	6	5	5	10	17%	20%	40%	30%
PENSACOLA CHRISTIAN COLL (99998)	4	7	5	4	50%	57%	40%	25%
SAINT LEO UNIV (1526)	8	8	11	15	25%	38%	9%	53%
STETSON UNIV (1531)	6	2	6	6	33%	50%	33%	33%
UNIV CENTRAL FL (3954)	44	37	39	48	59%	68%	36%	50%
UNIV FL (1535)	98	84	83	88	71%	82%	83%	72%
UNIV MIAMI (1536)	48	41	43	53	54%	73%	53%	64%
UNIV NORTH FL (9841)	13	15	11	15	54%	60%	45%	40%
UNIV SOUTH FL (1537)	52	38	44	46	60%	71%	61%	70%
UNIV TAMPA (1538)	20	8	19	15	60%	50%	47%	53%
UNIV WEST FL (3955)	3	5	4	4	33%	40%	50%	50%

Appendix D: Section Performance by Institution Attended - First-Time Testing Events

	Total Events per Section				Percent Pass			
	AUD	BEC	FAR	REG	AUD	BEC	FAR	REG
Georgia								
ALBANY ST UNIV (1544)	3	3	4	3	67%	67%	25%	33%
AMERICAN INTERCONT GA (21136)	1	1	2	5	0%	0%	50%	20%
AUGUSTA ST UNIV (1552)	9	11	5	9	33%	45%	60%	56%
BERRY COLL (1554)	7	5	8	6	57%	40%	38%	50%
BRENAU UNIV (1556)	3	5	4	4	0%	40%	25%	75%
CLARK ATLANTA UNIV (1559)	6	5	6	5	17%	20%	0%	20%
CLAYTON ST UNIV (8976)	16	12	12	13	56%	67%	33%	15%
COLUMBUS ST UNIV (1561)	4	3	5	3	50%	33%	20%	33%
DEVRY UNIV ALPHARETTA (666989)	2	5	0	3	0%	0%	0%	0%
DEVRY UNIV DECATUR (9224)	6	6	2	5	50%	0%	0%	20%
EMORY UNIV (1564)	33	29	33	36	55%	93%	67%	72%
GA COLL & ST UNIV (1602)	15	18	10	21	47%	28%	20%	48%
GA INST TECH (1569)	32	28	31	31	59%	64%	77%	42%
GA SOUTHERN UNIV (1572)	49	50	54	61	53%	52%	43%	39%
GA SOUTHWESTERN ST UNIV (1573)	6	5	7	8	33%	60%	14%	50%
GA ST UNIV (1574)	142	113	118	141	39%	47%	42%	43%
KENNESAW ST UNIV (1577)	61	60	47	69	44%	43%	45%	45%
LAGRANGE COLL (1578)	3	3	0	3	0%	67%	0%	67%
MACON ST COLL (7728)	9	10	7	9	44%	60%	57%	22%
MERCER UNIV ATLANTA (8419)	2	3	4	4	0%	100%	50%	25%
MERCER UNIV MACON (1580)	12	9	9	9	50%	56%	56%	44%
MOREHOUSE COLL (1582)	4	4	7	5	25%	75%	57%	60%
NORTH GA COLL & ST UNIV (1585)	15	14	19	18	80%	57%	42%	50%
OGLETHORPE UNIV (1586)	8	5	10	10	75%	60%	40%	40%
SHORTER COLL (1591)	7	4	5	5	29%	25%	40%	0%
UNIV GA (1598)	164	131	136	164	71%	88%	74%	66%
UNIV WEST GA (1601)	16	9	14	17	19%	33%	21%	18%
VALDOSTA ST UNIV (1599)	25	22	17	28	44%	32%	35%	57%
Guam								
UNIV GU (3935)	8	4	9	6	38%	25%	33%	33%
Hawaii								
BRIGHAM YOUNG UNIV HI (1606)	18	19	15	17	44%	58%	53%	29%
CHAMINADE UNIV HONOLULU (1605)	3	0	4	1	33%	0%	25%	0%
HI PACIFIC UNIV (7279)	15	10	12	20	20%	40%	50%	40%
UNIV HI HILO (1611)	4	5	4	2	50%	20%	25%	50%
UNIV HI MANOA (1610)	62	43	56	65	47%	33%	32%	48%
UNIV HI WEST OAHU (21078)	1	2	3	6	0%	0%	33%	50%
Idaho								
ALBERTSON COLL (1617)	5	5	5	4	20%	40%	20%	50%
BOISE ST UNIV (1616)	39	36	37	41	46%	44%	46%	44%
BRIGHAM YOUNG UNIV ID (1625)	32	29	36	42	50%	72%	53%	52%
ID ST UNIV (1620)	14	9	13	17	36%	56%	77%	35%
LEWIS CLARK ST COLL (1621)	7	9	7	6	43%	44%	43%	33%
UNIV ID (1626)	31	23	23	26	42%	61%	52%	42%
Illinois								
AMERICAN INTERCONT IL (666723)	6	8	3	5	0%	0%	0%	0%
AUGUSTANA COLL (1633)	9	6	6	9	67%	67%	67%	44%
AURORA UNIV (1634)	6	5	6	4	17%	20%	33%	25%
BENEDICTINE UNIV (1767)	9	10	10	14	33%	30%	20%	36%
BRADLEY UNIV (1641)	53	41	44	47	62%	66%	59%	55%
CHICAGO ST UNIV (1694)	7	4	5	9	14%	25%	20%	11%
DE PAUL UNIV (1671)	189	147	152	182	37%	46%	42%	41%
DEVRY UNIV ADDISON (22966)	25	15	19	23	24%	47%	47%	30%
DEVRY UNIV OAK BROOK TERRACE (1672)	12	7	12	10	0%	0%	17%	10%
DOMINCAN UNIV (1750)	8	9	8	8	25%	11%	13%	25%
EASTERN IL UNIV (1674)	27	25	27	27	56%	48%	52%	44%
ELMHURST COLL (1676)	14	11	18	14	50%	36%	39%	50%
GOVERNORS ST UNIV (9145)	14	13	11	20	14%	23%	18%	30%
IL INST TECH (1691)	4	3	4	3	75%	100%	50%	100%

Appendix D: Section Performance by Institution Attended - First-Time Testing Events

	Total Events per Section				Percent Pass			
	AUD	BEC	FAR	REG	AUD	BEC	FAR	REG
IL ST UNIV (1692)	96	89	84	104	63%	74%	64%	52%
IL WESLEYAN UNIV (1696)	31	25	26	34	65%	88%	58%	47%
KELLER GRAD SCHOOL DEVRY (20754)	89	75	70	86	30%	28%	30%	34%
LEWIS UNIV (1707)	10	4	8	11	50%	25%	25%	55%
LOYOLA UNIV CHICAGO (1710)	91	64	79	92	47%	58%	44%	48%
MCKENDREE UNIVERSITY (1722)	7	7	7	9	57%	71%	14%	33%
MILLIKIN UNIV (1724)	9	10	10	13	22%	30%	40%	38%
MONMOUTH COLL (1725)	3	4	3	3	67%	50%	67%	33%
NATIONAL LOUIS UNIV (1733)	4	2	0	1	25%	0%	0%	0%
NORTH CENTRAL COLL (1734)	13	14	14	18	54%	79%	43%	28%
NORTH PARK UNIV (1735)	2	5	2	6	100%	60%	100%	17%
NORTHEASTERN IL UNIV (1693)	26	27	20	19	42%	41%	50%	63%
NORTHERN IL UNIV (1737)	139	138	143	166	56%	70%	62%	45%
NORTHWESTERN UNIV (1739)	11	11	12	12	55%	73%	67%	50%
OLIVET NAZARENE UNIV (1741)	6	7	5	6	67%	100%	40%	50%
QUINCY UNIV (1745)	3	2	4	3	67%	50%	50%	67%
ROBERT MORRIS COLL (1746)	10	7	4	11	10%	29%	50%	18%
ROCKFORD COLL (1748)	3	4	3	5	67%	75%	0%	60%
ROOSEVELT UNIV (1749)	26	26	29	25	42%	38%	34%	44%
SAINT XAVIER UNIV (1768)	7	5	4	8	14%	60%	75%	63%
SOUTHERN IL UNIV CARBONDALE (1758)	35	29	40	41	34%	59%	33%	44%
SOUTHERN IL UNIV EDWARDSVILLE (1759)	40	33	34	46	60%	67%	47%	43%
TRINITY CHRISTIAN COLL (1771)	4	5	3	9	50%	60%	67%	78%
UNIV CHICAGO (1774)	12	8	8	10	33%	100%	50%	50%
UNIV IL CHICAGO (1776)	231	206	222	247	55%	80%	61%	60%
UNIV IL SPRINGFIELD (9333)	14	12	19	17	14%	25%	32%	24%
UNIV IL URBANA CHAMPAIGN (1775)	253	228	274	255	54%	76%	57%	55%
UNIV SAINT FRANCIS (1664)	4	3	2	4	50%	33%	50%	50%
WESTERN IL UNIV (1780)	20	13	13	18	45%	62%	38%	28%
WHEATON COLL (1781)	5	5	2	5	60%	80%	100%	40%
Indiana								
ANDERSON UNIV (1785)	5	2	7	5	80%	100%	57%	80%
BALL ST UNIV (1786)	51	31	39	48	37%	55%	51%	46%
BETHEL COLL (IN) (1787)	7	4	4	4	43%	75%	75%	50%
BUTLER UNIV (1788)	28	29	32	35	71%	72%	50%	54%
FRANKLIN COLL IN (1798)	9	6	9	6	22%	33%	33%	17%
GOSHEN COLL (1799)	12	9	13	14	58%	100%	77%	50%
GRACE COLL & SEMINARY (1800)	7	4	5	7	57%	100%	80%	86%
HUNTINGTON COLL (1803)	1	3	2	3	100%	0%	50%	0%
IN INST TECH (1805)	5	4	4	4	40%	25%	25%	50%
IN ST UNIV (1807)	11	14	13	14	27%	36%	23%	21%
IN UNIV BLOOMINGTON (1809)	282	230	255	275	59%	84%	68%	51%
IN UNIV NORTHWEST (1815)	6	3	7	4	50%	100%	29%	50%
IN UNIV PURDUE UNIV FORT WAYNE (1828)	15	8	10	11	40%	75%	50%	36%
IN UNIV PURDUE UNIV INDIANAPOLIS (1813)	67	57	65	65	45%	65%	48%	46%
IN UNIV SOUTH BEND (1816)	17	11	13	16	47%	45%	46%	50%
IN UNIV SOUTHEAST (1817)	11	9	11	9	27%	56%	36%	44%
IN WESLEYAN UNIV (1822)	23	17	19	20	39%	41%	21%	55%
MANCHESTER COLL (1820)	17	13	16	21	41%	62%	50%	38%
MARIAN COLL (1821)	6	6	6	6	33%	17%	33%	17%
PURDUE UNIV (1825)	131	107	113	125	32%	57%	44%	39%
SAINT JOSEPHS COLL (1833)	4	4	2	4	50%	25%	50%	25%
SAINT MARYS COLL (1836)	13	6	11	14	38%	50%	36%	21%
TAYLOR UNIV (1838)	8	5	6	7	88%	80%	50%	71%
TRINE UNIV (1839)	1	1	2	4	0%	0%	100%	25%
UNIV EVANSVILLE (1795)	5	6	8	8	60%	50%	13%	38%
UNIV INDIANAPOLIS (1804)	9	7	9	10	33%	43%	33%	40%
UNIV NOTRE DAME (1840)	162	139	156	176	72%	88%	73%	61%
UNIV SOUTHERN IN (1808)	21	12	20	21	48%	58%	40%	48%
UNIV ST FRANCIS (1832)	2	3	2	4	0%	33%	0%	25%
VALPARAISO UNIV (1842)	8	8	11	11	13%	88%	55%	36%

Appendix D: Section Performance by Institution Attended - First-Time Testing Events

	Total Events per Section				Percent Pass			
	AUD	BEC	FAR	REG	AUD	BEC	FAR	REG
Iowa								
AIB COLL BUSINESS (3963)	5	4	4	6	0%	0%	0%	33%
BRIAR CLIFF UNIV (1846)	3	4	6	4	67%	50%	33%	75%
BUENA VISTA UNIV (1847)	9	9	9	4	22%	0%	11%	50%
CLARKE COLL (1852)	2	1	1	3	50%	100%	0%	33%
COE COLL (1854)	4	5	5	5	50%	40%	60%	40%
DORDT COLL (1859)	5	3	4	7	60%	67%	50%	57%
DRAKE UNIV (1860)	23	19	19	28	52%	84%	53%	50%
GRAND VIEW UNIV (1867)	3	2	2	4	33%	100%	0%	25%
IA ST UNIV (1869)	78	72	66	75	38%	68%	62%	48%
KAPLAN UNIV (4586)	10	11	9	9	20%	27%	33%	44%
LORAS COLL (1873)	7	6	7	8	43%	83%	57%	63%
LUTHER COLL (1874)	14	14	13	17	36%	86%	46%	47%
MAHARISHI UNIV MANAGEMENT (11113)	3	1	2	3	0%	100%	50%	33%
MORNINGSIDE COLL (1879)	1	1	4	3	100%	100%	100%	0%
MOUNT SAINT CLARE COLL (1881)	3	2	4	4	67%	50%	0%	25%
NORTHWESTERN COLL IA (1883)	5	5	7	12	60%	80%	43%	50%
SAINT AMBROSE UNIV (1889)	11	7	9	10	27%	29%	56%	50%
SIMPSON COLL (1887)	10	7	6	8	40%	43%	50%	38%
UNIV DUBUQUE (1891)	7	8	7	10	29%	38%	14%	20%
UNIV IA (1892)	111	100	117	128	59%	83%	72%	73%
UNIV NORTHERN IA (1890)	78	79	84	86	65%	68%	65%	65%
UPPER IA UNIV (1893)	8	12	12	9	13%	50%	8%	44%
WARTBURG COLL (1896)	2	4	4	4	100%	100%	50%	75%
Kansas								
BAKER UNIV (1903)	5	6	3	7	0%	33%	0%	14%
BENEDICTINE COLL (10256)	7	6	8	5	14%	50%	38%	40%
EMPORIA ST UNIV (1927)	10	11	8	7	30%	18%	13%	14%
FORT HAYS ST UNIV (1915)	18	15	19	20	28%	33%	21%	30%
FRIENDS UNIV (1918)	2	3	4	5	0%	33%	25%	40%
KANSAS STATE UNIVERSITY (1928)	56	48	48	54	64%	77%	69%	57%
NEWMAN UNIV (1939)	3	4	2	5	0%	50%	0%	20%
OTTAWA UNIV (1937)	7	3	2	7	43%	0%	0%	29%
PITTSBURG ST UNIV (1926)	11	9	14	7	36%	33%	7%	0%
UNIV KS (1948)	120	99	116	125	48%	81%	60%	61%
WASHBURN UNIV (1949)	15	15	20	23	20%	67%	15%	35%
WICHITA ST UNIV (1950)	31	31	26	26	48%	58%	58%	69%
Kentucky								
ASBURY COLL (1952)	3	3	4	3	33%	100%	25%	33%
BELLARMINE UNIV (1954)	24	16	18	18	50%	56%	50%	50%
BEREA COLL (1955)	3	2	2	5	33%	100%	100%	20%
BRESCIA UNIV (1958)	2	3	4	1	0%	0%	75%	0%
EASTERN KY UNIV (1963)	17	10	10	10	47%	60%	30%	40%
GEORGETOWN COLL (1964)	2	1	4	2	0%	100%	25%	0%
KY ST UNIV (1968)	4	2	2	3	25%	0%	0%	0%
KY WESLEYAN COLL (1969)	5	6	3	3	40%	67%	33%	67%
LINDSEY WILSON COLL (1972)	3	4	3	5	33%	0%	67%	0%
MOREHEAD ST UNIV (1976)	6	5	7	5	67%	60%	29%	80%
MURRAY ST UNIV (1977)	21	12	23	19	24%	67%	43%	42%
NORTHERN KY UNIV (9275)	33	25	33	25	27%	60%	45%	32%
SPALDING UNIV (1960)	3	4	2	4	33%	25%	0%	25%
SULLIVAN UNIV (4619)	7	4	7	5	29%	0%	14%	20%
THOMAS MORE COLL (2001)	2	4	5	5	50%	50%	60%	20%
TRANSYLVANIA UNIV (1987)	14	11	16	7	64%	36%	31%	57%
UNIV KY (1989)	102	79	72	97	48%	63%	54%	56%
UNIV LOUISVILLE (1999)	44	32	35	36	34%	53%	26%	47%
UNIV OF CUMBERLANDS (1962)	3	2	0	2	100%	50%	0%	50%
WESTERN KY UNIV (2002)	28	25	28	33	46%	72%	61%	58%

Appendix D: Section Performance by Institution Attended - First-Time Testing Events

	Total Events per Section				Percent Pass			
	AUD	BEC	FAR	REG	AUD	BEC	FAR	REG
Louisiana								
DILLARD UNIV (2004)	1	3	4	1	0%	0%	0%	0%
GRAMBLING ST UNIV (2006)	6	6	4	3	33%	0%	0%	0%
LA ST UNIV AND A & M COLL (2010)	134	113	112	141	60%	57%	51%	46%
LA ST UNIV IN SHREVEPORT (2013)	9	9	5	8	33%	44%	40%	63%
LA TECH UNIV (2008)	25	21	20	27	44%	43%	45%	41%
LOYOLA UNIV NEW ORLEANS (2016)	10	18	16	17	40%	61%	63%	53%
MCNEESE ST UNIV (2017)	16	18	19	18	44%	39%	42%	44%
NICHOLLS ST UNIV (2005)	14	9	15	13	50%	22%	67%	54%
NORTHWESTERN ST UNIV (2021)	8	7	9	8	25%	43%	11%	50%
OUR LADY HOLY CROSS COLL (2023)	6	4	3	5	0%	0%	0%	0%
SOUTHEASTERN LA UNIV (2024)	52	37	36	37	33%	22%	25%	35%
SOUTHERN UNIV A&M BATON ROUGE (9636)	4	5	3	2	25%	0%	33%	0%
TULANE UNIV LA (2029)	36	30	38	53	64%	80%	71%	49%
UNIV LA LAFAYETTE (2031)	34	33	40	43	74%	64%	70%	72%
UNIV LA MONROE (2020)	17	19	15	19	41%	37%	47%	21%
UNIV NEW ORLEANS (2015)	37	36	50	47	32%	47%	32%	45%
XAVIER UNIV LA (2032)	1	1	3	0	0%	100%	0%	0%
Maine								
COLBY COLL (2039)	3	3	0	2	67%	67%	0%	50%
HUSSON UNIV (2043)	10	4	10	12	30%	25%	20%	33%
THOMAS COLL (2052)	5	2	6	6	80%	100%	33%	50%
UNIV ME (2053)	11	8	13	17	73%	88%	54%	65%
UNIV ME AUGUSTA (6760)	2	2	4	3	100%	50%	75%	67%
UNIV SOUTHERN ME (2054)	11	12	10	14	64%	58%	40%	64%
Maryland								
BOWIE ST UNIV (2062)	7	3	6	2	0%	0%	0%	0%
FROSTBURG ST UNIV (2072)	3	2	2	2	67%	50%	50%	100%
JOHNS HOPKINS UNIV (2077)	2	2	4	4	100%	100%	50%	50%
LOYOLA UNIVERSITY MD (2078)	32	30	25	34	53%	70%	72%	38%
MORGAN ST UNIV (2083)	1	4	2	3	0%	0%	0%	33%
MOUNT SAINT MARYS UNIV (2086)	1	3	1	3	0%	33%	0%	33%
SALISBURY UNIV (2091)	6	2	5	9	50%	50%	40%	56%
TOWSON UNIV (2099)	11	8	13	17	55%	75%	23%	53%
UNIV BALTIMORE (2102)	6	6	6	10	33%	33%	67%	40%
UNIV MD BALTIMORE COUNTY (2105)	6	4	7	6	17%	25%	29%	0%
UNIV MD COLL PARK (2103)	97	72	89	105	52%	72%	52%	47%
UNIV MD EASTERN SHORE (2106)	3	2	0	2	33%	0%	0%	0%
UNIV MD UNIV COLL (11644)	52	41	45	54	44%	46%	44%	35%
Massachusetts								
AMERICAN INTL COLL (2114)	5	4	5	3	60%	75%	40%	33%
ASSUMPTION COLL (2118)	24	24	21	25	42%	50%	43%	36%
BABSON COLL (2121)	40	34	39	49	63%	59%	62%	37%
BENTLEY COLL (2124)	175	141	148	152	50%	67%	52%	57%
BOSTON COLL (2128)	127	115	122	125	69%	90%	77%	71%
BOSTON UNIV (2130)	61	59	54	66	64%	76%	74%	56%
BRANDEIS UNIV (2133)	5	3	2	1	60%	67%	50%	100%
BRIDGEWATER ST COLL (2183)	9	5	8	8	56%	60%	38%	63%
CLARK UNIV (2139)	7	7	7	6	71%	86%	43%	50%
COLL HOLY CROSS (2141)	25	18	21	17	60%	89%	76%	65%
COLL OUR LADY OF THE ELMS (2140)	4	0	0	1	0%	0%	0%	0%
GORDON COLL (2153)	5	2	1	5	20%	50%	0%	20%
LASELL COLL (2158)	1	2	2	2	0%	0%	0%	50%
MA INST TECH (2178)	5	4	3	4	100%	100%	100%	75%
MERRIMACK COLL (2120)	13	7	10	16	23%	29%	20%	38%
NICHOLS COLL (2197)	7	8	6	7	43%	25%	17%	14%
NORTHEASTERN UNIV (2199)	125	106	108	133	56%	58%	45%	50%
SALEM ST UNIV (2188)	14	11	11	10	21%	45%	18%	30%
STONEHILL COLL (2217)	30	19	17	20	57%	63%	53%	45%
SUFFOLK UNIV (2218)	51	37	44	52	41%	54%	36%	40%

Appendix D: Section Performance by Institution Attended - First-Time Testing Events

	Total Events per Section				Percent Pass			
	AUD	BEC	FAR	REG	AUD	BEC	FAR	REG
TUFTS UNIV (2219)	4	4	3	5	75%	100%	100%	60%
UNIV MA AMHERST (2221)	111	91	109	108	45%	63%	43%	35%
UNIV MA BOSTON (2222)	32	33	36	33	44%	36%	31%	30%
UNIV MA DARTMOUTH (2210)	17	19	15	19	24%	26%	47%	37%
UNIV MA LOWELL (2161)	14	11	17	17	57%	55%	59%	29%
WESTERN NEW ENGLAND COLL (2226)	18	10	23	10	56%	40%	43%	30%
WESTFIELD ST COLL (2189)	5	5	6	8	60%	60%	33%	25%
WORCESTER ST COLL (2190)	5	3	5	4	60%	0%	20%	0%
Michigan								
ALBION COLL (2235)	7	8	8	9	57%	88%	63%	11%
ALMA COLL (2236)	4	4	4	5	50%	75%	50%	60%
ANDREWS UNIV (2238)	3	6	7	7	33%	67%	14%	29%
AQUINAS COLL (2239)	5	6	5	7	20%	50%	20%	43%
BAKER COLL FLINT (4673)	12	4	9	9	25%	75%	44%	44%
CALVIN COLL (2241)	26	18	21	27	69%	78%	71%	56%
CENTRAL MI UNIV (2243)	65	43	54	50	51%	56%	50%	58%
DAVENPORT UNIV (2249)	22	20	21	24	36%	35%	38%	38%
EASTERN MI UNIV (2259)	50	36	42	42	34%	56%	40%	48%
FERRIS ST UNIV (2260)	15	12	14	15	53%	67%	57%	47%
GRAND VALLEY ST UNIV (2268)	76	61	69	73	63%	84%	64%	73%
HILLSDALE COLL (2272)	7	7	8	9	29%	86%	13%	56%
HOPE COLL (2273)	13	12	14	14	54%	50%	57%	43%
LAKE SUPERIOR ST UNIV (2293)	5	6	8	9	40%	67%	13%	56%
MI ST UNIV (2290)	211	170	192	204	64%	77%	64%	61%
MI TECH UNIV (2292)	9	7	8	10	78%	71%	88%	60%
NORTHERN MI UNIV (2301)	10	7	8	8	20%	29%	25%	38%
NORTHWOOD UNIV (4072)	23	19	27	23	43%	53%	33%	39%
OAKLAND UNIV (2307)	42	34	38	40	57%	65%	63%	63%
SAGINAW VALLEY ST UNIV (2314)	19	13	22	16	26%	23%	27%	31%
SIENA HEIGHTS UNIV (2316)	7	5	8	6	43%	60%	50%	17%
SPRING ARBOR UNIV (2318)	0	1	3	4	0%	0%	33%	25%
UNIV DETROIT MERCY (2323)	2	0	2	3	50%	0%	0%	33%
UNIV MI ANN ARBOR (2325)	84	63	75	85	74%	92%	84%	74%
UNIV MI DEARBORN (2326)	37	32	40	35	62%	53%	63%	63%
UNIV MI FLINT (2327)	10	10	13	8	50%	10%	23%	25%
WALSH COLL (4071)	74	40	58	57	53%	63%	53%	53%
WAYNE ST UNIV (2329)	43	32	33	45	56%	53%	48%	33%
WESTERN MI UNIV (2330)	61	50	55	59	52%	54%	38%	41%
Minnesota								
AUGSBURG COLL (2334)	16	12	12	15	31%	50%	8%	40%
BEMIDJI ST UNIV (2336)	6	7	7	8	50%	57%	71%	63%
BETHEL COLL (MN) (9058)	12	17	11	13	50%	71%	73%	46%
COLL OF SAINT BENEDICT (2341)	11	11	10	14	73%	100%	90%	79%
COLL OF SAINT SCHOLASTICA (2343)	8	3	5	4	63%	0%	60%	0%
CONCORDIA COLL MOORHEAD (2346)	17	15	15	16	76%	87%	80%	56%
CONCORDIA UNIV MN (2347)	2	2	5	2	50%	50%	20%	50%
GUSTAVUS ADOLPHUS COLL (2353)	7	8	9	9	57%	63%	44%	33%
HAMLINE UNIV (2354)	3	1	3	4	33%	100%	33%	50%
METROPOLITAN ST UNIV (10374)	28	26	29	30	32%	54%	34%	37%
MN SCHOOL OF BUSINESS (4646)	2	4	3	4	0%	50%	33%	25%
MN ST UNIV MANKATO (2360)	43	35	49	50	42%	49%	49%	40%
MN ST UNIV MOORHEAD (2367)	15	15	15	15	53%	47%	27%	20%
NORTHWESTERN COLL MN (2371)	6	6	6	9	67%	67%	100%	56%
SAINT CATHERINE UNIV (2342)	4	2	4	3	75%	100%	50%	67%
SAINT CLOUD ST UNIV (2377)	48	55	47	53	67%	62%	68%	70%
SAINT JOHN'S UNIV (2379)	32	27	28	28	63%	74%	64%	61%
SAINT MARY'S UNIV OF MN (2380)	11	6	8	11	36%	0%	50%	18%
SOUTHWEST ST UNIV (2375)	6	5	9	7	50%	60%	56%	86%
UNIV MN DULUTH (2388)	43	35	37	45	40%	57%	41%	49%
UNIV MN TWIN CITIES (3969)	120	103	125	122	63%	79%	65%	53%

Appendix D: Section Performance by Institution Attended - First-Time Testing Events

	Total Events per Section				Percent Pass			
	AUD	BEC	FAR	REG	AUD	BEC	FAR	REG
UNIV ST THOMAS (2345)	66	62	61	69	48%	63%	54%	38%
WINONA ST UNIV (2394)	19	23	22	21	21%	35%	18%	33%
Mississippi								
ALCORN ST UNIV (2396)	4	2	1	1	25%	50%	0%	0%
BELHAVEN COLL (2397)	9	4	5	7	33%	25%	60%	29%
DELTA ST UNIV (2403)	7	6	5	4	43%	17%	40%	75%
JACKSON ST UNIV (2410)	11	11	8	8	27%	18%	0%	13%
MILLSAPS COLL (2414)	12	14	15	18	58%	43%	40%	50%
MS COLL (2415)	15	14	13	15	20%	29%	46%	47%
MS ST UNIV (2423)	56	54	52	70	45%	50%	52%	43%
MS UNIV FOR WOMEN (2422)	4	2	2	1	25%	50%	50%	0%
UNIV MS (2440)	100	85	88	105	43%	66%	63%	59%
UNIV SOUTHERN MS (2441)	34	27	26	25	38%	33%	38%	52%
Missouri								
AVILA UNIV (2449)	7	5	5	5	43%	60%	60%	80%
CENTRAL METHODIST UNIV (2453)	3	4	2	6	33%	0%	0%	33%
COLL OF OZARKS (2500)	1	0	4	4	0%	0%	25%	25%
COLUMBIA COLL (2456)	17	10	13	14	24%	20%	38%	29%
CULVER STOCKTON COLL (2460)	7	6	5	6	57%	67%	40%	67%
DEVRY UNIV KANSAS CITY (2455)	4	6	6	5	50%	17%	33%	0%
DRURY UNIV (2461)	17	16	19	13	29%	50%	47%	38%
FONTBONNE UNIV (2464)	4	4	3	6	0%	25%	33%	33%
LINCOLN UNIV (2479)	3	1	2	4	0%	100%	50%	25%
LINDENWOOD UNIV (2480)	13	12	10	12	23%	33%	30%	33%
MARYVILLE UNIV ST. LOUIS (2482)	11	7	11	8	36%	29%	18%	13%
MO BAPTIST UNIV (7540)	4	3	3	1	0%	33%	33%	0%
MO SOUTHERN ST UNIV (2488)	6	8	6	7	83%	63%	50%	57%
MO ST UNIV (2503)	49	45	61	51	45%	60%	48%	61%
MO VALLEY COLL (2489)	3	3	3	4	100%	0%	67%	25%
MO WESTERN ST UNIV (2490)	5	4	4	5	40%	25%	0%	20%
NORTHWEST MO ST UNIV (2496)	12	8	7	10	58%	50%	100%	60%
PARK UNIV (2498)	11	6	8	9	9%	33%	38%	44%
ROCKHURST UNIV (2499)	13	10	11	11	46%	30%	55%	18%
SOUTHEAST MO ST UNIV (2501)	20	9	19	20	55%	56%	53%	40%
SOUTHWEST BAPTIST UNIV (2502)	12	4	9	8	25%	25%	33%	13%
ST. LOUIS UNIV (2506)	63	61	56	60	54%	72%	48%	50%
TRUMAN ST UNIV (2495)	67	61	64	64	63%	93%	80%	81%
UNIV CENTRAL MO (2454)	26	23	19	23	31%	61%	53%	39%
UNIV MO COLUMBIA (2516)	116	108	115	122	63%	85%	74%	66%
UNIV MO KANSAS CITY (2518)	35	28	28	32	83%	71%	64%	72%
UNIV MO ST. LOUIS (2519)	51	34	46	49	49%	50%	43%	63%
WASHINGTON UNIV ST. LOUIS (2520)	29	24	27	29	86%	88%	78%	59%
WEBSTER UNIV (2521)	17	10	17	17	18%	40%	24%	29%
WESTMINSTER COLL (2523)	3	3	4	2	0%	67%	50%	0%
WILLIAM WOODS UNIV (2525)	1	3	1	3	0%	33%	0%	67%
Montana								
CARROLL COLL (MT) (2526)	4	7	5	6	50%	0%	20%	17%
MT ST UNIV BILLINGS (2530)	13	13	14	16	23%	38%	29%	31%
MT ST UNIV BOZEMAN (2532)	32	28	30	32	53%	54%	70%	59%
MT TECH UNIV (2531)	5	3	4	1	40%	33%	50%	0%
UNIV MT (2536)	43	31	35	43	49%	68%	83%	65%
Nebraska								
BELLEVUE UNIV (9743)	9	7	8	10	67%	43%	25%	30%
CREIGHTON UNIV (2542)	29	28	28	30	41%	68%	57%	50%
DOANE COLL (2544)	8	5	5	7	25%	60%	100%	29%
HASTINGS COLL (2548)	5	5	7	6	40%	60%	29%	33%
MIDLAND LUTHERAN COLL (2553)	7	8	10	6	57%	88%	60%	50%
NE WESLEYAN UNIV (2555)	7	5	5	7	71%	100%	60%	86%
PERU ST COLL (2559)	4	3	3	1	100%	100%	67%	100%
UNIV NE KEARNEY (2551)	16	7	10	5	44%	14%	60%	40%

Appendix D: Section Performance by Institution Attended - First-Time Testing Events

	Total Events per Section				Percent Pass			
	AUD	BEC	FAR	REG	AUD	BEC	FAR	REG
UNIV NE LINCOLN (2565)	39	45	39	49	44%	73%	69%	49%
UNIV NE OMAHA (2554)	21	18	29	27	57%	67%	62%	56%
WAYNE ST COLL (2566)	7	5	5	4	29%	40%	40%	25%
YORK COLL (2567)	4	1	4	2	25%	100%	50%	50%
Nevada								
UNIV NV LAS VEGAS (2569)	68	43	76	72	43%	56%	39%	51%
UNIV NV RENO (2568)	41	29	37	34	44%	41%	38%	41%
New Hampshire								
PLYMOUTH ST UNIV (2591)	5	6	9	3	20%	67%	11%	33%
SAINT ANSELM COLL (2587)	11	4	7	8	45%	50%	43%	13%
SOUTHERN NH UNIV (2580)	17	19	21	22	47%	37%	33%	45%
UNIV NH (2589)	43	28	36	42	53%	71%	61%	50%
New Jersey								
BERKELEY COLL (7502)	3	6	6	3	0%	0%	0%	33%
BETH MEDRASH GOVOHA (7947)	4	8	10	7	75%	38%	40%	57%
CALDWELL COLL (2598)	4	4	4	3	50%	25%	25%	67%
CENTENARY COLL (2599)	6	5	5	6	33%	20%	20%	50%
COLL NJ (2642)	60	47	57	60	57%	72%	67%	55%
FAIRLEIGH DICKINSON UNIV (2607)	38	38	37	45	42%	53%	35%	51%
FAIRLEIGH DICKINSON UNIV MADISON (4738)	8	10	8	8	50%	30%	38%	38%
FAIRLEIGH DICKINSON UNIV RUTHERFORD (2604)	10	10	10	7	50%	30%	50%	14%
FELICIAN COLL (2610)	6	4	4	5	17%	0%	0%	0%
GEORGIAN COURT UNIV (2608)	9	6	8	8	11%	33%	13%	13%
KEAN UNIV (2622)	27	24	24	39	26%	21%	21%	33%
MONMOUTH UNIV (2616)	35	42	32	37	26%	43%	28%	41%
MONTCLAIR ST UNIV (2617)	67	66	64	85	39%	36%	33%	26%
NJ CITY UNIV (2613)	17	8	11	15	24%	13%	9%	47%
NJ INST TECH (2621)	0	2	3	0	0%	0%	0%	0%
QUALIFYING CERTIFICATE (88822)	2	2	1	4	0%	0%	0%	50%
RAMAPO COLL NJ (9344)	39	33	32	49	41%	45%	34%	41%
RICHARD STOCKTON COLL NJ (9345)	31	30	23	30	39%	33%	39%	47%
RIDER UNIV (2628)	57	46	44	45	25%	26%	18%	42%
ROWAN UNIV (2609)	37	32	35	40	46%	38%	46%	48%
RUTGERS ST UNIV CAMDEN (4741)	34	30	43	37	38%	47%	37%	49%
RUTGERS ST UNIV NEW BRUNSWICK (6964)	97	79	91	91	42%	42%	41%	36%
RUTGERS ST UNIV NEWARK (2631)	110	88	130	132	33%	48%	34%	39%
SAINT PETERS COLL (2638)	8	9	15	11	13%	33%	27%	18%
SETON HALL UNIV (2632)	25	27	32	33	28%	37%	25%	21%
THOMAS EDISON ST COLL (21922)	11	7	6	5	55%	43%	67%	100%
WILLIAM PATERSON UNIV NJ (2625)	23	16	22	24	26%	25%	18%	42%
New Mexico								
COLL SANTA FE (2649)	4	1	2	3	0%	0%	0%	0%
EASTERN NM UNIV (2651)	6	3	6	6	50%	33%	17%	67%
NM HIGHLANDS UNIV (2653)	2	2	2	2	50%	50%	50%	0%
NM ST UNIV (2657)	17	15	20	27	24%	60%	30%	41%
SAINT JOHNS COLL (2093)	2	1	4	4	50%	100%	50%	25%
UNIV NM (2663)	39	29	48	41	46%	48%	23%	39%
WESTERN NM UNIV (2664)	4	3	4	2	50%	0%	0%	0%
New York								
ADELPHI UNIV (2666)	11	15	11	19	27%	20%	27%	42%
ALFRED UNIV (2668)	4	2	8	4	25%	50%	38%	25%
BERKELEY COLL NY (7394)	5	4	4	6	0%	0%	0%	17%
CANISIUS COLL (2681)	30	25	23	25	63%	80%	70%	60%
CLARKSON UNIV (2699)	6	3	2	3	50%	33%	50%	33%
COLGATE UNIV (2701)	5	1	2	1	40%	100%	50%	100%
COLL SAINT ROSE (2705)	8	5	10	6	25%	40%	10%	33%
COLUMBIA UNIV NY (2707)	10	9	7	8	60%	100%	86%	75%
CORNELL UNIV (2711)	32	27	24	30	75%	85%	54%	73%
CUNY BARUCH (7273)	256	210	263	289	48%	53%	51%	52%
CUNY BROOKLYN (2687)	89	74	70	78	45%	36%	37%	35%

Appendix D: Section Performance by Institution Attended - First-Time Testing Events

	Total Events per Section				Percent Pass			
	AUD	BEC	FAR	REG	AUD	BEC	FAR	REG
CUNY HERBERT H LEHMAN (7022)	16	24	18	15	19%	13%	22%	27%
CUNY HUNTER (2689)	48	33	39	46	17%	27%	28%	33%
CUNY MEDGAR EVERS (10097)	1	2	4	2	0%	0%	0%	0%
CUNY QUEENS (2690)	94	64	69	93	33%	28%	29%	33%
CUNY STATEN ISLAND (29040)	24	18	17	18	21%	28%	24%	22%
CUNY YORK COLL (4759)	4	4	4	7	0%	0%	25%	29%
DAEMEN COLL (2808)	6	5	5	4	50%	60%	20%	50%
DOWLING COLL (2667)	5	7	4	5	20%	0%	25%	20%
ELMIRA COLL (2718)	5	3	3	4	40%	100%	67%	50%
EXCELSIOR COLL (2834)	15	15	25	14	53%	33%	48%	64%
FORDHAM UNIV (2722)	76	63	64	72	42%	63%	38%	39%
HARTWICK COLL (2729)	7	5	2	8	29%	40%	0%	25%
HOFSTRA UNIV (2732)	78	56	67	82	37%	45%	28%	45%
HOUGHTON COLL (2734)	3	2	0	3	100%	50%	0%	33%
IONA COLL (2737)	14	15	13	11	43%	53%	15%	55%
ITHACA COLL (2739)	18	13	15	14	72%	85%	40%	36%
LE MOYNE COLL (2748)	18	22	22	17	33%	41%	45%	29%
LONG ISLAND UNIV BROOKLYN CENTER (4779)	7	6	4	5	14%	17%	50%	0%
LONG ISLAND UNIV CW POST (2754)	34	20	21	35	32%	40%	33%	37%
MANHATTAN COLL (2758)	19	14	23	18	32%	29%	13%	6%
MARIST COLL (2765)	21	19	16	26	38%	58%	44%	31%
MERCY COLL (2772)	6	2	6	3	17%	50%	50%	0%
MOLLOY COLL (2775)	4	7	2	7	0%	14%	0%	43%
MONROE COLL (4799)	7	8	4	6	0%	0%	0%	17%
MOUNT SAINT MARY COLL (2778)	7	1	4	4	0%	0%	0%	25%
NAZARETH COLL ROCHESTER (2779)	5	5	10	8	80%	80%	70%	38%
NIAGARA UNIV (2788)	16	13	14	15	38%	31%	36%	20%
NY INST TECH MANHATTAN (2782)	14	6	9	6	0%	33%	22%	50%
NY INST TECH OLD WESTBURY (4804)	3	3	2	5	0%	0%	0%	40%
NY UNIV (2785)	94	78	95	106	56%	88%	63%	47%
NYACK COLL (2790)	2	2	3	1	100%	0%	0%	0%
PACE UNIV NY (2791)	67	55	66	76	40%	51%	26%	36%
PACE UNIV PLEASANTVILLE (2792)	22	23	19	23	32%	48%	42%	30%
PACE UNIV WHITE PLAINS (2727)	4	5	2	2	75%	80%	50%	50%
ROCHESTER INST TECH (2806)	13	11	15	12	38%	64%	40%	33%
SAINT BONAVENTURE UNIV (2817)	28	19	19	22	50%	58%	26%	27%
SAINT FRANCIS COLL (2820)	14	8	6	7	43%	13%	33%	29%
SAINT JOHN FISHER COLL (2821)	17	18	17	16	41%	50%	47%	50%
SAINT JOHNS UNIV NEW YORK (2823)	111	88	94	94	30%	38%	38%	36%
SAINT JOSEPHS COLL NY (2825)	8	9	3	5	63%	22%	0%	40%
SAINT JOSEPHS COLL SUFFOLK (29081)	5	5	7	6	60%	60%	43%	33%
SAINT THOMAS AQUINAS COLL (2832)	3	2	4	4	33%	50%	25%	0%
SIENA COLL (2816)	41	34	25	28	49%	62%	32%	43%
SUNY OLD WESTBURY (7109)	31	18	31	33	29%	39%	29%	39%
SUNY ALBANY (2835)	99	69	91	94	39%	61%	48%	44%
SUNY BINGHAMTON (2836)	158	89	147	151	46%	70%	48%	43%
SUNY BROCKPORT (2841)	15	18	18	18	40%	50%	33%	44%
SUNY BUFFALO (2837)	91	75	102	96	60%	69%	51%	57%
SUNY BUFFALO (2842)	5	3	5	3	60%	33%	60%	100%
SUNY EMPIRE ST COLL (10286)	6	4	6	5	50%	100%	67%	60%
SUNY FREDONIA (2844)	8	7	7	8	38%	71%	71%	63%
SUNY GENESEO (2845)	36	33	43	42	58%	76%	63%	52%
SUNY INST TECH UTICA ROME (11678)	6	2	5	5	0%	50%	20%	20%
SUNY NEW PALTZ (2846)	14	20	16	19	50%	60%	63%	47%
SUNY ONEONTA (2847)	8	6	8	4	38%	33%	13%	75%
SUNY OSWEGO (2848)	27	24	26	24	37%	50%	23%	38%
SUNY PLATTSBURGH (2849)	16	9	15	13	31%	56%	13%	31%
SUNY STONY BROOK (2838)	20	20	23	25	45%	50%	35%	32%
SYRACUSE UNIV (2882)	74	62	56	89	41%	55%	43%	36%
TOURO COLL (10142)	52	39	51	42	50%	59%	59%	62%
UNIV ROCHESTER (2894)	11	7	9	6	64%	100%	56%	50%

Appendix D: Section Performance by Institution Attended - First-Time Testing Events

	Total Events per Section				Percent Pass			
	AUD	BEC	FAR	REG	AUD	BEC	FAR	REG
UTICA COLL (2883)	5	3	6	4	40%	67%	67%	50%
WAGNER COLL (2899)	18	14	17	12	17%	36%	12%	42%
YESHIVA UNIV (2903)	42	30	38	44	43%	57%	29%	32%
North Carolina								
APPALACHIAN ST UNIV (2906)	49	47	46	49	67%	66%	72%	53%
BARTON COLL (2908)	3	2	3	2	33%	0%	33%	50%
BELMONT ABBEY COLL (2910)	4	3	2	2	50%	0%	0%	0%
CAMPBELL UNIV (2913)	18	9	14	13	50%	44%	43%	38%
CATAWBA COLL (2914)	4	4	2	3	25%	50%	0%	67%
DAVIDSON COLL (2918)	6	6	7	6	83%	83%	57%	83%
DUKE UNIV (2920)	9	5	4	8	78%	100%	100%	63%
EAST CAROLINA UNIV (2923)	69	53	55	68	36%	43%	42%	37%
ELIZABETH CITY ST UNIV (2926)	4	2	2	2	0%	0%	0%	0%
ELON UNIV (2927)	38	28	35	37	37%	71%	37%	41%
FAYETTEVILLE ST UNIV (2928)	1	1	2	2	0%	0%	0%	0%
GARDNER WEBB UNIV (2929)	12	7	7	11	33%	29%	43%	55%
GUILFORD COLL (2931)	6	5	5	4	67%	60%	80%	25%
HIGH POINT UNIV (2933)	5	3	7	5	40%	67%	14%	60%
LENOIR RHYNE COLL (2941)	3	0	0	2	33%	0%	0%	0%
MEREDITH COLL (2945)	4	3	5	5	25%	100%	80%	80%
METHODIST UNIV (2946)	3	2	2	1	33%	0%	0%	0%
MOUNT OLIVE COLL (2949)	3	2	4	3	0%	0%	0%	0%
NC AGRICULTURAL & TECH ST UNIV (2905)	10	10	15	11	40%	20%	20%	18%
NC CENTRAL UNIV (2950)	5	5	6	1	0%	20%	33%	100%
NC ST UNIV RALEIGH (2972)	102	82	101	112	62%	68%	66%	56%
NC WESLEYAN COLL (2951)	3	6	4	4	33%	17%	50%	25%
PFEIFFER UNIV (2955)	4	4	1	4	25%	25%	0%	0%
UNIV NC ASHEVILLE (2907)	9	10	9	10	22%	40%	33%	40%
UNIV NC CHAPEL HILL (2974)	128	114	117	125	67%	90%	68%	66%
UNIV NC CHARLOTTE (2975)	39	43	38	39	51%	67%	45%	69%
UNIV NC GREENSBORO (2976)	30	22	30	26	63%	59%	60%	62%
UNIV NC PEMBROKE (2954)	3	3	3	4	67%	33%	67%	50%
UNIV NC WILMINGTON (2984)	75	74	60	65	47%	57%	52%	43%
WAKE FOREST UNIV (2978)	53	52	55	56	87%	92%	89%	86%
WESTERN CAROLINA UNIV (2981)	13	7	13	12	31%	57%	62%	42%
WINGATE UNIV (2985)	5	5	3	7	20%	20%	0%	29%
WINSTON SALEM ST UNIV (2986)	5	3	3	6	60%	0%	33%	33%
North Dakota								
DICKINSON ST UNIV (2989)	15	9	14	15	20%	44%	43%	47%
MINOT ST UNIV (2994)	6	4	7	7	33%	50%	86%	57%
ND ST UNIV (9265)	22	24	29	29	64%	63%	59%	66%
UNIV MARY (2992)	9	6	10	10	56%	50%	50%	50%
UNIV ND (3005)	57	41	45	63	63%	73%	71%	67%
Ohio								
ASHLAND UNIV (3012)	10	11	10	11	40%	73%	50%	45%
BALDWIN WALLACE COLL (3014)	19	19	26	26	42%	68%	42%	46%
BOWLING GREEN ST UNIV (3018)	65	44	36	65	52%	57%	53%	40%
CAPITAL UNIV (3023)	17	16	15	15	47%	50%	47%	33%
CASE WESTERN RESERVE UNIV (3024)	28	27	23	28	61%	93%	57%	46%
CEDARVILLE UNIV (3025)	7	5	8	8	71%	80%	63%	75%
CLEVELAND ST UNIV (3032)	44	44	53	52	55%	52%	53%	52%
COLUMBUS ST CC (6867)	5	2	3	2	40%	50%	33%	50%
DEFIANCE COLL (3041)	6	3	4	4	33%	67%	50%	50%
DEVRY UNIV COLUMBUS (3099)	9	7	5	8	44%	43%	40%	38%
FRANCISCAN UNIV STEUBENVILLE (3036)	2	5	1	5	50%	20%	0%	80%
FRANKLIN UNIV (3046)	50	36	38	32	24%	31%	26%	28%
HEIDELBERG COLL (3048)	3	4	2	2	0%	25%	0%	0%
HIRAM COLL (3049)	4	5	5	4	50%	20%	40%	50%
JOHN CARROLL UNIV (3050)	45	33	42	43	62%	76%	64%	58%
KENT ST UNIV (3051)	51	40	47	53	59%	65%	51%	55%

Appendix D: Section Performance by Institution Attended - First-Time Testing Events

	Total Events per Section				Percent Pass			
	AUD	BEC	FAR	REG	AUD	BEC	FAR	REG
MALONE COLL (3072)	4	2	4	4	50%	100%	25%	50%
MARIETTA COLL (3073)	4	2	2	3	50%	50%	50%	33%
MIAMI UNIV (3077)	190	171	165	182	59%	78%	62%	55%
MOUNT UNION COLL (3083)	4	5	5	4	50%	60%	100%	50%
MOUNT VERNON NAZARENE UNIV (7085)	8	7	5	6	38%	43%	20%	33%
MUSKINGUM COLL (3084)	3	2	1	4	67%	50%	0%	75%
NOTRE DAME COLL OH (3085)	6	6	5	4	0%	33%	40%	0%
OH DOMINICAN UNIV (3035)	9	7	11	7	22%	43%	9%	29%
OH NORTHERN UNIV (3089)	17	11	8	13	29%	45%	25%	15%
OH ST UNIV (6883)	227	183	212	233	57%	83%	63%	57%
OH UNIV (3100)	81	61	82	85	44%	64%	45%	35%
OH WESLEYAN UNIV (3109)	7	6	4	4	57%	83%	25%	25%
OTTERBEIN UNIV (3110)	7	3	5	6	43%	67%	60%	50%
UNIV AKRON (3123)	61	58	59	65	54%	62%	49%	48%
UNIV CINCINNATI (3125)	54	48	46	51	43%	50%	37%	55%
UNIV DAYTON (3127)	62	50	58	42	50%	76%	48%	33%
UNIV FINDLAY (3045)	7	7	5	12	43%	43%	80%	25%
UNIV NORTHWESTERN OH (4861)	4	2	1	3	50%	0%	0%	0%
UNIV TOLEDO (3131)	46	37	44	41	37%	62%	55%	51%
WALSH UNIV (3135)	5	4	5	5	20%	0%	20%	20%
WILMINGTON COLL (3142)	2	1	4	2	50%	0%	25%	50%
WITTENBERG UNIV (3143)	4	4	3	3	0%	75%	67%	33%
WRIGHT ST UNIV (3078)	29	28	27	28	62%	57%	63%	50%
XAVIER UNIV (3144)	31	30	28	31	65%	70%	54%	48%
YOUNGSTOWN ST UNIV (3145)	27	22	26	24	37%	45%	38%	29%
Oklahoma								
CAMERON UNIV (3150)	4	5	6	5	50%	20%	33%	20%
EAST CENTRAL UNIV (3154)	3	1	4	3	67%	0%	50%	67%
NORTHEASTERN ST UNIV (3161)	14	10	10	14	14%	30%	10%	36%
NORTHWESTERN OK ST UNIV (3163)	1	3	3	4	100%	33%	67%	50%
OK BAPTIST UNIV (3164)	3	3	2	3	33%	67%	50%	33%
OK CHRISTIAN UNIV (3165)	12	12	14	12	50%	75%	50%	75%
OK ST UNIV (3170)	99	88	95	106	65%	73%	61%	61%
OKLAHOMA CITY UNIV (3166)	10	4	7	6	40%	75%	29%	33%
ORAL ROBERTS UNIV (3985)	14	8	11	8	43%	50%	82%	50%
SOUTHEASTERN OK ST UNIV (3179)	2	3	2	2	50%	33%	0%	100%
SOUTHWESTERN OK ST UNIV (3181)	11	6	9	8	55%	67%	44%	38%
UNIV CENTRAL OK (3152)	43	30	29	45	47%	43%	45%	47%
UNIV OK NORMAN (3184)	70	56	54	75	54%	80%	57%	55%
UNIV TULSA (3185)	11	10	10	10	55%	70%	40%	50%
Oregon								
CONCORDIA UNIV (3191)	2	4	2	0	50%	0%	0%	0%
EASTERN OR UNIV (3193)	9	7	11	11	78%	71%	55%	45%
GEORGE FOX UNIV (3194)	8	6	6	4	13%	50%	33%	50%
LINFIELD COLL (3198)	19	20	20	24	47%	55%	40%	29%
OR ST UNIV (3210)	40	34	41	44	63%	68%	66%	50%
PACIFIC UNIV (3212)	2	3	6	2	100%	0%	33%	50%
PORTLAND ST UNIV (3216)	52	37	50	52	56%	73%	54%	63%
SOUTHERN OR UNIV (3219)	15	12	8	10	60%	58%	38%	50%
UNIV OR (3223)	78	64	77	81	56%	77%	62%	51%
UNIV PORTLAND (3224)	15	14	16	17	47%	64%	38%	29%
WESTERN OR UNIV (3209)	3	3	4	4	33%	33%	25%	25%
WILLAMETTE UNIV (3227)	3	3	3	3	100%	100%	100%	33%
Pennsylvania								
ALBRIGHT COLL (3229)	13	14	7	12	23%	14%	0%	25%
ALVERNIA COLL (3233)	6	6	3	6	17%	50%	33%	17%
ARCADIA UNIV (3235)	8	8	6	7	38%	50%	33%	29%
BLOOMSBURG UNIV PA (3315)	48	35	34	41	48%	60%	53%	44%
BUCKNELL UNIV (3238)	26	27	26	33	73%	85%	69%	48%
CA UNIV PA (3316)	7	10	6	10	29%	50%	17%	20%

Appendix D: Section Performance by Institution Attended - First-Time Testing Events

	Total Events per Section				Percent Pass			
	AUD	BEC	FAR	REG	AUD	BEC	FAR	REG
CABRINI COLL (3241)	5	5	7	9	20%	60%	29%	22%
CARLOW UNIV (3303)	2	3	3	3	50%	33%	33%	33%
CARNEGIE MELLON UNIV (3242)	6	4	4	8	50%	75%	25%	50%
CHATHAM UNIV (3244)	4	5	3	4	25%	40%	33%	25%
CHESTNUT HILL COLL (3245)	3	4	1	2	33%	25%	100%	0%
CLARION UNIV PA (9235)	9	6	4	10	67%	50%	25%	50%
COLL MISERICORDIA (3247)	4	1	0	5	0%	0%	0%	0%
DE VALLEY COLL (3252)	6	5	4	6	33%	20%	0%	33%
DESALES UNIV (3986)	17	17	11	20	24%	29%	27%	45%
DREXEL UNIV (3256)	84	84	68	87	36%	49%	32%	44%
DUQUESNE UNIV (3258)	67	47	35	60	42%	60%	54%	43%
EAST STROUDSBURG UNIV PA (3320)	8	3	6	5	38%	0%	33%	40%
EASTERN UNIV (3259)	5	7	6	6	40%	29%	50%	100%
EDINBORO UNIV PA (3321)	6	2	4	4	17%	0%	50%	0%
ELIZABETHTOWN COLL (3262)	21	12	10	12	29%	50%	10%	33%
FRANKLIN & MARSHALL COLL (3265)	5	2	4	4	80%	100%	75%	75%
GANNON UNIV (3266)	5	6	7	2	20%	33%	14%	0%
GENEVA COLL (3267)	9	3	4	7	44%	0%	25%	29%
GROVE CITY COLL (3269)	23	20	21	20	48%	60%	67%	60%
GWYNEDD MERCY COLL (3270)	8	3	6	10	25%	0%	33%	20%
HOLY FAMILY COLL (3275)	6	3	4	9	17%	33%	25%	11%
IMMACULATA UNIV (3276)	5	3	1	1	40%	33%	0%	0%
INDIANA UNIV PA (3277)	36	36	19	42	36%	33%	32%	31%
JUNIATA COLL (3279)	8	3	4	2	38%	67%	50%	100%
KEYSTONE COLL (3280)	6	5	1	3	0%	0%	0%	0%
KINGS COLL (3282)	24	27	19	18	29%	44%	42%	17%
KUTZTOWN UNIV PA (3322)	34	28	29	38	29%	54%	31%	37%
LA ROCHE COLL (3987)	5	8	2	9	0%	0%	0%	11%
LA SALLE UNIV (3287)	57	60	37	52	32%	33%	27%	17%
LAFAYETTE COLL (3284)	6	4	4	5	33%	75%	50%	0%
LEBANON VALLEY COLL (3288)	15	16	13	19	47%	56%	31%	32%
LEHIGH UNIV (3289)	74	67	71	84	68%	87%	66%	60%
LINCOLN UNIV (3290)	3	2	2	3	33%	0%	50%	0%
LOCK HAVEN UNIV PA (3323)	10	6	4	7	30%	17%	50%	43%
LYCOMING COLL (3293)	7	5	5	5	29%	60%	40%	40%
MARYWOOD UNIV (3296)	4	3	5	5	0%	33%	20%	20%
MERCYHURST COLL (3297)	17	10	8	11	24%	30%	38%	36%
MESSIAH COLL (3298)	25	21	18	21	48%	71%	56%	43%
MILLERSVILLE UNIV PA (3325)	13	13	14	13	38%	46%	29%	38%
MORAVIAN COLL (3301)	17	12	10	9	18%	33%	20%	33%
MOUNT ALOYSIUS COLL (3302)	2	5	1	1	50%	60%	0%	100%
MUHLENBERG COLL (3304)	25	21	23	21	48%	62%	57%	24%
NEUMANN UNIV (3988)	5	3	4	6	40%	33%	25%	50%
PA ST ERIE (3333)	2	3	3	3	50%	100%	67%	67%
PA ST UNIV PARK (3329)	276	277	227	272	47%	56%	44%	42%
PA ST UNIV PARK (6965)	11	5	6	10	45%	60%	67%	30%
PEIRCE COLL (3309)	3	2	1	2	100%	50%	0%	50%
PHILADELPHIA UNIV (3354)	10	11	10	10	20%	18%	10%	30%
POINT PARK UNIV (3357)	5	4	4	5	0%	25%	50%	20%
ROBERT MORRIS UNIV (3359)	39	30	25	32	31%	33%	32%	34%
SAINT FRANCIS UNIV (3366)	16	11	10	12	38%	18%	20%	33%
SAINT JOSEPHS UNIV (3367)	78	53	52	65	36%	68%	40%	23%
SAINT VINCENT COLL (3368)	16	22	10	14	31%	64%	30%	29%
SETON HILL UNIV (3362)	5	2	2	4	60%	50%	50%	25%
SHIPPENSBURG UNIV PA (3326)	35	32	32	34	71%	56%	50%	41%
SLIPPERY ROCK UNIV PA (3327)	19	16	9	17	21%	31%	22%	24%
SUSQUEHANNA UNIV (3369)	14	14	11	10	57%	43%	36%	40%
TEMPLE UNIV (3371)	184	162	149	164	32%	41%	30%	25%
THIEL COLL (3376)	8	6	6	8	13%	17%	33%	38%
UNIV PA (3378)	23	18	23	19	91%	89%	78%	84%
UNIV PITTSBURGH (3379)	154	128	116	124	51%	61%	51%	56%

Appendix D: Section Performance by Institution Attended - First-Time Testing Events

	Total Events per Section				Percent Pass			
	AUD	BEC	FAR	REG	AUD	BEC	FAR	REG
UNIV PITTSBURGH JOHNSTOWN (3382)	3	1	1	1	67%	0%	0%	100%
UNIV SCRANTON (3384)	27	32	24	20	59%	47%	54%	30%
URSINUS COLL (3385)	3	3	2	2	0%	0%	100%	0%
VILLANOVA UNIV (3388)	122	110	114	133	63%	82%	68%	47%
WASHINGTON & JEFFERSON COLL (3389)	19	18	18	17	42%	50%	50%	41%
WAYNESBURG COLL (3391)	3	4	2	4	0%	0%	0%	0%
WEST CHESTER UNIV PA (3328)	79	68	57	76	25%	34%	46%	39%
WESTMINSTER COLL (3392)	10	10	6	12	20%	30%	33%	33%
WIDENER UNIV PA (3313)	29	27	26	35	28%	33%	27%	20%
WILKES UNIV (3394)	15	15	10	14	27%	20%	20%	21%
YORK COLL PA (3399)	15	16	12	19	67%	31%	42%	47%
Puerto Rico								
INTER AMERICAN UNIV PR (8242)	4	8	11	7	0%	0%	9%	14%
INTER AMERICAN UNIV PR BARRANQUITAS (5027)	3	1	3	6	0%	0%	0%	0%
INTER AMERICAN UNIV PR BAYAMON (5028)	5	3	6	4	0%	0%	0%	0%
INTER AMERICAN UNIV PR METROPOLITAN (3940)	22	9	20	14	14%	0%	5%	14%
INTER AMERICAN UNIV PR PONCE (5029)	7	9	5	8	0%	0%	0%	0%
INTER AMERICAN UNIV PR SAN GERMAN (3938)	7	2	6	6	29%	0%	33%	0%
PONTIFICAL CATHOLIC UNIV PR (3936)	17	23	12	17	12%	9%	8%	12%
UNIV ESTE (3941)	4	6	8	3	0%	17%	13%	0%
UNIV METROPOLITANA (25875)	5	4	6	8	40%	0%	0%	25%
UNIV PR AGUADILLA (12123)	2	5	8	5	0%	0%	13%	0%
UNIV PR ARECIBO (7228)	10	7	9	9	30%	14%	0%	33%
UNIV PR BAYAMON (10975)	28	12	25	22	7%	8%	12%	9%
UNIV PR CAROLINA (30160)	6	3	5	4	17%	0%	20%	0%
UNIV PR CAYEY (7206)	12	18	14	16	0%	6%	14%	6%
UNIV PR HUMACAO (3943)	13	10	11	19	8%	10%	18%	21%
UNIV PR MAYAGUEZ (3944)	21	12	22	17	19%	17%	23%	12%
UNIV PR PONCE (9652)	13	10	14	10	15%	0%	14%	10%
UNIV PR RIO PIEDRAS (7108)	106	64	74	97	41%	27%	54%	29%
UNIV SACRED HEART (3937)	6	3	4	4	50%	33%	25%	25%
UNIV TURABO GURABO (11719)	8	5	6	3	0%	0%	0%	0%
Rhode Island								
BRYANT UNIV (3402)	96	59	83	91	52%	64%	49%	56%
JOHNSON & WALES UNIV (3404)	40	25	27	26	33%	28%	33%	42%
PROVIDENCE COLL (3406)	29	29	28	31	55%	72%	50%	42%
RI COLL (3407)	10	7	9	7	20%	14%	33%	43%
ROGER WILLIAMS UNIV (3410)	10	6	9	12	20%	17%	44%	33%
SALVE REGINA UNIV (3411)	5	10	6	12	40%	30%	17%	25%
UNIV RI (3414)	51	37	33	49	63%	70%	58%	51%
South Carolina								
BOB JONES UNIV (3421)	15	11	11	10	47%	64%	45%	70%
CITADEL MILITARY COLL SC (3423)	14	13	6	7	21%	23%	33%	14%
CLEMSON UNIV (3425)	55	38	44	52	64%	66%	64%	63%
COASTAL CAROLINA UNIV (3451)	8	7	9	7	13%	43%	44%	71%
COLL CHARLESTON (3428)	36	30	29	32	33%	63%	52%	56%
FRANCIS MARION UNIV (9226)	1	2	3	1	100%	50%	33%	0%
FURMAN UNIV (3434)	14	15	14	17	64%	80%	57%	53%
UNIV SC COLUMBIA (3448)	101	73	71	81	51%	70%	59%	49%
WINTHROP UNIV (3456)	11	7	8	11	73%	57%	63%	45%
WOFFORD COLL (3457)	15	15	14	14	47%	60%	71%	86%
South Dakota								
AUGUSTANA COLL (3458)	19	17	13	16	47%	59%	46%	56%
BLACK HILLS ST UNIV (3459)	6	4	4	7	33%	25%	50%	71%
CO TECHNICAL UNIV (666731)	3	5	5	4	67%	40%	20%	50%
NATIONAL AMERICAN UNIV (4057)	2	3	5	4	50%	33%	40%	50%
NORTHERN ST UNIV (3466)	4	4	6	5	25%	25%	17%	0%
SD ST UNIV (3471)	6	6	4	7	50%	50%	25%	57%
UNIV SD (3474)	18	12	17	21	61%	42%	71%	57%
UNIV SIOUX FALLS (3469)	9	10	7	8	44%	40%	71%	88%

Appendix D: Section Performance by Institution Attended - First-Time Testing Events

	Total Events per Section				Percent Pass			
	AUD	BEC	FAR	REG	AUD	BEC	FAR	REG
Tennessee								
AUSTIN PEAY ST UNIV (3478)	12	12	10	11	33%	33%	50%	36%
BELMONT UNIV (3479)	29	21	23	31	66%	57%	48%	45%
CARSON NEWMAN COLL (3481)	3	2	2	4	0%	50%	100%	50%
CHRISTIAN BROTHERS UNIV (3482)	4	3	8	4	25%	33%	0%	50%
CUMBERLAND UNIV (3485)	4	2	1	2	0%	0%	0%	50%
EAST TN ST UNIV (3487)	29	28	32	31	48%	46%	31%	48%
FISK UNIV (3490)	1	4	1	3	100%	25%	100%	33%
FREED HARDEMAN UNIV (3492)	4	6	4	4	0%	50%	50%	25%
LEE UNIV (3500)	12	6	11	6	67%	50%	73%	33%
LIPSCOMB UNIV (3486)	35	26	30	29	26%	46%	23%	34%
MIDDLE TN ST UNIV (3510)	71	54	55	64	42%	50%	56%	44%
RHODES COLL (3519)	11	9	16	15	45%	78%	56%	47%
SOUTHERN ADVENTIST UNIV (3518)	6	6	5	7	33%	83%	40%	29%
TN ST UNIV (3522)	13	7	8	12	31%	71%	13%	42%
TN TECH UNIV (3523)	31	33	26	26	35%	36%	27%	31%
TN WESLEYAN COLL (3525)	3	3	2	3	67%	67%	50%	33%
TREVECCA NAZARENE UNIV (3526)	4	1	2	6	75%	100%	100%	50%
TUSCULUM COLL (3527)	2	3	2	2	0%	0%	50%	50%
UNION UNIV (3528)	6	6	7	4	50%	50%	71%	75%
UNIV MEMPHIS (3509)	34	26	30	37	32%	31%	47%	30%
UNIV TN CHATTANOOGA (3529)	37	29	31	35	41%	41%	29%	49%
UNIV TN KNOXVILLE (3530)	100	84	88	106	62%	73%	74%	66%
UNIV TN MARTIN (3531)	16	9	15	9	19%	44%	20%	33%
VANDERBILT UNIV (3535)	37	37	33	36	70%	97%	73%	75%
Texas								
ABILENE CHRISTIAN UNIV (3537)	26	21	26	31	69%	62%	50%	55%
AMBERTON UNIV (22594)	0	1	1	4	0%	0%	100%	25%
ANGELO ST UNIV (3541)	21	17	12	17	38%	59%	58%	59%
BAYLOR UNIV (3545)	89	73	86	91	71%	89%	78%	69%
BAYLOR UNIV (6967)	9	7	5	10	33%	86%	20%	50%
DALLAS BAPTIST UNIV (3560)	9	12	8	11	22%	25%	25%	27%
DEVRY UNIV IRVING (10139)	8	2	6	8	25%	0%	33%	0%
HARDIN SIMMONS UNIV (3571)	4	3	1	2	25%	67%	0%	50%
HOUSTON BAPTIST UNIV (3576)	8	7	8	14	38%	29%	50%	36%
LAMAR COLL (3581)	15	8	16	9	53%	38%	50%	33%
LETOURNEAU UNIV (3584)	10	5	5	5	10%	60%	20%	20%
LUBBOCK CHRISTIAN UNIV (3586)	3	2	3	3	67%	50%	33%	67%
MIDWESTERN ST UNIV (3592)	15	12	8	13	33%	50%	75%	54%
OUR LADY THE LAKE UNIV (3598)	6	3	5	4	50%	33%	0%	0%
PRAIRIE VIEW A & M UNIV (3630)	4	3	3	3	0%	0%	0%	33%
RICE UNIV (3604)	8	7	7	9	75%	71%	57%	78%
SAINT EDWARDS UNIV (3621)	13	11	13	13	31%	45%	46%	46%
SAINT MARYS UNIV (3623)	13	5	8	4	46%	60%	25%	25%
SAM HOUSTON ST UNIV (3606)	43	29	35	51	53%	69%	43%	31%
SCHREINER UNIV (3610)	3	2	1	3	33%	0%	0%	0%
SOUTHERN METHODIST UNIV (3613)	75	62	71	74	64%	79%	70%	64%
SOUTHWESTERN UNIV (3620)	5	7	6	4	60%	86%	67%	75%
STEPHEN F AUSTIN ST UNIV (3624)	32	27	35	31	56%	48%	51%	23%
TARLETON ST UNIV (3631)	6	10	11	11	50%	10%	27%	73%
TRINITY UNIV (3647)	18	20	26	19	61%	75%	62%	68%
TX A&M INTL UNIV (9651)	5	7	6	6	20%	14%	17%	33%
TX A&M UNIV (3632)	279	248	259	278	65%	89%	78%	72%
TX A&M UNIV COMMERCE (3565)	13	13	13	15	38%	54%	38%	33%
TX A&M UNIV CORPUS CHRISTI (11161)	19	14	20	19	26%	50%	35%	47%
TX A&M UNIV KINGSVILLE (3639)	1	4	3	2	0%	0%	0%	50%
TX CHRISTIAN UNIV (3636)	47	42	44	49	60%	83%	70%	63%
TX LUTHERAN UNIV (3641)	9	7	8	6	67%	29%	75%	33%
TX SOUTHERN UNIV (3642)	4	7	4	2	0%	0%	0%	0%
TX ST UNIV SAN MARCOS (3615)	59	43	61	59	56%	67%	46%	41%

Appendix D: Section Performance by Institution Attended - First-Time Testing Events

	Total Events per Section				Percent Pass			
	AUD	BEC	FAR	REG	AUD	BEC	FAR	REG
TX TECH UNIV (3644)	108	73	104	97	50%	73%	59%	65%
TX WESLEYAN UNIV (3645)	7	4	9	6	29%	25%	22%	17%
TX WOMANS UNIV (3646)	9	8	6	9	33%	38%	17%	56%
UNIV DALLAS (3651)	8	9	9	17	50%	56%	56%	41%
UNIV HOUSTON (12826)	2	2	2	3	0%	0%	50%	33%
UNIV HOUSTON CLEAR LAKE (11711)	47	31	45	42	38%	32%	29%	40%
UNIV HOUSTON DOWNTOWN (3612)	51	40	53	41	39%	23%	26%	29%
UNIV HOUSTON UNIV PARK (3652)	174	130	135	160	40%	51%	37%	44%
UNIV HOUSTON VICTORIA (13231)	6	8	12	10	17%	63%	25%	10%
UNIV INCARNATE WORD (3578)	8	8	7	4	0%	0%	0%	25%
UNIV MARY HARDIN BAYLOR (3588)	9	9	10	12	44%	56%	50%	50%
UNIV NORTH TX (3594)	61	57	61	84	41%	58%	31%	46%
UNIV SAINT THOMAS (3654)	29	20	21	27	48%	45%	48%	41%
UNIV TX ARLINGTON (3656)	74	61	68	88	47%	51%	43%	45%
UNIV TX AUSTIN (3658)	262	233	249	265	65%	85%	78%	68%
UNIV TX BROWNSVILLE (30646)	6	6	3	4	50%	50%	33%	25%
UNIV TX DALLAS (9741)	142	107	127	139	43%	51%	39%	37%
UNIV TX EL PASO (3661)	11	16	5	17	73%	50%	40%	47%
UNIV TX PAN AMERICAN (3599)	11	9	12	9	36%	33%	50%	44%
UNIV TX PERMIAN BASIN (9930)	11	10	7	14	27%	40%	29%	64%
UNIV TX SAN ANTONIO (10115)	63	35	51	52	48%	54%	45%	48%
UNIV TX TYLER (11163)	13	20	14	17	31%	45%	50%	71%
WAYLAND BAPTIST UNIV (3663)	4	3	4	5	75%	33%	25%	40%
WEST TX A & M UNIV (3665)	18	10	16	16	28%	30%	13%	38%
Utah								
BRIGHAM YOUNG UNIV (3670)	206	185	194	221	72%	92%	74%	67%
SOUTHERN UT UNIV (3678)	35	24	23	28	37%	50%	52%	68%
UNIV UT (3675)	95	72	84	107	59%	78%	65%	67%
UT ST UNIV (3677)	50	30	47	58	48%	73%	53%	52%
UT VALLEY ST COLL (4027)	11	10	9	11	45%	40%	44%	55%
WEBER ST UNIV (3680)	27	22	31	38	67%	82%	48%	71%
Western Governors Univ (33394)	3	3	4	4	0%	33%	50%	25%
WESTMINSTER COLL (3681)	14	12	13	8	43%	58%	15%	13%
Vermont								
CASTLETON ST COLL (3683)	5	5	4	3	60%	80%	100%	100%
CHAMPLAIN COLL (3684)	14	9	12	13	43%	33%	17%	31%
SAINT MICHAELS COLL (3694)	18	8	13	11	56%	63%	69%	36%
UNIV VT (3696)	18	10	11	19	72%	80%	55%	47%
Virgin Islands								
UNIV VI (3946)	4	1	1	4	50%	0%	100%	0%
Virginia								
AVERETT UNIV (3702)	4	1	1	2	50%	0%	0%	0%
BRIDGEWATER COLL (3704)	6	5	7	4	33%	40%	0%	50%
CHRISTOPHER NEWPORT UNIV (3706)	10	7	4	11	40%	43%	75%	55%
COLL WILLIAM & MARY (3705)	70	60	65	65	54%	78%	66%	60%
EASTERN MENNONITE UNIV (3708)	5	4	4	5	60%	100%	75%	60%
FERRUM COLL (3711)	4	1	3	3	75%	0%	100%	33%
GEORGE MASON UNIV (3749)	114	84	105	122	44%	51%	52%	39%
HAMPDEN SYDNEY COLL (3713)	3	1	1	3	67%	0%	0%	67%
HAMPTON UNIV (3714)	17	15	7	12	12%	20%	29%	8%
JAMES MADISON UNIV (3721)	108	90	107	104	69%	82%	69%	62%
LIBERTY UNIV (20530)	22	21	22	28	59%	33%	32%	57%
LONGWOOD UNIV (3719)	8	6	8	8	25%	50%	50%	50%
LYNCHBURG COLL (3720)	4	2	4	3	50%	100%	100%	0%
MARYMOUNT UNIV (3724)	3	2	2	3	33%	100%	50%	67%
NORFOLK ST UNIV (3765)	3	1	3	3	33%	0%	33%	67%
NORTHERN VA CC (3727)	10	6	7	9	50%	50%	71%	33%
OLD DOMINION UNIV (3728)	32	25	37	37	59%	56%	43%	43%
RADFORD UNIV (3732)	14	9	6	9	29%	56%	33%	67%
RANDOLPH MACON COLL (3733)	7	10	8	8	29%	60%	25%	63%

Appendix D: Section Performance by Institution Attended - First-Time Testing Events

	Total Events per Section				Percent Pass			
	AUD	BEC	FAR	REG	AUD	BEC	FAR	REG
ROANOKE COLL (3736)	3	4	8	4	0%	100%	38%	0%
TIDEWATER CC (3712)	2	2	0	5	0%	50%	0%	40%
UNIV MARY WASHINGTON (3746)	10	6	8	7	50%	67%	38%	43%
UNIV RICHMOND (3744)	53	36	38	46	68%	92%	74%	48%
UNIV VA (3745)	87	78	78	96	78%	91%	87%	83%
UNIV VA COL WISE (CLINCH VALLEY COLL) (3747)	3	2	1	5	67%	50%	0%	80%
VA COMMONWEALTH UNIV (3735)	52	26	46	36	40%	38%	33%	42%
VA POLYTECHNIC INST & ST UNIV (3754)	137	117	121	143	55%	75%	60%	57%
WASHINGTON & LEE UNIV (3768)	20	18	22	21	60%	83%	77%	48%
Washington								
BELLEVUE CC (3769)	1	3	0	3	0%	100%	0%	0%
CENTRAL WA UNIV (3771)	61	63	57	66	41%	57%	35%	41%
CITY UNIV SEATTLE (13022)	12	9	10	13	25%	33%	20%	31%
EASTERN WA UNIV (3775)	31	27	30	27	39%	48%	30%	33%
GONZAGA UNIV (3778)	61	51	60	61	64%	80%	77%	64%
NORTH SEATTLE CC (9704)	5	3	7	5	60%	33%	71%	60%
PACIFIC LUTHERAN UNIV (3785)	9	8	13	10	0%	50%	15%	0%
SAINT MARTINS COLL (3794)	4	6	7	5	0%	33%	43%	40%
SEATTLE PACIFIC UNIV (3788)	18	14	10	16	44%	57%	50%	50%
SEATTLE UNIV (3790)	27	19	25	29	44%	53%	36%	41%
UNIV PUGET SOUND (3797)	3	3	5	2	33%	100%	100%	50%
UNIV WA (3798)	197	183	192	226	60%	77%	61%	60%
WA ST UNIV (3800)	60	67	68	70	47%	55%	46%	49%
WALLA WALLA UNIV (3799)	4	3	2	3	100%	33%	50%	67%
WESTERN WA UNIV (3802)	28	20	27	26	68%	70%	70%	69%
WHITWORTH COLL (3804)	6	5	5	6	50%	80%	60%	83%
West Virginia								
BETHANY COLL (3808)	4	0	1	3	75%	0%	100%	67%
CONCORD UNIV (3810)	1	5	2	6	0%	20%	50%	33%
FAIRMONT ST COLL (3812)	5	2	2	3	40%	0%	50%	67%
GLENVILLE ST COLL (3813)	3	1	2	0	33%	0%	0%	0%
MARSHALL UNIV (3815)	23	24	26	26	48%	38%	38%	38%
SALEM INTL UNIV (3820)	3	1	5	3	33%	100%	40%	33%
SHEPHERD UNIV (3822)	4	6	2	4	25%	50%	50%	75%
UNIV CHARLESTON (3818)	7	8	6	4	14%	25%	33%	50%
WEST LIBERTY ST COLL (3823)	5	5	8	6	20%	40%	13%	17%
WHEELING JESUIT UNIV (3831)	8	6	6	4	50%	67%	17%	0%
WV INST TECH (3825)	4	3	5	3	25%	33%	0%	0%
WV ST UNIV (3826)	9	10	4	10	33%	10%	0%	20%
WV UNIV (3827)	78	63	71	88	58%	41%	54%	49%
WV UNIV PARKERSBURG (3828)	4	4	4	4	50%	0%	50%	25%
WV WESLEYAN COLL (3830)	6	5	3	8	17%	80%	67%	63%
Wisconsin								
CARDINAL STRITCH UNIV (3837)	7	7	3	6	14%	57%	33%	33%
CARROLL UNIV (WI) (3838)	8	8	11	14	25%	63%	55%	57%
CARTHAGE COLL (3839)	7	8	8	5	14%	13%	0%	0%
CONCORDIA UNIV WI (3842)	8	6	7	6	38%	33%	57%	0%
EDGEWOOD COLL (3848)	7	8	6	9	14%	38%	33%	33%
LAKELAND COLL (3854)	25	19	26	29	36%	47%	58%	28%
MARQUETTE UNIV (3863)	72	59	55	70	65%	85%	80%	59%
MOUNT MARY COLL (3869)	5	2	4	2	20%	50%	0%	50%
SAINT NORBERT COLL (3892)	11	13	14	14	55%	69%	71%	64%
UNIV WI EAU CLAIRE (3917)	44	34	37	37	55%	71%	51%	57%
UNIV WI GREEN BAY (3899)	21	21	16	23	29%	29%	44%	35%
UNIV WI LA CROSSE (3919)	58	39	44	49	40%	79%	52%	57%
UNIV WI MADISON (3895)	139	115	122	123	66%	90%	79%	72%
UNIV WI MILWAUKEE (3896)	118	97	98	116	52%	63%	59%	53%
UNIV WI OSHKOSH (3920)	38	37	34	40	42%	70%	53%	55%
UNIV WI PARKSIDE (5015)	5	6	7	8	0%	50%	0%	0%
UNIV WI PLATTEVILLE (3921)	7	6	8	7	14%	83%	63%	57%

Appendix D: Section Performance by Institution Attended - First-Time Testing Events

	Total Events per Section				Percent Pass			
	AUD	BEC	FAR	REG	AUD	BEC	FAR	REG
UNIV WI RIVER FALLS (3923)	13	13	11	19	38%	85%	45%	58%
UNIV WI STEVENS POINT (3924)	8	8	5	10	38%	63%	60%	60%
UNIV WI SUPERIOR (3925)	9	6	7	7	44%	50%	29%	29%
UNIV WI WHITEWATER (3926)	108	100	106	100	48%	68%	62%	57%
Wyoming								
UNIV WY (3932)	36	29	27	38	44%	66%	67%	42%

ADVANCED DEGREE

ALL TESTING EVENTS

APPENDIX E

SUMMARY PERFORMANCE

Appendix E: Summary Performance for Advanced Degree - All Testing Events

	Candidates Total	Sections Total	Sections First-Time	Sections Re-Exam	Percent Pass	Average Score	Average Age
Alabama							
AUBURN UNIV (1009)	9	17	12	5	47.1%	73.8	30.8
TROY UNIV (1047)	26	53	29	24	34.0%	65.8	31.3
UNIV AL (1051)	15	43	22	21	55.8%	75.6	28.7
UNIV AL BIRMINGHAM (1052)	5	12	9	3	50.0%	68.3	33.9
UNIV AL HUNTSVILLE (1055)	5	11	11	0	45.5%	68.4	36.6
Arizona							
AZ ST UNIV (1081)	32	73	45	28	61.6%	75.1	31.9
GRAND CANYON UNIV (1074)	8	20	11	9	25.0%	58.2	34.8
THUNDERBIRD SCHOOL OF GLOBAL MGMT (1070)	16	37	24	13	40.5%	69.5	40.4
UNIV AZ (1083)	25	58	33	25	56.9%	75.1	30.3
UNIV PHOENIX (20988)	275	618	371	247	33.5%	63.9	37.6
Arkansas							
AR ST UNIV (1090)	13	30	16	14	40.0%	70.7	27.6
HENDERSON ST UNIV (1098)	7	18	12	6	33.3%	66.2	29.2
HENDRIX COLL (1099)	9	24	3	21	29.2%	65.6	26.1
UNIV AR (1108)	42	137	80	57	54.7%	73.1	26.0
UNIV AR LITTLE ROCK (1101)	14	39	14	25	53.9%	69.1	30.5
UNIV CENTRAL AR (1092)	22	55	32	23	41.8%	70.6	27.8
California							
CA LUTHERAN UNIV (1133)	8	22	9	13	27.3%	62.5	41.1
CA ST POLYTECH UNIV POMONA (1144)	6	19	5	14	52.6%	73.2	39.2
CA ST POLYTECH UNIV SAN LUIS OBISPO (1143)	26	54	39	15	46.3%	72.8	26.1
CA ST UNIV CHICO (1146)	9	27	14	13	51.9%	74.8	37.4
CA ST UNIV DOMINGUEZ HILLS (1141)	7	16	9	7	12.5%	57.8	36.5
CA ST UNIV EAST BAY (1138)	64	180	78	102	45.0%	71.9	37.6
CA ST UNIV FRESNO (1147)	16	44	22	22	52.3%	73.5	33.4
CA ST UNIV FULLERTON (1137)	48	122	64	58	45.1%	70.9	32.9
CA ST UNIV LONG BEACH (1139)	9	27	10	17	44.4%	68.9	36.0
CA ST UNIV LOS ANGELES (1140)	55	151	70	81	41.1%	70.2	33.6
CA ST UNIV NORTHRIDGE (1153)	21	48	24	24	41.7%	69.4	43.4
CA ST UNIV SACRAMENTO (1150)	33	88	56	32	50.0%	73.8	35.9
CA ST UNIV SAN BERNARDINO (1142)	21	39	27	12	51.3%	71.1	33.6
CA ST UNIV STANISLAUS (1157)	7	22	4	18	31.8%	68.3	38.0
CLAREMONT GRADUATE UNIV (1169)	5	7	7	0	14.3%	56.7	43.8
DEVRY UNIV LONG BEACH (666988)	14	43	17	26	20.9%	64.3	36.3
DEVRY UNIV POMONA (23329)	8	21	15	6	19.1%	53.2	32.8
GOLDEN GATE UNIV (1205)	167	404	216	188	39.4%	68.4	35.4
LA SIERRA UNIV (1215)	9	18	10	8	27.8%	57.3	30.0
LOYOLA MARYMOUNT UNIV (11649)	7	17	8	9	35.3%	72.6	33.8
NATIONAL UNIV (11460)	42	102	51	51	38.2%	68.1	39.3
PACIFIC ST UNIV (31633)	7	16	10	6	12.5%	55.2	42.2
PEPPERDINE (1264)	35	95	52	43	39.0%	69.3	37.1
SAN DIEGO ST UNIV (1151)	99	233	175	58	63.1%	76.9	31.1
SAN FRANCISCO ST UNIV (1154)	48	125	70	55	55.2%	75.1	34.6
SAN JOSE ST UNIV (1155)	63	158	121	37	60.8%	75.4	30.7
SANTA CLARA UNIV (1326)	14	28	17	11	39.3%	70.2	38.7
UNIV CA BERKELEY (1312)	5	14	13	1	78.6%	81.9	45.8
UNIV CA DAVIS (1313)	5	16	16	0	68.8%	79.3	35.0
UNIV CA IRVINE (1314)	12	25	13	12	56.0%	76.0	37.5
UNIV CA LOS ANGELES (1315)	13	33	31	2	75.8%	81.5	34.8

Appendix E: Summary Performance for Advanced Degree - All Testing Events

	Candidates Total	Sections Total	Sections First-Time	Sections Re-Exam	Percent Pass	Average Score	Average Age
UNIV CA RIVERSIDE (1316)	15	39	26	13	46.2%	71.1	31.8
UNIV CA SAN DIEGO (1317)	7	20	10	10	55.0%	73.0	32.9
UNIV CA SANTA BARBARA (1320)	7	20	14	6	55.0%	75.7	33.3
UNIV LA VERNE (1216)	16	30	20	10	23.3%	60.8	38.5
UNIV REDLANDS (1322)	5	17	11	6	23.5%	62.6	41.0
UNIV SAN DIEGO (10395)	32	88	56	32	48.9%	73.8	28.1
UNIV SAN FRANCISCO (1325)	13	32	22	10	53.1%	70.2	34.8
UNIV SOUTHERN CA (1328)	197	474	356	118	67.1%	77.3	29.1
WOODBURY UNIV (1343)	6	19	8	11	26.3%	68.3	37.1
Colorado							
CO ST UNIV (1350)	12	36	17	19	36.1%	67.9	40.6
REGIS UNIV (1363)	23	53	32	21	43.4%	69.2	40.2
UNIV CO BOULDER (1370)	20	51	28	23	52.9%	72.5	29.4
UNIV CO DENVER (6740)	13	28	21	7	39.3%	68.8	34.7
UNIV DENVER (1371)	38	77	39	38	45.5%	69.9	30.4
Connecticut							
FAIRFIELD UNIV (1385)	8	25	2	23	40.0%	69.4	30.7
QUINNIPIAC UNIV (1402)	6	23	11	12	39.1%	68.9	27.6
SACRED HEART UNIV (1403)	6	7	2	5	14.3%	61.1	33.1
UNIV BRIDGEPORT (1416)	6	19	7	12	21.1%	65.0	37.3
UNIV CT (1417)	22	67	21	46	38.8%	69.9	31.8
UNIV HARTFORD (1422)	18	41	23	18	41.5%	68.2	32.0
UNIV NEW HAVEN (1397)	10	30	9	21	13.3%	60.1	34.1
Delaware							
GOLDEY BEACOM COLL (1429)	5	14	9	5	42.9%	65.6	36.6
UNIV DE (1431)	10	18	15	3	44.4%	67.7	30.4
District of Columbia							
AMERICAN UNIV (1434)	23	54	33	21	50.0%	72.4	30.7
GEORGE WASHINGTON UNIV (1444)	52	128	90	38	60.2%	74.7	30.1
GEORGETOWN UNIV (1445)	8	18	9	9	50.0%	76.1	47.7
HOWARD UNIV (1448)	10	26	8	18	19.2%	67.3	33.5
SOUTHEASTERN UNIV (1456)	13	22	5	17	27.3%	68.0	37.7
STRAYER COLL (1459)	45	88	47	41	27.3%	61.5	37.8
Florida							
FL A&M UNIV (1480)	15	39	16	23	35.9%	68.4	26.5
FL ATLANTIC UNIV (1481)	17	49	27	22	32.7%	69.4	31.7
FL INTL UNIV (9635)	13	29	9	20	31.0%	67.8	40.5
FL ST UNIV (1489)	18	48	28	20	31.3%	67.6	32.7
NOVA SOUTHEASTERN UNIV (1509)	19	38	10	28	21.1%	60.7	34.5
SAINT LEO UNIV (1526)	7	14	11	3	21.4%	65.8	41.1
STETSON UNIV (1531)	5	10	6	4	40.0%	69.3	25.5
UNIV CENTRAL FL (3954)	13	41	28	13	61.0%	75.4	28.4
UNIV FL (1535)	19	49	37	12	67.4%	76.7	29.6
UNIV MIAMI (1536)	12	36	17	19	38.9%	71.9	31.4
UNIV NORTH FL (9841)	7	25	19	6	40.0%	72.8	28.4
UNIV TAMPA (1538)	5	17	5	12	35.3%	68.1	30.4
Georgia							
AMERICAN INTERCONT GA (21136)	7	21	4	17	23.8%	62.8	35.4
AUGUSTA ST UNIV (1552)	5	15	6	9	80.0%	79.5	33.7
CLARK ATLANTA UNIV (1559)	11	24	6	18	12.5%	62.5	31.6
GA COLL & ST UNIV (1602)	26	48	27	21	33.3%	68.8	29.4

Appendix E: Summary Performance for Advanced Degree - All Testing Events

	Candidates Total	Sections Total	Sections First-Time	Sections Re-Exam	Percent Pass	Average Score	Average Age
GA INST TECH (1569)	6	14	10	4	71.4%	80.4	36.8
GA SOUTHERN UNIV (1572)	32	82	34	48	32.9%	65.5	29.2
GA SOUTHWESTERN ST UNIV (1573)	5	11	5	6	27.3%	66.5	30.1
GA ST UNIV (1574)	45	117	84	33	66.7%	76.3	35.0
KENNESAW ST UNIV (1577)	43	90	49	41	48.9%	70.4	35.8
MERCER UNIV MACON (1580)	8	22	9	13	22.7%	70.7	36.2
UNIV GA (1598)	20	55	36	19	56.4%	77.4	30.7
UNIV WEST GA (1601)	9	14	8	6	35.7%	65.0	31.3
VALDOSTA ST UNIV (1599)	7	15	12	3	46.7%	71.9	35.2
Hawaii							
HI PACIFIC UNIV (7279)	11	31	12	19	35.5%	67.8	36.8
UNIV HI MANOA (1610)	17	55	17	38	49.1%	71.9	33.3
Idaho							
BOISE ST UNIV (1616)	14	37	23	14	62.2%	76.5	28.4
UNIV ID (1626)	14	31	23	8	54.8%	72.4	30.4
Illinois							
AMERICAN INTERCONT IL (666723)	5	11	8	3	18.2%	59.1	31.5
BENEDICTINE UNIV (1767)	10	16	8	8	25.0%	64.9	37.2
BRADLEY UNIV (1641)	32	85	67	18	76.5%	80.7	25.5
DE PAUL UNIV (1671)	72	194	119	75	50.5%	73.5	34.0
DOMINCAN UNIV (1750)	14	34	17	17	38.2%	69.6	35.5
EASTERN IL UNIV (1674)	15	32	26	6	62.5%	74.4	27.5
ELMHURST COLL (1676)	5	15	9	6	73.3%	78.5	27.8
GOVERNORS ST UNIV (9145)	14	36	25	11	11.1%	59.5	31.3
IL INST TECH (1691)	9	19	14	5	73.7%	74.2	30.2
IL ST UNIV (1692)	27	74	59	15	70.3%	76.6	27.4
KELLER GRAD SCHOOL DEVRY (20754)	148	313	191	122	25.6%	59.5	36.6
LEWIS UNIV (1707)	7	15	11	4	26.7%	65.7	34.7
LOYOLA UNIV CHICAGO (1710)	37	88	58	30	52.3%	72.6	31.7
NORTHEASTERN IL UNIV (1693)	9	16	9	7	43.8%	71.0	37.2
NORTHERN IL UNIV (1737)	58	163	96	67	49.1%	72.0	31.4
NORTHWESTERN UNIV (1739)	13	42	27	15	57.1%	75.6	39.9
ROOSEVELT UNIV (1749)	40	96	63	33	43.8%	68.9	32.1
SOUTHERN IL UNIV CARBONDALE (1758)	23	48	27	21	27.1%	65.6	26.4
SOUTHERN IL UNIV EDWARDSVILLE (1759)	33	79	61	18	62.0%	74.3	27.1
UNIV CHICAGO (1774)	22	42	30	12	54.8%	75.6	42.9
UNIV IL CHICAGO (1776)	65	149	100	49	52.4%	72.7	32.7
UNIV IL SPRINGFIELD (9333)	21	47	23	24	29.8%	67.9	33.6
UNIV IL URBANA CHAMPAIGN (1775)	85	195	123	72	58.0%	74.1	31.3
WESTERN IL UNIV (1780)	6	13	6	7	46.2%	70.8	28.1
Indiana							
BALL ST UNIV (1786)	15	40	12	28	47.5%	70.1	27.6
IN UNIV BLOOMINGTON (1809)	55	126	91	35	67.5%	76.2	30.3
IN UNIV PURDUE UNIV INDIANAPOLIS (1813)	32	68	40	28	45.6%	72.5	38.3
IN UNIV SOUTH BEND (1816)	5	13	6	7	53.9%	75.8	33.3
IN WESLEYAN UNIV (1822)	17	35	24	11	54.3%	69.0	36.1
PURDUE UNIV (1825)	22	48	34	14	45.8%	71.3	33.8
UNIV NOTRE DAME (1840)	81	199	113	86	55.8%	75.0	27.3
Iowa							
DRAKE UNIV (1860)	9	21	8	13	42.9%	68.9	30.2
IA ST UNIV (1869)	26	67	48	19	64.2%	75.0	29.4

Appendix E: Summary Performance for Advanced Degree - All Testing Events

	Candidates Total	Sections Total	Sections First-Time	Sections Re-Exam	Percent Pass	Average Score	Average Age
MAHARISHI UNIV MANAGEMENT (11113)	8	15	7	8	53.3%	70.3	32.9
SAINT AMBROSE UNIV (1889)	13	35	19	16	34.3%	67.3	26.5
UNIV IA (1892)	24	64	47	17	64.1%	77.6	31.4
UNIV NORTHERN IA (1890)	5	11	10	1	72.7%	77.5	31.9
UPPER IA UNIV (1893)	5	10	4	6	20.0%	60.3	46.0
Kansas							
EMPORIA ST UNIV (1927)	18	44	16	28	31.8%	69.9	27.8
KANSAS STATE UNIVERSITY (1928)	25	62	34	28	51.6%	74.3	29.7
PITTSBURG ST UNIV (1926)	6	21	9	12	42.9%	71.9	29.8
UNIV KS (1948)	48	111	66	45	62.2%	74.1	28.1
WASHBURN UNIV (1949)	5	14	4	10	42.9%	69.5	31.5
WICHITA ST UNIV (1950)	7	16	10	6	68.8%	77.8	28.2
Kentucky							
MURRAY ST UNIV (1977)	6	17	3	14	29.4%	70.2	41.0
NORTHERN KY UNIV (9275)	10	21	15	6	28.6%	69.2	29.7
UNIV KY (1989)	5	12	8	4	50.0%	74.4	30.7
Louisiana							
LA ST UNIV AND A & M COLL (2010)	68	175	101	74	53.1%	74.8	26.7
LA ST UNIV IN SHREVEPORT (2013)	5	12	7	5	25.0%	65.1	39.6
LA TECH UNIV (2008)	21	63	30	33	39.7%	71.3	26.3
MCNEESE ST UNIV (2017)	6	10	3	7	10.0%	62.9	32.6
NICHOLLS ST UNIV (2005)	6	16	8	8	31.3%	73.1	32.4
SOUTHEASTERN LA UNIV (2024)	21	71	26	45	28.2%	68.9	29.1
TULANE UNIV LA (2029)	56	146	78	68	55.5%	71.1	27.4
UNIV LA LAFAYETTE (2031)	5	16	8	8	37.5%	71.3	30.5
UNIV LA MONROE (2020)	5	22	13	9	54.6%	72.7	26.7
UNIV NEW ORLEANS (2015)	22	62	26	36	41.9%	72.4	29.2
Maine							
HUSSON UNIV (2043)	13	33	11	22	24.2%	66.2	27.7
THOMAS COLL (2052)	6	16	11	5	56.3%	76.6	25.1
UNIV ME (2053)	9	19	11	8	73.7%	77.2	26.5
UNIV SOUTHERN ME (2054)	8	22	13	9	45.5%	73.4	35.0
Maryland							
JOHNS HOPKINS UNIV (2077)	10	33	9	24	33.3%	68.7	39.0
UNIV BALTIMORE (2102)	6	10	8	2	60.0%	72.7	34.8
UNIV MD COLL PARK (2103)	17	43	32	11	51.2%	69.9	36.4
UNIV MD UNIV COLL (11644)	12	31	21	10	51.6%	74.8	34.0
Massachusetts							
BABSON COLL (2121)	17	56	28	28	39.3%	71.5	33.2
BENTLEY COLL (2124)	88	254	152	102	51.2%	74.3	29.4
BOSTON COLL (2128)	48	115	90	25	60.9%	76.0	28.0
BOSTON UNIV (2130)	9	14	10	4	78.6%	79.1	37.4
BRIDGEWATER ST COLL (2183)	6	14	6	8	35.7%	68.5	30.5
CLARK UNIV (2139)	11	26	11	15	57.7%	74.3	31.6
NORTHEASTERN UNIV (2199)	104	277	126	151	43.0%	71.1	29.1
SUFFOLK UNIV (2218)	56	142	79	63	47.2%	70.1	31.2
UNIV MA AMHERST (2221)	17	31	26	5	41.9%	71.2	28.9
UNIV MA BOSTON (2222)	26	63	44	19	52.4%	74.9	33.1
UNIV MA DARTMOUTH (2210)	8	18	13	5	38.9%	68.7	29.4
WESTERN NEW ENGLAND COLL (2226)	11	33	20	13	39.4%	73.2	31.2
WESTFIELD ST COLL (2189)	5	15	13	2	40.0%	69.4	25.9

Appendix E: Summary Performance for Advanced Degree - All Testing Events

	Candidates Total	Sections Total	Sections First-Time	Sections Re-Exam	Percent Pass	Average Score	Average Age
Michigan							
BAKER COLL FLINT (4673)	7	18	13	5	50.0%	67.7	38.6
CENTRAL MI UNIV (2243)	9	28	14	14	42.9%	66.6	36.2
DAVENPORT UNIV (2249)	13	33	28	5	36.4%	69.8	30.0
EASTERN MI UNIV (2259)	70	152	85	67	38.8%	69.3	31.8
GRAND VALLEY ST UNIV (2268)	34	101	68	33	60.4%	75.9	28.8
MI ST UNIV (2290)	48	104	56	48	54.8%	74.6	31.4
OAKLAND UNIV (2307)	17	37	22	15	43.2%	71.1	32.8
UNIV MI ANN ARBOR (2325)	24	65	45	20	76.9%	80.6	31.7
UNIV MI DEARBORN (2326)	8	20	16	4	65.0%	77.0	31.7
WALSH COLL (4071)	63	147	89	58	42.9%	71.9	34.1
WAYNE ST UNIV (2329)	44	122	66	56	48.4%	72.9	36.8
WESTERN MI UNIV (2330)	33	86	50	36	46.5%	72.4	29.2
Minnesota							
METROPOLITAN ST UNIV (10374)	5	10	10	0	50.0%	73.2	43.3
SAINT CLOUD ST UNIV (2377)	6	16	9	7	68.8%	81.3	33.3
SAINT JOHN'S UNIV (2379)	6	18	7	11	33.3%	68.3	28.8
UNIV MN TWIN CITIES (3969)	30	72	53	19	63.9%	75.5	33.8
UNIV ST THOMAS (2345)	14	40	29	11	52.5%	72.8	40.8
Mississippi							
JACKSON ST UNIV (2410)	6	27	4	23	22.2%	61.5	33.4
MILLSAPS COLL (2414)	16	39	28	11	48.7%	70.7	28.6
MS COLL (2415)	9	27	8	19	44.4%	69.5	32.8
MS ST UNIV (2423)	21	53	27	26	32.1%	67.3	29.8
UNIV MS (2440)	31	84	52	32	59.5%	74.3	27.7
UNIV SOUTHERN MS (2441)	8	14	6	8	7.1%	61.8	30.4
Missouri							
AVILA UNIV (2449)	5	18	11	7	27.8%	67.8	27.3
FONTBONNE UNIV (2464)	5	15	7	8	6.7%	61.1	31.8
LINCOLN UNIV (2479)	5	27	3	24	3.7%	66.1	35.4
LINDENWOOD UNIV (2480)	13	40	24	16	37.5%	67.4	34.7
MARYVILLE UNIV ST. LOUIS (2482)	5	17	5	12	23.5%	67.8	30.9
MO ST UNIV (2503)	50	114	68	46	51.8%	73.3	29.0
NORTHWEST MO ST UNIV (2496)	5	9	6	3	44.4%	76.4	27.9
ROCKHURST UNIV (2499)	7	13	9	4	53.9%	71.7	27.4
ST. LOUIS UNIV (2506)	39	99	63	36	51.5%	70.3	27.9
TRUMAN ST UNIV (2495)	14	26	12	14	53.9%	75.7	25.4
UNIV CENTRAL MO (2454)	9	29	19	10	34.5%	69.4	29.0
UNIV MO COLUMBIA (2516)	91	203	79	124	58.1%	74.3	25.8
UNIV MO KANSAS CITY (2518)	27	68	49	19	69.1%	76.6	33.1
UNIV MO ST. LOUIS (2519)	28	80	47	33	55.0%	74.9	32.2
WASHINGTON UNIV ST. LOUIS (2520)	22	54	36	18	57.4%	74.2	25.8
WEBSTER UNIV (2521)	29	61	43	18	26.2%	63.7	36.4
Montana							
MT ST UNIV BOZEMAN (2532)	7	8	7	1	75.0%	75.6	29.4
Nebraska							
BELLEVUE UNIV (9743)	6	17	11	6	47.1%	69.0	29.8
UNIV NE KEARNEY (2551)	6	18	10	8	33.3%	70.2	28.6
UNIV NE LINCOLN (2565)	30	91	58	33	60.4%	75.6	26.7
UNIV NE OMAHA (2554)	6	13	6	7	76.9%	78.8	37.3

Appendix E: Summary Performance for Advanced Degree - All Testing Events

	Candidates Total	Sections Total	Sections First-Time	Sections Re-Exam	Percent Pass	Average Score	Average Age
Nevada							
UNIV NV LAS VEGAS (2569)	40	94	44	50	46.8%	72.1	30.2
UNIV NV RENO (2568)	8	15	10	5	60.0%	79.0	32.5
New Hampshire							
SOUTHERN NH UN V (2580)	13	32	23	9	34.4%	68.3	40.0
UNIV NH (2589)	10	21	15	6	71.4%	79.5	24.9
New Jersey							
BETH MEDRASH GOVOHA (7947)	5	18	9	9	50.0%	72.9	32.1
FAIRLEIGH DICKINSON UNIV (2607)	64	137	104	33	48.2%	70.8	29.3
FAIRLEIGH DICKINSON UNIV MADISON (4738)	11	25	14	11	52.0%	75.9	36.9
FAIRLEIGH DICKINSON UNIV RUTHERFORD (2604)	21	43	22	21	51.2%	73.2	34.1
KEAN UNIV (2622)	12	27	14	13	44.4%	69.1	38.5
MONMOUTH UNIV (2616)	14	32	16	16	25.0%	63.0	33.3
MONTCLAIR ST UNIV (2617)	16	37	23	14	43.2%	70.0	32.2
NJ CITY UNIV (2613)	5	11	7	4	9.1%	62.6	41.7
NJ INST TECH (2621)	5	6	4	2	33.3%	67.5	35.5
RIDER UNIV (2628)	29	78	41	37	33.3%	67.9	29.5
RUTGERS ST UNIV CAMDEN (4741)	7	20	12	8	70.0%	77.5	31.6
RUTGERS ST UNIV NEW BRUNSWICK (6964)	28	79	45	34	41.8%	70.8	32.0
RUTGERS ST UNIV NEWARK (2631)	41	89	67	22	42.7%	68.7	31.7
SAINT PETERS COLL (2638)	9	21	12	9	33.3%	63.2	31.2
SETON HALL UNIV (2632)	13	38	17	21	36.8%	71.4	35.4
WILLIAM PATERSON UNIV NJ (2625)	6	13	10	3	15.4%	65.2	26.5
New Mexico							
NM ST UNIV (2657)	18	54	30	24	33.3%	69.6	30.4
UNIV NM (2663)	21	62	30	32	45.2%	73.3	32.3
New York							
ADELPHI UNIV (2666)	5	11	6	5	36.4%	60.5	29.0
CANISIUS COLL (2681)	7	29	14	15	27.6%	65.6	27.8
COLL SAINT ROSE (2705)	11	35	17	18	42.9%	68.2	26.6
COLUMBIA UNIV NY (2707)	7	18	17	1	88.9%	81.7	36.3
CORNELL UNIV (2711)	5	14	9	5	85.7%	80.5	28.8
CUNY BARUCH (7273)	129	306	209	97	61.4%	74.8	32.7
CUNY BROOKLYN (2687)	6	10	9	1	10.0%	54.6	40.1
CUNY QUEENS (2690)	7	17	12	5	47.1%	72.2	34.7
DAEMEN COLL (2808)	5	12	6	6	41.7%	65.7	24.8
FORDHAM UNIV (2722)	31	63	35	28	52.4%	74.0	31.5
HOFSTRA UNIV (2732)	30	78	45	33	34.6%	67.7	28.4
ITHACA COLL (2739)	6	18	8	10	55.6%	74.3	25.4
LE MOYNE COLL (2748)	10	21	14	7	28.6%	59.2	27.6
LONG ISLAND UNIV BROOKLYN CENTER (4779)	14	25	9	16	4.0%	56.0	32.9
LONG ISLAND UNIV CW POST (2754)	32	74	38	36	36.5%	67.6	34.8
MARIST COLL (2765)	5	10	9	1	10.0%	62.4	28.8
MERCY COLL (2772)	5	15	7	8	26.7%	69.6	37.4
NIAGARA UNIV (2788)	12	38	15	23	15.8%	66.2	24.7
NY INST TECH MANHATTAN (2782)	8	24	12	12	25.0%	67.7	36.3
NY UNIV (2785)	21	54	48	6	72.2%	78.1	36.6
PACE UNIV NY (2791)	77	200	91	109	38.0%	69.8	31.3
PACE UNIV PLEASANTVILLE (2792)	9	26	9	17	46.2%	71.7	28.0
PACE UNIV WHITE PLAINS (2727)	6	17	4	13	29.4%	72.5	43.7
ROCHESTER INST TECH (2806)	11	37	15	22	32.4%	69.1	33.4

Appendix E: Summary Performance for Advanced Degree - All Testing Events

	Candidates Total	Sections Total	Sections First-Time	Sections Re-Exam	Percent Pass	Average Score	Average Age
SAINT BONAVENTURE UNIV (2817)	30	79	42	37	38.0%	69.9	26.0
SAINT FRANCIS COLL (2820)	6	15	9	6	46.7%	71.9	24.7
SAINT JOHNS UNIV NEW YORK (2823)	130	283	147	136	32.2%	66.0	28.3
SAINT JOSEPHS COLL NY (2825)	6	12	10	2	33.3%	63.6	28.2
SIENA COLL (2816)	11	22	19	3	59.1%	74.2	23.9
SUNY OLD WESTBURY (7109)	5	10	6	4	50.0%	73.8	43.9
SUNY ALBANY (2835)	49	103	74	29	47.6%	70.8	29.4
SUNY BINGHAMTON (2836)	48	106	76	30	41.5%	67.4	27.6
SUNY BUFFALO (2837)	22	46	28	18	67.4%	75.3	30.0
SUNY GENESEO (2845)	8	16	10	6	12.5%	66.4	26.2
SUNY OSWEGO (2848)	18	48	21	27	33.3%	65.5	26.2
SUNY STONY BROOK (2838)	5	10	8	2	60.0%	69.8	28.6
SYRACUSE UNIV (2882)	20	49	22	27	28.6%	67.6	28.9
UNIV ROCHESTER (2894)	10	21	16	5	81.0%	82.0	32.7
WAGNER COLL (2899)	21	41	19	22	22.0%	60.1	29.1
North Carolina							
CAMPBELL UNIV (2913)	8	22	6	16	36.4%	70.6	35.0
DUKE UNIV (2920)	5	9	3	6	44.4%	69.7	37.9
EAST CAROLINA UNIV (2923)	35	86	28	58	37.2%	69.6	28.1
NC ST UNIV RALEIGH (2972)	10	25	22	3	72.0%	83.1	30.3
UNIV NC CHAPEL HILL (2974)	38	108	84	24	69.4%	77.9	27.8
UNIV NC CHARLOTTE (2975)	10	31	22	9	67.7%	81.1	28.8
UNIV NC GREENSBORO (2976)	12	28	18	10	78.6%	79.3	29.8
UNIV NC WILMINGTON (2984)	8	24	10	14	29.2%	69.7	35.4
WAKE FOREST UNIV (2978)	14	46	38	8	80.4%	80.0	26.8
Ohio							
ASHLAND UNIV (3012)	9	16	14	2	37.5%	65.9	39.4
BALDWIN WALLACE COLL (3014)	40	100	61	39	52.0%	71.7	29.6
BOWLING GREEN ST UNIV (3018)	45	129	66	63	47.3%	72.0	29.4
CAPITAL UNIV (3023)	7	11	7	4	36.4%	69.5	35.4
CASE WESTERN RESERVE UNIV (3024)	23	70	58	12	70.0%	76.3	30.8
CLEVELAND ST UNIV (3032)	60	139	97	42	45.3%	69.1	32.3
FRANKLIN UNIV (3046)	7	12	5	7	25.0%	68.5	31.3
JOHN CARROLL UNIV (3050)	22	65	39	26	60.0%	75.3	28.6
KENT ST UNIV (3051)	31	75	48	27	52.0%	73.2	29.1
MIAMI UNIV (3077)	23	57	38	19	59.7%	75.0	27.9
OH DOMINICAN UNIV (3035)	6	14	10	4	21.4%	67.0	29.7
OH ST UNIV (6883)	74	209	156	53	70.8%	79.7	26.1
OH UNIV (3100)	10	26	18	8	34.6%	63.9	29.9
UNIV AKRON (3123)	35	97	73	24	74.2%	77.4	30.8
UNIV CINCINNATI (3125)	22	50	19	31	46.0%	72.7	33.7
UNIV DAYTON (3127)	70	188	121	67	47.3%	71.7	24.9
UNIV FINDLAY (3045)	9	25	12	13	32.0%	67.6	33.5
UNIV TOLEDO (3131)	33	85	53	32	47.1%	71.3	31.5
WRIGHT ST UNIV (3078)	25	61	36	25	62.3%	76.8	30.0
XAVIER UNIV (3144)	17	37	27	10	56.8%	70.1	31.3
YOUNGSTOWN ST UNIV (3145)	11	32	15	17	46.9%	67.7	30.9
Oklahoma							
CAMERON UNIV (3150)	8	12	9	3	25.0%	61.4	35.9
NORTHEASTERN ST UNIV (3161)	8	19	11	8	31.6%	68.5	33.6
OK CHRISTIAN UNIV (3165)	9	30	20	10	66.7%	71.9	27.5

Appendix E: Summary Performance for Advanced Degree - All Testing Events

	Candidates Total	Sections Total	Sections First-Time	Sections Re-Exam	Percent Pass	Average Score	Average Age
OK ST UNIV (3170)	47	114	64	50	56.1%	73.8	30.0
OKLAHOMA CITY UNIV (3166)	23	52	22	30	38.5%	68.0	32.5
ORAL ROBERTS UNIV (3985)	9	24	6	18	58.3%	76.0	29.5
SOUTHWESTERN OK ST UNIV (3181)	7	14	11	3	14.3%	57.1	28.1
UNIV CENTRAL OK (3152)	18	38	16	22	36.8%	70.0	33.6
UNIV OK NORMAN (3184)	43	121	77	44	69.4%	77.6	26.8
UNIV TULSA (3185)	13	28	12	16	25.0%	65.3	33.1
Oregon							
OR ST UNIV (3210)	13	31	26	5	71.0%	78.4	30.7
PORTLAND ST UNIV (3216)	19	47	26	21	53.2%	73.9	36.2
UNIV OR (3223)	42	98	75	23	71.4%	77.2	28.0
WILLAMETTE UNIV (3227)	5	13	7	6	76.9%	78.6	30.6
Pennsylvania							
CARNEGIE MELLON UNIV (3242)	5	10	4	6	30.0%	70.4	35.9
DREXEL UNIV (3256)	25	48	33	15	54.2%	71.2	31.8
DUQUESNE UNIV (3258)	16	34	27	7	64.7%	76.9	31.5
INDIANA UNIV PA (3277)	9	18	10	8	38.9%	71.1	37.2
LA SALLE UNIV (3287)	21	50	21	29	36.0%	66.2	32.4
LEHIGH UNIV (3289)	11	26	18	8	46.2%	70.8	26.0
PA ST UNIV PARK (3329)	27	78	67	11	55.1%	74.6	27.5
PHILADELPHIA UNIV (3354)	7	18	8	10	27.8%	64.1	34.7
ROBERT MORRIS UNIV (3359)	9	22	12	10	54.6%	73.3	27.7
SAINT JOSEPHS UNIV (3367)	10	19	12	7	31.6%	66.9	40.1
TEMPLE UNIV (3371)	8	18	15	3	66.7%	72.6	33.2
UNIV PA (3378)	6	16	11	5	81.3%	82.1	36.7
UNIV PITTSBURGH (3379)	15	37	26	11	54.1%	72.8	31.9
UNIV SCRANTON (3384)	13	30	21	9	66.7%	75.3	25.3
VILLANOVA UNIV (3388)	19	53	26	27	47.2%	73.0	31.4
WIDENER UNIV PA (33[illegible]3)	9	17	10	7	41.2%	72.4	31.9
YORK COLL PA (3399)	5	9	6	3	33.3%	63.3	31.8
Puerto Rico							
INTER AMERICAN UNIV PR (8242)	9	12	11	1	8.3%	31.7	33.5
INTER AMERICAN UNIV PR METROPOLITAN (3940)	11	23	17	6	21.7%	56.9	34.0
INTER AMERICAN UNIV PR SAN GERMAN (3938)	5	11	7	4	9.1%	62.2	32.4
PONTIFICAL CATHOLIC UNIV PR (3936)	5	8	6	2	25.0%	54.5	31.3
UNIV PR RIO PIEDRAS (7108)	5	11	6	5	27.3%	67.7	36.4
Rhode Island							
BRYANT UNIV (3402)	29	68	42	26	51.5%	73.2	29.5
JOHNSON & WALES UNIV (3404)	17	31	24	7	41.9%	61.2	32.2
PROVIDENCE COLL (3406)	6	12	9	3	66.7%	80.2	28.9
UNIV RI (3414)	11	28	14	14	39.3%	70.9	34.4
South Carolina							
CLEMSON UNIV (3425)	5	12	11	1	83.3%	80.8	30.5
UNIV SC COLUMBIA (3448)	12	23	12	11	43.5%	75.7	36.2
South Dakota							
UNIV SD (3474)	32	85	41	44	50.6%	74.2	26.5
Tennessee							
BELMONT UNIV (3479)	27	75	30	45	30.7%	69.4	31.8
EAST TN ST UNIV (3487)	25	62	33	29	45.2%	71.3	29.5
LIPSCOMB UNIV (3486)	30	76	48	28	34.2%	66.7	26.0
MIDDLE TN ST UNIV (3510)	26	61	36	25	49.2%	71.5	27.8

Appendix E: Summary Performance for Advanced Degree - All Testing Events

	Candidates Total	Sections Total	Sections First-Time	Sections Re-Exam	Percent Pass	Average Score	Average Age
RHODES COLL (3519)	13	26	21	5	53.9%	76.0	24.5
TN ST UNIV (3522)	9	23	12	11	21.7%	64.0	33.4
TN TECH UNIV (3523)	26	67	48	19	28.4%	68.0	29.4
UNIV MEMPHIS (3509)	12	29	13	16	37.9%	70.1	30.6
UNIV TN CHATTANOOGA (3529)	22	55	38	17	34.6%	65.2	30.0
UNIV TN KNOXVILLE (3530)	26	74	40	34	54.1%	75.1	28.9
UNIV TN MARTIN (3531)	10	25	12	13	48.0%	71.0	29.5
VANDERBILT UNIV (3535)	18	43	23	20	58.1%	77.6	29.2
Texas							
ABILENE CHRISTIAN UNIV (3537)	38	98	49	49	44.9%	71.5	25.8
AMBERTON UNIV (22594)	5	12	3	9	16.7%	55.8	46.6
ANGELO ST UNIV (3541)	23	68	35	33	52.9%	73.6	32.5
BAYLOR UNIV (3545)	33	105	81	24	78.1%	80.2	25.7
BAYLOR UNIV (6967)	7	16	14	2	62.5%	73.7	26.8
DALLAS BAPTIST UNIV (3560)	17	51	17	34	21.6%	64.1	34.8
DEVRY UNIV IRVING (10139)	6	16	5	11	6.3%	53.9	38.8
HOUSTON BAPTIST UNIV (3576)	17	44	19	25	47.7%	72.7	29.0
LAMAR COLL (3581)	9	34	14	20	38.2%	70.3	29.3
MIDWESTERN ST UNIV (3592)	15	39	20	19	43.6%	70.5	29.6
OUR LADY THE LAKE UNIV (3598)	6	17	10	7	35.3%	70.6	41.0
RICE UNIV (3604)	8	14	7	7	64.3%	74.6	34.5
SAINT EDWARDS UNIV (3621)	12	42	25	17	52.4%	73.6	34.5
SAINT MARYS UNIV (3623)	5	9	8	1	44.4%	68.3	46.7
SAM HOUSTON ST UNIV (3606)	33	85	49	36	40.0%	70.5	28.7
SOUTHERN METHODIST UNIV (3613)	47	103	66	37	68.0%	77.4	29.3
STEPHEN F AUSTIN ST UNIV (3624)	38	82	42	40	48.8%	71.0	27.1
TRINITY UNIV (3647)	29	79	37	42	45.6%	71.4	25.9
TX A&M INTL UNIV (9651)	5	15	8	7	13.3%	54.7	34.1
TX A&M UNIV (3632)	69	164	99	65	59.2%	75.6	28.5
TX A&M UNIV COMMERCE (3565)	31	77	39	38	31.2%	65.7	33.4
TX A&M UNIV CORPUS CHRISTI (11161)	23	53	28	25	41.5%	67.6	29.0
TX CHRISTIAN UNIV (3636)	29	72	49	23	58.3%	77.8	26.9
TX SOUTHERN UNIV (3642)	6	8	3	5	12.5%	56.8	45.5
TX ST UNIV SAN MARCOS (3615)	74	188	96	92	52.7%	74.4	30.1
TX TECH UNIV (3644)	68	188	113	75	60.6%	75.0	26.6
TX WESLEYAN UNIV (3645)	8	20	15	5	25.0%	70.0	27.4
TX WOMANS UNIV (3646)	10	21	16	5	33.3%	63.0	33.1
UNIV DALLAS (3651)	33	85	35	50	32.9%	68.0	36.7
UNIV HOUSTON CLEAR LAKE (11711)	67	162	90	72	38.3%	66.7	32.4
UNIV HOUSTON UNIV PARK (3652)	137	326	198	128	50.3%	71.9	30.1
UNIV HOUSTON VICTORIA (13231)	16	45	15	30	35.6%	69.2	35.1
UNIV INCARNATE WORD (3578)	18	39	20	19	7.7%	53.9	32.2
UNIV NORTH TX (3594)	68	173	101	72	45.1%	71.3	30.9
UNIV SAINT THOMAS (3654)	56	122	64	58	41.8%	68.6	31.0
UNIV TX ARLINGTON (3656)	65	170	94	76	50.0%	73.0	31.9
UNIV TX AUSTIN (3658)	114	263	171	92	63.1%	76.6	29.4
UNIV TX DALLAS (9741)	136	328	189	139	41.5%	69.1	33.9
UNIV TX EL PASO (3661)	15	26	15	11	57.7%	74.2	33.7
UNIV TX PAN AMERICAN (3599)	11	24	12	12	20.8%	61.9	28.0
UNIV TX PERMIAN BASIN (9930)	5	16	8	8	75.0%	75.8	39.3
UNIV TX SAN ANTONIO (10115)	38	91	57	34	51.7%	72.2	31.6

Appendix E: Summary Performance for Advanced Degree - All Testing Events

	Candidates Total	Sections Total	Sections First-Time	Sections Re-Exam	Percent Pass	Average Score	Average Age
UNIV TX TYLER (11163)	11	30	19	11	33.3%	67.0	28.4
WEST TX A & M UNIV (3665)	37	108	45	63	33.3%	68.9	29.3
Utah							
BRIGHAM YOUNG UNIV (3670)	166	447	395	52	82.6%	82.6	27.3
SOUTHERN UT UN V (3678)	52	131	77	54	50.4%	72.9	28.2
UNIV UT (3675)	127	337	244	93	65.3%	77.1	30.3
UT ST UNIV (3677)	72	182	126	56	55.0%	75.1	30.7
WEBER ST UNIV (3680)	71	166	109	57	56.0%	73.5	31.3
WESTMINSTER COLL (3681)	31	61	32	29	41.0%	69.0	35.0
Vermont							
UNIV VT (3696)	5	13	12	1	84.6%	77.9	28.0
Virginia							
COLL WILLIAM & MARY (3705)	53	137	100	37	62.8%	75.7	26.4
GEORGE MASON UNIV (3749)	20	47	31	16	55.3%	73.8	32.5
HAMPTON UNIV (3714)	6	9	7	2	11.1%	58.9	25.5
JAMES MADISON UNIV (3721)	18	54	42	12	75.9%	80.7	24.1
LIBERTY UNIV (20530)	17	34	22	12	38.2%	67.2	30.7
OLD DOMINION UNIV (3728)	14	37	27	10	48.7%	74.0	31.2
UNIV VA (3745)	41	89	58	31	65.2%	75.7	27.7
VA COMMONWEALTH UNIV (3735)	17	42	24	18	47.6%	71.9	27.9
VA POLYTECHNIC INST & ST UNIV (3754)	35	93	55	38	63.4%	77.2	28.9
Washington							
CENTRAL WA UNIV (3771)	6	19	15	4	42.1%	69.9	28.6
GONZAGA UNIV (3778)	10	28	20	8	67.9%	76.2	30.1
SEATTLE UNIV (3790)	7	21	20	1	57.1%	77.2	32.4
UNIV WA (3798)	15	37	25	12	64.9%	77.1	35.0
WA ST UNIV (3800)	11	31	26	5	61.3%	76.5	27.0
WESTERN WA UNIV (3802)	6	12	12	0	66.7%	76.8	26.4
West Virginia							
MARSHALL UNIV (3815)	6	21	6	15	42.9%	72.9	38.5
WV UNIV (3827)	16	42	27	15	59.5%	75.2	28.4
WV WESLEYAN COLL (3830)	6	20	12	8	50.0%	70.8	24.6
Wisconsin							
EDGEWOOD COLL (3848)	8	20	8	12	50.0%	73.8	31.5
MARQUETTE UNIV (3863)	15	30	15	15	50.0%	73.5	30.0
UNIV WI MADISON (3895)	28	69	58	11	75.4%	79.2	29.0
UNIV WI MILWAUKEE (3896)	42	93	36	57	62.4%	76.4	30.0
UNIV WI WHITEWATER (3926)	78	199	85	114	49.8%	72.5	28.7
Wyoming							
UNIV WY (3932)	17	45	21	24	60.0%	76.3	29.8

BACHELOR'S DEGREE

ALL TESTING EVENTS

APPENDIX F

SUMMARY PERFORMANCE

Appendix F: Summary Performance for Bachelor's Degree - All Testing Events

	Candidates Total	Sections Total	Sections First-Time	Sections Re-Exam	Percent Pass	Average Score	Average Age
Alabama							
AL A&M UNIV (1002)	9	25	5	20	16.0%	57.4	30.5
AL ST UNIV (1005)	5	8	4	4	25.0%	64.9	34.5
ATHENS ST UNIV (1008)	23	42	15	27	26.2%	64.0	39.5
AUBURN UNIV (1009)	195	605	403	202	61.7%	75.8	26.6
AUBURN UNIV MONTGOMERY (8310)	37	91	32	59	30.8%	68.0	29.1
BIRMINGHAM SOUTHERN COLL (1012)	43	102	57	45	32.4%	66.9	27.2
HUNTINGDON COLL (1019)	9	24	17	7	50.0%	72.5	30.3
JACKSONVILLE ST UNIV (1020)	23	51	21	30	43.1%	67.9	29.0
OAKWOOD COLL (1033)	12	31	13	18	45.2%	68.8	29.8
SAMFORD UNIV (1036)	33	87	43	44	59.8%	75.1	25.6
SPRING HILL COLL (1041)	9	23	10	13	43.5%	70.4	28.5
TROY UNIV (1047)	69	165	96	69	35.2%	67.0	29.2
TUSKEGEE UNIV (1050)	7	19	8	11	21.1%	63.7	30.8
UNIV AL (1051)	241	717	427	290	49.1%	72.5	26.3
UNIV AL (8004)	7	15	2	13	53.3%	71.3	32.4
UNIV AL BIRMINGHAM (1052)	111	264	158	106	44.3%	71.4	30.1
UNIV AL HUNTSVILLE (1055)	21	48	22	26	27.1%	67.8	33.2
UNIV MONTEVALLO (1004)	15	31	19	12	48.4%	69.3	28.8
UNIV NORTH AL (1016)	20	51	31	20	60.8%	75.0	30.0
UNIV SOUTH AL (1057)	63	129	82	47	45.0%	71.3	31.2
UNIV WEST AL (1024)	7	16	9	7	25.0%	63.0	33.5
Alaska							
UNIV ALASKA ANCHORAGE (11462)	42	94	55	39	36.2%	66.2	30.1
UNIV ALASKA FAIRBANKS (1063)	12	23	17	6	34.8%	66.0	32.5
UNIV ALASKA SOUTHEAST (1065)	6	11	10	1	54.6%	71.7	35.8
Arizona							
AZ ST UNIV (1081)	370	889	588	301	54.7%	73.8	30.0
AZ ST UNIV WEST (66935)	16	40	15	25	52.5%	72.4	33.9
DEVRY UNIV PHOENIX (8322)	37	98	73	25	28.6%	63.5	35.6
GRAND CANYON UNIV (1074)	8	16	10	6	18.8%	64.9	32.5
NORTHERN AZ UNIV (1082)	81	196	112	84	40.8%	69.8	27.7
UNIV AZ (1083)	222	609	354	255	50.9%	72.5	28.1
UNIV PHOENIX (20988)	283	633	358	275	27.3%	63.3	39.4
WESTERN INTL UNIV (21715)	11	22	17	5	59.1%	72.9	40.6
Arkansas							
AR ST UNIV (1090)	35	83	48	35	32.5%	65.0	28.3
AR TECH UNIV (1089)	23	74	57	17	48.7%	70.9	30.9
HARDING UNIV (1097)	69	182	93	89	39.0%	70.1	25.8
HENDERSON ST UNIV (1098)	13	36	24	12	19.4%	63.8	27.4
HENDRIX COLL (1099)	8	16	11	5	18.8%	63.3	26.7
OUACHITA BAPTIST UNIV (1102)	22	45	22	23	42.2%	69.8	26.9
SOUTHERN AR UNIV (1107)	17	42	20	22	42.9%	69.3	30.8
UNIV AR (1108)	79	230	150	80	49.1%	71.4	27.1
UNIV AR LITTLE ROCK (1101)	35	87	33	54	41.4%	67.7	33.9
UNIV AR MONTICELLO (1085)	10	18	14	4	27.8%	65.2	27.7
UNIV AR PINE BLUFF (1086)	5	13	8	5	0.0%	53.0	32.2
UNIV CENTRAL AR (1092)	64	174	76	98	32.8%	68.7	30.4
California							
AZUSA PACIFIC UNIV (1117)	22	55	32	23	32.7%	66.0	25.3
BIOLA UNIV (1122)	34	76	41	35	38.2%	69.8	25.5
CA BAPTIST UNIV (1125)	21	38	21	17	21.1%	60.8	28.4

Appendix F: Summary Performance for Bachelor's Degree - All Testing Events

	Candidates Total	Sections Total	Sections First-Time	Sections Re-Exam	Percent Pass	Average Score	Average Age
CA LUTHERAN UNIV (1133)	28	79	30	49	40.5%	69.9	29.4
CA ST POLYTECH UNIV POMONA (1144)	171	394	218	176	27.9%	63.9	29.0
CA ST POLYTECH UNIV SAN LUIS OBISPO (1143)	279	658	372	286	51.1%	72.3	26.0
CA ST UNIV BAKERSFIELD (7993)	49	121	68	53	40.5%	69.3	29.8
CA ST UNIV CHICO (1146)	93	221	115	106	34.8%	69.8	30.0
CA ST UNIV DOMINGUEZ HILLS (1141)	56	142	51	91	22.5%	61.2	37.5
CA ST UNIV EAST BAY (1138)	206	491	247	244	36.7%	65.2	33.3
CA ST UNIV FRESNO (1147)	168	388	187	201	40.5%	70.1	30.4
CA ST UNIV FULLERTON (1137)	445	1,052	614	438	37.2%	67.7	29.8
CA ST UNIV LONG BEACH (1139)	268	641	358	283	37.6%	68.1	30.5
CA ST UNIV LOS ANGELES (1140)	231	592	278	314	30.4%	65.3	32.8
CA ST UNIV NORTHRIDGE (1153)	396	995	507	488	43.0%	70.6	31.7
CA ST UNIV SACRAMENTO (1150)	285	683	350	333	35.4%	67.4	30.1
CA ST UNIV SAN BERNARDINO (1142)	116	254	117	137	28.4%	66.6	30.9
CA ST UNIV SAN MARCOS (30113)	83	195	111	84	48.7%	72.8	30.6
CA ST UNIV STANISLAUS (1157)	57	126	51	75	32.5%	67.6	31.1
CHAPMAN UNIV (1164)	63	157	86	71	45.2%	72.0	27.8
CLAREMONT MCKENNA COLL (1170)	32	81	41	40	50.6%	73.2	25.0
CONCORDIA UNIV (20705)	7	20	6	14	15.0%	68.1	28.5
DEVRY UNIV LONG BEACH (666988)	15	35	20	15	20.0%	57.2	32.9
DEVRY UNIV POMONA (23329)	18	40	25	15	25.0%	60.4	34.1
FRESNO PACIFIC UNIV (1253)	15	42	18	24	50.0%	71.1	26.1
GOLDEN GATE UNIV (1205)	19	40	13	27	30.0%	63.9	38.7
HUMBOLDT ST UNIV (1149)	21	47	22	25	42.6%	71.0	32.3
LA SIERRA UNIV (1215)	7	20	9	11	10.0%	60.3	29.5
LOYOLA MARYMOUNT UNIV (11649)	105	266	157	109	48.9%	72.4	25.4
MASTERS COLL & SEMINARY (1220)	14	32	26	6	50.0%	71.5	24.2
MENLO COLL (1236)	6	12	9	3	25.0%	59.2	29.0
MOUNT SAINT MARYS COLL (1243)	15	44	20	24	27.3%	67.0	34.9
NATIONAL UNIV (11460)	28	65	34	31	35.4%	67.0	37.3
PACIFIC ST UNIV (31633)	6	15	5	10	26.7%	66.0	40.8
PACIFIC UNION COLL (1258)	11	26	17	9	50.0%	71.7	26.9
PEPPERDINE (1264)	26	68	41	27	51.5%	73.2	26.4
POINT LOMA NAZARENE UNIV (1262)	20	38	28	10	52.6%	73.9	24.1
SAINT MARYS COLL CA (1302)	49	120	66	54	33.3%	65.2	26.8
SAN DIEGO ST UNIV (1151)	319	762	412	350	44.1%	70.3	28.2
SAN FRANCISCO ST UNIV (1154)	252	597	303	294	33.5%	65.9	30.8
SAN JOSE ST UNIV (1155)	312	739	378	361	39.9%	68.5	31.2
SANTA CLARA UNIV (1326)	249	615	348	267	45.5%	71.1	24.9
SIMPSON UNIV (1291)	8	24	19	5	29.2%	61.5	25.4
SONOMA ST UNIV (1156)	122	276	148	128	28.6%	66.9	29.3
STANFORD UNIV (1305)	5	12	4	8	66.7%	79.9	33.9
UNIV CA BERKELEY (1312)	311	786	496	290	55.5%	73.3	26.9
UNIV CA DAVIS (1313)	123	284	160	124	48.6%	70.7	28.1
UNIV CA IRVINE (1314)	194	456	285	171	46.3%	69.6	26.9
UNIV CA LOS ANGELES (1315)	466	1,162	764	398	60.8%	74.8	26.5
UNIV CA RIVERSIDE (1316)	211	510	266	244	30.6%	66.0	26.8
UNIV CA SAN DIEGO (1317)	96	228	119	109	45.2%	70.4	28.2
UNIV CA SANTA BARBARA (1320)	550	1,326	724	602	50.8%	72.5	26.3
UNIV CA SANTA CRUZ (1321)	165	390	213	177	37.7%	69.3	26.3
UNIV LA VERNE (1216)	19	58	30	28	46.6%	69.8	30.3

Appendix F: Summary Performance for Bachelor's Degree - All Testing Events

	Candidates Total	Sections Total	Sections First-Time	Sections Re-Exam	Percent Pass	Average Score	Average Age
UNIV PACIFIC (1329)	40	94	49	45	44.7%	71.2	26.6
UNIV REDLANDS (1322)	28	60	33	27	25.0%	64.0	27.7
UNIV SAN DIEGO (10395)	139	314	201	113	50.3%	72.8	25.4
UNIV SAN FRANCISCO (1325)	85	197	105	92	30.0%	63.9	26.9
UNIV SOUTHERN CA (1328)	494	1,294	794	500	51.9%	72.9	26.1
VANGUARD UNIV SOUTHERN CA (1293)	6	18	10	8	55.6%	70.1	28.4
WOODBURY UNIV (1343)	9	20	4	16	15.0%	63.2	40.3
Colorado							
ADAMS ST COLL (1345)	12	22	4	18	45.5%	69.0	29.2
CO CHRISTIAN UNIV (9401)	5	10	5	5	0.0%	70.1	30.3
CO COLL (1347)	6	14	10	4	64.3%	75.6	42.6
CO ST UNIV (1350)	139	354	207	147	53.1%	73.6	28.1
FORT LEWIS COLL (1353)	43	101	47	54	34.7%	67.0	29.4
MESA ST COLL (1358)	20	58	34	24	43.1%	75.1	28.9
METRO ST COLL DENVER (1360)	93	232	131	101	32.3%	66.6	34.4
REGIS UNIV (1363)	73	179	98	81	44.1%	69.9	34.2
UNIV CO BOULDER (1370)	132	321	174	147	48.3%	73.4	28.5
UNIV CO COLORADO SPRINGS (4509)	42	108	56	52	41.7%	70.5	30.4
UNIV CO DENVER (6740)	85	188	106	82	41.5%	68.2	29.6
UNIV DENVER (1371)	55	118	56	62	55.1%	73.2	26.8
UNIV NORTHERN CO (1349)	66	167	75	92	37.7%	69.1	28.8
UNIV SOUTHERN CO (1365)	22	50	33	17	42.0%	68.8	32.7
WESTERN ST COLL (1372)	16	44	20	24	43.2%	70.6	30.6
Connecticut							
ALBERTUS MAGNUS COLL (1374)	5	9	5	4	11.1%	62.1	32.0
CENTRAL CT ST UNIV (1378)	59	131	70	61	44.3%	70.0	31.2
EASTERN CT ST UNIV (1425)	29	44	34	10	45.5%	69.2	31.6
FAIRFIELD UNIV (1385)	137	343	210	133	52.5%	73.2	24.6
QUINNIPIAC UNIV (1402)	75	207	120	87	37.2%	67.6	24.5
SACRED HEART UNIV (1403)	54	110	64	46	30.0%	64.7	27.6
SOUTHERN CT ST UNIV (1406)	27	58	39	19	32.8%	68.3	30.1
TEIKYO POST UNIV (1401)	12	27	16	11	29.6%	61.0	27.1
UNIV BRIDGEPORT (1416)	11	28	12	16	25.0%	64.0	33.4
UNIV CT (1417)	300	718	427	291	52.5%	73.8	25.0
UNIV HARTFORD (1422)	19	46	32	14	37.0%	64.3	26.4
UNIV NEW HAVEN (1397)	9	23	15	8	39.1%	69.7	28.2
WESTERN CT ST UNIV (1380)	21	57	37	20	45.6%	70.6	32.9
Delaware							
DE ST UNIV (1428)	11	36	10	26	16.7%	66.0	33.8
GOLDEY BEACOM COLL (1429)	32	67	30	37	22.4%	63.2	33.8
UNIV DE (1431)	221	598	387	211	53.0%	73.4	25.2
WESLEY COLL (1433)	5	12	4	8	41.7%	62.5	28.6
WILMINGTON COLL (7948)	26	61	43	18	36.1%	67.5	36.9
District of Columbia							
AMERICAN UNIV (1434)	67	162	109	53	51.9%	74.1	26.0
CATHOLIC UNIV OF AMERICA (1437)	8	18	8	10	33.3%	65.4	26.1
GEORGE WASHINGTON UNIV (1444)	66	173	103	70	53.2%	73.2	29.9
GEORGETOWN UNIV (1445)	44	123	97	26	69.1%	79.1	27.6
HOWARD UNIV (1448)	67	140	62	78	21.4%	61.6	30.5
SOUTHEASTERN UNIV (1456)	6	16	13	3	56.3%	73.1	27.3
STRAYER COLL (1459)	94	189	99	90	21.7%	60.2	36.3

Appendix F: Summary Performance for Bachelor's Degree - All Testing Events

	Candidates Total	Sections Total	Sections First-Time	Sections Re-Exam	Percent Pass	Average Score	Average Age
UNIV DC (1441)	15	32	17	15	12.5%	55.3	40.4
Florida							
BARRY UNIV (1466)	8	13	11	2	53.9%	70.5	31.8
BETHUNE COOKMAN COLL (1467)	8	13	3	10	23.1%	62.7	30.3
FL A&M UNIV (1480)	26	52	19	33	23.1%	63.0	30.0
FL ATLANTIC UNIV (1481)	58	133	73	60	43.6%	69.1	33.7
FL GULF COAST UNIV (32553)	11	29	19	10	37.9%	68.9	29.8
FL INTL UNIV (9635)	103	250	105	145	43.2%	71.7	30.9
FL MEMORIAL UNIV (1486)	5	9	4	5	0.0%	48.2	40.6
FL SOUTHERN COLL (1488)	5	17	3	14	29.4%	71.4	34.5
FL ST UNIV (1489)	91	234	145	89	54.7%	74.5	29.1
FLAGLER COLL (7893)	8	19	9	10	36.8%	68.5	32.0
NOVA SOUTHEASTERN UNIV (1509)	18	31	16	15	19.4%	58.4	34.1
PENSACOLA CHRISTIAN COLL (99998)	9	22	18	4	45.5%	69.6	27.0
SAINT LEO UNIV (1526)	24	54	31	23	51.9%	71.1	35.9
STETSON UNIV (1531)	9	22	14	8	45.5%	71.5	28.0
UNIV CENTRAL FL (3954)	92	219	136	83	48.0%	72.8	28.8
UNIV FL (1535)	108	291	186	105	60.8%	76.0	27.4
UNIV MIAMI (1536)	81	220	118	102	55.0%	74.8	26.8
UNIV NORTH FL (9841)	26	66	35	31	54.6%	74.3	32.0
UNIV SOUTH FL (1537)	111	266	163	103	55.6%	74.2	30.1
UNIV TAMPA (1538)	29	75	50	25	58.7%	73.5	26.1
UNIV WEST FL (3955)	13	24	12	12	37.5%	71.8	35.0
Georgia							
ALBANY ST UNIV (1544)	11	16	4	12	12.5%	59.7	32.4
AMERICAN INTERCONT GA (21136)	7	13	5	8	38.5%	68.1	36.2
AUGUSTA ST UNIV (1552)	23	53	27	26	35.9%	68.0	31.9
BERRY COLL (1554)	15	48	26	22	43.8%	72.1	26.1
BRENAU UNIV (1556)	9	18	10	8	22.2%	57.4	29.6
CLARK ATLANTA UNIV (1559)	13	28	16	12	25.0%	60.2	27.9
CLAYTON ST UNIV (8976)	32	88	49	39	39.8%	68.4	33.8
COLUMBUS ST UNIV (1561)	16	37	13	24	35.1%	66.6	36.3
DEVRY UNIV ALPHARETTA (666989)	6	9	8	1	0.0%	51.9	35.8
DEVRY UNIV DECATUR (9224)	17	30	18	12	16.7%	60.9	36.3
EMORY UNIV (1564)	59	159	99	60	57.2%	75.8	24.9
GA COLL & ST UNIV (1602)	23	57	32	25	42.1%	69.5	30.6
GA INST TECH (1569)	71	178	106	72	56.2%	75.3	26.6
GA SOUTHERN UNIV (1572)	113	282	173	109	46.8%	71.6	26.3
GA SOUTHWESTERN ST UNIV (1573)	15	35	20	15	48.6%	66.9	33.3
GA ST UNIV (1574)	325	752	413	339	37.2%	68.6	30.0
KENNESAW ST UNIV (1577)	156	354	184	170	42.9%	69.3	32.0
LAGRANGE COLL (1578)	7	11	9	2	36.4%	61.7	26.2
MACON ST COLL (7728)	21	52	35	17	46.2%	70.8	30.5
MERCER UNIV ATLANTA (8419)	7	14	10	4	42.9%	68.1	24.9
MERCER UNIV MACON (1580)	20	57	30	27	50.9%	71.7	30.1
MOREHOUSE COLL (1582)	18	44	20	24	36.4%	68.2	27.1
NORTH GA COLL & ST UNIV (1585)	45	112	63	49	45.5%	72.7	29.8
OGLETHORPE UNIV (1586)	23	41	19	22	58.5%	75.2	29.3
SHORTER COLL (1591)	11	29	19	10	41.4%	67.1	28.9
SPELMAN COLL (1594)	5	11	6	5	36.4%	71.1	29.8
UNIV GA (1598)	240	697	507	190	67.6%	77.2	26.5

Appendix F: Summary Performance for Bachelor's Degree - All Testing Events

	Candidates Total	Sections Total	Sections First-Time	Sections Re-Exam	Percent Pass	Average Score	Average Age
UNIV WEST GA (1601)	28	81	48	33	27.2%	64.8	28.3
VALDOSTA ST UNIV (1599)	59	144	79	65	41.7%	69.2	30.2
Guam							
UNIV GU (3935)	21	35	17	18	40.0%	65.2	34.3
Hawaii							
BRIGHAM YOUNG UNIV HI (1606)	36	88	67	21	47.7%	70.3	29.7
HI PACIFIC UNIV (7279)	29	72	36	36	27.8%	65.3	33.7
UNIV HI HILO (1611)	10	17	12	5	47.1%	72.9	28.7
UNIV HI MANOA (1610)	154	367	175	192	37.9%	68.4	29.2
UNIV HI WEST OAHU (21078)	10	20	11	9	40.0%	68.9	37.7
Idaho							
ALBERTSON COLL (1617)	8	23	19	4	39.1%	68.4	27.4
BOISE ST UNIV (1616)	82	188	105	83	43.1%	70.6	31.5
BRIGHAM YOUNG UNIV ID (1625)	89	195	134	61	48.7%	71.9	28.3
ID ST UNIV (1620)	41	88	51	37	47.7%	72.0	31.1
LEWIS CLARK ST COLL (1621)	16	40	27	13	35.0%	70.1	33.9
UNIV ID (1626)	53	139	79	60	41.0%	70.5	26.0
Illinois							
AMERICAN INTERCONT IL (666723)	6	19	14	5	0.0%	41.1	36.6
AUGUSTANA COLL (1633)	20	48	30	18	58.3%	73.3	26.5
AURORA UNIV (1634)	13	37	16	21	40.5%	68.8	28.3
BENEDICTINE UNIV (1767)	24	55	35	20	36.4%	63.3	30.5
BRADLEY UNIV (1641)	51	139	93	46	51.1%	73.6	27.6
CHICAGO ST UNIV (1694)	27	56	25	31	21.4%	65.0	38.0
DE PAUL UNIV (1671)	391	957	548	409	36.4%	68.2	27.8
DEVRY UNIV ADDISON (22966)	33	84	65	19	28.6%	60.0	32.5
DEVRY UNIV OAK BROOK TERRACE (1672)	31	78	40	38	10.3%	58.1	35.2
DOMINCAN UNIV (1750)	10	37	16	21	13.5%	60.6	27.6
EASTERN IL UNIV (1674)	50	125	80	45	42.4%	68.4	29.0
ELMHURST COLL (1676)	26	76	48	28	34.2%	68.3	27.8
GOVERNORS ST UNIV (9145)	26	71	33	38	49.3%	72.9	40.6
IL COLL (1688)	8	21	8	13	33.3%	70.0	28.5
IL ST UNIV (1692)	157	483	310	173	52.4%	73.6	26.8
IL WESLEYAN UNIV (1696)	55	181	100	81	60.2%	75.1	23.9
KELLER GRAD SCHOOL DEVRY (20754)	9	20	19	1	10.0%	56.1	40.1
LEWIS UNIV (1707)	16	46	22	24	50.0%	73.5	29.9
LOYOLA UNIV CHICAGO (1710)	174	450	263	187	44.7%	70.7	26.2
MCKENDREE UNIVERSITY (1722)	16	37	26	11	43.2%	68.9	28.7
MILLIKIN UNIV (1724)	23	67	39	28	37.3%	68.0	29.9
MONMOUTH COLL (1725)	7	21	13	8	42.9%	70.1	28.3
NORTH CENTRAL COLL (1734)	36	91	57	34	47.3%	73.5	28.6
NORTH PARK UNIV (1735)	8	26	15	11	61.5%	74.0	29.1
NORTHEASTERN IL UNIV (1693)	68	155	83	72	37.4%	66.8	35.1
NORTHERN IL UNIV (1737)	278	766	490	276	53.1%	73.5	27.4
NORTHWESTERN UNIV (1739)	10	24	19	5	66.7%	75.7	30.7
OLIVET NAZARENE UNIV (1741)	10	26	20	6	61.5%	76.6	24.6
QUINCY UNIV (1745)	10	17	11	6	47.1%	74.9	28.0
ROBERT MORRIS COLL (1746)	27	60	31	29	33.3%	67.1	32.2
ROCKFORD COLL (1748)	8	25	10	15	48.0%	72.5	33.4
ROOSEVELT UNIV (1749)	34	77	43	34	26.0%	65.7	37.6
SAINT XAVIER UNIV (1768)	15	31	20	11	45.2%	69.6	27.7

Appendix F: Summary Performance for Bachelor's Degree - All Testing Events

	Candidates Total	Sections Total	Sections First-Time	Sections Re-Exam	Percent Pass	Average Score	Average Age
SOUTHERN IL UNIV CARBONDALE (1758)	79	205	112	93	42.4%	70.0	29.0
SOUTHERN IL UNIV EDWARDSVILLE (1759)	55	131	92	39	47.3%	70.1	28.9
TRINITY CHRISTIAN COLL (1771)	14	29	21	8	62.1%	77.8	24.8
UNIV CHICAGO (1774)	7	21	8	13	47.6%	74.0	31.0
UNIV IL CHICAGO (1776)	413	1,241	802	439	57.2%	74.4	25.6
UNIV IL SPRINGFIELD (9333)	28	73	38	35	34.3%	68.0	31.9
UNIV IL URBANA CHAMPAIGN (1775)	461	1,336	869	467	53.7%	73.0	26.2
UNIV SAINT FRANCIS (1664)	6	16	13	3	50.0%	68.1	26.8
WESTERN IL UNIV (1780)	40	87	56	31	39.1%	69.8	29.9
WHEATON COLL (1781)	8	21	12	9	66.7%	77.8	30.6
Indiana							
ANDERSON UNIV (1785)	6	19	14	5	79.0%	79.4	24.8
BALL ST UNIV (1786)	101	280	147	133	36.4%	68.5	27.9
BETHEL COLL (IN) (1787)	11	31	19	12	51.6%	72.4	24.9
BUTLER UNIV (1788)	50	143	86	57	55.9%	73.1	26.8
FRANKLIN COLL IN (1798)	14	37	20	17	29.7%	68.7	25.5
GOSHEN COLL (1799)	20	46	42	4	67.4%	76.5	24.2
GRACE COLL & SEMINARY (1800)	13	34	15	19	50.0%	75.9	26.8
HUNTINGTON COLL (1803)	6	14	9	5	14.3%	58.8	26.7
IN INST TECH (1805)	7	20	10	10	30.0%	67.8	33.1
IN ST UNIV (1807)	35	77	52	25	29.9%	64.3	29.0
IN UNIV BLOOMINGTON (1809)	429	1,181	818	363	59.6%	75.0	26.0
IN UNIV EAST (1811)	5	6	3	3	16.7%	61.5	28.6
IN UNIV KOKOMO (1814)	6	22	8	14	54.6%	76.6	31.7
IN UNIV NORTHWEST (1815)	10	21	14	7	47.6%	67.2	31.9
IN UNIV- PURDUE UNIV - FORT WAYNE (1812)	6	13	2	11	23.1%	69.5	27.9
IN UNIV PURDUE UNIV FORT WAYNE (1828)	24	60	33	27	46.7%	72.1	26.9
IN UNIV PURDUE UNIV INDIANAPOLIS (1813)	118	294	177	117	41.8%	69.6	30.4
IN UNIV SOUTH BEND (1816)	21	62	38	24	40.3%	65.2	30.0
IN UNIV SOUTHEAST (1817)	24	65	40	25	35.4%	68.4	31.5
IN WESLEYAN UNIV (1822)	33	79	52	27	36.7%	67.3	31.2
MANCHESTER COLL (1820)	39	104	62	42	45.2%	70.3	24.8
MARIAN COLL (1821)	12	36	21	15	27.8%	66.1	28.8
OAKLAND CITY UNIV (1824)	5	14	9	5	57.1%	69.2	27.6
PURDUE UNIV (1825)	240	711	377	334	38.7%	68.7	26.7
SAINT JOSEPHS COLL (1833)	9	24	14	10	41.7%	65.9	26.9
SAINT MARYS COLL (1836)	30	91	44	47	30.8%	68.8	24.9
TAYLOR UNIV (1838)	12	32	22	10	59.4%	73.3	23.6
TRINE UNIV (1839)	9	22	7	15	40.9%	71.1	29.9
UNIV EVANSVILLE (1795)	21	52	27	25	32.7%	68.2	26.0
UNIV INDIANAPOLIS (1804)	21	66	26	40	28.8%	65.6	27.9
UNIV NOTRE DAME (1840)	196	612	486	126	73.7%	79.4	24.0
UNIV SOUTHERN IN (1808)	41	105	68	37	41.9%	71.2	27.5
UNIV ST FRANCIS (1832)	7	22	7	15	36.4%	72.9	25.2
VALPARAISO UNIV (1842)	23	56	29	27	41.1%	70.9	25.7
Iowa							
AIB COLL BUSINESS (3963)	12	25	17	8	28.0%	60.2	28.1
BRIAR CLIFF UNIV (1846)	9	19	17	2	52.6%	68.3	29.6
BUENA VISTA UNIV (1847)	21	50	29	21	26.0%	65.2	29.5
CLARKE COLL (1852)	7	11	5	6	36.4%	67.7	31.0
COE COLL (1854)	13	29	19	10	44.8%	70.5	26.0

Appendix F: Summary Performance for Bachelor's Degree - All Testing Events

	Candidates Total	Sections Total	Sections First-Time	Sections Re-Exam	Percent Pass	Average Score	Average Age
DORDT COLL (1859)	8	21	16	5	57.1%	76.2	23.7
DRAKE UNIV (1860)	35	88	59	29	51.1%	70.7	27.2
GRAND VIEW UNIV (1867)	6	14	11	3	42.9%	68.8	30.7
IA ST UNIV (1869)	118	351	231	120	49.3%	72.0	27.7
IA WESLEYAN COLL (1871)	8	12	5	7	25.0%	69.9	29.8
KAPLAN UNIV (4586)	19	52	38	14	25.0%	60.3	39.5
LORAS COLL (1873)	17	48	28	20	52.1%	72.6	24.2
LUTHER COLL (1874)	20	57	39	18	47.4%	72.8	26.9
MORNINGSIDE COLL (1879)	8	22	9	13	45.5%	68.2	35.8
MOUNT MERCY COLL (1880)	6	14	7	7	50.0%	75.6	29.9
MOUNT SAINT CLARE COLL (1881)	5	8	6	2	12.5%	55.8	27.5
NORTHWESTERN COLL IA (1883)	20	44	29	15	45.5%	69.6	25.5
SAINT AMBROSE UNIV (1889)	13	33	13	20	45.5%	70.2	26.6
SIMPSON COLL (1887)	18	46	30	16	39.1%	67.5	26.1
UNIV DUBUQUE (1891)	14	48	23	25	22.9%	66.7	25.1
UNIV IA (1892)	181	508	365	143	64.4%	76.4	26.5
UNIV NORTHERN IA (1890)	118	425	305	120	58.4%	75.5	25.2
UPPER IA UNIV (1893)	36	78	35	43	32.1%	65.1	34.7
WARTBURG COLL (1896)	7	22	14	8	59.1%	74.3	23.7
Kansas							
BAKER UNIV (1903)	11	25	16	9	12.0%	65.1	27.8
BENEDICTINE COLL (10256)	8	24	17	7	25.0%	65.1	27.8
EMPORIA ST UNIV (1927)	18	46	19	27	30.4%	70.3	29.1
FORT HAYS ST UNIV (1915)	44	104	62	42	32.7%	65.9	27.4
FRIENDS UNIV (1918)	5	21	14	7	38.1%	66.7	26.1
KANSAS STATE UNIVERSITY (1928)	72	216	147	69	61.6%	75.3	26.8
NEWMAN UNIV (1939)	6	15	10	5	26.7%	58.0	30.2
OTTAWA UNIV (1937)	10	24	17	7	33.3%	63.0	34.0
PITTSBURG ST UNIV (1926)	25	60	31	29	31.7%	66.6	26.9
UNIV KS (1948)	184	563	367	196	56.1%	74.5	25.8
WASHBURN UNIV (1949)	40	117	67	50	45.3%	70.6	29.2
WICHITA ST UNIV (1950)	59	157	103	54	47.1%	71.5	31.1
Kentucky							
ASBURY COLL (1952)	6	18	13	5	44.4%	71.7	27.8
BELLARMINE UNIV (1954)	43	102	69	33	52.0%	73.2	25.6
BEREA COLL (1955)	8	17	10	7	58.8%	72.7	27.4
BRESCIA UNIV (1958)	11	27	10	17	25.9%	67.7	27.4
EASTERN KY UNIV (1963)	35	65	42	23	44.6%	69.4	30.8
GEORGETOWN COLL (1964)	10	24	9	15	29.2%	64.0	26.6
KY ST UNIV (1968)	7	19	11	8	5.3%	60.1	28.7
KY WESLEYAN COLL (1969)	8	23	17	6	47.8%	70.3	23.9
LINDSEY WILSON COLL (1972)	9	28	15	13	35.7%	67.3	32.8
MOREHEAD ST UNIV (1976)	14	45	20	25	46.7%	70.3	30.0
MURRAY ST UNIV (1977)	53	116	67	49	44.8%	71.8	27.8
NORTHERN KY UNIV (9275)	67	171	98	73	42.7%	71.4	28.2
PIKEVILLE COLL (1980)	7	10	4	6	60.0%	68.0	29.4
SPALDING UNIV (1960)	8	19	13	6	42.1%	67.3	37.0
SULLIVAN UNIV (4619)	15	43	22	21	25.6%	62.0	38.1
THOMAS MORE COLL (2001)	17	43	16	27	27.9%	68.1	29.2
TRANSYLVANIA UNIV (1987)	28	72	48	24	51.4%	73.2	24.5
UNIV KY (1989)	207	578	334	244	50.5%	72.7	27.5

Appendix F: Summary Performance for Bachelor's Degree - All Testing Events

	Candidates Total	Sections Total	Sections First-Time	Sections Re-Exam	Percent Pass	Average Score	Average Age
UNIV LOUISVILLE (1999)	111	286	141	145	40.6%	69.4	31.6
UNIV OF CUMBERLANDS (1962)	5	9	7	2	55.6%	73.1	31.6
WESTERN KY UNIV (2002)	67	171	107	64	55.6%	74.5	28.5
Louisiana							
CENTENARY COLL LA (2003)	6	19	7	12	31.6%	72.0	30.2
DILLARD UNIV (2004)	10	24	9	15	8.3%	54.8	29.3
GRAMBLING ST UNIV (2006)	16	40	19	21	25.0%	61.8	29.7
LA COLL (2007)	5	7	5	2	57.1%	72.6	26.0
LA ST UNIV AND A & M COLL (2010)	223	578	364	214	49.1%	72.7	26.8
LA ST UNIV IN SHREVEPORT (2013)	25	50	24	26	46.0%	71.4	34.1
LA TECH UNIV (2008)	35	106	56	50	50.0%	71.6	29.3
LOYOLA UNIV NEW ORLEANS (2016)	34	87	57	30	52.9%	71.4	27.9
MCNEESE ST UNIV (2017)	42	123	68	55	43.1%	70.1	30.8
NICHOLLS ST UNIV (2005)	30	68	43	25	47.1%	70.9	30.3
NORTHWESTERN ST UNIV (2021)	22	49	32	17	30.6%	68.0	29.6
OUR LADY HOLY CROSS COLL (2023)	12	28	18	10	3.6%	42.9	36.4
SOUTHEASTERN LA UNIV (2024)	103	247	134	113	34.4%	67.3	29.7
SOUTHERN UNIV A&M BATON ROUGE (9636)	19	59	12	47	27.1%	68.8	35.1
SOUTHERN UNIV NEW ORLEANS (2026)	6	10	3	7	10.0%	52.1	37.0
TULANE UNIV LA (2029)	37	98	71	27	60.2%	73.8	26.9
UNIV LA LAFAYETTE (2031)	93	224	135	89	54.0%	75.2	27.9
UNIV LA MONROE (2020)	36	94	55	39	28.7%	66.2	27.8
UNIV NEW ORLEANS (2015)	107	254	139	115	37.4%	68.4	31.6
XAVIER UNIV LA (2032)	6	7	5	2	14.3%	41.9	35.8
Maine							
COLBY COLL (2039)	7	14	8	6	50.0%	73.3	37.2
HUSSON UNIV (2043)	12	19	12	7	31.6%	61.9	33.9
SAINT JOSEPHS COLL (2051)	7	13	7	6	38.5%	67.9	24.8
THOMAS COLL (2052)	8	20	7	13	40.0%	70.0	31.1
UNIV ME (2053)	26	59	36	23	55.9%	73.9	26.5
UNIV ME AUGUSTA (6760)	5	10	9	1	60.0%	76.5	36.0
UNIV SOUTHERN ME (2054)	23	51	30	21	51.0%	74.0	30.8
Maryland							
BOWIE ST UNIV (2062)	19	34	16	18	5.9%	59.2	33.6
FROSTBURG ST UNIV (2072)	7	18	8	10	44.4%	69.4	34.5
LOYOLA UNIVERSITY MD (2078)	63	173	113	60	48.6%	73.5	24.2
MORGAN ST UNIV (2083)	12	21	10	11	19.1%	62.3	32.2
MOUNT SAINT MARYS UNIV (2086)	6	8	3	5	37.5%	68.5	33.3
SALISBURY UNIV (2091)	18	40	19	21	45.0%	73.1	28.3
TOWSON UNIV (2099)	39	112	47	65	47.3%	71.4	30.2
UNIV BALTIMORE (2102)	16	40	20	20	27.5%	67.6	38.8
UNIV MD BALTIMORE COUNTY (2105)	13	37	18	19	27.0%	66.8	27.8
UNIV MD COLL PARK (2103)	211	492	318	174	50.4%	73.0	27.3
UNIV MD EASTERN SHORE (2106)	6	12	7	5	25.0%	70.8	28.1
UNIV MD UNIV COLL (11644)	94	226	137	89	31.4%	66.8	33.1
Massachusetts							
AMERICAN INTL COLL (2114)	6	14	10	4	50.0%	73.9	29.3
ASSUMPTION COLL (2118)	60	146	88	58	40.4%	68.5	25.4
BABSON COLL (2121)	65	176	108	68	50.6%	72.9	24.1
BENTLEY COLL (2124)	248	657	388	269	49.3%	71.6	25.6
BOSTON COLL (2128)	160	425	309	116	69.9%	78.2	24.3

Appendix F: Summary Performance for Bachelor's Degree - All Testing Events

	Candidates Total	Sections Total	Sections First-Time	Sections Re-Exam	Percent Pass	Average Score	Average Age
BOSTON UNIV (2130)	111	265	183	82	56.6%	74.3	24.6
BRIDGEWATER ST COLL (2183)	14	33	17	16	51.5%	73.0	34.5
CLARK UNIV (2139)	5	13	8	5	53.9%	67.1	29.0
COLL HOLY CROSS (2141)	37	102	73	29	60.8%	75.5	23.5
COLL OUR LADY OF THE ELMS (2140)	5	14	5	9	7.1%	61.4	25.5
FITCHBURG ST COLL (2184)	6	14	5	9	21.4%	67.7	30.8
GORDON COLL (2153)	8	21	11	10	23.8%	65.7	25.1
LASELL COLL (2158)	5	8	5	3	25.0%	61.0	26.9
MA INST TECH (2178)	5	12	12	0	91.7%	87.8	36.8
MERRIMACK COLL (2120)	30	68	33	35	39.7%	67.4	27.3
NICHOLS COLL (2197)	16	38	22	16	21.1%	63.8	28.1
NORTHEASTERN UNIV (2199)	136	348	219	129	44.0%	70.7	27.0
SALEM ST UNIV (2188)	34	76	37	39	29.0%	61.5	29.0
STONEHILL COLL (2217)	54	113	86	27	54.0%	72.8	24.5
SUFFOLK UNIV (2218)	52	113	71	42	30.1%	63.1	27.1
TUFTS UNIV (2219)	5	21	16	5	76.2%	80.4	32.8
UNIV MA AMHERST (2221)	196	495	319	176	46.5%	70.5	25.5
UNIV MA BOSTON (2222)	61	125	66	59	32.0%	64.8	32.0
UNIV MA DARTMOUTH (2210)	39	96	48	48	43.8%	68.1	28.2
UNIV MA LOWELL (2161)	35	85	51	34	51.8%	71.8	29.1
WESTERN NEW ENGLAND COLL (2226)	30	78	40	38	34.6%	68.0	27.2
WESTFIELD ST COLL (2189)	9	16	11	5	50.0%	69.8	29.5
WORCESTER ST COLL (2190)	16	28	15	13	25.0%	59.1	29.3
Michigan							
ALBION COLL (2235)	22	60	29	31	43.3%	71.1	24.5
ALMA COLL (2236)	10	25	17	8	48.0%	70.1	24.3
ANDREWS UNIV (2238)	15	35	21	14	34.3%	65.7	29.2
AQUINAS COLL (2239)	19	51	23	28	33.3%	66.5	26.4
BAKER COLL FLINT (4673)	18	33	18	15	36.4%	65.5	34.1
CALVIN COLL (2241)	42	129	84	45	58.9%	75.2	24.6
CENTRAL MI UNIV (2243)	122	330	178	152	50.0%	72.9	27.1
DAVENPORT UNIV (2249)	41	82	46	36	35.4%	65.3	32.3
EASTERN MI UNIV (2259)	39	118	65	53	44.1%	71.1	30.6
FERRIS ST UNIV (2260)	29	80	39	41	52.5%	71.4	27.8
GRAND VALLEY ST UNIV (2268)	112	294	193	101	66.7%	77.3	26.1
HILLSDALE COLL (2272)	21	50	30	20	38.0%	69.3	24.2
HOPE COLL (2273)	26	68	45	23	33.8%	66.7	24.0
LAKE SUPERIOR ST UNIV (2293)	18	53	27	26	39.6%	71.9	28.4
MI ST UNIV (2290)	376	1,003	694	309	61.4%	76.0	26.1
MI TECH UNIV (2292)	17	47	32	15	63.8%	76.3	26.7
NORTHERN MI UNIV (2301)	27	68	33	35	29.4%	67.3	28.2
NORTHWOOD UNIV (4072)	57	160	88	72	38.1%	67.9	28.9
OAKLAND UNIV (2307)	73	207	109	98	48.3%	72.8	28.6
SAGINAW VALLEY ST UNIV (2314)	42	111	59	52	34.2%	67.8	28.8
SIENA HEIGHTS UNIV (2316)	12	38	26	12	39.5%	67.4	28.8
SPRING ARBOR UNIV (2318)	8	22	7	15	27.3%	67.2	29.7
UNIV MI ANN ARBOR (2325)	103	321	237	84	72.6%	79.8	26.2
UNIV MI DEARBORN (2326)	74	196	124	72	53.6%	73.4	30.1
UNIV MI FLINT (2327)	28	60	36	24	33.3%	69.0	31.4
WALSH COLL (4071)	75	185	114	71	53.5%	72.6	32.4
WAYNE ST UNIV (2329)	55	140	78	62	45.0%	68.6	28.0

Appendix F: Summary Performance for Bachelor's Degree - All Testing Events

	Candidates Total	Sections Total	Sections First-Time	Sections Re-Exam	Percent Pass	Average Score	Average Age
WESTERN MI UNIV (2330)	118	330	172	158	38.5%	69.6	27.2
Minnesota							
AUGSBURG COLL (2334)	30	75	44	31	44.0%	71.3	30.4
BEMIDJI ST UNIV (2336)	17	41	19	22	43.9%	68.3	29.1
BETHEL COLL (MN) (9058)	20	51	38	13	51.0%	71.8	26.4
COLL OF SAINT BENEDICT (2341)	7	17	12	5	82.4%	81.1	24.8
COLL OF SAINT SCHOLASTICA (2343)	15	42	19	23	47.6%	70.5	27.4
CONCORDIA COLL MOORHEAD (2346)	28	64	38	26	60.9%	74.9	25.1
CONCORDIA UNIV MN (2347)	8	16	11	5	31.3%	59.0	31.2
GUSTAVUS ADOLPHUS COLL (2353)	20	50	29	21	50.0%	71.1	24.6
HAMLINE UNIV (2354)	5	13	8	5	61.5%	73.5	27.3
METROPOLITAN ST UNIV (10374)	67	154	83	71	34.4%	66.5	35.2
MN SCHOOL OF BUSINESS (4646)	8	18	10	8	33.3%	66.6	32.6
MN ST UNIV MANKATO (2360)	88	212	136	76	42.5%	69.3	28.2
MN ST UNIV MOORHEAD (2367)	29	74	40	34	37.8%	71.5	29.9
NORTHWESTERN COLL MN (2371)	14	35	22	13	54.3%	73.9	24.3
SAINT CATHERINE UNIV (2342)	8	20	11	9	50.0%	70.8	29.8
SAINT CLOUD ST UNIV (2377)	102	261	171	90	58.6%	75.1	27.3
SAINT JOHN'S UNIV (2379)	38	97	51	46	45.4%	72.0	25.5
SAINT MARY'S UNIV OF MN (2380)	16	45	26	19	37.8%	65.6	28.0
SOUTHWEST ST UNIV (2375)	10	30	22	8	63.3%	76.5	27.7
UNIV MN DULUTH (2388)	82	200	105	95	42.0%	70.2	27.0
UNIV MN TWIN CITIES (3969)	143	376	256	120	58.2%	75.2	28.3
UNIV ST THOMAS (2345)	107	265	150	115	44.9%	71.7	26.7
WINONA ST UNIV (2394)	52	136	73	63	34.6%	68.6	28.4
Mississippi							
BELHAVEN COLL (2397)	17	39	23	16	33.3%	69.8	38.0
DELTA ST UNIV (2403)	17	48	22	26	29.2%	65.1	28.3
JACKSON ST UNIV (2410)	39	82	34	48	14.6%	57.8	31.6
MILLSAPS COLL (2414)	21	57	31	26	50.9%	73.2	29.4
MS COLL (2415)	30	77	46	31	31.2%	64.9	31.2
MS ST UNIV (2423)	115	329	198	131	44.7%	69.8	27.9
MS UNIV FOR WOMEN (2422)	6	18	8	10	38.9%	71.7	29.2
UNIV MS (2440)	154	461	295	166	50.1%	72.5	26.8
UNIV SOUTHERN MS (2441)	86	196	106	90	36.2%	68.1	31.6
Missouri							
CENTRAL METHODIST UNIV (2453)	13	31	15	16	32.3%	66.8	27.8
COLL OF OZARKS (2500)	7	17	7	10	29.4%	70.6	25.1
COLUMBIA COLL (2456)	26	50	37	13	34.0%	61.7	36.2
CULVER STOCKTON COLL (2460)	8	29	24	5	58.6%	69.5	28.6
DEVRY UNIV KANSAS CITY (2455)	19	36	19	17	19.4%	65.1	31.3
DRURY UNIV (2461)	27	71	31	40	40.9%	68.5	26.7
EVANGEL UNIV (2463)	6	14	7	7	71.4%	71.9	29.5
FONTBONNE UNIV (2464)	6	12	7	5	41.7%	61.1	33.4
LINCOLN UNIV (2479)	5	10	7	3	30.0%	68.0	33.7
LINDENWOOD UNIV (2480)	15	36	23	13	30.6%	65.6	26.2
MARYVILLE UNIV ST. LOUIS (2482)	24	61	25	36	39.3%	69.0	28.0
MO SOUTHERN ST UNIV (2488)	19	41	26	15	53.7%	72.1	31.3
MO ST UNIV (2503)	70	195	103	92	46.2%	72.0	28.5
MO VALLEY COLL (2489)	6	16	13	3	50.0%	73.2	26.5
MO WESTERN ST UNIV (2490)	12	38	18	20	15.8%	58.8	41.5

Appendix F: Summary Performance for Bachelor's Degree - All Testing Events

	Candidates Total	Sections Total	Sections First-Time	Sections Re-Exam	Percent Pass	Average Score	Average Age
NORTHWEST MO ST UNIV (2496)	18	49	30	19	65.3%	75.2	28.4
PARK UNIV (2498)	30	69	32	37	37.7%	68.8	37.2
ROCKHURST UNIV (2499)	17	52	25	27	40.4%	69.7	24.7
SOUTHEAST MO ST UNIV (2501)	35	92	59	33	43.5%	69.0	30.9
SOUTHWEST BAPTIST UNIV (2502)	15	47	16	31	40.4%	71.7	25.1
ST. LOUIS UNIV (2506)	75	218	149	69	52.8%	72.3	25.9
TRUMAN ST UNIV (2495)	83	283	223	60	73.1%	78.9	25.1
UNIV CENTRAL MO (2454)	44	120	64	56	47.5%	71.6	32.0
UNIV MO COLUMBIA (2516)	24	53	28	25	39.6%	73.0	30.3
UNIV MO KANSAS CITY (2518)	31	85	51	34	52.9%	72.2	28.4
UNIV MO ST. LOUIS (2519)	72	165	112	53	46.7%	69.5	31.5
WASHINGTON UNIV ST. LOUIS (2520)	29	83	58	25	77.1%	80.0	27.8
WEBSTER UNIV (2521)	14	32	15	17	25.0%	61.5	29.0
WESTMINSTER COLL (2523)	10	35	8	27	22.9%	67.4	25.3
Montana							
CARROLL COLL (MT) (2526)	16	52	19	33	30.8%	65.1	26.4
MT ST UNIV BILLINGS (2530)	15	39	19	20	18.0%	64.8	32.6
MT ST UNIV BOZEMAN (2532)	52	152	92	60	52.6%	74.4	26.2
UNIV MT (2536)	52	161	91	70	55.3%	74.9	28.9
Nebraska							
BELLEVUE UNIV (9743)	11	26	15	11	26.9%	67.0	35.9
CHADRON ST COLL (2539)	5	13	6	7	38.5%	68.8	30.6
CREIGHTON UNIV (2542)	50	135	90	45	43.7%	69.7	25.2
DOANE COLL (2544)	17	51	20	31	39.2%	69.3	28.7
HASTINGS COLL (2548)	14	33	13	20	30.3%	65.8	28.0
MIDLAND LUTHERAN COLL (2553)	21	59	26	33	39.0%	70.3	28.0
NE WESLEYAN UNIV (2555)	14	38	20	18	65.8%	74.7	25.1
PERU ST COLL (2559)	7	19	10	9	57.9%	77.6	32.8
UNION COLL (2563)	5	15	8	7	40.0%	67.8	25.6
UNIV NE KEARNEY (2551)	21	50	26	24	46.0%	69.8	28.9
UNIV NE LINCOLN (2565)	66	160	79	81	43.1%	71.0	29.2
UNIV NE OMAHA (2554)	52	124	82	42	54.0%	74.2	27.7
WAYNE ST COLL (2566)	14	31	15	16	41.9%	69.1	27.6
YORK COLL (2567)	9	21	8	13	33.3%	66.0	33.6
Nevada							
UNIV NV LAS VEGAS (2569)	141	373	196	177	41.6%	69.1	30.1
UNIV NV RENO (2568)	77	215	124	91	37.2%	68.3	29.9
New Hampshire							
PLYMOUTH ST UNIV (2591)	16	25	16	9	52.0%	71.4	29.4
SAINT ANSELM COLL (2587)	17	45	30	15	37.8%	69.8	25.9
SOUTHERN NH UNIV (2580)	35	88	52	36	35.2%	66.8	33.9
UNIV NH (2589)	63	177	128	49	55.9%	74.2	25.8
New Jersey							
BERKELEY COLL (7502)	18	25	18	7	12.0%	56.1	29.3
BETH MEDRASH GOVOHA (7947)	10	22	14	8	45.5%	71.9	30.6
BLOOMFIELD COLL (2597)	7	11	5	6	18.2%	55.0	33.3
CALDWELL COLL (2598)	12	29	10	19	34.5%	68.0	29.5
CENTENARY COLL (2599)	7	19	15	4	31.6%	66.0	27.8
COLL NJ (2642)	108	275	184	91	58.6%	74.7	25.4
FAIRLEIGH DICKINSON UNIV (2607)	30	67	43	24	38.8%	65.6	28.7
FAIRLEIGH DICKINSON UNIV MADISON (4738)	12	34	19	15	29.4%	67.8	32.5

Appendix F: Summary Performance for Bachelor's Degree - All Testing Events

	Candidates Total	Sections Total	Sections First-Time	Sections Re-Exam	Percent Pass	Average Score	Average Age
FAIRLEIGH DICKINSON UNIV RUTHERFORD (2604)	9	29	12	17	17.2%	65.9	28.4
FELICIAN COLL (2610)	5	12	11	1	0.0%	54.7	31.5
GEORGIAN COURT UNIV (2608)	15	36	22	14	30.6%	63.6	32.7
KEAN UNIV (2622)	78	178	91	87	24.2%	62.9	31.5
MONMOUTH UNIV (2616)	71	187	115	72	31.0%	64.1	26.2
MONTCLAIR ST UNIV (2617)	159	411	201	210	33.3%	65.9	29.0
NJ CITY UNIV (2613)	35	75	37	38	26.7%	61.4	36.9
RAMAPO COLL NJ (9344)	84	232	127	105	39.7%	69.2	26.6
RICHARD STOCKTON COLL NJ (9345)	61	143	100	43	44.1%	70.4	28.6
RIDER UNIV (2628)	89	228	118	110	24.6%	63.9	28.7
ROWAN UNIV (2609)	79	189	109	80	43.4%	68.2	27.8
RUTGERS ST UNIV CAMDEN (4741)	84	217	116	101	33.2%	67.2	28.3
RUTGERS ST UNIV NEW BRUNSWICK (6964)	181	449	262	187	37.6%	67.4	27.1
RUTGERS ST UNIV NEWARK (2631)	280	620	341	279	38.2%	67.4	27.0
SAINT PETERS COLL (2638)	34	81	31	50	24.7%	63.0	29.9
SETON HALL UNIV (2632)	77	195	90	105	29.7%	65.6	26.1
THOMAS EDISON ST COLL (21922)	15	36	25	11	63.9%	77.9	34.1
WILLIAM PATERSON UNIV NJ (2625)	63	131	68	63	32.1%	67.5	29.3
New Mexico							
COLL SANTA FE (2649)	5	10	7	3	0.0%	43.7	34.0
EASTERN NM UNIV (2651)	13	25	16	9	36.0%	66.6	29.0
NM HIGHLANDS UNIV (2653)	8	18	8	10	38.9%	66.9	39.1
NM ST UNIV (2657)	47	105	47	58	34.3%	69.0	31.4
SAINT JOHNS COLL (2093)	6	13	11	2	38.5%	70.5	26.1
UNIV NM (2663)	96	264	124	140	39.8%	69.4	31.6
WESTERN NM UNIV (2664)	8	19	12	7	21.1%	61.5	27.6
New York							
ADELPHI UNIV (2666)	38	90	44	46	24.4%	64.5	27.7
ALFRED UNIV (2668)	8	12	11	1	41.7%	66.3	23.6
BARNARD COLL (2708)	5	9	6	3	44.4%	67.6	30.0
BERKELEY COLL NY (7394)	21	42	18	24	21.4%	57.6	31.4
CANISIUS COLL (2681)	32	90	63	27	72.2%	77.7	25.6
COLGATE UNIV (2701)	5	9	9	0	55.6%	73.6	30.3
COLL SAINT ROSE (2705)	5	15	4	11	26.7%	68.3	30.3
COLUMBIA UNIV NY (2707)	10	24	17	7	70.8%	73.8	30.2
CONCORDIA COLL (2709)	5	10	3	7	30.0%	66.0	29.4
CORNELL UNIV (2711)	42	97	76	21	72.2%	78.6	28.7
CUNY BARUCH (7273)	624	1,413	628	785	37.8%	68.5	30.0
CUNY BROOKLYN (2687)	159	361	213	148	33.8%	66.8	29.3
CUNY HERBERT H LEHMAN (7022)	51	80	47	33	18.8%	59.3	34.3
CUNY HUNTER (2689)	128	277	134	143	32.1%	66.2	29.6
CUNY MEDGAR EVERS (10097)	15	41	6	35	9.8%	57.0	34.9
CUNY QUEENS (2690)	249	541	230	311	30.5%	65.3	30.8
CUNY STATEN ISLAND (2698)	7	14	3	11	42.9%	69.3	31.2
CUNY STATEN ISLAND (29040)	57	108	60	48	26.9%	64.2	30.5
CUNY YORK COLL (4759)	20	32	15	17	18.8%	63.3	38.1
DAEMEN COLL (2808)	7	26	1	25	26.9%	68.2	32.1
DOWLING COLL (2667)	23	50	21	29	26.0%	65.6	33.6
ELMIRA COLL (2718)	8	19	10	9	63.2%	75.3	28.5
EXCELSIOR COLL (2834)	41	87	54	33	44.8%	68.6	34.3
FORDHAM UNIV (2722)	146	363	194	169	40.8%	70.3	25.3

Appendix F: Summary Performance for Bachelor's Degree - All Testing Events

	Candidates Total	Sections Total	Sections First-Time	Sections Re-Exam	Percent Pass	Average Score	Average Age
HARTWICK COLL (2729)	18	39	21	18	30.8%	69.3	28.7
HOFSTRA UNIV (2732)	143	350	176	174	36.0%	67.7	27.1
HOUGHTON COLL (2734)	6	10	8	2	70.0%	73.6	30.0
IONA COLL (2737)	39	113	47	66	28.3%	66.9	27.7
ITHACA COLL (2739)	32	88	51	37	45.5%	72.6	26.0
LE MOYNE COLL (2748)	35	94	41	53	39.4%	71.1	27.7
LONG ISLAND UNIV BROOKLYN CENTER (4779)	8	24	10	14	29.2%	67.8	29.2
LONG ISLAND UNIV CW POST (2754)	46	92	35	57	31.5%	66.3	29.4
MANHATTAN COLL (2758)	42	99	48	51	23.2%	60.1	27.4
MARIST COLL (2765)	49	131	69	62	44.3%	71.4	25.7
MERCY COLL (2772)	11	27	8	19	37.0%	68.3	37.3
MOLLOY COLL (2775)	15	37	16	21	21.6%	61.0	26.1
MONROE COLL (4799)	30	64	18	46	6.3%	55.8	34.2
MOUNT SAINT MARY COLL (2778)	7	15	13	2	6.7%	56.6	27.8
NAZARETH COLL ROCHESTER (2779)	12	35	25	10	68.6%	79.7	25.4
NIAGARA UNIV (2788)	27	66	33	33	34.9%	67.1	28.6
NY INST TECH MANHATTAN (2782)	18	30	21	9	23.3%	56.0	29.2
NY INST TECH OLD WESTBURY (4804)	13	25	12	13	20.0%	57.8	24.8
NY UNIV (2785)	119	312	194	118	53.2%	73.3	26.1
NYACK COLL (2790)	6	14	8	6	42.9%	67.8	27.3
PACE UNIV NY (2791)	120	287	109	178	27.9%	65.3	29.8
PACE UNIV PLEASANTVILLE (2792)	46	107	59	48	34.6%	66.5	28.6
ROBERTS WESLEYAN COLL (2805)	5	11	1	10	27.3%	69.2	27.4
ROCHESTER INST TECH (2806)	19	52	33	19	38.5%	70.1	29.3
SAINT BONAVENTURE UNIV (2817)	10	26	13	13	15.4%	62.0	30.6
SAINT FRANCIS COLL (2820)	12	29	11	18	41.4%	70.3	35.4
SAINT JOHN FISHER COLL (2821)	29	85	49	36	42.4%	72.0	26.4
SAINT JOHNS UNIV NEW YORK (2823)	143	351	179	172	31.9%	64.9	26.5
SAINT JOSEPHS COLL NY (2825)	7	12	11	1	50.0%	72.8	25.4
SAINT JOSEPHS COLL SUFFOLK (29081)	15	34	14	20	26.5%	66.9	30.7
SAINT THOMAS AQUINAS COLL (2832)	9	25	11	14	28.0%	67.0	27.4
SIENA COLL (2816)	78	188	88	100	35.1%	67.7	27.5
SKIDMORE COLL (2814)	7	19	10	9	42.1%	75.7	28.5
SUNY OLD WESTBURY (7109)	72	157	87	70	31.2%	63.4	32.3
SUNY ALBANY (2835)	194	456	253	203	41.7%	70.5	25.4
SUNY BINGHAMTON (2836)	252	632	366	266	45.1%	70.2	25.6
SUNY BROCKPORT (2841)	47	112	54	58	45.5%	72.9	28.9
SUNY BUFFALO (2837)	161	420	232	188	52.1%	73.3	27.3
SUNY BUFFALO (2842)	11	29	16	13	58.6%	75.0	30.0
SUNY EMPIRE ST COLL (10286)	12	34	20	14	55.9%	72.6	39.0
SUNY FREDONIA (2844)	18	36	27	9	63.9%	75.0	29.3
SUNY GENESEO (2845)	68	177	109	68	57.6%	74.7	25.3
SUNY INST TECH UTICA ROME (11678)	7	19	15	4	21.1%	64.5	32.8
SUNY NEW PALTZ (2846)	45	110	61	49	52.7%	74.3	28.5
SUNY ONEONTA (2847)	22	50	20	30	46.0%	70.1	26.9
SUNY OSWEGO (2848)	25	66	31	35	36.4%	69.8	28.1
SUNY PLATTSBURGH (2849)	41	116	49	67	27.6%	66.7	27.1
SUNY STONY BROOK (2838)	43	112	73	39	42.9%	69.6	28.5
SUNY UTICA-ROME (6792)	5	10	1	9	60.0%	76.1	31.5
SYRACUSE UNIV (2882)	159	409	220	189	42.8%	70.0	25.5
TOURO COLL (10142)	97	232	132	100	48.7%	72.4	26.4

Appendix F: Summary Performance for Bachelor's Degree - All Testing Events

	Candidates Total	Sections Total	Sections First-Time	Sections Re-Exam	Percent Pass	Average Score	Average Age
UNIV ROCHESTER (2894)	7	11	7	4	72.7%	79.2	31.3
UTICA COLL (2883)	12	35	13	22	40.0%	70.3	33.0
VASSAR COLL (2895)	5	11	9	2	72.7%	77.5	27.2
WAGNER COLL (2899)	25	59	39	20	35.6%	67.5	26.2
YESHIVA UNIV (2903)	90	209	103	106	42.1%	70.4	24.9
North Carolina							
APPALACHIAN ST UNIV (2906)	116	335	182	153	52.8%	74.3	27.5
BARTON COLL (2908)	9	21	10	11	28.6%	59.3	34.2
BELMONT ABBEY COLL (2910)	7	14	11	3	14.3%	65.3	34.6
CAMPBELL UNIV (2913)	34	83	48	35	48.2%	72.5	29.5
CATAWBA COLL (2914)	10	22	13	9	40.9%	62.6	29.7
DAVIDSON COLL (2918)	8	25	21	4	76.0%	82.4	25.0
DUKE UNIV (2920)	11	27	23	4	70.4%	80.2	29.6
EAST CAROLINA UNIV (2923)	107	324	212	112	43.5%	70.6	28.0
ELIZABETH CITY ST UNIV (2926)	7	14	10	4	0.0%	46.2	40.2
ELON UNIV (2927)	95	244	131	113	41.8%	69.5	24.9
FAYETTEVILLE ST UNIV (2928)	9	14	6	8	14.3%	58.3	36.8
GARDNER WEBB UNIV (2929)	13	30	21	9	36.7%	65.0	29.5
GREENSBORO COLL (2930)	10	24	7	17	37.5%	68.7	32.6
GUILFORD COLL (2931)	13	30	20	10	50.0%	75.0	36.1
HIGH POINT UNIV (2933)	24	59	13	46	28.8%	65.0	34.0
LENOIR RHYNE COLL (2941)	13	32	5	27	37.5%	71.0	29.5
MEREDITH COLL (2945)	10	31	17	14	45.2%	73.3	27.1
METHODIST UNIV (2946)	7	13	7	6	23.1%	65.6	36.4
MOUNT OLIVE COLL (2949)	7	15	12	3	6.7%	47.1	28.3
NC AGRICULTURAL & TECH ST UNIV (2905)	40	115	45	70	33.0%	67.6	28.5
NC CENTRAL UNIV (2950)	16	36	16	20	22.2%	58.4	32.9
NC ST UNIV RALEIGH (2972)	211	602	371	231	55.0%	74.5	27.0
NC WESLEYAN COLL (2951)	8	25	16	9	40.0%	57.7	40.6
PFEIFFER UNIV (2955)	6	20	9	11	15.0%	59.3	30.7
QUEENS UNIV CHARLOTTE (2957)	5	12	9	3	83.3%	78.7	29.6
UNIV NC ASHEVILLE (2907)	21	54	38	16	38.9%	72.1	35.1
UNIV NC CHAPEL HILL (2974)	166	530	398	132	66.8%	77.1	26.3
UNIV NC CHARLOTTE (2975)	94	243	136	107	47.3%	71.5	29.7
UNIV NC GREENSBORO (2976)	63	167	90	77	44.3%	70.9	29.3
UNIV NC PEMBROKE (2954)	9	21	13	8	47.6%	70.0	32.1
UNIV NC WILMINGTON (2984)	150	423	264	159	48.5%	72.6	26.6
WAKE FOREST UNIV (2978)	51	192	173	19	86.5%	84.8	24.1
WESTERN CAROLINA UNIV (2981)	20	51	41	10	37.3%	65.7	30.9
WINGATE UNIV (2985)	12	28	20	8	25.0%	66.2	25.5
WINSTON SALEM ST UNIV (2986)	15	48	17	31	20.8%	66.3	32.6
North Dakota							
DICKINSON ST UNIV (2989)	27	69	36	33	37.7%	63.9	28.1
JAMESTOWN COLL (2990)	5	13	7	6	38.5%	69.6	25.7
MINOT ST UNIV (2994)	10	19	14	5	52.6%	70.8	27.2
ND ST UNIV (9265)	39	103	52	51	52.4%	74.6	29.0
UNIV MARY (2992)	16	40	19	21	35.0%	66.3	28.8
UNIV ND (3005)	45	110	78	32	63.6%	77.1	26.7

Appendix F: Summary Performance for Bachelor's Degree - All Testing Events

	Candidates Total	Sections Total	Sections First-Time	Sections Re-Exam	Percent Pass	Average Score	Average Age
Ohio							
ASHLAND UNIV (3012)	14	45	26	19	42.2%	74.2	28.6
BALDWIN WALLACE COLL (3014)	20	52	29	23	40.4%	69.3	33.2
BOWLING GREEN ST UNIV (3018)	74	200	137	63	47.0%	71.8	27.9
CAPITAL UNIV (3023)	23	80	56	24	41.3%	67.3	24.9
CASE WESTERN RESERVE UNIV (3024)	23	65	42	23	58.5%	73.9	27.7
CEDARVILLE UNIV (3025)	22	64	26	38	54.7%	74.1	26.5
CENTRAL ST UNIV (3026)	5	12	5	7	25.0%	57.6	40.9
Chancellor University (3043)	8	24	8	16	29.2%	68.0	45.7
CLEVELAND ST UNIV (3032)	66	170	92	78	49.4%	72.6	31.5
DEFIANCE COLL (3041)	7	17	16	1	52.9%	70.9	26.3
DEVRY UNIV COLUMBUS (3099)	22	45	29	16	35.6%	62.0	38.4
FRANCISCAN UNIV STEUBENVILLE (3036)	7	17	13	4	41.2%	65.9	33.0
FRANKLIN UNIV (3046)	115	252	145	107	28.6%	62.0	36.0
HEIDELBERG COLL (3048)	10	31	11	20	22.6%	69.5	29.4
HIRAM COLL (3049)	12	42	18	24	35.7%	68.5	26.3
JOHN CARROLL UNIV (3050)	72	202	123	79	54.5%	74.9	25.5
KENT ST UNIV (3051)	91	234	137	97	52.1%	72.0	28.3
LAKE ERIE COLL (3066)	5	14	12	2	35.7%	65.7	31.5
MALONE COLL (3072)	6	20	14	6	50.0%	73.2	25.9
MARIETTA COLL (3073)	10	24	9	15	29.2%	65.2	28.6
MIAMI UNIV (3077)	311	864	636	228	59.4%	75.6	24.8
MOUNT UNION COLL (3083)	14	36	18	18	55.6%	75.2	25.9
MOUNT VERNON NAZARENE UNIV (7085)	8	22	17	5	31.8%	64.8	31.2
MUSKINGUM COLL (3084)	7	18	10	8	44.4%	66.7	29.9
NOTRE DAME COLL OH (3085)	11	29	21	8	13.8%	56.6	24.9
OH DOMINICAN UNIV (3035)	10	38	24	14	29.0%	64.3	26.7
OH NORTHERN UNIV (3089)	24	75	49	26	32.0%	67.3	25.2
OH ST UNIV (6883)	357	974	637	337	55.5%	73.9	26.8
OH UNIV (3100)	151	420	253	167	47.4%	71.9	25.5
OH WESLEYAN UNIV (3109)	14	33	21	12	45.5%	72.9	25.5
OTTERBEIN UNIV (3110)	12	31	21	10	48.4%	69.8	32.5
TIFFIN UNIV (3121)	6	17	9	8	23.5%	60.9	28.1
UNIV AKRON (3123)	95	267	160	107	46.1%	71.2	29.7
UNIV CINCINNATI (3125)	98	244	155	89	45.9%	70.6	29.1
UNIV DAYTON (3127)	54	149	83	66	45.0%	70.8	26.4
UNIV FINDLAY (3045)	10	37	19	18	48.7%	71.9	27.5
UNIV TOLEDO (3131)	57	150	105	45	47.3%	69.5	27.4
WALSH UNIV (3135)	15	38	15	23	23.7%	67.0	28.1
WILMINGTON COLL (3142)	6	12	8	4	33.3%	62.0	34.4
WITTENBERG UNIV (3143)	6	18	14	4	44.4%	70.5	28.7
WRIGHT ST UNIV (3078)	43	120	75	45	47.5%	71.2	29.1
XAVIER UNIV (3144)	57	151	89	62	55.0%	72.9	24.7
YOUNGSTOWN ST UNIV (3145)	52	127	79	48	45.7%	69.5	29.1
Oklahoma							
CAMERON UNIV (3150)	10	19	11	8	26.3%	58.2	34.7
EAST CENTRAL UNIV (3154)	20	38	6	32	31.6%	66.7	37.2
LANGSTON UNIV (3157)	20	29	4	25	13.8%	52.2	39.3
NORTHEASTERN ST UNIV (3161)	37	76	37	39	30.3%	62.8	31.2
NORTHWESTERN OK ST UNIV (3163)	7	14	8	6	28.6%	67.1	29.7
OK BAPTIST UNIV (3164)	7	19	11	8	47.4%	70.3	33.6

Appendix F: Summary Performance for Bachelor's Degree - All Testing Events

	Candidates Total	Sections Total	Sections First-Time	Sections Re-Exam	Percent Pass	Average Score	Average Age
OK CHRISTIAN UNIV (3165)	25	57	30	27	42.1%	70.6	26.2
OK ST UNIV (3170)	160	461	323	138	57.1%	74.9	27.0
OK ST UNIV OK CITY (9647)	6	9	4	5	33.3%	64.7	37.5
OKLAHOMA CITY UNIV (3166)	7	10	4	6	40.0%	70.2	33.4
ORAL ROBERTS UNIV (3985)	18	48	33	15	54.2%	72.4	28.3
SOUTHEASTERN OK ST UNIV (3179)	8	26	7	19	30.8%	65.8	34.1
SOUTHERN NAZARENE UNIV (3149)	10	24	2	22	33.3%	66.6	31.1
SOUTHWESTERN OK ST UNIV (3181)	30	73	23	50	35.6%	66.2	30.4
UNIV CENTRAL OK (3152)	122	264	126	138	39.4%	66.5	32.0
UNIV OK NORMAN (3184)	109	254	137	117	46.1%	70.7	29.2
UNIV TULSA (3185)	27	64	29	35	45.3%	72.8	28.9
Oregon							
CONCORDIA UNIV (3191)	5	12	8	4	8.3%	56.1	26.1
EASTERN OR UNIV (3193)	21	62	31	31	43.6%	70.6	30.7
GEORGE FOX UNIV (3194)	19	49	21	28	36.7%	68.8	25.8
LINFIELD COLL (3198)	49	139	82	57	40.3%	70.7	32.6
OR ST UNIV (3210)	92	212	131	81	53.3%	73.0	30.4
PACIFIC UNIV (3212)	12	27	13	14	48.2%	68.3	27.2
PORTLAND ST UNIV (3216)	116	265	157	108	55.9%	72.0	32.3
SOUTHERN OR UNIV (3219)	28	70	37	33	48.6%	73.1	31.0
UNIV OR (3223)	154	391	221	170	49.9%	71.8	28.9
UNIV PORTLAND (3224)	27	74	54	20	40.5%	69.9	24.2
Pennsylvania							
ALBRIGHT COLL (3229)	36	67	46	21	23.9%	65.7	32.4
ALVERNIA COLL (3233)	17	40	17	23	25.0%	66.2	32.6
ARCADIA UNIV (3235)	17	57	29	28	35.1%	65.7	25.5
BLOOMSBURG UNIV PA (3315)	108	279	147	132	47.3%	72.2	26.8
BUCKNELL UNIV (3238)	66	179	105	74	59.2%	76.0	25.3
CA UNIV PA (3316)	23	50	29	21	30.0%	64.2	32.9
CABRINI COLL (3241)	22	57	23	34	21.1%	56.9	29.0
CARLOW UNIV (3303)	9	17	11	6	41.2%	64.9	28.4
CARNEGIE MELLON UNIV (3242)	10	27	16	11	55.6%	73.9	30.7
CEDAR CREST COLL (3243)	5	11	3	8	36.4%	65.6	29.2
CHESTNUT HILL COLL (3245)	11	21	10	11	38.1%	64.7	30.6
CHEYNEY UNIV PA (3317)	5	8	5	3	0.0%	47.9	28.3
CLARION UNIV PA (9235)	28	64	29	35	50.0%	70.2	27.0
COLL MISERICORDIA (3247)	10	25	10	15	12.0%	59.2	30.8
DE VALLEY COLL (3252)	15	42	21	21	33.3%	65.8	26.2
DESALES UNIV (3986)	44	125	64	61	31.2%	66.6	28.2
DREXEL UNIV (3256)	219	538	285	253	36.6%	67.7	26.6
DUQUESNE UNIV (3258)	124	312	182	130	42.0%	69.8	25.1
EAST STROUDSBURG UNIV PA (3320)	19	39	20	19	41.0%	66.9	32.0
EASTERN UNIV (3259)	14	34	17	17	41.2%	71.9	26.5
EDINBORO UNIV PA (3321)	12	32	16	16	21.9%	64.5	29.6
ELIZABETHTOWN COLL (3262)	36	101	55	46	26.7%	65.1	27.8
FRANKLIN & MARSHALL COLL (3265)	8	21	15	6	76.2%	79.1	30.2
GANNON UNIV (3266)	18	41	16	25	22.0%	58.7	33.7
GENEVA COLL (3267)	18	44	23	21	34.1%	68.4	27.7
GETTYSBURG COLL (3268)	6	12	6	6	33.3%	67.2	28.9
GROVE CITY COLL (3269)	43	108	84	24	54.6%	74.1	25.8
GWYNEDD MERCY COLL (3270)	16	41	27	14	31.7%	63.3	28.5

Appendix F: Summary Performance for Bachelor's Degree - All Testing Events

	Candidates Total	Sections Total	Sections First-Time	Sections Re-Exam	Percent Pass	Average Score	Average Age
HOLY FAMILY COLL (3275)	14	23	19	4	13.0%	61.0	27.4
IMMACULATA UNIV (3276)	7	16	10	6	37.5%	63.9	27.1
INDIANA UNIV PA (3277)	81	227	122	105	31.7%	65.1	27.0
JUNIATA COLL (3279)	18	36	17	19	36.1%	65.7	26.9
KEYSTONE COLL (3280)	11	22	15	7	13.6%	60.4	26.3
KINGS COLL (3282)	71	153	82	71	30.7%	65.4	26.1
KUTZTOWN UNIV PA (3322)	75	185	128	57	39.5%	69.0	25.9
LA ROCHE COLL (3987)	26	59	24	35	17.0%	57.5	27.5
LA SALLE UNIV (3287)	137	340	183	157	29.4%	65.3	26.6
LAFAYETTE COLL (3284)	9	25	18	7	32.0%	63.0	29.4
LEBANON VALLEY COLL (3288)	34	88	61	27	40.9%	72.6	26.4
LEHIGH UNIV (3289)	139	367	257	110	62.4%	75.3	24.3
LINCOLN UNIV (3290)	11	27	10	17	25.9%	60.3	25.9
LOCK HAVEN UNIV PA (3323)	17	45	25	20	33.3%	59.4	28.8
LYCOMING COLL (3293)	14	39	22	17	41.0%	70.6	27.7
MARYWOOD UNIV (3296)	11	30	16	14	33.3%	67.0	35.5
MERCYHURST COLL (3297)	31	68	41	27	30.9%	63.1	26.0
MESSIAH COLL (3298)	42	120	85	35	55.0%	72.1	24.2
MILLERSVILLE UNIV PA (3325)	40	94	53	41	39.4%	66.6	28.1
MORAVIAN COLL (3301)	33	80	45	35	33.8%	66.9	26.2
MOUNT ALOYSIUS COLL (3302)	10	16	9	7	43.8%	71.4	28.1
MUHLENBERG COLL (3304)	55	154	86	68	44.2%	70.8	25.8
NEUMANN UNIV (3988)	13	29	18	11	34.5%	64.1	30.4
PA COLL TECH (3395)	6	11	8	3	18.2%	62.0	31.2
PA ST ERIE (3333)	6	14	11	3	71.4%	75.4	32.4
PA ST UNIV PARK (3329)	570	1,460	932	528	43.7%	69.7	25.7
PA ST UNIV PARK (6965)	62	182	30	152	29.7%	69.2	30.2
PEIRCE COLL (3309)	5	9	8	1	66.7%	69.8	34.6
PHILADELPHIA UNIV (3354)	30	87	31	56	29.9%	62.9	29.2
POINT PARK UNIV (3357)	11	21	14	7	9.5%	61.3	31.6
ROBERT MORRIS UNIV (3359)	99	214	114	100	31.8%	65.0	27.4
SAINT FRANCIS UNIV (3366)	38	86	46	40	23.3%	61.8	28.3
SAINT JOSEPHS UNIV (3367)	156	436	229	207	38.5%	69.0	25.0
SAINT VINCENT COLL (3368)	38	92	60	32	37.0%	69.3	24.5
SETON HILL UNIV (3362)	8	19	11	8	36.8%	67.0	25.9
SHIPPENSBURG UNIV PA (3326)	91	213	131	82	47.4%	71.0	26.6
SLIPPERY ROCK UNIV PA (3327)	43	97	60	37	24.7%	61.5	25.2
SUSQUEHANNA UNIV (3369)	24	65	39	26	33.9%	67.7	27.2
TEMPLE UNIV (3371)	435	1,023	626	397	31.4%	64.7	28.2
THIEL COLL (3376)	16	49	28	21	24.5%	61.8	25.3
UNIV PA (3378)	33	91	67	24	70.3%	77.2	30.5
UNIV PITTSBURGH (3379)	300	737	489	248	48.3%	72.0	26.1
UNIV PITTSBURGH JOHNSTOWN (3382)	9	21	6	15	23.8%	62.9	29.4
UNIV SCRANTON (3384)	67	139	69	70	35.3%	66.9	26.8
URSINUS COLL (3385)	11	24	10	14	25.0%	69.5	32.5
VILLANOVA UNIV (3388)	256	715	436	279	56.4%	74.5	24.7
WASHINGTON & JEFFERSON COLL (3389)	51	116	72	44	40.5%	70.6	25.4
WAYNESBURG COLL (3391)	12	24	13	11	8.3%	59.0	27.8
WEST CHESTER UNIV PA (3328)	209	503	278	225	37.2%	68.1	26.3
WESTMINSTER COLL (3392)	27	60	38	22	23.3%	60.6	26.0
WIDENER UNIV PA (3313)	82	202	107	95	25.7%	62.6	25.8

Appendix F: Summary Performance for Bachelor's Degree - All Testing Events

	Candidates Total	Sections Total	Sections First-Time	Sections Re-Exam	Percent Pass	Average Score	Average Age
WILKES UNIV (3394)	35	84	47	37	29.8%	62.6	28.1
YORK COLL PA (3399)	39	86	56	30	50.0%	72.2	26.9
Puerto Rico							
INTER AMERICAN UNIV PR (8242)	23	36	19	17	16.7%	51.2	34.0
INTER AMERICAN UNIV PR AGUADILLA (3939)	5	8	5	3	37.5%	62.9	35.1
INTER AMERICAN UNIV PR BARRANQUITAS (5027)	8	11	10	1	0.0%	35.3	28.0
INTER AMERICAN UNIV PR BAYAMON (5028)	8	14	11	3	0.0%	50.1	30.6
INTER AMERICAN UNIV PR METROPOLITAN (3940)	32	57	37	20	21.1%	55.0	30.7
INTER AMERICAN UNIV PR PONCE (5029)	16	35	29	6	0.0%	29.8	33.1
INTER AMERICAN UNIV PR SAN GERMAN (3938)	12	23	13	10	21.7%	58.0	32.5
PONTIFICAL CATHOLIC UNIV PR (3936)	37	84	60	24	17.9%	47.0	31.2
UNIV ESTE (3941)	8	15	14	1	13.3%	30.6	41.7
UNIV METROPOLITANA (25875)	9	19	16	3	15.8%	33.7	37.1
UNIV POLITECNICA DE PR (21000)	5	15	6	9	26.7%	67.3	34.9
UNIV PR AGUADILLA (12123)	17	26	20	6	3.9%	44.8	31.2
UNIV PR ARECIBO (7228)	26	47	32	15	17.0%	54.8	28.8
UNIV PR BAYAMON (10975)	64	143	79	64	18.2%	57.8	27.5
UNIV PR CAROLINA (30160)	12	25	18	7	12.0%	54.8	28.8
UNIV PR CAYEY (7206)	54	125	57	68	15.2%	56.4	27.8
UNIV PR HUMACAO (3943)	46	101	53	48	20.8%	57.7	27.1
UNIV PR MAYAGUEZ (3944)	55	118	62	56	24.6%	65.2	27.3
UNIV PR PONCE (9652)	23	65	47	18	16.9%	49.1	26.5
UNIV PR RIO PIEDRAS (7108)	233	589	305	284	38.0%	68.1	26.4
UNIV SACRED HEART (3937)	11	23	16	7	47.8%	72.0	27.3
UNIV TURABO GURABO (11719)	10	25	16	9	8.0%	47.1	30.2
Rhode Island							
BRYANT UNIV (3402)	178	434	282	152	50.2%	72.9	25.0
JOHNSON & WALES UNIV (3404)	43	111	87	24	29.7%	61.4	27.4
PROVIDENCE COLL (3406)	60	159	99	60	48.4%	73.1	25.4
RI COLL (3407)	16	45	30	15	31.1%	61.7	29.5
ROGER WILLIAMS UNIV (3410)	20	50	31	19	34.0%	64.6	23.4
SALVE REGINA UNIV (3411)	27	73	32	41	20.6%	62.9	26.4
UNIV RI (3414)	83	216	140	76	59.3%	74.2	26.2
South Carolina							
BOB JONES UNIV (3421)	14	33	19	14	48.5%	69.9	25.7
CITADEL MILITARY COLL SC (3423)	13	37	21	16	29.7%	62.6	26.3
CLEMSON UNIV (3425)	52	140	95	45	58.6%	74.4	26.1
COASTAL CAROLINA UNIV (3451)	13	31	16	15	35.5%	68.9	26.4
COLL CHARLESTON (3428)	32	87	57	30	58.6%	74.4	26.5
FURMAN UNIV (3434)	20	68	43	25	58.8%	77.1	24.3
UNIV SC COLUMBIA (3448)	86	247	174	73	49.4%	74.5	27.2
WINTHROP UNIV (3456)	20	39	18	21	43.6%	71.3	31.0
WOFFORD COLL (3457)	12	44	40	4	61.4%	73.9	26.5
South Dakota							
AUGUSTANA COLL (3458)	33	94	65	29	46.8%	72.8	25.8
BLACK HILLS ST UNIV (3459)	12	27	18	9	37.0%	69.4	30.4
CO TECHNICAL UNIV (666731)	9	18	10	8	22.2%	54.4	41.4
NATIONAL AMERICAN UNIV (4057)	11	22	14	8	27.3%	60.8	35.6
NORTHERN ST UNIV (3466)	12	30	14	16	30.0%	68.3	29.9
SD ST UNIV (3471)	15	32	23	9	40.6%	73.3	27.3
UNIV SD (3474)	16	41	25	16	61.0%	76.6	32.2

Appendix F: Summary Performance for Bachelor's Degree - All Testing Events

	Candidates Total	Sections Total	Sections First-Time	Sections Re-Exam	Percent Pass	Average Score	Average Age
UNIV SIOUX FALLS (3469)	18	41	33	8	53.7%	74.4	27.7
Tennessee							
AUSTIN PEAY ST UNIV (3478)	32	83	44	39	33.7%	64.6	29.1
BELMONT UNIV (3479)	36	81	62	19	54.3%	70.8	25.6
CARSON NEWMAN COLL (3481)	13	30	11	19	40.0%	68.7	33.4
CHRISTIAN BROTHERS UNIV (3482)	18	56	18	38	28.6%	67.6	28.8
CUMBERLAND UNIV (3485)	5	10	7	3	10.0%	58.5	25.1
EAST TN ST UNIV (3487)	48	110	72	38	33.6%	66.7	32.0
FISK UNIV (3490)	6	12	9	3	41.7%	68.0	25.3
FREED HARDEMAN UNIV (3492)	13	32	15	17	34.4%	65.8	30.4
LAMBUTH UNIV (3498)	6	18	8	10	22.2%	63.7	28.2
LEE UNIV (3500)	20	51	28	23	45.1%	67.3	30.1
LINCOLN MEMORIAL UNIV (3502)	6	23	4	19	39.1%	70.1	29.6
LIPSCOMB UNIV (3486)	35	87	50	37	25.3%	64.5	32.0
MIDDLE TN ST UNIV (3510)	104	295	175	120	46.1%	71.4	30.0
MILLIGAN COLL (3511)	5	13	5	8	30.8%	73.2	31.7
RHODES COLL (3519)	15	41	27	14	53.7%	72.1	24.7
SOUTHERN ADVENTIST UNIV (3518)	9	29	19	10	37.9%	69.2	26.2
TN ST UNIV (3522)	23	40	24	16	32.5%	63.2	34.1
TN TECH UNIV (3523)	42	103	57	46	30.1%	65.0	30.0
TN WESLEYAN COLL (3525)	10	22	11	11	45.5%	64.0	34.6
TREVECCA NAZARENE UNIV (3526)	7	28	11	17	46.4%	73.1	26.1
TUSCULUM COLL (3527)	7	12	9	3	33.3%	67.8	31.1
UNION UNIV (3528)	12	22	16	6	50.0%	71.5	27.4
UNIV MEMPHIS (3509)	57	128	68	60	28.1%	64.4	32.3
UNIV TN CHATTANOOGA (3529)	62	144	77	67	44.4%	70.6	29.8
UNIV TN KNOXVILLE (3530)	165	486	299	187	58.6%	74.1	27.6
UNIV TN MARTIN (3531)	28	79	36	43	27.9%	62.2	28.7
VANDERBILT UNIV (3535)	22	76	65	11	84.2%	82.5	25.7
Texas							
ABILENE CHRISTIAN UNIV (3537)	37	97	47	50	51.6%	73.9	26.6
AMBERTON UNIV (22594)	6	7	3	4	57.1%	72.1	42.9
ANGELO ST UNIV (3541)	17	56	31	25	41.1%	68.6	29.6
BAYLOR UNIV (3545)	93	244	137	107	54.5%	74.6	27.0
BAYLOR UNIV (6967)	8	29	17	12	48.3%	72.5	29.8
DALLAS BAPTIST UNIV (3560)	14	36	23	13	36.1%	66.6	29.0
DEVRY UNIV IRVING (10139)	13	25	19	6	20.0%	57.4	32.5
EAST TX BAPTIST UNIV (3564)	5	12	6	6	41.7%	62.6	30.1
HOUSTON BAPTIST UNIV (3576)	16	26	16	10	23.1%	61.2	31.5
LAMAR COLL (3581)	33	103	34	69	31.1%	67.7	30.8
LETOURNEAU UNIV (3584)	11	23	18	5	21.7%	65.5	35.8
LUBBOCK CHRISTIAN UNIV (3586)	8	23	11	12	39.1%	72.4	31.3
MIDWESTERN ST UNIV (3592)	20	44	28	16	54.6%	73.8	35.5
OUR LADY THE LAKE UNIV (3598)	7	10	8	2	30.0%	60.8	32.1
PRAIRIE VIEW A & M UNIV (3630)	8	16	5	11	37.5%	65.9	28.2
RICE UNIV (3604)	12	29	24	5	62.1%	77.4	31.4
SAINT EDWARDS UNIV (3621)	22	61	25	36	36.1%	71.2	34.1
SAINT MARYS UNIV (3623)	20	48	22	26	33.3%	68.7	29.3
SAM HOUSTON ST UNIV (3606)	97	265	109	156	38.1%	68.9	31.9
SCHREINER UNIV (3610)	8	22	9	13	27.3%	67.2	27.9
SOUTHERN METHODIST UNIV (3613)	102	320	212	108	57.8%	75.9	25.2

Appendix F: Summary Performance for Bachelor's Degree - All Testing Events

	Candidates Total	Sections Total	Sections First-Time	Sections Re-Exam	Percent Pass	Average Score	Average Age
SOUTHWESTERN ASSEMBLIES OF GOD UNIV (3616)	5	10	4	6	20.0%	66.2	32.6
SOUTHWESTERN UNIV (3620)	9	24	20	4	70.8%	77.3	30.3
STEPHEN F AUSTIN ST UNIV (3624)	32	64	42	22	42.2%	67.3	33.4
TARLETON ST UNIV (3631)	27	62	35	27	35.5%	68.2	32.6
TRINITY UNIV (3647)	30	77	46	31	62.3%	75.5	26.3
TX A&M INTL UNIV (9651)	14	25	15	10	24.0%	60.7	29.8
TX A&M UNIV (3632)	131	327	192	135	54.4%	73.2	30.2
TX A&M UNIV COMMERCE (3565)	10	27	15	12	48.2%	72.4	33.9
TX A&M UNIV CORPUS CHRISTI (11161)	26	61	36	25	42.6%	70.6	32.3
TX A&M UNIV KINGSVILLE (3639)	8	11	6	5	0.0%	55.7	37.7
TX CHRISTIAN UNIV (3636)	60	165	133	32	69.1%	77.5	25.3
TX LUTHERAN UNIV (3641)	32	62	30	32	45.2%	70.0	26.8
TX SOUTHERN UNIV (3642)	15	37	14	23	8.1%	54.3	35.9
TX ST UNIV SAN MARCOS (3615)	98	270	118	152	36.7%	69.4	30.6
TX TECH UNIV (3644)	122	338	217	121	47.9%	70.8	28.3
TX WESLEYAN UNIV (3645)	9	27	11	16	40.7%	65.1	37.1
TX WOMANS UNIV (3646)	13	41	16	25	39.0%	69.0	28.4
UNIV DALLAS (3651)	6	17	8	9	47.1%	73.4	30.5
UNIV HOUSTON (12826)	6	16	8	8	25.0%	67.6	34.0
UNIV HOUSTON CLEAR LAKE (11711)	69	135	75	60	36.3%	67.2	34.8
UNIV HOUSTON DOWNTOWN (3612)	159	318	181	137	28.0%	62.9	32.2
UNIV HOUSTON UNIV PARK (3652)	368	877	397	480	33.8%	67.4	30.6
UNIV HOUSTON VICTORIA (13231)	14	38	21	17	42.1%	70.2	32.6
UNIV INCARNATE WORD (3578)	9	20	7	13	25.0%	63.8	31.6
UNIV MARY HARDIN BAYLOR (3588)	21	53	39	14	47.2%	70.8	27.8
UNIV NORTH TX (3594)	103	251	122	129	34.7%	68.7	33.4
UNIV SAINT THOMAS (3654)	20	43	32	11	44.2%	69.7	28.2
UNIV TX ARLINGTON (3656)	138	355	179	176	42.3%	70.7	32.9
UNIV TX AUSTIN (3658)	122	314	209	105	57.0%	74.9	30.0
UNIV TX BROWNSVILLE (30646)	13	24	14	10	37.5%	68.3	30.0
UNIV TX DALLAS (9741)	184	530	287	243	37.4%	68.4	30.0
UNIV TX EL PASO (3661)	30	74	30	44	36.5%	68.0	29.6
UNIV TX PAN AMERICAN (3599)	27	43	23	20	48.8%	68.7	31.8
UNIV TX PERMIAN BASIN (9930)	27	57	34	23	36.8%	68.6	32.0
UNIV TX SAN ANTONIO (10115)	121	292	137	155	34.3%	66.9	33.3
UNIV TX TYLER (11163)	32	74	40	34	44.6%	68.8	30.4
WAYLAND BAPTIST UNIV (3663)	5	16	12	4	43.8%	71.3	32.0
WEST TX A & M UNIV (3665)	15	33	12	21	18.2%	64.3	30.1
Utah							
BRIGHAM YOUNG UNIV (3670)	172	424	293	131	59.0%	75.0	28.7
SOUTHERN UT UNIV (3678)	18	57	33	24	47.4%	74.3	30.6
UNIV UT (3675)	70	188	107	81	50.5%	72.2	31.4
UT ST UNIV (3677)	35	91	59	32	52.8%	71.4	29.9
UT VALLEY ST COLL (4027)	24	59	37	22	45.8%	71.5	32.2
WEBER ST UNIV (3680)	15	37	9	28	29.7%	72.4	33.9
Western Governors Univ (33394)	6	9	8	1	44.4%	64.7	33.3
WESTMINSTER COLL (3681)	8	23	14	9	21.7%	64.2	26.5
Vermont							
CASTLETON ST COLL (3683)	6	18	15	3	88.9%	82.1	28.5
CHAMPLAIN COLL (3684)	25	67	40	27	25.4%	67.1	29.2
SAINT MICHAELS COLL (3694)	32	80	49	31	41.3%	70.7	25.7

Appendix F: Summary Performance for Bachelor's Degree - All Testing Events

	Candidates Total	Sections Total	Sections First-Time	Sections Re-Exam	Percent Pass	Average Score	Average Age
UNIV VT (3696)	24	68	35	33	50.0%	73.3	29.3
Virgin Islands							
UNIV VI (3946)	9	12	8	4	25.0%	65.3	29.5
Virginia							
AVERETT UNIV (3702)	8	26	8	18	30.8%	67.6	35.5
BRIDGEWATER COLL (3704)	15	51	22	29	31.4%	65.7	24.9
CHRISTOPHER NEWPORT UNIV (3706)	22	53	31	22	34.0%	71.3	27.7
COLL WILLIAM & MARY (3705)	66	216	152	64	64.8%	76.7	25.2
EASTERN MENNONITE UNIV (3708)	5	19	18	1	68.4%	82.4	29.5
EMORY & HENRY COLL (3709)	10	22	6	16	45.5%	67.9	28.3
FERRUM COLL (3711)	8	15	11	4	60.0%	72.3	26.7
GEORGE MASON UNIV (3749)	287	667	385	282	42.9%	70.8	29.8
HAMPDEN SYDNEY COLL (3713)	5	11	8	3	63.6%	75.9	27.1
HAMPTON UNIV (3714)	38	109	43	66	21.1%	65.4	28.2
JAMES MADISON UNIV (3721)	165	497	358	139	60.6%	76.0	25.5
LIBERTY UNIV (20530)	48	107	68	39	47.7%	73.3	31.3
LONGWOOD UNIV (3719)	22	52	30	22	46.2%	68.4	25.9
LYNCHBURG COLL (3720)	8	22	13	9	54.6%	75.0	25.8
MARYMOUNT UNIV (3724)	5	17	8	9	52.9%	73.9	30.5
NORFOLK ST UNIV (3765)	15	29	7	22	41.4%	69.2	38.2
NORTHERN VA CC (3727)	11	25	20	5	56.0%	72.4	27.5
OLD DOMINION UNIV (3728)	75	160	103	57	45.0%	68.6	30.9
RADFORD UNIV (3732)	39	96	37	59	39.6%	69.3	27.6
RANDOLPH MACON COLL (3733)	20	57	33	24	43.9%	69.7	27.4
ROANOKE COLL (3736)	13	36	19	17	50.0%	73.1	26.2
TIDEWATER CC (3712)	5	11	8	3	27.3%	62.3	31.5
UNIV MARY WASHINGTON (3746)	19	40	31	9	45.0%	69.2	28.3
UNIV RICHMOND (3744)	92	269	170	99	63.9%	76.7	25.3
UNIV VA (3745)	109	330	275	55	83.0%	83.5	25.6
UNIV VA COL WISE (CLINCH VALLEY COLL) (3747)	11	22	11	11	50.0%	74.4	29.7
VA COMMONWEALTH UNIV (3735)	108	271	136	135	34.3%	67.4	29.5
VA MILITARY INST (3753)	5	15	7	8	53.3%	74.1	31.7
VA POLYTECHNIC INST & ST UNIV (3754)	251	698	454	244	55.3%	74.8	26.2
VA WESLEYAN COLL (3767)	6	18	7	11	38.9%	66.9	31.1
WASHINGTON & LEE UNIV (3768)	32	102	79	23	58.8%	76.0	24.8
Washington							
CENTRAL WA UNIV (3771)	103	256	185	71	45.7%	69.5	31.0
CITY UNIV SEATTLE (13022)	18	40	37	3	30.0%	61.4	37.4
EASTERN WA UNIV (3775)	52	129	80	49	35.7%	66.2	31.4
GONZAGA UNIV (3778)	73	205	157	48	64.9%	76.9	24.6
PACIFIC LUTHERAN UNIV (3785)	15	49	33	16	22.5%	61.7	24.8
SAINT MARTINS COLL (3794)	10	23	20	3	26.1%	60.3	33.6
SEATTLE PACIFIC UNIV (3788)	27	65	45	20	40.0%	71.7	25.2
SEATTLE UNIV (3790)	36	95	59	36	35.8%	68.2	27.4
UNIV PUGET SOUND (3797)	7	14	13	1	78.6%	77.1	33.4
UNIV WA (3798)	262	655	535	120	58.8%	74.5	28.1
WA ST UNIV (3800)	113	278	206	72	48.2%	72.2	27.7
WALLA WALLA UNIV (3799)	7	15	9	6	53.3%	75.8	25.1
WESTERN WA UNIV (3802)	44	107	77	30	64.5%	76.5	28.7
WHITWORTH COLL (3804)	12	28	20	8	60.7%	75.1	27.5
West Virginia							

Appendix F: Summary Performance for Bachelor's Degree - All Testing Events

	Candidates Total	Sections Total	Sections First-Time	Sections Re-Exam	Percent Pass	Average Score	Average Age
BETHANY COLL (3808)	6	11	8	3	72.7%	73.5	28.7
BLUEFIELD ST COLL (3809)	7	21	8	13	57.1%	75.2	34.6
CONCORD UNIV (3810)	17	35	14	21	31.4%	67.4	26.8
FAIRMONT ST COLL (3812)	12	30	12	18	40.0%	61.3	34.4
GLENVILLE ST COLL (3813)	5	8	6	2	12.5%	60.1	25.7
MARSHALL UNIV (3815)	76	184	93	91	41.9%	69.1	29.8
SALEM INTL UNIV (3820)	8	24	12	12	41.7%	71.3	36.6
SHEPHERD UNIV (3822)	13	40	16	24	60.0%	73.3	31.3
UNIV CHARLESTON (3818)	12	28	21	7	28.6%	60.7	27.4
WEST LIBERTY ST COLL (3823)	22	56	23	33	33.9%	66.4	28.3
WHEELING JESUIT UNIV (3831)	21	46	21	25	34.8%	67.0	27.2
WV INST TECH (3825)	13	33	15	18	15.2%	58.6	38.2
WV ST UNIV (3826)	32	75	32	43	24.0%	61.0	33.4
WV UNIV (3827)	183	460	273	187	47.0%	70.6	27.7
WV UNIV PARKERSBURG (3828)	10	21	16	5	42.9%	68.3	28.6
WV WESLEYAN COLL (3830)	6	13	10	3	46.2%	66.0	25.0
Wisconsin							
BELOIT COLL (3835)	5	11	8	3	45.5%	70.6	28.9
CARDINAL STRITCH UNIV (3837)	12	23	15	8	39.1%	68.9	31.6
CARROLL UNIV (WI) (3838)	21	49	26	23	51.0%	71.9	29.6
CARTHAGE COLL (3839)	19	54	28	26	20.4%	60.9	25.6
CONCORDIA UNIV WI (3842)	11	27	20	7	37.0%	65.2	24.8
EDGEWOOD COLL (3848)	13	38	22	16	23.7%	61.1	32.0
LAKELAND COLL (3854)	47	123	70	53	37.4%	70.2	37.5
Marion University (3861)	6	20	8	12	35.0%	67.6	25.4
MARQUETTE UNIV (3863)	98	287	200	87	61.3%	75.8	25.5
MOUNT MARY COLL (3869)	6	12	11	1	33.3%	61.7	42.8
SAINT NORBERT COLL (3892)	22	55	36	19	60.0%	71.0	24.9
UNIV WI EAU CLAIRE (3917)	87	198	114	84	56.1%	73.9	26.1
UNIV WI GREEN BAY (3899)	53	124	75	49	39.5%	70.7	27.4
UNIV WI LA CROSSE (3919)	84	229	147	82	49.3%	72.7	25.4
UNIV WI MADISON (3895)	159	490	366	124	72.2%	78.7	25.8
UNIV WI MILWAUKEE (3896)	135	382	248	134	49.5%	72.4	28.8
UNIV WI OSHKOSH (3920)	62	161	113	48	54.7%	74.0	26.0
UNIV WI PARKSIDE (5015)	22	37	25	12	13.5%	61.3	30.4
UNIV WI PLATTEVILLE (3921)	21	59	28	31	42.4%	71.2	28.5
UNIV WI RIVER FALLS (3923)	31	80	45	35	52.5%	72.5	28.9
UNIV WI STEVENS POINT (3924)	19	56	26	30	46.4%	73.1	30.4
UNIV WI SUPERIOR (3925)	12	34	21	13	35.3%	68.3	28.1
UNIV WI WHITEWATER (3926)	126	382	252	130	55.0%	74.2	26.3
VITERBO UNIV (3911)	5	13	4	9	23.1%	64.3	30.5
Wyoming							
UNIV WY (3932)	54	148	103	45	48.7%	72.8	28.2

ADVANCED DEGREE FIRST-TIME TESTING EVENTS

APPENDIX G

SUMMARY PERFORMANCE

Appendix G: Summary Performance for Advanced Degree - First-Time Events

	Candidates Total	Sections Total	Percent Pass	Average Score	Average Age
Alabama					
AUBURN UNIV (1009)	7	12	41.7%	74.2	30.7
TROY UNIV (1047)	18	29	37.9%	66.0	30.0
UNIV AL (1051)	10	22	59.1%	77.2	27.7
UNIV AL HUNTSVILLE (1055)	5	11	45.5%	68.4	36.6
Arizona					
AZ ST UNIV (1081)	24	45	73.3%	75.8	31.0
THUNDERBIRD SCHOOL OF GLOBAL MGMT (1070)	12	24	37.5%	69.3	40.9
UNIV AZ (1083)	18	33	63.6%	78.0	30.1
UNIV PHOENIX (20988)	206	371	31.8%	61.3	37.0
Arkansas					
AR ST UNIV (1090)	8	16	56.3%	72.7	28.3
HENDERSON ST UNIV (1098)	5	12	41.7%	70.3	29.6
UNIV AR (1108)	29	80	60.0%	72.5	24.4
UNIV AR LITTLE ROCK (1101)	9	14	64.3%	72.6	38.0
UNIV CENTRAL AR (1092)	15	32	56.3%	73.9	28.9
California					
CA LUTHERAN UNIV (1133)	5	9	44.4%	65.3	36.2
CA ST POLYTECH UNIV SAN LUIS OBISPO (1143)	21	39	43.6%	72.2	26.2
CA ST UNIV CHICO (1146)	5	14	64.3%	76.8	40.2
CA ST UNIV DOMINGUEZ HILLS (1141)	5	9	22.2%	61.0	35.9
CA ST UNIV EAST BAY (1138)	40	78	46.2%	72.5	36.5
CA ST UNIV FRESNO (1147)	11	22	77.3%	79.4	35.7
CA ST UNIV FULLERTON (1137)	33	64	51.6%	73.4	31.9
CA ST UNIV LONG BEACH (1139)	6	10	60.0%	74.4	38.1
CA ST UNIV LOS ANGELES (1140)	39	70	45.7%	71.2	33.5
CA ST UNIV NORTHRIDGE (1153)	14	24	37.5%	68.3	48.8
CA ST UNIV SACRAMENTO (1150)	25	56	53.6%	74.9	33.2
CA ST UNIV SAN BERNARDINO (1142)	19	27	48.2%	70.6	32.6
CLAREMONT GRADUATE UNIV (1169)	5	7	14.3%	56.7	43.8
DEVRY UNIV LONG BEACH (666988)	9	17	5.9%	58.8	34.0
DEVRY UNIV POMONA (23329)	7	15	13.3%	45.1	35.1
GOLDEN GATE UNIV (1205)	116	216	43.5%	67.5	34.2
LA SIERRA UNIV (1215)	8	10	10.0%	58.0	30.2
LOYOLA MARYMOUNT UNIV (11649)	5	8	50.0%	75.1	35.3
NATIONAL UNIV (11460)	27	51	45.1%	68.8	39.6
PACIFIC ST UNIV (31633)	7	10	20.0%	48.9	39.1
PEPPERDINE (1264)	26	52	38.5%	69.1	36.8
SAN DIEGO ST UNIV (1151)	87	175	68.6%	78.0	30.6
SAN FRANCISCO ST UNIV (1154)	39	70	70.0%	78.8	32.9
SAN JOSE ST UNIV (1155)	53	121	62.8%	76.3	30.4
SANTA CLARA UNIV (1326)	10	17	41.2%	69.2	41.9
UNIV CA BERKELEY (1312)	5	13	84.6%	82.9	45.6
UNIV CA DAVIS (1313)	5	16	68.8%	79.3	35.0
UNIV CA IRVINE (1314)	9	13	61.5%	78.3	35.0
UNIV CA LOS ANGELES (1315)	12	31	74.2%	81.6	34.3
UNIV CA RIVERSIDE (1316)	11	26	50.0%	69.6	31.9
UNIV CA SAN DIEGO (1317)	5	10	70.0%	74.8	30.1
UNIV CA SANTA BARBARA (1320)	6	14	71.4%	78.6	34.2
UNIV LA VERNE (1216)	14	20	20.0%	55.4	41.3
UNIV REDLANDS (1322)	5	11	27.3%	61.2	46.0
UNIV SAN DIEGO (10395)	24	56	51.8%	74.0	28.1

Appendix G: Summary Performance for Advanced Degree - First-Time Events

	Candidates Total	Sections Total	Percent Pass	Average Score	Average Age
UNIV SAN FRANCISCO (1325)	11	22	59.1%	72.0	33.0
UNIV SOUTHERN CA (1328)	163	356	71.1%	78.0	28.7
Colorado					
CO ST UNIV (1350)	9	17	52.9%	67.5	38.4
REGIS UNIV (1363)	17	32	37.5%	66.4	41.7
UNIV CO BOULDER (1370)	12	28	67.9%	77.1	26.8
UNIV CO DENVER (6740)	11	21	38.1%	66.5	35.1
UNIV DENVER (1371)	24	39	38.5%	65.3	30.0
Connecticut					
QUINNIPIAC UNIV (1402)	5	11	54.6%	74.3	26.3
UNIV CT (1417)	14	21	47.6%	73.7	30.8
UNIV HARTFORD (1422)	11	23	43.5%	65.7	33.0
UNIV NEW HAVEN (1397)	6	9	11.1%	52.9	31.7
Delaware					
UNIV DE (1431)	9	15	46.7%	66.6	30.4
District of Columbia					
AMERICAN UNIV (1434)	19	33	54.6%	73.1	29.2
GEORGE WASHINGTON UNIV (1444)	44	90	65.6%	75.9	29.9
GEORGETOWN UNIV (1445)	7	9	66.7%	77.7	44.1
SOUTHEASTERN UNIV (1456)	5	5	60.0%	67.4	32.8
STRAYER COLL (1459)	33	47	25.5%	56.4	36.8
Florida					
FL A&M UNIV (1480)	8	16	25.0%	67.3	24.7
FL ATLANTIC UNIV (1481)	14	27	29.6%	67.6	32.5
FL INTL UNIV (9635)	6	9	33.3%	64.1	48.0
FL ST UNIV (1489)	14	28	42.9%	67.7	31.8
NOVA SOUTHEASTERN UNIV (1509)	8	10	30.0%	57.5	33.9
SAINT LEO UNIV (1526)	6	11	9.1%	63.0	40.2
STETSON UNIV (1531)	5	6	50.0%	69.5	25.8
UNIV CENTRAL FL (3954)	12	28	75.0%	79.3	28.7
UNIV FL (1535)	17	37	67.6%	76.4	29.9
UNIV MIAMI (1536)	9	17	52.9%	75.1	30.2
UNIV NORTH FL (9841)	7	19	36.8%	72.7	28.5
Georgia					
CLARK ATLANTA UNIV (1559)	5	6	16.7%	56.5	32.7
GA COLL & ST UNIV (1602)	18	27	40.7%	67.7	29.7
GA SOUTHERN UNIV (1572)	20	34	29.4%	60.4	29.4
GA ST UNIV (1574)	40	84	67.9%	76.3	33.0
KENNESAW ST UNIV (1577)	28	49	53.1%	70.4	36.1
MERCER UNIV MACON (1580)	6	9	22.2%	71.0	35.3
UNIV GA (1598)	17	36	58.3%	78.1	29.2
UNIV WEST GA (1601)	7	8	12.5%	55.6	31.3
VALDOSTA ST UNIV (1599)	6	12	50.0%	71.3	35.2
Hawaii					
HI PACIFIC UNIV (7279)	8	12	50.0%	67.4	38.8
UNIV HI MANOA (1610)	10	17	52.9%	68.7	32.8
Idaho					
BOISE ST UNIV (1616)	11	23	60.9%	76.1	28.6
UNIV ID (1626)	11	23	56.5%	72.5	29.3
Illinois					
AMERICAN INTERCONT IL (666723)	5	8	0.0%	54.5	32.0
BENEDICTINE UNIV (1767)	6	8	0.0%	62.8	32.8

Appendix G: Summary Performance for Advanced Degree - First-Time Events

	Candidates Total	Sections Total	Percent Pass	Average Score	Average Age
BRADLEY UNIV (1641)	28	67	73.1%	80.9	25.2
DE PAUL UNIV (1671)	63	119	54.6%	75.1	32.8
DOMINCAN UNIV (1750)	9	17	35.3%	67.9	31.7
EASTERN IL UNIV (1674)	13	26	65.4%	74.4	27.8
GOVERNORS ST UNIV (9145)	10	25	4.0%	56.0	31.6
IL INST TECH (1691)	7	14	78.6%	76.1	29.4
IL ST UNIV (1692)	24	59	76.3%	77.5	26.4
KELLER GRAD SCHOOL DEVRY (20754)	109	191	20.4%	57.2	36.0
LEWIS UNIV (1707)	6	11	27.3%	66.6	32.3
LOYOLA UNIV CHICAGO (1710)	29	58	44.8%	70.5	30.6
NORTHEASTERN IL UNIV (1693)	7	9	55.6%	74.0	31.6
NORTHERN IL UNIV (1737)	44	96	54.2%	73.1	30.9
NORTHWESTERN UNIV (1739)	10	27	63.0%	76.9	42.1
ROOSEVELT UNIV (1749)	30	63	47.6%	69.6	31.3
SOUTHERN IL UNIV CARBONDALE (1758)	16	27	25.9%	61.4	25.6
SOUTHERN IL UNIV EDWARDSVILLE (1759)	25	61	65.6%	74.9	26.6
UNIV CHICAGO (1774)	16	30	60.0%	77.7	43.4
UNIV IL CHICAGO (1776)	52	100	57.0%	73.3	32.1
UNIV IL SPRINGFIELD (9333)	15	23	13.0%	61.8	30.6
UNIV IL URBANA CHAMPAIGN (1775)	60	123	65.0%	75.8	29.2
WESTERN IL UNIV (1780)	5	6	50.0%	69.8	28.4
Indiana					
BALL ST UNIV (1786)	8	12	58.3%	68.3	27.3
IN UNIV BLOOMINGTON (1809)	42	91	70.3%	76.9	30.4
IN UNIV PURDUE UNIV INDIANAPOLIS (1813)	22	40	50.0%	72.7	37.2
IN WESLEYAN UNIV (1822)	16	24	45.8%	65.3	34.9
PURDUE UNIV (1825)	18	34	50.0%	71.6	32.0
UNIV NOTRE DAME (1840)	61	113	58.4%	75.4	26.7
Iowa					
DRAKE UNIV (1860)	5	8	37.5%	62.5	31.3
IA ST UNIV (1869)	20	48	64.6%	74.7	27.9
MAHARISHI UNIV MANAGEMENT (11113)	5	7	42.9%	68.1	35.1
SAINT AMBROSE UNIV (1889)	9	19	31.6%	63.7	26.0
UNIV IA (1892)	19	47	70.2%	78.2	32.3
UNIV NORTHERN IA (1890)	5	10	70.0%	76.8	31.8
Kansas					
EMPORIA ST UNIV (1927)	10	16	31.3%	67.8	28.3
KANSAS STATE UNIVERSITY (1928)	15	34	67.7%	78.3	27.1
PITTSBURG ST UNIV (1926)	5	9	33.3%	74.3	29.3
UNIV KS (1948)	31	66	56.1%	72.0	28.3
Kentucky					
NORTHERN KY UNIV (9275)	8	15	40.0%	72.7	30.3
Louisiana					
LA ST UNIV AND A & M COLL (2010)	46	101	57.4%	75.7	26.0
LA TECH UNIV (2008)	16	30	40.0%	70.9	26.3
SOUTHEASTERN LA UNIV (2024)	14	26	26.9%	67.8	30.4
TULANE UNIV LA (2029)	38	78	62.8%	71.9	27.1
UNIV NEW ORLEANS (2015)	16	26	46.2%	70.4	28.8
Maine					
HUSSON UNIV (2043)	6	11	36.4%	69.2	25.9
UNIV ME (2053)	7	11	90.9%	79.5	26.7
UNIV SOUTHERN ME (2054)	5	13	38.5%	73.1	36.5

Appendix G: Summary Performance for Advanced Degree - First-Time Events

	Candidates Total	Sections Total	Percent Pass	Average Score	Average Age
Maryland					
UNIV BALTIMORE (2102)	6	8	50.0%	70.9	33.1
UNIV MD COLL PARK (2103)	13	32	53.1%	68.2	35.9
UNIV MD UNIV COLL (11644)	10	21	52.4%	74.7	33.4
Massachusetts					
BABSON COLL (2121)	13	28	35.7%	70.9	31.1
BENTLEY COLL (2124)	71	152	57.2%	75.0	28.9
BOSTON COLL (2128)	41	90	64.4%	77.0	27.6
BOSTON UNIV (2130)	6	10	80.0%	82.0	38.9
CLARK UNIV (2139)	7	11	54.6%	74.2	30.3
NORTHEASTERN UNIV (2199)	74	126	43.7%	70.6	29.1
SUFFOLK UNIV (2218)	41	79	53.2%	70.2	31.2
UNIV MA AMHERST (2221)	15	26	42.3%	71.3	29.3
UNIV MA BOSTON (2222)	21	44	52.3%	74.5	32.0
UNIV MA DARTMOUTH (2210)	7	13	23.1%	64.8	29.9
WESTERN NEW ENGLAND COLL (2226)	9	20	50.0%	75.3	31.1
WESTFIELD ST COLL (2189)	5	13	38.5%	68.8	25.9
Michigan					
BAKER COLL FLINT (4673)	5	13	46.2%	65.8	36.6
CENTRAL MI UNIV (2243)	7	14	35.7%	58.9	37.5
DAVENPORT UNIV (2249)	11	28	32.1%	68.7	29.6
EASTERN MI UNIV (2259)	51	85	37.7%	69.7	31.3
GRAND VALLEY ST UNIV (2268)	29	68	67.7%	78.0	29.2
MI ST UNIV (2290)	33	56	60.7%	75.4	30.2
OAKLAND UNIV (2307)	11	22	45.5%	70.2	31.1
UNIV MI ANN ARBOR (2325)	19	45	84.4%	82.2	30.9
UNIV MI DEARBORN (2326)	8	16	56.3%	76.9	31.2
WALSH COLL (4071)	47	89	50.6%	72.2	34.3
WAYNE ST UNIV (2329)	35	66	45.5%	71.6	35.2
WESTERN MI UNIV (2330)	23	50	54.0%	74.0	28.7
Minnesota					
METROPOLITAN ST UNIV (10374)	5	10	50.0%	73.2	43.3
UNIV MN TWIN CITIES (3969)	24	53	58.5%	75.2	32.6
UNIV ST THOMAS (2345)	12	29	44.8%	71.7	40.2
Mississippi					
MILLSAPS COLL (2414)	12	28	46.4%	70.6	27.3
MS COLL (2415)	6	8	62.5%	70.1	29.9
MS ST UNIV (2423)	14	27	22.2%	64.0	30.3
UNIV MS (2440)	22	52	61.5%	74.1	26.4
UNIV SOUTHERN MS (2441)	5	6	16.7%	62.8	33.7
Missouri					
FONTBONNE UNIV (2464)	5	7	0.0%	53.3	32.4
LINDENWOOD UNIV (2480)	12	24	33.3%	66.3	30.7
MO ST UNIV (2503)	31	68	54.4%	72.6	27.7
ROCKHURST UNIV (2499)	6	9	55.6%	72.6	27.3
ST. LOUIS UNIV (2506)	30	63	55.6%	71.7	26.8
TRUMAN ST UNIV (2495)	6	12	58.3%	78.5	24.5
UNIV CENTRAL MO (2454)	7	19	31.6%	69.5	27.6
UNIV MO COLUMBIA (2516)	37	79	68.4%	75.4	26.4
UNIV MO KANSAS CITY (2518)	22	49	77.6%	78.2	32.1
UNIV MO ST. LOUIS (2519)	21	47	66.0%	77.0	30.2
WASHINGTON UNIV ST. LOUIS (2520)	18	36	58.3%	74.8	25.4

Appendix G: Summary Performance for Advanced Degree - First-Time Events

	Candidates Total	Sections Total	Percent Pass	Average Score	Average Age
WEBSTER UNIV (2521)	22	43	25.6%	61.0	36.6
Montana					
MT ST UNIV BOZEMAN (2532)	6	7	71.4%	75.3	29.4
Nebraska					
UNIV NE LINCOLN (2565)	24	58	63.8%	77.8	26.5
UNIV NE OMAHA (2554)	5	6	83.3%	80.3	33.8
Nevada					
UNIV NV LAS VEGAS (2569)	27	44	38.6%	70.5	30.6
UNIV NV RENO (2568)	5	10	60.0%	79.5	31.9
New Hampshire					
SOUTHERN NH UNIV (2580)	10	23	34.8%	66.1	39.8
UNIV NH (2589)	8	15	73.3%	79.5	24.4
New Jersey					
FAIRLEIGH DICKINSON UNIV (2607)	57	104	51.9%	70.6	29.5
FAIRLEIGH DICKINSON UNIV MADISON (4738)	9	14	35.7%	74.9	39.1
FAIRLEIGH DICKINSON UNIV RUTHERFORD (2604)	11	22	45.5%	73.7	35.6
KEAN UNIV (2622)	10	14	57.1%	69.3	37.8
MONMOUTH UNIV (2616)	9	16	25.0%	57.8	29.8
MONTCLAIR ST UNIV (2617)	13	23	47.8%	69.5	32.1
NJ CITY UNIV (2613)	5	7	14.3%	62.3	42.1
RIDER UNIV (2628)	21	41	31.7%	65.3	30.4
RUTGERS ST UNIV NEW BRUNSWICK (6964)	25	45	42.2%	71.5	30.8
RUTGERS ST UNIV NEWARK (2631)	38	67	37.3%	66.4	30.1
SAINT PETERS COLL (2638)	5	12	33.3%	62.8	29.1
SETON HALL UNIV (2632)	11	17	41.2%	71.9	33.2
WILLIAM PATERSON UNIV NJ (2625)	5	10	10.0%	62.8	26.3
New Mexico					
NM ST UNIV (2657)	14	30	36.7%	69.7	30.7
UNIV NM (2663)	14	30	33.3%	72.1	33.5
New York					
ADELPHI UNIV (2666)	5	6	16.7%	47.5	33.0
COLL SAINT ROSE (2705)	7	17	29.4%	64.1	26.7
COLUMBIA UNIV NY (2707)	7	17	88.2%	81.8	36.2
CUNY BARUCH (7273)	105	209	66.5%	75.3	31.6
CUNY BROOKLYN (2687)	6	9	11.1%	55.7	40.8
CUNY QUEENS (2690)	7	12	50.0%	71.9	29.5
FORDHAM UNIV (2722)	23	35	51.4%	72.0	29.8
HOFSTRA UNIV (2732)	25	45	24.4%	66.1	27.8
LE MOYNE COLL (2748)	9	14	42.9%	64.9	24.5
LONG ISLAND UNIV BROOKLYN CENTER (4779)	8	9	0.0%	54.9	35.6
LONG ISLAND UNIV CW POST (2754)	24	38	36.8%	65.1	33.5
MARIST COLL (2765)	5	9	11.1%	61.4	26.3
NIAGARA UNIV (2788)	7	15	0.0%	60.3	23.9
NY INST TECH MANHATTAN (2782)	6	12	8.3%	63.3	33.2
NY UNIV (2785)	19	48	79.2%	79.3	35.3
PACE UNIV NY (2791)	59	91	45.1%	69.8	31.6
PACE UNIV PLEASANTVILLE (2792)	5	9	33.3%	67.4	25.8
ROCHESTER INST TECH (2806)	7	15	53.3%	66.9	33.1
SAINT BONAVENTURE UNIV (2817)	20	42	45.2%	70.1	24.1
SAINT FRANCIS COLL (2820)	6	9	33.3%	66.4	24.3
SAINT JOHNS UNIV NEW YORK (2823)	97	147	37.4%	65.8	27.3
SAINT JOSEPHS COLL NY (2825)	6	10	20.0%	60.6	28.7

Appendix G: Summary Performance for Advanced Degree - First-Time Events

	Candidates Total	Sections Total	Percent Pass	Average Score	Average Age
SIENA COLL (2816)	10	19	52.6%	72.5	23.8
SUNY ALBANY (2835)	44	74	50.0%	70.7	29.4
SUNY BINGHAMTON (2836)	38	76	42.1%	66.4	27.8
SUNY BUFFALO (2837)	14	28	60.7%	74.3	30.3
SUNY GENESEO (2845)	8	10	10.0%	63.1	26.7
SUNY OSWEGO (2848)	13	21	33.3%	63.0	25.1
SUNY STONY BROOK (2838)	5	8	62.5%	72.5	28.7
SYRACUSE UNIV (2882)	12	22	27.3%	65.0	29.7
UNIV ROCHESTER (2894)	8	16	87.5%	84.8	33.9
WAGNER COLL (2899)	13	19	21.1%	55.4	27.2
North Carolina					
EAST CAROLINA UNIV (2923)	15	28	42.9%	70.0	29.2
NC ST UNIV RALEIGH (2972)	10	22	72.7%	83.2	29.4
UNIV NC CHAPEL HILL (2974)	33	84	73.8%	78.8	27.1
UNIV NC CHARLOTTE (2975)	9	22	77.3%	83.4	29.8
UNIV NC GREENSBORO (2976)	10	18	88.9%	83.3	30.4
UNIV NC WILMINGTON (2984)	6	10	10.0%	63.0	31.7
WAKE FOREST UNIV (2978)	13	38	79.0%	78.9	26.5
Ohio					
ASHLAND UNIV (3012)	8	14	35.7%	64.9	40.7
BALDWIN WALLACE COLL (3014)	30	61	54.1%	70.7	29.6
BOWLING GREEN ST UNIV (3018)	33	66	57.6%	72.7	28.6
CAPITAL UNIV (3023)	5	7	57.1%	71.3	37.1
CASE WESTERN RESERVE UNIV (3024)	23	58	72.4%	77.4	29.3
CLEVELAND ST UNIV (3032)	49	97	49.5%	69.5	32.7
JOHN CARROLL UNIV (3050)	16	39	66.7%	75.8	28.2
KENT ST UNIV (3051)	21	48	54.2%	73.7	28.6
MIAMI UNIV (3077)	16	38	68.4%	76.2	25.5
OH ST UNIV (6883)	59	156	78.9%	81.7	25.6
OH UNIV (3100)	9	18	27.8%	61.4	30.4
UNIV AKRON (3123)	27	73	78.1%	78.8	29.3
UNIV CINCINNATI (3125)	12	19	36.8%	69.0	34.2
UNIV DAYTON (3127)	50	121	52.9%	73.3	24.2
UNIV FINDLAY (3045)	6	12	33.3%	62.7	31.2
UNIV TOLEDO (3131)	24	53	54.7%	71.6	30.3
WRIGHT ST UNIV (3078)	18	36	66.7%	77.9	30.2
XAVIER UNIV (3144)	14	27	59.3%	69.4	31.5
YOUNGSTOWN ST UNIV (3145)	8	15	46.7%	63.7	30.4
Oklahoma					
CAMERON UNIV (3150)	6	9	33.3%	58.9	36.5
NORTHEASTERN ST UNIV (3161)	6	11	18.2%	64.8	31.3
OK CHRISTIAN UNIV (3165)	7	20	80.0%	75.6	27.0
OK ST UNIV (3170)	28	64	67.2%	77.8	29.9
OKLAHOMA CITY UNIV (3166)	14	22	40.9%	68.9	30.7
UNIV CENTRAL OK (3152)	12	16	31.3%	69.5	32.1
UNIV OK NORMAN (3184)	34	77	75.3%	78.1	25.8
UNIV TULSA (3185)	8	12	25.0%	63.3	35.9
Oregon					
OR ST UNIV (3210)	12	26	73.1%	78.8	30.1
PORTLAND ST UNIV (3216)	13	26	65.4%	77.1	36.4
UNIV OR (3223)	37	75	72.0%	78.1	27.2

Appendix G: Summary Performance for Advanced Degree - First-Time Events

	Candidates Total	Sections Total	Percent Pass	Average Score	Average Age
Pennsylvania					
DREXEL UNIV (3256)	23	33	42.4%	67.9	30.0
DUQUESNE UNIV (3258)	14	27	74.1%	78.6	31.7
INDIANA UNIV PA (3277)	7	10	30.0%	67.3	42.0
LA SALLE UNIV (3287)	14	21	57.1%	69.9	29.6
LEHIGH UNIV (3289)	9	18	50.0%	73.1	25.5
PA ST UNIV PARK (3329)	24	67	59.7%	76.6	24.8
PHILADELPHIA UNIV (3354)	5	8	12.5%	55.3	40.0
ROBERT MORRIS UNIV (3359)	6	12	33.3%	68.9	28.1
SAINT JOSEPHS UNIV (3367)	10	12	16.7%	63.4	39.3
TEMPLE UNIV (3371)	7	15	60.0%	71.1	33.3
UNIV PA (3378)	5	11	81.8%	84.5	42.3
UNIV PITTSBURGH (3379)	12	26	69.2%	77.2	28.4
UNIV SCRANTON (3384)	13	21	66.7%	74.7	25.5
VILLANOVA UNIV (3388)	13	26	46.2%	72.4	28.1
WIDENER UNIV PA (3313)	7	10	40.0%	71.2	31.1
Puerto Rico					
INTER AMERICAN UNIV PR (8242)	8	11	9.1%	32.9	34.1
INTER AMERICAN UNIV PR METROPOLITAN (3940)	9	17	5.9%	47.6	34.8
INTER AMERICAN UNIV PR SAN GERMAN (3938)	5	7	0.0%	55.7	33.9
PONTIFICAL CATHOLIC UNIV PR (3936)	5	6	33.3%	50.7	30.5
UNIV PR RIO PIEDRAS (7108)	5	6	16.7%	62.2	36.5
Rhode Island					
BRYANT UNIV (3402)	22	42	57.1%	74.1	27.4
JOHNSON & WALES UNIV (3404)	14	24	41.7%	60.5	32.2
PROVIDENCE COLL (3406)	5	9	66.7%	80.7	28.0
UNIV RI (3414)	8	14	42.9%	72.3	34.4
South Carolina					
UNIV SC COLUMBIA (3448)	9	12	58.3%	79.8	33.3
South Dakota					
UNIV SD (3474)	23	41	53.7%	76.9	25.9
Tennessee					
BELMONT UNIV (3479)	16	30	40.0%	70.9	31.6
EAST TN ST UNIV (3487)	16	33	60.6%	73.9	28.4
LIPSCOMB UNIV (3486)	24	48	33.3%	64.7	25.2
MIDDLE TN ST UNIV (3510)	20	36	47.2%	70.4	27.3
RHODES COLL (3519)	12	21	47.6%	74.7	24.1
TN ST UNIV (3522)	6	12	33.3%	68.0	32.7
TN TECH UNIV (3523)	23	48	29.2%	69.0	30.4
UNIV MEMPHIS (3509)	7	13	30.8%	69.1	30.3
UNIV TN CHATTANOOGA (3529)	17	38	34.2%	64.0	29.9
UNIV TN KNOXVILLE (3530)	18	40	70.0%	77.4	28.1
UNIV TN MARTIN (3531)	6	12	50.0%	71.3	29.0
VANDERBILT UNIV (3535)	7	23	73.9%	81.1	29.1
Texas					
ABILENE CHRISTIAN UNIV (3537)	26	49	49.0%	72.0	25.2
ANGELO ST UNIV (3541)	15	35	65.7%	77.2	31.1
BAYLOR UNIV (3545)	27	81	87.7%	82.7	24.8
BAYLOR UNIV (6967)	7	14	57.1%	72.6	27.1
DALLAS BAPTIST UNIV (3560)	10	17	11.8%	58.9	37.0
HOUSTON BAPTIST UNIV (3576)	10	19	52.6%	73.5	31.7
LAMAR COLL (3581)	7	14	50.0%	73.2	26.6

Appendix G: Summary Performance for Advanced Degree - First-Time Events

	Candidates Total	Sections Total	Percent Pass	Average Score	Average Age
MIDWESTERN ST UNIV (3592)	12	20	35.0%	69.3	27.6
OUR LADY THE LAKE UNIV (3598)	5	10	20.0%	68.3	41.0
RICE UNIV (3604)	5	7	85.7%	79.7	36.4
SAINT EDWARDS UNIV (3621)	10	25	44.0%	72.1	36.1
SAINT MARYS UNIV (3623)	5	8	50.0%	68.0	48.9
SAM HOUSTON ST UNIV (3606)	26	49	44.9%	70.1	26.9
SOUTHERN METHODIST UNIV (3613)	31	66	71.2%	78.3	28.3
STEPHEN F AUSTIN ST UNIV (3624)	23	42	47.6%	68.8	27.1
TRINITY UNIV (3647)	18	37	54.1%	72.4	24.8
TX A&M UNIV (3632)	52	99	67.7%	78.3	28.4
TX A&M UNIV COMMERCE (3565)	19	39	38.5%	63.2	30.0
TX A&M UNIV CORPUS CHRISTI (11161)	18	28	35.7%	63.9	28.6
TX CHRISTIAN UNIV (3636)	21	49	63.3%	78.3	26.3
TX ST UNIV SAN MARCOS (3615)	49	96	68.8%	77.0	30.2
TX TECH UNIV (3644)	53	113	69.0%	76.8	26.2
TX WESLEYAN UNIV (3645)	7	15	26.7%	70.2	27.1
TX WOMANS UNIV (3646)	9	16	25.0%	60.8	34.1
UNIV DALLAS (3651)	22	35	40.0%	69.0	38.1
UNIV HOUSTON CLEAR LAKE (11711)	56	90	37.8%	64.7	33.2
UNIV HOUSTON UNIV PARK (3652)	106	198	56.1%	73.4	29.5
UNIV HOUSTON VICTORIA (13231)	9	15	20.0%	67.5	34.5
UNIV INCARNATE WORD (3578)	12	20	5.0%	48.2	31.8
UNIV NORTH TX (3594)	53	101	47.5%	71.5	30.6
UNIV SAINT THOMAS (3654)	37	64	45.3%	69.8	30.6
UNIV TX ARLINGTON (3656)	54	94	51.1%	73.5	31.1
UNIV TX AUSTIN (3658)	86	171	70.8%	78.2	29.4
UNIV TX DALLAS (9741)	94	189	45.0%	69.4	33.4
UNIV TX EL PASO (3661)	11	15	60.0%	73.3	34.0
UNIV TX PAN AMERICAN (3599)	8	12	16.7%	57.7	26.2
UNIV TX PERMIAN BASIN (9930)	5	8	75.0%	74.8	47.5
UNIV TX SAN ANTONIO (10115)	31	57	63.2%	74.3	30.4
UNIV TX TYLER (11163)	9	19	42.1%	69.6	26.6
WEST TX A & M UNIV (3665)	27	45	28.9%	66.8	30.2
Utah					
BRIGHAM YOUNG UNIV (3670)	157	395	85.8%	83.4	27.1
SOUTHERN UT UNIV (3678)	41	77	50.7%	72.4	27.6
UNIV UT (3675)	109	244	69.7%	77.9	29.6
UT ST UNIV (3677)	59	126	54.0%	75.3	30.6
WEBER ST UNIV (3680)	55	109	66.1%	75.2	30.8
WESTMINSTER COLL (3681)	20	32	43.8%	66.9	34.8
Vermont					
UNIV VT (3696)	5	12	83.3%	77.3	27.8
Virginia					
COLL WILLIAM & MARY (3705)	42	100	62.0%	75.8	25.7
GEORGE MASON UNIV (3749)	16	31	51.6%	72.9	32.2
HAMPTON UNIV (3714)	5	7	0.0%	54.1	25.9
JAMES MADISON UNIV (3721)	15	42	85.7%	83.1	24.0
LIBERTY UNIV (20530)	14	22	36.4%	64.9	31.9
OLD DOMINION UNIV (3728)	14	27	44.4%	72.9	31.3
UNIV VA (3745)	29	58	65.5%	77.0	27.3
VA COMMONWEALTH UNIV (3735)	16	24	54.2%	70.8	27.3
VA POLYTECHNIC INST & ST UNIV (3754)	25	55	69.1%	77.8	27.4

Appendix G: Summary Performance for Advanced Degree - First-Time Events

	Candidates Total	Sections Total	Percent Pass	Average Score	Average Age
Washington					
CENTRAL WA UNIV (3771)	6	15	46.7%	69.5	28.8
GONZAGA UNIV (3778)	9	20	65.0%	75.8	31.5
SEATTLE UNIV (3790)	7	20	60.0%	77.7	32.3
UNIV WA (3798)	11	25	76.0%	79.2	36.5
WA ST UNIV (3800)	11	26	57.7%	75.5	26.8
WESTERN WA UNIV (3802)	6	12	66.7%	76.8	26.4
West Virginia					
WV UNIV (3827)	13	27	74.1%	77.1	28.2
WV WESLEYAN COLL (3830)	6	12	66.7%	72.5	23.9
Wisconsin					
EDGEWOOD COLL (3848)	5	8	50.0%	73.0	28.0
MARQUETTE UNIV (3863)	11	15	46.7%	74.0	28.0
UNIV WI MADISON (3895)	26	58	74.1%	78.9	28.9
UNIV WI MILWAUKEE (3896)	22	36	63.9%	78.2	31.7
UNIV WI WHITEWATER (3926)	45	85	42.4%	69.8	28.9
Wyoming					
UNIV WY (3932)	11	21	61.9%	76.1	29.5

BACHELOR'S DEGREE

FIRST-TIME TESTING EVENTS

APPENDIX H

SUMMARY PERFORMANCE

Appendix H: Summary Performance for Bachelor's Degree - First-Time Events

	Candidates Total	Sections Total	Percent Pass	Average Score	Average Age
Alabama					
ATHENS ST UNIV (1008)	12	15	20.0%	58.8	40.4
AUBURN UNIV (1009)	149	403	68.7%	77.6	25.6
AUBURN UNIV MONTGOMERY (8310)	20	32	12.5%	62.8	28.9
BIRMINGHAM SOUTHERN COLL (1012)	29	57	29.8%	65.1	26.0
HUNTINGDON COLL (1019)	8	17	58.8%	73.3	29.9
JACKSONVILLE ST UNIV (1020)	11	21	52.4%	67.9	27.0
OAKWOOD COLL (1033)	8	13	38.5%	65.8	25.6
SAMFORD UNIV (1036)	20	43	69.8%	76.9	24.6
TROY UNIV (1047)	49	96	28.1%	64.5	29.9
UNIV AL (1051)	173	427	56.4%	73.8	25.1
UNIV AL BIRMINGHAM (1052)	75	158	45.6%	71.9	29.2
UNIV AL HUNTSVILLE (1055)	15	22	40.9%	70.6	32.7
UNIV MONTEVALLO (1004)	11	19	47.4%	68.4	29.3
UNIV NORTH AL (1016)	12	31	58.1%	73.8	29.9
UNIV SOUTH AL (1057)	44	82	39.0%	70.4	31.1
Alaska					
UNIV ALASKA ANCHORAGE (11462)	36	55	29.1%	63.9	30.7
UNIV ALASKA FAIRBANKS (1063)	9	17	41.2%	67.1	33.3
UNIV ALASKA SOUTHEAST (1065)	6	10	50.0%	71.3	34.8
Arizona					
AZ ST UNIV (1081)	284	588	59.0%	74.8	29.1
AZ ST UNIV WEST (66935)	9	15	53.3%	71.4	33.8
DEVRY UNIV PHOENIX (8322)	32	73	27.4%	61.1	34.2
GRAND CANYON UNIV (1074)	6	10	20.0%	60.1	30.6
NORTHERN AZ UNIV (1082)	61	112	44.6%	69.9	27.6
UNIV AZ (1083)	166	354	53.1%	72.6	27.9
UNIV PHOENIX (20988)	201	358	27.4%	61.2	38.2
WESTERN INTL UNIV (21715)	9	17	58.8%	72.1	40.8
Arkansas					
AR ST UNIV (1090)	24	48	18.8%	61.5	27.3
AR TECH UNIV (1089)	22	57	54.4%	71.1	28.5
HARDING UNIV (1097)	43	93	43.0%	71.5	25.0
HENDERSON ST UNIV (1098)	10	24	16.7%	63.1	25.7
HENDRIX COLL (1099)	6	11	18.2%	59.5	26.5
OUACHITA BAPTIST UNIV (1102)	14	22	45.5%	69.6	25.0
SOUTHERN AR UNIV (1107)	12	20	20.0%	61.7	30.5
UNIV AR (1108)	59	150	53.3%	73.1	26.8
UNIV AR LITTLE ROCK (1101)	19	33	42.4%	66.0	35.3
UNIV AR MONTICELLO (1085)	9	14	35.7%	64.9	27.0
UNIV CENTRAL AR (1092)	40	76	34.2%	68.3	30.4
California					
AZUSA PACIFIC UNIV (1117)	18	32	25.0%	62.3	24.6
BIOLA UNIV (1122)	24	41	29.3%	66.3	25.0
CA BAPTIST UNIV (1125)	15	21	14.3%	57.6	29.1
CA LUTHERAN UNIV (1133)	15	30	23.3%	64.3	27.7
CA ST POLYTECH UNIV POMONA (1144)	126	218	26.2%	61.7	28.2
CA ST POLYTECH UNIV SAN LUIS OBISPO (1143)	204	372	51.1%	72.1	25.2
CA ST UNIV BAKERSFIELD (7993)	35	68	45.6%	67.9	30.2
CA ST UNIV CHICO (1146)	68	115	37.4%	68.4	28.4
CA ST UNIV DOMINGUEZ HILLS (1141)	32	51	27.5%	59.5	37.2
CA ST UNIV EAST BAY (1138)	134	247	37.7%	64.4	32.7

Appendix H: Summary Performance for Bachelor's Degree - First-Time Events

	Candidates Total	Sections Total	Percent Pass	Average Score	Average Age
CA ST UNIV FRESNO (1147)	114	187	36.9%	68.1	29.3
CA ST UNIV FULLERTON (1137)	324	614	36.5%	66.1	29.2
CA ST UNIV LONG BEACH (1139)	198	358	39.7%	67.3	30.1
CA ST UNIV LOS ANGELES (1140)	154	278	25.5%	61.2	32.1
CA ST UNIV NORTHRIDGE (1153)	270	507	46.6%	70.3	30.4
CA ST UNIV SACRAMENTO (1150)	194	350	35.7%	65.1	29.8
CA ST UNIV SAN BERNARDINO (1142)	72	117	20.5%	63.3	30.2
CA ST UNIV SAN MARCOS (30113)	61	111	55.0%	72.9	29.1
CA ST UNIV STANISLAUS (1157)	34	51	31.4%	65.3	31.7
CHAPMAN UNIV (1164)	46	86	54.7%	73.3	26.7
CLAREMONT MCKENNA COLL (1170)	22	41	68.3%	79.3	24.0
DEVRY UNIV LONG BEACH (666988)	12	20	10.0%	48.9	33.5
DEVRY UNIV POMONA (23329)	12	25	24.0%	59.0	32.7
FRESNO PACIFIC UNIV (1253)	11	18	44.4%	66.6	26.4
GOLDEN GATE UNIV (1205)	7	13	23.1%	55.7	34.8
HUMBOLDT ST UNIV (1149)	14	22	40.9%	68.5	30.4
LA SIERRA UNIV (1215)	6	9	0.0%	51.9	31.3
LOYOLA MARYMOUNT UNIV (11649)	73	157	52.9%	73.3	24.4
MASTERS COLL & SEMINARY (1220)	12	26	46.2%	70.5	23.8
MENLO COLL (1236)	5	9	11.1%	55.6	28.4
MOUNT SAINT MARYS COLL (1243)	10	20	40.0%	69.2	26.1
NATIONAL UNIV (11460)	20	34	35.3%	65.0	39.9
PACIFIC UNION COLL (1258)	8	17	58.8%	72.6	25.0
PEPPERDINE (1264)	23	41	51.2%	72.5	25.6
POINT LOMA NAZARENE UNIV (1262)	17	28	53.6%	74.4	23.8
SAINT MARYS COLL CA (1302)	35	66	31.8%	64.8	26.4
SAN DIEGO ST UNIV (1151)	236	412	44.9%	69.4	27.3
SAN FRANCISCO ST UNIV (1154)	173	303	35.3%	64.3	30.1
SAN JOSE ST UNIV (1155)	209	378	41.0%	67.2	29.6
SANTA CLARA UNIV (1326)	193	348	48.6%	70.6	24.3
SIMPSON UNIV (1291)	7	19	31.6%	63.0	25.5
SONOMA ST UNIV (1156)	90	148	26.4%	65.6	27.6
UNIV CA BERKELEY (1312)	236	496	62.1%	75.4	26.3
UNIV CA DAVIS (1313)	89	160	52.5%	71.6	27.5
UNIV CA IRVINE (1314)	153	285	46.7%	68.6	26.4
UNIV CA LOS ANGELES (1315)	372	764	65.3%	76.1	25.5
UNIV CA RIVERSIDE (1316)	140	266	31.2%	65.8	26.2
UNIV CA SAN DIEGO (1317)	72	119	46.2%	69.0	27.6
UNIV CA SANTA BARBARA (1320)	389	724	51.4%	71.9	25.4
UNIV CA SANTA CRUZ (1321)	126	213	39.9%	68.6	26.0
UNIV LA VERNE (1216)	14	30	40.0%	65.5	28.6
UNIV PACIFIC (1329)	26	49	53.1%	72.0	26.1
UNIV REDLANDS (1322)	21	33	24.2%	60.0	25.6
UNIV SAN DIEGO (10395)	106	201	52.2%	73.0	24.5
UNIV SAN FRANCISCO (1325)	53	105	24.8%	59.9	26.9
UNIV SOUTHERN CA (1328)	368	794	56.9%	73.9	25.0
VANGUARD UNIV SOUTHERN CA (1293)	5	10	80.0%	78.6	27.6
Colorado					
CO COLL (1347)	6	10	70.0%	77.3	42.2
CO ST UNIV (1350)	103	207	64.3%	75.6	27.9
FORT LEWIS COLL (1353)	29	47	27.7%	63.3	29.8
MESA ST COLL (1358)	18	34	41.2%	74.0	27.4

Appendix H: Summary Performance for Bachelor's Degree - First-Time Events

	Candidates Total	Sections Total	Percent Pass	Average Score	Average Age
METRO ST COLL DENVER (1360)	70	131	34.4%	65.3	34.7
REGIS UNIV (1363)	45	98	48.0%	69.2	34.6
UNIV CO BOULDER (1370)	87	174	49.4%	73.7	28.6
UNIV CO COLORADO SPRINGS (4509)	30	56	48.2%	69.3	31.2
UNIV CO DENVER (6740)	67	106	33.0%	64.3	28.8
UNIV DENVER (1371)	32	56	60.7%	73.8	26.0
UNIV NORTHERN CO (1349)	40	75	34.7%	67.8	29.0
UNIV SOUTHERN CO (1365)	17	33	42.4%	72.2	30.1
WESTERN ST COLL (1372)	9	20	70.0%	75.3	29.7
Connecticut					
CENTRAL CT ST UNIV (1378)	39	70	44.3%	67.7	31.6
EASTERN CT ST UNIV (1425)	23	34	41.2%	67.5	31.2
FAIRFIELD UNIV (1385)	109	210	54.3%	73.6	24.1
QUINNIPIAC UNIV (1402)	56	120	40.0%	68.4	24.0
SACRED HEART UNIV (1403)	40	64	25.0%	63.3	26.4
SOUTHERN CT ST UNIV (1406)	23	39	28.2%	66.3	28.3
TEIKYO POST UNIV (1401)	9	16	37.5%	59.3	24.4
UNIV BRIDGEPORT (1416)	8	12	25.0%	61.8	29.5
UNIV CT (1417)	227	427	54.8%	74.3	24.3
UNIV HARTFORD (1422)	16	32	34.4%	62.9	26.8
UNIV NEW HAVEN (1397)	9	15	20.0%	66.7	27.5
WESTERN CT ST UNIV (1380)	20	37	51.4%	71.4	32.3
Delaware					
DE ST UNIV (1428)	7	10	20.0%	66.7	27.9
GOLDEY BEACOM COLL (1429)	20	30	13.3%	58.1	31.2
UNIV DE (1431)	180	387	56.9%	73.9	24.7
WILMINGTON COLL (7948)	19	43	30.2%	64.9	37.5
District of Columbia					
AMERICAN UNIV (1434)	50	109	55.1%	75.0	24.8
CATHOLIC UNIV OF AMERICA (1437)	5	8	12.5%	53.5	25.0
GEORGE WASHINGTON UNIV (1444)	47	103	61.2%	75.9	28.4
GEORGETOWN UNIV (1445)	40	97	72.2%	80.0	27.0
HOWARD UNIV (1448)	36	62	17.7%	59.9	28.3
SOUTHEASTERN UNIV (1456)	5	13	61.5%	72.7	27.5
STRAYER COLL (1459)	66	99	16.2%	53.7	35.6
UNIV DC (1441)	10	17	0.0%	48.5	41.6
Florida					
BARRY UNIV (1466)	7	11	63.6%	71.2	31.9
FL A&M UNIV (1480)	14	19	5.3%	57.4	27.3
FL ATLANTIC UNIV (1481)	43	73	45.2%	68.3	33.8
FL GULF COAST UNIV (32553)	9	19	36.8%	69.2	28.0
FL INTL UNIV (9635)	66	105	46.7%	72.1	30.8
FL ST UNIV (1489)	71	145	55.9%	74.9	28.5
FLAGLER COLL (7893)	5	9	44.4%	65.2	32.0
NOVA SOUTHEASTERN UNIV (1509)	13	16	25.0%	55.7	33.6
PENSACOLA CHRISTIAN COLL (99998)	8	18	38.9%	67.0	26.3
SAINT LEO UNIV (1526)	18	31	41.9%	67.1	33.9
STETSON UNIV (1531)	8	14	28.6%	68.4	29.7
UNIV CENTRAL FL (3954)	72	136	48.5%	72.4	28.8
UNIV FL (1535)	87	186	70.4%	77.9	27.4
UNIV MIAMI (1536)	54	118	62.7%	76.2	25.3
UNIV NORTH FL (9841)	18	35	57.1%	74.5	30.8

Appendix H: Summary Performance for Bachelor's Degree - First-Time Events

	Candidates Total	Sections Total	Percent Pass	Average Score	Average Age
UNIV SOUTH FL (1537)	83	163	64.4%	75.6	29.0
UNIV TAMPA (1538)	24	50	54.0%	72.3	25.7
UNIV WEST FL (3955)	7	12	41.7%	73.0	33.7
Georgia					
AUGUSTA ST UNIV (1552)	15	27	33.3%	66.4	30.8
BERRY COLL (1554)	11	26	46.2%	73.8	26.0
BRENAU UNIV (1556)	6	10	30.0%	53.0	29.2
CLARK ATLANTA UNIV (1559)	7	16	12.5%	50.3	28.0
CLAYTON ST UNIV (8976)	25	49	40.8%	68.3	33.5
COLUMBUS ST UNIV (1561)	7	13	38.5%	64.6	37.5
DEVRY UNIV ALPHARETTA (666989)	5	8	0.0%	49.5	36.2
DEVRY UNIV DECATUR (9224)	13	18	22.2%	55.3	36.8
EMORY UNIV (1564)	46	99	66.7%	79.2	24.0
GA COLL & ST UNIV (1602)	17	32	37.5%	67.3	29.5
GA INST TECH (1569)	47	106	60.4%	76.6	26.1
GA SOUTHERN UNIV (1572)	74	173	49.7%	71.9	25.5
GA SOUTHWESTERN ST UNIV (1573)	11	20	45.0%	63.3	32.9
GA ST UNIV (1574)	230	413	37.5%	67.3	28.7
KENNESAW ST UNIV (1577)	111	184	42.4%	67.3	31.6
LAGRANGE COLL (1578)	6	9	44.4%	62.9	26.8
MACON ST COLL (7728)	18	35	45.7%	68.3	29.9
MERCER UNIV ATLANTA (8419)	6	10	60.0%	71.2	24.3
MERCER UNIV MACON (1580)	14	30	60.0%	71.3	28.3
MOREHOUSE COLL (1582)	10	20	55.0%	71.6	26.1
NORTH GA COLL & ST UNIV (1585)	32	63	55.6%	73.9	29.8
OGLETHORPE UNIV (1586)	12	19	68.4%	76.6	27.3
SHORTER COLL (1591)	9	19	26.3%	63.2	29.4
UNIV GA (1598)	195	507	74.0%	78.3	25.8
UNIV WEST GA (1601)	22	48	22.9%	61.8	27.3
VALDOSTA ST UNIV (1599)	48	79	43.0%	67.6	28.1
Guam					
UNIV GU (3935)	14	17	41.2%	61.4	35.7
Hawaii					
BRIGHAM YOUNG UNIV HI (1606)	30	67	47.8%	70.3	28.7
HI PACIFIC UNIV (7279)	20	36	30.6%	63.4	32.6
UNIV HI HILO (1611)	7	12	41.7%	72.2	27.6
UNIV HI MANOA (1610)	98	175	37.7%	66.7	28.8
UNIV HI WEST OAHU (21078)	7	11	36.4%	66.7	39.1
Idaho					
ALBERTSON COLL (1617)	8	19	31.6%	66.8	27.2
BOISE ST UNIV (1616)	51	105	45.7%	70.3	29.8
BRIGHAM YOUNG UNIV ID (1625)	69	134	55.2%	73.8	27.8
ID ST UNIV (1620)	27	51	51.0%	71.7	30.1
LEWIS CLARK ST COLL (1621)	12	27	44.4%	71.5	31.1
UNIV ID (1626)	40	79	45.6%	71.1	26.1
Illinois					
AMERICAN INTERCONT IL (666723)	6	14	0.0%	37.4	37.6
AUGUSTANA COLL (1633)	15	30	60.0%	71.9	25.7
AURORA UNIV (1634)	8	16	25.0%	65.6	29.1
BENEDICTINE UNIV (1767)	18	35	37.1%	59.6	28.6
BRADLEY UNIV (1641)	41	93	58.1%	74.4	25.8
CHICAGO ST UNIV (1694)	18	25	16.0%	62.0	36.6

Appendix H: Summary Performance for Bachelor's Degree - First-Time Events

	Candidates Total	Sections Total	Percent Pass	Average Score	Average Age
DE PAUL UNIV (1671)	290	548	38.3%	67.5	26.5
DEVRY UNIV ADDISON (22966)	29	65	29.2%	59.9	32.4
DEVRY UNIV OAK BROOK TERRACE (1672)	20	40	5.0%	52.6	35.0
DOMINCAN UNIV (1750)	7	16	0.0%	53.6	26.6
EASTERN IL UNIV (1674)	37	80	45.0%	67.5	27.8
ELMHURST COLL (1676)	22	48	39.6%	68.3	26.6
GOVERNORS ST UNIV (9145)	18	33	36.4%	71.2	37.0
IL ST UNIV (1692)	113	310	59.7%	75.0	26.1
IL WESLEYAN UNIV (1696)	36	100	64.0%	76.4	23.0
KELLER GRAD SCHOOL DEVRY (20754)	8	19	10.5%	55.2	40.7
LEWIS UNIV (1707)	13	22	50.0%	72.7	28.8
LOYOLA UNIV CHICAGO (1710)	130	263	50.6%	71.7	25.4
MCKENDREE UNIVERSITY (1722)	13	26	42.3%	67.7	28.3
MILLIKIN UNIV (1724)	19	39	35.9%	65.4	30.4
MONMOUTH COLL (1725)	6	13	53.9%	72.4	26.6
NORTH CENTRAL COLL (1734)	29	57	50.9%	73.7	26.4
NORTH PARK UNIV (1735)	6	15	53.3%	73.5	25.4
NORTHEASTERN IL UNIV (1693)	46	83	47.0%	67.7	33.6
NORTHERN IL UNIV (1737)	215	490	58.2%	74.8	26.8
NORTHWESTERN UNIV (1739)	8	19	57.9%	74.2	29.0
OLIVET NAZARENE UNIV (1741)	8	20	65.0%	77.1	23.9
QUINCY UNIV (1745)	7	11	54.6%	76.7	28.5
ROBERT MORRIS COLL (1746)	21	31	22.6%	61.5	30.1
ROCKFORD COLL (1748)	6	10	50.0%	71.8	29.8
ROOSEVELT UNIV (1749)	24	43	27.9%	63.9	34.6
SAINT XAVIER UNIV (1768)	11	20	45.0%	67.5	26.7
SOUTHERN IL UNIV CARBONDALE (1758)	59	112	44.6%	69.3	27.6
SOUTHERN IL UNIV EDWARDSVILLE (1759)	44	92	45.7%	69.9	28.7
TRINITY CHRISTIAN COLL (1771)	11	21	66.7%	79.2	24.7
UNIV CHICAGO (1774)	5	8	37.5%	73.0	28.0
UNIV IL CHICAGO (1776)	308	802	64.0%	75.7	25.1
UNIV IL SPRINGFIELD (9333)	16	38	31.6%	63.9	29.7
UNIV IL URBANA CHAMPAIGN (1775)	342	869	59.4%	74.2	25.3
UNIV SAINT FRANCIS (1664)	6	13	46.2%	66.1	25.6
WESTERN IL UNIV (1780)	27	56	41.1%	70.2	29.0
WHEATON COLL (1781)	7	12	75.0%	80.4	32.4
Indiana					
ANDERSON UNIV (1785)	5	14	78.6%	79.6	24.9
BALL ST UNIV (1786)	67	147	44.2%	69.2	27.1
BETHEL COLL (IN) (1787)	7	19	57.9%	73.9	24.3
BUTLER UNIV (1788)	35	86	62.8%	74.2	27.3
FRANKLIN COLL IN (1798)	11	20	25.0%	68.5	25.5
GOSHEN COLL (1799)	18	42	66.7%	76.4	24.1
GRACE COLL & SEMINARY (1800)	8	15	66.7%	79.8	24.7
HUNTINGTON COLL (1803)	5	9	22.2%	55.4	28.1
IN INST TECH (1805)	6	10	40.0%	66.2	30.8
IN ST UNIV (1807)	29	52	26.9%	62.9	28.4
IN UNIV BLOOMINGTON (1809)	334	818	64.1%	75.8	25.6
IN UNIV NORTHWEST (1815)	7	14	50.0%	67.9	31.3
IN UNIV PURDUE UNIV FORT WAYNE (1828)	17	33	45.5%	71.7	26.7
IN UNIV PURDUE UNIV INDIANAPOLIS (1813)	87	177	46.3%	70.9	30.4
IN UNIV SOUTH BEND (1816)	15	38	44.7%	64.3	30.0

Appendix H: Summary Performance for Bachelor's Degree - First-Time Events

	Candidates Total	Sections Total	Percent Pass	Average Score	Average Age
IN UNIV SOUTHEAST (1817)	19	40	40.0%	68.9	30.0
IN WESLEYAN UNIV (1822)	26	52	34.6%	65.6	30.6
MANCHESTER COLL (1820)	28	62	43.6%	68.4	24.3
MARIAN COLL (1821)	11	21	23.8%	66.1	30.2
PURDUE UNIV (1825)	161	377	41.6%	67.6	26.7
SAINT JOSEPHS COLL (1833)	5	14	35.7%	63.4	26.8
SAINT MARYS COLL (1836)	22	44	34.1%	69.5	23.8
TAYLOR UNIV (1838)	10	22	68.2%	76.1	22.9
TRINE UNIV (1839)	6	7	28.6%	68.6	29.6
UNIV EVANSVILLE (1795)	15	27	37.0%	70.2	25.5
UNIV INDIANAPOLIS (1804)	13	26	30.8%	65.5	28.4
UNIV NOTRE DAME (1840)	167	486	75.1%	80.1	23.5
UNIV SOUTHERN IN (1808)	32	68	47.1%	71.4	26.6
UNIV ST FRANCIS (1832)	5	7	28.6%	69.9	24.7
VALPARAISO UNIV (1842)	14	29	51.7%	71.6	24.6
Iowa					
AIB COLL BUSINESS (3963)	9	17	5.9%	52.4	26.5
BRIAR CLIFF UNIV (1846)	8	17	52.9%	69.5	29.6
BUENA VISTA UNIV (1847)	13	29	13.8%	64.1	28.9
CLARKE COLL (1852)	5	5	20.0%	62.0	36.2
COE COLL (1854)	9	19	47.4%	71.2	25.4
DORDT COLL (1859)	6	16	50.0%	75.2	23.6
DRAKE UNIV (1860)	27	59	54.2%	71.3	26.3
GRAND VIEW UNIV (1867)	6	11	36.4%	67.1	31.1
IA ST UNIV (1869)	94	231	51.5%	72.5	26.4
KAPLAN UNIV (4586)	16	38	31.6%	59.5	40.0
LORAS COLL (1873)	11	28	60.7%	74.9	24.2
LUTHER COLL (1874)	18	39	53.9%	74.1	27.1
MORNINGSIDE COLL (1879)	5	9	66.7%	74.9	38.4
NORTHWESTERN COLL IA (1883)	16	29	55.2%	75.0	25.7
SAINT AMBROSE UNIV (1889)	8	13	38.5%	70.6	24.8
SIMPSON COLL (1887)	15	30	43.3%	67.3	25.4
UNIV DUBUQUE (1891)	8	23	8.7%	62.0	25.8
UNIV IA (1892)	148	365	72.3%	78.6	26.1
UNIV NORTHERN IA (1890)	89	305	64.9%	77.2	24.2
UPPER IA UNIV (1893)	22	35	31.4%	63.4	33.9
WARTBURG COLL (1896)	6	14	78.6%	75.4	23.5
Kansas					
BAKER UNIV (1903)	8	16	12.5%	63.3	28.4
BENEDICTINE COLL (10256)	7	17	23.5%	63.8	26.9
EMPORIA ST UNIV (1927)	12	19	10.5%	65.1	27.7
FORT HAYS ST UNIV (1915)	33	62	30.7%	65.8	26.8
FRIENDS UNIV (1918)	5	14	28.6%	62.5	25.6
KANSAS STATE UNIVERSITY (1928)	50	147	66.0%	76.6	26.1
NEWMAN UNIV (1939)	5	10	30.0%	61.9	30.7
OTTAWA UNIV (1937)	8	17	23.5%	57.6	34.8
PITTSBURG ST UNIV (1926)	18	31	16.1%	61.7	25.9
UNIV KS (1948)	132	367	62.7%	76.0	25.5
WASHBURN UNIV (1949)	28	67	32.8%	67.7	30.5
WICHITA ST UNIV (1950)	50	103	54.4%	72.1	29.5

Appendix H: Summary Performance for Bachelor's Degree - First-Time Events

	Candidates Total	Sections Total	Percent Pass	Average Score	Average Age
Kentucky					
ASBURY COLL (1952)	5	13	46.2%	70.9	28.1
BELLARMINE UNIV (1954)	33	69	49.3%	72.0	24.9
BEREA COLL (1955)	5	10	50.0%	70.4	25.7
BRESCIA UNIV (1958)	7	10	30.0%	67.3	26.6
EASTERN KY UNIV (1963)	28	42	42.9%	69.5	29.7
GEORGETOWN COLL (1964)	5	9	22.2%	55.6	26.4
KY ST UNIV (1968)	6	11	9.1%	57.0	28.2
KY WESLEYAN COLL (1969)	7	17	52.9%	70.2	24.0
LINDSEY WILSON COLL (1972)	8	15	20.0%	61.7	34.0
MOREHEAD ST UNIV (1976)	8	20	55.0%	73.5	26.6
MURRAY ST UNIV (1977)	43	67	40.3%	70.6	27.1
NORTHERN KY UNIV (9275)	44	98	39.8%	70.3	27.8
SPALDING UNIV (1960)	6	13	23.1%	62.8	39.8
SULLIVAN UNIV (4619)	12	22	18.2%	55.9	37.7
THOMAS MORE COLL (2001)	8	16	43.8%	68.8	26.0
TRANSYLVANIA UNIV (1987)	23	48	45.8%	72.1	23.9
UNIV KY (1989)	152	334	54.5%	73.6	26.3
UNIV LOUISVILLE (1999)	81	141	37.6%	66.2	31.2
UNIV OF CUMBERLANDS (1962)	5	7	71.4%	75.4	28.1
WESTERN KY UNIV (2002)	49	107	58.9%	75.2	28.5
Louisiana					
DILLARD UNIV (2004)	5	9	0.0%	50.2	27.1
GRAMBLING ST UNIV (2006)	13	19	10.5%	55.3	28.6
LA ST UNIV AND A & M COLL (2010)	175	364	52.2%	73.3	26.0
LA ST UNIV IN SHREVEPORT (2013)	15	24	50.0%	69.9	34.2
LA TECH UNIV (2008)	25	56	48.2%	72.1	29.4
LOYOLA UNIV NEW ORLEANS (2016)	27	57	56.1%	71.3	28.1
MCNEESE ST UNIV (2017)	35	68	42.7%	68.5	29.9
NICHOLLS ST UNIV (2005)	23	43	55.8%	72.2	29.2
NORTHWESTERN ST UNIV (2021)	19	32	31.3%	65.3	28.0
OUR LADY HOLY CROSS COLL (2023)	9	18	0.0%	38.9	34.6
SOUTHEASTERN LA UNIV (2024)	75	134	29.9%	64.9	28.6
SOUTHERN UNIV A&M BATON ROUGE (9636)	9	12	16.7%	61.6	38.6
TULANE UNIV LA (2029)	32	71	63.4%	74.2	26.4
UNIV LA LAFAYETTE (2031)	63	135	70.4%	78.7	26.9
UNIV LA MONROE (2020)	27	55	27.3%	64.3	27.1
UNIV NEW ORLEANS (2015)	75	139	36.0%	66.4	30.8
XAVIER UNIV LA (2032)	5	5	20.0%	39.8	29.8
Maine					
COLBY COLL (2039)	5	8	62.5%	79.0	32.3
HUSSON UNIV (2043)	10	12	41.7%	62.2	35.2
UNIV ME (2053)	22	36	61.1%	74.3	26.9
UNIV ME AUGUSTA (6760)	5	9	66.7%	77.6	36.3
UNIV SOUTHERN ME (2054)	19	30	63.3%	77.9	30.7
Maryland					
BOWIE ST UNIV (2062)	11	16	0.0%	60.6	34.5
LOYOLA UNIVERSITY MD (2078)	50	113	58.4%	74.9	23.5
MORGAN ST UNIV (2083)	8	10	10.0%	54.4	32.3
SALISBURY UNIV (2091)	10	19	47.4%	73.8	25.4
TOWSON UNIV (2099)	25	47	48.9%	69.7	30.7
UNIV BALTIMORE (2102)	12	20	40.0%	69.5	36.0

Appendix H: Summary Performance for Bachelor's Degree - First-Time Events

	Candidates Total	Sections Total	Percent Pass	Average Score	Average Age
UNIV MD BALTIMORE COUNTY (2105)	9	18	22.2%	64.9	26.2
UNIV MD COLL PARK (2103)	166	318	55.0%	73.6	26.7
UNIV MD EASTERN SHORE (2106)	5	7	14.3%	69.4	27.8
UNIV MD UNIV COLL (11644)	67	137	34.3%	66.0	30.3
Massachusetts					
AMERICAN INTL COLL (2114)	6	10	50.0%	73.8	29.9
ASSUMPTION COLL (2118)	46	88	43.2%	67.1	24.7
BABSON COLL (2121)	53	108	55.6%	74.4	23.5
BENTLEY COLL (2124)	191	388	53.9%	72.4	25.0
BOSTON COLL (2128)	132	309	80.3%	80.8	23.8
BOSTON UNIV (2130)	86	183	63.4%	75.8	24.4
BRIDGEWATER ST COLL (2183)	10	17	58.8%	73.7	33.3
COLL HOLY CROSS (2141)	30	73	68.5%	76.8	23.3
COLL OUR LADY OF THE ELMS (2140)	5	5	0.0%	53.2	24.3
GORDON COLL (2153)	6	11	27.3%	63.4	26.0
MA INST TECH (2178)	5	12	91.7%	87.8	36.8
MERRIMACK COLL (2120)	20	33	36.4%	65.0	26.9
NICHOLS COLL (2197)	11	22	13.6%	60.8	26.9
NORTHEASTERN UNIV (2199)	103	219	48.9%	71.0	26.3
SALEM ST UNIV (2188)	21	37	27.0%	59.8	27.9
STONEHILL COLL (2217)	46	86	54.7%	72.8	24.3
SUFFOLK UNIV (2218)	37	71	31.0%	62.8	26.0
TUFTS UNIV (2219)	5	16	81.3%	81.9	33.4
UNIV MA AMHERST (2221)	149	319	45.5%	69.9	25.0
UNIV MA BOSTON (2222)	39	66	27.3%	60.8	30.7
UNIV MA DARTMOUTH (2210)	25	48	37.5%	64.8	28.3
UNIV MA LOWELL (2161)	29	51	51.0%	72.3	28.1
WESTERN NEW ENGLAND COLL (2226)	22	40	42.5%	70.0	25.6
WESTFIELD ST COLL (2189)	7	11	45.5%	71.3	28.8
WORCESTER ST COLL (2190)	10	15	26.7%	59.8	28.3
Michigan					
ALBION COLL (2235)	17	29	51.7%	72.5	24.0
ALMA COLL (2236)	7	17	58.8%	72.0	23.7
ANDREWS UNIV (2238)	12	21	33.3%	63.0	30.5
AQUINAS COLL (2239)	11	23	34.8%	66.5	27.3
BAKER COLL FLINT (4673)	12	18	44.4%	64.3	33.7
CALVIN COLL (2241)	33	84	66.7%	75.5	23.9
CENTRAL MI UNIV (2243)	86	178	55.1%	73.4	26.4
DAVENPORT UNIV (2249)	24	46	30.4%	61.2	31.7
EASTERN MI UNIV (2259)	30	65	43.1%	70.9	29.8
FERRIS ST UNIV (2260)	19	39	56.4%	70.3	25.4
GRAND VALLEY ST UNIV (2268)	89	193	72.5%	78.4	25.1
HILLSDALE COLL (2272)	15	30	46.7%	69.8	24.1
HOPE COLL (2273)	19	45	42.2%	66.6	23.4
LAKE SUPERIOR ST UNIV (2293)	13	27	44.4%	72.6	27.5
MI ST UNIV (2290)	303	694	66.6%	77.1	25.2
MI TECH UNIV (2292)	12	32	71.9%	77.0	26.4
NORTHERN MI UNIV (2301)	16	33	27.3%	66.2	26.7
NORTHWOOD UNIV (4072)	40	88	38.6%	67.4	28.5
OAKLAND UNIV (2307)	50	109	57.8%	74.6	27.8
SAGINAW VALLEY ST UNIV (2314)	31	59	28.8%	65.4	27.5
SIENA HEIGHTS UNIV (2316)	10	26	42.3%	66.1	28.7

Appendix H: Summary Performance for Bachelor's Degree - First-Time Events

	Candidates Total	Sections Total	Percent Pass	Average Score	Average Age
SPRING ARBOR UNIV (2318)	6	7	28.6%	65.6	25.4
UNIV MI ANN ARBOR (2325)	83	237	80.6%	82.0	25.5
UNIV MI DEARBORN (2326)	58	124	60.5%	74.6	28.7
UNIV MI FLINT (2327)	20	36	27.8%	68.3	31.3
WALSH COLL (4071)	59	114	55.3%	72.0	31.7
WAYNE ST UNIV (2329)	44	78	47.4%	67.2	27.5
WESTERN MI UNIV (2330)	83	172	43.0%	70.1	26.6
Minnesota					
AUGSBURG COLL (2334)	25	44	36.4%	69.0	31.2
BEMIDJI ST UNIV (2336)	9	19	68.4%	73.4	29.0
BETHEL COLL (MN) (9058)	16	38	50.0%	70.5	26.9
COLL OF SAINT SCHOLASTICA (2343)	11	19	42.1%	64.6	26.1
CONCORDIA COLL MOORHEAD (2346)	19	38	65.8%	74.0	23.9
CONCORDIA UNIV MN (2347)	5	11	36.4%	60.3	33.3
GUSTAVUS ADOLPHUS COLL (2353)	13	29	55.2%	70.3	23.8
METROPOLITAN ST UNIV (10374)	47	83	30.1%	63.3	34.3
MN SCHOOL OF BUSINESS (4646)	5	10	20.0%	61.9	27.4
MN ST UNIV MANKATO (2360)	70	136	39.7%	67.5	28.1
MN ST UNIV MOORHEAD (2367)	23	40	35.0%	70.3	30.4
NORTHWESTERN COLL MN (2371)	9	22	68.2%	75.8	24.2
SAINT CATHERINE UNIV (2342)	5	11	63.6%	72.7	29.6
SAINT CLOUD ST UNIV (2377)	73	171	65.5%	76.4	26.2
SAINT JOHN'S UNIV (2379)	25	51	52.9%	73.6	24.6
SAINT MARY'S UNIV OF MN (2380)	10	26	30.8%	63.2	27.6
SOUTHWEST ST UNIV (2375)	9	22	68.2%	77.6	28.2
UNIV MN DULUTH (2388)	54	105	36.2%	67.9	25.8
UNIV MN TWIN CITIES (3969)	108	256	62.1%	76.1	27.8
UNIV ST THOMAS (2345)	69	150	47.3%	72.8	25.7
WINONA ST UNIV (2394)	36	73	30.1%	66.3	27.8
Mississippi					
BELHAVEN COLL (2397)	14	23	34.8%	68.7	33.9
DELTA ST UNIV (2403)	12	22	40.9%	65.5	27.1
JACKSON ST UNIV (2410)	21	34	17.7%	51.7	29.0
MILLSAPS COLL (2414)	13	31	48.4%	72.6	27.7
MS COLL (2415)	21	46	32.6%	63.5	31.0
MS ST UNIV (2423)	82	198	50.0%	70.6	26.5
UNIV MS (2440)	111	295	56.3%	73.8	25.6
UNIV SOUTHERN MS (2441)	61	106	41.5%	69.3	31.6
Missouri					
CENTRAL METHODIST UNIV (2453)	11	15	20.0%	58.5	26.6
COLL OF OZARKS (2500)	5	7	28.6%	71.7	23.8
COLUMBIA COLL (2456)	22	37	21.6%	56.9	38.4
CULVER STOCKTON COLL (2460)	8	24	58.3%	69.9	28.9
DEVRY UNIV KANSAS CITY (2455)	14	19	26.3%	63.1	32.9
DRURY UNIV (2461)	14	31	35.5%	64.7	26.9
LINDENWOOD UNIV (2480)	14	23	26.1%	62.9	25.9
MARYVILLE UNIV ST. LOUIS (2482)	14	25	20.0%	62.9	28.9
MO SOUTHERN ST UNIV (2488)	13	26	61.5%	72.3	31.8
MO ST UNIV (2503)	47	103	46.6%	71.4	26.9
MO VALLEY COLL (2489)	6	13	46.2%	72.7	26.2
MO WESTERN ST UNIV (2490)	8	18	22.2%	58.6	37.2
NORTHWEST MO ST UNIV (2496)	12	30	70.0%	74.7	27.4

Appendix H: Summary Performance for Bachelor's Degree - First-Time Events

	Candidates Total	Sections Total	Percent Pass	Average Score	Average Age
PARK UNIV (2498)	16	32	31.3%	63.8	39.1
ROCKHURST UNIV (2499)	11	25	28.0%	66.6	24.1
SOUTHEAST MO ST UNIV (2501)	27	59	50.9%	70.6	28.7
SOUTHWEST BAPTIST UNIV (2502)	9	16	31.3%	68.1	25.0
ST. LOUIS UNIV (2506)	60	149	54.4%	73.6	25.4
TRUMAN ST UNIV (2495)	68	223	80.7%	80.6	24.3
UNIV CENTRAL MO (2454)	27	64	48.4%	71.4	32.4
UNIV MO COLUMBIA (2516)	15	28	46.4%	75.7	32.0
UNIV MO KANSAS CITY (2518)	24	51	66.7%	76.7	26.6
UNIV MO ST. LOUIS (2519)	55	112	45.5%	68.6	29.9
WASHINGTON UNIV ST. LOUIS (2520)	24	58	86.2%	82.1	27.8
WEBSTER UNIV (2521)	9	15	20.0%	56.7	27.5
Montana					
CARROLL COLL (MT) (2526)	8	19	21.1%	64.2	23.9
MT ST UNIV BILLINGS (2530)	9	19	15.8%	62.1	29.6
MT ST UNIV BOZEMAN (2532)	37	92	57.6%	75.1	25.4
UNIV MT (2536)	37	91	65.9%	78.7	28.9
Nebraska					
BELLEVUE UNIV (9743)	8	15	20.0%	64.7	34.0
CREIGHTON UNIV (2542)	37	90	48.9%	70.1	24.3
DOANE COLL (2544)	10	20	45.0%	65.9	29.2
HASTINGS COLL (2548)	8	13	30.8%	61.5	27.1
MIDLAND LUTHERAN COLL (2553)	13	26	61.5%	74.1	25.6
NE WESLEYAN UNIV (2555)	7	20	85.0%	79.2	23.8
PERU ST COLL (2559)	5	10	90.0%	84.6	36.3
UNIV NE KEARNEY (2551)	14	26	38.5%	66.7	27.3
UNIV NE LINCOLN (2565)	44	79	48.1%	70.9	28.4
UNIV NE OMAHA (2554)	39	82	57.3%	75.1	27.6
WAYNE ST COLL (2566)	7	15	20.0%	60.8	25.1
YORK COLL (2567)	5	8	62.5%	72.6	29.6
Nevada					
UNIV NV LAS VEGAS (2569)	101	196	45.4%	69.1	29.3
UNIV NV RENO (2568)	60	124	41.1%	69.6	28.7
New Hampshire					
PLYMOUTH ST UNIV (2591)	12	16	37.5%	68.3	29.5
SAINT ANSELM COLL (2587)	14	30	36.7%	69.3	25.4
SOUTHERN NH UNIV (2580)	27	52	40.4%	65.3	33.9
UNIV NH (2589)	56	128	58.6%	74.1	25.1
New Jersey					
BERKELEY COLL (7502)	13	18	5.6%	53.4	28.9
BETH MEDRASH GOVOHA (7947)	8	14	50.0%	73.8	31.6
CALDWELL COLL (2598)	7	10	40.0%	66.8	25.9
CENTENARY COLL (2599)	6	15	40.0%	66.4	28.4
COLL NJ (2642)	87	184	60.3%	75.3	24.9
FAIRLEIGH DICKINSON UNIV (2607)	22	43	37.2%	63.9	27.6
FAIRLEIGH DICKINSON UNIV MADISON (4738)	8	19	36.8%	64.7	33.5
FELICIAN COLL (2610)	5	11	0.0%	53.5	30.9
GEORGIAN COURT UNIV (2608)	10	22	13.6%	56.5	32.4
KEAN UNIV (2622)	52	91	17.6%	58.3	31.6
MONMOUTH UNIV (2616)	49	115	38.3%	63.8	25.4
MONTCLAIR ST UNIV (2617)	105	201	29.9%	62.1	27.1
NJ CITY UNIV (2613)	21	37	24.3%	55.8	36.1

Appendix H: Summary Performance for Bachelor's Degree - First-Time Events

	Candidates Total	Sections Total	Percent Pass	Average Score	Average Age
RAMAPO COLL NJ (9344)	63	127	41.7%	69.1	25.8
RICHARD STOCKTON COLL NJ (9345)	48	100	40.0%	69.5	28.4
RIDER UNIV (2628)	54	118	25.4%	62.9	26.9
ROWAN UNIV (2609)	60	109	45.9%	67.1	26.8
RUTGERS ST UNIV CAMDEN (4741)	55	116	35.3%	67.8	28.7
RUTGERS ST UNIV NEW BRUNSWICK (6964)	138	262	38.6%	66.4	26.2
RUTGERS ST UNIV NEWARK (2631)	197	341	38.4%	66.3	26.1
SAINT PETERS COLL (2638)	22	31	19.4%	58.1	30.2
SETON HALL UNIV (2632)	51	90	24.4%	62.2	24.6
THOMAS EDISON ST COLL (21922)	12	25	72.0%	80.8	32.4
WILLIAM PATERSON UNIV NJ (2625)	45	68	33.8%	66.8	27.6
New Mexico					
EASTERN NM UNIV (2651)	11	16	31.3%	63.6	27.3
NM HIGHLANDS UNIV (2653)	5	8	37.5%	62.9	43.2
NM ST UNIV (2657)	30	47	38.3%	67.9	29.8
SAINT JOHNS COLL (2093)	5	11	45.5%	71.9	25.9
UNIV NM (2663)	76	124	39.5%	67.4	31.0
WESTERN NM UNIV (2664)	7	12	16.7%	58.6	26.9
New York					
ADELPHI UNIV (2666)	26	44	29.6%	63.0	27.4
ALFRED UNIV (2668)	7	11	45.5%	66.7	23.6
BERKELEY COLL NY (7394)	10	18	5.6%	42.9	29.9
CANISIUS COLL (2681)	25	63	77.8%	78.8	24.3
COLGATE UNIV (2701)	5	9	55.6%	73.6	30.3
COLUMBIA UNIV NY (2707)	7	17	70.6%	73.9	29.3
CORNELL UNIV (2711)	37	76	71.1%	79.0	27.8
CUNY BARUCH (7273)	394	628	43.2%	68.1	28.9
CUNY BROOKLYN (2687)	124	213	35.7%	65.9	28.2
CUNY HERBERT H LEHMAN (7022)	37	47	14.9%	56.0	32.4
CUNY HUNTER (2689)	88	134	29.1%	63.3	29.1
CUNY MEDGAR EVERS (10097)	5	6	0.0%	63.7	33.0
CUNY QUEENS (2690)	156	230	29.1%	62.3	29.9
CUNY STATEN ISLAND (29040)	40	60	23.3%	59.2	30.9
CUNY YORK COLL (4759)	13	15	13.3%	59.3	32.3
DOWLING COLL (2667)	14	21	14.3%	61.3	33.1
EXCELSIOR COLL (2834)	32	54	50.0%	69.2	34.5
FORDHAM UNIV (2722)	100	194	45.9%	70.3	24.0
HARTWICK COLL (2729)	14	21	23.8%	65.9	29.0
HOFSTRA UNIV (2732)	95	176	41.5%	67.3	26.9
HOUGHTON COLL (2734)	5	8	62.5%	71.3	28.2
IONA COLL (2737)	23	47	38.3%	63.9	25.5
ITHACA COLL (2739)	22	51	58.8%	75.4	23.9
LE MOYNE COLL (2748)	21	41	36.6%	69.7	26.0
LONG ISLAND UNIV BROOKLYN CENTER (4779)	6	10	30.0%	63.5	28.0
LONG ISLAND UNIV CW POST (2754)	26	35	20.0%	61.7	29.0
MANHATTAN COLL (2758)	30	48	14.6%	53.0	27.0
MARIST COLL (2765)	37	69	44.9%	71.3	25.4
MERCY COLL (2772)	5	8	50.0%	73.4	43.5
MOLLOY COLL (2775)	10	16	18.8%	53.4	22.9
MONROE COLL (4799)	14	18	0.0%	42.6	32.8
MOUNT SAINT MARY COLL (2778)	6	13	7.7%	58.5	28.0
NAZARETH COLL ROCHESTER (2779)	10	25	64.0%	80.5	24.9

Appendix H: Summary Performance for Bachelor's Degree - First-Time Events

	Candidates Total	Sections Total	Percent Pass	Average Score	Average Age
NIAGARA UNIV (2788)	15	33	39.4%	66.2	26.3
NY INST TECH MANHATTAN (2782)	13	21	28.6%	53.0	29.2
NY INST TECH OLD WESTBURY (4804)	8	12	8.3%	53.6	24.6
NY UNIV (2785)	96	194	54.6%	73.7	25.4
NYACK COLL (2790)	5	8	25.0%	65.0	26.3
PACE UNIV NY (2791)	68	109	28.4%	64.3	29.6
PACE UNIV PLEASANTVILLE (2792)	33	59	42.4%	66.7	27.0
ROCHESTER INST TECH (2806)	15	33	42.4%	72.2	29.7
SAINT BONAVENTURE UNIV (2817)	6	13	0.0%	57.4	33.7
SAINT FRANCIS COLL (2820)	8	11	36.4%	65.9	30.5
SAINT JOHN FISHER COLL (2821)	22	49	49.0%	73.0	26.3
SAINT JOHNS UNIV NEW YORK (2823)	96	179	34.6%	63.6	25.2
SAINT JOSEPHS COLL NY (2825)	7	11	45.5%	71.6	25.4
SAINT JOSEPHS COLL SUFFOLK (29081)	7	14	50.0%	74.0	30.1
SAINT THOMAS AQUINAS COLL (2832)	5	11	27.3%	66.1	23.8
SIENA COLL (2816)	51	88	40.9%	68.9	26.8
SUNY OLD WESTBURY (7109)	56	87	28.7%	59.8	32.1
SUNY ALBANY (2835)	138	253	47.0%	71.2	24.8
SUNY BINGHAMTON (2836)	197	366	50.3%	71.2	24.4
SUNY BROCKPORT (2841)	31	54	48.2%	73.3	28.4
SUNY BUFFALO (2837)	109	232	57.3%	74.5	26.5
SUNY BUFFALO (2842)	7	16	62.5%	75.3	27.8
SUNY EMPIRE ST COLL (10286)	12	20	70.0%	74.3	35.7
SUNY FREDONIA (2844)	15	27	66.7%	75.4	28.8
SUNY GENESEO (2845)	53	109	66.1%	77.0	23.9
SUNY INST TECH UTICA ROME (11678)	7	15	20.0%	64.5	31.6
SUNY NEW PALTZ (2846)	33	61	59.0%	76.5	27.4
SUNY ONEONTA (2847)	13	20	35.0%	63.5	26.1
SUNY OSWEGO (2848)	19	31	51.6%	73.0	28.9
SUNY PLATTSBURGH (2849)	28	49	30.6%	66.2	27.0
SUNY STONY BROOK (2838)	35	73	39.7%	67.6	28.1
SYRACUSE UNIV (2882)	110	220	45.5%	70.0	24.7
TOURO COLL (10142)	80	132	53.8%	73.3	26.1
UNIV ROCHESTER (2894)	5	7	71.4%	79.0	33.0
UTICA COLL (2883)	7	13	46.2%	72.2	28.5
WAGNER COLL (2899)	22	39	23.1%	64.7	25.3
YESHIVA UNIV (2903)	64	103	35.9%	67.5	24.7
North Carolina					
APPALACHIAN ST UNIV (2906)	75	182	64.8%	76.3	26.6
BARTON COLL (2908)	6	10	30.0%	55.4	35.6
BELMONT ABBEY COLL (2910)	5	11	18.2%	65.0	31.8
CAMPBELL UNIV (2913)	24	48	39.6%	70.3	28.0
CATAWBA COLL (2914)	5	13	38.5%	56.8	30.1
DAVIDSON COLL (2918)	6	21	71.4%	81.7	24.4
DUKE UNIV (2920)	10	23	78.3%	81.7	28.3
EAST CAROLINA UNIV (2923)	83	212	37.7%	68.8	27.0
ELIZABETH CITY ST UNIV (2926)	5	10	0.0%	40.2	40.5
ELON UNIV (2927)	62	131	42.8%	70.1	24.4
FAYETTEVILLE ST UNIV (2928)	5	6	0.0%	39.7	39.8
GARDNER WEBB UNIV (2929)	9	21	38.1%	64.0	28.7
GUILFORD COLL (2931)	10	20	60.0%	76.1	37.2
HIGH POINT UNIV (2933)	9	13	23.1%	59.4	37.2

Appendix H: Summary Performance for Bachelor's Degree - First-Time Events

	Candidates Total	Sections Total	Percent Pass	Average Score	Average Age
LENOIR RHYNE COLL (2941)	5	5	20.0%	67.2	33.4
MEREDITH COLL (2945)	6	17	70.6%	77.9	24.5
MOUNT OLIVE COLL (2949)	5	12	0.0%	43.8	27.6
NC AGRICULTURAL & TECH ST UNIV (2905)	23	45	24.4%	66.0	28.4
NC CENTRAL UNIV (2950)	9	16	18.8%	49.1	32.1
NC ST UNIV RALEIGH (2972)	146	371	62.5%	76.3	26.1
NC WESLEYAN COLL (2951)	6	16	31.3%	48.2	35.6
UNIV NC ASHEVILLE (2907)	18	38	34.2%	71.2	35.5
UNIV NC CHAPEL HILL (2974)	132	398	72.6%	78.5	25.8
UNIV NC CHARLOTTE (2975)	63	136	55.9%	73.8	30.2
UNIV NC GREENSBORO (2976)	44	90	55.6%	73.3	28.8
UNIV NC PEMBROKE (2954)	6	13	53.9%	70.5	31.1
UNIV NC WILMINGTON (2984)	106	264	51.1%	73.1	25.6
WAKE FOREST UNIV (2978)	47	173	91.3%	86.4	23.9
WESTERN CAROLINA UNIV (2981)	18	41	43.9%	66.4	29.9
WINGATE UNIV (2985)	9	20	20.0%	64.9	25.0
WINSTON SALEM ST UNIV (2986)	9	17	35.3%	65.0	32.4
North Dakota					
DICKINSON ST UNIV (2989)	18	36	38.9%	60.6	26.2
MINOT ST UNIV (2994)	8	14	57.1%	71.8	27.3
ND ST UNIV (9265)	26	52	63.5%	77.0	28.8
UNIV MARY (2992)	12	19	42.1%	66.6	29.9
UNIV ND (3005)	38	78	69.2%	78.5	26.5
Ohio					
ASHLAND UNIV (3012)	10	26	57.7%	75.9	29.0
BALDWIN WALLACE COLL (3014)	14	29	37.9%	67.1	31.1
BOWLING GREEN ST UNIV (3018)	63	137	47.5%	72.3	27.7
CAPITAL UNIV (3023)	18	56	42.9%	65.8	24.9
CASE WESTERN RESERVE UNIV (3024)	19	42	54.8%	73.4	26.9
CEDARVILLE UNIV (3025)	14	26	73.1%	77.1	24.6
CLEVELAND ST UNIV (3032)	44	92	55.4%	72.8	29.8
DEFIANCE COLL (3041)	6	16	50.0%	70.1	26.4
DEVRY UNIV COLUMBUS (3099)	17	29	41.4%	62.1	38.3
FRANCISCAN UNIV STEUBENVILLE (3036)	6	13	46.2%	64.6	32.1
FRANKLIN UNIV (3046)	80	145	25.5%	60.9	35.7
HEIDELBERG COLL (3048)	6	11	9.1%	68.4	28.0
HIRAM COLL (3049)	8	18	38.9%	67.2	25.5
JOHN CARROLL UNIV (3050)	57	123	63.4%	77.0	24.9
KENT ST UNIV (3051)	64	137	59.1%	73.6	27.3
MALONE COLL (3072)	5	14	50.0%	73.1	25.2
MARIETTA COLL (3073)	5	9	33.3%	63.8	28.8
MIAMI UNIV (3077)	253	636	62.9%	76.6	24.5
MOUNT UNION COLL (3083)	9	18	66.7%	79.2	25.3
MOUNT VERNON NAZARENE UNIV (7085)	7	17	29.4%	62.9	31.5
MUSKINGUM COLL (3084)	6	10	60.0%	73.2	26.3
NOTRE DAME COLL OH (3085)	9	21	19.1%	60.4	25.0
OH DOMINICAN UNIV (3035)	9	24	20.8%	61.1	26.8
OH NORTHERN UNIV (3089)	19	49	28.6%	65.2	24.8
OH ST UNIV (6883)	271	637	59.5%	75.0	25.8
OH UNIV (3100)	108	253	49.0%	71.9	25.0
OH WESLEYAN UNIV (3109)	12	21	52.4%	74.6	24.9
OTTERBEIN UNIV (3110)	9	21	52.4%	68.3	29.1

Appendix H: Summary Performance for Bachelor's Degree - First-Time Events

	Candidates Total	Sections Total	Percent Pass	Average Score	Average Age
UNIV AKRON (3123)	67	160	41.3%	70.3	28.8
UNIV CINCINNATI (3125)	75	155	46.5%	69.6	27.8
UNIV DAYTON (3127)	36	83	50.6%	72.0	26.1
UNIV FINDLAY (3045)	8	19	47.4%	72.5	25.5
UNIV TOLEDO (3131)	46	105	45.7%	68.5	27.0
WALSH UNIV (3135)	6	15	20.0%	67.3	30.4
WITTENBERG UNIV (3143)	6	14	42.9%	69.9	29.2
WRIGHT ST UNIV (3078)	35	75	54.7%	73.4	27.4
XAVIER UNIV (3144)	37	89	57.3%	74.4	24.6
YOUNGSTOWN ST UNIV (3145)	40	79	36.7%	67.0	29.0
Oklahoma					
CAMERON UNIV (3150)	8	11	27.3%	60.5	32.9
NORTHEASTERN ST UNIV (3161)	24	37	24.3%	57.4	31.6
NORTHWESTERN OK ST UNIV (3163)	5	8	37.5%	69.3	27.5
OK BAPTIST UNIV (3164)	6	11	45.5%	71.7	35.4
OK CHRISTIAN UNIV (3165)	17	30	50.0%	73.0	24.8
OK ST UNIV (3170)	121	323	64.4%	76.6	26.0
ORAL ROBERTS UNIV (3985)	14	33	54.6%	72.1	26.9
SOUTHWESTERN OK ST UNIV (3181)	12	23	65.2%	72.7	26.6
UNIV CENTRAL OK (3152)	69	126	49.2%	70.7	30.8
UNIV OK NORMAN (3184)	67	137	49.6%	72.4	27.4
UNIV TULSA (3185)	16	29	65.5%	77.2	27.7
Oregon					
CONCORDIA UNIV (3191)	5	8	12.5%	59.0	25.7
EASTERN OR UNIV (3193)	12	31	54.8%	70.5	29.4
GEORGE FOX UNIV (3194)	11	21	28.6%	68.2	24.3
LINFIELD COLL (3198)	39	82	42.7%	70.4	33.9
OR ST UNIV (3210)	71	131	58.8%	74.1	29.1
PACIFIC UNIV (3212)	8	13	38.5%	64.6	25.3
PORTLAND ST UNIV (3216)	77	157	60.5%	73.5	30.9
SOUTHERN OR UNIV (3219)	19	37	56.8%	75.1	32.0
UNIV OR (3223)	109	221	56.6%	73.6	27.1
UNIV PORTLAND (3224)	23	54	46.3%	71.5	23.2
Pennsylvania					
ALBRIGHT COLL (3229)	32	46	17.4%	62.3	32.3
ALVERNIA COLL (3233)	13	17	17.7%	61.9	30.8
ARCADIA UNIV (3235)	11	29	37.9%	64.2	24.0
BLOOMSBURG UNIV PA (3315)	83	147	50.3%	72.3	26.1
BUCKNELL UNIV (3238)	47	105	68.6%	77.9	24.5
CA UNIV PA (3316)	17	29	34.5%	61.8	31.7
CABRINI COLL (3241)	12	23	21.7%	59.6	24.8
CARLOW UNIV (3303)	6	11	36.4%	59.0	28.4
CARNEGIE MELLON UNIV (3242)	8	16	62.5%	72.9	31.5
CHESTNUT HILL COLL (3245)	6	10	30.0%	55.7	34.6
CLARION UNIV PA (9235)	19	29	51.7%	71.0	27.7
COLL MISERICORDIA (3247)	8	10	0.0%	50.1	29.2
DE VALLEY COLL (3252)	12	21	23.8%	58.5	26.3
DESALES UNIV (3986)	34	64	32.8%	64.4	27.1
DREXEL UNIV (3256)	159	285	40.4%	67.2	25.8
DUQUESNE UNIV (3258)	97	182	44.5%	70.4	24.6
EAST STROUDSBURG UNIV PA (3320)	12	20	30.0%	60.8	28.5
EASTERN UNIV (3259)	9	17	47.1%	72.0	27.7

Appendix H: Summary Performance for Bachelor's Degree - First-Time Events

	Candidates Total	Sections Total	Percent Pass	Average Score	Average Age
EDINBORO UNIV PA (3321)	10	16	18.8%	58.8	29.9
ELIZABETHTOWN COLL (3262)	32	55	30.9%	63.7	25.9
FRANKLIN & MARSHALL COLL (3265)	6	15	80.0%	81.0	29.1
GANNON UNIV (3266)	12	16	12.5%	51.4	31.6
GENEVA COLL (3267)	14	23	30.4%	65.5	27.8
GROVE CITY COLL (3269)	37	84	58.3%	74.6	25.9
GWYNEDD MERCY COLL (3270)	13	27	22.2%	57.8	28.6
HOLY FAMILY COLL (3275)	13	19	15.8%	62.3	26.6
IMMACULATA UNIV (3276)	6	10	30.0%	57.6	27.1
INDIANA UNIV PA (3277)	63	122	33.6%	63.2	26.8
JUNIATA COLL (3279)	12	17	52.9%	64.9	25.8
KEYSTONE COLL (3280)	10	15	0.0%	55.4	24.8
KINGS COLL (3282)	49	82	32.9%	65.4	25.3
KUTZTOWN UNIV PA (3322)	64	128	37.5%	68.0	25.7
LA ROCHE COLL (3987)	17	24	4.2%	47.0	24.5
LA SALLE UNIV (3287)	89	183	23.5%	61.9	25.8
LAFAYETTE COLL (3284)	7	18	38.9%	63.7	27.3
LEBANON VALLEY COLL (3288)	28	61	42.6%	72.5	25.7
LEHIGH UNIV (3289)	110	257	68.9%	76.9	23.5
LINCOLN UNIV (3290)	6	10	20.0%	54.8	24.7
LOCK HAVEN UNIV PA (3323)	12	25	36.0%	55.9	27.9
LYCOMING COLL (3293)	9	22	40.9%	70.1	25.6
MARYWOOD UNIV (3296)	9	16	18.8%	62.0	28.4
MERCYHURST COLL (3297)	22	41	34.2%	63.0	25.4
MESSIAH COLL (3298)	37	85	54.1%	71.6	23.8
MILLERSVILLE UNIV PA (3325)	31	53	37.7%	66.0	26.9
MORAVIAN COLL (3301)	24	45	24.4%	62.7	24.4
MOUNT ALOYSIUS COLL (3302)	7	9	55.6%	73.8	29.4
MUHLENBERG COLL (3304)	41	86	47.7%	70.8	25.0
NEUMANN UNIV (3988)	9	18	38.9%	65.7	33.6
PA ST ERIE (3333)	5	11	72.7%	76.0	34.2
PA ST UNIV PARK (3329)	457	932	45.0%	69.5	25.5
PA ST UNIV PARK (6965)	19	30	43.3%	71.2	29.7
PEIRCE COLL (3309)	5	8	62.5%	67.5	35.1
PHILADELPHIA UNIV (3354)	12	31	22.6%	56.5	27.0
POINT PARK UNIV (3357)	8	14	7.1%	58.9	33.8
ROBERT MORRIS UNIV (3359)	72	114	32.5%	62.9	27.7
SAINT FRANCIS UNIV (3366)	29	46	23.9%	61.3	26.9
SAINT JOSEPHS UNIV (3367)	105	229	41.9%	69.4	24.4
SAINT VINCENT COLL (3368)	27	60	40.0%	70.7	24.0
SETON HILL UNIV (3362)	6	11	45.5%	66.1	25.1
SHIPPENSBURG UNIV PA (3326)	65	131	55.0%	71.6	26.2
SLIPPERY ROCK UNIV PA (3327)	34	60	25.0%	60.0	24.6
SUSQUEHANNA UNIV (3369)	21	39	35.9%	66.5	27.6
TEMPLE UNIV (3371)	335	626	30.7%	63.4	27.5
THIEL COLL (3376)	11	28	25.0%	60.1	23.7
UNIV PA (3378)	27	67	85.1%	82.0	30.7
UNIV PITTSBURGH (3379)	248	489	54.2%	73.1	25.4
UNIV PITTSBURGH JOHNSTOWN (3382)	5	6	50.0%	62.2	30.6
UNIV SCRANTON (3384)	42	69	39.1%	67.7	26.5
URSINUS COLL (3385)	8	10	20.0%	67.2	32.4
VILLANOVA UNIV (3388)	187	436	65.1%	76.5	24.0

Appendix H: Summary Performance for Bachelor's Degree - First-Time Events

	Candidates Total	Sections Total	Percent Pass	Average Score	Average Age
WASHINGTON & JEFFERSON COLL (3389)	41	72	45.8%	71.7	24.8
WAYNESBURG COLL (3391)	10	13	0.0%	52.4	29.8
WEST CHESTER UNIV PA (3328)	146	278	34.9%	66.8	25.9
WESTMINSTER COLL (3392)	21	38	29.0%	61.3	25.7
WIDENER UNIV PA (3313)	60	107	25.2%	60.9	25.1
WILKES UNIV (3394)	29	47	19.2%	61.6	27.5
YORK COLL PA (3399)	30	56	50.0%	72.0	25.4
Puerto Rico					
INTER AMERICAN UNIV PR (8242)	14	19	5.3%	39.4	38.8
INTER AMERICAN UNIV PR BARRANQUITAS (5027)	7	10	0.0%	32.5	28.5
INTER AMERICAN UNIV PR BAYAMON (5028)	6	11	0.0%	49.0	30.8
INTER AMERICAN UNIV PR METROPOLITAN (3940)	25	37	10.8%	48.9	30.2
INTER AMERICAN UNIV PR PONCE (5029)	14	29	0.0%	25.6	33.2
INTER AMERICAN UNIV PR SAN GERMAN (3938)	8	13	30.8%	65.0	31.7
PONTIFICAL CATHOLIC UNIV PR (3936)	30	60	8.3%	37.2	31.8
UNIV ESTE (3941)	8	14	14.3%	28.5	40.9
UNIV METROPOLITANA (25875)	9	16	12.5%	31.4	37.0
UNIV PR AGUADILLA (12123)	14	20	5.0%	40.6	30.7
UNIV PR ARECIBO (7228)	21	32	21.9%	54.2	27.9
UNIV PR BAYAMON (10975)	48	79	5.1%	49.9	27.2
UNIV PR CAROLINA (30160)	10	18	11.1%	53.1	29.2
UNIV PR CAYEY (7206)	37	57	7.0%	47.1	27.4
UNIV PR HUMACAO (3943)	31	53	15.1%	50.8	26.4
UNIV PR MAYAGUEZ (3944)	39	62	9.7%	58.8	27.0
UNIV PR PONCE (9652)	20	47	10.6%	43.7	26.4
UNIV PR RIO PIEDRAS (7108)	161	305	37.1%	65.5	25.6
UNIV SACRED HEART (3937)	9	16	37.5%	71.1	27.5
UNIV TURABO GURABO (11719)	8	16	0.0%	43.6	30.8
Rhode Island					
BRYANT UNIV (3402)	143	282	55.0%	73.5	24.5
JOHNSON & WALES UNIV (3404)	39	87	29.9%	60.8	27.4
PROVIDENCE COLL (3406)	46	99	54.6%	74.9	24.4
RI COLL (3407)	12	30	26.7%	60.1	27.6
ROGER WILLIAMS UNIV (3410)	17	31	32.3%	62.6	23.4
SALVE REGINA UNIV (3411)	18	32	28.1%	63.9	26.4
UNIV RI (3414)	67	140	66.4%	75.0	25.4
South Carolina					
BOB JONES UNIV (3421)	9	19	68.4%	74.1	23.3
CITADEL MILITARY COLL SC (3423)	9	21	23.8%	58.7	26.5
CLEMSON UNIV (3425)	40	95	61.1%	75.6	25.4
COASTAL CAROLINA UNIV (3451)	10	16	25.0%	63.8	25.3
COLL CHARLESTON (3428)	24	57	61.4%	75.9	25.6
FURMAN UNIV (3434)	15	43	60.5%	78.0	23.7
UNIV SC COLUMBIA (3448)	72	174	54.0%	75.4	26.1
WINTHROP UNIV (3456)	11	18	61.1%	75.0	31.1
WOFFORD COLL (3457)	12	40	65.0%	74.5	25.6
South Dakota					
AUGUSTANA COLL (3458)	27	65	52.3%	74.4	25.6
BLACK HILLS ST UNIV (3459)	9	18	50.0%	71.7	32.2
CO TECHNICAL UNIV (666731)	6	10	30.0%	53.2	33.5
NATIONAL AMERICAN UNIV (4057)	7	14	42.9%	63.4	36.2
NORTHERN ST UNIV (3466)	8	14	21.4%	67.0	30.3

Appendix H: Summary Performance for Bachelor's Degree - First-Time Events

	Candidates Total	Sections Total	Percent Pass	Average Score	Average Age
SD ST UNIV (3471)	12	23	47.8%	75.0	26.4
UNIV SD (3474)	13	25	68.0%	77.6	30.8
UNIV SIOUX FALLS (3469)	16	33	57.6%	74.5	27.3
Tennessee					
AUSTIN PEAY ST UNIV (3478)	20	44	38.6%	63.5	28.1
BELMONT UNIV (3479)	30	62	58.1%	71.8	25.1
CARSON NEWMAN COLL (3481)	9	11	45.5%	66.7	27.5
CHRISTIAN BROTHERS UNIV (3482)	9	18	22.2%	65.1	27.0
EAST TN ST UNIV (3487)	37	72	33.3%	66.6	32.3
FISK UNIV (3490)	5	9	44.4%	68.3	23.5
FREED HARDEMAN UNIV (3492)	9	15	26.7%	64.4	28.3
LEE UNIV (3500)	15	28	57.1%	71.0	28.6
LIPSCOMB UNIV (3486)	27	50	20.0%	62.0	32.1
MIDDLE TN ST UNIV (3510)	77	175	49.1%	71.5	29.3
RHODES COLL (3519)	12	27	55.6%	72.6	24.1
SOUTHERN ADVENTIST UNIV (3518)	8	19	42.1%	69.5	25.1
TN ST UNIV (3522)	17	24	37.5%	62.2	32.8
TN TECH UNIV (3523)	30	57	28.1%	61.2	27.2
TN WESLEYAN COLL (3525)	7	11	54.6%	58.5	34.5
TREVECCA NAZARENE UNIV (3526)	6	11	63.6%	74.0	25.5
TUSCULUM COLL (3527)	7	9	22.2%	64.9	30.3
UNION UNIV (3528)	8	16	62.5%	73.4	26.1
UNIV MEMPHIS (3509)	36	68	29.4%	61.0	32.1
UNIV TN CHATTANOOGA (3529)	42	77	42.9%	69.5	27.2
UNIV TN KNOXVILLE (3530)	117	299	70.6%	76.8	26.2
UNIV TN MARTIN (3531)	19	36	19.4%	52.7	29.4
VANDERBILT UNIV (3535)	20	65	83.1%	83.0	25.2
Texas					
ABILENE CHRISTIAN UNIV (3537)	26	47	61.7%	75.8	26.1
ANGELO ST UNIV (3541)	14	31	35.5%	68.6	30.6
BAYLOR UNIV (3545)	65	137	59.9%	75.7	26.2
BAYLOR UNIV (6967)	7	17	41.2%	69.8	29.1
DALLAS BAPTIST UNIV (3560)	11	23	34.8%	66.5	28.5
DEVRY UNIV IRVING (10139)	9	19	21.1%	54.6	31.4
HOUSTON BAPTIST UNIV (3576)	11	16	25.0%	62.4	33.0
LAMAR COLL (3581)	17	34	44.1%	72.1	29.8
LETOURNEAU UNIV (3584)	11	18	27.8%	66.2	34.5
LUBBOCK CHRISTIAN UNIV (3586)	5	11	54.6%	77.4	32.3
MIDWESTERN ST UNIV (3592)	15	28	60.7%	74.9	35.6
OUR LADY THE LAKE UNIV (3598)	7	8	25.0%	57.6	32.5
RICE UNIV (3604)	11	24	66.7%	78.8	31.0
SAINT EDWARDS UNIV (3621)	14	25	40.0%	69.6	33.2
SAINT MARYS UNIV (3623)	13	22	36.4%	69.9	30.3
SAM HOUSTON ST UNIV (3606)	63	109	47.7%	69.8	30.6
SCHREINER UNIV (3610)	7	9	11.1%	61.4	28.3
SOUTHERN METHODIST UNIV (3613)	71	212	67.5%	78.4	24.3
SOUTHWESTERN UNIV (3620)	7	20	70.0%	77.2	30.1
STEPHEN F AUSTIN ST UNIV (3624)	26	42	47.6%	67.3	32.5
TARLETON ST UNIV (3631)	17	35	40.0%	68.0	32.4
TRINITY UNIV (3647)	22	46	76.1%	78.8	25.9
TX A&M INTL UNIV (9651)	10	15	26.7%	60.5	29.1
TX A&M UNIV (3632)	101	192	64.6%	75.0	29.5

Appendix H: Summary Performance for Bachelor's Degree - First-Time Events

	Candidates Total	Sections Total	Percent Pass	Average Score	Average Age
TX A&M UNIV COMMERCE (3565)	8	15	46.7%	72.3	35.5
TX A&M UNIV CORPUS CHRISTI (11161)	21	36	47.2%	70.9	30.8
TX A&M UNIV KINGSVILLE (3639)	5	6	0.0%	54.0	30.8
TX CHRISTIAN UNIV (3636)	49	133	70.7%	78.0	25.2
TX LUTHERAN UNIV (3641)	19	30	53.3%	71.3	25.8
TX SOUTHERN UNIV (3642)	9	14	0.0%	42.2	37.1
TX ST UNIV SAN MARCOS (3615)	65	118	38.1%	67.9	29.4
TX TECH UNIV (3644)	97	217	52.1%	70.7	28.0
TX WESLEYAN UNIV (3645)	6	11	18.2%	54.5	38.4
TX WOMANS UNIV (3646)	8	16	50.0%	69.6	25.5
UNIV HOUSTON CLEAR LAKE (11711)	46	75	32.0%	64.8	32.9
UNIV HOUSTON DOWNTOWN (3612)	118	181	29.8%	61.9	32.6
UNIV HOUSTON UNIV PARK (3652)	238	397	35.3%	66.4	30.3
UNIV HOUSTON VICTORIA (13231)	10	21	33.3%	68.8	32.4
UNIV INCARNATE WORD (3578)	7	7	0.0%	46.1	33.8
UNIV MARY HARDIN BAYLOR (3588)	18	39	51.3%	71.2	27.0
UNIV NORTH TX (3594)	71	122	39.3%	68.1	32.3
UNIV SAINT THOMAS (3654)	17	32	43.8%	69.5	28.1
UNIV TX ARLINGTON (3656)	99	179	43.0%	70.1	32.6
UNIV TX AUSTIN (3658)	99	209	66.5%	76.8	29.6
UNIV TX BROWNSVILLE (30646)	9	14	50.0%	69.1	28.7
UNIV TX DALLAS (9741)	121	287	38.3%	67.7	28.8
UNIV TX EL PASO (3661)	17	30	46.7%	70.2	29.8
UNIV TX PAN AMERICAN (3599)	17	23	47.8%	66.7	32.0
UNIV TX PERMIAN BASIN (9930)	21	34	35.3%	68.9	29.2
UNIV TX SAN ANTONIO (10115)	85	137	40.9%	67.6	32.0
UNIV TX TYLER (11163)	22	40	52.5%	70.2	30.6
WAYLAND BAPTIST UNIV (3663)	5	12	41.7%	71.0	33.9
WEST TX A & M UNIV (3665)	10	12	0.0%	59.5	31.2
Utah					
BRIGHAM YOUNG UNIV (3670)	134	293	61.8%	75.3	28.0
SOUTHERN UT UNIV (3678)	14	33	51.5%	74.2	28.3
UNIV UT (3675)	53	107	58.9%	73.2	29.9
UT ST UNIV (3677)	27	59	55.9%	70.7	29.5
UT VALLEY ST COLL (4027)	18	37	48.7%	72.9	31.4
WEBER ST UNIV (3680)	8	9	66.7%	74.0	28.5
Western Governors Univ (33394)	5	8	50.0%	64.1	32.5
WESTMINSTER COLL (3681)	6	14	14.3%	60.2	26.9
Vermont					
CASTLETON ST COLL (3683)	6	15	86.7%	82.4	28.1
CHAMPLAIN COLL (3684)	24	40	35.0%	67.9	28.7
SAINT MICHAELS COLL (3694)	26	49	55.1%	72.9	25.5
UNIV VT (3696)	17	35	60.0%	74.3	30.5
Virgin Islands					
UNIV VI (3946)	6	8	25.0%	65.3	29.8
Virginia					
AVERETT UNIV (3702)	5	8	25.0%	66.6	34.2
BRIDGEWATER COLL (3704)	10	22	27.3%	61.2	24.0
CHRISTOPHER NEWPORT UNIV (3706)	15	31	48.4%	73.3	26.2
COLL WILLIAM & MARY (3705)	56	152	67.1%	77.3	24.4
EASTERN MENNONITE UNIV (3708)	5	18	72.2%	82.9	29.8
FERRUM COLL (3711)	6	11	63.6%	74.5	26.0

Appendix H: Summary Performance for Bachelor's Degree - First-Time Events

	Candidates Total	Sections Total	Percent Pass	Average Score	Average Age
GEORGE MASON UNIV (3749)	216	385	45.7%	70.4	28.7
HAMPDEN SYDNEY COLL (3713)	5	8	50.0%	75.9	27.0
HAMPTON UNIV (3714)	24	43	18.6%	62.7	29.5
JAMES MADISON UNIV (3721)	126	358	68.7%	78.3	24.8
LIBERTY UNIV (20530)	37	68	50.0%	73.4	31.7
LONGWOOD UNIV (3719)	17	30	43.3%	67.2	25.5
LYNCHBURG COLL (3720)	7	13	61.5%	75.8	25.3
NORFOLK ST UNIV (3765)	6	7	57.1%	62.9	35.8
NORTHERN VA CC (3727)	10	20	50.0%	71.1	27.4
OLD DOMINION UNIV (3728)	52	103	51.5%	69.4	30.1
RADFORD UNIV (3732)	23	37	43.2%	68.9	26.2
RANDOLPH MACON COLL (3733)	15	33	45.5%	69.6	26.9
ROANOKE COLL (3736)	11	19	36.8%	69.9	25.8
TIDEWATER CC (3712)	5	8	25.0%	61.1	33.0
UNIV MARY WASHINGTON (3746)	16	31	48.4%	72.0	28.2
UNIV RICHMOND (3744)	64	170	68.8%	78.3	24.8
UNIV VA (3745)	96	275	88.7%	85.4	24.7
UNIV VA COL WISE (CLINCH VALLEY COLL) (3747)	7	11	63.6%	75.0	28.6
VA COMMONWEALTH UNIV (3735)	76	136	35.3%	66.2	28.8
VA POLYTECHNIC INST & ST UNIV (3754)	197	454	60.6%	75.7	25.5
WASHINGTON & LEE UNIV (3768)	31	79	65.8%	77.9	24.4
Washington					
CENTRAL WA UNIV (3771)	89	185	44.3%	68.5	31.0
CITY UNIV SEATTLE (13022)	17	37	27.0%	60.1	37.9
EASTERN WA UNIV (3775)	42	80	40.0%	67.7	31.1
GONZAGA UNIV (3778)	64	157	68.8%	77.6	24.5
PACIFIC LUTHERAN UNIV (3785)	13	33	12.1%	57.3	24.8
SAINT MARTINS COLL (3794)	9	20	30.0%	60.9	32.7
SEATTLE PACIFIC UNIV (3788)	22	45	46.7%	73.0	24.9
SEATTLE UNIV (3790)	30	59	32.2%	65.4	27.0
UNIV PUGET SOUND (3797)	7	13	76.9%	76.8	33.3
UNIV WA (3798)	238	535	60.2%	74.8	27.9
WA ST UNIV (3800)	98	206	48.5%	71.7	27.2
WALLA WALLA UNIV (3799)	5	9	55.6%	77.0	24.1
WESTERN WA UNIV (3802)	38	77	67.5%	76.6	27.7
WHITWORTH COLL (3804)	11	20	70.0%	76.9	28.7
West Virginia					
BETHANY COLL (3808)	5	8	75.0%	76.0	29.3
CONCORD UNIV (3810)	9	14	28.6%	68.1	26.6
FAIRMONT ST COLL (3812)	5	12	41.7%	62.6	31.4
GLENVILLE ST COLL (3813)	5	6	16.7%	59.5	26.1
MARSHALL UNIV (3815)	54	93	40.9%	67.8	27.1
SALEM INTL UNIV (3820)	5	12	41.7%	67.2	37.9
SHEPHERD UNIV (3822)	7	16	50.0%	68.1	26.4
UNIV CHARLESTON (3818)	9	21	33.3%	61.2	23.4
WEST LIBERTY ST COLL (3823)	11	23	21.7%	64.4	28.4
WHEELING JESUIT UNIV (3831)	13	21	42.9%	64.5	28.6
WV INST TECH (3825)	7	15	13.3%	54.9	40.1
WV ST UNIV (3826)	21	32	15.6%	56.6	28.8
WV UNIV (3827)	132	273	48.4%	70.9	26.7
WV UNIV PARKERSBURG (3828)	9	16	31.3%	64.8	28.5
WV WESLEYAN COLL (3830)	5	10	40.0%	64.5	25.0

Appendix H: Summary Performance for Bachelor's Degree - First-Time Events

	Candidates Total	Sections Total	Percent Pass	Average Score	Average Age
Wisconsin					
CARDINAL STRITCH UNIV (3837)	9	15	53.3%	69.1	34.4
CARROLL UNIV (WI) (3838)	12	26	50.0%	68.5	29.0
CARTHAGE COLL (3839)	13	28	7.1%	54.0	25.5
CONCORDIA UNIV WI (3842)	10	20	35.0%	63.3	25.1
EDGEWOOD COLL (3848)	9	22	22.7%	59.2	33.1
LAKELAND COLL (3854)	30	70	38.6%	69.3	40.9
MARQUETTE UNIV (3863)	80	200	70.0%	77.6	25.1
MOUNT MARY COLL (3869)	5	11	27.3%	60.4	44.1
SAINT NORBERT COLL (3892)	16	36	63.9%	71.9	24.9
UNIV WI EAU CLAIRE (3917)	58	114	58.8%	74.2	25.8
UNIV WI GREEN BAY (3899)	33	75	33.3%	70.5	26.8
UNIV WI LA CROSSE (3919)	62	147	51.0%	72.9	25.2
UNIV WI MADISON (3895)	130	366	76.0%	80.5	24.9
UNIV WI MILWAUKEE (3896)	99	248	53.2%	73.3	28.0
UNIV WI OSHKOSH (3920)	50	113	53.1%	73.4	25.4
UNIV WI PARKSIDE (5015)	16	25	12.0%	59.3	29.8
UNIV WI PLATTEVILLE (3921)	13	28	53.6%	71.8	29.1
UNIV WI RIVER FALLS (3923)	23	45	57.8%	73.7	28.3
UNIV WI STEVENS POINT (3924)	13	26	50.0%	73.5	30.3
UNIV WI SUPERIOR (3925)	10	21	38.1%	66.4	28.9
UNIV WI WHITEWATER (3926)	89	252	61.1%	75.9	25.6
Wyoming					
UNIV WY (3932)	48	103	50.5%	73.3	27.3

Glossary

Data Definitions

Below are brief descriptions for the data fields and terms found in this publication. With the exception of the multi-year trends, the data presented in this publication represents the statistics and performance for only those candidates and testing events during the calendar year 2011.

Advanced Degree: The number or percentage of sections associated with an application listing an advanced degree (graduate or post graduate) as the primary degree. Because the degree is associated with an application and not the candidate, a single candidate can be reported under multiple degree types during his/her examination process. Data associated with jurisdictions allowing a certificate of enrollment (COE) are most affected by this reporting methodology.

Age: All ages used for calculations at the time of a given testing event for each candidate. If a candidate sits for multiple sections in a given year, his/her age is calculated four separate times.

Age Rank: Ranking of jurisdictions based on the average age of its candidates. The youngest average age jurisdiction was arbitrarily given the ranking of 1. A higher or lower ranking is provided as a relative reference only and not intended to denote a level of performance.

Average: All averages (mean) are calculated at the testing event level.

Candidate: A unique (distinct) individual participating in the examination process during the reported testing window and, if applicable, within the reported category. For example, a candidate who sat for a two sections in each of the 4 quarters would count as 1 candidate in the respective quarter and as 1 candidate for the year.

Degree Type: Candidate degrees are recorded at the time of application and are associated with the testing event. The degree for that event will remain the same even if the candidate earns a different degree prior to passing all 4 sections.

FICE Code: The Federal Interagency Committee on Education (FICE) code is a 6-digit identifier assigned to every institute of higher education (2-year degree or higher) in the U.S.

First-Time: First-Time (FT) refers to sections that were taken for the first time by a given unique candidate.

Foreign: The number or percentage of candidates with an international address who applied to sit for the exam. These candidates can include U.S. citizens who are living or studying abroad at the time of application.

Gender: A candidate's gender is determined by salutation entered during the application process (Mister, Misses, etc...). This field is not captured by all jurisdictions.

In-State Address: The number or percentage of candidates who applied to sit for the exam in the same jurisdiction in which they reside.

Institution: A place of higher learning, typically a college or university, is referred to as an institution.

Jurisdiction: The 50 States plus the District of Columbia, Puerto Rico, Northern Mariana Islands, U.S. Virgin Islands and Guam.

New Candidate: A candidate who has not sat for ANY testing event prior to the testing window in which they are being reported.

Out of State Address: Refers to a candidate with a mailing address in one of the 55 jurisdictions but is applying to sit for the exam in a different jurisdiction.

Pass Rate or Percent Pass: The pass rate is calculated directly by dividing the count of testing events passed by the total testing events.

Passing 4th Section: A candidate who successfully passes his/her final section of the exam during the reported period is counted in this metric.

Program: The title program refers to the part of an educational institution that produces/prepares CPA candidates. The rankings of institutions are based on the size of these programs and not necessarily the size the institution. Program size is determined by the number of CPA candidates listing that institution in a given reporting period or testing window.

Re-Exam: Re-Exam (RE) refers to all testing events subsequent to the First-Time testing event.

Score: The numerical score received for each testing event.

Section: Refers to one of the four areas of the Examination: AUD, BEC, FAR or REG. The term Section(s) is also synonymous with Testing Event(s) for this and other NASBA reports.

11615908R00173

Made in the USA
Charleston, SC
10 March 2012